W9-CKC-479

COLLEGE ENGLISH AND COMMUNICATION

Marie M. Stewart, Ph.D.
Former Head of the
Business Education Department
Stonington High School
Stonington, Connecticut

Frank W. Lanham, Ph.D.
Professor of Vocational and
Applied Arts Education
Wayne State University
Detroit, Michigan

Kenneth Zimmer, Ed.D.
Professor of Business Education
and Office Administration
California State University
Los Angeles, California

COLLEGE ENGLISH AND COMMUNICATION

THIRD EDITION

GREGG AND COMMUNITY COLLEGE DIVISION
McGraw-Hill Book Company

New York St. Louis Dallas San Francisco
Auckland Düsseldorf Johannesburg Kuala Lumpur
London Mexico Montreal New Delhi
Panama Paris São Paulo Singapore
Sydney Tokyo Toronto

DESIGNER: Carol Inouye
PHOTOGRAPHER: Sebastian Milito
SPONSORING EDITOR: Joseph Tinervia
SENIOR EDITING MANAGER: Elizabeth Huffman
EDITING SUPERVISOR: Evelyn Belov
PRODUCTION SUPERVISOR: Gary Whitcraft

COLLEGE ENGLISH AND COMMUNICATION, Third Edition

4 5 6 7 8 9 0 KPKP 7 8 4 3 2 1 0 9 8 7

Library of Congress Cataloging in Publication Data

Stewart, Marie M date.
College English and communication.

Bibliography: p.
Includes index.
1. English language—Rhetoric. I. Lanham, Frank
Wesley, date. joint author. II. Zimmer, Kenneth,
date. joint author. III. Title.
PE1408.S763 1975 808′.066′6514 74-23459
ISBN 0-07-061401-6

Preface

Managers, secretaries, accountants, sales representatives—these and virtually all other business workers spend a great deal of their on-the-job time speaking, reading, writing, and listening in order to perform their specialized job duties. Invariably, the men and women who achieve the greatest success in their business careers are those who have mastered these four language arts as well as the specialized skills that their jobs require. *College English and Communication, Third Edition,* provides a comprehensive program to help students master the fundamental principles of effective communication and develop the proficiency in reading, writing, listening, and speaking they will need to enter upon and progress in their careers.

LEARNING THE FUNDAMENTAL PRINCIPLES

To develop a high level of effectiveness in reading, writing, listening, and speaking, the business worker must know how to apply the fundamental principles of word usage, grammar, and style.

Skillful word usage is implicit in effective communication; therefore, *College English and Communication* provides for continual vocabulary expansion and refinement. Chapter 1 (Sections 1 through 4) erects a platform for vocabulary building and spelling improvement. To reinforce this platform, the end-of-section activities in each of the following chapters include an exercise to help students further develop their spelling and other vocabulary skills.

The principles of grammar which every business worker must apply in writing and in speaking are fully discussed in Chapter 3 (Sections 7 through 21). Those principles that are most often misunderstood or forgotten receive special attention in *Memory Hooks.* The *Twilight Zones,* which treat language-usage principles that are in a state of transition, give the instructor an opportunity to accept or to reject alternative principles as he or she thinks appropriate. Within each section of this chapter, *Checkup* exercises provide immediate practice in applying the principles.

A consistent application of the principles of writing style helps the reader to interpret a message. In Chapter 4 (Sections 22 through 30), the student masters the style of expressing numbers and of using punctuation, capitalization, and abbreviations in business communications. As in the preceding chapter, frequent *Checkup* exercises provide immediate reinforcement of principles.

IMPROVING LISTENING AND READING SKILLS

Effective listening and efficient reading are as important on the job as they are in the classroom. Chapter 2 (Sections 5 and 6) establishes a continuing program for listening and reading improvement.

Section 5 outlines the need for active listening in business situations and presents a self-improvement program to help students become better listeners. As the first step in this listening-improvement program, students determine their listening weaknesses by answering a series of questions and evaluating their answers. The program then helps students to correct their weaknesses and to develop habits that contribute to effective listening.

The guides to reading improvement presented in Section 6 will enable students to increase their reading speed and to improve their reading comprehension. Students learn to adjust their reading rate according to the materials they are reading, to read in thought units, to scan or preview materials, and to apply other techniques that will improve their reading skills.

MASTERING WRITING PRINCIPLES

College English and Communication presents a thorough program on written business communications. The specialized principles and techniques covered in Chapters 5 through 8 (Sections 31 through 48) are designed to put students in complete control of any writing assignment they encounter on the job.

Chapter 5 (Sections 31 through 33) emphasizes structural principles and writing techniques that the business writer can use to help the reader interpret a letter, memo, or other message quickly and correctly.

Chapter 6 (Sections 34 and 35) inspires students to think creatively in preparation for writing the various types of business communications that will be discussed in Chapter 7. The presentation of basic psychological drives that motivate human behavior (Section 34) gives students the insights they need in order to get positive responses to their letters and memos. In Section 35, students acquire the skills of planning and organizing messages.

Special-purpose letters require special coverage. Chapter 7 (Sections 36 through 44) covers the common but important letters written for special purposes and offers principles and procedures for writing them creatively. As a preface to this project, Section 36 presents a complete discussion of the elements of style characteristic of all business letters.

Chapter 8 (Sections 45 through 48) gives full attention to communications within a company and presents specialized types of written communications: memos in Section 45; informal reports in Section 46; formal reports in Section 47; and news releases, minutes, and telegrams in Section 48.

DEVELOPING SPEAKING TECHNIQUES

Telephoning clients, greeting visitors, asking and answering questions in ordinary business conversation, participating in meetings—these are but a few of the many on-the-job activities that require skill in communicating orally. Chapter 9 (Sections 49 through 54) offers a practical approach to mastering speaking techniques, an approach that will prepare the student for short-term and long-term oral communication needs.

PREPARING FOR AND ADVANCING ON THE JOB

Business communication skills are put to their first real test when the student applies for a job. Chapter 10 (Sections 55 and 56) prepares the student for this important test by emphasizing the principles and techniques of writing to get a job and of communicating successfully during face-to-face interviews. Chapter 11 (Sections 57 and 58) identifies and helps the student develop the communication skills needed to advance on the job.

COMMUNICATION PROJECTS

In addition to the *Checkup* exercises that appear within the sections in Chapters 3 through 5, *College English and Communication, Third Edition,* provides a variety of *Communication Projects* at the end of each of the 58 sections of the text.

The *Practical Application* exercises immediately reinforce the principles presented in the section the student has just studied and review those covered in previous sections.

The *Editing Practice* exercises help the student acquire the ability to detect —and to correct—errors in English usage.

The *Case Problem* generally emphasizes the human relations aspects of successful business communication and develops the student's ability to make sound judgments and decisions in typical on-the-job situations.

SUPPORTING MATERIALS

Communication Problems Correlated With College English and Communication, Third Edition, presents additional skill-building activities for each section of the textbook. Each worksheet includes carefully planned exercises that reinforce, review, and enrich the principles presented in the corresponding section of the text.

The *Instructor's Guide and Key* is a valuable source of help for planning and presenting a successful communications course. It includes 32 pages of test masters, which the instructor may duplicate for classroom use, as well as a complete key to the text, the *Communication Problems,* and the test exercises.

Marie M. Stewart
Frank W. Lanham
Kenneth Zimmer

Contents

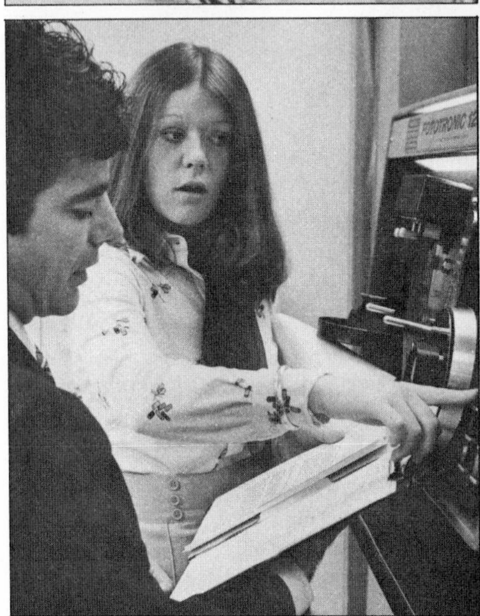

Rio

INTRODUCTION

Communicating in the World of Business

To an accountant, job success depends on more than a knowledge of accounting. To a secretary, proficiency requires more than good typing and shorthand skills. And to a sales representative, excellence means more than just meeting the monthly sales quota. For these employees, and for all other office personnel, job success cannot be measured solely in terms of special training or particular experience. Instead, success on the job can be measured by each employee's ability to communicate.

The accountant need not know how to type, the secretary may never learn to operate a calculator, and the sales representative may not be able to take dictation; but everyone who works in an office *must* excel in communicating. Office workers must *write* memos and letters; must *speak* to co-workers, customers, and clients; must *read* memos, letters, reports, invoices, and bills; and must *listen* to managers and executives, co-workers and customers. Skill in all communications media is important to every office worker, for most of everyone's business day is spent in communicating.

Even on your first job you will need skill in communicating; certainly, if you would like to advance to better positions, you must master the basic principles of writing, reading, listening, and speaking. This book will help you to acquire and develop the needed skills; it will also guide you in using these skills most effectively.

THE SCOPE OF BUSINESS COMMUNICATION

Millions of words are spoken and listened to, written and read, every business day. These daily communications are directed either outside the company or within the company, and the range of these communications is wide.

Communication *outside* the company is usually very broad in scope: many channels of communication—from direct mail campaigns to press releases—are available. Outside the company, communication is directed to other companies, to government agencies, to stockholders, to suppliers, to customers, to the press, and to the general public.

Communication *within* the company may take the form of departmental meetings, interdivisional conferences, memorandums, and other written and verbal messages of all kinds. Without such communication, there could be no advertising, no sales, no marketing plan, no budget. In fact, there could be no business without communication.

The scope of any company's communications system—whether it be international or local, large or small—depends more on the nature of the company's business than on its size. There are many obvious differences from company to company in operations, functions, purposes, but what is essential to *all* companies is an effective system of communication.

HOW TO COMMUNICATE

Communication is the lifeline of any business. We know it today in many sophisticated forms, but initially communication was simply face-to-face conversation. The earliest written communication was accomplished with symbols, or word-pictures, which depicted rather than spelled out the message. As languages developed, and with them writing systems, patterns of written communications evolved. These patterns, or forms, of writing have been refined and added to over the centuries, so that today we have a wide choice of media for transmitting written messages. Messages such as telegrams can be transmitted via electrical impulses, and electronic data communications can be transmitted with exceptional rapidity from any terminal that is hooked up to a central storage area.

Means of transmitting oral messages have also become increasingly sophisticated. The telephone, of course, has for a long time been considered basic equipment in any office; today it is a very versatile instrument, capable of providing many different services.

Whether we wish to communicate in print, in sound, or through an audio-visual combination, we have a wealth of choices. It has become as easy to send a message to the other side of the globe as it always has been to send a message around the corner.

Sending Messages Orally

Face-to-Face Contact Face-to-face communication is particularly important in dealing with customers, with sales representatives, and with co-workers. Often face-to-face conversation is taken for granted and treated as if communicating orally requires little or no skill. As a matter of fact, this method requires an exceptional amount of skill if the message is to be transmitted clearly and convincingly.

The Telephone The telephone is used by every business worker to communicate with others both inside and outside the business office. The use of the telephone facilitates receiving messages from outside the office and sending messages to other locations speedily and almost effortlessly.

The Speakerphone utilizes a microphone and a speaker so that a group may participate in a telephone conversation. The Picturephone adds a viewing screen to the audio equipment, so callers can see each other and show diagrams, blueprints, products, and other items while discussing them. The Magicall dialer is only one of several kinds of automatic dialers that store phone numbers on magnetic or motorized tape or on pre-punched plastic cards, to be used to dial numbers automatically.

When great distances are involved, however, the use of the telephone is expensive, and the communicator must determine whether the cost is justified.

When a great many calls are placed between various branch offices of one firm or between two or more separate firms, direct telephone lines may be installed to connect the callers. By using these direct lines, calls do not have to be transmitted through the telephone office.

Interoffice Communication Devices Although the telephone is frequently used for interoffice communication, other devices are available. Loudspeaker systems enable a speaker to address a group rather than each individual separately. Some interoffice communication systems are designed to connect two or more offices in the same building.

Meetings Meetings or conferences are an integral aspect of every business office. Meetings are used to orient new employees, to train both new and experienced personnel, and to provide information on new policies and products. Sometimes they are used for "brainstorming," a technique often used for developing new ideas. Because business leaders must often lead conferences as well as participate in them, they should be familiar with discussion-leading techniques and parliamentary procedure. These techniques can save valuable time and make conferences more productive.

Speeches Though not all business workers are called on to give formal speeches, many of them are required to do so at one time or another. This activity is not limited to the top executives of a business firm; secretaries, sales representatives, accountants, and others are sometimes invited to address school groups, professional and civic organizations, and church and social groups. Even the fields of radio and television are within the realm of possibility. A businessman or businesswoman must remember that when he or she speaks to a group, the firm—not the individual—is being represented. Often members of the audience will have little or no other contact with the company; therefore, they will judge the firm by the impression given by the speaker. Here is a valuable public-relations opportunity. People who make the most of this type of opportunity are almost certain to enhance their chances for success in business.

Dictation Devices Although the dictation disc, tape, belt, cylinder, or wire is usually thought of as a means of recording dictation that a stenographer will later transcribe into letter or report form, the practice of mailing these recordings directly to the correspondent is growing in popularity. Of course, this technique is most informal and should be used only for communicating within one company or with business associates with whom the dictator is well acquainted. The disadvantage of sending the recorded message directly to the addressee is that no written record of the message is provided.

Sending Written Messages

Memorandums A memorandum is actually a form of letter or report, even though it differs in appearance from either of these forms of communication. Memorandums are usually neither so formal nor so long as either the

business letter or the report, but this fact does not decrease their importance as a medium of communication. Memorandums are the most frequently used form of interoffice communication.

Letters Letters are used for every conceivable type of business communication. They are used to communicate with those who buy from a firm and with those who sell to a firm. They are used for sales promotion, for giving or requesting information, for requesting credit, for granting (or refusing) credit, for requesting payment on overdue accounts, and for social-business purposes. A complete list of the purposes served by business letters would be almost endless. Letters may be written and prepared individually, or they may be written in a form-letter style designed for a mass mailing.

Telegrams Domestic and international telegrams are used by business workers when speed is essential in transmitting written messages. In domestic communications, telegrams are often used because they attract more attention than other types of messages. Since the cost of telegrams is based on the number of words used, special skill in writing highly condensed, yet clear, messages is required.

Reports The modern business world depends heavily on reports to give facts or to report progress to business owners and to individuals at various operating levels. The length and formality of a report will vary with its purpose. One report may be a hundred pages long; another may be only one page long. The skillful writer must know the form and style most suitable for each particular report. There are several types of reports that business workers may have to prepare, but one special type of report with which they should be familiar is the report of what transpires at meetings, usually referred to as *minutes*.

Business Literature Books, newspapers, magazines, and pamphlets provide excellent opportunities for creative business writers to express their views on various phases of business. Executives often contribute to books and periodicals; in fact, some magazines depend entirely on the contributions of executives for the articles they publish.

News Releases A business likes to keep its name before the public. One way of doing so is to inform the public about changes in personnel, new product or service innovations, participation of its personnel in business or civic activities, and other such newsworthy items. For such events, news releases are written and are sent to newspapers and to radio and television stations. Naturally, news releases will receive more favorable attention if they are prepared in a style acceptable to the medium to which they are sent.

Advertising Copy Advertising copy for newspapers, magazines, radio, television, pamphlets, folders, and sales letters accounts for an enormous volume of business communications. Such material is usually prepared by people especially trained for this kind of writing, although business workers in the fields of advertising, marketing, or sales are very frequently given this responsibility. Even if they do not actually prepare the copy, such employees must evaluate the material prepared by others.

DATA COMMUNICATIONS IN BUSINESS

The development of automation and electronic data processing has led to a new field of communication called *data communications*. What makes data communications different from any other form of communication? First of all, whatever information is transmitted must first be translated into a special code, of which there are over sixty in operation today. This code, usually referred to as *language*, takes the place of the words that you and I would ordinarily use in sending a message. In reality, the code is the language of the machine, just as English is the language of people.

The second distinguishing characteristic of data communications is that the data are transmitted by some electronic means—for example, a telephone line that may connect two computers. One computer is sending the information and the other is receiving it. Here are some examples of data communications at work in business:

> The Holiday Inn in New York confirms an executive's room reservation in Los Angeles by its direct teleprinter communication (Holidex) with Holiday Inn's central office.
>
> The branch office manager submits sales information to the company's home office computer, using a magnetic-tape or punched-card transmission system.
>
> On the first of the month, a sales manager receives a report of the preceding month's sales by means of a teleprinter service from the company's data processing center.

Data communications makes it possible to store vast amounts of information in one place and to select and rapidly transmit this information to another place. The information that is stored, therefore, must be accurate and must also be clear to the user. Otherwise, costly mistakes may result. If Holiday Inn makes a reservation for an executive when there actually is no space available, ill will and the loss of that company's future business may be the outcome.

The effectiveness of any data communications system depends on accuracy and clarity at the time the information is programmed, as well as at the time the information is retrieved. Undoubtedly, the person who needs the information wants it in order to make some important decision that must be put into writing, probably in the form of a report. Therefore, the business worker should be familiar with business report writing and should be able to communicate data in a manner that will be understood by the reader. One of the functions of this book is to teach you how to write such reports.

YOU AS A BUSINESS COMMUNICATOR

No matter how extensive or elaborate a communications system may be, effective communication still depends on the individual's skill in using written and spoken words.

Rio

Because nearly every business employee is involved in communicating, as a business worker you must be able to speak and write with clarity, confidence, and knowledge. You must also be able to read and to listen with understanding. To ensure personal success, as well as the success of your company, you and every other employee must be a skilled business communicator.

In recent years, business people and the general public have become increasingly aware of the need for improving every business worker's communication skills—particularly the skills of workers who come in contact with the public. Today, courses in effective speaking and writing, as well as in reading improvement, are offered not only by colleges and universities but also by companies themselves. Businesses know that the time and money spent to improve the communication skills of their employees represent dollars saved in time and understanding in day-to-day business operations.

DEVELOPING COMMUNICATION SKILLS

A skilled communicator is a person who can communicate facts, ideas, opinions, and instructions with a minimum of effort. To become a skillful communicator, you must know how to use language correctly. Therefore, you must command a broad vocabulary, which involves not only the ability to spell and pronounce words but also the knowledge of how to use words precisely. You must be able to speak and write without error, with as much clarity and in as few words as possible. Not only must you be familiar with the many media available for communicating, but you must also have the ability to select the best medium to convey a particular message. If you are to be considered a skilled business communicator, you must be well read and well informed about your field of work, your company, and your particular function in that company. You must be able to think creatively. You must use research techniques effectively when resource materials are called for, and you must know how to outline, draft, and perfect your message so that it is well fitted to both the purpose you wish to achieve and the medium you have chosen to convey it.

HUMAN RELATIONS AND COMMUNICATION

Your work in this course and your study of this book will be directed toward helping you achieve this goal—becoming a skillful communicator. However, one skill that cannot be overlooked and that is essential to success in all aspects of your job, not just in communication, is skill in human relations, the ability to understand and deal with people. Skill in human relations cannot be learned mechanically as can structure and usage or vocabulary and spelling. Although these mechanics contribute to skill in human relations, they are basically tools for making communication in any human relations situation more effective.

Employees who are skilled in human relations have learned to consider carefully each situation in which they are dealing with others, taking time to consider the feelings and goals of those with whom they are dealing. They remember that every person believes that his or her own opinion is founded

TOTRONIC 1200

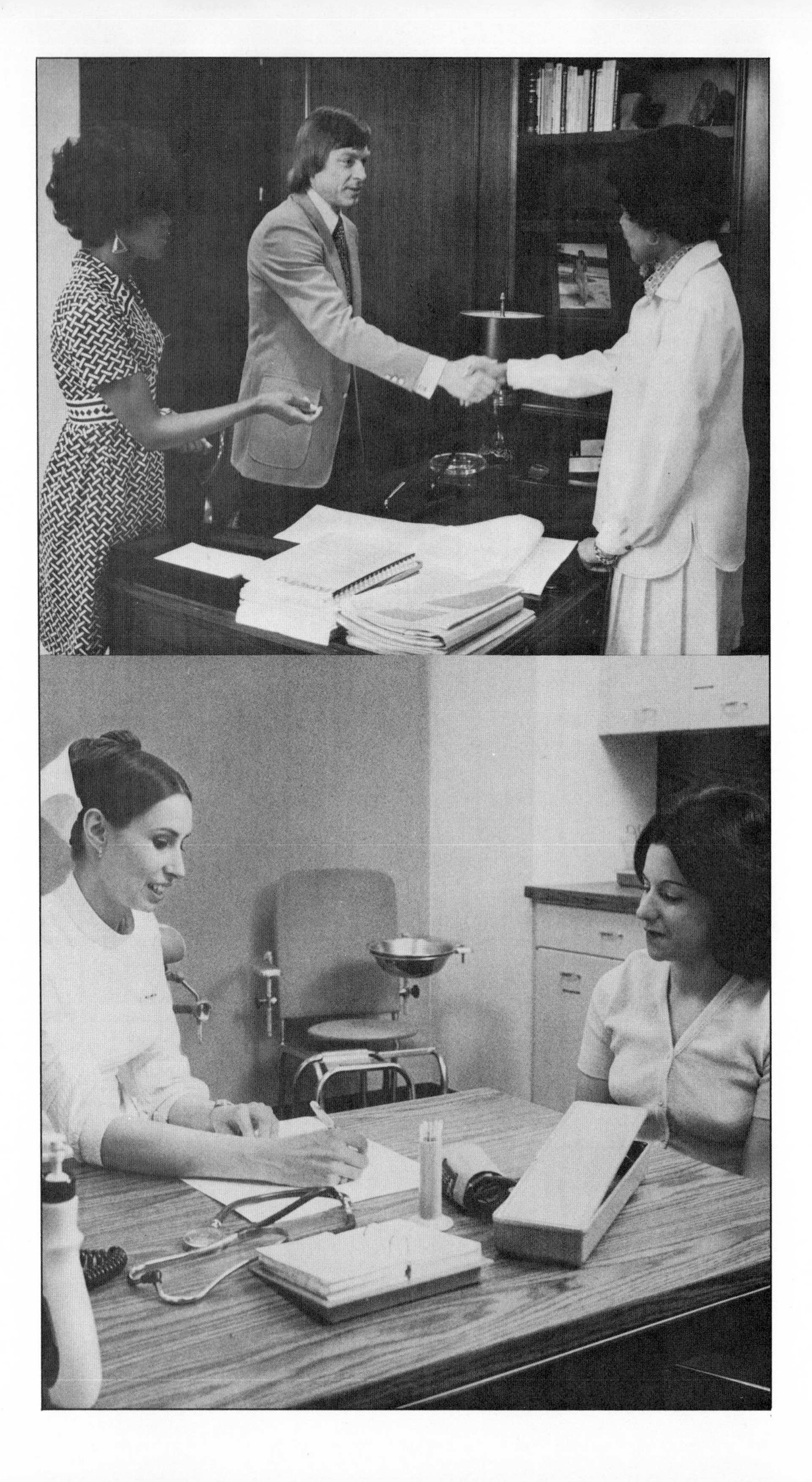

on good reasons. They give instructions clearly and carefully, taking time to make sure that they are correct. We might say that they practice "business diplomacy."

Sales representatives dealing with irate customers hear the customers out and then try to satisfy both the customers and their companies by understanding both sides of the issue. Employers dealing with employees who have a grievance try to show the workers that they understand their problems, and they remember to give reasons for the company policies they must uphold. Supervisors who must change the jobs of employees let the workers know why they are being given a different kind of work. In all phases of activity today, the business community is interested in improving human relations. That is why studies of personnel relations, labor relations, management relations, and public relations are being given a great deal of attention.

WHY COMMUNICATION SKILLS ARE IMPORTANT TO YOU

Perhaps the way you can best prove your ability to accept leadership responsibilities is through communication. By your facility in expressing ideas, you can convince others of your merits.

As you study the material presented in this book and obtain valuable practice in building your communication skills, keep in mind the important role that communications can play in helping you achieve a successful future in the business world. And remember, too, that every hour of study is time spent in working for yourself, for your own personal advancement.

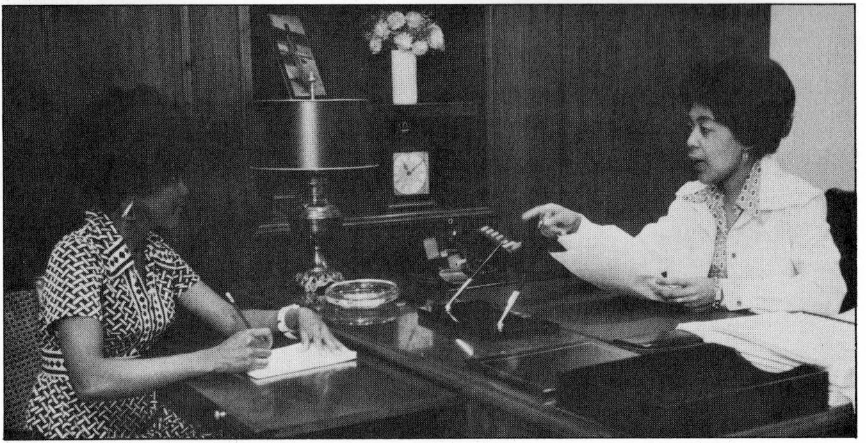

USING WORDS EFFECTIVELY

1 References for Building Your Vocabulary

The marvelous variety of the English language enables us to present our ideas exactly as we think of them. Our language offers us many, many words to choose from, and our ability to choose the precise word determines how well we convey our meaning to our readers and to our listeners. Words are the fundamental units of communication, and the effective writer or speaker is the one most skillful in joining the appropriate words together to get ideas across.

The effective communicator, therefore, requires an extensive vocabulary. Speakers and writers must continually strive to improve their vocabularies; the best of them supplement the words they already know with three excellent references: a dictionary, a thesaurus, and a dictionary of synonyms. The people who have a flair for speaking or writing know that the English language is rich in choices and that they need not settle for less than the precise word, less than the word that adds color, or less than the word that creates an image. Of the three, the reference you are likely to reach for most often is the dictionary.

THE DICTIONARY

The most useful reference for those who deal in words is the dictionary. The sooner the writer or speaker learns to make the best use of the dictionary, the sooner he or she learns to use words precisely. Every successful writer, secretary, editor, proofreader, executive, and student keeps a dictionary within easy reach and uses it often.

Those who work extensively with the written and spoken word should select a reliable dictionary. For ordinary office and school use, a standard abridged (concise) dictionary is adequate. A pocket-sized dictionary is not recommended for business use because the number of word entries it contains is necessarily limited, it provides little word information, and it lacks the "extras" to be found in a larger dictionary.[1]

For our purposes we will categorize dictionary information into two groups: "Word Information" and "Other Information."

Word Information

The dictionary is used primarily, of course, to look up information about specific words—spellings, definitions, synonyms, and the like. As an example of the extensive information provided by a good dictionary, consider the dictionary entry for *college* shown at the top of page 17.

[1] The dictionary used as the source for this discussion is, except where noted, *Webster's New Collegiate Dictionary*, G. & C. Merriam Co., Springfield, Massachusetts, 1974.

> **col·lege** \ˈkäl-ij\ *n* [ME, fr. MF, fr. L *collegium* society, fr. *collega* colleague — more at COLLEAGUE] **1 :** a body of clergy living together and supported by a foundation **2 :** a building used for an educational or religious purpose **3 a :** a self-governing constituent body of a university offering living quarters and instruction but not granting degrees <Balliol and Magdalen *Colleges* at Oxford> **b :** a preparatory or high school **c :** an independent institution of higher learning offering a course of general studies leading to a bachelor's degree **d :** a part of a university offering a specialized group of courses **e :** an institution offering instruction usu. in a professional, vocational, or technical field <war ~> <business ~> <barber ~> **4 :** COMPANY, GROUP; *specif* **:** an organized body of persons engaged in a common pursuit or having common interests or duties **5 a :** a group of persons considered by law to be a unit **b :** a body of electors — compare ELECTORAL COLLEGE **6 :** the faculty, students, or administration of a college — **college** *adj*

Spelling First, the dictionary tells how the word *college* is spelled. Many people, however, are unable to use a dictionary because they do not know what letters stand for specific sounds. The topics presented in Section 4, "Spelling Improvement," provide the hearing and seeing skills needed for finding words in the dictionary. Some additional tips for verifying the spelling of words are these:

Be sure that you see the letters in their correct order; for example, *niece,* not *neice.*

Be sure that you have not inserted letters that are not there, as *athaletic* instead of *athletic.*

Be sure that you have included all the letters that are in the word; for example, *embarrass,* not *embarass.*

Be sure that the word is not some other word that is spelled somewhat like the one you are seeking. *Read the definition.* Suppose you are writing this sentence: "Mr. Harris sent me a compl?mentary copy of his book." You need to verify the spelling of *compl?mentary.* In the dictionary you will find *complEmentary,* followed by the definition "serving to fill out or complete." This definition is not the meaning you want. But look under *complImentary* and you will find "given free as courtesy or favor." Now you know that the word you seek is *complimentary.*

Many words have more than one spelling. The dictionary shows spellings that are equally correct by joining them by *or.* For example, the dictionary entry for *traveler* reads "traveler *or* traveller." This indicates that both spellings are standard, both are commonly used. When one spelling is less commonly used, the dictionary joins them by *also*: "lovable *also* loveable" shows that both spellings are used, but the second less commonly so.

Pay particular attention to compound words to determine whether they are written as one word (*shortcut*), two words (*sales check*), or a hyphenated word (*left-handedness*).

Be sure to include any accent marks that are part of a word. For example, *résumé* is a noun that means "a summary"; but *resume* is a verb that means "to assume or take again."

Hyphenation If a word must be divided at the end of a line of writing, the writer must know where the word can be correctly divided. Dictionary entries indicate, by centered periods, where words can be hyphenated: *col·lege; ap·pre·ci·ate,* but *ap·pre·cia·tive.*

Capitalization The dictionary shows if a word is to be capitalized when it is not the first word of a sentence. For example, the word *south* is usually not capitalized, but when it refers to a specific region, it *is* capitalized.

Pronunciation and Syllabic Division Immediately after the regular spelling of a word is its phonetic spelling, which indicates where the word is accented and where syllabic divisions occur in pronunciation. If you are unfamiliar with phonetic symbols, refer to the dictionary section that explains them. The dictionary shows that the pronunciation of *appreciate* is ə-prē'-shē-āt. The hyphens indicate syllable breaks. (*Webster's New Collegiate Dictionary* and some other dictionaries show major and minor stresses by placing an accent mark *before* the stressed syllable. In this text we place an apostrophe *after* a syllable to show the syllable is stressed; and we show only major, not minor, stresses.)

Part of Speech The abbreviations following the word entries, *n, adj, adv, vi* or *vt,* and so on, indicate that the word is a *n*oun, *adj*ective, *adv*erb, or *v*erb (*i*ntransitive or *t*ransitive). Knowing the part of speech can often help you to spell a word correctly. For example, the dictionary lists *upside down* as an adverb, *upside-down* as an adjective. If you wanted to write "The upside-down picture made all of us laugh," knowing that the word you need is an adjective (to describe *picture*) will help you to find the proper spelling: *upside-down*(adj), not *upside down*(adv).

Etymology A word's etymology is its origin or derivation. Very often readers skip or skim the etymologies, although they can be both interesting and informative and can act as reminders in the future. For example, the etymology of *radar* reads "*ra*dio *d*etecting *a*nd *r*anging," which tells us that *radar* is a word formed from the initial letters of a compound term (called an "acronym").

Definition A good dictionary lists all the various definitions a word may have, usually in the order in which they developed, and labels special definitions. For example, a special definition under *dead* reads "*Sports.* Out of play."

Inflectional Forms and Derivatives The dictionary shows the irregular plurals of nouns, the past tense and participial forms of irregular verbs, and the comparative and superlative forms of irregular adjectives and adverbs. For example, after the definition of the noun *contract* are its derivative noun *contractibility* and its derivative adjective *contractible.* Look at the entry on page 19 for the irregular verb *teach* and note its past, *taught,* its present participle, *teaching,* and its third person singular present tense, *teaches.*[2]

Synonyms For many entries the dictionary also lists synonyms (words that have almost the same meanings as the entry). Note, however, that each synonym listed above for *teach* (*teach, instruct, educate, tutor, train, school, discipline, drill*) has its own distinct flavor.

Illustrations Many word entries are further clarified by accompanying drawings, charts, or tables. Such illustrations are particularly useful when

[2] *The American Heritage Dictionary of the English Language* lists all verb forms, whether regular or irregular.

teach (tēch) *v.* **taught** (tôt), **teaching, teaches.** —*tr.* **1.** To impart knowledge or skill to; give instruction to. **2.** To provide knowledge of; instruct in. **3.** To cause to learn by example or experience: *Her rebuff taught him never to ask again.* **4.** To advocate; preach. —*intr.* To give instruction, especially as an occupation. [Teach, taught; Middle English *techen, tahte,* Old English *tǣcan, tǣhte* (past tense), *getǣht* (unattested past participle). See **deik-** in Appendix.*]
Synonyms: *teach, instruct, educate, tutor, train, school, discipline, drill.* These verbs mean to impart knowledge or skill. *Teach* is the most widely applicable, since it can refer to any such act of communicating. *Instruct* usually suggests methodical direction in a specific subject or area. *Educate* is comprehensive and implies a wide area of learning, achieved either by experience or, more often, by formal instruction in many subjects. *Tutor* usually refers to private instruction of one student or a small group. *Train* generally implies concentration on particular skills intended to fit a person, or sometimes an animal, for a desired role. *School* and *discipline* now usually refer to training in modes of behavior. *School* often implies indoctrination, not necessarily in an unfavorable sense, and an arduous learning process. *Discipline* usually refers to teaching of control, especially self-control. *Drill* implies rigorous instruction or training, often by repetition of a routine.

they help to delineate or define a word. For example, good dictionaries illustrate, near the definition of the noun *cross,* some of the many different types of crosses; these illustrations help the reader visualize the types of crosses better than the definitions do.

Other Information

A good dictionary provides much more than just word information. For instance, a good abridged dictionary contains a guide to the organization and use of the dictionary, explanatory notes about the kinds of information contained at each entry, a key to phonetic symbols, a guide to correct punctuation, a list of abbreviations used in the word entries, and more. Here are some of the extra aids you may find helpful.

Signs and Symbols This section comprises signs and symbols frequently used in such fields as astronomy, biology, business, chemistry, data processing, mathematics, medicine, philately, physics, and weather.

Biographical Names The names of famous people, each with the proper spelling and pronunciation, are listed under this heading. Such biographical data as dates of birth and death, nationality, and occupation are also given. This section may be used, for example, to check the pronunciation of names to be used in a speech or to identify unknown names encountered in reading or conversation.

Geographical Names This section provides information about places—names, pronunciation, location, population, and so on. This section, therefore, can be helpful when checking the spelling of places to which correspondence is to be addressed.

Handbook of Style This very useful section contains rules on punctuation, italicization, capitalization, and plurals; sample footnotes; forms of address; and style in business correspondence.

Foreign Words and Phrases This guide to some words and phrases commonly encountered offers both pronunciation and spelling assistance.

A good dictionary is an invaluable resource. Invest in a good abridged dictionary—and use it often.

THESAURUS

A thesaurus is a book of words arranged according to ideas. Unlike the dictionary, in which you seek information about a specific word, the thesaurus is a reference in which you seek various ways of expressing a concept or an idea. Whether you are looking for *the* precise word to express your idea or for synonyms to give it nuance and color, the thesaurus is indispensable.

The thesaurus is divided into two sections: an alphabetical list of words, each with a key number, serves as a guide to the main, or numbered, section. If, for example, you are looking for ways of describing or using the word *creative*, look in the alphabetical section for entries under *creative*.

creative
productive 164.9
originative 166.23
inventive 533.18

Three basic synonyms are listed: *productive, originative,* and *inventive.* Let us say that *inventive* is closest to the idea you want to express; the other two words have different connotations. Therefore, use the number after *inventive,* 533.18, as your guide and refer to paragraph 18 in the section numbered 533. There you will find these synonyms for *creative*:

ADJS. **18. imaginative, inventive, original,** originative, **creative, ingenious; productive, fertile,** fecund, prolific; **inspired,** visioned.

Here are some situations in which the thesaurus is especially helpful.

To Find the Most Suitable Word for a Given Idea

You are describing the qualifications for a certain position in your company and you wish to emphasize that the applicant must be reliable. In the alphabetical section of your thesaurus you find these categories under *reliable*: *stable, sure, safe, solvent, trustworthy.* Of these words, *trustworthy* is the word with the meaning closest to the one you want to convey, so you follow the guide numbers after it and find these adjectives: *trustworthy, trusty, trustable, faithworthy, reliable, dependable, responsible,* and more. You consider and choose *dependable.*

To Avoid Repeating a Word

In describing job qualifications, you have used the word *skillful* twice and do not want to repeat it. Of the choices under *skillful* in the alphabetical index you follow *expert* and choose from among the following adjectives: *skillful, expert, proficient, dexterous, adroit, deft, adept, apt, handy,* and others.

To Locate the Right Word for Something Vaguely Remembered

In describing a Mexican scene, you want to identify the typical high-crowned felt or straw hat worn by many of the men. You have forgotten its name, so you turn to *hat* in the alphabetical guide. There you find a reference to "types of hats" in the numbered section, and you find the word that eluded you—*sombrero.*

To Find an Appropriate Phrase

You are looking for a substitute for *cooperate fully* to use in a memo you are writing. Under *cooperate* you find the following phrases: *work together, act together, pull together, hold together, hang together, keep together, stand together, stand shoulder to shoulder, lay one's heads together, band together, be in league with, unite one's efforts, act in concert, join in, work to one end.* Which would you choose?

Roget's International Thesaurus is the classic thesaurus. It is available in a paperback, pocket-size edition. Experienced writers and fledgling writers both consult Roget when they are stymied for the exact words to express their thoughts, when they want to add flavor and color to their writing, when they would like to create a fresh image with words.

DICTIONARY OF SYNONYMS

A reference book like *Webster's Dictionary of Synonyms* is valuable to the business writer, the speech writer, and the writer of advertising copy. (How to use synonyms and antonyms is explained fully in Section 3.)

Communication Projects

PRACTICAL APPLICATION

A For a speech she was preparing, Mildred James referred to the following people. She used a dictionary to check the pronunciation of their names. For each name, write the pronunciation she found and give some identifying information about the person.

1. da Vinci
2. Fessenden
3. Malthus
4. Nkrumah
5. Thyssen

B The firm you have just joined imports goods from all over the world. You begin to jot down place names that are unfamiliar to you so that you can look them up in the dictionary, learn exactly where they are, and master their pronunciation. What do you find for the following?

1. Gloucester
2. New Delhi
3. Kuala Lumpur
4. Istanbul
5. Dubrovnik

C The following words should be part of your vocabulary. For each, write the correct pronunciation and the most common definition. Then use each word in a sentence.

1. excise
2. ecology
3. morale
4. bankruptcy
5. depreciation
6. lien
7. mortgage
8. emanate
9. franchise
10. monopoly

D The writer of the following sentences confused two similar words. Replace any incorrect word with the correct one. Define both the correct and the incorrect word.

1. At the reception each person will be formerly introduced to the guest of honor.
2. The speaker we have chosen is an imminent author and lecturer.
3. Should supervisors advice their subordinates?
4. The vice president notified all personal of the early closing.
5. The report on the new factory sight was submitted to the board today.

E Are you sure which of the two spellings for each word below is the preferred spelling? Check your decision against the dictionary.

1. saleable, salable
2. labeled, labelled
3. center, centre
4. envelope, envelop (noun)
5. instalment, installment
6. advisor, adviser
7. judgement, judgment
8. acknowledgement, acknowledgment

EDITING PRACTICE

Hidden Pairs From each group of words below two can be matched because they are similar or opposite in meaning. Find each pair. Jot down the letters of your choice and indicate whether the words are synonyms or antonyms.

Example: (a) practice (b) proscribe (c) placate (d) preempt (e) retaliate
Answer: c and e; antonyms

1. (a) wield (b) procure (c) wither (d) obfuscate (e) obtain
2. (a) circumstance (b) sanitation (c) cenotaph (d) situation (e) accident
3. (a) dispense (b) depreciate (c) spend (d) disburse (e) disperse
4. (a) devalue (b) give (c) locate (d) retain (e) indicate
5. (a) unlawful (b) illegible (c) ineligible (d) unreadable (e) uncouth
6. (a) deny (b) alleviate (c) aggravate (d) solder (e) obfuscate
7. (a) wretched (b) rotated (c) obsolete (d) antiquated (e) meticulous
8. (a) imitative (b) exemplary (c) despicable (d) deplorable (e) showy
9. (a) fireplace (b) decease (c) abundance (d) dearth (e) bravery
10. (a) preempt (b) prescribe (c) replace (d) prejudge (e) remunerate

CASE PROBLEM

Problem Solving You are a transcription pool supervisor, and Mr. Edgar, who draws on the pool for stenographic assistance, has asked you not to send him Patricia or Ann. His reason is that they change his punctuation and wording; consequently, time is wasted and nerves are frayed because he insists that they retype the letters exactly as he dictated them.

What steps would you take to solve this problem and to ensure that there will be no similar problem in the future?

2 Precision in Word Usage

Words stir the emotions. They can lift the heart, persuade one to act, or enlighten the mind. They can bewilder, cause despair, or evoke anger. The words you use in writing and speaking can build the respect and admiration of those with whom you are communicating; or they can mark you as unimaginative—and uneducated. If your word resources are limited, you have no stockpile from which you can choose words that will communicate precise shades of meaning. However, having a good vocabulary is not simply a matter of knowing many words. Skillful business communicators know that they must use the *right* word at the *right* time. They must be concerned with correctness in the words they use, and they must also be concerned with the interpretations that readers or listeners will make of the words. Therefore, they follow certain guides that help them use words precisely.

THE CORRECT WORD

Careful speakers and writers are aware of the difference between correct usage and illiterate usage, and they opt for what is correct. The first step is to avoid using words that do not exist. For example, the writer of "irregardless of the amount" is using a nonword and, therefore, is guilty of illiterate usage. The correct choice would have been *regardless,* or perhaps *irrespective of,* but the two somehow came out as the illiterate *irregardless.*

Mispronunciation of a correct word may be responsible for the creation of an illiterate word. For example, if *irrep'arable* is mispronounced *irrepair'able,* an illiterate word has been created. Other illiteracies are *renumeration* for *remuneration* (although *enumeration* is correct); *hunderd* for *hundred; strinth* for *strength; revelant* for *relevant; compare'able* for *com'parable.*

Checking the dictionary to find if a word is indeed a word and, if it is, to learn how it is pronounced can prevent many illiterate usages.

HOMONYMS

Words that look or sound alike—but have different meanings—are known as homonyms. Choosing the incorrect word (although it may sound or even look correct) is one of the most frequently committed errors of word usage.

For example, the tenants of a large apartment house receive a letter urging that "All the *residence* should protest the increased tax rate." This important message might be ignored simply because the writer cannot distinguish people, *residents*, from places, *residences*. Another letter writer may request a ream of *stationary*, much to the amusement of the *stationer* supplying it.

Below are some homonyms that every business writer should know.

aisle, isle
allowed, aloud
altar, alter
ascent, assent
assistance, assistants
attendance, attendants
bail, bale
brake, break
canvas, canvass
cereal, serial
cite, site, sight
coarse, course
complement, compliment
correspondence, correspondents
dependence, dependents
desert, dessert
dual, duel
foreword, forward
forth, fourth
grate, great
hear, here
instance, instants
intense, intents
lean, lien
leased, least
lesser, lessor
loan, lone
mail, male
medal, meddle
miner, minor
overdo, overdue
pain, pane
passed, past
patience, patients
peace, piece
presence, presents
principal, principle
raise, raze
rap, wrap
right, write
sole, soul
some, sum
stake, steak
stationary, stationery
strait, straight
their, there, they're
threw, through
to, too, two
wait, weight
waive, wave
weak, week

Pseudohomonyms

Pseudohomonyms are words that sound somewhat alike but have different meanings. They are called "pseudo" because, when pronounced correctly, these words do *not* sound exactly alike. For example, the statement "Smith, Jones, and Hill earned $300, $500, and $800, respectfully" is incorrect. The communicator has confused the word *respectfully* (meaning "courteously") with *respectively* (meaning "in the order given"). The pseudohomonyms that give the most trouble are listed on page 25.

accept, except
access, excess
adapt, adopt
addition, edition
adverse, averse
advice, advise
affect, effect
allusion, illusion
appraise, apprise
carton, cartoon
cooperation, corporation
dairy, diary
decent, descent, dissent
deceased, diseased
deference, difference
detract, distract
device, devise
disburse, disperse
disprove, disapprove
elicit, illicit
eligible, illegible
emigrate, immigrate
eminent, imminent
expand, expend
extant, extent
facilitate, felicitate
fiscal, physical
formally, formerly
ingenious, ingenuous
later, latter
liable, libel
persecute, prosecute
personal, personnel
precede, proceed
reality, realty
recent, resent
respectfully, respectively
statue, statute
suit, suite

Spelling

Business executives complain more about employees' poor spelling than about any other single language handicap. Since there is little excuse for misspelling words, that fault will surely mark the communicator as careless or, worse, ignorant. You can steadily improve your spelling by giving careful attention to the similarities and differences between homonyms or pseudohomonyms and to the suggestions in Section 4 and at the end of this chapter—and by developing the dictionary habit.

WORDS SUITED TO THE AUDIENCE

In a speech addressed to a purely social club, an architect would be unwise to discuss technical aspects of architecture and to use such terms as *cantilever, interstice, porosity, stress,* and *tenon.* The speaker would lose the audience as soon as it could not follow the presentation. But if the speech included such nontechnical terms as *living space, elevation, ventilation,* and *safety,* the audience would understand. In other words, genuine communication occurs when a speaker chooses words geared to the knowledge level and to the interests of the audience.

WORDS WITH DIFFERENT SHADES OF MEANING

The English language is rich in words expressing many shades of meaning, and the skilled communicator chooses the exact word to convey precisely the meaning that is intended. The wrong choice may distort the speaker's or the writer's intention. For example, only an unskilled writer or speaker uses the word *cheap* to express *inexpensive.* A successful salesperson certainly would know that to most people, the word *cheap* means "worthless or shoddy"—*inexpensive* does not. An *inexpensive* suit may be considered a bargain; a *cheap* suit never is. The difference in shades of meaning here means dollars and cents to salespeople.

A guest speaker introduced as "notorious for initiating legislation to improve equal-employment opportunities" is being given an unintentionally ludicrous buildup. The word that took the introduction so far off course is the fancy synonym for "famous," *notorious*, which means "*un*favorably known"! Skilled communicators always check the dictionary for meanings of words they do not know.

WORDS TO AVOID

One of the aims of communicating in business is to build goodwill. Because words play an important part in building business friendships, a successful communicator uses words that are positive and pleasant to hear or to read, eliminates unnecessary words and phrases to save the reader's time, and uses up-to-date words to build reader confidence and avoid an old, stale sound.

Avoid Negative Words

Which of the following paragraphs is more likely to retain customer goodwill?

> You omitted to state the quantity and the colors of the slacks you ordered. We cannot ship with such incomplete order information.
>
> The size 36 slacks you ordered will be on their way to you just as soon as you tell us how many pairs you want and in what colors—tan, gray, navy, or maroon.

Although the second paragraph is the obvious selection, note that both paragraphs try to say the same thing. The second paragraph is positively worded and avoids such unpleasant expressions as "you omitted" and "cannot ship with such incomplete information." Negative words are almost sure to evoke a negative response. The customer reading these may cancel the order.

Words create negative responses when the reader feels blamed or accused. Most expert business writers consider *failed, careless, delay,* and *inexcusable* negative words, regardless of how the words are used, and recommend avoiding these words. Actually, such words are unpleasant primarily when they are accompanied by *you* ("you failed") or *your* ("your delay"). "Your oversight," "your error," "your claim" signal the reader to react negatively; but "our oversight," "our error"—though not necessarily wise choices of words—carry a different impression entirely.

The following words can sound only negative when used with *you* or *your* and thus cannot promote good business relationships.

blunder	defective	inability	regret
claim	delay	inadequate	trouble
complaint	dissatisfaction	inferior	unfavorable
criticism	error	mistake	unfortunate
damage	failure	neglected	unsatisfactory

Delete Unnecessary Words

Some writers and speakers spoil otherwise correct English by adding unnecessary and repetitious words—words that merely clutter the message. The italicized words in the following expressions are unnecessary and should be omitted.

adequate *enough*
as yet
at about
up above
both alike
new beginner
cooperate *together*
same identical
lose *out*
meet *up* with
modern methods *of today*
over *with*
customary practice
connect *up*
continue *on*
and etc.
as to whether
past experience
free gratis
inside *of*
my *personal* opinion
rarely (seldom) *ever*
repeat *back* or *again*
refer *back*
true facts

Avoid Out-of-Date Words

The practiced communicator avoids using words that are out of date. For example, do not use words such as these:

advise or state (for *say, tell*)
beg
duly
esteemed
herewith (except in legal work)
kindly (for *please*)
party (for *person*, except in legal work)
same ("and we will send you same")
trust (for *hope, know, believe*)
via

BUILDING AN EFFECTIVE VOCABULARY

If you look through a book written for children, you will notice that the same words are repeated throughout the story. Because children's vocabularies are limited, the writer of children's books must communicate with a limited vocabulary. Although children's books look simple—both to read and to create—they are very difficult to write. The point here is simple: The more limited a writer's vocabulary is, the more difficult the job of communicating becomes. With fewer tools, or words, to work with, the writer is clearly at a disadvantage.

Conversely, the richer your vocabulary, the easier it will be for you to write, to speak, to read, and to listen. An effective vocabulary enables you to choose the best word, the most exact word, when you speak or write; it will also help you to understand the words you hear or read.

If you constantly strive to increase your vocabulary, you will become aware that opportunities for daily vocabulary building are present all around us. Following the suggestions below will noticeably increase your word power.

Become Word-Conscious

Be alert to new and different words; learn how they are spelled, how they are pronounced, what they mean, and how to use them correctly. Listen for new words in class, on the job, from radio and television, from movies, and in the theater. When you read textbooks, newspapers, magazines, fiction or nonfiction, watch for new words that will enrich your vocabulary. It is often helpful to record new words in a special notebook for study and future reference.

Sometimes you will learn new and specialized words because you need to know them as the working vocabulary for a new subject you are studying or for a new job you are learning. At other times you will learn words almost by accident, simply because you see or hear them so often. Frequently you will find yourself learning a new word merely because it interests you. Take advantage of every opportunity to expand your word power. But discriminate between good English and slang. In business situations, a large vocabulary of slang is a poor vocabulary.

Learn to Use Word Tools

A dictionary, a thesaurus, and a dictionary of synonyms are the tools needed for vocabulary building. Your consistent use of these tools should increase your word power. (See Section 1 for a discussion of these references.)

Practice Using New Words

Unless you practice using new words you will not remember them. Use them when you speak. Use new and different words when you write business or social material. Be sure, of course, that you understand the meanings and possible shades of meanings of any new words you use. Aim constantly for variety and precision in the use of words.

Communication Projects

PRACTICAL APPLICATION

A Do you know these words well enough to pronounce each correctly and use it meaningfully in a sentence? If not, consult the dictionary. Then try using each in a sentence—or several in one sentence.

exonerate	morale
loquacious	vindictive
mesmerize	ubiquitous

B From the choices in parentheses, select the word that best completes the meaning of the sentence.

1. The rioters were (disbursed, dispersed) by the use of tear gas.
2. As one of the signers of the contract, he is not a/an (disinterested, uninterested) party to the negotiations.

3. The document will not be signed until all the heirs (ascent, assent) to its provisions.
4. All the (fiscal, physical) assets of the company are to be sold at auction.
5. He was appointed (council, counsel) in the company's tax division.
6. The work was done without the (assistance, assistants) of the clerks.
7. Mr. Kent was asked to prepare a (bibliographical, biographical) description to be used to introduce the speaker to the audience.
8. He waited (awhile, a while) before reporting her tardiness.
9. Your account is long (passed, past) due.
10. The printer made a (sleight, slight) change in the style of type.

C Recast each of the following negative sentences to achieve a positive message.

1. Your letter was not received until today, too late for our special offer, which ended yesterday.
2. We aren't able to send the three pillows you ordered because you didn't specify a second color choice and we are all out of orange.
3. You still owe us $9.57 from your last order, which you failed to send with the payment we received today.
4. We cannot understand how you did not follow the instructions for putting together the "Handy Andy" repair kit and had five pieces left over.
5. This equipment will not operate on 110-volt power, so do not use that voltage or you will burn out the motor.

D Study the following excerpts from advertisements, and write on a separate sheet of paper the descriptive words you find.

1. Australia . . . cut off from the rest of the world . . . developed into a world of its own . . . where you'll meet implausible creatures from centuries ago. The land itself resembles nothing so much as a set for a science fiction movie. From a distance, for example, the Mount Olga Range appears to be a herd of enormous elephants, sleeping in the desert. In Australia there's not only room to breathe. There's room to gasp!
2. In the can't-wait world of business, there's a need for a big bank that rolls up its sleeves and gets the job done. Business lives in a microsecond world. A quick, competent, yes-or-no decision can make the difference between success or failure . . . for a program, for a product, even for an entire company. At ______ Bank, we've structured our whole decision-making process on quickness and competence. We've a minimum of committees and a maximum of authority for our individual bankers . . . and almost no room at all for corporate "formality." For instance, we've pulled together financing packages in excess of $100 million—virtually overnight—for some of the nation's top corporations. And we were able to do it because our decision makers weren't behind closed doors when the decision was needed.
3. Let's shield roadside pillars before they become killers! Too many solid concrete obstructions are being left completely unshielded, and they're taking too many lives. But there's a way to correct this deadly hazard before it results in a needless disaster. A properly placed guardrail or an energy-absorbing crash cushion shielding these pillars would give an errant motorist a good chance of survival. We'll never eliminate human error on our highways. But with enough public awareness and concern, we can reduce the number of roadside deathtraps that kill and maim thousands of Americans every year.

E Suppose you were asked to prepare a sales promotion letter to older people announcing a "See America Now" tour service. Choose any part of the country for your "tour"—or all of it—and for each point below, write a brief paragraph using a variety of descriptive, picture-making words.

1. Be adventurous.
2. Relive American history.
3. Be economical.

Plan and present a two-minute description of a product you'd like to sell. Use specific words, utilizing all the vocabulary know-how you've acquired so far in this course.

EDITING PRACTICE

Making Sense Suppose you need to supply a word missing in transcription or in a rough draft. Study the context of each sentence below and supply a suitable word.

1. Since keypunch operators must work rotating shifts, any applicant for such a job needs to have a _______ schedule.
2. A person who can do many different things well can be described as _______.
3. We have your request for _______ of materials for covering porch furniture.
4. We are working as hard as possible to discover the _______ of the trunk that should have been delivered to you on Monday.
5. Have your _______ draw up your will so that it is clear and legal.

CASE PROBLEM

Tactful Words The office manager of the Casko Company found, when she examined letters written by Rudy Blake, that Rudy was not very tactful when he wrote to customers of the company. He frequently used expressions like *your error, you claim,* and *you failed.* In discussing this problem with Rudy, the office manager learned that Rudy did not understand that these expressions were negative and could result in the loss of goodwill—or even customer business. "After all," said Rudy, "when customers are at fault, why shouldn't we tell them so?" How should the office manager answer Rudy?

3 Variety in Word Usage

You are far more likely to win and keep the undivided attention of your reader or listener if you dispense with worn-out words and phrases. The liveliness and freshness of your message can be killed by using the same old trite words and expressions. Your success as a business communicator depends largely upon your imaginative use of expressions.

WHAT TO AVOID

A writer or speaker who has been working at the same job for years may lose some enthusiasm and freshness of outlook. To prevent communication from reflecting this loss, every writer and every speaker must be alert to ways of avoiding stale communications. One way is to avoid using hackneyed or worn-out words and expressions.

Avoid Overused Words

Retiring overused words can change a flat, dull communication into one that attracts the reader. The adjective *nice* is an example of an overused word: a *nice*-looking hat; a *nice* time at a party; a *nice* person to work with; a *nice* steak for dinner. How much more interesting would be these word choices: a *stunning, chic, smart,* or *lovely* hat; a *lively, gay, stimulating,* or *splendid* party; an *amiable, good-natured, friendly, cooperative,* or *pleasant* person to work with; a *tender, delicious, mouth-watering,* or *sizzling* steak.

Adjectives such as *good, awful, bad,* and *fine* are overused. The following sentences show how meaningless these words can be.

1. Friction among staff members can result in a *bad* situation.
2. The party last Saturday was *good,* and the food was *good* too.
3. We have an *awful* backlog of orders.
4. The company gave a *fine* luncheon for him when he retired.

Now see what words could have been substituted—words that impart zest and life to the sentences.

Sentence 1: *unfortunate, troublesome,* or *difficult* situation

Sentence 2: *delightful, enjoyable,* or *pleasant* party; *delicious, savory, delectable, tasty, appetizing,* or *rich* food

Sentence 3: *tremendous, enormous, gigantic,* or *annoying* backlog

Sentence 4: *delightful, pleasant,* or *splendid* luncheon

By substituting more precise adjectives for the commonly relied on *good, awful, bad,* and *fine,* you have created more accurate descriptions too. Analyze your speech and writing to discover the words *you* habitually overwork!

Avoid Overused Expressions

Just as generalized, overworked words are ineffective in communication, so also are trite expressions. Such phrases as "better late than never," "free and easy," "let's face it," "last but not least," "at all times," "in the near future," and a host of similar clichés have grown stale. Their use exposes a definite lack of imagination. Avoid them.

Some commonly overused words and expressions, together with suggested substitutions for them, are listed below.

For	Substitute
along the lines of	like
asset	advantage, gain, possession, resource
at all times	always
deal	agreement, arrangement, transaction
factor	event, occurrence, part
field	branch, department, domain, point, question, range, realm, region, scene, scope, sphere, subject, theme
fix	adjust, arrange, attach, bind, mend, confirm, define, establish, limit, place, prepare, repair
inasmuch as	since, as
in the near future	soon (or state the exact time)
line	business, merchandise, goods, stock
matter	situation, question, subject, point (or mention what is specifically referred to)
our Mr. Smith	our representative, Mr. Smith,
proposition	proposal, undertaking, offer, plan, affair, recommendation, idea
say	exclaim, declare, utter, articulate, express, assert, relate, remark, mention
reaction	opinion, attitude, impression
recent communication	letter of (give exact date)
run	manage, direct, operate

WHAT TO STRIVE FOR

Identifying and thus avoiding hackneyed words and expressions are relatively easy—a *minor* accomplishment. Achieving variety in word usage, however, requires creativity—a *major* accomplishment. To develop creativity you need to understand, study, and apply the following suggestions.

Select Suitable Synonyms

Choosing suitable synonyms is an excellent means of supplying variety. A synonym, as you know, is a word that has the same or nearly the same meaning as another word; for example, *level, plane, smooth, even,* and *flat* are synonymous. Although synonyms have the same basic meaning, each synonym has a different shade of meaning. To select the synonym that best expresses a specific idea, you must develop word discrimination and language sense.

For example, instead of using that overworked catchall *bad,* you look in the dictionary and find these synonyms: *evil, ill, wicked,* and *naughty.* All are synonyms, but you would not use them interchangeably. The dictionary entry is instructive:

> [1]**bad** \'bad\ *adj* **worse** \'wərs\; **worst** \'wərst\ [ME] **1 a** : failing to reach an acceptable standard : POOR **b** : UNFAVORABLE <make a ~ impression> **c** : not fresh or sound : SPOILED, DILAPIDATED <~ fish> <the house was in ~ condition> **2 a** : morally objectionable **b** : MISCHIEVOUS, DISOBEDIENT **3** : inadequate or unsuited to a purpose <a ~ plan> <~ lighting> **4** : DISAGREEABLE, UNPLEASANT <~ news> **5 a** : INJURIOUS, HARMFUL **b** : SEVERE <a ~ cold> **6** : INCORRECT, FAULTY <~ grammar> **7 a** : suffering pain or distress <felt generally ~> **b** : UNHEALTHY, DISEASED <~ teeth> **8** : SORROWFUL, SORRY **9** : INVALID, VOID <a ~ check> — **bad** *adv* — **bad·ly** *adv* — **bad·ness** *n*
>
> ***syn*** BAD, EVIL, ILL, WICKED, NAUGHTY *shared meaning element* : not ethically or morally acceptable. BAD, a very general term, is applicable to anyone or anything reprehensible for whatever reason and to whatever degree <such a *bad* boy, he won't stay in the yard> <almost as *bad* . . . as kill a king, and marry with his brother —Shak.> EVIL may add to *bad* a strong suggestion of the sinister or baleful <watched silently with an *evil* glow in his eyes> <an *evil* deed> ILL may suggest an active malevolence or vicious intent <misled by *ill* counsel> or it may merely attribute objectionableness or inferiority to someone or something <a man held in *ill* repute> WICKED usually implies serious moral reprehensibility <the *wicked* sorcerers who have done people to death by their charms —J. G. Frazer> or it may suggest malevolence and malice <a brooding *wicked* spirit> NAUGHTY, once a close synonym of *wicked,* is now usually restricted to trivial misdeeds (as of children) or used to suggest reprehensibility in a light or playful way <a very *naughty* story> ***ant*** good

An appropriate word to describe the character of Lady Macbeth might be *evil,* certainly not *naughty.* However, *naughty* is also a synonym for *bad,* the word originally chosen. When you choose one rather than another synonym, be sure you know exactly what nuance of meaning you wish to convey.

Sometimes a dictionary will refer you to another entry for synonyms. For example, when looking for synonyms under the adjective *exact,* you will read "see *correct.*" There, under the entry for *correct,* are listed the synonyms *correct, accurate, exact, precise, nice,* and *right.* If no synonyms are listed for the word you seek and there is no reference to another entry, you can create a phrase to achieve variety. Under the word *explore,* for example, the dictionary lists no synonyms, but look at its definition: "to search through or into; to examine minutely; to penetrate into; to make or conduct a systematic search." Thus, instead of using *explore,* you can make a phrase to fit: "*search* the area *thoroughly,*" "*examine* the records *minutely,*" "*systematically search* the files."

An excellent source of synonyms, of course, is the thesaurus. With the help of the thesaurus you can avoid trite expressions and develop variety in word usage. For instance, suppose you are preparing a report in which you claim "Capable office workers are few and far between." You wish to avoid the expression *few and far between,* partly because it is trite and partly because it does not exactly express the thought you would like to convey.

The dictionary will provide limited assistance here. The word *few* is defined as "not many; consisting of or amounting to a small number." The thesaurus, on the other hand, gives many additional similar words and phrases; for example, *sparseness, handful, meager, small number, hardly any, scarcely any, scant, rare,* and *minority.* So you might say, "Capable office workers are in scant supply."

Use Appropriate Antonyms

An antonym is a word that means exactly the opposite of another word. For example, *light* is an antonym of *dark.* Antonyms may also be "created" by using such prefixes as *il-, in-, ir-, non-,* and *un-* before a word. For instance, *legible* becomes *illegible; credible, incredible; trustworthy, untrustworthy; expensive, inexpensive; delivery, nondelivery; responsible, irresponsible;* and so on.

Facility in the use of antonyms sometimes helps the communicator make a telling point. An advertisment for 7–Up, a soft drink, tries to capitalize on being different from the popular, common cola drinks; the advertising copy boasts of "the *un*cola."

Choose Picture-Making Words

Picture-making words make readers or listeners "see" what is being described —often with themselves in the picture. Picture-making words raise word usage to the highest level; achieving it requires imagination as well as creativity. A thesaurus is a treasure house of picture-making words. Even if *the* exact word you seek is not there, some other word or words will act like a spark, illuminating the very idea you want to convey.

To an advertising copywriter, each word must contribute to the message, because each word is costly to the client. The copywriter makes pictures for readers and does so in the fewest possible words. Notice the colorful words used in the following advertisements:

> This compact car is a gas-sipper, not a gas-guzzler.
>
> Drive along a coastline that curves past endless ocean into never-ending sunsets.
>
> Our new acoustical ceiling soaks up excess noise.

Read the last one aloud and note that not only does it create a picture, it has enough *s* sounds to provide its own "noise."

Skillfully used picture-making words will improve your messages, whether spoken or written, but it requires much work and practice to develop this skill.

Communication Projects

PRACTICAL APPLICATION

A The following sentences contain italicized words or phrases that are weak or colorless. Substitute a more meaningful (picture-making) word or phrase for each.

1. The contractor made some *good* suggestions for remodeling the office.
2. Staff members expect a *big* announcement soon about the new procedures.

3. The report he prepared was *awful.*
4. My boss had a *nice* vacation in Mexico.
5. We have a *fine* bowling team this year.
6. Miss Jameson had her typewriter *fixed* last week.
7. The office manager *said* that he would not tolerate office gossip.
8. At our office picnic, *a good time was had by all.*
9. A *bad* error must have been made in coding the letter.
10. The mail clerk *walked slowly* through the office.

B Complete each of the following sentences by supplying, at the point marked by a question mark, the best descriptive word at your command.

1. These imported folding bicycles should appeal to ? buyers.
2. The "worldwide" cookbook we are preparing has ? recipes.
3. Her duties are more ? since her promotion.
4. It is ? to keep such detailed records of incoming mail.
5. As a sales executive, he is ?

C Match each word in Column I with a word or phrase from Column II which has a similar meaning.

I	II
a. reliable	1. happen again
b. stubborn	2. judge
c. procrastinate	3. minor
d. confirm	4. considerable
e. recur	5. allusion
f. goods	6. trustworthy
g. evaluate	7. put off
h. incidental	8. validate
i. reference	9. merchandise
j. precarious	10. illusion
	11. unsafe
	12. obstinate

D The verb *fix* is overused by many people, as are the adjectives *fine* and *good.* In the following phrases, substitute a precise word for *fix* and list substitute descriptive terms for *fine* and *good.*

1. fix the vending machine
2. a good meeting
3. a fine program
4. fix the letter
5. a good presentation
6. a fine supervisor
7. a good secretary
8. fix the broken space bar
9. a fine building
10. fix this error

E What words or phrases may be substituted for each of the following italicized expressions? For each expression, write a sentence using the word or phrase suggested.

1. a worker who never *leaves you in the lurch*
2. must stop *passing the buck*
3. get it done *somehow or other*
4. *ironing out the bugs* in our procedure
5. thought about *calling it quits*
6. he *gets on his high horse*
7. she *racked her brains*
8. he *sets no store by*
9. she *made short work of* it
10. likes to *toot her own horn*

F Write an antonym for each of the following words.

1. pedantic 2. sensitive 3. pretentious 4. courageous 5. sensational

EDITING PRACTICE

Picture-Making Words Rewrite these sentences, substituting an exact picture-making word for the italicized word or words in each item.

1. Her description of taking her nephew to the zoo was *funny*.
2. From the plane we had a *grand* view of the mountains.
3. Don't decide until you consider all *sides* of his offer.
4. A career in ecology requires *good* preparation.
5. Moving into our new building gave our morale a *big* boost.

CASE PROBLEM

The Uninformed Employees The Warner Paper Manufacturing Company makes cardboard boxes, as well as other paper products. The vice president in charge of production, Tom Stewart, saw a demonstration of a new machine that folds boxes more efficiently than the one now owned by the company. While this new machine would not reduce labor, it would do a better job of folding. Mr. Stewart decided to order the new machine on a trial basis. When the machine was delivered to the room where it would be used, it was not unpacked because the manufacturer's representative could not set it up until the following week. Of course, most of the employees noticed the box and could see from the markings on the crate that it was a new folding machine. Soon rumors began to spread that this new machine would replace many of the employees and that they had better start looking for new positions.

Within one week after the machine arrived, Bill Brown, the head supervisor, came to Tom Stewart and told him of the discontent arising in the department, all because of lack of information about the new machine. Bill emphasized that the employees had many reasonable questions about the machine and the effect it would have on their work.

1. Who should handle this problem—Bill Brown or Tom Stewart?
2. What can he tell the employees in order to allay their fears?
3. What should have been done to prevent this problem from occurring?

4 Spelling Improvement

A spelling error is like a hole in the paper, a grease stain on the page, an upside-down word, because it diverts the reader's attention from your message. Readers find spelling errors intrusive, a waste of their reading time. Your spelling errors also tell your readers this about you: You do not have sufficient regard for your readers to take the trouble to spell correctly for them.

We often base our judgments on our visual impressions. We label a man wearing a stained shirt as slovenly. We note a woman's wrinkled dress and think of her as sloppy. Perhaps you do not judge so hastily, but others might. Spelling errors may be just enough "visual evidence" to cause negative judgments about you and your company. The best course is to deprive your readers of that opportunity.

In business, your ability, or inability, to spell words correctly can affect your status and your job advancement. To overcome your spelling difficulties, you should study and apply the principles presented in this section. You will learn some guides to correct spelling, and you will be alert to the spelling pitfalls that make consulting a dictionary imperative.

GUIDES TO CORRECT SPELLING

Because there are so many variations in the spelling of English words, a writer must first know the principles that almost always hold true. Following are the basic guides to correct spelling. Every writer must know and be able to apply them.

Final *Y*

Many common nouns end in *y*: *baby, lady, company, attorney, monkey.* The spelling of the plurals of these common nouns depends on whether the *y* is preceded by a consonant or a vowel. If preceded by a consonant, the *y* is changed to *i* and *es* is added: *baby, babies; lady, ladies; company, companies.* If preceded by a vowel, only *s* is added: *attorney, attorneys; monkey, monkeys.*

Ei and *Ie* Words

Among the most frequently misspelled words are these: *believe, belief, deceive, deceit, perceive, conceive, conceit, receive, receipt, relieve,* and *relief.* The word *Alice* is a clue to their correct spelling. In *Alice* we see the combinations *li* and *ce*. These combinations can help you remember that the correct spelling after *l* is *ie* (*believe*); after *c*, *ei* (*receive*).

Endings *Ful, Ous, Ally, Ily*

To spell the endings *ful, ous, ally,* and *ily* correctly, a writer needs to know that:

The suffix *ful* has only one *l*: *careful, skillful, sorrowful.*

An adjective ending with the sound "us" is spelled *ous*: *glorious, gracious, monotonous, serious.*

The ending *ally* has two *l*'s: *incidentally, accidentally, usually.*

The ending *ily* has one *l*: *merrily, necessarily, readily.*

Doubling a Final Consonant

Knowing when to double and when not to double a final consonant is easy for the person who can determine the sound. The only aid needed is this: If the last syllable of the base word is accented, if the vowel sound in the last syllable is *short*, and if the suffix to be added begins with a vowel, double the final consonant.

compel	compelled, compelling	omit	omitted, omitting
equip	equipped, equipping	prefer	preferred, preferring
occur	occurred, occurrence, occurring	regret	regretted, regretting

In each of the following words, the accent is on the *first* syllable; therefore, in the preferred spelling, the final consonant is *not* doubled.

benefit	benefited, benefiting
cancel	canceled, canceling (*but* cancellation)
differ	differed, differing
equal	equaled, equaling
marvel	marveled, marveling, marvelous
travel	traveled, traveler, traveling

Words of One Syllable

If you can differentiate long and short sounds of vowels, you can determine whether or not to double the final consonant of a one-syllable word. If the vowel sound is long, do *not* double; if short, double the final consonant.

hope	hoping *(long vowel)*	hop	hopping *(short vowel)*
mope	moping *(long)*	mop	mopping *(short)*
plane	planing *(long)*	plan	planning *(short)*
pine	pining *(long)*	pin	pinning *(short)*

⊙ **CHECKUP 1** Correct any spelling errors in these sentences.

1. We are not permited to release the figures you requested.
2. Retailers have had a very successfull year.
3. Mr. Lynch's reference is not quite clear.
4. Unless we recieve your check by May 1, we must take legal action.
5. The strikers are hopping for an early settlement.
6. We hope your latest venture turns out satisfactorily.
7. Do you have all the supplys you need for this project?
8. Your action placed us in a most ridiculus position.

DICTIONARY "ALERTS"

Most good spellers do not pluck out of their memories the correct spelling of all words they write. They know where the spelling pitfalls lie and therefore are alert to the need for consulting a dictionary.

The most common spelling pitfalls are presented here so that you, too, will be alert to the tricky combinations that are the nemeses of so many writers. Remember: If you are not sure how to spell words containing these prefixes and suffixes, *use your dictionary.*

Word Beginnings

Words beginning with the prefixes *per, pur* and *ser, sur* present a spelling obstacle because they sound alike. If you are not absolutely certain of the correct spelling of any given word, check a dictionary. Study the following words:

perimeter	purloin	serpent	surmount
perplex	purpose	servant	surplus
persist	pursuit	service	surtax

Word Endings

The following groups of word endings are tricky because they have similar sounds or because they may be pronounced carelessly. The spellings of these endings, however, differ. Do not try to guess at spellings of words with the following ending sounds.

"Unt," "Uns" If these endings were always clearly enunciated as *ant, ance, ent, ence,* they would present no problem. However, because they are so often sounded "unt" and "uns" and because there are so many words with these endings, they are spelling danger spots. They must be spelled by eye, not by ear. Some common words having these endings are the following:

accountant	maintenance	incompetent	existence
defendant	perseverance	dependent	independence
descendant	remittance	permanent	interference
tenant	resistance	silent	violence

"Uhble," "Uhbility" The sound "uhble," which might be spelled *able* or *ible,* is another trap. The alert writer consults a dictionary in order to avoid misspelling this ending. Some common "uhble" and "uhbility" words are the following:

enjoyable	availability	collectible	flexibility
payable	capability	deductible	plausibility
receivable	mailability	reversible	possibility
returnable	probability	ineligible	visibility

"Shun," "Shus" Words ending in "shun" might be spelled *tion, sion,* or even *cian, tian, sian, cion,* or *xion.* The ending "shus" might be *cious* or *tious.* Learn the spelling of the words listed here, but at the same time, remember never to trust a "shun" or a "shus" ending.

audition	dietitian	conscious	complexion
collision	Caucasian	suspicious	conscientious
connection	suspension	technician	pretentious
ignition	suspicion	statistician	propitious

"Shul," "Shent" The ending that sounds like "shul" is sometimes spelled *cial* and sometimes *tial.* A "shent" ending might be *cient* or *tient.* Look at the following words and learn how they are spelled, but never take chances on the spelling of any word ending in "shul" or "shent."

artificial	essential	incipient	impatient
beneficial	partial	deficient	proficient
judicial	substantial	efficient	quotient

"Ize," "Kul" The ending "ize" might be spelled *ize, ise,* or even *yze (analyze).* A "kul" ending could be *cal* or *cle.* An expert writer, therefore, consults a dictionary for these word endings. Study the following "ize" and "kul" words:

apologize	advertise	identical	obstacle
criticize	enterprise	mechanical	particle
realize	improvise	statistical	spectacle
temporize	merchandise	technical	vehicle

Ar, Ary, Er, Ery, Or, Ory *Stationary* and *stationery* end with the same sound, but they are spelled differently. Words that end in *ar, ary, er, ery, or,* or *ory* should be recognized as spelling hazards; you should always verify each spelling. Memorize the spellings of the following words:

calendar	advertiser	debtor
customary	adviser	inventory
grammar	customer	realtor

"Seed" Although only a few words have "seed" endings, they are frequently written incorrectly because the ending has three different spellings. When studying the following list of "seed" words, memorize these facts: (1) The *only* word ending in *sede* is *supersede,* and (2) the *only* words ending in *ceed* are *exceed, proceed,* and *succeed.* All other "seed" words, then, must be spelled *cede.*

sede	**ceed**	**cede**	
supersede	exceed	accede	precede
	proceed	cede	recede
	(*but* procedure)	concede	secede
	succeed	intercede	

⊙ **CHECKUP 2** What is the correct spelling of the words in parentheses?

1. You are to (proseed) in accordance with the (preseeding) directions.
2. (Reversuhble) raincoats do double duty.
3. We are all prone to (critisize) public officials.
4. Bill's outstanding characteristic is his (perseveruns).
5. We are unable to grant you any (extenshun) of time.
6. Are those signatures (identikul)?

YOUR SPELLING VOCABULARY

Business writers cannot afford the time-consuming interruptions caused by verifying spellings too frequently. They must, therefore, be sure of the correct spellings of the words used most often in their communications.

The list of Words Often Misspelled (see the Appendix) will serve as a foundation for developing a good spelling vocabulary. But knowing how to spell these words requires more than memorization. You must analyze each word and fix in your mind its peculiarities, as illustrated by the analyses of the following twenty words.

accommodate (two *c*'s, two *m*'s)
aggressive (two *g*'s, two *s*'s)
believe (*ie*)
chief (*ie*)
convenient (*ven, ient*)
definite (*fi*)
develop (no final *e*)
embarrass (two *r*'s, two *s*'s)
forty, fortieth (only *four* words without *u*)
ninth (only *nine* word without *e*)
occasion (two *c*'s, one *s*)
occurred (two *c*'s, two *r*'s)
precede (*cede*)
privilege (*vile*)
proceed (*ceed*)
receive (*ei*)
recommend (one *c*, two *m*'s)
repetition (*pe*)
separate (*par*)
until (only one *l*)

Communication Projects

PRACTICAL APPLICATION

A Without using a dictionary, write the appropriate forms of the words enclosed in parentheses. Then check your answers in a dictionary.

1. Several rare (monkey) have been imported by the zoo.
2. Rising gold prices forced the (scrap) of expansion plans.
3. You will find thread, zippers, and other (sundry) in the Notions Department.
4. (Scrape) off the excess paint with a wet sponge is best.
5. He phoned me (incident), just after you left.
6. Your (defer)-payment plan is excellent.
7. Mirrors with (bevel) edges were missing from the June 8 shipment.
8. The (pulley) we ordered have not yet been delivered.
9. We think that your advertisement is (deceive) the public.
10. This is a most (moment) decision for us.
11. There is no substitute for (care) checking.
12. A correspondence consultant can make many (help) suggestions.
13. You would do well not to act too (hasty).
14. Your account is (pay) on the first of each month.
15. We did not intend that our statement be taken (literal).

B Make any spelling corrections needed in these sentences.

1. We plan to develope a list of sources for free travel posters.
2. Streamlining our proceedures will reduce overhead costs.
3. He did not realize that his humorous remarks would be taken seriously.
4. Applicants who are over fourty often feel at a disadvantage.
5. Confirmation of our accomodations at the ski lodge came today.
6. The speaker's mispronunciation of his name embarrassed my boss.
7. Make a list of the accounts that we consider uncollectible.
8. We recommend that you make a servay.
9. Eleanor is an exceptionally competant secretary.
10. All advertisers will be exhibitors at the boat show.
11. Mr. O'Brien's contention is that the expansion plans are not complete.
12. Please write the city and the state on seperate lines.
13. On file cards, the last name preceeds the first name.
14. Mr. Gray handles all our technicle problems.
15. Doing business with you is indeed a privelege.

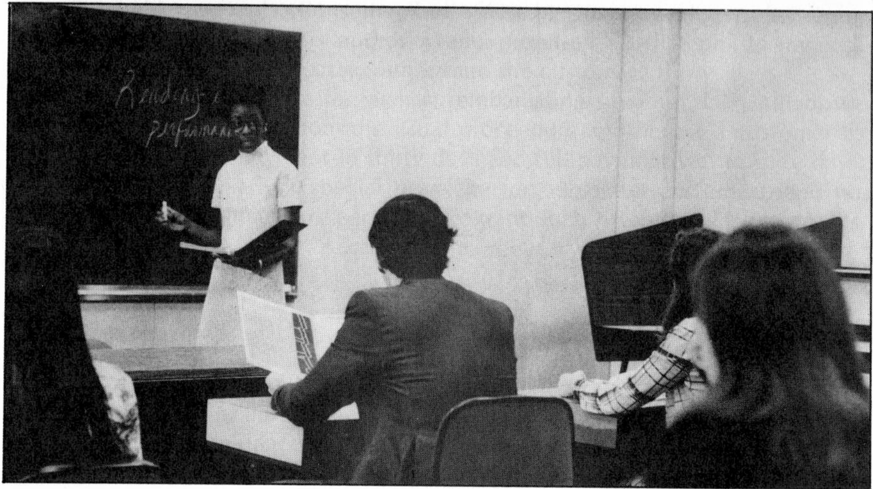

CHAPTER 2

RECEIVING COMMUNICATIONS

5 Developing Listening Skill

Communication is a two-way process—it is both the sending and the receiving of a message. Transmitting information is only half of the process; a message sent but not received has not been communicated. Reading and listening are the two most common ways of receiving communications; there can be no communication, of course, through a book or a letter if its message is not read and understood. Nor can there be communication when the speaker addresses the deaf or speaks in a language incomprehensible to the listener. In short, communication in any medium depends on the sender's ability to transmit a message and the receiver's ability to accept and comprehend it.

THE NEED FOR LISTENING SKILL

Most people recognize the importance of reading skill. However, surveys of communication habits reveal that *the majority of business people spend most of their communication time in listening.*[1] The average business employee spends approximately 70 percent of the workday in verbal communication, and nearly half of this time is spent in listening; however, research indicates that most of us listen with only about 25 percent efficiency.[2]

LISTENING AND THE BUSINESS WORKER

Since most of our communication time in business is spent in listening, it is important to be a skillful listener. Some business workers rely on listening skill for the success of their daily assignments; telephone operators, receptionists, and salesclerks lead the list. There are many others. Certainly every business worker—secretary, typist, accountant, machine operator, clerk—receives oral instructions and information from co-workers, superiors, and customers. Failure to listen properly can create misunderstanding, cause errors, waste time and money, and lessen goodwill. A survey by a retail-stores organization indicated that 68 percent of customers lost were lost because of indifferent salespeople—salespeople who probably did not listen to their customers' wishes.[3] Obviously, listening skill pays off.

ACTIVE VERSUS PASSIVE LISTENING

Listening can be active or passive. When we listen passively, we absorb just enough of the speaker's words to keep the conversation going. We can get by with passive listening in a casual conversation with friends, in a telephone

[1]William F. Keefe, *Listen, Management*, McGraw-Hill Book Company, New York, 1971, p. 9.

[2]Ralph G. Nichols and Leonard A. Stevens, *Are You Listening?* McGraw-Hill Book Company, 1957, pp. ix, 6, 8.

[3]*Ibid.*, pp. 167-168.

chat with a relative, or in a discussion while playing cards. In such situations, it may make little difference whether or not we actually hear and absorb every word. However, in the business office and in all other business settings, active listening is required.

Active listening means concentrating on what is being said, absorbing as much as possible, and participating mentally in what is heard. The listener participates by summarizing the speaker's words mentally while listening.

You must be able to determine when you must be an active listener. Will it be to your advantage to remember what is being said? Are the speaker's remarks likely to result in your taking some sort of action? If the answer to either of these questions is "Yes," you must listen actively. The salesclerk who must remember the customer's wishes, the bank teller who has been asked for certain denominations of bills, the airline reservation agent who asks where a traveler is going and when the traveler would like to arrive—all must listen actively.

HOW TO IMPROVE YOUR LISTENING SKILL

When we read we may occasionally lapse into a daydream, allowing our minds to wander from the page, even though our eyes may be riveted to it. When we listen, we may also find our concentration drifting and realize we are thinking of something else. In reading, we can return to the point where we left off. In listening, we cannot. It is too late.

The reasons we take these mental side trips may vary from person to person and from day to day, depending on our foremost thoughts of the day, the people we are trying to listen to, and so on. One common reason is that the average person speaks between 125 and 150 words a minute, but a good listener can comprehend about 300 words a minute.[4] Thus, it is easy for any listener's brain to take a nap occasionally.

But whatever the reasons for not listening, listening skill, like reading skill, can be improved. Reading-improvement programs, increasingly popular in recent years, are helping many people better their comprehension and increase their reading rate. Listening-improvement programs, too, are now being included in high school and in college courses and in employee-development programs.

Determine Your Listening Strengths and Weaknesses

The first step toward improving your listening skill is to determine your listening strengths and weaknesses. To start, answer the following questions; then use the answers to decide where to begin your self-improvement program.

1. Have you recently had your hearing acuity tested?
2. Do you avoid being distracted by outside sights and sounds when listening to someone speak?
3. Do you make it a point not to interrupt before a speaker finishes a thought?

[4]*Ibid.*, p. 78.

4. Do you avoid doing something else (reading, for example) at the same time you are trying to listen?
5. When people talk to you, do you concentrate on what they are saying, or do you permit yourself to take brain naps and mental excursions?
6. Do you listen for ideas and for feelings as well as for facts?
7. Do you look at the person who is talking to you?
8. Do you feel that other people have something to contribute to your knowledge?
9. If something is not clear to you, do you ask the speaker to repeat or to explain the point again?
10. Do you avoid being prejudiced by words and phrases used by the speaker?
11. When someone is talking to you, do you try to make the person think that you are paying attention even if you are not?
12. Can you tell by a person's appearance and delivery that whatever is said will not be of interest to you?
13. Do you turn your attention elsewhere when you believe a speaker will not have anything of interest to say to you?
14. Do you have to ask the speaker to repeat because you cannot remember what was said?
15. If you feel that it takes too much time and effort to understand something, do you try to avoid hearing it?

You should have answered "Yes" to the first ten questions and "No" to the last five questions. If you did not have a perfect score, perhaps the following suggestions can help you to begin your own listening-improvement program.

Develop the Proper Attitude Toward Listening

Listening is strictly a voluntary activity; no one can be forced to listen. The main purpose of a lecture or a class discussion is learning; the student who wants to learn listens. The stenographer who wants to record all the words of the dictator listens. And the supervisor who is eager to help employees solve their problems also listens. Every good listener tries to find something of interest in the speaker's message and attempts to sustain this interest. The supervisor who listens halfheartedly to employees' complaints doesn't really listen.

To be a good listener—to want to hear what the other person has to say—you must first respect the speaker and the speaker's right to have a point of view. Sometimes you will find it difficult to go along with ideas that are contrary to yours. Whether or not you should stick to your own point of view or change your thinking can be determined only after you have listened to what the speaker has to say. If you can learn the reasons for the ideas presented, you will be in a better position to make a decision. Such decisions may call for either changing your own thinking or influencing the thinking of the other person by showing specifically where his ideas or her ideas are factually inaccurate or illogical.

Finally, a good listener is objective about personalities and does not let mannerisms, voice, speech patterns, or other personality characteristics diminish what the speaker is saying. A good listener focuses attention on the *words* and *ideas* of the speaker rather than on the speaker's appearance or manner of speaking.

Prepare Yourself Physically for Effective Listening

Here are some suggestions you can easily follow in physically preparing yourself to listen effectively:

If you have difficulty hearing, have a doctor check your hearing acuity and suggest any necessary corrective measures.

Sit where the conditions for hearing will be best for you. If your mind wanders easily, try to find a place where you will not have visual or auditory distractions.

Look at the speaker while you are listening.

Have the seating arrangement and room ventilation as comfortable as possible.

Learn to recognize nonverbal forms of communication, such as the speaker's inflection, gestures, posture, and facial expressions.

Prepare Yourself Mentally for Effective Listening

An effective listener is mentally prepared to listen. This statement implies several things. The listener must understand what the speaker is saying. Therefore, the listener must have a vocabulary that includes not only words in general usage but also words common to the trade. One unfamiliar word can mean that the listener will not understand the whole message or will incorrectly interpret all or part of the message. For example, a secretary asked an office clerk to bring a *ream* of typewriting paper. The office clerk did not know the meaning of the word *ream*—all the packages in the supply room were marked "500 Sheets"—and had to go back to the secretary to ask what *ream* meant. An efficient listener should, if possible, ask a speaker to explain unfamiliar words. However, if such interruptions are frequent, the listener may be embarrassed.

The efficient listener prepares for attending a lecture or a speech by reading about the topic so as to listen better and to derive greater benefit from the speaker's message.

Many words in the English language have multiple meanings, and the efficient listener realizes that it isn't always possible to know which of several meanings the speaker intends. For example, a secretary may be requested to *duplicate* a letter. Of course, a letter may be duplicated by using carbon paper, by photocopying, or by running off copies on a fluid or a stencil duplicator. To make certain of the intention of the speaker, a good listener should ask questions rather than make assumptions that may be incorrect. By asking either "Is this what you mean?" or "Did I understand you correctly?" the listener avoids problems of misinterpretation. The secretary in the example above should have asked a question such as, "Would you like five photocopies?"

Develop Habits That Contribute to Effective Listening

Skill in any activity is based on acquiring habits that contribute to the development of that skill. A skilled typist develops correct habits of sitting, key stroking, and reaching, among others. A skilled swimmer practices correct habits of movement and breathing. So, too, the effective listener must develop habits that contribute to improving listening skill. What do these habits include?

Ability to concentrate
Alertness in grasping ideas
Ability to coordinate ideas
Ability to take notes when necessary

Concentrating Because the typical listener can comprehend at a much faster rate than most speakers talk, the listener frequently has difficulty in concentrating and, as a result, "tunes out" the speaker. The listener daydreams, relaxes, and notes all distractions, such as noises and movements. A distracted listener, therefore, can become too hopelessly confused to "tune in" again, having lost part of what has been said. Concentration, therefore, requires discipline and sustained, undivided attention. What, then, *should* you be doing during the time when your mind is waiting for the speaker's words to catch up to it?

Grasping Ideas When you listen, try to think along with the speaker and to recognize the main points of the message. Take an essential idea, fact, or piece of information and rephrase it mentally in your own words. This process will help you to understand and to remember what you hear. For example, the following selection demonstrates what you might be thinking while the speaker is talking.

What the Speaker Is Saying	What You Are Saying to Yourself
I have read many books on selling. There are books that bring up every possible selling situation and give you ways and means to meet those situations—several hundred of them perhaps. But when you get in the presence of a prospect, you cannot recall any of them. However, you *can* remember this formula: ask yourself the simple question, "Just what does this prospect *want*?" If you cannot find out any other way, ask him. It is often that simple. Too many salesmen think they must do *all* of the talking. Avoid it. Listen at least half the time and ask questions. It is only in this way you can uncover unsatisfied wants.[5]	You can't memorize ways of meeting every selling situation presented in books. You should find out what the prospect wants. Ask him what he wants, if necessary. You don't need to do all the talking—listen half the time and ask questions.

As you hear each idea presented, weigh it in terms of its validity. To yourself, you might ask and answer such questions as "What has this to do with me?" "Are things exactly as the speaker says?" "Is anything left out? If so why?" "How can I use this material?" "Why is the speaker pounding the table?" "Has the speaker confused solid evidence with emotionalism?" "Is the illustration typical, or is it an exaggerated example?" "Is the illustration out of date and no longer applicable?"

When the speaker takes time to move from one point to another, review mentally what was said. In this way, you can improve both your comprehen-

[5]William Phillips Sandford and Willard Hayes Yeager, *Effective Business Speech*, McGraw-Hill Book Company, New York, 1960, p. 176.

sion and your retention of the message while keeping your mind from wandering.

Another way to use extra listening time is to think ahead and to anticipate what the speaker is going to say next. If you select a point that is actually made by the speaker, you will remember it longer. If you select a point that the speaker does not make, you can compare the speaker's point with the one you selected. In this way, you will learn by comparison and contrast.

Coordinating Ideas Besides perceiving the speaker's main idea, try to coordinate ideas and information that contribute to the main idea. For example, read the speech excerpt below. Note that only the first sentence, the italicized words, is part of the main idea. The other sentences are not separate ideas but are sidelights that add color, interest, and details to the main idea.

> *One of the major cost factors in operating a modern business office is absenteeism and tardiness.* For instance, if an office with one thousand employees averages fifty absences a month and the average daily rate of pay is $25, the company loses $1,250 a month or $15,000 a year. Such a loss takes a big bite out of company profits.

In this paragraph, notice the words *For instance*. Speakers often provide the listener with cues that indicate whether an idea is a new one or whether it merely adds support to an idea already presented. *For instance* tells us that what follows will support an idea already presented.

Note-Taking In many instances, the listener must take notes in order to retain the information for future reference. The student who attends a lecture, the secretary who takes a telephone message, and the accountant who receives a set of oral instructions from the head accountant are but a few examples of people who must take notes as they listen. Taking notes is actually an extension of active listening participation and consists of putting on paper, in your own words, the essential ideas and information provided by the speaker. Do not spend too much time taking notes, or you will miss the heart of the message. Never attempt to take verbatim notes. Proper note-taking can contribute to effective concentration, to learning, and to remembering. Here are some suggestions for taking notes:

1. Prepare in advance by reading as much as you can about the subject on which you are to hear someone speak.
2. Sit in a location where you can hear and see without strain.
3. Come equipped for note-taking with plenty of notepaper, a good pen, and an extra pencil or two.
4. Use a firm, uncluttered writing surface.
5. Label your notes so that you can identify them later without difficulty.
6. Listen for such speaker's cues as "first," "second," and "third"; "another important consideration"; "finally"; "the most significant thing"; "on the other hand"; "in summary"; as well as questions posed by the speaker, pauses, voice intonations, and gestures.
7. Flag important parts of your notes with brackets, underscores, arrows, or indentions.
8. Listen for special instructions.
9. Read over your notes promptly after the speech.

Efficient listening, like efficient reading, requires practice. Take every opportunity to practice the suggestions just given. Remember that to listen successfully, you must concentrate, review mentally what has been said, coordinate ideas, and take notes.

Communication Projects

PRACTICAL APPLICATION

A Reexamine the questions used to determine your listening strengths and weaknesses (pages 47–48). Indicate the reason for the "Yes" or "No" answer to each question.

B Your instructor will read a selection to you. Listen very carefully, but do not take notes. After the reading, your instructor will ask you to answer several questions about the selection.

C A good listener is able to distinguish facts from opinions. On a separate sheet of paper indicate which of the following statements are opinions and which are "facts."

1. The film we saw on pollution control was very thought-provoking.
2. He was offered $500 for his old car.
3. The owner of a car parked on the street after midnight is likely to be given a parking ticket.
4. A girl with red hair should never wear pink.
5. Some service stations are limiting gasoline sales to their customers.
6. Your choice of a Nu-Day home freezer is the wisest decision you ever made.
7. We will have fun at the party this weekend.
8. This clock will run for 40 hours without rewinding.
9. No other typewriter has such a beautiful design as this one.
10. They will have a wonderful time at the family reunion.

D Your instructor will give you a set of directions. Listen to them very carefully but take no written notes. You will then follow the directions given.

E List twenty words that affect you emotionally by evoking such feelings as pleasure, sadness, satisfaction, or horror. Be prepared to discuss the following questions.

1. Why do certain words emotionally affect individuals?
2. Why might words of this type have different connotations to different people?

F Your instructor will give you directions for an exercise to determine the span of your listening attention.

EDITING PRACTICE

Contextually Speaking Some of the following sentences contain words that are out of context. Correct each sentence that contains a contextually incorrect word. Write *OK* for any correct sentence.

1. The alleged murderer is to be arranged in court next Monday.
2. He accused the company of infringing his patent rights.
3. Any discrimination of confidential information is prohibited.
4. Our fund-raising plans required the continued corporation of everyone.
5. Personality is a very important fact in securing and holding a job.

CASE PROBLEM

The Careless Clerk Tom Williams was a reservation clerk for Westcoast Airlines. One afternoon he answered the telephone in his customary fashion by asking, "May I help you?" He was told that Mrs. Roberta Powell would like to make reservations on a flight to Seattle, Washington, that would get her there in time for a 5 p.m. dinner meeting with a very important client. Tom checked the flight bookings for the date and time requested and found that the only space he had available was on a flight leaving at 7 a.m. the same day. There was a 2:10 p.m. flight, arriving in Seattle at 4:15 p.m., but there was no space available. Mrs. Powell had a meeting to attend that morning and could not leave before noon.

Tom said he would put Mrs. Powell's name on the waiting list for the 2:10 flight and would notify her if there were any cancellations. He told Mrs. Powell that there was a good chance of getting a seat on the 2:10 flight, since her name would be the first one on the waiting list. Mrs. Powell thought this arrangement would be fine, gave Tom the necessary information about contacting her, and hung up. Just as soon as Tom hung up, the customer standing in front of him started asking for information regarding other flights, and Tom neglected to record Mrs. Powell's name on the proper waiting list.

When Mrs. Powell had not received any word regarding her reservation by the day preceding the flight, she asked her secretary to check with the airline office. The clerk who answered the telephone referred to the waiting list but, of course, did not find Mrs. Powell's name among the nine or ten names listed. Because there were so many names already on the waiting list, it was extremely doubtful whether more than the first two or three could be accommodated on that flight. When Mrs. Powell heard the news from her secretary, she became extremely angry and telephoned the general manager of Westcoast Airlines to register her complaint.

1. Was Mrs. Powell justified in her complaint? Why or why not?
2. What should the general manager say to Mrs. Powell in an attempt to smooth out the situation?
3. What advice should the general manager give to Tom Williams?

6 Developing Reading Skill

The inability to read would be too limiting a handicap for anyone entering business to even contemplate. Because reading is so fundamental a part of daily life, perhaps we sometimes take reading skill for granted. Actually, like most other skills, reading skill can be developed. Proficiency in reading is a prerequisite for anyone entering a business career. For example, to succeed in business, a typist must be able to read copy accurately and rapidly. A secretary requires reading skill to proofread typed letters. An executive requires excellent reading skill to cope with a seemingly endless stream of letters, reports, periodicals, and books. An accountant needs reading skill to check one set of figures against another. A supervisor or a manager must read countless status reports, forms, memos, schedules, evaluations, and requisitions.

Your reading skill directly affects how well and how rapidly you understand written communications and how successful you will be on the job. It would be difficult to overestimate the importance of reading as a communication skill. The guides presented in this section will help you improve your reading skill.

ELEMENTS OF READING SKILL

Two elements make up reading skill—speed and comprehension. How fast you are able to read will determine how much material you can cover in the time you can devote to reading. As a student, you have often been required to read a great deal for your courses. The slow reader must spend every evening and many hours on weekends to cover all the assigned reading—and still may not be able to complete it all! The fast reader would undoubtedly have time left over for personal pleasure and relaxation.

The business worker is paid for producing, whether what is produced is a typewritten business letter or a decision to establish a branch store in Kalamazoo. Therefore, the worker cannot devote the entire working day to reading only, no matter how important the reading matter may be. And, of course, the more a business worker can read and absorb, the more information is available for making decisions or performing a particular task.

Even more important than speed is comprehension, understanding what you read. Regardless of how fast you read, if you don't comprehend what you are reading, you achieve nothing. Therefore, you must fully understand the meanings of the words used and the implications of the thoughts expressed by the writer.

Do you fully comprehend the material that you read? Or does a poor vocabulary or improper reading habits block your ability to receive accurately the message conveyed? Unless you can answer "Yes" to the first question and "No" to the second, you should improve your reading skill. Any improvement you make will contribute to your success as a business worker.

Is it too late to improve your reading skill? Not if you are willing to work at it. Many people have vastly improved both their reading speed and their comprehension through reading-improvement courses offered by schools, by business organizations, and by private institutes devoted specifically to reading improvement. Those who have serious reading deficiencies or those who wish to make great strides in reading improvement should enroll in one of these organized programs. However, there are several things you can do on your own to improve your reading skill.

GUIDES TO READING IMPROVEMENT

Study the following four-step program for improving your reading skill.

Check Physical Factors

The condition of your eyes plays an important role in reading effectiveness. You should have your eyes checked regularly by a competent eye specialist, particularly if you wear glasses or show any signs of difficulty, such as blurred vision, smarting eyes, or the need to hold copy either very close to your eyes or at arm's length.

Lighting conditions also affect the ease with which you read. Natural light, of course, is preferred. The best artificial light for reading is an indirect light. In either case, the light should fall on the copy, not on your eyes, and there should be no glaring or shiny spots anywhere near you.

For the best reading conditions, you should sit comfortably in a well-ventilated, not overheated room. The room should be free of distracting sights and sounds.

Whether or not you wear glasses, you should practice good eye hygiene. Here are some suggestions:

Rest your eyes every half hour or so either by looking into the distance or by closing them for a few minutes.

Exercise your eyes, especially when you are doing close work and your eyes begin feeling tired. One good exercise for strengthening the eye muscles is to rotate the eyeballs slowly without moving your head. Try to see far to the right; then to the left; then up; and finally, down.

Avoid reading when you are in bright sunlight or while you are riding in a vehicle.

Have eye injuries or sties attended to immediately by a physician.

Adjust Reading Rate to Material and Purpose

You should adjust your reading speed to the material you are reading and to your purpose for reading it.

Reading for Pleasure If you are reading novels, magazine articles, newspaper items, and the like, you do not need to absorb every detail or remember many specific facts. Therefore, you should be able to read quite rapidly, at a rate of around 400 words a minute.

Reading for Specific Data When you are looking for a specific name, date, or other item of information, you should be able, by skimming a page, to locate the item without reading every word. When you wish to determine the principal ideas in reading matter, perhaps in order to decide whether or not to read it, skim each page and stop only to read significant phrases.

Reading for Retention or Analysis This kind of reading includes textbook reading or other study reading requiring either the memorization of facts or a thorough understanding of the meaning so that you can interpret, explain, or apply it to other situations. Reading for retention or analysis calls for active participation by the reader and may require a slower reading rate. Active participation in reading is discussed on page 58.

Copying and Checking This kind of reading includes proofreading typewritten or printed copy, checking invoices, copying material to prepare punched cards or tapes, and so on. Such reading must be carefully done, with full concentration and attention to meaning and accuracy. One undetected error may be very costly. Unless the following were read for meaning, the error would not be discovered.

> The principle of $324 must be paid by January 5. (*Principal* is the proper word.)

Checking one copy against another or one column of figures against another calls for a high degree of concentration, for one must read and compare two sets of items.

Increase Reading Speed

How rapidly you should read depends upon the type of material you are reading and the purpose for which you are reading. Most "light" reading should be read at the rate of at least 400 words a minute. Most studying and other serious reading should be read at the rate of at least 200 to 250 words a minute. Here are six suggestions for helping you improve your reading speed.

Add to Your Vocabulary Enlarging your vocabulary will help you read faster and understand better. You will not need to stop to look up word meanings so often, and you will not be so likely to misinterpret the meaning that is intended of a word that has many shades of meaning.

Read in Thought Units Read in thought units rather than word by word. Remember that all words are not of equal importance. Develop your visual span by forcing your eyes to take in more words at each pause. With fewer pauses on each line of print, you naturally read faster. For example, read the following lines:

1. t m l q w z
2. books chair driver down
3. read in thought units

Certainly you had no difficulty in reading each of these lines, but each succeeding line should have been read faster. In the first line, you had to read individual letters; in the second, you read individual words; but in the third, your eyes could encompass and read the whole phrase with one glance.

You should be able to read a line in a newspaper column with only one or two eye pauses and to read a book-width line with not more than four or five pauses. Read the following sentence, and notice the difference in speed when you read word by word and when you read in thought units.

Word by Word	Good / readers / are / more / likely / to / understand / and / remember / what / they / read / if / they / actively / participate / in / what / they / are / reading.
Phrases	Good readers / are more likely / to understand and remember / what they read / if they actively participate / in what they are reading.

Keep Your Eyes Moving From Left to Right Do not allow yourself to go back and read a phrase a second time. These backward movements of the eyes, called *regressions,* slow the reader and are often habit-forming. Force yourself to concentrate and to get the meaning of a phrase the first time. To do so demands practice, discipline, and the elimination of all distractions that might interfere with your reading.

Avoid Vocalization Don't spell or pronounce the words you are reading, not even silently. Such vocalization limits you to reading only as fast as you can read aloud.

Read Only Word Beginnings Many words can be identified by reading only the beginnings. For example, you can easily identify the complete words, from these first syllables: *remem—, sepa—, funda—, educa—.* You can tell from the rest of the sentence what the exact ending of each word should be; for example, *remembering, remembrance; separate, separately, separation: He remem—* (*remembered*) *how to sepa—* (*separate*) *the parts.*

Practice Rapid Reading By exercising your willpower and by continually practicing rapid reading, you are certain to increase your reading speed. Reading, like any other skill, will improve with proper practice.

Improve Reading Comprehension

Even more important than reading speed to the student and business worker are comprehension (understanding) and retention (remembering). Many of the suggestions made for increasing reading speed will also contribute to greater comprehension. Some additional aids follow.

Scan or Preview the Material Look over the material to be read, noting the main headings and subheadings, looking at illustrations, and reading captions and numbered portions. This preliminary survey will help you determine your purpose in reading, and it will also help reinforce the important points you want to remember.

Participate Actively in Your Reading Try to relate what you are reading to what you already know. Keep in mind the problem you wanted to solve when you started to read. Concentrate!

Study all the illustrations—the pictures, graphs, and charts—and read the footnotes; all are designed to further explain and amplify the main ideas. Pay special attention to the author's examples; they have been specifically added to clarify ideas and to help the reader remember.

Take Notes If you own the book or magazine you are reading, you may wish to underline or otherwise mark key words or phrases. You may also want to make marginal notes. If the publication is not yours, you may take notes in a notebook that you can refer to later.

How do you select the essential material for note-taking? Just record main ideas and related ideas. Never take verbatim notes, even if you know shorthand.

How do you find the main ideas? Usually, writers convey only one idea per paragraph. Often this main idea is in the first sentence, but sometimes it may be in the last sentence. Occasionally there may be two central ideas expressed in a key phrase or sentence within the paragraph. If you have difficulty finding a central idea, you may need to read the paragraph carefully two or three times. In addition to the central idea, you should also note facts, examples, and other ideas that explain, support, and develop the main idea.

Reread and Review How often you reread or review material will depend on its difficulty and on the use you plan to make of it. Often a quick skimming or rereading of your notes will be adequate for review if the first reading was done carefully.

If you will follow the suggestions made in this section and immediately begin a definite plan for reading improvement, you will find that not only will you be able to read more in the same amount of time, but you will also get more from what you read.

Communication Projects

PRACTICAL APPLICATION

A To test your reading speed, have someone time you with a stopwatch (or a watch with a second hand) as you read the following selection.

Hot-rodders were once a menace to safety on the public highways, but most of them have now become both respectable and well respected for their help to other motorists. As a sport, hot-rodding got off to a hazardous start in the forties, when old cars were made into steel rams and the young drivers collected dents the way the outlaws used to collect notches on their guns. Some aimed their rolling junk heaps at one and all, and even at each other. A driver who might flinch from a collision was called a quitter. It was a bad nightmare, and it was getting worse until, at last, parents and their friends got excited and began corrective actions.

One step taken in some towns was to set up, on a local airfield, a drag strip where hot-rodders could hold driving contests and exhibits. Civic leaders in some cities formed clubs at whose meetings young drivers could get help in the mechanics of building and driving a hot rod safely; some of the clubs issued neat plaques for the cars of members. Fine new magazines, with as much stress on safety and on service to stranded motorists as on the inventing of new paint jobs and body angles, caused interest in the sport to jump ahead and did much at the same time to attract many of the finest young drivers into a legion of Sir Galahads of the highway.

But the fate of our hot-rodders is a question mark for the future. Each time there is a driving discourtesy or an accident involving a young driver, fuel is lent to the fury of those who feel that hot-rodding is a hazard, that it expands to the danger point the ego of its fans, that it must be suppressed. Yet there are others who believe this sport can be kept safe and useful and that it should be developed further. They protest that it is not fair to criticize the entire field for the bad judgment of a few mavericks. They point proudly to the thousands of "wreckless" young drivers who star in the campaign to bring courtesy back into motoring and who know infinitely more than most of their dads do about what goes on under the hood of the modern automobile.[6] (380 words)

Note how long you took to read the selection above. Check your reading speed with the following chart. For example, if you read the above paragraphs in one minute, your reading speed is 380 words per minute; if it took you two minutes, your speed is 190 words per minute.

30 seconds	760 wpm	2½ minutes	152 wpm
1 minute	380 wpm	3 minutes	127 wpm
1½ minutes	253 wpm	3½ minutes	109 wpm
2 minutes	190 wpm	4 minutes	95 wpm

B One good reading habit that will help you gain speed is to look only at the beginnings of familiar words rather than at the entire words. Test your ability to do this by reading as rapidly as possible the following paragraph, in which the endings of some familiar words have been omitted.

The right atti__ makes all the diff__ in the out__ expres__ of your pers__: atti__ toward your work, tow__ your co__, tow__ your emp__, tow__ life in gen__. You reveal your atti__ tow__ people in the way you resp__ to sugg__. You can reject them in a self-righ__, almost indig__ manner. Or you can adopt an indiff__, "don't care" atti__. These are both neg__ resp__. The pos__ resp__ is to accept sugg__ and crit__ thought__ and graciously. Then you can act upon them acc__ to your best judg__, with resul__ self-impr__.

[6]John L. Rowe et al., *Vocational Office Typing*, 191 Series Edition, Book Two, McGraw-Hill Book Company, New York, 1967, p. 20.

C Secretaries, typists, clerical workers, copy editors, and advertising copywriters must learn how to proofread carefully. Proofreading calls for the reading of each word not only for spelling but also for its meaning within the sentence. Proofread the following letter, and on a separate sheet of paper make a list of all the errors. Then rewrite the letter so that it is free from error.

> In accordance with our telephone conservation, we are senting you corected specifacations. Note that instalation of a two-way comunication systems is now required. Also, the thermastat is to be re-located to the upstair hall.
>
> Please send us your revise bid propperly typed on your company stationary, not latter then Oct. 1.

D Checking amounts of money and other figures often results in errors because of reading carelessness. Compare the following two lists. Indicate which pairs of items do not agree.

List A	List B
1. 838754B	838754B
2. 2243887	2243387
3. $4697.54	$46979.54
4. 6833T79	6833T79
5. SM178871	SM178187
6. 654V133	645V133
7. WTRZK	WTZRK
8. January 17, 1946	January 17, 1964
9. 115 dozen at 61¾¢	115 dozen at 63¼¢
10. T168V142L987	T168V142L897

EDITING PRACTICE

Digesting a Letter Secretaries and administrative assistants often read all incoming letters for their employers. When employers are especially busy, they may ask their assistants or secretaries to prepare a short digest (or summary) of each letter so that they won't have to read the entire message. Using incomplete sentences, write a digest of the following letter.

> Gentlemen:
>
> Your check for $868 is overdue in payment of additional repairs we have already completed in the remodeling of your offices.
>
> You will remember that when we found structural weakness in the corridor walls, we pointed this out to you as a violation of the building code. You authorized us to proceed with the necessary strengthening of the walls. We did so and notified you that the additional charges totaled $868, which was not covered in the original contract.
>
> May we have your check by return mail.
>
> Very truly yours,

CASE PROBLEM

The Talkative Visitor Sally Bowman is a receptionist and switchboard operator at the Lincoln Electrical Supply Company. One afternoon Michael Graham, who had an appointment to discuss a new product with Sally's boss, arrived at the office. However, because Sally's boss was in conference and would not be available for about ten minutes, Sally asked Mr. Graham to be seated until her boss was free. For a minute or two, Mr. Graham thumbed through one of the magazines lying on the table in the reception room. Then he started talking to Sally, who was not occupied at the switchboard that moment. Soon, however, the board lit up, but Mr. Graham continued talking to Sally. The flashing of the lights indicated that the calling parties were getting impatient because of the delay, but Sally did not know how to get Mr. Graham to stop talking to her so that she could attend to her duties.

1. What could Sally say to Mr. Graham so that he would not be offended when she interrupted him?
2. Suppose Mr. Graham continued talking. What should Sally do?

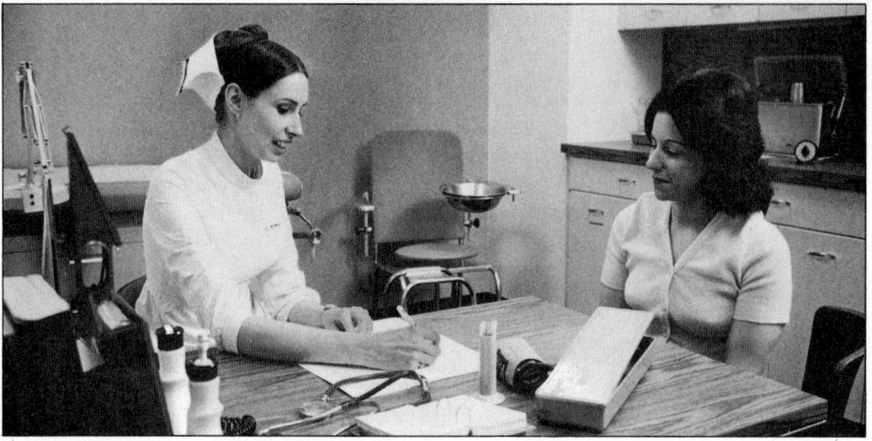

CHAPTER 3 LANGUAGE STRUCTURE

7 These Changing Times

Over the past forty or fifty years advances in technology have so changed American business and industry that progress in these areas seems revolutionary. The nation's economic progress reflects these changes too—and will probably do so for some time to come.

An astonishing number of new devices and methods serve us in business and industry. For example, only a generation or two ago, accountants did computations in their heads and recorded them in longhand. When the first calculators appeared on the market, they were considered the ultimate aids to accurate and rapid reckoning. Today, computers of the most awesome intricacy perform the most complex computations; tomorrow, further advancements in computer wizardry will be applied.

Great changes have also taken place in transportation, in mass communication, in service professions, in food packaging and distribution, in pollution control, and in many other fields. Teenagers have grown up with changes that seem miraculous to the older generation, such as faster and faster planes capable of carrying more and more passengers and freight. "Live by Satellite" television enables people to see programs from foreign countries while those events are taking place.

Without communication, however, there can be no progress. Every change, no matter how slight, is dependent on language—writing, speaking, reading, listening. You can readily understand that providing new safety features in an automobile, for instance, requires more than blueprints. Numerous letters and reports must be written; whatever is written must be read and studied; frequent conferences must be held. And when you consider that planning is concerned with marketing as well as with manufacturing the product, the number and kinds of communications almost overwhelm the imagination.

Logically, then, we must expect that language itself has changed with these changing times, and it has. Whenever you hear the term *standard English*, you will know it refers to the clear, but also correct, English used by expert modern communicators.

STANDARD ENGLISH

Changes are worthwhile only when they serve a purpose—producing better goods more quickly, reducing the margin of error, promoting efficiency, building goodwill, and so on. Consequently, we can assume that there are good reasons for any changes made in the English language.

The assumption is correct. The purpose of standard English, the language of today, is to ensure the utmost clarity and accuracy in communication.

Achieving this purpose will increase profits by saving the time and money wasted on messages that confuse a listener or reader. Communicating clearly and accurately not only prevents incidents that cause ill will but also helps to build goodwill.

If you will read thoughtfully the following discussion of standard English, you will know what it is—and what it is *not*.

Outdated Usage

Some of the English principles that were taught early in this century are no longer a part of our English courses—and with good reason. Some of these principles required learning many rules for alternate usages, but the differences were so unimportant that insistence on learning and following these rules fell into the category of "nitpicking." Because the intelligent mind rejects any unnecessary learning burden, the rules for unimportant differences were forgotten, and the words whose usages they governed were used interchangeably.

As an illustration, consider the use of *shall* and *will*. The writer of today does not have to stop to review rules before deciding which is correct—"*Shall* (or *Will*) you attend the banquet on Friday?" Furthermore, if you received a letter containing the question "Shall you attend the banquet on Friday?" the *shall* would strike you as being a little stilted. Yet, according to one out-of-style rule, *shall* would be the correct choice for this particular question.

There are other rules that are also now out of style; for instance, this rule: "Do not use the apostrophe and *s* to form the possessive of inanimate things; use an *of* phrase." Applying this rule would mean that the title *Nation's Business* is incorrect and must be written *The Business of the Nation*. Observing this apostrophe rule would destroy the effectiveness, the pungency, of much of our writing. We would have to write "The secretary of today has challenging job opportunities," instead of the smoother and more forceful "Today's secretary has challenging job opportunities."

In the Twilight Zone

Just as each day has a period that is neither night nor day, but somewhere between, so are there English principles that are in the process of changing from "definitely incorrect" to "well, maybe," and in time the change may very well be considered "correct." Their place in the Twilight Zone is dictated by common usage, which means their increasing use by educated persons.

Changes in the English language, however, take place very slowly; it may be many years before common usage is universal enough to promote any principle to the status of being correct. In the meantime, a knowledgeable communicator conforms to a common-usage trend only when such conformity suits an audience or when it accomplishes some clear purpose.

Using the preposition *like* for the conjunction *as* is a prime example of a Twilight Zone principle. As you probably know, a conjunction, not a preposition, must be used to introduce a clause; yet frequently you hear or read such expressions as these: "*like* I said before," "*like* you did yesterday," "*like* it was going to rain." Although quite commonly heard, the use of *like* for *as* is not universally accepted, as witness the nationwide storm of criticism that arose when a leading tobacco company used as part of its slogan "*like* a cigarette should" instead of "*as* a cigarette should." Most interesting is the thought that the protesters provided an enormous amount of free advertising, though many of the protesters probably made the same mistake in their own everyday speech.

A lesson to be learned here is that a Twilight Zone expression might pass unnoticed when used orally, but that the same expression when written could expose the writer to censure.

Nonstandard English

Do not let the preceding discussion lead you into thinking that, as far as English usage is concerned, "Anything goes." While it is true that some principles are no longer in use and that other principles may be in the process of change, it is also true that a standard of quality in English usage does exist.

In fact, the business world puts a premium on the ability to write and speak standard English. Why? Well, a business writer or speaker wants the readers or audience to pay attention to the message, not to its grammar. Hence standard English, the usage customarily associated with business communication, is the usage that is the least likely to attract attention to itself. Mastery of standard English, therefore, is a key factor to success in business.

YOU AND YOUR ENGLISH

Your college training will be an advantage when you are applying for a position and whenever you are considered for an on-the-job promotion. Remember, though, that a high quality of performance will be expected of you.

Communication of all kinds—speaking, writing, listening, or reading—will play an important part in your job performance. Since the basis of all communication is language, the excellence of your performance will depend to a great extent on your command of the English language.

The language-structure presentation in this chapter will provide you with a solid foundation in modern English usage. You will not study principles that have fallen into disuse. Twilight Zone principles will be pointed out to you, and you may wish to use them in *informal* writing or speech. Your *formal* communication efforts, however, must be presented in standard English.

To paraphrase the objective of a leading newspaper, "All the News That's Fit to Print," this chapter teaches "All the Language Principles You Need to Know."

Communication Projects

PRACTICAL APPLICATION

A In the following paragraphs, see whether you can spot any instances of substandard English. If you do, write your corrections. This exercise previews the points of grammar that will be discussed in Sections 8 to 21.

1. We were sorry to learn of the inconvenience you was caused by our being out of stock of the Paul Revere stainless steel cutlery we had advertised. Our salesclerk should have offered to take your order at the sale price and to notify you when the new stock is received. Each of our customers are important to us. Please give us the opportunity soon to serve you more satisfactory.
2. The procedure for returning unsold consignment items are confusing. Yet all of we sales supervisors are expected to interpret all of them rules to our staffs. I request, therefore, that we have a meeting to clarify these procedure.
3. Thank you very much for the courtesy you showed Mr. Hill and I during our visit to your office on June 3. Installing a Telefax in our plant would involve a great deal of money, and we felt that we must be sure of its value to our particular operation before considering such a step. The opportunity of seeing your Telefax and its picture-sending advantages was of real help to us, and we come away with much valuable information.

B Correct any spelling errors you find here.

Thanks for your note of comendation about my proposals for next year's convention. As our plans develope, I will keep you informed.

EDITING PRACTICE

The Right Word in the Right Place The words *complete, operation, further,* and *running* are used in the following letter, but are they used in the right places? Rewrite the letter and, if these words are not in the right places, put them where they belong.

Gentlemen:

Last January we sold you one of our Rapid Knitting machines. We guarantee our machines, for we know that they are in perfect operation condition when they leave our factory. We presume that your machine is giving further satisfaction.

We should be grateful to you, however, for filling out the enclosed blank form. You will note that the form asks for details about the running of the machine. If you have complete details or if you have any remarks, please write them on the back of the form.

Very sincerely yours,

CASE PROBLEM

Embarrassing Moment Raymond Mullins belongs to one of the local civic clubs and attends its meetings regularly. During the social hour at one of the meetings, one of his best customers greets Mr. Mullins by name. However,

Mr. Mullins has to return the greeting without mentioning the customer's name—he cannot remember it. During the conversation with the customer, another member of the organization, Frank Whelan, approaches both men. "Hello, Ray; it's good to see you again—and I'd like to welcome your guest to our meeting." Now Mr. Mullins must introduce the two men, and he still cannot remember the name of the customer whom Frank Whelan has mistaken for his guest.

1. What should Mr. Mullins say?
2. What might the customer have said, when he first appeared, to protect Mr. Mullins from being embarrassed?
3. What is a good way to remember names?

8 The Sentence

The sentence is the thought unit with which writers or speakers express themselves. Quite possibly the writer may be able to identify nouns, verbs, and other parts of speech. The writer may also know the principal parts of verbs, the case forms of pronouns, the rules governing parallel construction, and many other pertinent details. This knowledge is worthless, however, unless it effectively expresses the writer's thoughts, ideas, and convictions. Effective expression can be achieved only through the medium of the sentence. Logically, then, a review of the mechanics of communication should start with the sentence.

The topics presented in this section, although few in number, are important because their correct usage lays the foundation for both written and oral communication.

DEFINITION

The traditional definition of a sentence, "A sentence is a group of words expressing a complete thought," cannot be improved upon. However, because so many people write sentence fragments instead of complete sentences, the following Memory Hook is presented as an aid to immediate understanding and correct application of the definition of a sentence.

▣ **MEMORY HOOK** A group of words starting with a capital letter and ending with a period is a sentence only if the words express a complete thought—that is, make sense. This principle may be condensed: *No Sense—*

No Sentence. A writer who makes the sentence-fragment error usually does not see that the fragment is part of a preceding or a following sentence.

> As requested, we are shipping your Order 468 on Thursday of this week. (These words make sense, have meaning, express a complete thought; therefore, this is a sentence.)
>
> As requested. We are shipping your Order 468 on Thursday of this week. (The first group of words is a "no sense" group. The writer did not see that the sentence fragment is the introduction to the main thought: *As requested, we . . .*)
>
> Your appointment has been changed to 10 a.m. on May 6. Because Mr. Ames will not return to the office until May 5. (The second group, the sentence fragment, is the explanatory part of the main message. The sentence should be written as follows: *Your appointment has been changed to 10 a.m. on May 6 because Mr. Ames will not return to the office until May 5.*)

SUBJECT AND PREDICATE

In order to construct a sentence correctly, a speaker or a writer must be able to recognize its subject and predicate. Every sentence has a subject and a predicate. Once you select the subject, you know that the predicate is the rest of the sentence. The subject is that part of the sentence that shows who *is speaking* or *is spoken to* or *is the person or thing spoken about.* The predicate, then, is what is being said about the subject.

The complete subject may be a single word or a group of words, such as:

> *He* announced the winners. (*He* is the complete subject of the sentence, the *person speaking.*)
>
> *You* must report all violations. (*You* is the complete subject, the *person spoken to.*)
>
> *The secretary in the outer office* also acts as receptionist. (*The secretary in the outer office* is the complete subject, the *person spoken about.*)
>
> *Pictures for the new brochure* will be taken tomorrow. (*Pictures for the new brochure* is the complete subject, the *things spoken about.*)

⊙ **CHECKUP 1** Checkups appear at intervals throughout Chapters 3 and 4. The purpose of these checkups is to help you measure your knowledge of the rules covered and to pinpoint the areas in which you need additional study.

Indicate whether the following groups of words are sentences or sentence fragments. Then rewrite the sentence fragments to make sentences.

1. After we found the missing information.
2. The Sky-Lab program has been very successful.
3. We expect to rent an apartment in the new housing project.
4. All the needy children in our town.
5. We are thinking of hiring an additional store detective.
6. When you address by electronic tape.
7. Information in our files is on microfilm.
8. Which saves much office space.
9. The contract for launching pads has been awarded to Bell & Owen.

SIMPLE AND COMPOUND SUBJECTS

A *simple subject* is the most important single word in the complete subject. For example:

> The *girl* in the blue dress is a new employee. (The complete subject is *The girl in the blue dress.* The most important single word is *girl;* therefore, *girl* is the simple subject.)
>
> Essential *elements* of the sentence are presented in this lesson. (*Essential elements of the sentence* is the complete subject. The most important single word in the complete subject is *elements,* which is the simple subject.)

A *compound subject* consists of two or more words that are equally important and are joined usually by a conjunction such as *and, or,* or *nor.*

> The *debits and credits* in the trial balance must be equal. (The complete subject is *The debits and credits in the trial balance.* The most important words, *debits* and *credits,* are equally important and are joined by the conjunction *and.* The compound subject is *debits and credits.*)
>
> *Boxes* containing stationery *or crates* containing spare parts are not to be stored in Warehouse 7. (*Boxes containing stationery or crates containing spare parts* is the complete subject. *Boxes* and *crates* are the most important words, are equally important, and are joined by the conjunction *or.* The compound subject, therefore, is *boxes or crates.*)

NORMAL AND INVERTED SENTENCE ORDER

Many glaring errors in grammar are caused by the inability to identify true subjects of sentences, especially when sentences are in inverted order. The ability to recognize inverted sentence order and to change inverted order to normal order will help you to avoid making such errors when writing or speaking. As given here, the presentation of normal and inverted order promotes immediate recognition of sentence subjects.

A sentence is considered in *normal order* when the complete subject precedes the complete predicate. When the complete subject does not precede the complete predicate, the sentence is said to be in *inverted order.* To change inverted order to normal order, rearrange the words so that the complete subject is written first, followed by the complete predicate. You should know that most questions are in inverted order. Here are some illustrations:

> The staff is no longer required to work overtime during inventory. (Because the complete subject precedes the complete predicate, this sentence is in normal order.)
>
> During inventory, the staff is no longer required to work overtime. (Here the complete subject does not precede the complete predicate; therefore, the sentence is in inverted order.)
>
> Where did you get your information? (This question is in inverted order. Why? Because the subject is *you,* and *you* does not precede the predicate. Normal order is this: *You did get your information where?*)

Now consider this sentence: "Where's your shoes?" Knowledge of inverted and normal order, plus the ability to change inverted order to normal order, would have prevented this serious error in grammar. Changed to normal order, the sentence is this: "Your shoes is where?" Surely, no educated person would write or say "Shoes *is*." Mentally, we would have changed the question to normal order and would have written or said "Where *are* your shoes?"

A letter containing the sentence "In the following pages appear a full explanation of our reasons for not joining the Association" would lessen the prestige of the writer and the writer's company. In normal order, the sentence is this: "A full explanation of our reasons for not joining the Association appear in the following pages." Obviously, *A full explanation appear* is wrong; the plural verb *appear* has been incorrectly used instead of the singular *appears*.

⊙ **CHECKUP 2** In each of the following sentences, write the complete subject and draw a line under the simple or the compound subject. If a sentence is in inverted order, change it to normal order before making the selection.

1. Do you react favorably to most abstractionist painting?
2. The Senate is expected to confirm the appointment soon.
3. To be eligible for compensation, an employee must be injured on the job.
4. The Common Market is seeking lower tariffs on its exports to the United States.
5. To reach the top in a secretarial career, you must acquire an extensive vocabulary.
6. What is the difference between the words *recession* and *depression*?
7. Somewhere in the spacecraft is a radar screen.
8. Efficiency and industry are important qualifications for success.
9. On the shelf behind my desk are paper clips, typewriter ribbons, and staplers.

Communication Projects

PRACTICAL APPLICATION

A If one of the sentences below is a fragment, make it a complete sentence. If a sentence is in inverted order, write it in normal order. Then write the complete subject for each sentence and draw a line under the simple or the compound subject.

1. Syllabi and notebooks are available for everyone who registered for the course.
2. Despite the very poor attendance at the exhibition.
3. Stretched out on the grass at the edge of the road lay two blanket-covered bodies.
4. Another receptionist or a part-time clerk-typist is to be hired soon.
5. Excited over their chance to win the company bowling team championship when they met last night.
6. A course for high-speed shorthand writers is being offered this year.
7. Is youth unemployment a growing problem?
8. In clerical testing programs, five-minute typing tests are most frequently used.
9. What is your opinion of sympathy strikes?
10. Students who are graduated from our college are well trained.

11. Because we are making a very small profit.
12. Did Mr. Evans buzz for his secretary?
13. Time and tide wait for no man.
14. Hundreds of packages of seeds were shipped today.
15. Do the type bars on that typewriter stick in damp weather?

B For each correct sentence, write *OK* on your paper. For each incorrect sentence, make the necessary correction.

1. The modifications of the new contract is expected in today's mail.
2. Has his monthly installment payments been made on time?
3. Have you read the latest newspaper report on the fuel oil crisis?
4. There is more clerks than any other classification of employees.
5. Were there any more resignations requested at the meeting?
6. In the right margin was typed the identification initials.
7. Do you think his reasons for refusing the promotion is valid?
8. Enclosed is the names that you requested in your letter.
9. In which of our letters was the serial numbers you quoted?
10. Where is the point of no return in this situation?

EDITING PRACTICE

Revising Telegrams Rewrite the following telegrams, and use no more than 15 words to express each message clearly.

1. Urgent we have new model electric ranges at once. Advertising already printed. Let us know when you will ship us more ranges.
2. Changing arrival time of L. M. Corson to 2:30 Monday afternoon, United Flight 141 at O'Hare Airport. Please arrange rental of a car for that time.
3. Change your plans and proceed directly to western sales meeting in Denver, without stopover in Detroit. Your presentation has been switched to the opening meeting.
4. Your contract approved today. Sending it to you by special delivery. Proceed according to the plan agreed upon.
5. Retail price of our Frosty refrigerator still $395. Rumored that price increase will go into effect next month.

Proofreading for Spelling Errors Write the correct spelling for any misspelled words in the following paragraph.

> We were glad to learn that you plan to exibit at the Housewares Show at the Hotel James on May 9. Your company has been assigned a booth on the mezzanine floor, which is easily accessable from the lobby. If there is anything we can do beforehand to help you set up your display quickly, please do not hesitate to call on us.

CASE PROBLEM

Making Introductions At the annual office picnic for employees and members of their families, George Adams would like to introduce his wife and his mother and father to his boss, John Harvey, president of the company.

1. How should George make these introductions?
2. What might be a good source of information on how to introduce people?
3. How would you make these introductions to the president and his wife and to the vice president, Robert Thompson, and his wife?

9 Verbs

To convey meaning effectively, a speaker or a writer must be comfortable in using correct verbs and verb forms. The guidelines for verb usage in this section will help you avoid the more common verb errors.

DEFINITION

A *verb* is defined as a word that asserts or assumes action, a condition, or a state of being. You can identify a verb quickly by looking for the word that sparks the sentence into motion. Without a verb as a spark, a sentence is incomplete—an inert, lifeless group of words. For instance:

His secretary the letter. (These words mean nothing.)

His secretary (wrote, transcribed, misfiled, retyped) the letter. (See how each verb makes the words come to life in a different way.)

When you can quickly and unerringly identify the word that sparks a sentence into motion, you are ready to learn how to use verbs correctly.

⊙ **CHECKUP 1** Identify the verbs in the following sentences. If the verb is missing in any group of words, supply a verb that makes sense.

1. The West Coast distribution center stocks all our books.
2. He was sorry to learn of your serious accident.
3. The company's annual report is beautifully printed.
4. How soon these orders for Scranton?
5. Color balance is an essential factor in home decorating.
6. Where is the next convention to be held?
7. Did you the report on Miss Rosa's desk?
8. Our purchasing department places all our orders.
9. At the annual office picnic for employees and members of their families, Tina and Gary all the prizes.

VERB PHRASES

To communicate accurately, a speaker or writer sometimes needs a phrase consisting of two or more verbs to give life to a sentence. Verb phrases are composed of a main (principal) verb and one or more helping (auxiliary) verbs, such as *may have written, had spoken, is going, would have been lost, should have been seen.*

Study the following list of some of the more common helping verbs.

is	will	will have	might have been
was	has been	could have	will have been
has	had been	should have	could have been
had	may have	would have	should have been
shall	might have	may have been	would have been

The *main* verb in any verb phrase is always the *last* verb, and the preceding verb or verbs are the helpers.

> Our files *must be kept* in perfect order. (Main verb, *kept*; helping verbs, *must* and *be*.)
>
> All communications *must be* clear and accurate. (Main verb, *be*; helping verb, *must*.)
>
> You *should have checked* those figures. (Main verb, *checked*; helping verbs, *should* and *have*.)

Note that in the second sentence *be* is the main verb but that in the first sentence *be* is a helper. The verbs *be* and *been* will present no problem if you remember that the *last* verb is the *main* verb and the preceding verb or verbs are helpers.

⊙ **CHECKUP 2** Identify the verb phrases, main verbs, and helping verbs.

1. The board meeting has been postponed until Friday.
2. She was entirely justified in her refusal.
3. Has anyone seen my red pen?
4. Our lawyers are meeting next week.
5. How many are going to the convention?
6. It would be well for you to proofread more carefully.
7. Those specifications should have gone out yesterday.
8. She will have arrived by then.
9. Is this the entire report?
10. Will all the members attend tomorrow's meeting?
11. She wrote a very detailed summary.
12. Mrs. Jensen has already asked for a transfer.

REGULAR AND IRREGULAR VERBS

Verbs are classified as either *regular* or *irregular* according to the way their principal parts are formed. The principal parts of verbs are the present, past, and past participle. These principal parts of verbs are used to express the time of action, or tense, of a verb.

Regular Verbs

A regular verb forms the past tense and the past participle by adding *ed*, as in *walk, walked, walked* and *call, called, called*. The principal parts of regular verbs do not need special study because a mistake in the use of those verbs is rarely made.

Irregular Verbs

Irregular verbs, however, form the past tense and past participle in various ways—frequently by changing to a different word. Errors in the use of irregular verbs occur so often, particularly in speech, that facility in handling these verbs is a "must" for effective communication. Therefore, careful study of the chart of irregular verb forms on page 75 is recommended.

PRINCIPAL PARTS OF IRREGULAR VERBS

Present	Past	Past Participle
am	was	been
bear	bore	borne
begin	began	begun
bid (to command)	bade	bidden
bid (to offer to pay)	bid	bid
bite	bit	bitten
blow	blew	blown
break	broke	broken
bring	brought	brought
burst	burst	burst
catch	caught	caught
choose	chose	chosen
come	came	come
do	did	done
draw	drew	drawn
drink	drank	drunk
drive	drove	driven
eat	ate	eaten
fall	fell	fallen
fight	fought	fought
flee	fled	fled
fly	flew	flown
forget	forgot	forgotten
freeze	froze	frozen
get	got	got
give	gave	given
go	went	gone
grow	grew	grown
hang (to put to death)	hanged	hanged
hang (to suspend)	hung	hung
hide	hid	hidden
know	knew	known
lay	laid (*not* layed)	laid (*not* layed)
leave	left	left
lend	lent	lent
lie	lay	lain
pay	paid (*not* payed)	paid (*not* payed)
ride	rode	ridden
ring	rang	rung
rise	rose	risen
run	ran	run
see	saw	seen
set	set	set
shake	shook	shaken
sit	sat	sat
speak	spoke	spoken
steal	stole	stolen
strike	struck	struck
take	took	taken
tear	tore	torn
throw	threw	thrown
wear	wore	worn
write	wrote	written

As you study irregular verbs, remember that an irregular verb in the past tense never has a helping verb, whereas a past participle always has at least one helping verb. For example, "Has the bell rang yet?" is obviously incorrect. The past tense of *ring* is *rang,* and a verb in the past tense never has a helper. But in this sentence there is a helper, *has;* therefore, the past participle *rung* should be used: "Has the bell *rung* yet?"

◇ **TWILIGHT ZONE: *Lend, Loan*** Although *lend* is a verb and *loan* is a noun, you will very often see or hear *loan* used as a verb, as in "The bank will surely *loan* you enough to tide you over." If you choose to join the increasing number of persons who *loan,* rather than *lend,* you should know that you are making a minor error.

⊙ **CHECKUP 3** Find and correct all principal-part errors in the following sentences. Justify your corrections on the basis of whether or not the main verb requires a helping verb.

> The bus had went before we reached the station. (The correction is "*gone*—helper." The correct verb is *gone* because the helper *had* is used. *Went* is incorrect because the past tense of irregular verbs is never used with a helper.)

1. She had drove four hours through the storm.
2. I should have wrote her last week.
3. As soon as he come into the room, he saw she was angry.
4. Will you loan me some stamps, please?
5. We'd just began to think that you weren't coming after all.

◇ **TWILIGHT ZONE: Split Infinitives** An infinitive is a verb usually preceded by *to,* such as *to run, to say, to do, to think.* When writers place a word or words between the *to* and the verb, they "split an infinitive." Infinitive splitting was once considered a major error. Today, however, split infinitives such as *to actually do, to emphatically state,* and *to loyally pledge* are sometimes used to make a statement more emphatic or to avoid an awkwardly constructed sentence. Nonetheless, as a beginning writer, you should avoid splitting an infinitive whenever your doing so will not substantially alter the sentence.

IF, AS IF, AS THOUGH, WISH

Speakers and writers often have difficulty choosing the correct verb to follow *if, as if, as though,* and *wish.* Here is a simple rule to follow: After *if, as if, as though,* and *wish,* use *were* where ordinarily *was* would be used.

> Mr. Ready looks *as if* he *were* ill. (But he is not ill.)
>
> Miss York acted *as though* she *were* disappointed. (But she may not be disappointed.)
>
> I *wish* it *were* possible to grant your request. (But it is not possible.)

A minor problem occurs with the use of *was* or *were* after *if. Were* is used if the expression is not true, is doubtful, or is not possible. However, *was* is used if the expression is true or could be true. Study the examples illustrated below.

If I *were* you, I would ask for a transfer. (But I am not you.)

If Washington *were* living, he would be amazed at the growth of our nation. (But Washington is not living.)

If Mr. Leary *was* here (and he may have been), I did not see him.

⊙ **CHECKUP 4** Make any needed corrections in the following sentences. If you correct a split infinitive, indicate the infinitive and the word or group of words that cause the split.

1. If her car was bigger, she would take all of us.
2. To accurately predict the finishing date, she needs more information.
3. I wonder if she wishes she was going.
4. Miss Grayson always walks as if she was in a hurry.
5. Everyone else's job looks as though it was easy.
6. She admits that she would request a transfer if she were you.
7. If Harriet were to suddenly leave, we would require three people to replace her.
8. As though his taking two days off wasn't enough, Bill arrived two hours late this morning!
9. Please ask Pat to carefully retype this draft copy.
10. Max could answer your question if he were here.

Communication Projects

PRACTICAL APPLICATION

A In each of the following sentences *(a)* indicate the verb, *(b)* underline the main verb if there is a verb phrase, and *(c)* supply a verb for any group of words where the verb is missing.

1. Our lawyer is filing a lien against the Adams property.
2. An improved ultrasonic security system has been in the experimental stage.
3. Colored transparencies will better capture your viewers' attention.
4. Has she previously conducted a market survey?
5. Her assistant should have asked permission for the schedule change.
6. The market value of that stock has suddenly decreased.
7. The minutes of the meeting must have been mislaid.
8. Has the bulletin been read by the entire staff?
9. Have you written reminders to all delinquent customers?
10. Ann the best file clerk we ever had.
11. The foreign delegation will arrive tomorrow.
12. Our company periodic surveys.
13. What has been your outstanding personnel problem?
14. Whom have you appointed to fill the vacancy?
15. The Williams letter should have been mailed yesterday.
16. Has there been any change in his feeling about the strike?
17. Mr. Haynes his arm.
18. How fast can you take dictation?
19. Yesterday Mr. Hill the sales record.
20. Evidence of scientific advances can be seen everywhere.

B If a sentence is correct, write *OK* on your paper. If incorrect, write the correction and your reason for making it. If you correct a split infinitive, indicate the word or words that cause the split.

1. Why did you loan your copy of the report to her?
2. I would not have chose such a bright color for the new lounge.
3. Negotiations for a change in grievance procedures have broke down.
4. To better understand the requirements, please read the following explanation.
5. The shipping department staff would not need overtime if the flow of work was better planned.
6. I don't think the bell has rang yet.
7. If the price was lower, we would place a large order.
8. Some persons find it impossible to clearly reason when under pressure.
9. If I were an economist, I would be better able to answer your question.
10. Did you know that we run that advertisement last week?
11. Five-minute typing tests are most frequently used. In clerical testing programs.
12. For several years now, Mr. Mason has sang in the company chorus.
13. Does it look as though the snow were melting?
14. Have you ever spoke before a group?
15. Somewhere in the outgoing mail tray is the letters on which you forgot to make carbon-copy notations.

EDITING PRACTICE

Editing for Vocabulary Errors Write your correction for any vocabulary errors you find in the following paragraph.

> Thank you very much for sending us an advance copy of your report on consumer trends during the passed ten years. A study of your findings has given us confidence in the soundness of the planned promotion program for our new low-calorie deserts. We now know that we are in line with current public interest and demand.

CASE PROBLEM

The Straw That Broke the Camel's Back Bob Haynes is the supervisor of one office section in which tardiness is a serious problem. Bob's boss was so disturbed by the excessive tardiness in this section that he suggested that Bob call a meeting of his people to see what could be done about the problem. Bob called the group together, explained the situation to them, and together they set up a plan to control the tardiness. They agreed that anyone who was tardy would remain at work twice the amount of time of the lateness. In addition, each member of the group pledged to be at work on time. The very next morning following this meeting, Mildred Anson, one of the clerks in Bob's section, was fifteen minutes late. When Bob talked to Mildred and reminded her that she was to remain thirty minutes after the regular time, Mildred explained that she lived beyond the bus line and had to ride with someone who worked for another company and who was on a different time schedule. Consequently, she said, she was not responsible for being late.

1. What should Bob Haynes do about this situation?
2. What should he say to Mildred?

10 More About Verbs

A professor of English once conducted a most illuminating, though informal, study. He was interested in finding out which elements of English grammar were stumbling blocks to his students, despite their years of grammar study. Each semester, over a period of ten years, he asked entering students to list the grammar principles that they still did not understand. When the study was completed, he found that usage of *lie* and *lay, sit* and *set,* and *rise* and *raise* ranked among the top three areas of difficulty. This section on verbs, therefore, concentrates on clearing up cloudiness about the correct usage of *lie* and *lay, sit* and *set, rise* and *raise.*

CLASSIFICATION OF VERBS

In order to use the correct forms of *lie* and *lay, sit* and *set, rise* and *raise,* it is first necessary to know how verbs are classified. Verbs may be divided into three classifications: (1) "being" verbs, (2) transitive verbs, and (3) intransitive verbs.

"Being" Verbs

The different forms of the verb *to be* are as follows:

> *am, is, are, was, were*
>
> *be* with a helper: *shall be, will be, may be, can be, would be, might be,* and so on
>
> *been* with a helper or helpers: *has been, have been, had been, shall have been, will have been, could have been, might have been,* and so on

These are the seven "being" verbs. Because of the need for instant recognition of "being" verbs, they should be memorized, preferably in this order: *am, is, are, was, were,* helper *be,* helper(s) *been.*

Note: A single-word "being" verb can be classified easily. In a verb phrase, however, remember that a verb is "being" only when it is the main verb, the *last* verb in the phrase. If it is not the last verb, it is a helping verb.

> The minutes *are* in that green notebook. (Since *are* is the only verb, it is obviously a "being" verb.)
>
> She *would have been* at the meeting except for another appointment. (Since *been* is the last verb in the verb phrase, it is a "being" verb.)
>
> The folders *were placed* correctly in the file. (*Placed* is the last verb in the phrase, and it is not a "being" verb. Therefore, *were* is a helping verb.)
>
> Mr. Betts *is going* to Chicago tomorrow. (*Going* is the main verb; *is* is a helping verb; *is going* is not a "being" verb.)

⊙ **CHECKUP 1** Select the verb or verb phrase in each of the following sentences, and identify the "being" verbs.

1. The increasing number of careers open to women is encouraging.
2. The production figures for this quarter are running behind the same period last year.
3. The possibility of a fuel oil shortage has been much discussed recently.
4. Were all survey results filed yesterday?
5. Well-prepared business writers are in demand.
6. The main vault must have been locked before closing hours.

Transitive and Intransitive Verbs

A *transitive verb* is a verb that takes an object; an *intransitive verb* is a verb that does not take an object. To ensure rapid and accurate selection of transitive and intransitive verbs, study the following Memory Hook.

▣ **MEMORY HOOK** A transitive verb is a verb that is followed by an answer to the question "What?" or "Whom?" If no answer can be found, the verb is intransitive. Set up a thinking procedure like the following:

1. Say the verb.
2. Ask "What?" or "Whom?"
3. If there is an answer to either question, the verb is transitive. If not, the verb is intransitive.

See how this thought process is applied in the following illustrations:

1. The supervisor *relayed* the order immediately. (Relayed what? Answer—*order*. Since there is an answer, *relayed* in the sentence is a transitive verb.)
2. Mrs. Anton *left* sometime during the forenoon. (Left what? No answer. Left whom? No answer. In this sentence *left* is an intransitive verb.)
3. *Do you know* Jim Bonnell? (Do know what? No answer. Do know whom? Answer—*Jim Bonnell. Do know*, then, is a transitive verb.)

Always Transitive

Whenever a past participle has one of the "being" verbs as a helper—*was done, has been broken, might be chosen, is burned*—that verb is always transitive because the subject is acted upon.

> The "Top Secret" papers *should have been hidden* from public gaze. (*Hidden* is a past participle; *should have been* is a "being" verb, but in this sentence it is used as a helper. *Should have been hidden* is automatically a transitive verb.)

In the next example, note that the main verb is not a past participle:

> The wind *was blowing* with hurricane force. (Although there is a "being" verb helper here, the main verb is not a past participle. For this verb, therefore, ask the questions "What?" and "Whom?" Since neither question can be answered, *was blowing* is an intransitive verb.)

⊙ **CHECKUP 2** In the following sentences, identify each verb as "being," transitive, or intransitive. Use *B* for "being," *T* for "transitive," *I* for "intransitive." Watch for any past participles that have "being" verb helpers.

1. She should have authorized a refund to that customer.
2. The staff members are anticipating substantial raises.
3. The messenger was not here at all yesterday.
4. Surely, the check should have been sent on Friday.
5. Did you look at all the letters?
6. Did you see any packages?

LIE, LAY; SIT, SET; RISE, RAISE

The foundation for correct use of *lie* and *lay, sit* and *set,* and *rise* and *raise* has now been laid. In each pair, one of the verbs is transitive; the other, intransitive. To choose the correct verb form, a speaker or writer needs to determine which of the pair is transitive and which is intransitive. Use the following Memory Hook for split-second recognition of the correct verb.

▣ **MEMORY HOOK** Notice that there is a letter *i* or an *i* sound in the present form of one member of each pair of verbs. These *i* verbs are *lie, sit,* and *rise*. The word *intransitive* starts with the letter *i*. Therefore, remember that the *i* verbs *lie, sit,* and *rise* are intransitive.

Present	Past	Past Participle	Present Participle	Infinitive
lie	lay	lain	lying	to lie
lay	laid	laid	laying	to lay
sit	sat	sat	sitting	to sit
set	set	set	setting	to set
rise	rose	risen	rising	to rise
raise	raised	raised	raising	to raise

Obviously, once the intransitive verb is identified, the other member of the pair must be transitive. Remember, however, that a past participle that has a "being" verb helper is always transitive.

Observe and adopt the line of reasoning set up in each of the following illustrations:

Marie (lay, laid) the new magazine on her desk. (Which is needed here, a transitive or an intransitive verb? Answer—*transitive*. How do you know? Answer—because "magazines" answers the question "What?" Which verb is transitive? Answer—*Laid*. Which form is correct? Answer—*Laid*.)

My father (lies, lays) down for a short nap before dinner. (The verb has no object; therefore, an intransitive verb is needed. The intransitive verb *lies* is the correct verb.)

The package was (sat, set) on the top shelf. (There is no problem here. *Set* is correct because a past participle with a "being" verb helper is always transitive.)

⊙ **CHECKUP 3** For each of the following sentences, determine whether a transitive or an intransitive verb is needed and tell why. Then name the correct verb.

1. Train that dog not to (lie, lay) on the rug.
2. (Sit, Set) your marginal stops at 15 and 70.
3. The water has (risen, raised) to the top of the pier.
4. Those machines have (lain, laid) idle for a month.
5. Did you know that the salary maximum has been (risen, raised)?
6. Mr. Tarny's new house (sits, sets) on a hilltop.
7. You left your belongings (lying, laying) on all the chairs.
8. The engineers' reports were (lain, laid) on the bottom shelf.

Communication Projects

PRACTICAL APPLICATION

A Identify the verb in each of the following sentences, and indicate whether it is transitive, intransitive, or "being." Use *B* for "being," *T* for "transitive," *I* for "intransitive."

1. His equity in the land has been legally conveyed to his nephew.
2. I dislike overuse of the word *contact* as a verb.
3. Are government price controls being successfully applied?
4. Did your secretary sign the requisition?
5. They are contesting his rights in a patent infringement suit.
6. We surely cannot be at our desks every minute of the day!
7. There were often a dozen or more callers in our small office.
8. All letters were finished before noon, despite interruptions.
9. A business correspondent writes many different kinds of communications.
10. You should have been here before 8:30.
11. Are you buying a new automatic typewriter?
12. That sentence should have been changed to normal order.
13. Opposition makes Mr. Benson more persistent.
14. A set of form letters has finally been prepared.
15. A digest of the letters should be on my desk today.

B For the rest of this chapter and throughout Chapter 4, Practical Application B will review material from earlier lessons as well as from the current lesson. If a sentence is correct, write *OK* on your paper; if incorrect, make the necessary correction.

1. Her umbrella, raincoat, and boots were lying there ready for the next storm.
2. All the competitive price information was laid on his desk this morning.
3. He decided to lie his questions before the committee at its next meeting.
4. Does the camping area we chose lay north or west of Yellowstone Park?
5. We should be laying plans now for the new operations manual.
6. To really be convincing, you yourself must believe in what you say.
7. A gentleman always rises to his feet when a lady enters the room.
8. The work schedule was lain out just last week.
9. Your portfolio is lying in readiness for the meeting.
10. Yesterday the stencils laid on the top shelf.

11. That particular objection has been risen many times.
12. In our library is many books on the subject of nuclear fission.
13. Behind the machine is the boxes of key-punch cards.
14. When your currect account is payed, we shall be glad to open a new one.
15. Loan me a few sheets of carbon paper, please.
16. In the dictionary is many synonyms for nouns.
17. Both soldiers are laying now in Flanders Field.
18. Was the flagpole set securely in cement?
19. Please let that book lay where you found it.
20. He had laid down to rest after his long trip.

EDITING PRACTICE

Wanted: An Editor Who Can Spell If you are that editor, you will be able to find and correct any spelling errors in this paragraph.

> May we send you a sample casette of our new sales training material? You will find this material invaluable in motivating your sales representatives. Just drop the enclose reply card in the mail today, and we will rush your sample casette, together with details of our complete course, "Sell Your Way to Success."

CASE PROBLEM

The Helpful Employee Irma Mattell recently gave notice of her intention to resign from her position as secretary in the Bell Manufacturing Company's office. Her replacement is coming in tomorrow, two days before Irma will be leaving, to be oriented to the new position. Irma has decided that a brief, typed summary of her duties would be helpful for the replacement.

1. Why would such a summary be helpful, even though Irma will be spending two days with the secretary who is to replace her?
2. What should the summary contain?

11 Nouns—Plurals

Its inconsistencies make English a difficult language to speak and to write. One of the difficulties presented by the English language is the correct spelling of the plurals of nouns. Plurals are formed in many ways. For example, consider the following sentence: "Embargoes on the importation of pianos are unknown today." The plural of *embargo* is *embargoes,* but the plural of *piano* is *pianos.* Although both singulars end in *o,* one adds *es* to form its plural but the other adds only *s.* Here is another illustration: "*Attorneys* for the steel *companies* were consulted about the merger." *Attorney* ends in *y;* its plural is formed by adding *s. Company* also ends in *y,* but its plural is formed by changing the *y* to *i* and adding *es*. The plurals of nouns are formed in such a variety of ways that only a skilled writer is always correct in forming plurals. This section will help you in developing the high level of skill needed to form noun plurals correctly by (1) presenting solutions to the most difficult plural problems, (2) reviewing rules that you may have forgotten, (3) pointing out plurals that sometimes require dictionary help, and (4) analyzing plurals that cause frequent errors in grammar.

KEYS TO CORRECT PLURALS

Analysis of the difficulties in forming plurals shows that four plural formations evidently are not understood by some business writers. These four problems and keys to their solutions will now be discussed.

Plurals of Names

Most common nouns form the plural by adding *s* to the singular form—*book, books; letter, letters.* However, common nouns ending in *s, sh, ch, x,* and *z* form their plurals by adding *es* to the singular form.

lens	lenses	tax	taxes
brush	brushes	topaz	topazes
bench	benches		

Few writers make errors using *s* or *es* to form the plurals of common nouns. If they understand that the plurals of proper nouns or *names* are formed in exactly the same way, they will also make few errors when writing plurals of names.

farmer	farmers	Palmer	the Palmers
carton	cartons	Barton	the Bartons
brass	brasses	Ellis	the Ellises
dish	dishes	Walsh	the Walshes
branch	branches	Stritch	the Stritches
fox	foxes	Wilcox	the Wilcoxes
chintz	chintzes	Schlitz	the Schlitzes

Plurals of Titles With Names

When a title accompanies a name, make either the name or the title plural. Never make both the name and the title plural.

Singular	Plural
Mr. Carlin	*Messrs.* Carlin, the *Messrs.* Carlin, or the two Mr. *Carlins* (*Messrs.* is the abbreviation for *Messieurs,* French for "Misters.")
Mrs. Fort	The Mrs. *Forts* or *Mesdames* Fort (*Mesdames* is the French word that means more than one "Mrs.")
Miss York	*Misses* York or the two Miss *Yorks*
Professor Weber	*Professors* Weber or the Professor *Webers*

Plurals With Apostrophes

Over the years, usage had dictated some changes in forming certain plurals. It is not necessary to use an apostrophe every time you add an *s* or an *es* to form a plural, as you will see from the following guidelines:

1. Form the plural of capitalized letters and of abbreviations containing all-capital letters by adding only a lowercase *s*.
2. Form the plural of lowercase letters and of abbreviations using lowercase letters by adding an apostrophe and *s*.
3. Form the plural of numbers used as numbers and of words used as words by adding only an *s* or *es*; however, if the plural form might be misread, add an apostrophe and *s*.

She sent far too many *SOSs*.

I always stay home when I am expecting *c.o.d.'s*.

Her *g's* and *f's* are poorly written.

The *ups* and *downs* of the company's earnings are shown in the chart.

Try not to give a learner too many *don'ts*.

The temperature was in the *80s*.

Plurals of Compound Nouns

A compound noun is a noun consisting of two or more words. It may be either hyphenated or unhyphenated. The rule to remember is this: The plural of a compound noun is formed on the important, or main, word.

chief of police	*chiefs* of police
editor in chief	*editors* in chief
major general	major *generals*
personnel manager	personnel *managers*
son-in-law	*sons*-in-law

Note: In a very few compounds, the plural is added to both parts: *gentlemen ushers, Knights Templars.*

⊙ **CHECKUP 1** Correct any errors in the following sentences, and be able to justify your corrections.

1. There are only two Roxy's in the telephone book.
2. All his cars have been Buicks.
3. Including aunts and cousins, we have four Margaret's in our family.
4. Both his daughter-in-laws are attorneys.
5. In fifty years our firm has had only three editors in chief.
6. His IOU's were all too frequent.
7. The Wallaces are being honored on their wedding anniversary.
8. Wouldn't you know that the Jones's would make the lowest bid!
9. The Misses Stewarts have won the trip to Paris.
10. Modern typewriters have plus's on the top row of keys.
11. The Doctors Smiths have opened an office on Main Street.
12. Bill and Jack were the runner-ups in the tournament.

PLURALS TO REVIEW

The following three rules for forming noun plurals are so generally well understood that they need to be reviewed only briefly.

Plurals of Nouns Ending in *Y*

When a singular noun ends in *y* and the *y* is preceded by a consonant, the plural is formed by changing the *y* to *i* and adding *es*; when the *y* is preceded by a vowel, the plural is formed by adding *s*. See the following illustrations:

supply	supplies	*but*	valley	valleys
facility	facilities		foray	forays

Note: This rule does not apply to proper names. All proper names ending in *y* form the plural by adding *s*; for example, *three Marys, the Averys.*

Nouns With Two Plurals With Different Meanings

A few nouns have two plurals, each of which has a different meaning. Here are some examples of such nouns:

brother	brothers (blood relatives)
	brethren (members of a society)
staff	staffs (personnel)
	staves (sticks, poles)
index	indexes (to books)
	indices (symbols)

Vowel Changes and *En* Endings

Some nouns form the plural by changing a vowel instead of adding *s*. A few other plurals end in *en*. Although these rules generally seem to be well understood, a brief refresher is needed to fill in the "plurals" picture.

Vowel Change:	man	men	woman	women
	goose	geese	mouse	mice
***en* Ending:**	child	children	ox	oxen

Note: In a very few words ending in *man*, the plural is formed by adding *s*; for example, *German, Germans; talisman, talismans; ottoman, ottomans.*

⊙ **CHECKUP 2** Study the following sentences, and make any needed corrections.

1. The facultys of all three schools will attend the conference.
2. If the usual indices are to be believed, the stock market will soon rise.
3. Is it humane to use monkies for laboratory research?
4. A metropolitan area is composed of several communitys.
5. Alaska and Hawaii were originally territorys of the United States.
6. We are returning this order because barrels with loose staffs are of no use to us.

DICTIONARY ALERTS

Plural forms of singular nouns ending in *o* and in *f* or *fe* vary so much that there is doubtful value in memorizing exceptions to the rules. You should be sure of the plurals of *o*- and *f*- or *fe*-ending nouns that occur frequently in your writing. You should also know that these plurals are tricky; therefore, if you are not absolutely sure, you should consult a dictionary.

Plurals of Nouns Ending in *O*

Singular nouns ending in *o* preceded by a *vowel* form the plural by adding *s*. Some nouns ending in *o* preceded by a *consonant* form the plural by adding *s*; others, by adding *es*. Do not guess at the correct spelling of the plural of a noun ending in *o* when that *o* is preceded by a consonant; look it up in a dictionary.

It is interesting to note that nouns that relate to music and end in *o* always form their plurals by adding *s*; for example, *piano, pianos*; *alto, altos*; *oratorio, oratorios*.

Some examples of plurals of nouns ending in *o* are given below. Make a habit of consulting a dictionary to determine the correct plurals of nouns ending in *o*.

Final *o* preceded by a vowel:

studio	studios	cameo	cameos
folio	folios	ratio	ratios

Final *o* preceded by a consonant, adding *s* for the plural:

domino	dominos	zero	zeros
dynamo	dynamos	lasso	lassos
tobacco	tobaccos	albino	albinos

Final *o* preceded by a consonant, adding *es* for the plural:

mosquito	mosquitoes	cargo	cargoes
potato	potatoes	echo	echoes
motto	mottoes	hero	heroes
volcano	volcanoes	veto	vetoes

Plurals of Nouns Ending in *F* or *Fe*

Some nouns ending in *f* or *fe* change the *f* or *fe* to *v* and add *es* to form their plurals; others simply add *s*. The plural of a noun ending in *f* or *fe*, therefore, should be recognized as a spelling hazard. Study the following illustrations and observe that there is neither a rule nor a pattern for these plurals.

Final *f* or *fe*, changing to *v* and adding *es*:

shelf	shelves	self	selves
life	lives	knife	knives
half	halves	leaf	leaves
loaf	loaves	thief	thieves

Final *f* or *fe*, adding *s*:

handkerchief	handkerchiefs	safe	safes
plaintiff	plaintiffs	gulf	gulfs
roof	roofs	grief	griefs
belief	beliefs	chef	chefs
proof	proofs	strife	strifes
bailiff	bailiffs	chief	chiefs

⊙ **CHECKUP 3** Make the needed corrections in the following sentences.

1. He was injured by the horse's hooves.
2. I think we should all take several leafs from his book.
3. He has made a thorough study of albinos.
4. The scores of piano concertos can be obtained from the library.
5. Tomatos from Florida are now in the market.
6. The newer motels have radioes in all rooms.

PLURALS FOR CORRECT GRAMMAR

One reason for learning how to form the plurals of nouns is that such knowledge improves spelling. A mastery of the four rules presented here, however, also can help a speaker or a writer avoid making errors in grammar. For instance, when you know that *news* is always singular, you will say or write "News *is*," not "News *are*." If you know that *scissors* is always plural, you will say "Scissors *are*," not "Scissors *is*."

To be correct in grammar usage, a writer or speaker needs to know (1) the nouns that have the same form in both the singular and the plural, (2) the nouns that are always singular, (3) the nouns that are always plural, and (4) the foreign nouns that follow the foreign spelling in the plural.

Same Form Singular and Plural

The following are illustrations of nouns that have the same form regardless of whether their meaning is singular or plural:

Chinese	deer	odds	sheep
cod	Japanese	politics	vermin
corps (pronounced "korz" in the plural)	moose	salmon	wheat

When modified by another number, the following nouns usually have the same form to denote either a singular or a plural number:

three *thousand* orders	four *score* years
two *yoke* of oxen	two *dozen* apples
six *hundred* chairs	

Always Singular

Here are some illustrations of nouns that are always singular and with which a singular verb must be used:

statistics (science)	molasses
mathematics	civics
economics (science)	milk
news	music

Always Plural

The following nouns are always plural and must therefore always take a plural verb:

statistics (facts)	auspices	tidings
scales (for weighing)	trousers	thanks
headquarters	proceeds	riches
credentials	winnings	antics
belongings	premises	goods
hysterics	scissors	tongs

Foreign Nouns

Some nouns of foreign origin, mainly Latin and Greek, have been given English plurals; some have only foreign plurals; and still others have two plurals, English and foreign. When there is a choice, the foreign forms are used mainly in formal, scientific, and technical writing. Usually, the endings of foreign nouns indicate they are singular or plural. Some common endings for Latin nouns are as follows:

Singular Ending	Plural Ending
um (candelabrum)	a (candelabra)
is (thesis)	es (theses)
us (stylus)	i (styli)
a (alumna)	ae (alumnae)

Words of Greek origin like *criterion* and *phenomenon* take the plural ending *a—criteria, phenomena.*

Keeping singular and plural endings in mind, study the following illustrations of plurals of foreign nouns:

Singular	Foreign Plural	English Plural
addendum	addenda	
alumna	alumnae	
alumnus	alumni	
analysis	analyses	
axis	axes	
basis	bases	
crisis	crises	
criterion	criteria	criterions
curriculum	curricula	curriculums
datum	data	
formula	formulae	formulas
hypothesis	hypotheses	
index	indices	indexes
medium	media	mediums
memorandum	memoranda	memorandums
nucleus	nuclei	nucleuses
oasis	oases	
parenthesis	parentheses	
stadium	stadia	stadiums
stimulus	stimuli	
terminus	termini	terminuses
vertebra	vertebrae	vertebras

◇ **TWILIGHT ZONE: *Data*** Many writers now treat *data* as a collective noun with a singular idea; therefore, *data* with a singular verb is considered correct. Some writers, accustomed to *data* as a plural noun, are reluctant to give it up. Their solution, or compromise, is to make a distinction between singular and plural; hence they are careful to say: "These data were compiled from several reports. However, the significant data is from the HEW study."

⊙ **CHECKUP 4** Find and correct any errors in the following sentences.

1. She has written a book about the lives of famous mediums.
2. All our textbooks contain well-prepared indexes.
3. The new ambassador's credentials are to be presented to the President tomorrow.
4. Some newspapers print more than all the news that are fit to print.
5. Parentheses is to be used to enclose references.
6. Has the goods been stored in the bin?
7. The alumni is interested in a winning football team.

Communication Projects

PRACTICAL APPLICATION

A For each correct sentence in the following group, write *OK* on your paper. For each incorrect sentence, write the correction.

1. All the relatives of the Barneses are invited to the reception.
2. The prize was awarded to the Misses Ransomes.
3. The two terminuses have been chosen for the new truck route.
4. Children should never play with knifes.
5. All the peace proposals have met with vetos by the great powers.
6. New recreational facilities are planned for senior citizens.
7. The Jones's have the most entries in the directory.
8. Mr. York's letters are full of *ands*.
9. The Vargas's are relocating their factory.
10. Chief Murphy is attending the state convention of chief of polices.
11. In your ten years of hunting, how many deers have you shot?
12. Since we have three Ann's in our office, we have resorted to nicknames.
13. Privates think that brigadiers general have easy lives.
14. There are three sixes in my license number.
15. Mr. Kelly says that all Kellies are intelligent.
16. File De Beaumont's correspondence with the Ds.
17. Here are the news from WNBI.
18. The Fitchs will have no trouble floating the loan.
19. Young attornies spend much of their time preparing briefs.
20. Verbs are the dynamoes of sentences.

B If a sentence is correct, write *OK* on your paper. If it is incorrect, write the correction.

1. I know she wishes she was eligible for the position.
2. Where are the styli for signing these stencils?
3. The analyses of the operating statements was expected today.
4. His winnings from any gambling is taxable.
5. The advertisements appealed to woman's interests.
6. She begins too many sentences with *and's*.
7. You should be lying your plans now for your summer vacation.
8. Have we payed all operating costs for this month?
9. In some states, civics are required for graduation.
10. On the card was printed, "Christmas Greetings from the Davis's."
11. At the last regular meeting, your proposal was lain on the table.
12. We all wished that Mr. Allen were present at the meeting.
13. Sit the vase on the table in the living room.
14. At the head table was seated the senior section managers.
15. The combinations on all the saves have been changed.

EDITING PRACTICE

Editing for Context Rewrite each sentence that contains a word that is contextually incorrect. Write *OK* for any contextually correct sentence.

1. Please do not let another two-week period elevate before sending in your monthly payment.
2. We have no covenant with other manufacturers.
3. This service is given as a gesture of friendship, not with any thought of financial removal.
4. Our federal government continually operates at a deficit.
5. Rationing was necessary during the war years because of the scarcity of many commodities.

Homonyms, Anybody? Correct any homonym or pseudohomonym error you may find in the following paragraph. Before you start, be sure that you know the meaning of the word *homonym*.

> The insoluble condition of the company led to its bankruptcy. All creditors were notified so that they could file liens against the company's tangential assets. For instants, Ace Hardware has already filed a lien.

CASE PROBLEM

The Correspondence Consultant You have been hired by Blanton, Inc., to study its correspondence and to make recommendations for improving letters written by its personnel. List the details of the preliminary planning that would be necessary to do a top job.

Nouns and Pronouns—Possessive Forms

This section provides a thorough review of the possessive forms of nouns and pronouns. Study it carefully to understand the most common use of the apostrophe, to know how to use it in certain special ownership situations, and to have greater facility in using personal pronoun possessives. Your skill in the use of possessive forms will develop as you practice—and master—the principles explained in this section.

MOST COMMON USE OF THE APOSTROPHE

The apostrophe is most commonly used to show possession as applied to a noun; for example, *ladies' clothing, children's books, student's tuition.* Three simple rules govern the use of the apostrophe to show possession.

1. For a word that does not end in *s,* add an apostrophe and *s.*

   The *child's* request was granted.

   The *children's* request was granted. (Because neither *child* nor *children* ends in *s,* add an apostrophe and *s* to show possession. The same rule applies to other words that do not end in *s.*)

2. For a word that does end in *s,* add only an apostrophe.

   Ladies' clothing is sold by all department stores.

   Policemen often sponsor *boys'* clubs.

3. For a word ending in *s* which has an added syllable when its possessive is pronounced, add an apostrophe and *s.*

   The *actress's* behavior received more attention than it deserved.

   The *witness's* testimony was easily refuted. (There is one more syllable in *actress's* than in *actress;* there is one more syllable in *witness's* than in *witness.* Therefore, add an apostrophe and *s* to each word to form its possessive.)

If you need help in determining which word denotes ownership, use the following Memory Hook to bring it into focus.

MEMORY HOOK Remember that the ownership word precedes whatever is owned by that word. For instance: "The man's hats were lost in the fire." The meaning is "the hats belonging to the man." *Man,* then, is the ownership word, and since it does not end in *s,* an apostrophe and *s* are added. Consider this sentence: "Children's toys should be durable." The meaning is "toys belonging to children." *Children,* then, is the word that takes the apostrophe.

To isolate the ownership word, say the word that represents what is owned. Next say "belonging to" or "of the," and then say the word that you think is the ownership word. This procedure will immediately identify the ownership word and will prevent using the apostrophe with the incorrect word. Study the Memory Hook procedures used in the following illustrations:

> The *secretaries'* desks are all grouped together. ("Desks belonging to secretaries." *Secretaries* is the ownership word, and since it ends in *s*, only an apostrophe is added.)
>
> The *hero's* role is usually played by a famous star. ("Role of the hero." *Hero* is the ownership word and does not end in *s*; therefore, an apostrophe and *s* are added.)

Note: The trend is to omit the apostrophe in names of organizations and institutions, except when the name ends in *men*, such as *Lions Club, Teachers College*, but *Businessmen's Club*.

⊙ **CHECKUP 1** Use the rule and the Memory Hook to determine how the possessive case of each noun should be written in the sentences below.

1. Childrens rights are guarded by the state.
2. An exception was made in Mr. Whitbys case.
3. The employees grievance procedures are being revised.
4. New chairs have been ordered for all the transcribers work stations.
5. The judge listened to the prosecuting attorneys arguments.
6. Womens organizations often provide counseling services.

ADDITIONAL USES OF THE APOSTROPHE WITH NOUNS

In addition to the basic rule, the following special rules cover the formation of certain types of possessives.

Possessive of a Compound Noun

The *last word* of a compound noun is the word that takes the apostrophe. Therefore, if the last word does not end in *s*, use an apostrophe and *s*. If the last word does end in *s*, use only an apostrophe.

> My *sisters-in-law's* families have many advantages. ("Families belonging to my sisters-in-law." *Law*, the last word, does not end in *s*.)
>
> You are using *somebody else's* stapler. ("Stapler belonging to somebody else." *Else*, the last word, does not end in *s*.)
>
> The two *vice presidents'* reports were confidential. ("Reports belonging to two vice presidents." The last word, *presidents*, ends in *s*.)

Joint or Separate Ownership

Joint ownership is shown by using the apostrophe with the last member of the combination, such as:

> *Jane and Sue's* mother is a college professor. ("The mother of Jane and Sue." Note the singular noun *mother* and the singular verb *is*.)
>
> There are no chairs for visitors in *Bob and Mark's* office. ("Office belonging to Bob and Mark." Note the singular noun *office*.)

Separate ownership is indicated by placing an apostrophe with each member of the combination. Always remember that separate apostrophes must be used to show separate ownership.

> *Jane's and Sue's* mothers are very good friends. ("The mother of Jane *and* the mother of Sue." Note the plural noun *mothers* and the plural verb *are*.)
>
> There are no chairs for visitors in *Bob's and Mark's* offices. ("Office belonging to Bob *and* office belonging to Mark." Note the plural noun *offices*.)

Possessive Case Before a Gerund

A gerund is a verb form ending in *ing* that is used as a noun; for example, "*Walking* to work would be beneficial," "*Dancing* is a form of poetry." A noun or a pronoun that precedes a gerund must be in the possessive case.

> Did you find *Ray's* checking of your returns a real help? (Possessive *Ray's* before the gerund *checking*.)
>
> We should appreciate *your* sending a check immediately. (Possessive *your* before the gerund *sending*.)

Appositive Showing Possession

Sometimes a noun that would ordinarily be in the possessive is followed by an appositive—a word or a group of words used to explain, or to give additional information about, a preceding word or phrase. In such cases, the apostrophe is used *only* with the appositive.

> That is Miss Forbes, the file *clerk's*, responsibility. (The appositive, *clerk*, takes the apostrophe. Note that there is no apostrophe following *Forbes*.)

⊙ **CHECKUP 2** Correct any errors in the use of the possessive case in the following sentences.

1. All secretary's-treasurers' reports are due tomorrow.
2. The keys to Allen's and Dave's car are missing.
3. Their mothers-in-law's friendship with each other is amazing.
4. Gale and Ellen's jobs are very different.
5. Bill's watching the clock is beginning to annoy Mr. Dunham.
6. Checking the time cards is someone's else job.
7. Mr. Barr disapproves of you using a worn-out typewriter ribbon.
8. Have you the key to David and Mike's lockers?

PERSONAL PRONOUN POSSESSIVES

The following rule has no exceptions: Personal pronoun possessives *never* take an apostrophe. Yet the error of using an apostrophe in a personal pronoun possessive (*my, your, his, their,* and so on) or in the pronoun *whose* is frequently found in business correspondence. Any writer who knows the rule can avoid this error. Study the following examples:

> The river was slowly meandering on *its* way. ("Way belonging to it.")
>
> Are you sure that these identification initials are *hers*? (Never *her's*.)

Confusion in Use of Personal Pronoun Possessives

Several of the pronoun possessives are pronounced exactly like other words that have entirely different meanings. Such words are known as homonyms. Master the following explanations to prevent any confusion.

Its The personal pronoun possessive *its*, meaning "belonging to it," is often misused for *it's*, meaning "it is"—and vice versa. If the difference in meaning is understood, the error will not be made.

> *It's* a good idea to put an apostrophe in *its* proper place. ("It is a good idea . . . place belonging to it.")

Their These three words have the same sound: *their, they're,* and *there. Their* means "belonging to them." *They're* is the contraction of *they are.* If the meaning is neither of these, *there* is the correct word to use.

> *They're* having trouble finding *their* places over *there.* ("They are having trouble finding places belonging to them over there." The last word, "there," is correct because the meaning is neither "they are" nor "belonging to them.")

Your *Your* and *you're* sound alike, but their meanings are different. *Your* means "belonging to you"; *you're* means "you are."

> When *you're* well trained, *your* job will go well. ("When you are well trained, the job belonging to you will go well.")

Our Clearly enunciated, *our* and *are* do not have precisely the same sounds, but because of careless enunciation, they are often confused. *Our* means "belonging to us." *Are* should be remembered as one of the "being" verbs.

> The union delegates *are* conferring about *our* salary increments. ("The union delegates are (the verb) conferring about salary increments belonging to us.")

Whose *Whose* is a possessive pronoun meaning "belonging to whom." This possessive must not be confused with *who's*, which is the contraction of *who is.*

> *Who's* the applicant *whose* recommendations are unsigned? ("Who is the applicant . . . recommendations belonging to whom.")

⊙ **CHECKUP 3** Make the necessary corrections in the following sentences, and explain your changes in terms of the meaning of the sentence.

1. Our thanks are due the sponsors of this contest.
2. She must know whose going to attend before she reserves rooms.
3. The one whose name is first on the list will receive the award.
4. There to announce there new location after visiting there next week.
5. If your interested, call and make an appointment.
6. Do not separate a letter from it's envelope if an enclosure is missing.
7. Who's telephone was reported out of order?
8. You know full well that its worth more than you paid for it.
9. The stationery lay right there on his desk.
10. When there ready, the printers will ask for the rest of the copy.
11. Do you know who's wallet this is?

Communication Projects

PRACTICAL APPLICATION

A Make the necessary corrections in the following sentences. If a sentence is correct, write *OK* on your paper.

1. Its too soon to know if its going to rain tomorrow.
2. The clerks-typist's pay scales vary considerably.
3. Salesmens compensation usually includes an incentive plan.
4. The sale of both Darbys and Jones houses is expected soon.
5. The Lewis' daughters are attending the same college.
6. You will find no cameos on there jewelry counter.
7. Where shall we store the shipment of stenographers notebooks?
8. When your writing an office communication, always make a carbon copy.
9. Have you bought your ticket for the policemens' ball?
10. There is a good reason for their cutting down overhead.
11. Please send are regrets to the Bindlosses.
12. Their is no reason for you to be discouraged.
13. Julia is forever criticizing somebody's else English.
14. On which floor of this store is the woman's clothing department?
15. Cleo's and Maureen's hair is always well groomed.
16. Mr. Abbot commented on you taking too long a coffee break.
17. Every job has it's advantages and disadvantages.
18. A new porch is being built on the Ellis' house.
19. Mr. Ford appreciated you sending a sales representative to call on him.
20. Do you know who's going to operate the computer?

B Correct the following sentences wherever necessary. If a sentence is correct, write *OK* on your paper.

1. The drought will drive the price of potatos even higher.
2. Miniature firemens hats were given away at the toy store.
3. He was pleased at Carmen receiving such well-deserved recognition.
4. The scent of lily of the valleys is used in a famous perfume.
5. Kelly and Shelleys' names are often assumed to be masculine rather than feminine.
6. Has anybody elses painting been sold?
7. Grand pianoes are displayed on the second floor of the store.
8. My stapler was loaned without my permission.
9. Some supervisors do not give there directions clearly.
10. The cornerstone for our new factory was lain last Monday.
11. Students complaints are often based on faulty premises.
12. Consult the Davises whenever you have any question about etiquette.
13. Mr. North's son is living in a boys dormitory.
14. Was the message lying on Mrs. Gregg's desk when she returned?
15. We will give you our answer in three weeks time.
16. The *w*s on that stencil were not struck hard enough.
17. There are many doctors offices in our building.
18. Did the Black's attend the Christmas party?
19. From the lobby could be heard the shrill sound of lady's voices.
20. Your data regarding income tax reductions is incorrect.

EDITING PRACTICE

Call an Editor! Rewrite the following letter, editing it to make the necessary corrections.

Dear Howard:

It looks as though Fred was right about the Kelly's. They have admitted their assets are froze.

Do you think that we should call for a meeting of the chief of staffs of all the other companys affected by the Kelly's misfortune? Do you know of any plans that were lain in anticipation of such an occurrence?

I expect to be in Boston on Monday of next week. May be we should meet for lunch and pool our information. As presidents of vitally concerned firms, you and I must corporate if we are to protect our company's interests.

Sincerely yours,

The Pool Supervisor Check to see if there are any spelling errors in the following paragraph, which was transcribed by one of your pool stenographers. If there are errors, write the correct spelling or spellings.

We are not satisfied with the prooves of the pictures for our new housing development and ask that you retake them. The fact that each house has a fireplace is a strong selling point; therefore, all pictures for our brochure should be taken from an angle that shows fireplace chimnies. We should appreciate your getting the new pictures to us by May 9.

CASE PROBLEM

The Correspondence Consultant In Section 11, you outlined your preliminary plan for improving letters written by the personnel of Blanton, Inc. One phase of that plan was to study samples of letters currently being written. What are some of the weaknesses you expect to find?

13 | Pronouns—Nominative and Objective Forms

Suppose the business letters you received in today's mail contained the following sentences:

Please let any of our officers or myself know when you hear from the contractor.

The higher prices will affect we retailers' sales projections.

You can depend on John and I to back up your proposal at the meeting.

Can your impression of these writers and, by association, of their companies be anything but negative? Why not? Because the use of incorrect case forms is offensive to anyone who cares about grammar.

The ability to use pronouns correctly is another hallmark of the successful communicator. Study and practice, not guesswork, are required. But, first, the business writer must understand the term *case* to be able to use the correct case form with almost automatic proficiency. The following discussion of cases concentrates on those pronouns most subject to error.

CASE

Case describes the form of a noun or a pronoun and indicates its relation to other words in the sentence. There are three cases: nominative, objective, and possessive. You have already studied pronoun possessives. To reduce learning time, emphasis is placed here on nominative-case principles: The writer who is thoroughly grounded in nominative-case usage knows immediately that a pronoun not conforming to a nominative-case rule must be in the objective case. There is, then, no real need to memorize the rules for using the objective case.

NOMINATIVE- AND OBJECTIVE-CASE FORMS OF PRONOUNS

The pronouns that have different forms in the nominative and in the objective case are *I, he, she, we, they,* and *who.* Accurate selection of correct pronouns is based upon knowing which is the nominative and which is the objective form of each pronoun. The forms are as follows:

Nominative:	I	he	she	we	they	who
Objective:	me	him	her	us	them	whom

NOMINATIVE CASE

Among the many rules for using the nominative case, only three are really needed for correct use of the nominative case of pronouns.

Subject of a Verb

Any pronoun that is the subject of a verb, either the simple subject or part of a compound subject, is in the nominative case.

> *I* will go to the bank. (Why not "Me will go to the bank"? Because *I*, the nominative form, must be used as the subject of a verb. *Me* is the objective form.)

Predicate Nominative

A predicate nominative is a noun or a pronoun that completes the meaning of a "being" verb. The "being" verbs, as you know, are *am, is, are, was, were,* helper *be,* and helper(s) *been.* Any pronoun that follows and completes the meaning of any one of these "being" verbs must always be in the nominative case.

> If I were (he? him?), I would correct the error. (*Were* is a "being" verb. A pronoun that completes the meaning of a "being" verb is in the nominative case. Therefore, the nominative *he* is correct.)
>
> It must have been (they? them?) whom we saw. (Do you see *must have been*? Then you know at once that *they*, the nominative case, is correct.)

Complement of the Infinitive *To Be* When *To Be* Has No Subject

Any pronoun that follows and completes the meaning of the infinitive *to be* when *to be* has no subject of its own is in the nominative case. To apply this rule correctly, you must understand that (1) the rule applies *only* to the infinitive *to be* and must not be used in any other situation, and (2) the infinitive *to be* has a subject of its own only if a noun or a pronoun immediately precedes it.

Study the thinking process used in the following illustrations:

> Who would ever wish to be (I? me?)? (Do you see *to be*? Is there a noun or a pronoun directly before it? No. Then this *to be* has no subject of its own, and the nominative *I* is correct.)
>
> In the dark, Ann thought Harry to be (I? me?). (Is there a noun or a pronoun immediately preceding *to be*? Yes. Then the subject of *to be* is *Harry*, and the objective *me* is correct.)
>
> The receptionist mistakenly thought the visitors to be (we? us?). (Do you see *to be*? Is there a noun or a pronoun directly before it? Yes, *visitors*. This *to be*, then, does have a subject of its own, *visitors*; and the nominative-case form after it would be incorrect. Obviously, the objective *us* is correct in this sentence.)

MEMORY HOOK For a Memory Hook on which to hang the *to be* rule, make this connection:

> NO subject—NOminative case

NO is the word to remember, and *NO* starts the word *NOminative*. Hooking up the two *No*s makes for immediate, correct application of the rule.

CHECKUP 1 Correct the pronoun forms in these sentences. If the correction is a nominative-case form, give your reason. Do not attempt to give a reason for choosing an objective-case form. (Your only reason would be that, as the pronoun could not be the nominative form, the objective form must be correct.)

1. My supervisor thought the culprit to be I.
2. Do you know whom is taking over her job?
3. She and her sister Ellen look so alike that Ellen is often thought to be her.
4. When I knock at his door, I always say, "It is me."
5. I wouldn't want to be him, would you?
6. Who made the last touchdown?
7. Why did you say that it must be me who was ill?
8. The telephone operator is often taken to be her.
9. If you were me, would you look for another position?
10. The most trustworthy workers are them who accept responsibility.

OBJECTIVE-CASE FORMS OF PRONOUNS

The efficient way to select objective-case forms of pronouns is to know that the objective case is correct whenever a pronoun does not conform to one of the nominative-case principles. Some writers, however, might like to be able to quote the rules for use of the objective case. For that reason, principles governing use of the objective case are given here.

Use the objective-case forms of personal pronouns and of *who* when the pronoun is:

The object of a verb, a preposition, or an infinitive.
The subject of an infinitive.
The complement of the infinitive *to be* when *to be* has a subject of its own.

PRONOUN USAGE PROBLEMS

Selecting the correct pronouns is often a problem in five different situations. Solutions to three of these problem situations are given in this section, and to the remaining two problems, in Section 14. Follow closely the presentation and the explanations given here.

Ross and I or *Ross and Me*?

A compound subject or object is composed of two like elements joined by a coordinate conjunction, such as *Sara or Suzanne, Mr. Dunn and I, Bob or me, you and him*. When a pronoun is part of a compound subject or object, the case of the pronoun is frequently incorrect. For instance: "Sue and (she? her?) tabulated the data." "Miss Gray sat in front of Ruth and (I? me?)." You will be able to select instantly the correct case form of a pronoun occurring in a compound subject or object if you learn the following Memory Hook.

MEMORY HOOK Whenever a compound subject or object contains a pronoun—*Ann and she, Frank or him*—mentally omit everything in the compound except the pronoun. Then read or say the sentence, and the correct form stands out like a beacon light.

Mr. Ryan and (I? me?) will find the discrepancy. (Omit *Mr. Ryan and*, and you must say, "*I* will find the discrepancy.")

I should like to sit in front of Frank or (he? him?). (Omit *Frank or*, and you must say, "I should like to sit in front of *him*.")

We Students or *Us Students*?

The correct pronoun is seldom used in such expressions (called "restrictive appositives") as *we girls, us fellows, we writers, us teachers*. For this situation, too, there is a Memory Hook that will solve the problem—and solve it fast!

MEMORY HOOK When you are about to use a pronoun in a restrictive appositive, mentally omit the noun and retain only the pronoun. Read or say the sentence and use only the pronoun. The correct form will immediately become apparent.

(We? Us?) writers must use imagination. (Omit the noun *writers*, read the sentence, and you come up with this: "*We* must use imagination." *We* is correct because it is the subject of the verb *must use*.)

Mr. Sibley told (we? us?) writers to use imagination. (Omitting *writers* and rereading the sentence forces out the correct pronoun form: "Mr. Sibley told *us* to use imagination.")

⊙ **CHECKUP 2** Use the Memory Hooks just learned to determine whether the correct pronoun forms are used in the following sentences. If a nominative-case form is used to correct a sentence, be sure to quote the rule that justifies this choice.

1. Would you let Miss Jansen or I know if you can come.
2. Richard and me are going to help her.
3. Us secretaries should have been notified first.
4. Would you like we girls to type the tabs?
5. Was that David or him in the elevator?
6. It must have been us accountants who mixed up the assignments.

Which Case Form After *Than* or *As*?

A pronoun that follows *than* or *as* in a statement of comparison frequently appears in an incomplete clause, such as "You are more skilled than (I? me?)." "Proofreading bores Miss Riley as much as (I? me?)." The correct pronoun form can be determined by mentally supplying the words that are not expressed; for example, "You are more skilled than *I (am)*." *I* stands out as the subject of the understood verb. "Proofreading bores Miss Riley as much as (*it bores*) *me*."

With the solution to the problem in mind, study the following examples:

Jane thinks that she types faster than (I? me?). (Supply the unexpressed words, as follows: "Jane thinks that she types faster than *I* (*do*)." *I* is correct because it is the subject of the understood verb, *do*.)

Unnecessary waste distresses Mr. Reed as much as (I? me?). (The complete meaning is this: "Unnecessary waste distresses Mr. Reed as much as (*it distresses*) *me*.")

Sometimes the pronoun form depends on the meaning given by voice emphasis. Italics are used for written emphasis, and italics are used in the practice sentences where voice emphasis shows the meaning that determines the selection of the correct pronoun. For example, see sentences 5 and 6 in Checkup 3.

⊙ **CHECKUP 3** The following sentences provide practice in applying solutions to the three problem situations just presented. If you choose a nominative-case form, give the reason for your choice.

1. Carson or me will have to stay late tonight.
2. It should be Miss Kelley or him who gives permission.
3. All of we employees will benefit from the new plan.
4. Our trainees often surprise we supervisors by their quickness.
5. I do hope they give *you* better treatment than we.
6. I do hope *they* give you better treatment than us.
7. Do you think you have been as faithful as him?
8. Our office force works much harder than them.

Communication Projects

PRACTICAL APPLICATION

A Make any needed corrections in the following sentences. Use these short forms to indicate your reasons for selecting nominative-case forms: *sov* (for "subject of the verb"), *pn* (for "predicate nominative"), or *tbns* (for "this *to be* has *no subject* of its own").

1. Bert and him disagree on even trivial matters.
2. The missing girls were thought to be Marta and me.
3. His wife understands legal language as well as him.
4. Karen swims better than either my sister or me.
5. Please see Mrs. Alden or I before using the new copier.
6. The sales manager asked we six girls to attend the meeting.
7. All us older employees are checking our retirement benefits.
8. Both the manager and us girls missed the five o'clock bus.
9. Whom has the answer to this problem?
10. It must have been her whom you saw in the foyer.
11. Sam is often taken to be me.
12. The telephone call was for Mr. Sheedy or I.
13. Was it him who released the information?
14. On closer acquaintance, I find that I like *Roy* better than he.
15. Mr. Sims took the movie star to be she.
16. I should like to have you and her retype these papers.
17. Do you think that us men have a chance to win the tournament?
18. It would be me who would make such a silly mistake!
19. Would you trust *Ellen* rather than she?
20. Please let us accounting clerks check our own figures.

B Correct the following sentences wherever necessary. If a sentence is correct, write *OK* on your paper.

1. If it depended on you and I, the work would be done by now.
2. The bank notified all us depositors of the new procedures.
3. I would not want to be him, despite his power and position.
4. She told me they're expecting to finish their stock-taking next week.
5. I think *she* is a better claim agent than him.
6. All the memos' he received were improperly signed.
7. It could not have been her who found the error.
8. The accident victim was lying in the road.
9. All bidders specifications' have been mailed.
10. Now that the painters are here, our office is all tore up.
11. Who did you take me to be?
12. Are *you* as friendly with Simon as him?
13. Have the Ellises answered our letter?
14. Did you know that us operators are in line for a bonus?
15. Our linen handkerchieves are imported from Ireland.
16. If he were I, he would surely say the same thing.
17. Mrs. Bolton plans to take her secretary and I to the meeting.
18. Mr. Cotter and us other executives will work next Saturday.
19. Find out about the Rosses' credit rating before you answer their letter.
20. Please give these schedules to Bob and he.

EDITING PRACTICE

Plurals and Possessives Indicate any errors in plurals or in possessives. Write *OK* for any correct sentence.

1. Customers often confuse the two Jessys' in our store.
2. Mrs. Carlin and her two sister-in-laws all work for our firm.
3. The Davis' children all have first names beginning with *D*.
4. Notary publics usually charge a small fee for their services.
5. His whereabouts has been a mystery ever since Monday.
6. I believe the Barnes' are moving to Houston.
7. The scissors we manufacture is made of highest-quality steel.
8. They're so sure that their billfolds will stay there untouched.
9. Boys shoes' cost as much as grown men's.
10. I dislike his voice, but I like hers.
11. The cafeteria sandwiches' are a little stale.
12. The sixes in this copy must have been struck too lightly.

Only One Word The polish of a letter can sometimes be marred by just one word, as is the case in this letter. Can you find the word and make the correction?

> Your analysis of the buying habits of our charge-account customers is very well done and will be of help to all of us here at Blanton's.
>
> The only suggestion I have to make is that you delete pages 5 and 6. These pages list details that are irrevelant, minutiae that serve only to obscure the points brought out in the first four pages.
>
> If I can be of further help, please let me know.

CASE PROBLEM

The Correspondence Consultant Now that you have completed your study of the letters written by the staff of Blanton, Inc., you should be ready to make recommendations for improvement. What would be your recommendations?

14 Pronouns—Additional Usage Problems

Comparable only to the commonly misused *lie* and *lay, sit* and *set*, and *rise* and *raise* is the confusing choice between *who* and *whom*. Knowing when to use *who* (nominative case) and when to use *whom* (objective case) is one of the obstacles to mastering the use of pronouns. Another stumbling block is the correct usage of those pronouns ending in *self* or *selves* (also known as compound personal pronouns).

SELF-ENDING PRONOUNS

Myself, yourself, himself, herself, itself, ourselves, yourselves, and *themselves* are the pronouns ending in *self.* These pronouns are often mistakenly used in place of the nominative- or objective-case form of a personal pronoun. For instance, in the sentence "Mrs. Cole and myself will be happy to accept your invitation," the writer, unsure about *I* or *me,* avoids both and uses the *self* pronoun as an escape. Actually, this is just as serious an error as writing "Mrs. Cole and *me* will be happy. . . ." The *self* pronouns are correctly used only to intensify or to reflect a noun or another pronoun.

Intensive Use

A *self*-ending pronoun is used to intensify—that is, to emphasize—the meaning of a statement. To illustrate:

> Mr. Myers told me the news. (This is an unemphatic statement.)
>
> Mr. Myers *himself* told me the news. (The word *himself* intensifies the meaning.)

A word of caution is needed here. Take care to place a *self*-ending pronoun where it will perform its emphasizing function. Careless placement might result in something like the following:

> She said that the home economics teacher cannot sew *herself.* (Written correctly and with a less painful implication, the sentence reads: "She said that the home economics teacher *herself* cannot sew.")

Reflexive Use

A *self* pronoun may also be used to reflect some noun or pronoun that has already been named.

> I could not bring *myself* to look at the accident. (*Myself* refers to *I.*)
>
> Legislators should not vote *themselves* increases in salary. (*Themselves* refers to *legislators.*)

CASE OF PRONOUN APPOSITIVES

An appositive is a word or a group of words used to explain, or to give additional information about, a preceding word or phrase.

> Our secretaries, Miss Howe and Miss Shea, will make the appointments. (*Miss Howe and Miss Shea* gives additional information about *secretaries;* therefore, *Miss Howe and Miss Shea* is an appositive.)

Note the comma before and the comma after the appositive. An important punctuation rule is this: *A nonrestrictive appositive is set off by commas.*

The case rule for appositives is the following: *An appositive is the same case as the word with which it is in apposition.* The case form of an appositive is a problem only when that appositive is a compound containing a pronoun, such as "Our secretaries, Miss Howe and (she? her?), will make the appointments." To solve this problem, use the following Memory Hook.

⊡ **MEMORY HOOK** Refer to the Memory Hook for compound subjects or objects on page 100. Follow the advice given there—to omit the noun in the compound. Also omit the word or words with which the compound is in apposition, like this:

> Our secretaries, Miss Howe and (she? her?), will make the appointments. (*Miss Howe and* would be omitted because there is a pronoun in the compound. Now omit *our secretaries,* the words with which the compound is in apposition. The result is this: *She will make the appointments.*)
>
> Mr. Baker commended our junior executives, Bill and (he? him?). Using the Memory Hook results in the following: *Mr. Baker commended him.*)

⊙ **CHECKUP 1** Which sentences are incorrect? Why?

1. The inseparable friends, Tom and him, are no longer so inseparable.
2. Both my neighbor and myself heard prowlers last night.
3. The two best workers, Marie and her, are to receive raises.
4. The manager suspected the loafers to be the three girls, Pam Jan, and she.
5. Jim and I will treat ourselves to a good lunch.
6. We are not ready to ship ourselves.
7. Both Mr. Senay and myself have been working steadily all day.
8. The successful candidates were the first two, Selden and him.
9. The machine is operated by Paul and myself.
10. Mr. Myers put us, Brian and myself, in charge.

WHO AND *WHOM; WHOEVER* AND *WHOMEVER*

The pronouns *who* and *whoever* are nominative-case forms; *whom* and *whomever* are objective-case forms. If the pronoun is the subject of a verb, a predicate nominative, or the complement of a *to be* that has no subject of its own, use the nominative form. If the pronoun is none of these, use the objective form. The selection process, however, can be considerably sped up by using the following Memory Hook.

⊡ **MEMORY HOOK** When faced with a choice between *who* and *whom* or between *whoever* and *whomever,* do this: Mentally substitute *he* or *him.* If *he* could be substituted, the correct pronoun is *who* or *whoever.* If *him* could be substituted, the correct pronoun is *whom* or *whomever.*

> The lawyer (who? whom?) Mr. King mentioned is known as a tax expert. (Make the substitution: *Mr. King mentioned (him).* The correct pronoun is *whom* because *him* can be substituted.)
>
> I don't care (who? whom?) she visits. (Make the substitution: *She visits (him).* The correct pronoun is *whom* because *him* can be substituted.)

Who or *Whom* in an Interrogative Sentence

A question containing *who* or *whom* is usually in inverted order. First, change the order from inverted to normal order. Then apply the Memory Hook at the bottom of page 105. Here are some additional illustrations.

> (Who? Whom?) is the man wearing tennis shoes? (Normal order: *The man wearing tennis shoes is (he). Who* is correct because it is a predicate nominative.)
>
> (Who? Whom?) do you take me for? (Normal order: *You do take me for (him). Whom* is correct because *him* can be substituted.)

A few *who, whom* questions are not in inverted order because there is no way that the order can be changed. In such questions, use the Memory Hook at the bottom of page 105 to pinpoint the correct pronoun.

> (Who? Whom?) is supposed to revise the filing system? (Make the substitution: *(He) is supposed. . . . Who* is correct because it is the subject of the verb.)
>
> (Whoever? Whomever?) would believe your fantastic story? (*(He) would believe. . . . Whoever* is correct because it is the subject of the verb.)

⊙ **CHECKUP 2** Use the Memory Hook to decide whether or not the pronouns are correct. If you use *who,* quote the nominative-case rule that applies.

1. Who did he ask to be chairperson?
2. Who has been responsible for spreading such rumors?
3. Who will the company appoint to the new position?
4. Who did you meet at the convention?
5. Who did you bring with you?

Who, Whom; Whoever, Whomever in a Dependent Clause

Most *who, whom* errors are made when either pronoun is used in a dependent clause. The selection procedure given here has been carefully thought out and tested. If you follow it exactly as presented, your error count will be zero. There are two steps to the procedure.

Step 1 Isolate, or take out, the clause. The pronoun is part of the dependent clause to which it belongs, and the case form is determined by the function of that pronoun in the dependent clause. When isolating a clause, start with the word *who, whom, whoever,* or *whomever.*

> Edgar talks to (whoever, whomever) he meets on the bus. (Isolate the clause: *(whoever, whomever) he meets on the bus.*)
>
> I do not know (who, whom) the caller could have been. (Isolate the clause: *(who, whom) the caller could have been.*)
>
> Be gracious to (whoever, whomever) calls on the telephone. (Isolate the clause: *(whoever, whomever) calls on the telephone.*)

Step 2 If the isolated clause is in inverted order, change it to normal order. The order of the clause can be seen at a glance. If only the *who* pronoun appears before the verb, the clause is in normal order. If a *who* pronoun *plus* a noun or another pronoun appear before the verb, the clause is in inverted order. To make Step 2 absolutely clear, consider the clauses that were isolated in the Step 1 illustrations.

> (whoever, whomever) he meets on the bus. (The *who* pronoun plus the pronoun *he* appear before the verb. This clause, therefore, is out of order. The normal order is this: *he meets (him) on the bus. Whomever* is correct because *him* can be substituted.)
>
> (who, whom) the caller could have been. (The *who* pronoun plus the noun *caller* appear before the verb; therefore, the clause is in inverted order. The normal order is this: *the caller could have been (he). Who* is correct because it is a predicate nominative.)
>
> (whoever, whomever) calls on the telephone. (Since only the *who* pronoun appears before the verb, the clause is in normal order. Using the Memory Hook, make the substitution: *(he) calls on the telephone. Whoever* is correct because it is the subject of the verb.)

⊙ **CHECKUP 3** When studying these sentences, be sure to follow the Step 1 and Step 2 procedure. Select the correct pronouns and justify your selections.

1. The newly elected senator is a woman (who, whom) we all respect.
2. The lawyer (who, whom) we heard is a noted courtroom orator.
3. Jeffrey Bennon, (who, whom) defended the case yesterday, is a famous trial lawyer.
4. Do you know (who, whom) will be awarded the top sales prize?
5. This question is for (whoever, whomever) has the correct data.
6. Do you know (who, whom) will be awarded the honorary title?
7. (Whoever, Whomever) draws the short straw will have to clean the machines.
8. My brother, (who, whom) you met last week, has leased an appartment in your building.
9. (Whoever, Whomever) told you that is incorrect.
10. The person (who, whom) we elected is Carla Robbins.

Clause Within a *Who, Whom* Clause Sometimes confusion is caused by a parenthetical clause—*I think, he says, we believe*—that occurs within a *who, whom* clause. Whenever you see a clause like this, mentally omit it. Omitting the parenthetical clause will enable you to select the correct pronoun more quickly.

> Is that the man (who, whom) you said I should introduce to Mr. Abbot? (Step 1—Isolate the clause: *(who, whom) you said I should introduce to Mr. Abbot.* Step 2—Omit the parenthetical clause *you said.* The normal order of the resulting clause is this: *I should introduce (him) to Mr. Abbot. Whom* is correct because *him* can be substituted.)

However, the process of selecting the correct pronoun is the same even if the parenthetical clause is retained. Consider the clause discussed above.

> (who, whom) you said I should introduce to Mr. Abbot. (The normal order of the clause is this: *you said I should introduce (him) to Mr. Abbot.* Again, *whom* is correct because *him* can be substituted.)

⊙ **CHECKUP 4** Make any necessary corrections, and explain your reasons for making them. If a nominative form is selected, give the rule that governs its use.

1. Give the award to whoever you think best deserves it.
2. She was one of those people whom her boss called "fidgeters."
3. You must ask whoever you think will do the best job.
4. The group elected John, whom we all agreed is well qualified to be president.
5. Do you know who they will select?
6. You may give these records to whoever you choose.
7. You may give the records to whomever asks for them.
8. Todd is a man whom I believe will do fine work.

Communication Projects

PRACTICAL APPLICATION

A Make the necessary corrections in the following sentences. Give reasons for nominative-case choices.

1. The chairman appointed Judy and myself as tellers for the election.
2. At parties Sam ignores people whom he thinks are likely to be bores.
3. To his amazement, the first two prizes were won by Richard and himself.
4. Craig is the one person whom I am sure would never say such a thing.
5. We three, Dave and Lance and myself, tried out for the bowling team.
6. Any complaints about scheduling must have come from them, Miss Ashton and she.
7. Two branch managers, Clayton Jones and me, are being promoted.
8. Whom shall I ask to sit at this desk?
9. Wait a minute; I'm just going to leave myself.
10. Whom do you think will win the prize?
11. I have listed the names of all who she said had the best recommendations.
12. Who is the better typist, Barbara or she?
13. Tell whomever is first to arrive to unlock all the doors.
14. Our very best friends are they, Amy and her.
15. The promotion will be given to whoever we think deserves it.
16. Mr. Kain asked Fred and myself to sell tickets for the game.
17. Who does Mr. Tubbs outrank in seniority?
18. Where are the repairmen, Mr. Tate and him?
19. Was that assignment supposed to be for us, Dennis and myself?
20. Whom do you think you are?

B Correct the following sentences wherever necessary. If a sentence is correct, write *OK* on your paper.

1. Why do I make more errors than her?
2. What he earns is no business of her's.
3. I have not read as widely as him.
4. Company B offers better opportunities for Barbara and I to advance.
5. She pleaded for another chance for Rachel and herself.

6. Do you think that teacher's jobs are as plentiful as ever?
7. Written authorization can be given only by Mrs. Johnson or me.
8. Who did they take Joseph to be?
9. Whose the new stenographer in the pool?
10. If it were possible, who would you wish to be?
11. Surely you do not expect us drivers to take another test!
12. Whom did you think him to be, Bob or he?
13. The election is a question of whom conducts the best campaign.
14. I left the pen with the girl whom I thought had charge of lost articles.
15. The fastest operators are Andy and him.
16. Whom do you consider is the best scientist in our plant?
17. The visitor who you saw in the office this morning came to see Mr. Byrne and me.
18. You should select whoever you think will work well with our group.
19. Our favorite researchers, Mr. Carr and he, have found the answer to our problem.
20. A good receptionist does not become too friendly with a caller who she does not know.

EDITING PRACTICE

Spelling and Possessives Indicate any errors in spelling or in the use of the possessive case. Write *OK* for any correct sentences.

1. Do not become dependent on other people to help you do your work.
2. The very existence of our company is threatened by the paper shortage.
3. The players wives' eagerly awaited their return from the road trip.
4. There remittance was already overdue.
5. Please tell us what its all about.
6. "A full day's work for a full day's pay" is a slogan that is worth adopting.
7. Did you know that there receiving an additional week's wages?
8. Be sure to send a letter of transmital with each contract.
9. Since we pay by check, we do not need a receipt.
10. The extra bonus was a surprise to all of us.

The Sour Note Somewhere in this paragraph is one word or phrase that jars. It could almost pass undetected, but it shouldn't be permitted to. Find the error and correct it.

> Thank you for telling us so soon that you are unable to except an appointment as trustee for the Community Center. We realize that you give your services to many civic and religious organizations, and we can understand that there must be a cutoff place somewhere; but we did hope that you might be able to take on just one more—the Community Center. Do you think you could find time to be a "consultant-at-large," a person on whom we could call for advice on some particularly knotty problem?

CASE PROBLEM

The Wrong Impression Fred Clay was being interviewed by William Dalton, general manager, for a position as office supervisor with the Economy Printing Company. In the interview, Mr. Dalton asked about two important points: (1) the formal training in supervision that Fred had and (2) Fred's experience as a supervisor. Fred proudly mentioned his ten years of work experience and emphasized the value of this phase of his background for the office supervisor's job. He casually told Mr. Dalton that he had no formal training in supervision but that his work experience taught him all he needed to know.

Later on, Mr. Dalton asked Fred for his philosophy of supervision. Fred replied tartly: "I believe a supervisor's job is to keep close tabs on everybody so that they get their work done and don't get out of line. It is certainly not necessary to let them in on everything. What they don't know doesn't hurt them."

A few days after the personal interview with Mr. Dalton, Fred received a letter from the Economy Printing Company thanking him for making application with them, but indicating that someone else had been hired for the position. Naturally, Fred was disappointed and tried to determine whether something had gone wrong in the interview, since his experience was exactly what the company wanted.

1. What went wrong in the interview that cost Fred this job?
2. What might Fred have said regarding training in supervision that might have helped him get this job?

15 Predicate Agreement—With Simple Subject

An amusing feature of a well-known magazine was called "Your Slip Is Showing." It contained spelling and grammatical errors that had slipped past proofreaders and into print, often with ludicrous results. In conversation, grammatical errors might slip by unnoticed or they might be quickly forgotten. But a spelling or a grammatical error in business writing would not escape a reader. Such an error would be seen, read, and reread. Moreover, it would remain visible for a long time.

Lack of agreement between the subject and the predicate is one frequently made error. This and similar errors are so serious and so noticeable that they warrant discussion of the rules for proper agreement throughout this section and the next two sections.

Rules of agreement are so specific that each rule applies only to a particular type of subject. This section presents the basic rule of agreement and the rule for predicate agreement with two different types of simple subjects. Study and practice these rules thoroughly before advancing to Section 16, where the rules for predicate agreement with the four remaining types of simple subjects are presented.

BASIC PRINCIPLE OF AGREEMENT

The basic agreement rule for all sentences that have a simple subject is this: *A predicate must agree in number and person with the simple subject.* The following examples illustrate subject-verb agreement.

> The employees who relocated to our new plant (is? are?) receiving company funds for moving expenses. (The simple subject is *employees,* which is plural; therefore, the plural verb *are* agrees with the plural subject.)
>
> A supervisor with these desirable personality traits (is? are?) hard to find. (The simple subject is *supervisor,* which is singular; therefore, the singular verb *is* agrees with the singular subject.)

Agreement Preliminaries

Before you can correctly apply the rules for agreement, you must understand the following four elements.

Predicate Verb and Pronoun(s) The basic principle states that "a predicate must agree." The meaning is that the *predicate verb* and any *predicate pronoun or pronouns* referring to the simple subject must agree with that subject.

> The conference room, including furniture, lamps, and paintings, (has? have?) been completely redecorated for (his? her? its? their?) new users. (The simple subject is *conference room,* which is singular in number and neuter in gender. Therefore, to agree with *conference room,* the correct predicate verb and predicate pronoun are *has* and *its.*)
>
> Our company (prefers? prefer?) to have meetings for all (his? her? its? their?) staff every Monday morning. (The simple subject is *company,* which is singular in number and neuter in gender. The predicate verb and predicate pronoun are *prefers* and *its,* to agree with *company.*)

Correct Pronoun Choice Whenever the gender of a simple subject is clearly masculine or feminine, choosing the correct pronoun is no problem. Many simple subjects, such as *employee, citizen,* and *nobody,* could be either masculine or feminine. Which pronoun is correct?

The "traditional" rule was to choose *he* whenever the simple subject could be either masculine or feminine, a rule that ignored women. But in actual practice, writers would choose *he* to agree with simple subjects such as *executive, doctor,* and *treasurer,* and *she* to agree with simple subjects such as *nurse, secretary,* and *receptionist,* a practice that typecast men and women into very definite, limited roles. This practice is perhaps worse than ignoring women!

To avoid (not solve) this problem, use *he or she* or a similar combination of pronouns to refer to a simple subject that could be either masculine or feminine.

> An executive must depend on *his or her* assistants for accurate information.
>
> A secretary must be able to transcribe *his or her* shorthand precisely.

When *he or she* or similar combinations are used too often, the message will be difficult to read. In such cases, the above examples, for instance, might be revised as follows:

> Executives must depend on *their* assistants for accurate information.
>
> Secretaries must be able to transcribe *their* shorthand precisely.

Singular or Plural Verb Sometimes agreement errors are made because writers forget that a verb that ends in *s* or *es* is singular. The confusing fact is that both singular verbs and plural nouns most often end in *s* or *es*. Remember that *s* or *es* is a signal that the verb is singular. Say or write:

> The men *go*; but the man *goes*.
>
> Children *have talked*; but the child *has talked* or the child *talks*.
>
> Contestants *guess*; but the contestant *guesses* or *has guessed*.

Inverted Order To find the subject more easily, change sentences that are in inverted order to normal order. This principle, taught in Section 8 and practiced in succeeding lessons, is repeated here because failure to make the change often causes errors in predicate agreement, as shown by the following examples.

> Above the bookshelves (was? were?) a newly painted mural. (The careless person sees *bookshelves* and uses the plural verb *were*. *Mural*, however, is the simple subject; therefore, the correct verb is *was*.)
>
> In this notebook (is? are?) samples of the style for informal reports. (Mentally changing this sentence to normal order shows *samples* to be the simple subject. Therefore, the correct verb is *are*.)

⊙ **CHECKUP 1** Make the necessary corrections in the following sentences, using the answer form shown below.

> Sentence: If a poorly dressed stranger call, treat them courteously.
> Answer: *calls* and *him or her*, to agree with *stranger*.

1. Among our company's top sales representatives are Jack Jones.
2. A customer can apply for their special holiday money tokens until December 1.
3. Ahead in the way of exciting events are our annual staff outing to Silver Falls.
4. A new collection of imported handbags are on display in our store.
5. The entire plant, with all their buildings, are for sale.
6. A shipment of automobile parts are on their way to us now.
7. Each of us have our own desk.
8. Mr. Foley, as well as you, are being asked to test the machine.

THERE AT THE BEGINNING OF A SENTENCE OR CLAUSE

A sentence or clause that begins with *there—there is, there are, there has been, there have been*, and like expressions—is in inverted order. The subject follows the verb. In accordance with the basic principle, the predicate must agree with the simple subject.

His secretary reports that there (is? are?) three interviews scheduled today. (The simple subject of the clause is the plural noun *interviews*. The verb, therefore, is *are*, to agree with *interviews*.)

There (is? are?) many workers who have difficulty with (his or her? their?) hearing. (Changing to normal order shows the plural noun *workers* to be the simple subject. Therefore, your selection is *have* and *their*, to agree with *workers*.)

⊙ **CHECKUP 2** Make the necessary corrections in these sentences, giving your answers in the form shown in Checkup 1.

1. Among those helping in the campaign there is several members of our organization.
2. The contractor replied that there is no ceramic tiles of that color available.
3. We think that there is more goods coming in tomorrow.
4. We realize that there is grave danger of a crisis.
5. Did you know that there is ten questions still to be answered?

COLLECTIVE-NOUN SIMPLE SUBJECT

A collective noun is a word that refers to a group or collection of persons or things, such as *class, faculty, herd, jury, committee, audience,* and *company*. The correct number, singular or plural, of a collective noun is not always easily recognized. If the group or collection is considered to be acting as a whole, the subject is singular; if considered to be acting separately, the subject is plural. To interpret the group as acting separately, the sentence context must be such that only a plural predicate could be used. For instance:

A jury (does? do?) not give (its? their?) verdict carelessly. (*Jury* is a collective noun and in this sentence is acting as a whole, as one unit. Your selection would be *does* and *its*, to agree with *jury*.)

The jury (is? are?) arguing vehemently. (To argue, more than one person is needed. The plural verb *are* is correct because the jury members are acting separately.)

⊙ **CHECKUP 3** These sentences provide practice in all the agreement principles studied thus far. Make the necessary corrections, giving your answers in the form used in Checkups 1 and 2.

1. Have you noticed that a secretary soon learns to assign priorities in their duties?
2. How is it that one of them seem so undecided about joining us for lunch?
3. You will see that there are three photographs to be mailed.
4. A registered nurse, as well as a teacher and a lawyer, are licensed by the state.
5. Every nation looks to their leaders for guidance.
6. The committee was consulting with their individual attorneys.
7. The principal announced that the faculty was excused from attendance at the assembly.
8. Our company have completed their twentieth year in business.
9. On my desk are staplers that do not belong to me.
10. The class were preparing to leave on their field trip.

Communication Projects

PRACTICAL APPLICATION

A Correct the following sentences, following the answer form shown below.

Sentence: All employees of the institution does not take its vacation during the summer.

Answer: *do* and *their*, to agree with *employees*

1. The bowling team is planning to compete in the regional tournament.
2. We do not think that even one of the cashiers have been given building plans.
3. The donor, as well as the trustees, are satisfied with the building plans.
4. During what month was these people forced to stay at a motel because of flood damage to their homes?
5. There is several acceptable styles for typing a business letter.
6. Each officer of the League of Women Voters use their own letterheads.
7. Of all the types of business letters, there is only a few that a secretary is likely to compose.
8. Mathematics, as well as history and English, are required of all students.
9. After the introductory remarks come the prepared speech.
10. No administrative assistant will leave until they finish their work.
11. The agency reported that there was several openings for file clerks.
12. The complete list of desks, tables, and chairs shows a need for additional equipment.
13. The council was evidently quarreling among themselves.
14. There is always two sides to every question.
15. The public has widely differing opinions about secondary-school education.
16. Four carbons, as well as the original, is to be typed for all letters to Barr & Company.
17. You, as well as I, are eligible for the appointment.
18. The chairperson said that each group must make its own rules.
19. Has there been many sales representatives in the store today?
20. The news about Social Security increases have just reached us.

B Correct the following sentences. If a sentence is correct, write *OK* on your paper.

1. Has the lieutenant governor's speech been taped yet?
2. We cannot understand why Mr. Howard thought Leslie to be me.
3. My boss, together with other senior executives, enjoys their being included in the bonus-sharing plan.
4. Have the Kuress's found a suitable name yet for their new line of hand tools?
5. The employee who serves beyond twenty-five years receives additional pension benefits.
6. The faculty signed their full names to their contracts.
7. Doesn't his balance check with your's?
8. Is the president's whereabouts a secret?
9. Is there ten reams in that package?
10. No body of men have rendered finer service to the country.

11. Every man in the locker rooms have their special complaints about the service.
12. The duplicator lay on it's side in the machines room.
13. When your looking for advancement, be sure that you are qualified for a promotion.
14. The survey showed that there is enough jobs for everyone.
15. Every one of we women has her own correspondence routine.

EDITING PRACTICE

Editor Needed! Rewrite this letter, making the necessary corrections.

Gentlemen:

Mr. Dunn and myself have carefully considered your application for further credit. In our company, however, many policies designed to cover every aspect of the business is in effect. According to one company policy, the credit officers may not extend credit beyond a $1,000 limit.

Mr. Dunn, as well as me, wishes he was able to grant your request. Until such time as your account is reduced below $1,000, however, we shall be happy to do business with you on a cash basis.

Very sincerely yours,

Pseudohomonyms As you know, pseudohomonyms are words that sound somewhat alike but have different meanings. Correct any pseudohomonym errors you find in the following paragraph.

In the name of all the personal connected with the Community Center, I thank you for accepting our invitation to act in an advisory capacity whenever legal problems arise. Your willingness to help has effected the morale of the entire staff, for we are now relieved of all worry about conforming to the numerous local ordnances. You are filling a real need, Mr. Marr, and we are glad to have your services available to us.

CASE PROBLEM

The Perplexed Secretary Mary Lou Jones is private secretary to an executive. One day her boss, Mrs. Merriwether, indicated that she had to work all day on a speech she had to give the following day. "Do not disturb me under any circumstances," Mrs. Merriwether cautioned Mary Lou. Just one hour later the telephone rang and a voice asked to speak to Mrs. Merriwether. "May I ask who is calling?" Mary Lou inquired. In a slightly angered tone, the voice indicated that it was Mr. Sells, Mrs. Merriwether's boss, and that he wanted to speak to Mrs. Merriwether immediately.

In view of Mrs. Merriwether's instructions, what should Mary Lou say to Mr. Sells? Give a reason for your answer.

16 Predicate Agreement—Other Types of Simple Subjects

The basic principle of agreement—that the predicate must agree in number and person with the simple subject—holds true for all cases of simple-subject agreement. However, a specific rule for each of the six types of simple subjects must be learned and applied to that one type only. Keep this fact in mind when studying the following separate rules for the remaining four types of simple subjects.

FOREIGN-NOUN SUBJECT

From the discussion on the formation of plurals, in Section 11, you learned that the number of a foreign noun is shown by its *ending*; for example, *crisis, crises; stylus, styli; alumna, alumnae.* Therefore, when the simple subject of a sentence is a foreign noun, the singular or plural ending of that noun will govern predicate agreement.

> The basis for his statements *was* unsound. (The predicate must be singular to agree with the singular subject *basis.*)
>
> The bases for his statements *were* unsound. (The predicate must be plural to agree with the plural subject *bases.*)

⊙ **CHECKUP 1** Select the simple subject in each of these sentences, and identify the rule applying to it such as *basic* (for subjects that are obviously singular or plural), *sentence or clause beginning with* there, *collective noun,* or *foreign noun.* Then make any corrections that may be needed.

1. Does his analyses of the market surveys reveal need for changes in the product?
2. Interplanetary travel, with its technical and ethical implications, seem possible in our children's lifetime.
3. The hospital personnel below the supervisory level is voting on the new contract next week.
4. The criteria for executive selection has been announced today.
5. The administrative staff is not in agreement.
6. There was no reasons given for his dismissal.
7. Fungi in profusion are found in the tropics.
8. There seems to be some differences of opinion about the worth of the proposal.
9. Janet, as well as the other correspondents, were invited to express their opinions freely.
10. The class has varying ideas about study procedures.

PART, PORTION, OR AMOUNT SUBJECT

Sometimes a simple subject is a word that means a part, a portion, or an amount of something, such as *all, half, some, two-thirds.* With a subject of this type, the number of the predicate cannot be determined until the following questions are answered: Part of what? Portion of what? Amount of what? For instance:

> Some (is? are?) missing. (Which is correct, *is* or *are*? Without additional information, you cannot select either verb as correct.)
>
> Some of the report (is? are?) missing. (*Is* is correct, because the subject is *some* of *one thing*.)
>
> Some of the reports (is? are?) missing. (*Are* is correct in this sentence, because the subject is *some* of *more than one thing*.)

Here is the rule that governs this type of subject: When the simple subject of a sentence is a word that means part, portion, or amount, the number of the predicate is determined by the meaning of the complete subject, not the simple subject alone.

CHECKUP 2 Make your selection of the correct word or words, and indicate the word that influenced your choice. Follow this example:

> Sentence: Three-fifths of the space (is? are?) occupied by desks.
> Answer: *is, space*

1. Over half the records (was? were?) damaged by fire and smoke.
2. Some of the office (is? are?) used for a visitors' reception area.
3. Part of the new components (was? were?) found defective when (it? they?) (was? were?) first tested.
4. Half the shipments (has? have?) been rerouted.
5. All the typewriters (needs? need?) to have (its? their?) (ribbon? ribbons?) changed.
6. Nine-tenths of our office (was? were?) formerly poorly lighted.

A NUMBER, THE NUMBER SUBJECT

A number has a plural meaning, and the predicate must be plural; *the number* has a singular meaning, and the predicate must be singular. An adjective between the *a* or *the* and *number* does not affect this principle. Here are some illustrations:

> A number of applicants (was? were?) interviewed today. (*Were*, because *a number* is plural.)
>
> The number of clerks in business offices (outnumbers? outnumber?) all other employees. (*Outnumbers*, because *the number* is singular.)
>
> A great number of inquiries about our new product (comes? come?) into the office each week. (*Come*, because *a number* is plural.)

Business writers must be able to apply the correct principles of grammar instantly. They have no time to sit and ponder. Trying to remember whether *a number* or *the number* is singular could waste thinking time, but understanding the following Memory Hook can make the correct application of *a number, the number* quick and easy.

MEMORY HOOK When confronted with the choice of the correct predicate for *a number* or *the number*, picture the following:

Plural: a
Singular: the

Which is the shorter word, *plural* or *singular*? Which is the shorter word, *a* or *the*? The shorter word *a* goes with the shorter word *plural*; the longer word *the* goes with the longer word *singular*. Therefore, *a number* is *plural*; *the number* is *singular*.

INDEFINITE-WORD SUBJECT

The indefinite words *each, either, neither, everyone, everybody, someone, somebody, anyone, anybody, no one, nobody,* and *a person* are singular in meaning. Therefore, whenever one of these indefinite words is the subject of a sentence, the predicate must be singular.

Each of us (has? have?) (his or her? their?) own private beliefs. (*Has* and *his or her*, to agree with the singular subject *each*.)

Everybody (is? are?) to take (his or her? their?) (place? places?) on the platform. (*Is, his or her, place,* to agree with *everybody*.)

A person (resents? resent?) having (his or her? their?) legal rights challenged. (*Resents* and *his or her*, to agree with *a person*.)

CHECKUP 3 These sentences provide comprehensive practice for the rules studied in Sections 15 and 16. Follow these directions: (1) name the subject, (2) identify that subject according to type, (3) make corrections where needed, and (4) give reasons for making corrections.

1. The number of exemptions he claims are far more than mine.
2. The parentheses on my typewriter does not align properly when I type rapidly.
3. Everyone seems pleased at the news of their acceptance into membership.
4. The entire advisory council is to be seated at the speaker's table.
5. Our family are always the last to give up time-honored tradition.
6. No one expects their room assignment for the convention before next week.
7. The number of available stenographers are fewer than the government needs.
8. Part, but not all, of the papers was in the safe.
9. Miss Dean, together with the pool typists, have posted their first win in the bowling match.
10. All the money have not yet been accounted for.
11. Neither of the proposed solutions are acceptable.
12. A number of persons has been asking for you.

Communication Projects

PRACTICAL APPLICATION

A Make all necessary corrections in the following sentences, and indicate your reason for making each correction. The following example shows you how to write your answers.

Sentence: Nobody are to have their lunch hour curtailed.
Answer: *is, his or her,* to agree with *nobody*

1. A number of serious accidents has occurred at that dangerous intersection.
2. Incorrect diagnoses are sometimes made even by trained specialists.
3. Owing to a failure of the store's air conditioning, some of the fruit in the display cases were spoiled.
4. Has the alumni of our school reached its financial goal for this year?
5. The number of people willing to work on these service projects are surprisingly large.
6. Neither of the branch managers admits they erred in predicting higher sales this month.
7. When the game ended, the entire team was jumping up and down with excitement at their hard-won victory.
8. A number of different magazines comes into this office every week.
9. Anyone who pleases only themselves will soon lack friends.
10. Some bacteria is found in all liquids.
11. Only half the people in this country speaks English correctly.
12. Is the sanatorium open for inspection?
13. The large number of absences has held up production.
14. Incorrect analysis of contributing causes are the reason for the protest.
15. The number of staff members are known only by the personnel department.
16. None of the books has been returned to its special section.
17. Everyone will please tidy their own desk each night.
18. If anybody from the main office calls, be sure to get their number.
19. Three-fourths of the time were spent in research.
20. Neither of the applicants were chosen for the position.

B Correct the following sentences wherever necessary.

1. The leads in the school play, Audrey and him, are very well suited for their parts.
2. Some of our stockroom supplies, especially shorthand notebooks, needs replenishing.
3. Everyone are expected to be punctual in returning to work after lunch.
4. Do you know the Schmitzes' new address?
5. Some of our branch offices are to be closed permanently.
6. The audience was so unruly that they were asked to leave the hall.
7. All us businessmen hear is taxes, taxes, and more taxes.
8. When I unlocked the door, I found all the confidential records laying open on my desk.
9. Every one of our products are tested thoroughly before they are offered to the public.
10. A number of sets of dishes is included in the sale.
11. Bill said that there were present at the meeting only Jack, Walt, and he.

12. Mr. Jacobs, as well as his assistants, are trying to beat a deadline.
13. Neither of you are receiving a duplicate income tax withholding statement.
14. The Board of Education recognize the need for increased school facilities.
15. The number of mediocre workers are greater than one would think.
16. Has the data been checked by your chief accountant?
17. Neither of the secretaries are good at computations.
18. Why don't the plant manager hire his own workers?
19. The focus of our thoughts have been on the strong points in the program.
20. In the locker rooms were stored all the missing umbrellas.

EDITING PRACTICE

Editing for Triteness Rewrite these sentences, using more direct statements for the italicized trite expressions.

1. Announcing the winner before the program begins would be *letting the cat out of the bag.*
2. *Last but not least,* one signature is missing on the enclosed contract.
3. We can say *without fear of contradiction* that our work is always satisfactory.
4. It *goes without saying* that we must collect from customers in order to meet our own obligations.
5. In the past year our sales have increased *by leaps and bounds.*
6. Any plan that involves increased overhead must be *nipped in the bud.*

The Spelling-Conscious Proofreader Find and correct any spelling errors there may be in this paragraph.

> We should like very much to accomodate your group at our hotel for your banquet on June 2, but all our dining rooms are taken for that night. However, the thought has occurred to us that you might try the Meadow Inn, where there are rooms large enough to be adequate for your purpose. Please continue to keep us in mind whenever you need banquet facilities.

CASE PROBLEM

The Beginning Dictator Ronald G. Moore has been recently promoted to a supervisory job where, for the first time, he is responsible for writing letters to customers. He has been assigned a part-time stenographer. Rather than dictate letters to the stenographer, Ronald writes them out in longhand and asks the stenographer to type them in letter form.

1. Do you think this is an efficient procedure? Why or why not?
2. What would you suggest?

17 Predicate Agreement—With Compound Subject

As we know from Section 8, the subject of a sentence may be either simple or compound. Predicate agreement with simple subjects was discussed in Sections 15 and 16. Agreement with compound subjects is presented in this section. Only two types of compound subjects are considered here—those joined by *and* and those joined by *or* or *nor*. Although there are only two rules to be learned, many writers are confused about the correct predicate to use with a compound subject. Perhaps they do not realize that a *separate rule* covers each kind of compound subject and that there is no relationship, or carryover, between the rules. They do not understand that when they see a compound subject joined by *and*, they should use the rule that applies *only* to a compound subject joined by *and*. By the same token, when they see a compound subject joined by *or* or *nor*, they should use the *or*, *nor* rule.

A third topic presented later in this section, the relative-pronoun rule, might be called the "orphan" rule. The rule for agreement of the predicate in a relative-pronoun clause makes no mention of a simple or a compound subject. Your mastery of agreement rules, however, would not be complete without an understanding of this topic.

SUBJECTS JOINED BY *AND*

A compound subject joined by *and* takes a plural predicate.

> Eileen *and* I *are* going. (Not *is going*.)
>
> Jack *and* Bill *have* made their plans.

Applying this rule is almost automatic. However, there are two instances when a compound subject joined by *and* takes a singular predicate. Watch for these exceptions.

Exception 1

When a subject consisting of two nouns joined by *and* refers to the same person or thing, a singular predicate is used.

> The end *and* aim of my existence *is* a happy old age. (Both *end* and *aim* refer to the same thing; therefore, the predicate is singular.)
>
> Pie *and* ice cream *is* my favorite dessert. (This is *one* dessert, consisting of a piece of pie with a scoop of ice cream on top of it.)

Mastery of this agreement principle enables a writer to convey the meaning exactly. Look at the following illustration.

> Pie *and* ice cream *are* my favorite desserts. (Note the plural verb *are* and the plural noun *desserts*. The meaning here is that there are two kinds of desserts that the writer favors: pie is one; ice cream is the other.)

Exception 2

When two subjects joined by *and* are modified by *each, every,* or *many a,* a singular predicate is used.

> *Every* truck driver, relief driver, *and* assistant *is* required to have a valid driver's license as part of *his* qualifications. (The singular verb *is* and the subject pronoun *his* are correct because the compound subject joined by *and* is modified by the word *every.*)
>
> *Many an* ambitious secretary *and* stenographer *has earned* rapid promotion. (The singular verb *has earned* is correct because the compound subject joined by *and* is modified by *many an.*)

⊙ **CHECKUP 1** Make any needed corrections in these sentences. Give an explanation for each correction you make.

1. The long and the short of it were that we all left early.
2. Ham and eggs is a favorite item in our cafeteria.
3. Dependability and initiative is important in superior job performance.
4. Both Marie and her sister always looks well groomed.
5. In the early days of this nation, the bow and arrow were a formidable weapon.
6. Many a tenant and landlord have protested the proposed tax increase.
7. Each man, woman, and child in the city were on the street today.
8. The letter and the envelope has been separated.

SUBJECTS JOINED BY *OR* OR *NOR*

The rules for predicate agreement when a compound subject consists of words joined by *or* or *nor* can be boiled down to this: Match the predicate with the part of the subject nearer (or nearest) the verb. The following Memory Hook provides an even quicker way of applying this rule.

▣ **MEMORY HOOK** When the words in a subject are joined by *or* or *nor,* start with the part of the subject before the verb and read the rest of the sentence.

> Neither the *parents nor* the *child* (was? were?) watching traffic signals. (Do you see a compound subject joined by *nor*? The part of the subject next to the verb is *child.* Say "child" and read the rest of the sentence. *Was* stands out instantly as the correct verb.)
>
> Neither the *child nor* the *parents* (was? were?) watching traffic signals. (*Parents* is the part of the subject next to the verb. Say "parents" and read the rest of the sentence. *Were* is immediately seen as the correct verb.)
>
> Either *Bill or* his *brothers* (is? are?) to be asked to exhibit (his? their?) workshop products. (*Brothers* is next to the verb. Starting with *brothers,* the sentence reads as follows: *brothers* are . . . *to exhibit* their *workshop products.* The selections are *are* and *their* to agree with *brothers.*)

⊙ **CHECKUP 2** For practice in applying the Memory Hook for compound subjects joined by *or* or *nor,* select the correct words in the following sentences and give the reasons for your selections.

1. Neither the new employee nor the older employees (likes? like?) the change in (her? their?) working hours.
2. Neither the older employees nor the new employee (likes? like?) the change in (her? their?) working hours.
3. Either you or he (is? are?) to be transferred to the main office.
4. Either he or you (is? are?) to be transferred to the main office.
5. Neither Mark nor his helpers (has? have?) (his? their?) (mind? minds?) on (his? their?) work.
6. Neither his helpers nor Mark (has? have?) (his? their?) (mind? minds?) on (his? their?) work.

⊙ **CHECKUP 3** Test yourself to see whether you can apply the two compound subject rules correctly. Make any needed corrections in these sentences and tell why you make them.

1. Either Janet or Hazel are to answer my phone during lunch hour.
2. Each transparency, tape, and cassette are to be relabeled for our new filing system.
3. Neither Miss Gurney nor Miss Harrison feel ready to announce their retirement plans.
4. Mercury or alcohol are used in most thermometers.
5. What were the sum and substance of her remarks?

RELATIVE-PRONOUN CLAUSE

Before you learn and apply the important "orphan" rule for predicate agreement in a relative-pronoun clause, the following facts must be established.

1. The relative pronouns are *who, which,* and *that.*
2. A relative pronoun is called *relative* because it relates back to a word that is called an *antecedent.*
3. The antecedent is usually the noun or the pronoun appearing immediately before the relative pronoun.

Recognizing Relative Pronouns and Antecedents

The following illustrations will help you recognize relative pronouns and their antecedents:

> Mr. Berry is one of those administrators *who* think their methods are the most efficient. (Do you see a relative pronoun? Name it. How do you know that it is a relative pronoun? Answer: *Who* is a relative pronoun because it relates back to its antecedent *administrators.*)
>
> Where can I buy one of those erasers *that* have brushes attached to them? (What is the relative pronoun, and why is it a relative pronoun? Answer: *That* is a relative pronoun because it relates back to its antecedent *erasers.*)

In the following examples, can you see that *who, which,* and *that* are not relative pronouns? They cannot be, because they do not relate to anything. They have no antecedents.

> Who is that woman at the desk by the door?
>
> Do you know which story is true?
>
> Mr. Cable said that Lisa is being considered for a promotion.

Relative-Pronoun Rule

The rule that governs predicate agreement in clauses introduced by relative pronouns is this: The predicate of a clause introduced by a relative pronoun agrees with the antecedent of that pronoun, *not* with the relative pronoun itself. Study the following Memory Hook for help in remembering this rule.

▣ MEMORY HOOK When you see a relative pronoun introducing a clause, omit the pronoun and use the antecedent as the subject of the clause.

> Ralph is one of those employees who (thinks? think?) (he? they?) can earn much while doing little. (Omit *who;* start with the antecedent *employees,* and read on. Your selections must be *think* and *they,* to agree with *employees.*)
>
> Mrs. Berry is one of those administrators who (likes? like?) to have (her? their?) work attended to at once. (Omit *who* and start with the antecedent *administrators.* Your selections are *like* and *their,* to agree with *administrators.*)
>
> Where can I buy one of those erasers that (has? have?) (a brush? brushes?) attached to (it? them?)? (Omit *that,* start with the antecedent *erasers,* and read on. The selections are *have, brushes, them,* to agree with *erasers.*)

⊙ CHECKUP 4 In the following sentences, make corrections wherever necessary. Explain why you made your corrections.

1. The newest worker is the one who is assigned the earliest lunch hour.
2. Cheese and crackers are always an excellent dessert.
3. My brother is one of the drivers who has a perfect safety record this year.
4. A large banquet or small luncheons seem to be the best choice for our fund-raising efforts.
5. The carbon copy had some faint letters, which often is a signal to discard the carbon paper.
6. Neither you nor she are in danger of being transferred.
7. Please check the bills of lading that is in the "urgent" basket.
8. Not every writer and editor enjoy rewriting assignments.

Communication Projects

PRACTICAL APPLICATION

A Write *OK* on your paper for any correct sentence. For any incorrect sentence, write the correction and your reason for making it.

1. Each work station, filing area, and supply cabinet were relocated in our new offices.
2. My boss bought one of those paper shredders that does a thorough job of destroying confidential papers.
3. Every plant, vase, and ornament on her table were broken.
4. Either the lawyer or his legal clerks is able to notarize documents.
5. In the new shopping center are the best florist and the best music store in our town.
6. Waffles and sausages are my favorite Sunday breakfast.
7. Neither the programmer nor the keyboard operators realize the significance of this rush work.
8. Jim and I am to proofread the whole report.

9. The comma or the semicolon is required between the parts of a compound sentence.
10. Neither he nor you are expected to be an experienced writer.
11. Your job is to paint the fence posts, which are being delivered today.
12. A block and tackle are of great help to construction workers.
13. Mr. Kenyon is one of those persons who is always late in keeping his appointments.
14. The tiger is one animal that is noted for pacing restlessly in its cage.
15. Many a man, woman, and child were frightened when the plane broke the sound barrier.
16. Each man and woman in this office are expected to do their best.
17. Our sales manager is one of those men who makes friends wherever he goes.
18. Both the recorder and the treasurer submits his reports to the president.
19. Either you or Mr. Oats are to write the news release.
20. Both the editors and Mr. Kain has his wits about him today.

B Correct the following sentences wherever necessary.

1. Every apostrophe and hyphen are to be inserted by the transcriber.
2. There are the book of parliamentary order and the minute books that he asked for.
3. The Messrs. Johansen are celebrating the thirtieth anniversary of their actuarial firm.
4. Mastery of language fundamentals was considered the most important of the requirements that is demanded of a business writer.
5. There was a bankruptcy petition and a tax lien to be filed by last Monday.
6. We newcomers wish to be represented on the standing committees as well as them.
7. Neither Carol nor the other officers has been asked for their resignations.
8. Mr. Buchanan is one of the few corporate officers who have a legal degree.
9. The minority was arguing among themselves about the wording of their report.
10. Two-thirds of the consignment were lost in the railroad wreck.
11. Admittance slips or other identification are required by the guard at the main entrance gate.
12. The vallies in the graph show up very clearly.
13. Each typing error and poor erasure are noticed by Mr. Dole.
14. Who said that nobody is to eat their lunch in the office?
15. Mr. Marsh bought one of those houses that was built last spring.
16. Do you know that neither Earl nor Henry attend classes?
17. Bananas and orange juice are the special reducing diet recommended in the magazine advertisement.
18. The number of delinquent accounts is scarcely surprising.
19. Did either John or Martin hand in their resignation?
20. Have the Duggan's been notified about the change of date?

EDITING PRACTICE

Editing for Correct Grammar Indicate any grammatical errors in these sentences. Write *OK* for any correct sentence.

1. Neither the auditors nor I am pleased with the changes in the format of our annual report.

2. Everybody means to do their best to prevent a recurrence of such errors.
3. Undoubtedly, there was a great many candidates considered for this job.
4. Every one of our salespeople, however, are trained to report suspected shoplifters.
5. We agreed that this was the moment for we legal secretaries to announce our preferences.
6. The number of customers who ask for our products are increasing steadily.
7. We do realize that you know more than us about the public's buying habits.
8. You might be interested to know that my friend and business competitor concurs in this opinion.
9. Undoubtedly, ours is only one of many like reports that has come to you since you made your announcement.
10. In our last consignment was only two cartons of the size for which we receive so many requests.

The Proofreader's Vocabulary You are proofreading this paragraph for vocabulary errors. Write your correction for any such error you find.

> The starting point of the mail promotion plan for our new shampoo is the envelope we use. If our envelope does not have some devise that will capture the interest or pique the curiosity of the person receiving the promotional material, it will not be opened. Please work up some ideas for an effective envelope; then you and I can get together and chose the one that we think will best suit our purpose.

CASE PROBLEM

The Emergency Ellen Burton and Irene Day are stenographers in the office of Baxter and Allen, Certified Public Accountants. In addition to their regular stenographic duties, Ellen is responsible for monthly billings to clients, and Irene is responsible for maintaining the correspondence files. All billings to customers are supposed to be mailed by the second day of each month. Ellen was absent from work for a week in late April because of illness and returned to the office April 29. Today is May 1, and the bills are far from ready to be mailed. The supervisor is away, and the problem must be resolved by Ellen.

1. Should Ellen ask Irene for help with the billing? Why or why not?
2. If she asks Irene for help, what should Ellen say to her?
3. What might be done by the department supervisor to avoid such bottlenecks?

18 Adjectives

Adjectives are words that describe, enhance, limit—or in some other way *modify*—nouns or pronouns. If the noun is the substantive word, the factual and essential word, it is the adjective that colors it, that sparks it with life and interest. A perfunctory reply to a letter might begin: "Your letter of May 1 suggests . . ." Dull, isn't it? The addition of an adjective immediately adds color to the sentence: "Your *thoughtful* letter . . ." or "Your *puzzling* letter . . ." Either of these opening sentences would engage the reader; it is unlikely that the original sentence could.

Important as it is to select appropriate adjectives, it is still more important to use them correctly. Extensive vocabulary notwithstanding, the writer or speaker guilty of "those kind," "them reports," or "more better plans" is considered illiterate.

To communicate effectively and correctly, master the following rules governing the use of adjectives.

COMPARISON OF ADJECTIVES

Most adjectives change their forms to express different degrees of quality. This modification is called *comparison*. There are three forms or degrees of adjective comparison: (1) *positive*, used when the adjective is not compared with anything else; (2) *comparative*, used to express a higher or a lower degree than is expressed by the positive degree; and (3) *superlative*, used to denote either the highest or the lowest degree.

Forms of Adjective Comparison

Adjectives may be compared in any one of the three following ways:

1. By adding *er* to the positive to form the comparative degree and *est* to the positive to form the superlative degree.

Positive	Comparative	Superlative
quick	quicker	quickest
happy	happier	happiest
late	later	latest

2. By inserting the word *more* or *less* before the positive to form the comparative degree, and *most* or *least* before the positive to form the superlative degree.

Positive	Comparative	Superlative
patient	more (less) patient	most (least) patient
punctual	more (less) punctual	most (least) punctual
responsible	more (less) responsible	most (least) responsible

3. By changing the form of the word completely.

Positive	Comparative	Superlative
much, many	more	most
little	less	least
good	better	best
bad	worse	worst

Selection of Correct Forms of Comparison

Adjectives of *one* syllable are compared by adding *er, est*; adjectives of *three or more* syllables, by adding *more, less* or *most, least*. Some adjectives of *two* syllables are compared by adding *er, est,* and others by adding *more, less* or *most, least.* Selection of the correct form of comparison for adjectives of two syllables presents no problem because the incorrect form offends the ear.

The electric typewriter is *more useful* than the manual machine. (*Usefuler* would offend the ear.)

Jane is the *prettiest* girl in the class. (Not *most pretty*.)

Double Comparison

Note that adjectives may be compared in any one of three ways. A common error, double comparison, occurs when *two* forms of comparison are used for *one* adjective.

The union leaders agreed that this was the *fairest* contract. (Not *most fairest*.)

This box has *smoother* edges. (Not *more smoother*.)

⊙ **CHECKUP 1** Test your understanding of the rules for comparing adjectives by making any needed corrections in the following sentences.

1. In typing, the most commonest errors are in word division.
2. The office looked worser before it was repainted.
3. The most handsomest man at the party was her brother Martin.
4. I feel more stronger since my week's vacation at the lake.

Choice of Comparative or Superlative Degree

When referring to *two* persons, places, or things, use the comparative degree; but when referring to *more than two* persons, places, or things, use the superlative degree.

Both ideas are good, but I think this is the *better*. (Referring to two in number.)

All the ideas are good, but I think this is the *best*. (Referring to more than two in number.)

◇ **TWILIGHT ZONE: Absolute Adjectives** Absolute adjectives are adjectives that cannot be compared because in the positive degree they are already tops. For instance, if you have a *full* glass of water, nobody else could have one that is *fuller;* nor could someone have the *fullest* glass of all. Here are some examples of absolute adjectives:

complete	empty	perfect	supreme
correct	full	perpendicular	unanimous
dead	immaculate	round	unique

To express the degree to which a person or thing approaches the ultimate, the positive degree, use *more nearly* or *most nearly.* If, for example, three persons were drawing circles, John's could be *more nearly* round than Bob's, and Tom's could be the *most nearly* round.

Many modern writers, however, do not always use the *more nearly* and *most nearly* degrees of comparison for absolute adjectives. They feel that such usage makes their writing stilted and weakens the effectiveness of a message. For instance, they would write, "Ours is the *most complete* reference book on the market." And, in all fairness, we must concede that the "punch" would be lost by writing, "Ours is the *most nearly complete* reference book on the market."

⊙ **CHECKUP 2** Make any needed corrections, and be prepared to give reasons for all corrections you make.

1. Which sales representative is the more successful, Larsen or Coray?
2. I had the most nearly correct answer to the crossword puzzle.
3. Janet is to decide the kind of drapes she likes better.
4. Which painting is the largest, hers or his?

ADJECTIVE PITFALLS

Anyone trying to use adjectives correctly should be aware of the following five adjective pitfalls.

Other, Else, and *All* in Comparisons

When comparing a particular person or thing with other members of the group to which it belongs, use the words other or else with the comparative degree. Compare the following sentences:

> Jack is *more* dependable than *any* member of our staff. Jack is *more* dependable than *any other* member of our staff. (Without the word *other,* the first sentence suggests that Jack is not a staff member but an outsider who is being compared with staff members. The word *other* makes it clear that Jack belongs to the staff and is being compared with the rest of the staff.)
>
> Betsy is *more* imaginative than *anyone else* in our class. (The word *else* is required here to show that Betsy is part of the class.)

With the superlative degree, however, use the word *all,* not *any.*

> Jack is the *most* dependable of *all* the correspondents on our staff.

Omission of the Modifier

When a modifier such as *a, the,* or *my* is repeated before each noun in a series, two or more persons or things are clearly indicated. If the modifier is not repeated, only one person or thing is meant.

> My friend and neighbor (is? are?) moving to Boston. (Since the adjective *my* is not repeated, *friend and neighbor* is one person. *Is* is the correct verb.)
>
> My friend and my neighbor (is? are?) moving to Boston. (Since the adjective is repeated, there are two different persons here. *Are* is the correct verb.)

Compound Adjectives

When two or more words are combined before a noun to form one adjectival idea—to make a compound adjective—they should be joined by a hyphen or hyphens.

first-quality product	air-conditioned office
well-ventilated room	800-meter race
no-fault insurance	up-to-date methods
pollution-conscious group	coast-to-coast telecast
duty-free goods	fund-raising efforts

One exception to this rule involves certain well-known compounds that, through usage, have lost the hyphen.

life insurance coverage	real estate broker
high school teacher	social security benefits

The following terms are usually not hyphenated when they follow a noun because they no longer function as one-idea adjectives.

> His book is *well known.* (*Known* is simply a predicate adjective modified by the adverb *well.*)

However, if the words still combine to form one idea, they are hyphenated even after the noun.

> The group is *pollution-conscious.*
>
> The bank is *air-conditioned.*

⊙ **CHECKUP 3** These sentences call for application of the three rules just presented. Can you find the errors?

1. Eleanor transcribes more of his work than anyone in our office.
2. The tile we chose is available in 4 inch squares or 6 inch ones.
3. An indignant looking woman opened the door when he rang the bell.
4. Susan is more adept at telephone selling than any member of our sales staff.
5. He was amazed at how she achieved out of the ordinary solutions to ordinary problems.
6. Mr. Coe's friend and neighbor borrow the tools they need.
7. A center is usually the tallest of all the players on the team.
8. A center is usually taller than any player on the team.
9. Mr. Coe's brother and his neighbor borrow whatever tools they need.
10. Your suggestion is the best of any that we have received.

This (These), That (Those)

The adjectives *this* and *these* indicate nearness to the speaker; *that* and *those* indicate distance from the speaker. Never use the pronoun *them* as an adjective to replace *these* or *those*.

> Did you deposit *those* checks for Mr. Barr? (Not *them checks*.)
>
> Are you finished working with *these* files? (Not *them files*.)

This (These), That (Those) With *Kind(s)* or *Sort(s)*

Kind and *sort* are singular nouns; *kinds* and *sorts*, plural nouns. A singular noun is modified by a singular adjective; a plural noun, by a plural adjective. Study the following illustrations:

> Why waste your time reading (this? these?) kinds of books? (The plural adjective *these* should modify the plural noun *kinds*.)
>
> Mr. Kent has little patience with (that? those?) sort of caller. (The singular adjective *that* should modify the singular noun *sort*.)

The expressions *kind of* and *sort of* should not be followed by the article *a*(*n*).

> What *kind of* pen are you using? (Not *what kind of a pen*.)
>
> What *sort of* education do you think she has had? (Not *what sort of an education*.)

⊙ **CHECKUP 4** Find and correct the errors in these sentences.

1. Please total the overtime hours on them timecards.
2. We did not expect her to make those sort of errors.
3. She remembered them enclosures only after she sealed the letters.
4. I shall attend to them as soon as I possibly can.
5. These kinds of machines are a complete puzzle to me.
6. Mr. Hewitt is not in favor of those kind of discussions.
7. That clerk always has a sort of a smile on his face.

FOR ADDED POLISH

Two more rules govern the choice of words when referring to two or to more than two in number. Although these rules are not directly related to a study of adjectives, they are fine points that writers and speakers need to know.

Each Other, One Another

Use *each other* when referring to two in number; use *one another* when referring to more than two in number.

> Fred and Jim enjoy working with *each other*. (Two in number.)
>
> All the accountants must be ready to check *one another's* figures. (More than two in number.)

Either, Neither; Any, Any One, No One, Not Any

Either and *neither* refer to one of two persons or things. *Any* or *any one, no one,* and *not any* should be used to refer to one of three or more persons or things, such as:

> *Either* of the stenographers will take your dictation. (Since *either* is used, there must be only two stenographers.)
>
> *Any one* of the stenographers will take your dictation. (Since *any one* is used, there must be more than two stenographers.)

⊙ **CHECKUP 5** Make any needed corrections, and justify any correction you make.

1. Of the two supervisors, not any was available to handle the emergency.
2. My boss and her boss enjoy one another's company at lunch
3. Neither of the four applicants has all the qualifications we want.
4. Fred, Don, and Ken are very good about sharing one another's supplies.
5. Either of those four typists will type your rough draft.
6. All our secretaries are forever borrowing each other's dictionaries.

Communication Projects

PRACTICAL APPLICATION

A In the following sentences, write the corrections for all incorrect sentences and write *OK* for all correct sentences.

1. For door to door soliciting one must obtain a permit.
2. Do you think we should have the same kind of a program as we had last time?
3. Handling these kind of complaint letters tries my patience.
4. The new bulbs we imported are much more hardier than those we sold last year.
5. All them employment applications should be given to Joyce Adams.
6. The new shopping mall is larger than any in the entire state.
7. The cochairpersons, Janet and Ann, are well aware of one another's preferences.
8. After examining both machines, I think that we should purchase the smallest one.
9. Ours is the building nearest the subway entrance.
10. Which member of the board of directors is the oldest?
11. Can you make that skirt more circular?
12. All the advertised computers are good, but neither is exactly suited to our needs.
13. Napoleon is the greatest of any general in the history of France.
14. You will be allowed full credit for them books you returned Monday.
15. Are these kinds of appliances going to be on sale?

B Correct the following sentences wherever necessary.

1. The only ones who understood his allusions were Gregory and I.
2. Her absences are fewer than any person in the department.

3. The founder and director of the organization is to be the banquet speaker.
4. Neither the discussion leader nor we members of the committee thinks the plan is workable.
5. The sales manager asked Dave and she to conduct a consumer survey.
6. He chose to invest some of his inheritance in tax exempt bonds.
7. After an exhausting day, it is wise to lay down for a while before dinner.
8. Everyone who devises a production shortcut is encouraged to share their discovery with the rest of us.
9. One-half the books on the shelf have not been cataloged.
10. Check these figures with whomever has time to help you.
11. Your argument is much more stronger than Jerry's.
12. Secretary's voices should be low and well modulated.
13. Which do you think is better—high wages, security, or happiness?
14. Which has the better ribbon, this machine or that one?
15. Why doesn't the highway department make those corners rounder?
16. The memoranda on the desk was from Mr. Lamb.
17. The main contributors to the bulletin were Ashby and I.
18. The plan can be put into effect without anyone objecting to it.
19. Do not take them remarks of his so seriously.
20. Our three junior executives help each other whenever they can.

EDITING PRACTICE

Plurals and Possessives Edit the following sentences, correcting all errors. Write *OK* for any correct sentence.

1. My brother-in-law's car is a special model.
2. The Flaherties are experts in human relations.
3. Bob and Jack's fathers are scientists.
4. It's a good idea, but it needs further study.
5. I think that there very much pleased with the outcome of the research.
6. We appreciate Mr. Curtin taking the time to answer our question.
7. Do you know who's car is in front of the hydrant?
8. Are you in favor of an office employee's union?
9. All the engineers have made there reports.
10. Try to avoid our landlords' dog.

Executives Also Proofread You have dictated the following memo and are now proofreading it. Identify and correct any errors you find.

> For mailing purposes, file categorys are to be set up according to ZIP Codes. The post office requires that all bulk mailing be seperated into bundles, each of which contains mail that goes to one particular ZIP Code number. In this office, then, address files must be kept in ZIP Code numerical order, not alphabetical order.

CASE PROBLEM

A Tactful Correction When Robert Whiting, a clerk, filled out a cash sales slip for a customer, he entered the total as $7 instead of $9. The customer took the slip to the cashier, Edith Lake, for payment; and Edith discovered the error.

1. What should Edith say to retain the customer's goodwill?
2. What should Edith say, if anything, to Robert about his error?

19 Adverbs

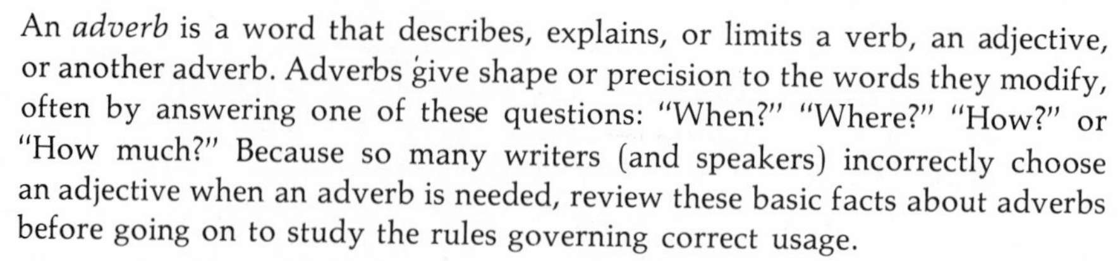

An *adverb* is a word that describes, explains, or limits a verb, an adjective, or another adverb. Adverbs give shape or precision to the words they modify, often by answering one of these questions: "When?" "Where?" "How?" or "How much?" Because so many writers (and speakers) incorrectly choose an adjective when an adverb is needed, review these basic facts about adverbs before going on to study the rules governing correct usage.

1. Adverbs, like adjectives, have three degrees: the positive, the comparative, and the superlative.
2. Although most words ending in *ly* are adverbs, not all adverbs end in *ly*. For example, *lovely* is an adjective.
3. An adverb usually answers one of the following questions: "When?" "Where?" "How?" "Why?" "How much or how little?" "To what extent?"

TYPES OF ADVERBS

Adverbs are classified as *simple* or *conjunctive*, depending on how they are used. Also under consideration here are adverbial clauses, which function as adverbs.

Simple Adverbs

A simple adverb is used as a modifier only. Here is a list of some of the most common simple adverbs:

always   immediately   now   then
clearly   much   quite   there
hard   nearly   right   too
here   never   soon   very

The correct route is indicated *clearly* on this map. (The simple adverb *clearly* modifies the verb *is indicated* and answers the question "How?")

Conjunctive Adverbs

A conjunctive adverb connects two independent clauses in one sentence and acts as a regular adverb in the second clause. The following adverbs are often used as conjunctive adverbs. You will need to recognize them in order to punctuate properly.

accordingly   however   nevertheless   therefore
consequently   likewise   otherwise   thus
furthermore   moreover   then   yet

Completion by the target date is doubtful; *nevertheless*, we will try our best to finish by then. (The conjunctive adverb *nevertheless* connects the two independent clauses and acts as a regular adverb in the second clause.)

Adverbial Clauses

An adverbial clause is a dependent clause that functions as an adverb in a sentence. An adverbial clause modifies a verb, an adjective, or an adverb in the main clause. The words in the following list introduce dependent clauses that usually function as adverbs.

after	because	if	until
although	before	since	when
as	for	unless	while

No improvement can be expected *unless the law is strictly enforced.* (The adverbial clause *unless the law is strictly enforced* modifies the verb *can be expected.*)

Your speech will be more effective *if you include a slide presentation.* (The adverbial clause *if you include a slide presentation* modifies the adjective *more effective.*)

⊙ **CHECKUP 1** Make the needed adverb corrections in the following sentences. Identify the conjunctive adverbs and adverbial clauses.

1. All contestants competed fair.
2. The winners will be announced today after all the votes are tallied.
3. He drove faster than any other racing car driver.
4. I enjoy swimming; however, I tire easily.
5. Time passes quick while I am on vacation.
6. From her position in the lobby, our receptionist can see plain anyone who uses the elevators.
7. Please remain seated until the results are verified.
8. I'll be waiting when you get there.
9. The project must be completed on time; therefore, we shall ask for volunteers to work late tonight.
10. The sun was shining bright until we arrived on the beach.

ADVERB OR ADJECTIVE AFTER VERB

To the already acknowledged problems of choosing between *lie* and *lay* and between *who* and *whom,* we can now add another confusing pair of choice—*bad* and *badly*. Do you feel *bad,* or *badly,* about not always making the right choice? The difficulty here is in knowing whether to use an adjective (*bad*) or an adverb (*badly*) after certain kinds of verbs. This section is designed to make it easy for you to decide when to use each modifier.

Linking Verb or Not a Linking Verb?

Not all verbs denote action. When verbs such as *seem, appear, look, sound, feel, taste,* and *smell* do not express action; they are properly considered linking verbs. When they do express action, they cannot be classed as linking verbs. Linking verbs are always no-action verbs.

Don said that the coffee *tasted* strong. (In this sentence, *tasted* is a linking verb, a no-action verb. After all, the coffee is not doing the tasting!)

Bob *felt* bad when his suggestion was rejected. (*Felt* here is a linking verb, a no-action verb. Bob is not feeling anything with his hands; he is not acting.)

Now study the following examples and note that these same verbs can also be action verbs.

> Don *tasted* the coffee gingerly before drinking it. (Here *tasted* is an action verb. Don has a tongue and is using it. Action is taking place.)
> Bob *felt* stealthily in his pocket for the memorandum. (*Felt* here is an action verb. Bob is acting; he is feeling with his fingers.)

The Rule

An adverb is used after an action verb; an adjective after a no-action verb. In the previous illustrations, note that when *tasted* was a no-action verb, the adjective *strong* was used. In the second set of illustrations, when *tasted* was an action verb, the adverb *gingerly* was used. The following Memory Hook is helpful for remembering the rule.

▣ **MEMORY HOOK** Hook up *action—adverb* and *no action—adjective* by retaining a mental picture of the following pairs:

Action	No Action
Adverb	Adjective

Action and *adverb* have the same number of letters, and *no action* and *adjective* match in number of letter spaces.

⊙ **CHECKUP 2** Keeping in mind *action—adverb* and *no action—adjective*, make any necessary corrections in these sentences.

1. When he opened the kitchen door, he smelled escaping gas distinct.
2. The edges of my new chair feel roughly even after they were rubbed down.
3. That red and black jacket looks strikingly on her.
4. Although the juice smelled sweetly, we could not drink it.
5. Did your secretary look careful through the incoming correspondence?
6. The police car appeared suddenly around the corner.

ADVERB PITFALLS

Five rules governing the correct use of adverbs are frequently violated—both in speech and in writing. Knowing these rules, and their correct application, should enable you to bypass the most common problems.

Position of the Adverb

An adverb should be placed as close as possible to the word it modifies. Failure to do so may cause the meaning of a sentence to be clouded—or even changed entirely.

> *Only* I changed the ribbon on that typewriter. (No one else changed it.)
>
> I changed *only* the ribbon on the typewriter. (I didn't change anything else on that typewriter.)
>
> I changed the ribbon *only* on that typewriter. (I didn't change the ribbon on any other typewriter.)

Double Negative

Scarcely, only, hardly, but, and *never* are negative in meaning; do not use another negative with them.

Ken *scarcely has* time to do his work. (Not *Ken hasn't scarcely.*)

Mr. Todd *could hardly* wait for his secretary to answer the buzzer. (Not *Mr. Todd couldn't hardly.*)

We *couldn't help smiling* at his astonishment. (Not *couldn't help but smile.*)

⊙ **CHECKUP 3** Correct all errors in adverb usage in the following sentences.

1. Despite the delay, we hadn't but one complaint.
2. They only drove there to see the view, not to have a picnic.
3. Without experience, you can't hardly find a good job.
4. He couldn't help but laugh at her antics.
5. The lines were so busy that we couldn't get scarcely one call through.
6. Did you know that Lucy hasn't never before done this kind of work?
7. I thought that the applicants for the job had only been interviewed yesterday, not three days ago.
8. There wasn't but one shipping clerk in the stockroom on Wednesday morning.

Never or *Not*

Never and *not* are both adverbs, but they should not be used interchangeably, for their meanings are quite different. *Never* means "not ever; at no time; not in any degree, way, or condition." It is a strong word. *Not* is simply a word that expresses negation. *Never* is frequently used incorrectly instead of *not*. Study the following examples:

Mr. Lyons said that he did *not* receive your letter. (Not *that he never received.*)

We have *never* been late with an interest payment. (*Never,* meaning "not ever," is correct in this sentence.)

Where for *That*

The subordinate conjunction *that,* not the conjunctive adverb *where,* should be used after such expressions as "I saw in the paper," "We read in the magazine," "The announcement notes," and so on.

Did you read in the paper *that* our company is expanding? (Not *read in the paper where.*)

The memo states *that* Tom is to have an assistant. (Not *states where.*)

Badly or *Worst Way* for *Very Much*

Too often, *badly* and *worst way* are used when what is really meant is *very much.* Study the following illustrations:

Bob's reason for taking extra lunch time was that he (very much? badly?) wanted a haircut. (Who would ever want a haircut *badly*? The correct meaning, of course, is that he *very much* wanted a haircut.)

David wanted to learn shorthand (in the worst way? very much?). (David would never be able to write shorthand if he learned it *in the worst way*. The correct answer, therefore, is *very much*.)

⊙ **CHECKUP 4** Find and correct any errors in these sentences.

1. He says he never saw the stop sign at that intersection.
2. Did you see in the paper where we are going to have a severe winter this year?
3. She badly wanted to earn extra money so as to afford a trip to Europe.
4. Sue needed money in the worst way.
5. I read in the annual report where our dividend is to be increased next year.

ADVERB AND ADJECTIVE CONFUSION

Many adverbs derive from adjectives, simply through the addition of *ly*, but the two cannot be used interchangeably. For example, the adjective *real* should not be used to modify another adjective, *happy*. An adverb is needed here to correctly state that someone is *really happy*.

Five pairs of words often cause confusion, possibly because one member of each pair is an adjective; the other, an adverb. In each pair discussed below, the first word is an adjective; the second, an adverb.

Sure, Surely; Real, Really

When an adjective is needed, use *sure* or *real*. When an adverb is required, use *surely* or *really*. The following Memory Hook will help you in selecting the correct word.

▣ **MEMORY HOOK** If the word *very* or *certainly* can be substituted for the word in question, use *surely* or *really*. Hook up the final *y* in *very* or *certainly* with the final *y* in *surely* or *really*.

> The boss was (real? really?) angry this morning. (*The boss was very angry. Very* ends in *y; really* ends in *y. Really* is correct.)
>
> You (sure? surely?) have been a success as an executive. *(You certainly have been a success. Certainly* ends in *y; surely* ends in *y. Surely,* then, is correct.)

Good, Well

Good is the adjective and *well* is the adverb, except when referring to health. If the question "How?" can be answered, use *well*; if not, use *good*. Remember, though, that *well* is always used when speaking of health.

> The new correspondent does *good* work. (*Good* is an adjective modifying the noun *work*. It does not answer the question "How?")
>
> The new correspondent works *well*. (Works how? The adverb *well* answers the question and is, therefore, correct.)
>
> The new correspondent complained of not feeling *well*. (When speaking of health, always use *well*.)

Some, Somewhat

Some is an adjective; *somewhat*, an adverb. For rapid selection of the correct word, learn the following Memory Hook.

▣ **MEMORY HOOK** Use *somewhat* if you can substitute the words *a little bit*; otherwise, use *some*.

Mr. King was (some? somewhat?) doubtful about approving the plan. (Mr. King was *a little bit* doubtful; therefore, *somewhat* is correct.)

We gave Mr. King (some? somewhat?) plans for his approval. (*Some* is correct because *a little bit* cannot be substituted.)

Most, Almost

Most is an adjective, the superlative of *much* or *many*, as in *much, more, most. Almost* is an adverb meaning "not quite" or "very nearly."

We have (most? almost?) enough data for our statistical report. (*We have* not quite *or* very nearly *enough. Almost* is correct.)

(Most? Almost?) secretaries have transcribed (most? almost?) all their dictation by three o'clock. (Many, more, *most secretaries have transcribed* very nearly *all. Most* is correct for the first choice; *almost*, for the second.)

⊙ **CHECKUP 5** Correct any errors you find in the following sentences.

1. Most anyone can learn to operate this machine in one lesson.
2. The sudden decrease in our sweater sales is real alarming.
3. The bonus incentive plan seems to be working good.
4. The movers were sure careless in taking out the file cabinets.
5. Wasn't she somewhat hesitant about asking for an appointment?
6. A few of our typists are some careless about proofreading.
7. Why don't you see the nurse if you don't feel good?
8. After hearing your story, I felt you were sure justified in protesting.

Communication Projects

PRACTICAL APPLICATION

A Write the corrections for any adverb errors in the following sentences. Write *OK* for any correct sentence.

1. We all sure felt badly about her moving so far away.
2. If you want the job done real good, hire Mr. Kemp.
3. The company's sales decreased some last month.
4. The flu made me feel miserably all this week.
5. She appeared quite tearfully during the trial.
6. Miss Kane never told us when our raises would begin.
7. The accident victim badly needed immediate attention.
8. Our quarterly sales contest is almost finished.
9. They never told us they were going to close the Newton plant.
10. The letter was typed so poorly that Mr. Forbes refused to sign it.

11. Do not serve us the syrup that tastes so bitter.
12. Our ad writer does his best work in a real quiet office.
13. Prospects for increased sales during the next month surely look well.
14. Mr. Kent didn't hardly notice the stacks of outgoing mail.
15. The new secretary's letters scarcely contain a single erasure.
16. Did you see in today's paper where taxes are to be lowered?
17. Church bells sound clear on a frosty day.
18. Dick would like to work for our firm in the worst way.
19. Mr. Jeffers cannot breathe good unless the windows are open.
20. For as long as I have worked for him, Mr. Barr hasn't never lost his temper.

B Correct the following sentences wherever necessary.

1. His hard experiences have helped him to be self reliant.
2. With new indirect lighting, that dark room looks beautifully now.
3. The sales' offices he has rented are the most expensive of any in the whole town.
4. No business can afford those kind of customer complaints.
5. Them hand painted trays will please the particularest shopper.
6. I only told she, not her whole family.
7. Jim admitted he had never seen them estimates.
8. Leonore read in the company newspaper where Mr. Tompkins was elected president of the camera club.
9. With his new hearing aid, Paul can hear most as well as me.
10. Weren't you surprised that our supervisor hadn't only one change to suggest?
11. On which floor are lady's suits sold?
12. Bill will surely receive a fine recommendation, for he has always performed his duties faithful.
13. May I have one of those pens that have retractable points?
14. That correspondent badly needs a refresher course in grammer.
15. We owe our success to the fact that our employees cooperate so well with one another.
16. Experience is sure a good teacher.
17. Your carbons would look better if you used a more sharper typing stroke.
18. Is Ronald doing good in his new position?
19. Every business needs those kind of word-of-mouth advertising.
20. All the applicants were somewhat nervous and ill at ease.

EDITING PRACTICE

Editor, Editor! Rewrite the following letter, correcting whatever errors it contains.

Dear Mrs. Gibson:

FRUITY-BLEND is a most refreshing drink. It tastes deliciously and has all those kind of nutrients that dietitians recommend.

FRUITY contains less sugar than any soft drink on the market. It is tested regular for caloric content by our up to date research department. Your diet is safe with FRUITY.

If you have not yet tried FRUITY-BLEND, your first sip will make you wish you had tried it sooner. Act quick and buy the drink that is absolutely the best of any beverage of it's kind!

Cordially yours,

Did I Say That? Your boss proofreads this paragraph and questions a word you have used. Actually, you transcribed exactly what was dictated, but you should have made the correction. What is this word?

> You will be able to work in comfort this summer if you install a Kool Air Conditioner now. And you will also be able to maintain your production record, for you will not be hampered by the stickiness caused by undue prespiration. Shortly after you have read the enclosed "Kool" literature, you may expect a visit from our air-conditioner expert, Mr. Ray T. Hyde.

CASE PROBLEM

Introducing Yourself You have just arrived at a reception for new students by the college president. You meet the members of the faculty who are in the receiving line and then help yourself to some refreshments. The students and various faculty members who arrived earlier are clustered in many small groups around the room, and you do not know whether to stand by yourself until someone comes over to you or whether to approach one of the groups.

1. What do you think you should do? Why?
2. If you decided to approach one of the groups, what would you say?
3. If you were responsible for arranging this reception, what would you do to make it easier for a newcomer to mix with others?

Prepositions

The misuse of prepositions is frequently responsible for awkward locutions, that is, for an awkward way of expressing something. This section should make it easier for you to spot commonly made errors—more important, it should help you to avoid making them.

DEFINITIONS

A *preposition* is a connecting word that shows the relation between a noun or a pronoun and some other word in the sentence. Here is a list of some of the more commonly used prepositions:

about	but (meaning "except")	off
above	by	on
after	except	over
among	for	to
at	from	under
before	in	up
below	into	upon
beside	like	until
between	of	with

A preposition always begins in a prepositional phrase—*in* the office, *at* our bank, *around* the next corner, *with* him, and so on. A *prepositional phrase* consists of a preposition with its noun or pronoun object, together with any modifiers.

Keeping in mind the definitions and the fact that a preposition never stands alone, give close attention to the following rules of correct usage.

WORDS REQUIRING SPECIFIC PREPOSITIONS

Idiomatic usage requires that some words be followed by specific prepositions. Other words require one preposition for one meaning and an entirely different preposition for another meaning. Failure to use the correct preposition with a certain word or failure to use the preposition that applies to the context of a particular sentence is a common error that spoils the effect of a finished performance. The words that require specific prepositions, together with those prepositions and examples of their use, are listed below.

abhorrence *of*
abhorrent *to*
abide *by* a decision
abide *with* a person
abounds *in* or *with*
accompanied *by* (attended by a person)
accompanied *with* (attended by something)
acquit *of*
adapted *to* (adjusted to)
adapted *for* (made over for)
adapted *from* a work
affinity *between*
agree *to* a proposal
agree *with* someone
agreeable *to* (*with* is permissible)
angry *at* a thing or condition
angry *with* a person
attend *to* (listen)
attend *upon* (wait)
beneficial *to*
bestow *upon*
buy *from*
compare *to* the mirror image (assert a likeness)
compare *with* the reverse side (analyze for similarities or differences)
compliance *with*
comply *with*
confer *on* or *upon* (give to)
confer *with* (talk to)
confide *in* (place confidence in)
confide *to* (entrust to)
conform *to* (in conformity *to* or *with*)
consist *in* (exists in)
consist *of* (made up of)
convenient *for* (suitable for, easy for)
convenient *to* (near)
conversant *with*
correspond *to* or *with* (match; agree with)
correspond *with* (exchange letters)
credit *for*
deal *in* goods or services
deal *with* someone
depend or dependent *on* (but independent *of*)
derogatory *to*
different *from* (not *than* or *to*)
disappointed *in* or *with*
discrepancy *between* two things
discrepancy *in* one thing
dispense *with*
employ *for* a purpose
employed *at* a stipulated salary
employed *in*, *on*, or *upon* a work or business
enter *into* (become a party to)
enter *into* or *upon* (start)
enter *in* a record
enter *at* a given point
exception *to* a statement
familiarize *with*
foreign *to* (preferred to *from*)
identical *with*
independent *of* (not *from*)
inferior or superior *to*
need *of* or *for*
part *from* (take leave of)
part *with* (relinquish)
plan or planning *to* (not *on*)
profit *by*
in regard *to*
with regard *to*
as regards
retroactive *to* (not *from*)
speak *to* (tell something to a person)
speak *with* (discuss with)
wait *for* a person, a train, an event
wait *on* a customer, a guest

⊙ **CHECKUP 1** Supply the missing preposition in each of the following sentences.

1. She waited (?) that bus half an hour in the pouring rain.
2. His petty cash totals do not correspond (?) mine.
3. The blanket we manufacture consists (?) equal parts of polyester and wool.
4. The new research building is not convenient (?) the old cafeteria.

SPECIFIC PREPOSITIONS MOST USED IN BUSINESS

Because of their frequent occurrence in business communications, nine of the words requiring specific prepositions are presented below for special study.

Agree With, Agree To

Use *agree with* when the object of the preposition is a person; use *agree to* when the object is not a person, such as:

> Don thinks it good policy to *agree with* the boss. (The object of the preposition is a person; therefore, *with* is correct.)
>
> Don will not *agree to* any proposal made by Todd. (Since *proposal,* the object of the preposition, is not a person, *to* is correct.)

Angry With, Angry At

Use *angry with* when the object of the preposition is a person; use *angry at* when the object is not a person, such as:

> We were *angry with* the waiter who served our lunch. (*With* is correct because the object of the preposition is a person.)
>
> We were *angry at* the poor service of the waiter at lunch. (*At* is correct because *service,* the object of the preposition, is not a person.)

Part From, Part With

Part from means "to take leave of"; *part with* means "to relinquish, to give up." *Part from* is generally used when the object of the preposition is a person; and *part with,* when the object is not a person.

> At what time last night did you and Kent *part from* each other? (*From* is correct. The meaning is "take leave of.")
>
> Jack seemed loath to *part with* the picture. (*With* is correct. *Picture,* the object of the preposition, is not a person.)

Discrepancy In, Discrepancy Between

Use *discrepancy in* when the object of the preposition is singular; use *discrepancy between* when the object denotes exactly *two* in number.

> I found several *discrepancies in* Bill's report. (*Report* is singular; therefore, *in* is correct.)
>
> Did you notice any *discrepancy between* Bill's story and Fred's? (There are exactly two stories; therefore, *between* is correct.)

In Regard To, With Regard To, As Regards

These three phrases are equally correct, but *regards* cannot be used with *in* or *with*. Whenever *regards*, the word ending in *s*, is used, it must be paired with *as*, the word that also ends in *s*.

> This is the third time we have notified you (in? with? as?) regard to broken items in your shipments to us. (*Regard* does not end in *s*; therefore, *with* or *in* is correct.)
>
> *As regards* boiler insurance, we suggest that you talk with Mr. Wahl. (Since *regards* ends in *s*, the *s*-ending word *as* is correct.)

Different From, Identical With, Plan To, Retroactive To

The correct prepositions to be used after *different, identical, plan,* and *retroactive* should be memorized. These expressions are used so frequently that you should not need to continually check a reference manual. Study the following illustrations:

> Do you have any carbons that are *different from* these? (Not *different than*.)
>
> Check to see whether your total is *identical with* Peter's. (Not *identical to*.)
>
> Is Mr. West *planning to* have a general meeting on Friday? (Not *planning on having*.)
>
> Can a law be made *retroactive to* some previous date? (Not *retroactive from*.)

⊙ **CHECKUP 2** Make whatever corrections are necessary.

1. The rest of the group did not agree with Wayne's proposals.
2. These new bookends are identical to the ones I saw in Stanton's.
3. Her mailing procedures are different than the ones I know.
4. Dan was not angry at the other members of the team.
5. While listening to the taped conversation, I noted several discrepancies in it and the typescript.
6. Frank parted with Barbara at the entrance to her building.
7. We have no plans as regards future expansion.
8. We should like to talk with you in regards to your proposal.
9. Do you plan on having an office of your own?
10. This directive is retroactive from May 1.

PREPOSITION PITFALLS

Preposition pitfalls trap the person who cannot choose correctly between two prepositions or who does not know when a preposition should be used and when it should be omitted. To avoid these snares, study the following seven guides to correct preposition usage.

Between, Among

Between is commonly used when referring to two persons, places, or things; *among* when referring to more than two.

> We are finding it difficult to choose *between* Jack and Harry. (Since there are two persons, *between* is correct.)
>
> Were the notices distributed *among* all members of the staff? (*All* connotes "more than two"; therefore, *among* is correct.)

Between may also express the relation of one thing to each and all of several related things.

> The new contract is *between* the teacher's union and each of the seven school districts in the county.

Beside, Besides

Beside means "by the side of"; *besides* means "in addition to." Study the following illustrations:

> As chairperson, I was seated *beside* the guest of honor at dinner. (Meaning "by the side of" the guest of honor.)
>
> How many members of the committee *besides* you were seated at the speaker's table? (Meaning "in addition to" you.)

Inside, Outside

The preposition *of* is not used after *inside* or *outside*. When referring to time, use *within*, not *inside of*.

> The receptionist's desk is just *inside* the main entrance. (Not *inside of*.)
>
> We have a thermometer *outside* the east window. (Not *outside of*.)
>
> Our reports must be finished *within* a week. (Not *inside of*.)

All, Both

Use *of* after *all* or *both* only when *all* or *both* refers to a pronoun. Omit *of* if either word refers to a noun.

> *All of* them have saved *all* their stamps. (*All of* is followed by the pronoun *them*, and *all* precedes the noun *stamps*.)
>
> *Both of* us knew that *both* the packages should have been mailed yesterday. (*Both of us*, but *both the packages*.)

At, To; In, Into

At and *in* denote position; *to* and *into* signify motion.

> After I arrived *at* your office, I found that I had come *to* the wrong place. (*At* for position; *to* for motion.)
>
> As he went *into* the park, he saw an oriole sitting *in* a tree. (*Into* for motion; *in* for position.)

Note: When either *at* or *in* refers to a place, use *in* for larger places and *at* for smaller.

> Mark lives *in* Chicago and works *at* the Marshall Bond store. (*In* Chicago, the larger place; *at* the store, the smaller place.)

Behind, Not *In Back Of*

Use *behind*, not *in back of*. *In front of*, however, is correct.

> This folder should be filed *behind*, not *in front of*, the guide. (*Behind*, not *in back of*.)

From, Off

From is generally used with persons; *off* is used with things. *Off* can be used with persons only when something that is physically resting on them is being lifted away. Never use *of* or *from* after *off*.

> You may borrow a coat *from* Bill.
>
> Take your books *off* the desk.
>
> Please take your foot *off* mine. (Your foot is resting on mine; please lift it away.)

⊙ **CHECKUP 3** Correct the preposition errors in the sentences below.

1. We go to the library outside of our regular school schedule.
2. The tie score meant that the first prize was divided between the two teams.
3. I drove in the garage before I noticed someone lurking in the shadows.
4. Stack the letters besides the tray marked "Outgoing Mail."
5. A conference is going on in back of those locked doors.
6. Have you hidden all the money?

PREPOSITION ILLITERACIES

Some preposition errors are so serious that the person who makes them may be considered either uneducated or extremely careless. Avoid illiteracies such as the following.

Should Of

Of is a preposition; *have* is a verb. Writing *of* for *have* is a very serious error that may be charged to poor diction. "Shuduv" is often heard instead of "should have"; consequently *should of* is often written instead of *should have*. Study these illustrations.

> Knowing that you were in a hurry, we *should have* replied sooner. (Not *should of*.)
>
> You *ought not to have* paid the bill before May 2. (Not *ought not to of*.)

Where . . . At; Where . . . To

The use of *at* or *to* with *where* is illiterate.

> Do you know *where* Mr. Kidd is? (Not *where Mr. Kidd is at*.)
>
> *Where* did she go? (Not *Where did she go to?*)

Help From

Another illiteracy is the use of *from* after the word *help*.

> I could not *help* complimenting them on their sales records. (Not *help from*.)
>
> I couldn't *help* expressing my pleasure at the news. (Not *help from*.)

Opposite To

The use of *to* after *opposite* is incorrect.

Your locker is the one *opposite* mine. (Not *opposite to*.)

Like For

Adding *for* after *like* to make *like for* is incorrect. Omit the *for*.

We should *like* you to attend the meeting as our guest. (Not *like for*.)

⊙ **CHECKUP 4** See if you can find the illiteracies in the following sentences.

1. In rearranging the room, make sure the bookcase is opposite to the table.
2. He could of answered her question but he chose not to do so.
3. Do you know where the new sales manuals are at?
4. Joyce cannot help asking all those questions.
5. Do you think that we hadn't ought to of mentioned the incident to the boss?
6. That error should of been corrected immediately.
7. Where have all the supplies gone to?

Communication Projects

PRACTICAL APPLICATION

A Correct the sentences in which prepositions are used incorrectly. Write *OK* for any correct sentence.

1. Put all the damaged pieces into this box.
2. If you sit in back of that pillar, you will not be able to see the receptionist.
3. No one told her that her name had been taken from off the list.
4. Will you please speak with Gerry about her lengthy personal phone calls.
5. He plans on landing a job independent from his father's help.
6. He would like for you to be his guest at the next club luncheon.
7. The way Miss Hagen answers the phone is almost identical to the way you do.
8. Answering the telephone during the lunch hour is shared between Jenny, Sally, and James.
9. We can't expect reimbursement inside of three weeks.
10. Everyone agreed with the suggestion of working fewer days per week.
11. Where in the world did that caller go to?
12. Ann dislikes parting with any of her possessions.
13. Who, beside Bob, is being promoted?
14. Remember that the increase is retroactive to June 1.
15. The Herald Building is opposite ours.
16. There seems to be some discrepancy in your total and mine.
17. We surely should of checked those figures.
18. When he makes an error, Bill becomes angry with his calculator.
19. Peter could not help from stating his position on the question.
20. Mr. Taylor has no statement to make in regards to the merger.

B Find the errors in the following sentences. Write *OK* for any correct sentence.

1. These new specifications do not conform with the old ones.
2. Back-ordering them parts will not be convenient to our schedule.
3. He is expected to return inside of a week.
4. For safety's sake, let's keep this matter a secret between you and I.
5. Miss Conlon has not been to the office all this week.
6. The cartons are too heavy for her to lift from off the table.
7. Most of us have almost finished our special assignments.
8. I have never seen Mr. McHale look so good.
9. This photocopier works differently to the one I have always used.
10. We very much appreciate your loaning us a copy of your sales manual.
11. You sure like to operate that machine, don't you?
12. Because every man and boy did their best, the affair was a success.
13. The defendant was acquitted from the charge.
14. If I were he, I would delegate some of the minor jobs.
15. Which of the twins is the more dependable?
16. You should of studied the layout before starting to write the copy.
17. We should like to confer with you in regards to your credit rating.
18. The Harrises' order has priority for tomorrow.
19. The staff should attend upon every instruction Mr. Dunn gives.
20. Whom have you chosen to head the steering committee?

EDITING PRACTICE

Make the Blanks Make Sense Write a word that would make sense if inserted in the blank space within the sentence.

1. To help us determine your credit rating, please see that we get a copy of your current . . . statement.
2. We feel that we can recommend your new cleaner without . . . .
3. Next week the . . . are coming to examine our books, and you, of course, would prefer them to see that your account is paid in full.
4. We think that your machine is far . . . to all others now on the market.
5. It is almost impossible to dye two hides . . . the same shade.
6. Have you in imagination ever . . . passage on some fast ocean liner and traveled to far-off lands?
7. We know that you must have been prevented from settling your account by some . . . over which you had no control.
8. There has been a great deal of illness at home, resulting in many . . . expenses.
9. Because of the difference in price, shipping and billing from Erie would . . . the displeasure of our customers.
10. Our firm no longer operates under the name listed in the present . . . of the Red Book.

Oops! You have typed the following paragraph and are now proofreading it. Did you make any spelling errors?

Your copy for advanced advertising of our new complexion soap is somewhat agressive and should be toned down a little. As I read what you had written, I got the feeling that you were trying to *make* me buy. Please rewrite it, presenting your material from the viewpoint of what our soap will do for the reader—give health and beauty reasons, for instance.

CASE PROBLEM

A Case of Ethics There is a rule at the Burns Office Equipment Company that personal mail may not be sent through the company's postage meter machine. Jack Thompson, who is in charge of the mail room, receives a batch of mail from Mary Weston, secretary to the vice president, that contains some obviously personal letters written by Mary. Jack is not sure whether Mary inadvertently placed her personal mail among the company correspondence or whether Mary was trying deliberately to slip her personal letters in with the other letters.

1. What should Jack do about the situation? Why?
2. What should Jack say to Mary?

Conjunctions

A conjunction is a word used to *connect* words, phrases, or clauses within a sentence.

> The original *and* the carbon are lying on your desk. (In this sentence, the conjunction *and* connects the words *original* and *carbon*.)
>
> You will find them on your blotter *or* in the tray. (The conjunction *or* connects the phrases *on your blotter* and *in the tray*.)
>
> Bill usually attends to the outgoing mail, *but* he is not in the office today. (The conjunction *but* connects the two main clauses.)

Conjunctions, like the other parts of speech, must be studied to ensure correct usage. A thorough understanding of conjunctions and their functions should make it easier for you to learn the rules of punctuation and sentence structure in Chapters 4 and 5. In this section on conjunctions, their classification is considered first, then pitfalls in usage, and last, parallel structure.

CLASSIFICATION OF CONJUNCTIONS

Conjunctions are classified as *coordinate, correlative,* and *subordinate.* The first two can be used only to connect elements of equal rank, or kind; the third, as its name suggests, joins a subordinate clause with a main clause.

Coordinate Conjunctions

The coordinate conjunctions are *and, but, or,* and *nor.* Their function is to connect *like* elements of grammar—two or more *words,* two or more *phrases,* or two or more *clauses.* These conjunctions must not be used to connect *unlike* elements.

> The photocopier *and* the copying paper are now in Mary's office. (The conjunction *and* connects the words *photocopier* and *paper.*)
>
> He was late leaving for the airport, *but* he arrived in time to board the plane. (The conjunction *but* connects two independent clauses.)
>
> We shall leave for Detroit on Friday morning *or* on Saturday. (The conjunction *or* connects the phrases *on Friday morning* and *on Saturday.*)

Correlative Conjunctions

Correlative conjunctions are used in pairs to connect *like* grammatical elements. The most common correlative conjunctions are the following:

both . . . and	not only . . . but also
either . . . or	whether . . . or
neither . . . nor	

Note that *or* is paired with *either,* and *nor* is paired with *neither.*

Although the words, phrases, or clauses connected by a correlative might instead be connected by a coordinate, the paired conjunctions are sometimes chosen to convey a slightly different meaning or emphasis. For example, the coordinate *and* means "in addition to" or "also," just as the correlatives *not only . . . but also* do. But note how the second sentence tells more about the situation described than the first sentence does.

> The audience *and* the actors cheered when the playwright walked onstage.
>
> *Not only* the audience *but also* the actors cheered when the playwright walked onstage.

Subordinate Conjunctions

Subordinate conjunctions join clauses of *unequal* rank. A subordinate conjunction introduces a dependent (subordinate) clause and connects it to an independent (main) clause.

> *Although* the contract does not meet all our demands, it seems to be an acceptable compromise. (The subordinate conjunction *although* introduces the dependent clause *although the contract does not meet all our demands* and connects it to the main clause.)
>
> Let us know at once *if* you think the idea has value. (The subordinate conjunction *if* introduces the dependent clause *if you think the idea has value* and connects it to the main clause.)

Study the following list of commonly used subordinate conjunctions. Not only will you need to use them correctly, but also you will need to punctuate them accurately.

after	before	provided that	when
although	even if	since	whenever
as	for	so that	where
as if	how	than	wherever
as soon as	if	that	whether
as though	in case that	unless	while
because	in order that	until	why

⊙ **CHECKUP 1** Identify the conjunctions in these sentences, and classify them as coordinate, correlative, or subordinate.

1. Mr. Bryan told me that he may fly to Denver next week.
2. I expected either Jane or one of the other typists to answer the phone.
3. The order can be shipped next week if we ask the men to work overtime.
4. Write at once if you wish to take the special discount.
5. When you arrive in Seattle, call immediately for an appointment.
6. A correspondent cannot afford to be weak in spelling and in grammar.
7. Are you satisfied with both the job and the salary?

CONJUNCTION PITFALLS

Errors in the use of conjunctions occur when a writer or a speaker, faced with a choice, is unable to select the conjunction that best conveys the intended meaning. Another problem arises when there is doubt about whether it would be correct to use a preposition instead of a conjunction. Study the following rules in order to avoid these pitfalls. In the following discussion, the emphasis is on learning to select the conjunction that is correct in each instance.

But or *And*?

Whenever there is a contrasting or an opposing idea, no matter how faint, use the conjunction *but*—not *and*.

> Ann is our fastest typist, *but* Sue is more accurate. (*But*, for contrast.)

Who, Which, or *That*?

The relative pronouns *who, which,* and *that* are correctly used as follows: *who*, to refer to persons; *which*, to refer to objects; *that*, to refer to persons, animals, or objects. Never use *and who* or *and which*.

> Barr is the man *who* knows how to operate the machine. (*Who*, referring to a person.)
>
> I have chosen the 21-day tour, *which* offers substantial savings. (*Which*, referring to an object.)
>
> The children's zoo has young animals *that* can be touched and petted. (*That*, referring to animals.)
>
> The company is made up of three highly successful divisions, which (not *and which*) are all located in Chicago.

Since or *Because,* not *Being That*

The use of *being that* when *since* or *because* is meant is an illiteracy. There is no such conjunction as *being that*.

> *Because* the bill was not paid within the discount period, we will expect your check for $14.10. (Obviously, *because* is correct.)

That,* not *Because* or *Like

Say *reason is that,* not *reason is because; pretend that,* not *pretend like.* See the following illustrations:

> The *reason* I was late *is that* our bus was stalled. (Not *reason is because.*)
> When David arrives, *pretend that* you do not see him. (Not *pretend like.*)

◇ **TWILIGHT ZONE: *As . . . As; So . . . As*** The rule concerning the use of the correlatives *as . . . as* and *so . . . as* has fewer adherents today than it once had. However, some writers still make a distinction when choosing between these pairs of correlatives. To be precise and correct, then, use *as . . . as* when making a *positive* statement and *so . . . as* when making a *negative* statement.

> Bill writes just *as* well *as* I do. (*As . . . as* for a positive statement.)
> Bill does not write *so* well *as* Jerry. (*So . . . as* for a negative statement.)

⊙ **CHECKUP 2** Make any needed corrections.

1. We failed to find the tapes that were mailed to us from Boston.
2. Ethel can't handle a rush assignment as well as Jane.
3. Being that the mailing rates have increased sharply, the new catalogs will be much smaller.
4. The reason for my failure to check the enclosures is because the letter contained no enclosure notation.
5. Your job is difficult, and you are not pressed for time.
6. Can you pretend like you do not understand English?
7. Mimeographed letters have never been so effective as typewritten letters.

Distinguishing Between Conjunctions and Prepositions

As you know, a preposition always occurs in a prepositional phrase, which consists of the preposition and its noun or pronoun object, together with any modifiers. A subordinate conjunction, however, is used to introduce a clause, which is a group of words containing a subject and a predicate. With this review as background, the following discussion points out how to avoid common confusions between conjunctions and prepositions.

Unless,* not *Without* or *Except *Without* and *except* are prepositions that are frequently used incorrectly for the conjunction *unless.*

> Mr. Burr said that you are not to leave the office *unless* you get permission. (Not *without you get permission. You get permission* is a clause and must be introduced by a conjunction.)
>
> Mr. Burr said that you are not to leave the office *without* getting permission. (*Without* is correct in this sentence because it is part of the prepositional phrase *without getting permission.*)

◇ **TWILIGHT ZONE: *As, As If, As Though,* not *Like*** *Like* is a preposition, and a preposition should not introduce a clause. However, so many persons use *like* as a conjunction that such usage is now in the Twilight Zone. If you want to be technically correct, you should not use *like* for *as, as if,* or *as though.*

> You looked *as if* you were angry. (Not *like you were angry.* The clause *you were angry* should be introduced by a conjunction.)
>
> Do you wish you had talent *like* his? (Here the preposition *like* is correct. *Like* introduces the prepositional phrase *like his.*)

⊙ **CHECKUP 3** Correct any errors that occur in these sentences.

1. Do not give the wholesale discount to new buyers without you ask the sales manager.
2. It seems like we are going to have a mild winter.
3. Please don't leave without you tell him good-bye.
4. The letters would have been mailed yesterday except I had interruptions.
5. Never change any wording without you consult me.
6. Bill never opens the safe except I tell him to do so.

PARALLEL STRUCTURE

Observance of parallel structure is one of the earmarks of a well-trained communicator. Ideas of equal importance should be expressed in parallel structure; for instance, a noun should be paralleled with a noun, an adjective with an adjective, a phrase with a phrase, and so on.

> Mr. Betts works quietly and quickly. (The word before the conjunction *and* is an adverb, and the word after the conjunction *and* is an adverb. This is parallel structure.)
>
> Mr. Betts works quietly and with speed. (Parallel structure is violated here because the conjunction *and* connects an adverb and a prepositional phrase—unlike elements.)
>
> Did you place the letter on top of the desk or in the drawer? (The coordinate conjunction *or* connects two prepositional phrases.)

Coordinate and correlative conjunctions are the pivots for application of the principle of parallel structure, and the presentation here is divided into a discussion of the pivotal uses of each type of conjunction.

With Coordinate Conjunctions

Coordinate conjunctions must connect *like elements.* For instance, if an adjective is used before a coordinate conjunction, an adjective must also follow that conjunction. The elements that are written *before* and *after* a coordinate conjunction must match. Study these illustrations:

> The executives seem alert and (to be ready? ready?) to adopt new ideas. (An adjective occurs before *and,* the pivot; the principle of parallel structure demands that an adjective follow the *and. Ready* is therefore correct.)
>
> Which job do you prefer—typing, filing, or (to take? taking?) dictation? (Before the conjunction *or* there are two gerunds, *typing* and *filing.* Therefore, a gerund must follow the conjunction *or. Taking* is correct.)

⊙ CHECKUP 4 Can you balance the following sentences?

1. The Ajax computer is famous for its precision-made components and because it can be adapted to many different situations.
2. Trimflex plastic sheets can be bent, rolled, or even are immersible in water.
3. Applicants must be personable, adaptable, and can meet people easily.
4. Fast typing is one thing, but to cut a stencil is quite another.
5. You may cash your check at the cashier's window, at the main office, or go to the bank.

With Correlative Conjunctions

Earlier in this lesson, you learned that correlative conjunctions are conjunctions used in pairs. Parallel structure requires that parallel statements be expressed in parallel form. The element that *follows* the *first* of the paired conjunctions must agree with the element that *follows* the *second* member of the pair.

> Mr. Olsen wishes *either* Tom *or* me to take the message. (The first member of the pair, *either*, is followed by the noun *Tom*. The second member, *or*, is followed by the pronoun *me*. Nouns and pronouns are considered to be like elements; therefore, the structure is parallel.)
>
> *Not only* had the office been cleaned, *but also* it had been freshly painted. (The structure is parallel because the correlative conjunctions *not only* and *but also* join two independent clauses. Do not be misled because the first independent clause is in inverted order.)

⊙ CHECKUP 5 Correct these sentences so that elements used with correlative conjunctions are correctly matched.

1. The agenda for the meeting will either be prepared by Miss Allen or her assistant.
2. Does your boss both like to travel and to meet new people?
3. Because of the fuel shortage, we were neither allowed to drive alone to work nor staying after closing time.

Communication Projects

PRACTICAL APPLICATION

A Correct each incorrect sentence. Write *OK* for any correct sentence.

1. The reason that sales decreased this last quarter is because customers hesitated to invest in new equipment.
2. The budget for next year is not as high as we requested.
3. Don't plan on buying new typewriters without you see if they are provided for in the budget.
4. Mrs. Marlow always acts like she is not satisfied with my work.
5. These requisition forms are not as easy to use as the old ones.
6. Finding an opening is easy, but to get the job is sometimes not so easy.

7. We are going on vacation tomorrow, and today we have work to do.
8. John was not able to attend the meeting because he had to go to the dentist.
9. The article about undersea life is both well written and has colorful illustrations.
10. No applications by minors will be considered without their parents sign the applications.
11. The lawyers should decide not only what their fees will be, but also they should let their clients know.
12. According to rumors, it looks like our boss will be transferred to Houston.
13. The shipping department manager neither wants more help nor more overtime.
14. Expert writers like them are hard to find.
15. The reason I came early is because my appointment has been changed.
16. The salesroom is 50 feet wide, 80 feet in length, and 18 feet high.
17. We wish we could grant your request, being that you are such a good customer.
18. This year's edition of the manual is just as accurate as last year's edition.
19. We shall not be able to show a profit unless there is a sharp upturn in the market.
20. Such extensions of credit are neither allowed to the large customer nor to the small customer.

B List the changes needed to correct each sentence that contains errors.

1. The questionnaires are not in the files, and I saw them there yesterday.
2. The speaker sounded like he was suffering from a cold.
3. I wrote three times to complain about my hospital bill, but I never received an answer.
4. He neither looked at the interviewer nor at his notes.
5. Without your totals agree with mine, we will both have to stay tonight until they do.
6. Has anyone seen the truck drivers, Ray and he?
7. I thought she looked pale and that she was about to faint.
8. Our family has never before enjoyed a vacation so much as we did this summer.
9. There are eight legal holidays next year, and five of them fall on Mondays.
10. They ought to of asked us what we preferred instead of deciding it themselves.
11. The work will be done quickly if you divide the assignment among the three correspondents.
12. Did you know that there is a chefs' union?
13. We have neither the time or the money to do much experimentation.
14. You would do well not to trust them kind of proposals.
15. In our business, typewritten letters produce no more sales than using printed ones.
16. Being that Mr. Park made up the payroll, he can answer your questions.
17. Are you most ready to check these statements?
18. Did you see in the paper where Gold Company has filed a bankruptcy petition?
19. The applicant agreed to accept the position and that he would start Monday.
20. Don't you wish that you had an extra income like Bob and me?

EDITING PRACTICE

Editing for Correct Grammar Indicate the grammatical errors in these sentences. Write *OK* for any correct sentence.

1. No one thinks she should of been blamed for the mistake.
2. We sent out ten thousand direct mail pieces, and which are proving very successful in increasing sales.
3. Your system for filing punch cards is not much different than ours.
4. Inside of a month the contractor will write us in regards to the date for completion of the work.
5. An intelligent, industrious young graduate will do good in a business office.
6. I received the notice, and I have not yet had time to study the agenda.
7. Your job is to edit, write headings, and the assembling of graphs for these reports.
8. It looks like we shall have to revise our form letters.
9. Between the three of us, I think we can push the project to completion.
10. We can readily see that your opinions are identical with ours.

Proofreading for Spelling Errors Write the correct spelling for any misspelled words in the following paragraph.

> We are sending you a free copy of our populer booklet, *How to Increase the Affectiveness of Your Advertising.* At The Ad House, advertising is our only business. Weather you need media specialsts and techinical copywriters or just a convenient agency to buy magazine space for your coupon ads, you will find that The Ad House will provide you with expert servise.

Plurals and Possessives Edit the following sentences, correcting all errors and writing *OK* for any correct sentence.

1. The New School is considered the best childrens' school in our area.
2. My sister-in-laws and my brothers flew in for our wedding, and they all stayed as guests in my father-in-law house.
3. Economics are one of the few courses I disliked in college.
4. She had a beautiful reading room that was completely lined with bookshelfs.
5. Ella and Mike are the two dynamoes of the Accounting Department.
6. The Bradford Hotel did not have the proper facilities for our banquet.
7. I sincerely hope that the Misses Joneses agree to act as our consultants.
8. The painting I admire most is her's.
9. Plagued by mosquitos, we ended our picnic at noon.
10. In statistical typing, the periods before the zeroes must be aligned.
11. Of all the news that I heard today, yours are the most interesting.
12. More than half of the cameras that we sell are manufactured by the Japaneses.
13. The ratioes reported are obviously typographical errors!
14. We will need at least three dozens chairs, don't you agree?
15. The little girl in the first row knows the mottoes of all fifty states.
16. Marys' new plane is a small, light, easy-to-control model.
17. They are the United State's principal ally in Africa.
18. Benson's and Carter's Card Shop is the largest in our town.

19. The Professors Weber, tonights' guest speakers, are my sisters-in-law.
20. Please give the scissors to Joan when you are finished with it.

CASE PROBLEM

The Pool Supervisor Executives of the Hammett Company who use stenographers from the pool are complaining that their letters have to be retyped because of errors in spelling. What steps would you take to remedy the situation?

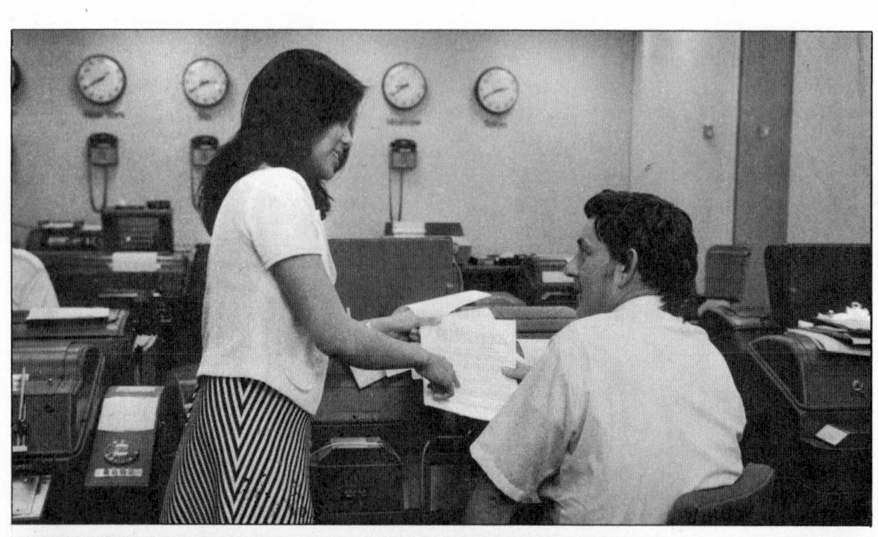

THE MECHANICS OF STYLE

22 Period, Question Mark, Exclamation Point

Writers use punctuation marks to help their readers better understand a message. Just as speakers use pauses, changes in voice pitch, and gestures to help interpret verbal messages for their audiences, so writers use punctuation marks to guide their readers into correctly interpreting their written messages. The period, the question mark, and the exclamation point have several functions; however, their main function is to signify that one thought is completed and that another thought is about to begin. In this section we will discuss this main function and some auxiliary functions of the period, the question mark, and the exclamation point.

PERIOD

The following discussion is divided into three main topics—when to use a period, when not to use a period, and pitfalls in the use of the period. Use a period (1) to end a declarative or an imperative sentence and (2) to end a request that is phrased as a question simply for the sake of courtesy.

After Declarative and Imperative Sentences

A declarative sentence makes a statement; an imperative sentence orders or entreats.

> Your order will be shipped tomorrow. (Declarative sentence.)
> Ship our order on or before June 1. (Imperative sentence.)

After Requests Phrased as Questions

Because such wording as "Send us your check immediately" is abrupt and peremptory, requests or suggestions are often phrased as questions, just to be polite; for instance: "Will you please send us your check immediately." This sentence requests the reader to act rather than to answer a question and is followed by a period, not by a question mark. Compare the following sentences:

> Will you be able to give us your decision by May 1? (Here the writer wants a "Yes" or "No" answer.)
>
> May we have your decision by May 1. (No question is intended here. The writer actually means: "Get busy and see to it that we have your decision by May 1.")

⊙ **CHECKUP 1** Decide whether or not to use periods to end these sentences.

1. Have you had these figures checked
2. Did you receive the new rug samples yet
3. Please mail your report by the end of next week
4. We had a hectic day yesterday
5. May we have your revised bid by Monday, June 5
6. Would you please try to return from lunch early today, Joan
7. I asked him if he wanted to come with us
8. May we attend the seminar at Temple Hall
9. May we have your completed questionnaire by the end of the week
10. Rush our order to us as soon as possible, Mr. James

When Not to Use a Period

Do not use a period to end any but a declarative or an imperative sentence or a request phrased as a question. Therefore, do not use a period in the following five cases.

After a Sentence Ending in an Abbreviation Only one period is used to indicate the end of a sentence; therefore, if a sentence ends with an abbreviation, do not use a second period

We are shipping your future orders c.o.d. (Not *c.o.d..*)

Please be sure to be there at 6 p.m. (Not *p.m..*)

Then, on the line below, type *R.S.V.P.* (Not *R.S.V.P..*)

After a Heading or Title; After a Roman Numeral Written With a Name A period should not follow any centered heading or any roman numeral used with a name or a title.

Chapter Four: The Mechanics of Style (Chapter heading)

Huckleberry Finn (Centered title)

Henry VIII was a much-married man. (Not *Henry VIII. was . . . .*)

After Numbers or Letters Enclosed in Parentheses In paragraphs or in outlines, do not use periods with numbers or letters enclosed in parentheses.

My reasons for declining your offer are these: (*a*) . . . , (*b*) . . . , and (*c*) . . . . (No period with letters enclosed in parentheses.)

The topics are:

1. The dictating machine
2. The telephone
    a. Placing calls
    b. Answering calls

After Items in Tabulated Lists or in Outlines Do not use a period after short phrases unless the phrases are essential to the grammatical completeness of the statement introducing the list. *Do* use a period after independent clauses, dependent clauses, or long phrases appearing on separate lines in a list. If the list includes both short and long phrases, use periods.

Section 1 is organized as follows: (No period after short phrases.)
1. Use of period
2. Period pitfalls

Section 1 demonstrates: (Period following short phrases that complete the statement introducing the list.)
1. The use of the period.
2. Period pitfalls.

Keep in mind the following: (Period following independent clauses.)
1. A well-written letter increases prestige.
2. A well-written letter promotes goodwill.

After Even Amounts of Dollars Except in tabulations, do not use periods or zeros after even amounts of dollars.

We have your check for $50, which is the final payment on your refrigerator. (Note *$50*, not *$50.*, not *$50.00.*)

⊙ **CHECKUP 2** Find the errors and make the needed corrections in these sentences.

1. Was George III. the last of the Hanoverians?
2. Our catalogs are printed by Colorama Press, Inc..
3. This endorsement increases your policy coverage to $15,000. and adds only $110 to your annual premium.
4. We must refuse to (1.) accept the shipment, (2.) pay the freight, or (3.) place a duplicate order.
5. The following are headings or titles. How would you punctuate them?
   Business Communications and On-the-Job Requirements
   The World Around Us
   Chapter VI
6. For only $1.00 you will know the convenience of instant hot water.
7. Verbs may be divided into three classifications:
   1. "Being" verbs.
   2. Transitive verbs.
   3. Intransitive verbs.

Period Pitfalls

Even some experienced writers fall into one or both of the following pitfalls: (1) using a period to end an incomplete thought or (2) using a comma when the correct punctuation is a period. These serious errors can be avoided by mastering the following guides to punctuation.

The Period Fault The period fault is the use of a period after words that do not express a complete thought and therefore are not sentences. They are the "no-sense" groups discussed in Chapter 3, Section 8.

We are not quoting prices just now. As our increased costs have not been determined. (The second group of words illustrates the period fault. Correctly written, the sentence is as follows: *We are not quoting prices just now, as our increased costs have not been determined.*)

The use of a period after a condensed expression—such as an answer to a question or a phrase that leads into another thought—is *not* a period fault. These expressions do not rightly belong in another sentence. If a condensed expression is declarative or imperative, it is followed by a period.

Do we have a reference manual for secretaries? Not at present. (*Not at present* is the answer to a question and is not part of a preceding or a following sentence. It is correctly followed by a period and can stand alone.)

The Comma-for-Period Fault The comma-for-period fault is the use of a comma to join two separate, distinct, and different thoughts. The correct punctuation in this construction is a period, because two different thoughts should be expressed as two separate sentences.

Our correspondents are attending a workshop, they are being sent at company expense. (These separate and different thoughts must be written as separate sentences.)

For years we have ordered supplies from you, we have never had cause to complain about quality or about your service. (Here, too, there are two separate thoughts joined by a comma. They should be written as two separate sentences.)

The book you ordered is not available now, we are temporarily out of stock. (Here, again, there are two separate thoughts joined by a comma. They should be written as separate sentences.)

⊙ **CHECKUP 3** Are there any period or comma-for-period faults in these sentences?

1. Our computer programming courses are listed in the enclosed folder, this year we have added a new brush-up course.
2. Although oil shipments have been drastically curtailed. We expect the situation to improve by next month.
3. Computer time sharing has proved economical for many small companies, the needs of our company might be served in this way.
4. We call your attention to your overdue account. No doubt, in the rush of business, you have overlooked payment.
5. Please join us for lunch on Monday, we are leaving at one o'clock.
6. Our new sales representative made ten calls yesterday. Receiving six orders.

QUESTION MARK

Use a question mark after a *direct* question, after a short direct question following a statement, and in a series of questions.

After a Direct Question

A question mark ends any sentence that asks a direct question. Some examples of direct questions are as follows:

Why has our note been discounted?
When do you plan to make the change?
The salesclerk asked, "When did you buy that suit?"

After a Short Direct Question Following a Statement

When a sentence begins as a statement and closes with a short direct question, the end punctuation must be a question mark.

> You are expecting Mr. Young on Monday, are you not?
>
> He has been invited to lunch with you, hasn't he?

In a Series of Questions

If a sentence contains a series of questions, a question mark should be used after each member of the series. Do not capitalize the separate items.

> Do you plan to vacation in Boston? in New York? in Chicago?
>
> Who is to accept the plaque—the president? the editor in chief? the personnel manager?

Question Mark Pitfall

Some writers, upon seeing the word *ask* or *why* or *how* in a sentence, automatically end that sentence with a question mark. Not recognizing the so-called "indirect question" that such words signify is the question mark pitfall. An indirect question is a statement and should end with a period.

> We are frequently asked whether we hire college students for summer jobs. (This is a statement, not a question.)
>
> Mr. Syme asks how soon we intend to join the association. (This, too, is a statement and properly ends with a period.)

⊙ **CHECKUP 4** In which of the following sentences is the question mark used incorrectly? In which is the period used incorrectly?

1. Jim asked Miss Johnson if she could suggest a better title for his report?
2. Most of us are becoming pollution-conscious, aren't we.
3. The sales manager asks when we prefer to meet next week?
4. Are you acquainted with the president of the company? the comptroller? the plant manager?
5. When will you have your report ready, Fred?

EXCLAMATION POINT

The exclamation point is popularly thought of as a mark indicating strong feeling. This is true, of course, but the writer or the speaker is the one who must decide whether to give greater emphasis to a statement or a question by using an exclamation point.

> Who would ever interpret my request in such a way? (This is a question, as the writer indicates by using the question mark.)
>
> Who would ever interpret my request in such a way! (Now the writer is somewhat irked, as evidenced by the exclamation point.)
>
> Where in the world is our Order 876 (Without an end punctuation mark, the reader cannot tell whether this is a question or an exclamation. If a question mark is used, the writer is just seeking information; if an exclamation point is used, the writer is expressing irritation or anger.)

Although the use of the exclamation point depends on the emotion the writer wishes to express, every writer should be familiar with the following two correct usages of the exclamation point.

After a Single Word or a Short Phrase

The exclamation point may be correctly used after a single word or a short phrase. The sentence that follows the exclamation, however, is punctuated in the usual way.

Fine! You have our authorization to proceed. (The exclamation is followed by a declarative sentence.)

Well! Did you see what happened? (The exclamation is followed by a question.)

Great Scott! What a relief that was! (The first exclamation is followed by a second exclamation.)

After the Word *Oh*

The exclamation point is used after *oh* when *oh* is the entire exclamation. If a group of words containing *oh* is the exclamation, *oh* is followed by a comma. Capitalize *oh* only at the beginning of a sentence.

Oh! What have I done?

The play was good—but, oh, how sad! (Note, also, that a comma precedes the *oh* occurring within the sentence.)

⊙ **CHECKUP 5** What exclamation point corrections are needed in these sentences?

1. All this repetition is necessary, but, oh, so tiresome.
2. Wonderful. We are moving to our new headquarters next week!
3. What an adventure awaits you when you take one of our "mystery" tours.
4. How glad I am that you are joining our staff.
5. What. Have you been idle all morning?
6. Oh! What wonderful news this is!
7. I am eager to know what firm in this state does the most business!

Communication Projects

PRACTICAL APPLICATION

A For the following sentences, make any needed period, question mark, or exclamation point corrections. Write *OK* for any correct sentence.

1. Would you please send me a cash refund instead of a credit memorandum?
2. If you want to study forest management, have you considered the schools in Montana? In Washington? In Oregon?
3. Because of the fuel shortage we are setting our office thermostat at 68° F.

4. The trade-in value of the old car is $1,100, and the price of the new car is $4,800.
5. The repairman asked when the Multilith had been purchased?
6. All federal funds available under Title IV. have been exhausted.
7. Oh no! Both meetings I must attend are scheduled for the same time!
8. Those two books are on the reference shelf, the others you asked about are not in the library.
9. Please let us know by May 1. We cannot wait beyond that date.
10. This ribbon is very faint. Although it was changed only last week.
11. I do not have the authority to make this decision. I wish that Mr. Watts were here.
12. You will be sure to enclose a check, will you not?
13. Well done! We are all happy about your promotion.
14. Our president is expected to return Tuesday. On the evening plane.
15. The customer asked if we would wrap her purchase for mailing.
16. Sweaters are selling very well. So well that we can hardly meet the demand.
17. May we expect a reply by Monday of next week?
18. Peter has superior writing skill—but, oh, what a drab personality!
19. Your subscription has expired, there is still time, however, to renew it.
20. Some suggestions for good study habits are as follows:
    1. Read the entire assignment to get an overview of the task ahead of you
    2. Take each phase separately, study it, and think about it
    3. Once more, read the assignment as a whole

B Correct the following sentences wherever necessary.

1. Gifts certainly should not be sent c.o.d.
2. The examination was much more harder than I expected.
3. Well done! Your promotion to district manager is certainly well deserved.
4. They entered the room quickly and they took a long time finding their seats.
5. Sign and return each copy of the contract. We will add our signatures and return one copy to you.
6. Pope John XXVI. was a most unusual man.
7. The new interchanges on Route 80 are better designed than any in the country.
8. Have you ever seen a live koala bear? Which is a small bear native to Australia.
9. Whom do you think is most likely to be chosen?
10. The craftsmen chose to resign rather than accepting lower wages.
11. May we ask you to report immediately on these claims for damages.
12. I do not mind anyone criticizing my writing.
13. The officer asked who owned the car with the flat tire?
14. We were late because the storm disrupted the schedules of commuter's trains.
15. Our maintenance crew is exceptionally efficient.
16. The price of $55.00 is net, not list.
17. Labor Day is one of those holidays that has meaning for all workers.
18. Dick was asked whether the blueprints had been filed.
19. How many copys of the bulletin are to be duplicated?
20. Our company makes silverware that is of outstanding beauty, of unusual design, and is sterling of the best quality.

EDITING PRACTICE

The Ad Writer The following sentences are taken from ads written to promote the sale of "Smoothee," a new hair preparation. Rewrite any sentences that need revision.

1. SMOOTHEE *forces* your hair to lay flat!
2. SMOOTHEE—like it's name—smooths away hair problems!
3. No hair preparation does the job that SMOOTHEE does!
4. SMOOTHEE develops resistance to dandruff!
5. Buy one bottle of SMOOTHEE, and you'll never buy another!

Any Spelling Corrections Needed? If there are spelling errors in the following paragraphs, write the correct spelling.

> Your long and outstanding record of interest in civic affairs prompts us to invite you to become a promoter or a sponser of the Bellville Choral Club concert scheduled for June 9. As you probably know, the procedes will be used to help finance the Head Start project planned for this summer. We shall be happy to list you on the program as a sponser (contribution of $50 or more) or as a promoter (contribution of $25).

CASE PROBLEM

Retaining Goodwill Fred James is supervisor of the adjustment department of a large department store. In reviewing the carbons of letters sent to customers by some of his correspondents, Fred found the following two statements: (1) "Really, Mrs. Whitehouse, you can't blame us if you don't follow the instructions included with each mixer." (2) "You should know that we can't allow a refund unless you return the merchandise within a reasonable time."

1. Do you find anything wrong with either of these statements?
2. If so, what would you have written?

23 Semicolon, Colon, Dash

The semicolon, the colon, and the dash are tools that the writer uses to "hold" the reader at some point within the sentence. With these tools, the writer guides the reader into pausing for a short rest before going on to complete the sentence. All three punctuation marks discussed here arrest, or hold, the reader, but each one has its own particular holding function. For that reason, each "hold" punctuation mark will be discussed separately in this section.

SEMICOLON

By forcing the reader to pause, the semicolon directs the reader to phrase a sentence so that its message can be clearly understood. Study the following discussion to learn when a semicolon is properly used.

To Indicate Omission of a Conjunction

A compound sentence is a sentence that contains two or more independent clauses. In such a sentence the clauses are usually connected by a comma and a conjunction.

> Special orders are drop-shipped if they total $10 or more, but this service is offered to charge customers only. (In this compound sentence, the clauses are connected by a comma and the conjunction *but.*)

Whenever a conjunction in a compound sentence is omitted, a semicolon is used in its place.

> Special orders are drop-shipped if they total $10 or more; this service is offered to charge customers only.

Before a Second Clause Starting With an Introductory Word

In some compound sentences, the second clause starts with an introductory word such as:

accordingly	consequently	moreover
again	furthermore	nevertheless
also	however	otherwise
besides	indeed	therefore

In a sentence of this kind, the reader must pause briefly, first to assimilate the meaning of the first clause, and then to prepare to connect it with the meaning of the rest of the sentence. That is why a semicolon is used before a second independent clause that starts with an introductory word instead of with a coordinating conjunction.

> A catalog is costly to produce; nevertheless, it is essential to our mail order business. (A semicolon and an introductory word are used in place of a comma and a coordinating conjunction to separate the two independent clauses.)
>
> All tickets for the May 7 performance have been sold; however, we shall be glad to call you if we receive any late cancellations. (Here, too, a semicolon and an introductory word are used in place of a comma and a coordinating conjunction to separate the two independent clauses.)

Before Explanatory or Enumerating Words

A semicolon precedes such expressions as *for example, for instance, that is,* and *that is to say* when these expressions introduce an independent clause, an enumeration, or an explanation that is incidental to the rest of the sentence.

> When I was in college, my father was my greatest handicap; that is to say, he was too free with his checkbook. (*That is to say* introduces an explanation that is incidental to the rest of the sentence.)

As Exceptions to Comma Rules

Three additional uses of the semicolon may be considered exceptions to comma uses. These rules are presented with the rules for commas in Section 24.

⊙ **CHECKUP 1** Make any necessary corrections in the use of semicolons in the following sentences.

1. This country does not produce sufficient fuel for its needs, therefore, it is dependent upon imported fuel.
2. Delays occurred throughout the production cycle, consequently, the target date for announcing the new product had to be changed.
3. One importer specializes in handicrafts from Spain, another imports only leather goods from Italy.
4. The multimedia presentation of the story of textiles was fascinating, moreover, it was very informative.
5. Reading broadens the mind therefore, the person who continues to read continues to be educated.
6. On cold days, Jim's hands are too cold to write, on warm days, they are too hot.
7. Your work shows an uneven typing touch, for instance, all carbon copies are difficult to read.

COLON

A colon stops the reader for an express purpose: to signal that something important is coming. The function of the colon, therefore, is to give a reader time to get ready for something that merits special consideration. To use the colon effectively, a writer must know the rules that govern its application.

Colon Before Listed Items

A colon is used before listed items in both sentence and outline form. Expressions such as *the following, as follows, this, these,* and *thus* are the words most often used to introduce a list.

> The four methods of filing are as follows: alphabetic, numeric, geographic, and subject. (This is a listing in sentence form.)
>
> The proper procedure is this:
> 1. Read the entire lesson first.
> 2. Study each item intensively.
> 3. Study the lesson as a whole.
>
> (This is a listing in outline form.)

Colon Instead of Semicolon

You have learned that a semicolon is used before such expressions as *for example* and *that is* when these expressions introduce an independent clause, an enumeration, or an explanation that is incidental to the rest of the sentence. However, when the explanation or enumeration is anticipated, a colon is used instead of a semicolon.

> A good conversationalist must remember two things: namely, when to speak and when to keep silent.

Colon to Emphasize

Probably the most important reason for using a colon as a sign for the reader to pause is to emphasize, to point up, a thought that the writer considers important. Study the following illustrations:

> You should always remember that punctuation is the tool of the writer. (There is no particular "punch" in this sentence.)
>
> Remember this: Punctuation is the tool of the writer. (Do you see how the revision makes the message emphatic?)

Capitalization After Colon

The rule for capitalizing after a colon is this: The first word of a *complete* sentence following a colon should be capitalized if the sentence requires special emphasis or if the sentence states a formal rule.

> The three "hold buttons" are these: the semicolon, the colon, and the dash. (Not a complete sentence, not capitalized.)
>
> Remember this: Use a colon to emphasize a point. (Complete sentence capitalized because it requires special emphasis.)
>
> Learn the following rule: Use a colon before listed items. (Complete sentence capitalized because it states a formal rule.)

Colon or Period?

If the last words in a sentence do not directly lead into a listing or a statement, use a period after those words, not a colon. A period, not a colon, is also used if an "interrupting" sentence appears between the lead-in sentence and the listing.

> The following sentences will help you to recognize independent clauses when you see them. (Period, not a colon, because the sentence does not lead directly into a listing.)
>
> Sentences that test your understanding of colon usage are as follows: (Colon, because the last words lead directly into a listing.)
>
> Please send me the following items. You will, of course, ship by parcel post. (Correct, with a period rather than a colon after *items*, because the lead-in sentence and the listing are interrupted by another sentence.)

⊙ **CHECKUP 2** Apply your knowledge of the "stop" uses of the colon by making any needed corrections in the following sentences.

1. The following supplies are needed: fine-line black pens, half-inch-wide cellophane tape, red file folders.
2. One fact is most significant: all the thefts took place during the holiday weekend.
3. Our air tours include many extras for example; airport limousine service, discount theater tickets, and reduced rates at well-known restaurants.
4. The following are my reasons for resigning. Please note that there is no dissatisfaction with the company or with working conditions.
5. We are offering the following fringe benefits paid vacations, paid life and health insurance, and discount privileges on many purchases.
6. Words frequently misspelled are these: *Accommodate, definite, separate, embarrass.*

DASH

The specific purpose of the dash is to break the thought abruptly and thus call special attention to the words following it. Because the dash is the most forceful of the three "stop" or "hold" punctuation marks, reserve it for writing situations requiring extra force.

Dash or Semicolon or Colon?

It is the writer who decides whether to use a semicolon, a colon, or a dash, for only the writer knows what effect is intended. If the writer wants the reader to pause long enough to assimilate the first part of a message before going on to the second part, the punctuation to use is a semicolon. If the writer wants to signal to the reader that the second part of the sentence contains something important, something to be noted, the punctuation to use is a colon. And if the writer wants to interrupt a message to introduce another with special impact, the best way to do it is with a dash.

> Your advertising dollar will bring you the greatest return if you buy time on OKTV; this is the television network that statistics prove is tuned in by most viewers in this area. (A good sentence, but not a forceful one.)
>
> For the best return on your advertising dollar, do this: Buy time on OKTV, the television network that statistics prove is tuned in by most viewers in this area. (This is a better sentence; a more forceful one.)
>
> Your advertising dollar will bring you the greatest return if you buy time on OKTV—the television network that statistics prove is tuned in by most viewers in this area. (The dash snaps off the main thought and thereby adds power to the rest of the message. This is the most forceful sentence.)

Forceful Summarizing, Forceful Repetition

Do you feel that by summarizing what was already written (or said), you will make your message more easily remembered? If you do, use a dash to separate the summary from the rest of the sentence. Do you hope that by repeating a message, you will make a deeper impression with it? Again, if you do, then use a dash to separate the repetition from the rest of the sentence.

> Road maps, hotel reservations, credit cards—these must be ready before Saturday. (The dash in this sentence is used for forceful summarizing.)
>
> Your train leaves from the lower level of Grand Central Station—from the lower level, notice. (Forceful repetition. The writer wishes *lower level* to stick in the reader's mind.)

The Dash With an Afterthought

A good writer may *plan* afterthoughts in order to add variety to the writing, to soften a statement that might give offense, or to arouse the reader's curiosity. The dash is the mark used before a planned afterthought.

> Each of the words omitted—and there are several—is very important. (For variety in style.)
>
> We are unable to take advantage of your offer—at least, not for a few months. (To soften a refusal.)
>
> The merger seems to be shaping up—but more about this later. (This will keep the reader "in suspense.")

⊙ **CHECKUP 3** Correct whatever dash errors there may be in the following sentences.

1. Are you satisfied with your vocabulary—with the words at your command?
2. Our new dictionary offers a clear, concise guide to anyone who speaks or writes—and that is everyone.
3. Send for your examination copy—without cost or obligation—and see for yourself.
4. Every morning during vacation, the Perrys climbed the hill, played tennis, and went swimming—all before breakfast.
5. I wish I had time to tell you about—but I must stop dictating now.

Punctuating Words Set Off by Dashes

No punctuation is used before an opening dash, with the exception of quotation marks or a period following an abbreviation. If words set off by dashes come at the end of a sentence, the closing dash should be replaced by the punctuation needed to end the sentence.

> Our offices are air-conditioned—a necessity in this climate. (No punctuation before dash; period used to end declarative sentence.)
>
> This artifact dates back to 400 B.C.—an exciting discovery indeed! (Period following the abbreviation *B.C.* precedes opening dash; exclamation point follows exclamatory expression.)

The question mark or the exclamation point may be used before a closing dash when such punctuation is needed. However, if a declarative sentence is set off by dashes, a period does not precede the closing dash.

> Your customer—what is his name?—must have kept you waiting a long time.
>
> Our football team—and what a team!—won the championship.
>
> Mr. Williams—he's the gentleman you met yesterday—will call again next week. (No period before the closing dash.)

Commas Within Groups of Words Set Off by Dashes Use commas where needed within groups of words set off by dashes. The point to remember is that the commas may be used within the group of words—not at the beginning, not at the end.

> Most of our writers—and Bill, of course, will bear me out—have had excellent training.

⊙ **CHECKUP 4** Correct any punctuation errors in the following sentences.

1. All aspects of the work—the poor hardware, the cheap paint, the sloppy workmanship,—are far below acceptable standards.
2. The men have been moving the drafting room equipment,—and what a heavy job it is, too—ever since they came in this morning.
3. Have you visited any foreign cities—London, Paris, Rome, to mention a few.
4. It is the love of learning—or is it the love of good grades—that marks the real student.
5. Innate curiosity and a longing to express beauty,—these were primary forces in Leonardo's genius.

Communication Projects

PRACTICAL APPLICATION

A Correct all the incorrect sentences in this group.

1. Some students read so slowly that they fall hopelessly behind, others read so fast that they tackle extra assignments.
2. The catalog offers the following tempting delicacies, truffles from France, marmalade from England, shortbread from Scotland.
3. Are the following rights guaranteed by the Constitution, the right to worship, the right to work, the right to privacy?
4. Decentralization of corporate operations has these advantages: less congested commuting, lower taxes, better housing.
5. The following changes in retirement benefits will take effect January 1: You will receive a personal letter later with the figures that apply to you.
6. The sample kits have not yet been made up, however, they should be ready by February 1.
7. The new turret lathes—shipment has been delayed because of a flood at factory.—are now expected within the next two weeks.
8. The legal situation is this: the contract has been breached and we are suing for damages.
9. The latest improvements in camera design, faster shutter speed, wider lens opening, special double-exposure feature, have been incorporated in the new Rollo-15.
10. Would you like to know more about your camera—how to take better pictures, what's new in equipment and techniques?
11. Sometimes money is made by saving money; for instance, payment of bills within the discount period saves the amount of the discount.
12. A receptionist should not be too friendly actually, most employers prefer a little reserve.
13. The dash—do you remember?—is used effectively by few writers.
14. They uttered no cry; not a sound escaped from their lips.
15. The chairman arrived at the meeting quite unprepared that is to say, he had forgotten to bring his notes.
16. Would you be interested in: seeing a play or hearing a concert?
17. She is a charming person,—charming and very interesting, too.
18. A writer must know the uses of punctuation tools; for instance, the semicolon "holds" the reader at some point within the sentence.
19. Your service is poor in the following areas: acknowledging orders, making satisfactory adjustments, shipping promptly.
20. Which type of money order do you mean—postal, express, or telegraph.

B Correct the following sentences wherever necessary.

1. She should of asked for written confirmation.
2. Mrs. Hansen has several assistants, if you can call them assistants.
3. There only fault is that they are too eager.
4. I warn you for the last time; such conduct is not acceptable in this office.
5. Affluence was the watchword of our society, now it is scarcity.
6. A few overdue library books have been returned, the rest are incurring heavy fines.
7. All unneeded lights were to be dimmed, nevertheless, the reception area is still bright.

8. Have you used these kind of punched cards before?
9. I wish this aerial map were clearer.
10. The witness seemed to completely evade the last question she was asked.
11. For his tardiness, Harry offered the following excuses: The rain, the traffic, the scarcity of taxis.
12. May we have your reply before the market closes on Friday.
13. We are sure of this one thing: we will grant him no further credit.
14. It is often said—I am not sure how true the statement is—that real music lovers prefer to sit in the upper balcony.
15. Correct the errors in the following sentences: Some of the sentences are correct.
16. We have many calls for steam irons in fact, we sold 175 last week.
17. In our office we can choose our vacation time furthermore, we are paid in advance at vacation time.
18. Bert feels that he cannot spare time to study science, literature, history—all the fascinating topics that make for good conversation.
19. In our opinion, your fields should lay fallow for an entire year.
20. Learn to avoid the common grammar pitfalls; for instance, do not confuse plurals and possessives.

EDITING PRACTICE

The Editorial Supervisor One of your writers overuses the italicized words in the following sentences. Supply two synonyms for each overworked word.

1. We are fully *cognizant* of your sales promotion difficulties.
2. This statement is not intended to be *dogmatic*.
3. Evans was never known to *shirk* his responsibilities.
4. The increased fringe benefits will have a *terrific* effect on morale.
5. Please let me know how you feel about the *matter*.
6. A sales representative's card should indicate his or her *line*.

Robot Secretary Your new secretary, Susan Barrett, has been with you only a week, but already you are beginning to think she is a robot. She does your work fast and efficiently—but she doesn't use her head! What support for your opinion can you find in this paragraph?

> The day after your visit to the Gift Shoppe, we received a shipment of very beautiful glassware. In that shipment was a handsome reproduction of an old Irish bowel that can be used for flowers or fruit; and the price is within the range you specified. This item is being set aside until you have a chance to see it. Won't you pay us another visit—soon?

CASE PROBLEM

Addressing Your Boss John Teller was recently hired as junior accountant in the office of the Boswell Manufacturing Company. There is an air of informality in the office, and John notes that his co-workers refer to the president, James J. Castle, as Jim. John has been saying "Mr. Castle" whenever speaking to him or referring to him in any way.

1. Should John call the president by his first name or continue to use "Mr. Castle"?
2. Under what circumstances do you think employees should call their co-workers by their first names and under what circumstances by a courtesy title, such as *Mr.* or *Miss*?

24 The Comma

The comma's special function is to slow the reader, and it accomplishes that by providing a logical place to pause before continuing to read. Sometimes a sentence contains elements that need to be separated so that the reader won't misinterpret the message. The writer inserts a comma to do the separating.

> Underneath the desk was all rotted away. (What was rotted away? This sentence is ambiguous.)
>
> Underneath, the desk was all rotted away. (By slowing the reader, the writer shows plainly that the desk, not the floor, was rotted away.)
>
> If Tom comes to work late, once more he will be discharged. (Comma placement can alter the meaning of a sentence. The meaning here seems to be that Tom is repeatedly fired. But the meaning intended is closer to the example below.)
>
> If Tom comes to work late once more, he will be discharged. (Making the reader pause after *more* shapes the correct thought unit.)

The comma is used so often and in such a variety of situations that lack of facility in using it can spoil the effectiveness of any written communication. Therefore, the next three sections will discuss the many uses of the comma.

IN A COMPOUND SENTENCE

A compound sentence is a sentence that contains two or more independent clauses. When the clauses are joined by a conjunction such as *and, but, or,* or *nor,* a comma is used before the conjunction. For a better understanding of the rule, study the line of reasoning developed in the following Memory Hook.

▣ **MEMORY HOOK** Concentrate on four words—*and, but, or, nor.* Whenever you see one of these words following an independent clause, look to see whether there is a stated subject of another independent clause after it. If so, use a comma before the *and, but, or,* or *nor.*

In slogan style, the rule is *No Subject, No Comma.* For example:

> Your order was received today, and shipment will be made tomorrow. (Here we have *and,* and the noun *shipment* is the expressed subject of the following clause. The comma, therefore, is correctly used.)
>
> Your order has been received and will be shipped tomorrow. (Do not use a comma in this sentence. There is no expressed subject after the *and—No Subject, No Comma.*)

Although the comma is usually required to separate the parts of a compound sentence, there are the following minor exceptions.

Very Short Clauses

If the clauses of a compound sentence are very short, the comma may be omitted.

> We sent the check but we received no acknowledgment.
> Tim writes the copy and Dick edits it.

Semicolon Instead of Comma

When a longer pause than a comma affords is desired between the parts of a compound sentence, use a semicolon to separate the parts.

When an Additional Comma Might Be Misleading If either clause of a compound sentence already contains a comma (or commas) and a misreading is likely, use a semicolon to separate the clauses. However, if no misreading is likely, a comma may be used instead to separate the clauses. For instance:

> The purpose of the week-long session is to improve our skills in writing business letters, memos, and informal reports; and formal reports, too, will be covered if time permits. (The semicolon prevents the misreading *informal reports, and formal reports* by holding the reader after *informal reports.*)
>
> I was in Washington, D.C., last Tuesday, and thinking that I might catch a glimpse of the President, I visited the White House. (The two parts of the sentence are so closely related that a comma is sufficient to make the break between clauses.)

When Clauses Are Unusually Long When the clauses of a compound sentence are unusually long, a brief pause for a comma may not give the reader time enough to understand the different parts of the sentence. In such sentences, the writer may want a stronger break than the comma creates and so may use a semicolon. Note, however, that the clauses are still linked by a coordinating conjunction.

> Punctuation is important to business people who depend on their writing to communicate on the job; and complete mastery of the use of punctuation tools will help business writers to create more effective communications and to advance on their jobs.

⊙ **CHECKUP 1** What are the errors in these sentences?

1. You may agree but I disagree.
2. The specifications which we received today, are clear but we cannot possibly meet the deadline for bids.
3. Any necessary repairs to your air conditioner are covered by the service contract but we cannot send a mechanic to repair it until next Wednesday or Thursday.
4. Although our product is new, it is giving satisfaction and the two-year testing period is paying off.
5. Do you ever stop for a moment to think of the advancement opportunities in this company?
6. The paper is not durable enough for our documents nor is it of the right size.
7. If you pay within ten days, you may take the discount but if you wait a month, you must pay the full amount.

IN A SERIES

A series consists of at least three items in sequence. The items may be words, phrases, or clauses. Use commas to separate the parts of a series; also use a comma before the conjunction that precedes the last item in a series.

> English, shorthand, and typewriting are the foundation courses for a stenographer. (Series of words.)
>
> Will the new branch be located in Buffalo, in Cleveland, or in Gary? (Series of phrases.)

Use of the comma to separate the parts of a series is the most frequently used series rule, but it is not the only one. The following discussion completes the *series* picture.

Etc. Ending a Series

When *etc.* (meaning "and so forth") ends a series, it must be set off by commas —a comma before and a comma after. If *etc.* ends a sentence, the period denoting the abbreviation is also the ending punctuation mark. (Do not use *and etc.* The word *and* is superfluous before *and so forth.*)

> An employer considers grooming, manners, work habits, etc., when promoting a person to an executive position.
>
> Every typist should be able to type manuscripts, outlines, statements, etc.

Semicolon Instead of Comma in a Series

A comma slows; a semicolon "holds." Logically, then, if the items in a series are long independent clauses or if they already contain commas, a semicolon should be used to separate these items.

> We should like you to do the following: arrange our goods into shipping units; transport them to the place where they are to be consumed; store them there if storage is necessary; and obtain a signed receipt showing the time of delivery and the condition of the goods. (You can see that a long pause is needed between the items.)
>
> During our vacation trip last year, we stopped at the following places: Oil City, Pennsylvania; Ann Arbor, Michigan; Gary, Indiana; Kansas City, Missouri; and Santa Fe, New Mexico. (A semicolon to separate the parts of the series holds the reader long enough to grasp the meaning immediately.)

Do Not Use a Comma

Commas must not be used, however, in certain series situations.

End of Series No comma is used at the end of a series that has a conjunction immediately before the last item—unless the sentence structure demands a comma at that point. Such instances are rare.

> Water, heat, and electricity are services for which payment must be made promptly. (A comma after *electricity* would be incorrect.)

Repeated Conjunction If the conjunction is repeated before each item in a series, no commas are used to separate the items.

You can get the information from Bill or Tom or Ray.

In a Firm Name When a series of three or more names connected by an ampersand (&) constitutes a firm name, no comma is used before the ampersand.

Our investments are handled by Mell, Lyons, Pierce & Dunn.

⊙ **CHECKUP 2** Keeping the word *series* in mind, find the errors in the following sentences.

1. We could find no information about him in the encyclopedia, in a biographical dictionary or in *Who's Who.*
2. A sales manual, a catalog, and a discount sheet, were placed before each sales representative at the first training session.
3. She could not decide whether to invest her savings in mutual funds, or in an annuity, or in savings certificates.
4. Do this immediately: prepare a data sheet, write a covering letter of application, and write me when you have mailed them.
5. Hats, shoes, handbags, etc., will be on sale Saturday.
6. The name Veal, Chop, & Eaton belongs in the "odd-name" category.
7. Advancement is more likely if you are careful about grammar, punctuation, enunciation, and etc.

FOLLOWING AN INTRODUCTORY WORD, PHRASE, OR CLAUSE

A comma is used after an introductory word, phrase, or clause as a signal to the reader to slow down to prevent confusion and misinterpretation of messages.

Introductory Word

An introductory word at the beginning of a sentence or a clause is followed by a comma. Some of the most commonly used introductory words are the following:

accordingly	fortunately	naturally	otherwise
actually	further	next	perhaps
also	however	nevertheless	personally
besides	indeed	no	say
consequently	meanwhile	now	theoretically
finally	moreover	obviously	therefore
first	namely	originally	yes

Fortunately, the assignment is an easy one. (Here the introductory word falls at the beginning of the sentence.)

I did not enjoy the play; nevertheless, I stayed for the entire performance. (The introductory word introduces a clause within the sentence.)

However high the price, we feel that the purchase is justified. (In this sentence *however* is not introductory. It is essential to the message *however high the price* and, therefore, is not followed by a comma.)

Introductory Phrase

An infinitive phrase at the beginning of a sentence is followed by a comma unless the phrase is the subject of the sentence.

> To do a good editing job, one must have a fine background in English. (Introductory infinitive phrase.)
>
> To do a good editing job is imperative. (Here the infinitive phrase is the subject of the sentence.)

An introductory participial phrase is always followed by a comma. However, don't confuse an introductory participial phrase with a gerund phrase that serves as subject.

> Standing on the platform, Mr. Kain could check the attendance of his staff members. (Introductory participial phrase.)
>
> Checking the time cards is someone else's job. (Here the gerund phrase *checking the time cards* is the subject of the sentence.)

Whether or not to use a comma after an initial prepositional phrase presents a problem. If the phrase is very short or if it flows into the main thought, do not use a comma. Use a comma, however, if the phrase is very long, if it is clearly introductory, or if it contains a verbal (participle, infinitive, or gerund) or a dependent clause.

> In winter our store does not close on Wednesday afternoons. (No comma because the phrase is very short and flows into the main thought.)
>
> In the third drawer of the desk near the window, you will find the letter. (Long introductory phrase.)
>
> After seeing Jane, I took a short walk in the park. (Prepositional phrase containing a gerund, *seeing*.)

Introductory Clause

An introductory clause is a subordinate clause that precedes the main thought. To slow the reader, a comma is placed after an introductory clause.

> When I give the signal, start the presses rolling. (Without the comma to slow the reader, the eye might see as a thought unit the words *when I give the signal start*.)

Ability to recognize on sight the words or phrases that begin introductory clauses will enable you to apply this comma rule correctly. Study the following list carefully:

after
although
as
as if
as soon as
as though
because
before
even if
for
how
if
inasmuch as
in case that
in order that
otherwise
provided
since
so that
supposing
then
till
though
unless
until
when
whenever
where
whereas
wherever
whether
while

⊙ **CHECKUP 3** Find the errors in "introductions" in these sentences.

1. Of course, I am stating only my personal opinion.
2. Moving the carriage by hand, is not necessary when you use an electric typewriter.
3. Despite the economic situation people are still spending money freely.
4. Obviously Miss Ames cannot attend the conference in Dallas if she must be in Chicago on that date.
5. Sitting so close to the speaker I noticed he was pale and perspiring.
6. When your warehouse is finished, we should like to rent floor space.
7. Costs are mounting steadily; consequently our prices must be raised.
8. To find the percentage rate divide the smaller number by the larger number.
9. If you prefer the bill can be sent weekly, instead of monthly.

NEVER, NEVER

There are five comma pitfalls that the writer must avoid. You will avoid these pitfalls if you observe the "never, nevers" presented here and in the following two sections. The first is this: Never, never separate the parts of a compound subject, a compound object, or a compound verb by a *single* comma. Use at least *two* commas—or none at all.

Carter or Barton can supply the special paper you need. (No single comma separates the parts of the compound subject *Carter or Barton*.)

You have my permission to experiment with Plan A and Plan B. (No single comma separates the parts of the compound object of the preposition *with*.)

Simply sign and mail the renewal card. (No single comma separates the parts of the compound verb *sign and mail*.)

Our special services and, of course, full credit privileges are yours for the asking. (This sentence does not violate the "never, never" rule because *two* commas separate an element that interrupts the compound subject *special services and full credit privileges*.)

Communication Projects

PRACTICAL APPLICATION

A Correct each incorrect sentence in the following group.

1. Disregarding the advice of his staff, he plunged ahead with his wild scheme.
2. Personally I would prefer to wait at least a month.
3. Whenever we find a new supplier he or she seems to be just ready to retire.
4. Janet scored high on the placement test, however her poor grooming counts against her.
5. Please rush this order by air express, and wire me when you have shipped it.
6. All branch offices will be closed evenings, Wednesday afternoons, and all day Saturday.
7. Miss Carter has been appointed director of market research, but she will not assume her new duties until she tours all our plants.

8. Do you know the difference between a certified check and a cashier's check and a bank check?
9. The price you quoted is within reason, but, before placing an order, we must see some samples.
10. We can ship your order by freight or we can send it by one of our trucks.
11. We asked for it and we got it.
12. Corn, wheat, and soybeans, are important crops in our country.
13. In addition to the introduction, how much of the report has Don written?
14. Our store is now open on Friday nights, and will continue to be so for the rest of the summer.
15. Johnson, Johnson, & Barr are management consultants.

B Correct the following sentences wherever necessary.

1. Mortgage loans are difficult to obtain, and are becoming increasingly so even at higher interest rates.
2. The contractor asked how many doors we wanted rehung?
3. Surprisingly, she disposed of all the handknit sweaters at a good profit.
4. You and Mr. Harris will both visit the proposed plant site, won't you.
5. Replacement parts are available at our downtown store or you will find them at our Liberty Street branch.
6. Since your balance is past due, we must withhold shipping your current order until your account is paid in full.
7. Her regular reports are always very well prepared, that is why she was asked to write the annual report.
8. The director of research has formed his own consulting firm; furthermore his wife has joined him in this new venture.
9. This restriction is covered under Section XIX, of the statute.
10. The new computer course will not be offered until next spring, but, in the event of heavy demand, it might be introduced this fall.
11. What a relief. You were most kind to let us know so soon.
12. Will you please send us the requested information immediately.
13. The supplies needed for painting a room are brushes, paint, turpentine etc.
14. To make up for lost time we must work evenings all next week.
15. These pills are not recommended for general use, that is, they should be taken only on the advice of a doctor.
16. On our May 2 order, we did not receive the bath towels, color green, the face cloths, rose, or the hand towels, blue.
17. You will enjoy the books we have listed below. They are instructive, and entertaining.
18. Mr. Crowley insists that all of us are divided into two general classes,— those who do and those who don't.
19. On the other hand, our supply of refrigerators is low.
20. Our office is an ideal place to work quite different from the average office.

EDITING PRACTICE

The Rewrite Desk Edit and rewrite the following paragraph to correct all mistakes.

Of all the skirts we placed on sale last week the azure ones were in greatest demand. Your order was received on the forth day of the sale which was

> after our stock of azure skirts were sold out. The quality of these garments is so good so unusual that we wanted you to have one of them at the low, sale price. Therefore we are sending you a skirt in your size in the new popular ice-blue color. If you are not pleased with the choice we have made for you please do not hesitate to return the skirt.

The Blue-Ribbon Speller If you are a blue-ribbon speller, you will be able to find and correct any spelling errors in this paragraph.

> Although we know that the use of *loan* as a verb is considered permissable, we are reluctant to sanction such usage in the letters sent by our executives. As bankers, we should project an image of conservatism and stability; therefore, we cannot afford to go along with any Twilight Zone changes. And bankers, of all people, should most certainly know the differance between *lend* and *loan*.

CASE PROBLEM

Telephone Technique Criticize the following telephone conversation. Then rewrite it to avoid the types of errors you criticized.

> *Person answering.* Hello.
> *Caller.* Who is this?
> *Person answering.* Who do you want?
> *Caller.* I was trying to get the credit department.
> *Person answering.* This is the credit department.
> *Caller.* Is George Becker there?
> *Person answering.* Yes, he is.
> *Caller.* May I speak with him, please?

25 The Comma (Continued)

In some sentences the meaning is made clear through the use of the comma; in others, the meaning is made clear by not using a comma. Knowing when and when not to use a comma enables a writer to express what is meant in a clear, direct way. The first step in knowing when to use a comma and when to refrain from using it is to understand the traditional terms restrictive and nonrestrictive. Restrictive means "essential to the meaning"; nonrestrictive means "not essential to the meaning."

The comma rule that governs such situations is this: *Use commas to set off any word or words that are not essential to the clarity of the message.* Quite obviously, then, commas are not used if the words *are* essential to message clarity.

Practically speaking, in this section you will learn to set off by commas any word or words that give additional information or that are "excess baggage." To determine whether or not commas should be used, just ask yourself: "Are these words necessary to the meaning? Can they be omitted without affecting the clarity of the message?" If the words can be omitted, they are set off by commas; if they cannot, no commas are used.

> Our new policy, as we wrote you two weeks ago, goes into effect June 1. (Why are the words *as we wrote you two weeks ago* set off by commas? Because they are not essential to the message.)
>
> The report is to be set up as we outlined in our June 1 letter. (Why is no comma used before the clause starting with *as*? Because the clause is a necessary part of the message.)

SUBORDINATE CLAUSE FOLLOWING MAIN CLAUSE

We know that a subordinate clause that precedes a main thought is always set off by a comma. (This is discussed in Section 24.) Use of the comma with an introductory clause, therefore, presents no problem. When a subordinate clause follows a main clause, however, there is a question about using a comma. The problem is solved by determining whether or not the subordinate clause is necessary to the meaning. If it is necessary, no commas are used; if it is not necessary, commas are used.

> They will draw up the contract after we have confirmed the details. (Are the words *after we have confirmed the details* necessary to the meaning? Yes, they are. Therefore, they should not be set off by commas.)
>
> They will draw up the contract tomorrow, after we have confirmed the details. (Is the clause starting with *after* necessary to this meaning? No. Then it is correctly set off by a comma.)

INTERRUPTING, PARENTHETIC, EXPLANATORY ELEMENTS

Interrupting

An interrupting element does exactly what its name indicates—it interrupts a message. Since an interruption is not essential to the meaning of a sentence, such an interruption is set off by commas.

> Our service, moreover, includes gift wrapping of all purchases made in the gift department. (*Moreover* can be omitted without affecting the clarity of the message.)
>
> The additional discount, however, can be taken only on lots of five hundred or more. (*However* is set off by commas because it interrupts the meaning of the sentence.)

Parenthetic

A parenthetic element is any expression in words, phrases, or clauses that is inserted by way of comment. Such words may be used to qualify or to amend the message. The writer may wish to soften a harsh statement, sharpen a fuzzy one, or point up a contrast. Whatever the reason, the parenthetic words are not essential to the meaning and are, therefore, set off by commas.

> The most controversial item, as I see it, should be placed at the end of the agenda. (The qualifying parenthetic expression, *as I see it,* is set off by commas.)
>
> The gift, but not the bill, is to be sent to Mrs. Carr. (The parenthetic expression, *but not the bill,* is used to emphasize a contrast.)

Explanatory

An explanatory element is not essential to the meaning, but it does give additional information. When you want an expression to be construed as additional information, set it off by commas. If you would like those words to be interpreted as an essential part of the message, do not use commas. An explanatory element need not be a clause; rather, it may be any group of words giving additional information.

> Mr. Coe, who is the senior member of the staff, has been promoted to the chief executive position. (Can *who is the senior member of the staff* be omitted without affecting the main message? Does the clause constitute additional information? "Yes" is the answer to both questions; therefore, the clause has been set off by commas.)
>
> The man who will be promoted to the chief executive position is the senior member of the staff. (Use of the question procedure shows that this "who" clause is necessary to the meaning. Commas, therefore, are not used.)
>
> The manager, sensing the tension, stepped in and averted a dispute. (The group of words giving additional information is a participial phrase. This explanatory element is correctly set off by commas.)

⊙ **CHECKUP 1** Are the commas used correctly in these sentences?

1. Mrs. Parsons, unwilling to wait any longer hung up the telephone.
2. The clearance sale will end on Saturday, unless bad weather prevents shoppers from coming to the store this week.
3. Joanne's new job is not so high paying as, but is much more interesting than her previous position.
4. A business transaction, if mutual satisfaction is your object, should benefit both the seller and the buyer.
5. The best thing to do therefore is to wait for the auditors' report.
6. We are accepting your application, although we do think that you should have been sponsored by a club member.
7. My mother, who is a tax attorney, handles our family's finances.
8. The judge was forced, therefore to declare a mistrial.
9. The typist, whom you want for statistical reports, is Pat Henley.

APPOSITIVES AND RELATED CONSTRUCTIONS

The rules for using commas with appositives and commas with three closely related constructions can be grouped for this discussion. Studying these rules as a unit will aid in learning, in retaining, and in using them correctly.

Appositives

An appositive is a group of words or a single word that gives more information about a preceding word or phrase. If appositives are not essential to the meaning, they are set off by commas.

> The manager of data processing services, Miss Ada Garner, has been promoted to vice president. (The appositive, *Miss Ada Garner*, is additional information and is correctly set off by commas.)
>
> Our first caller, a middle-aged woman, had a real problem. (The appositive, *a middle-aged woman*, is set off by commas.)

Sometimes the appositive is very closely connected with the noun that precedes it. In such cases, commas are not used because the closely connected term cannot be omitted without clouding the message.

> His brother Tom is an accomplished writer. (If *Tom* is omitted, the message is not complete. Therefore, *Tom* is a closely connected word and is not set off by commas.)
>
> The year 1066 will always stand out in my memory. (Omission of *1066* would obscure the meaning of the sentence. An expression that is essential to the meaning is not set off by commas.)

Degrees, Titles, and Other Explanatory Terms

When *M.D.* is written after a name, additional information is given about a person—namely, that he or she is a doctor of medicine. *Inc.* after a firm name gives the added information that the firm has been incorporated. *Jr.* after a man's name informs everybody that this man is the son, not the father, of the same name. Degrees, titles, *Inc.*, *Ltd.*, and other explanatory terms are like appositives in that they give additional information. For this reason, they are set off by commas.

> The Reverend James Kenny, D.D., conducted the services.
>
> Otto Gross, Sr., is one of our best customers.
>
> Make the check out to Benton & Company, Inc., and send it by registered mail.

Calendar Dates

A year included in a date is explanatory, telling, for example, which May 1 is meant or which May, if the day is not given. Because it gives additional information, the year included in a date is set off by commas.

> August 14, 1945, is a date frequently mentioned in history books.
>
> In August, 1945, the electrifying news was flashed to the world.

States, Cities

The name of a state written after the name of a city gives additional information; for example, it tells which Springfield or which Columbus is meant. Because it serves an additional-information function, the name of the state is set off by commas.

> Mr. Davis calls Springfield, Ohio, his native city.
>
> Which is the larger town—Forest, Iowa, or Forest, Idaho?

⊙ **CHECKUP 2** What comma errors are there in these sentences?

1. Creative Interiors Inc. is the name of a new interior decorating firm.
2. The company's legal counsel, Ann King and Paul Brown, are graduates of the same law school.
3. Please reserve a single room for the president of our society, Dr. Barry Farmer for Sunday through Tuesday, May 5–7.
4. The appointment of Miss Elizabeth Jenkins Ph.D., as adjunct professor of chemistry, was announced today.
5. When did Ivan the Terrible rule in Russia?
6. "John B. Watts Manager" is the correct typed signature.
7. In April, 1917 the United States entered World War I.
8. Would you rather live in Tampa, Florida, than in Tempe, Arizona?
9. The announcement, that Mr. Greene's boat had been wrecked off Anderson Island, was confirmed by Coast Guard officials.

◈ **TWILIGHT ZONE** When a majority of so-called "authorities" no longer adhere to what was formerly a rule of correct usage, that principle can surely be said to be in the Twilight Zone. One such principle is that of distinguishing between the use of *that* and *which.*

The meticulous writer, however, knows and observes the following rule: Clauses that are not necessary to the meaning are introduced by *which.* Clauses that are necessary are introduced by *that.* Commas are used with "which" clauses; commas are not used with "that" clauses.

⊡ **MEMORY HOOK** Which is the longer word, *which* or *that*? Does it take longer to type a comma or not to type a comma? Hook up the longer word *which* with the longer time it takes to type commas. Obviously, commas are not used with the shorter word *that.*

> The handbags on the first counter, which are real bargains, should make a fine sales leader. (Additional-information "which" clause is correctly set off by commas.)
>
> The handbags that are on the first counter should make a fine sales leader. ("That" clauses cannot be omitted without clouding the meaning, and no commas are used with them.)

NEVER, NEVER

The second and third "never, nevers" are these:

Subject From Predicate

Never, never separate a subject from its predicate by a single comma.

> The missile experiments conducted by Dr. Grove, were described in a special bulletin. (Here the subject is separated from its predicate by a single comma, thus violating a "never, never" rule. No comma should be used.)
>
> Experiments with missiles, including those conducted by Dr. Grove, were described in a special bulletin. (This sentence is correct. Note that there are two commas in the subject and that they are used to set off words that give additional information.)

Verb or Infinitive From Object or Complement

Never, never separate a verb or an infinitive from its object or complement by a *single* comma.

> All members of the staff know full well that Mr. Watts has always been, the "thinker" for our organization. (Because a single comma separates the verb *has been* from its complement, a "never, never" rule is violated.)
>
> We are very glad to hear, that you are interested in purchasing our patio furniture. (This sentence is incorrect because a *single* comma separates the infinitive *to hear* from its object.)

⊙ **CHECKUP 3** Find and correct the errors in the following sentences.

1. That both players were guilty of unsportsmanlike conduct, is all too apparent.
2. The mannerism that I dislike most is his continually rubbing his nose.
3. Any reimbursement, which is claimed by an employee, must be approved by the office manager.
4. Commas are used to indicate, that the words they enclose are not essential to the meaning.
5. Paul learned at an early age, the necessity for budgeting.
6. Results of the survey definitely show, that the morale of our staff is high.
7. Our organizational plan, which you are free to use, was prepared by the office manager.

Communication Projects

PRACTICAL APPLICATION

A Correct the sentences in which commas are used incorrectly. Write *OK* for any correct sentence.

1. His name appears as Julius Polk Esq. on the printed letterhead which means that he is an attorney.
2. The replacement tiles, that we ordered today, are priced higher than in our last order.
3. My boss is sending a gift copy of his new book *Travels to Everywhere* to his mother-in-law.
4. Did you know that my cousin, Marie, has an adopted sister?
5. Our employee newspaper aims to build up rather than tear down employee morale.
6. Incidentally Theodore O. Warren Sr. is my uncle's full name.
7. It will be September 19, 1987 before there is a solar eclipse in our area.
8. All merit increases therefore will be reviewed by the personnel manager.
9. The catalog of Barnett, Ltd. lists such typically British goods as silverware and china.
10. Their forecast in view of present market conditions is discouragingly gloomy.
11. Mr. Lunt's decision is closely connected with but in no way dependent on that of his competitor.
12. Please return to us for our files, the personal data on Mark Hagen.

13. I should accept such a fine offer, if it were made to me.
14. A great fortune in the hands of an inexperienced person, may turn out to be a great misfortune.
15. Mrs. Knott, who is our good friend, has devised a better method.
16. Please retype this article whenever you have some spare time.
17. My thesaurus which always helps with word problems has been mislaid.
18. Mrs. Daniels carefully explained, that the accident was unavoidable.
19. Pittsburgh, Pennsylvania, is spelled differently from other cities by that name.
20. Mr. Hunter exhausted by the pressures of the day canceled the afternoon meeting.

B Correct the following sentences wherever necessary.

1. Leisure Town is a self-contained community; with no outside maintenance required of its residents.
2. Students with excellent study habits and high grades may be considered bookworms, but their later achievements and financial success are often the result of this earlier self-discipline.
3. Students are no longer as interested in sewing, in cooking or in the other so-called domestic arts.
4. Our profit-sharing plan does I believe distribute surplus earnings fairly.
5. May we have your renewal order by the end of January.
6. The custodian too is relieved of his duties.
7. One draftsman asked who authorized the alterations in his blueprint?
8. We regret the inconvenience you were caused by the late arrival of the "Skyway Limited" on January 2, furthermore, we enclose a discount slip you may apply toward your next trip.
9. The entire nonpartisan board, all citizens of the best reputation, are in complete agreement, and we affirm our complete faith in the mayor's decision.
10. Miss Logan, training director for our company, has been chosen to receive the award.
11. *Its* is possessive; *it's* is a contraction of *it* and *is*.
12. What is the correct salutation for a governor? a judge. a clergyman.
13. The court upheld us, and the weight of public opinion was on our side.
14. We shall be glad to ship your order if you will send us a check for $134.
15. Mr. Quinn is an excellent accountant, he qualified as a CPA.
16. However hard we work, we cannot keep abreast of the orders.
17. Our aims at all times are these to please our customers, to satisfy our bankers, and to treat our employees fairly.
18. Names must be checked carefully, not just casually inspected, if the directory is to be of any value.
19. Skill, courage, daring all of these qualities are required of Olympic athletes.
20. The lawyer whose office is on the first floor is trying a very important case.

EDITING PRACTICE

The Editing Desk Your job is to edit this paragraph, correcting all errors.

Miss Ayres and myself are very happy to give you additional information about our training program for secretaries. Miss Ayres as you probably

> allready know is our correspondence consultant, and she carries on the training program. She analyzes carbons of outgoing letters for such errors as punctuation, spelling, case forms of pronouns, etc. and discusses her findings with the secretaries concerned. In order to make the corrections stick the secretaries are scheduled for meetings about once a month. The purpose of the meetings are to clear up questions about the errors, that are most frequently made by most of the secretaries.

Mispronunciation Because of your extensive vocabulary, you would transcribe correctly any word mispronounced by a dictator. Is any such correction needed in the following paragraph?

> May I take a rain check on your invitation to speak to the Blanton sales staff on March 18? Right now I am under medical care for a bronical condition that has affected my voice, and the doctor has ordered that I curtail all speaking engagements for at least a month. But please keep me in mind for future assignments, for I particularly enjoy talking to Blanton employees.

CASE PROBLEM

Correcting the Boss Ethel Nelson, secretary to Joseph Foster, has just placed a set of letters on her employer's desk for signature. In glancing over the letters, Mr. Foster reads the following sentence in one of the letters: "We will mail the package before January 6, 19—, so that you will have it in time."

Mr. Foster takes his pen and draws a line through the comma following "19—" and tells Ethel that the comma does not belong there.

1. Who is correct? Why?
2. What should Ethel do about the situation?
3. How should Mr. Foster make corrections so that the entire letter does not have to be retyped?

The value of the comma in making written communication effective is shown by the fact that three sections of this textbook are devoted to a discussion of its use. Because the comma is used so frequently and in so many different situations, lack of facility in handling it results in a high error score for a business writer. The confusion and misinterpretation caused by inept use of commas may destroy customer and vendor goodwill.

Additional letters may have to be written to clarify a message that should have been stated clearly in the original letter. When such letters have to be written, a company loses money. Skilled writers, therefore, build goodwill and make money for their employers because they know all the mechanics of written communication.

In this section, the remaining six rules that govern the use of the comma will be presented. Mastery of these rules and of those already presented in Sections 24 and 25 can help you achieve proficiency in comma usage.

WITH MODIFYING ADJECTIVES

When two or more adjectives separately modify a noun, a comma is used to separate the adjectives.

> All of us agree that Miss Kostanik is the most dynamic, most personable, most experienced executive in our company. (Miss Kostanik is *the most dynamic executive, the most personable executive, the most experienced executive.* Commas are used because each adjective separately modifies the noun *executive.*)
>
> Mr. Allen is a fair, conscientious, brilliant man. (Mr. Allen is a *fair man,* a *conscientious man,* a *brilliant man.* Commas are used because each adjective separately modifies the noun.)

Many writers who know this rule are unable to apply it correctly. The difficulty is in determining whether or not each adjective *separately* modifies the noun. Here is a Memory Hook to help you apply correctly the rule for commas with modifying adjectives.

▣ **MEMORY HOOK** If the word *and* can be correctly used between the adjectives, a comma must separate those adjectives. If *and* cannot be correctly inserted, no comma is needed. Study the following illustrations and explanations:

> Dick is a diligent, reliable, accurate accountant. (The commas are correct because you can say "diligent *and* reliable *and* accurate." A comma after *accurate* would obviously be incorrect because you would not say "accurate *and* accountant.")
>
> Ellen is acquainted with the latest scientific discoveries. (No comma is used here. You would not say "latest *and* scientific discoveries." *Latest,* the first adjective, modifies the unit *scientific discoveries,* which consists of the second adjective plus the noun.)

⊙ **CHECKUP 1** Use the "and" Memory Hook to see how quickly you can insert the correct punctuation in the following sentences.

1. Does the photocopier produce clean legible copies?
2. Have you seen the new insulated opaque drapes?
3. After we reach Chicago, we shall make arrangements for some lengthy personal interviews.
4. We are enclosing a list of bonds suitable for conservative private investment.
5. Next week our lightweight thermal blankets will be on sale.

FOR OMISSIONS, WITH REPEATED EXPRESSIONS, AND IN DIRECT ADDRESS

The comma is also used to save time and words, to emphasize an important thought, and to set off names and terms in direct address. These are the uses discussed in this section.

Omissions

Whenever possible, writers save reading and writing time. Sometimes, for example, writers do not repeat words that, once stated in the sentence, are implicit thereafter. To make such an omission, insert a comma to make the reader pause long enough to mentally supply the omitted words.

> Call loans must be paid on demand; time loans, at the end of a stated period. (The comma after *time loans* slows the reader long enough to supply the omitted words *must be paid.*)
>
> According to this month's travel schedule, Mr. Gold will be out of the office on June 3; Miss Roberts, June 6; Mr. DuBois, June 13; and Ms. Blakiston, June 20. (The comma after each of the last three names slows the reader long enough to supply the omitted words *will be out of the office on.*)

Repeated Expressions

Repetition will often emphasize an important point, will add power to the statement. Such repetition, however, must be planned; and the writer adds strength by using a comma to set off the repetition.

> Never, never use a single comma to separate a subject from its predicate. (This is repetition planned to emphasize a very important rule. The comma, by slowing the reader, adds power to the statement.)

Direct Address

Names or terms used in speaking directly to a particular person or group of persons should be set off by commas.

> Mr. Bennett, we are asking you to give us the benefit of your experience.

⊙ **CHECKUP 2** The following sentences illustrate use of commas for omissions, for planned repetition, and for direct address. Make whatever corrections are needed.

1. This country seems to be running out of fuel all types of fuel.
2. Thank you Mr. Ellison for sending the announcement of the opening of your research lab.
3. In the new planned development, one-eighth of the land will be used for high-rise apartments; one-half for recreational areas.
4. Harvard was founded in 1636; Yale in 1701.
5. Paul writes that he is happy in his new job very happy.
6. You will surely understand, gentlemen, why this information is confidential.
7. The first part of the shipment was made on June 1; the second on July 1.
8. To prevent errors, Don should set up a routine, a work routine.

IN NUMBERS AND BETWEEN UNRELATED NUMBERS

Use a comma to separate thousands, hundred thousands, millions, and so on, in numbers of four or more digits. This function of the comma prevents misreading of numbers.

> Our municipal debt of $1,500,000 is relatively small. (When the number is written correctly, there is little excuse for misreading it.)

When two unrelated numbers are written together, a comma must be used to separate them. Without some means of slowing the reader, the numbers tend to be read together.

> By January 30, 450 stockholders had returned their proxy notices. (A comma between *January 30* and *450* slows the reader and prevents confusion.)

NEVER, NEVER

Our "never, never" discussion ends with the following two principles. Any study of the use of commas would be incomplete without discussing the situations in which a comma must *not* be used; hence, this "never, never" series in Sections 24, 25, and 26 is important.

In Numbers

Never, never use a comma in years, page numbers, house and telephone numbers, ZIP Code numbers, serial numbers, and decimals, even if such numbers consist of four or more digits. These items are written as follows:

in 1975	1402 Main Street	Ames, Iowa 50010	2.3874
page 1212	(617) 847-3562	RA 11167099	

In Weights, Capacities, Measurements

Never, never use a comma to separate the parts of *one* weight, *one* capacity, or *one* measurement. The numbers must be comprehended as a unit.

> The jet record for cross-country flight is said to be 2 hours 13 minutes 7 seconds. (Since there is no comma, the reader understands that this is *one* time unit.)

⊙ **CHECKUP 3** Apply the rules for using and for not using commas in numbers by making the needed corrections in these sentences.

1. The installment contract calls for a down payment of $1800.
2. Each drafting table is 9 feet, 4 inches long.
3. Please attach this endorsement to Policy 55,804.
4. On Invoice 751, 6 items are listed instead of 14.
5. Please change my address to 7,481 Southern Boulevard.
6. The quotation we used appears on page 1,623.
7. We made the trip in exactly 3 hours, 50 minutes, 4 seconds.
8. In 1974 898 new accounts were added.

Communication Projects

PRACTICAL APPLICATION

A Write the correction for each incorrect sentence in this group. Write *OK* for each correct sentence.

1. At the door was a stocky surly disheveled man in shirt-sleeves.
2. Is it possible Miss Scanlan that you have mislaid our last three statements?
3. Ever since we changed accountants, we have had troublesome inaccurate quarterly statements.
4. Your signature must be notarized on all copies of the contract, all three copies.
5. To place your order, please telephone our Teleservice number, 744-4000.
6. The fragile glassware was packed in special reinforced double-bottomed cartons.
7. Hilltop Haven features sunny large well-furnished rooms.
8. The first baby born in our town this year weighed exactly 8 pounds, 3 ounces.
9. Fund-raising efforts last year brought in a total of $5000.
10. Memory Hooks promote instant, accurate, application of rules.
11. Irving was born in 1783; Longfellow in 1807; and Holmes in 1809.
12. Yours was a good report an excellent report.
13. The words of the Gettysburg Address may be forgotten; the spirit, never.
14. We like Mr. York's calm unemotional approach to problem solving.
15. You, Mrs. Carson, are one of our most valued customers.

B Correct each incorrect sentence in the following exercise.

1. This memo is for Theodora Klemer not for Theodore Clemmer.
2. Straight-leg waistbandless polyester knit slacks are new for spring.
3. As shown in Table 14., 28 communities were surveyed for this study.
4. These plaid slacks, for example have their own color-coordinated jackets.
5. Just think, you can slip on this wrinkle-free dress as soon as you unpack but don't wait to place your order until too late.
6. All maintenance work such as washing windows, polishing floors, and vacuuming rugs is to be handled by Tidy Cleaners.
7. Anyway they have billed us twice for the same work.
8. The Reed catalog lists only first-quality high-fashion imported clothing.
9. The therapists, who have completed a refresher course, will qualify for immediate work.
10. Please you are not to say another word in his defense.
11. November, 1918, was an important month in our history.
12. Always remember, young man, that people make their own "breaks."
13. After all fellow workers unreasonable demands will defeat our purpose.
14. Just a month before the same sharp reminder was necessary.
15. The first lot of returned goods was sold in the basement store; the second in the housewares department.
16. However, much we are opposed, we will abide by the majority vote.
17. In the first month of 1975, 2,642 motorbikes rolled off our assembly lines.
18. We do not have the candlestick in brass; however, we do have the same design in pewter.
19. Genius is not so much intellect as it is the capacity for hard work perseveringly hard work.
20. The package, lying on the table, belongs to Mr. Ames.

EDITING PRACTICE

Proofreading for Spelling Errors Because of your reputation as a good speller, you are often asked to proofread for spelling errors. Make the necessary corrections in this paragraph.

> Yes, it is true that Mr. Kane has definitely committed himself to helping with this year's United Fund drive—but in an advisory capacity only. He will be an ex *officio* member of the steering committee and will act as a resource person for the initial-gifts phase of the program.

CASE PROBLEM

The Mumbling Dictator Jean Walker recently has been hired as a secretary in the law firm of Beatty and Barnes. Mrs. Barnes does most of her dictating to a recording machine, and Jean transcribes the dictation as soon as possible. Although Mrs. Barnes' voice is loud enough, Jean has difficulty understanding her; many of her words are garbled. Jean suspects that Mrs. Barnes dictates with a hard candy in her mouth, but she is not really sure.

1. How should Jean handle this situation?
2. If you were Mrs. Barnes, would you object to Jean's criticizing your dictation technique?

27 Quotation Marks, Parentheses, Apostrophes

We are all so aware of words—reading them, writing them, speaking them, and hearing them—that we may not realize how attuned we are, too, to signs and symbols. Yet we respond to signs, and follow their wordless directions, almost daily. The most familiar signs are easy to recognize and to identify with their messages. To the driver, for example, a curving arrow signals the direction in which the road curves; a blinking light warns the driver to slow down; still other signs alert the driver to "read" other messages.

Writers, too, use signs to convey certain messages. To indicate to the reader that some expressions are special and different in some way, the writer can use quotation marks, parentheses, and apostrophes. Any of these marks can be considered a signal, then, and the reader should be as aware of its significance as of the word or words affected by it.

Written communications may actually be misleading if writer and reader do not share an expert's knowledge of these three important signals.

QUOTATION MARKS

Quotation marks are used primarily to signal the reader thus: "The speaker or the writer used these exact words." Although this symbol, the quotation mark, usually signifies direct quotations, writers—and readers—must also be familiar with several other uses for quotation marks.

Direct Quotations

A direct quotation is the word-for-word record of something that has been said or written, and quotation marks are the symbols that signal a direct quotation. In most instances, a comma precedes a direct quotation that comes at the end of the sentence.

> Mr. Smith said, "I am leaving for Chicago tonight." (Note comma following *said.*)
>
> The letter read, "Your order of May 16 has been received." (Quotation marks signal that these are the exact words appearing in the letter. Note comma following *read.*)

If the quotation is introduced by an independent clause, however, a colon should be used in place of a comma.

> The letter read as follows: "Your order of May 16 has been received and will be shipped before May 20."

A colon should also be used if the quotation is long or consists of several sentences.

> Mr. Smith said: "I am leaving for Chicago tonight, and tomorrow morning I will meet with Mr. Brown to discuss the signing of the contract. If he signs it immediately, I will spend the rest of the day sightseeing."

When a direct quotation falls at the beginning of a sentence, the punctuation that ends the quotation depends on whether the quotation is a declaration, a question, or an exclamation.

> "I am so glad to meet you," said Mr. Howe. (In a declaration, a comma, rather than a period, is placed before the closing quotation marks.)
>
> "When may I see you again?" he asked. (In a question, retain the question mark before the closing quotation marks.)
>
> "What a remarkable play!" he exclaimed. (In an exclamation, retain the exclamation point before the closing quotation marks.)

Note: All quoted material must be copied exactly as it was written. If any change is made, the material is not a direct quotation. Never use quotation marks to enclose indirectly quoted words (usually introduced by *that*).

Interrupted Quotations

When a direct quotation is interrupted, only the quoted words are enclosed in quotation marks.

> "Whenever possible," read the directive, "file all carbon copies before closing time." (The commas set off the interruption.)

Any semicolon or period that would be used if the quotation were not interrupted is placed after the interrupting words.

"Bob will be the manager," said Miss Scott; "Fred, the assistant."

"I am resigning my position," wrote Mr. King. "It is time for a younger person to take over."

Quotation Within a Quotation

When quotation marks are needed within a quotation, use single quotation marks.

Frank asked, "Did you say '16' or '60'?"

The end punctuation for a quotation within a quotation is handled this way: Periods and commas are set within both the single and the double quotation marks. (When you type single and double quotation marks, do not allow for a space between them.)

She answered, "Their offer is a perfect example of 'Hobson's choice.'"

"We shall, of course, reject their 'ultimatum,'" Mr. Daly quipped.

⊙ **CHECKUP 1** Find and correct all errors in the following sentences.

1. "What a wonderful place for a vacation" exclaimed Miss Howard!
2. Here are the bid requirements: "All bids must be submitted, sealed, in duplicate, by 4 p.m. Friday, February 15."
3. Mrs. Simpson said that "no one is permitted to stay after office hours."
4. "Will there be any exceptions to this rule I asked?
5. Richard explained, "I said 'I do agree,' not 'I disagree.'"

Quoting Terms and Expressions

Writers often signal their readers that certain expressions or terms are particularly significant by enclosing the significant words in quotation marks. The first word within the quotation marks is capitalized if the expression is a complete sentence or, of course, if the word would be capitalized normally. The following are some of the ways quotation marks are used to denote expressions and terms having special significance.

For Explanations, Definitions, and Unusual Terms Words and phrases accompanied by their definitions or introduced by such expressions as *so-called, known as, marked, signed,* and similar expressions are enclosed in quotation marks.

In the printing trade, a *widow* is simply "a short last line of a paragraph."

Working regularly at a second job is known as "moonlighting."

It was signed "Laura B. Sheng."

Terms that may be unfamiliar to the general reader or that are unusual when used in certain contexts should be set off so that the reader is prepared to recognize them. In the next examples, the signals are the quotation marks around the rather commonplace words *flat* and *tailor-made,* since each is used in a rather uncommon way.

> The photo-offset printer will have to make an entirely new "flat." (Technical term that may be unfamiliar to the reader.)
>
> Each letter in the series will be "tailor-made" to your needs. (Unusual term when referring to letters.)

For Translation of Foreign Words The translation of any foreign word or expression is enclosed in quotation marks.

> One meaning of *laissez-faire* is "noninterference."

For Slang, Humor, or Poor Grammar A writer who wishes to "perk up" the message occasionally uses slang, poor grammar, or an expression that is intended to be funny. In such cases, enclosing the words in quotation marks signals the reader that their use is intentional.

> We are so glad to hear "them things" about your progress.
>
> An "authority" is any person who is a hundred miles from home.

Note: When *etc.* is used at the end of a quotation, the *etc.* should be placed outside the quotation marks.

> "We, the people of the United States," etc., is the beginning of the Preamble to the Constitution of the United States.

⊙ **CHECKUP 2** Is the use or nonuse of quotation marks correct in these sentences?

1. We agreed that he was a "master" in certain areas, but we did not say which areas.
2. When archaeologists talk about a "dig," they mean the site of their explorations.
3. Did you know that *modus operandi* means manner of working?
4. She joined that so-called panel of experts reluctantly.
5. The part of the upper deck of a ship forward of the foremast is known as the forecastle.
6. Such white lies are rather common and are considered horn-tooting.

Quoting Titles

The rules for quoting titles are as follows:

Quote titles of the following: parts and chapters of books (but *not* titles of books), lectures, articles, essays, sermons, toasts, mottoes, paintings, poems, sculptures, and names of ships.

> Part Seven, "Writing Craft," contains three sections.
>
> "There's always room at the top" is my motto.
>
> We are sailing on the "Queen Anne."

Titles of complete works published and bound separately, such as books, booklets, long poems, magazines, and newspapers, should be underscored.

The titles of plays, operas, and movies are also underscored. Underscoring in typewritten copy is the counterpart of *italics* in printed publications.

> The title of this book is <u>College English and Communication.</u>
>
> I read the story in <u>The New York Times.</u>
>
> *The Sound of Music* delighted audiences for years.

When such words as *preface, introduction, contents, appendix,* or *index* refer to respective parts of a specific book, they are capitalized, not quoted.

Punctuating at End of Quoted Material

Are punctuation marks occurring at the end of quotations placed inside or outside the quotes? To answer this question, study the following three rules.

Periods and commas are *always* placed *inside* the closing quotes.

> Charging interest at a higher rate than is allowed by law is called "usury."
>
> A.D., meaning "in the year of our Lord," precedes the year.

Colons and semicolons are *always* placed *outside* the closing quotes.

> Please "rush": 1 dozen packages mixed flower seeds, 4 lawn mowers, and 6 garden rakes.
>
> The friendly feeling of the public for a firm is known as "goodwill"; without it, no business can long endure.

Question marks and exclamation points may be placed inside or outside the closing quotes, depending on whether the quoted material or the entire sentence is the question or the exclamation. If only the quoted words are the question or the exclamation, the punctuation is placed *inside* the ending quotes.

> The personnel manager asked, "What qualifications does the applicant have?" (The quote is the question; therefore, the question mark is placed with the question, *inside* the closing quotation marks.)
>
> A voice boomed over the loudspeaker, "Attention, please!" (The quote is the exclamation.)
>
> Mr. Cook's directive, "Cut down overhead!" must not be disregarded. (The quote is the exclamation. Note also that the exclamation point following *overhead* takes the place of a comma.)

If the entire sentence is a question or an exclamation, the question mark or the exclamation point is placed at the very end, *outside* the quotation marks.

> Is this stock one of the "blue chips"? (The entire sentence, not the quote, is the question.)
>
> What a horrible example of "featherbedding"! (The entire group of words, not just "featherbedding," is the exclamation.)

⊙ **CHECKUP 3** In the following sentences, make any needed corrections in the use of quotation marks.

1. He has had several articles printed in Flying Saucer Review.
2. A whole room in the Museum is occupied by Monet's Water Lilies.
3. How tragic was the burning of the ship Morro Castle!
4. Do you know what is meant by the expression "under the counter?"
5. Kipling's "If" merits many a rereading.

PARENTHESES

The expert writer realizes that no two words are truly the same. There is a subtle distinction that shades the meaning of each word and makes it different from other words. The expert writer chooses carefully, never casually, the specific word required for each occasion.

Commas, dashes, and parentheses share certain functions in common. From among these three distinct forms of punctuation the expert writer chooses the one that best fits the specific writing situation. The specific uses of parentheses are discussed in this section. Study it carefully so that when you use parentheses you will not be making an arbitrary choice.

Enclosing Words That Give Additional Information

Although commas and dashes are also used to enclose "additional information" words, parentheses have a different and special function. Words that are set off by commas or dashes may be omitted, although they supplement the main thought of a message. Words in parentheses, on the other hand, are clearly extraneous.

> Mr. Bell, one of our most efficient auditors, will be in charge of the audit. (Although the words enclosed in commas *may* be omitted, they do add something to the main thought.)
>
> Each of the words omitted—and there are several—is most important. (The words set off by dashes *may* be omitted, but without them the sentence lacks emphasis.)
>
> The executor named in a will by the testator (the person who made the will) is to carry out the provisions of the will. (The words in parentheses make no contribution to the main thought.)

Indicating References

Parentheses are of great value for enclosing a reference, a direction, or the name of an authority for a statement.

> Use of parentheses in enumerated items has already been discussed (see Part 1). (Parentheses enclose a reference.)
>
> Insert the carbon pack (be sure that sides and top of pack are straightened), and start typing on line 15. (Parentheses enclose directions.)
>
> Business communication involves reading, writing, speaking, and listening. (Kenneth Steele) (Parentheses enclose the name of the authority.)

Punctuating Words in Parentheses

No mark of punctuation is used immediately *before* an opening parenthesis when the parenthetical words are within a sentence.

> Call me tomorrow (Thursday) for confirmation of these figures. (No mark of punctuation before *Thursday*.)
>
> A complete list of parts is included in the Appendix (see pages 143 through 157), but the specifications of the parts are in another booklet. (No mark of punctuation before the opening parenthesis.)

Words in Parentheses Within a Sentence Any regular sentence punctuation—comma, period, colon, and so on—is placed *after* the closing parenthesis.

> Call me tomorrow (Thursday), and I will give you the figures. (The sentence calls for a comma to separate the independent clauses, and that comma is placed after the closing parenthesis.)
>
> We sent our check (as promised); however, we have heard nothing from him. (The semicolon is placed after the closing parenthesis.)

However, if the word or words in parentheses require a question mark, a colon, or a period to end an abbreviation, that punctuation is placed *before* the closing parenthesis.

> All reports must be finished this week (can you beat it!), and we thought the deadline was next week.
>
> The newest fabrics made of synthetic fibers (Dacron, Acrilan, etc.) are our specialties.

The first word of an expression in parentheses within a sentence is capitalized only when that first word is a proper noun. This is true even when the expression is a complete sentence. For example:

> Use the enclosed envelope (it is all ready to go), and send us your check by return mail.

Words in Parentheses Standing Alone When words enclosed in parentheses are not part of a sentence, but are entirely independent, the first word is capitalized and the end punctuation is placed before the closing parenthesis.

> Corporate sales have advanced rapidly in the past year. (See our annual report for details.)
>
> Please return the entry blank as soon as possible. (You might win a big prize!)

⊙ **CHECKUP 4** Edit the following sentences for correct parentheses usage.

1. A company's income statement, (formerly called the profit and loss statement), indicates its financial condition.
2. Place trays in refrigerator at any desired height (first remove masking tape from edges of trays).
3. Your fruit-of-the-month gift will arrive, (as explained in the enclosed schedule) at the same time each month.
4. Would you be interested in our introductory offer of twelve issues for $10 (regularly $1.50 an issue?)
5. All bids must be in by Friday of this week (whew), not a week from Friday.
6. If Hicks accepts the offer (It looks as if he will), he will have to leave within the next four weeks.

APOSTROPHES

Apostrophes, as discussed earlier, are used to show possession. They are also used to form the plurals of letters, signs, symbols, and words used as words. (See Section 11.) Three additional usages are discussed here.

In Contractions

An apostrophe is used to indicate a shortened form of one or more words, such as: *nat'l* for *national*; *don't* for *do not*; and *o'clock* for *of the clock*. Some words formerly considered contractions are now accepted as complete words: for example, *phone* and *cello*.

For Omission of Figures

Use an apostrophe to signal the omission of the first figures of a date: '75 for 1975.

My youngest daughter will be graduated from college with the class of '91.

For Invented Words

A verb form that is made up from a letter or an abbreviation must be signaled as an invention. To do this, add an apostrophe and *d* or *ing* to the coined verb.

The manager *OK'd* the shipment.

⊙ **CHECKUP 5** Can you find the errors in apostrophe usage?

1. My fathers class, the class of '41, was the last to graduate before World War II.
2. You shouldnt spend so much money on gifts for me.
3. She laboriously wrote "contd" at the top of each page.
4. Life in the 20s must have been very hectic.
5. Has Mr. Banks OKd your proposal?

Communication Projects

PRACTICAL APPLICATION

A Make any needed corrections in the use of quotation marks, parentheses, or apostrophes.

1. The most amusing slogan I know is this one for a sausage manufacturer: "Our wurst is the best."
2. "Great news," Jane shouted; "we have won first prize"!
3. To a psychiatrist and to a musician, "fugue" means entirely different things.
4. His conversation is loaded with he don't's and you wasn't's.
5. "Your word command can be your key to success," begins a sales letter for a new dictionary; it then asks, "are you comfortable with the words you write, speak, and read"?
6. Hadnt we better decide on a date for our next meeting?
7. To save on fuel bills, we keep our thermostat set in the upper 60s.

8. Wouldn't a little knowledge of Latin reveal that *in loco parentis* means in the place of a parent?
9. The heavyweight contender KO'd the champion in the second round of the fight.
10. "In registering this package, Cora asked, shall I mark it "Return Receipt Requested"?
11. "Theoretically, you are right," said Bob; "practically, you are wrong."
12. The latest directive (and its a beauty!) will shake up the entire staff.
13. Turning from the telephone, Mr. Hill declared "that somebody had given him the wrong information."
14. "Call for Mr. Ward" rang through the lobby!
15. Yours for only $10 (tax included)!
16. Thrifty people estimate their income and expenses for a given period. (This is known as "budgeting").
17. After receiving news of the disaster (Or was it a catastrophe?) the Red Cross rushed help to the area.
18. For the latest news, listen to WNAD 9890 on your dial every hour on the hour.
19. The information you seek appears in the section "Judging Cottons".
20. The truth of the matter is (Haven't you guessed it?) that there are no flying saucers.

B Correct all errors in the following sentences.

1. Nowadays children don't seem to know what it means to "mind your ps and qs."
2. Statistical exhibits will be found in the "Appendix" of this report.
3. BBD&Os bookings are higher this year than last.
4. Brancusi's sculpture *Bird in Space* is in the museum's permanent collection.
5. The applicant asked if she might 'phone her previous employer to verify certain dates?
6. That new rug is worth every penny of the $500.00 we paid for it.
7. Federal funds should not be allocated by the "pork barrel" method.
8. The college will qualify for a Phi Beta Kappa chapter when it increases the number of Ph.D.s on its faculty.
9. The editor asked the author: "Just what do you mean by "psi" in your case notes"?
10. "Sixteen Puritan Poets" is an anthology of little-known American poets (all from the seventeenth century).
11. The discussion will cover the following topics: (1.) the population, (2.) the political party in control, and (3.) the recent bond issue.
12. "For growth, buy stocks," said the consultant; "for safety, bonds."
13. The steps in the selling process have already been discussed (see page 1,710).
14. "A *non sequitur,*" he said, "is a statement that does not follow."
15. The storm ravaged the entire Atlantic coast—from Eastport, Maine, to Key West, Florida,—at hurricane force.
16. The bank may refuse to honor (pay) the check when it is presented.
17. J. P. Lunt, editor of "Fashion Magazine," will address the convention.
18. Because of the delay, (they claim it was unavoidable) we are embarrassed.
19. This is what Mr. King said: "The estimates must be ready by Monday."
20. *Nom de plume* is translated as pen name.

EDITING PRACTICE

The Editing Desk Another assignment has come in. Edit the following paragraph.

> Yes we do give continuing communication training to our secretaries. As most of our staff members have been out of school for many years they have forgotten much of the fundamental training that is for them essential absolutely essential. We find too that some of the recent graduates are not as well prepared as they might be. We firmly believe that the letters that go out from our office advertise the quality of our company, therefore, we insist that those letters be technically correct.

Word Confusions Word confusions are hazards for the writer who doesn't know the difference in meaning between words that sound alike. Can you straighten out any word confusions in this paragraph?

> Your good friend and mine, Professor Link, suggested that I write and ask you about the advisability of taking a journalism course during my senior year at the University. In preparation for a career as a business writer, I am taking all the prescribed courses. Journalism, however, is not included in this list of courses. I know that your correspondence write news releases, but is this part of their work important enough to warrant specialized training in journalism? I should be very grateful for any advice you can give me.

CASE PROBLEM

Solving Problems by Discussion The small-group discussion technique is often used to solve problems. Shared ideas and experiences of a group often provide better solutions to problems than the limited ideas and experiences of an individual. Here is the way this technique works: (1) Divide the group into small sections of four, five, or six. (2) Make certain everyone in each group is acquainted. (3) Elect a chairperson and a recorder for each group. The recorder will take notes and will later report the major points of the discussion to the entire class. (4) Make certain that everyone understands the problem to be discussed. (5) Be sure that everyone enters into the discussion.

Here is the problem: What are the most important subjects (besides those "majored in") for business students? Why?

28 Capitalization

To make words stand out as more important, to emphasize words, to show that some words are distinctive, the writer must know the fundamental, arbitrary rules of capitalization. Some of these rules are so well known they are virtually always followed. But there are capitalization pitfalls which every business writer should know. Study this section carefully to be sure you will always correctly apply the rules of capitalization.

ARBITRARY RULES

Arbitrary rules govern the mechanical aspects of capitalization, those situations where a writer always capitalizes or never capitalizes. These rules are explained below.

First Words

Capitalize the first word of (1) a sentence or a group of words used as a sentence; (2) each line of poetry; (3) each item in an outline; (4) a sentence in a direct quotation; (5) a complete sentence after a colon, in order to emphasize a statement or to state a formal rule; and (6) a complimentary closing. For example:

1. Correct capitalization is the mark of a polished writer. (Complete sentence.)
   No, not now. (Group of words used as a sentence.)
2. Loveliest of trees, the cherry now
   Is hung with bloom along the bough.
   —A. E. Housman
   (Each line of poetry.)
3. Be sure to remember that:
   a. Proper nouns are always capitalized.
   b. A business may have its own rules for capitalization. (First word of items in an outline.)
4. Mark Twain once said, "Everybody talks about the weather." (First word of a quoted sentence.)
5. The idea is this: Meaningful repetitive practice builds skill. (Capitalization of a complete sentence after a colon in order to emphasize a statement.)
6. Very sincerely yours, (First word of a complimentary closing.)

⊙ **CHECKUP 1** Check your understanding of the rule for capitalizing first words by making any needed corrections in these sentences.

1. He pointed excitedly to the door and shouted, "Stop that thief!"
2. Do I think UFOs are "real"? yes and no.
3. Carl Sandburg's poem "Chicago" has these famous lines:
   "Stormy, husky, brawling,
   City of the big shoulders."

4. An appropriate closing for this letter is "yours sincerely."
5. Two types of responses to be expected are these:
   a. the reflex response
   b. the reason response

Headings and Titles of Publications

The arbitrary rule for the capitalization of headings and titles of publications is this: *Capitalize all main words, but do not capitalize articles, conjunctions, and short prepositions.* A "short preposition" consists of three or fewer letters. Obviously, if the preposition has four or more letters, it will be capitalized. This rule applies also to the words in any hyphenated expression in a title or heading. The first and last words of a title should be capitalized, even if they are articles or short prepositions.

Their experiences are related in an article entitled "Two Men and an Army." (*And* is a conjunction; *an* is an article.)

The Nebraska state motto is "Equality Before the Law." (*Before* is a preposition containing six letters.)

The title of the book is *Use Up-to-Date Typing Methods.* (The hyphenated compound follows the capitalization rule.)

Have you read the essay entitled "The World We Live In"? (Here both the article and the short preposition are capitalized because they are the first and last words of the title.)

PROPER ADJECTIVES

A proper adjective is an adjective formed from a proper noun; for example, *Mexican, South American, Lenten, Victorian.* Proper adjectives are capitalized.

Note: Through long use, certain adjectives are no longer capitalized because they have lost their association with the proper nouns from which they were derived; for example, *venetian* blind, *turkish* towel, *india* ink, *panama* hat. Always consult a dictionary to decide whether or not to capitalize such adjectives.

Seasons of the Year

Seasons of the year are not capitalized; for example, the *spring* styles, our *fall* opening, sales during the *winter* months.

⊙ **CHECKUP 2** What are the errors in the following sentences?

1. The play we saw was a comedy, "Sam and the Knights-errant Cut up."
2. Pan-Americanism was once very popular in most Latin American countries.
3. The advertising slogan for a silent burglar alarm is "Will You be the Next Victim of a Hit-and-Run Robber?"
4. David's mother is French; his father, Irish.
5. In May we begin to plan for our Winter business.

NAMES OF PERSONS, PLACES, THINGS

A capital letter is used by the writer to say: "This is a specific person, place, or thing, and this name is exclusively the property of this particular person, place, or thing."

> Bob attends the First Methodist Church. (Capitalization shows that this is the official name of a specific church.)
>
> Bob attends the first church that was built in our city. (Here there is no name that is exclusively the property of any specific person, place, or thing; therefore, no capitalization.)

Names of Persons

To all of us, the sound of our own name is sweet music. Therefore, a mistake in spelling or in capitalizing someone's name may jeopardize goodwill. Names should be written *as the owners wish them to be written*, regardless of the rules. Only if there is no way of finding out the specific spelling that a person prefers are the following rules to be used.

O', Mc, Mac The prefixes *O'* and *Mc* are followed by a capital letter without spacing; for example, *O'Brien, McCaffrey*. The prefix *Mac* may or may not be followed by a capital, as: *MacMillan, Macmillan*.

D, Da, De, Della, Di, Du, La, Le, Lo, Van, Von These prefixes are capitalized only when the surname is written alone, without a first name, title, or initials; for example, *De Frias, Van Hoven, Du Mont*. When a first name, an initial, or a title appears with the surname, the prefix is not capitalized unless the individual person prefers a capital letter.

> We enjoyed La Follette's speech. (*La* is capitalized because only the surname is written.)
>
> Did you enjoy Senator la Follette's speech? (*La* is not capitalized because a title is written with the surname.)
>
> We always enjoy Von Hoffman's lectures. (*Von* is capitalized because only the surname is written.)
>
> Are you registered for any of Professor von Hoffman's classes? (Because a title is written with the surname, *von* is not capitalized.)
>
> I voted for De Luca. (*De* is capitalized because only the surname is written.)
>
> In her victory speech, Governor-elect de Luca vowed to continue her fight for judicial reform. (Because a title is written with the surname, *de* is not capitalized.)

Names of Places

Capitalize names of geographical localities, streets, parks, rivers, buildings, and so on, such as *South America, Main Street, Bryant Park, Delaware River, Medical Arts Building*.

Capitalize the word *city* only when it is part of the corporate name of a city; *Dodge City*, but *the city of Boston*.

Capitalize the word *state* only when it follows the name of a state: *Kansas State*, but the *state of Kansas*.

Capitalize the word *the* in names of places only when *the* is part of the official name: *The Hague*, but *the Maritime Provinces*.

Names of Things

Capital letters designate an official name that is the exclusive property of specific companies, associations, committees, bureaus, schools, clubs, governmental bodies, and so on. For example:

> Our children have all been graduated from Wilson Junior High School. (*Wilson Junior High School* is the official name of a specific junior high school.)
>
> Our children have all been graduated from a junior high school in Wilson. (In this sentence there is no name that is the official name of a specific junior high school.)
>
> Are you a member of the National Education Association? (Capitalizing the official title of a specific organization.)
>
> We have had no word from the State Department of Education. (Capitalizing the official title of a specific department.)
>
> Please cancel our subscription to *The Evening Sun*. (Because *The* is capitalized, it must be part of the official name of the paper. Otherwise, the sentence would be written as follows: "Please cancel our subscription to the *Evening Sun*.")

Capitalize names of historical events and documents, of holidays and religious days.

> Mr. Bell was wounded in the Battle of the Bulge. (Historical event is capitalized.)
>
> Hitler bitterly resented the provisions of the Treaty of Versailles. (Historical document is capitalized.)
>
> Manufacturing as we know it today started with the Industrial Revolution. (Period in history is capitalized.)
>
> Did you know that Easter and Passover occur at the same time of year? (Religious days are capitalized.)

⊙ **CHECKUP 3** Are the names of persons, places, and things capitalized correctly in these sentences?

1. The highest mountain in the United States is Mount McKinley in the State of Washington.
2. The new employee's name is Anita Von Fischer.
3. Was the Constitutional Convention held in 1778?
4. The sandstone in Monument Valley, Utah, is made up of rocks from the Paleozoic era.
5. Martin Luther's appearance before the Diet of Worms was a turning point in the reformation.
6. Do you prefer the Green mountains to the White mountains?
7. Real Estate Enterprises owns the Herald Building.

CAPITALIZATION PITFALLS

Capitalization pitfalls result from uncertainty about the use of capitals in certain situations. For instance, in the sentence "Chicago is west of New York," the problem is whether or not to capitalize *west*. A problem also arises with a sentence like this: "The Governor (governor?) has made his appointments." Logical and explicit solutions to the most frequent problems are presented in this section.

Points of the Compass

Capitalize points of the compass—*North, West, Southeast,* and so on—when those names denote a *specific section* of the country. When compass points refer simply to direction, do not capitalize them.

> That candidate is very popular in the East and in the South. (Points of the compass capitalized because they are names of specific sections of the country.)
>
> Is Seattle north, west, or northwest of Chicago? (Points of the compass are not capitalized because they indicate direction.)

Substitutions

Substitutions, much like nicknames, are terms used in place of official names. These terms may be used for both persons and places, and they are capitalized if (1) they are generally known and recognized and (2) they can be lifted out of the sentence and replaced by a complete, official name.

> Germany was very proud of the brilliance of the Desert Fox. (General Rommel was known by the descriptive term *Desert Fox.* The term *Desert Fox* can be lifted out of the sentence and replaced by the name *General Rommel.*)
>
> Mr. Martin has gone to the Windy City for a few days. (*Windy City,* describing *Chicago,* is a term that is generally known.)

Shortened Forms

Instead of writing out the complete name of some particular person, place, or thing, a writer will sometimes use a shortened form of that name. A shortened form of a name is capitalized when it is used to indicate that a *particular, specific* person, place, or thing is meant.

> Make an appointment for Mr. Owen to see the Admiral. (A *specific* admiral is meant, and his complete name can be supplied.)
>
> Among our customers we number an admiral and a general. (These are not meant to be shortened forms for a specific admiral and a specific general; therefore, they are not capitalized.)
>
> We are going to California by way of the Canal. (Here *Canal* is a shortened form of *Panama Canal.*)

Terms such as *company, college, association, club,* and so on, are not usually capitalized when they stand alone, even though they are specifically used in place of the full official name of an organization.

> Our company offers a training program for new employees.

However, if one is a member of the organization and is writing formally or officially about the organization, it is customary to capitalize the shortened form.

> The Company will not submit a bid for this contract. (An official statement; therefore, *Company* is capitalized.)

Capitalize the word *federal* only when it occurs in official names of federal agencies, as in *Federal Communications Commission.* The terms *government* and *federal government* (referring specifically to the United States government) are not usually capitalized except in formal writing.

⊙ **CHECKUP 4** Test your understanding of the preceding three principles by making the necessary corrections in the following sentences.

1. She enjoys the milder winters in the South.
2. The Federal agency handling the investigation is the Internal Revenue service.
3. The heavy storms extended as far West as Chicago.
4. We visited the United States Mint in the City of Brotherly Love.
5. The spoils system was introduced by old hickory.
6. You will save time by using the Skyway.

Commercial Products

Some writers have difficulty recognizing the difference between the proper nouns that are part of the official name of a commercial product and the common nouns that name the general class of the product. For instance, which capitalization is correct—*Arch Saver Shoes* or *Arch Saver shoes?* Because *Arch Saver* is the official name of that brand, *Arch Saver shoes* would be correct. Whenever there is doubt, check the official name.

> Most of our calls are for International Electric appliances. (For *appliances* made by *International Electric*.)
>
> Everywhere one turns, there seems to be an advertisement for Lightning Television. (Capitalization shows that the official name of this product is *Lightning Television*.)

Personal and Official Titles

A title written *before* a name is always capitalized.

> Invitations were extended to Dr. Carlin, Admiral Shafer, and Captain McCaffrey.

Except in addresses, a title written *after* a name is capitalized only when it belongs to a person who holds a nationally or universally recognized high position—a member of congress, a high government official, a reigning monarch.

> Warren Burger, Chief Justice of the Supreme Court, wrote a dissenting opinion. (*Chief Justice* is capitalized because the title is that of a high government official.)
>
> The rise of Peter Blake, president of Commercial Enterprises, has been phenomenal. (*President* is not capitalized because, while Mr. Blake might be "top brass" to the employees of Commercial Enterprises, his title has no significance to the nation at large.)

When *ex-* and *-elect* are joined to titles, they are not capitalized. *Former* and *late* used with titles are also not capitalized.

> Political science students were happy to hear that ex-Senator Porter will teach a course on foreign affairs.
>
> We have not yet heard from Mayor-elect Walsh.
>
> Woodrow Wilson, former President of the United States, was at one time a professor at Princeton.
>
> The new book on the late President Johnson will concentrate on his domestic policies.

⊙ **CHECKUP 5** Can you find and correct the capitalization errors in these sentences?

1. Taster's Choice Coffee is my choice too.
2. The service center for Sunbeam Electric Toasters is nearby.
3. Haile Selassie became emperor of Ethiopia in 1930.
4. When Lyndon B. Johnson died, there was no other living former president.
5. Mr. Canty, Superintendent of Schools, attended a national meeting of educators.
6. Not long after World War II, general Eisenhower became President.
7. Have Nabisco Products been on the market for many years?

Communication Projects

PRACTICAL APPLICATION

A Write the corrections for the capitalization errors in these sentences. Write *OK* for any correct sentence.

1. Automobile prices are somewhat higher on the west coast.
2. Have you read Oscar Wilde's play, *The Importance of being Earnest?*
3. We have decided to order Venetian blinds for the sunny side of the office.
4. The soprano had sung at the Metropolitan Opera house.
5. Current fashions emphasize nostalgia for The Roaring Twenties.
6. The woman who wrote that book is a former Professor of Mathematics at Old Eli.
7. The procedure for confirming a Vice President by vote of Congress is the subject of her report.
8. Although Armistice day in 1918 brought wild rejoicing in the streets of London, today it is almost forgotten.
9. The Corn Belt comprises such States as Iowa, Nebraska, and Illinois.
10. We shall all be sorry to see the General retire from active duty.
11. Jane Eston has a new Byrd convertible.
12. Before he joined our staff, Bates worked for the Wright Aeronautical corporation.
13. The Turnpike is one of America's best superhighways.
14. The Autumn styles reflect the brilliant colors of the changing leaves.
15. The country around Garden city is rather flat.
16. "Very Sincerely yours" is frequently used to close a letter.
17. The message is this: "your sales approach was commented on favorably."
18. Did you know that the constitution state is noted for its scenery?
19. You should write to Fred Watkins, president of the Chamber of Commerce.
20. Will the Senator be at City Hall on Tuesday?

B Correct all errors in the following sentences.

1. The committee hearings were marred by unprovoked, vitriolic, emotional, outbursts.
2. Every possible courtesy and assistance, has been pledged to our international visitors.
3. Scientific exploration continues year-round at the South pole.

4. Independence, Missouri, was Former President Truman's home when he first became a United States senator.
5. The South is famous for such regional food as corn pone and hominy grits.
6. He prefers the title "Psychiatric evaluation of UFO contactees" for Chapter VII.
7. The matanuska valley in the State of Alaska was the site of a short-lived Federal homesteading project.
8. The letters were signed by President Jamison of the Retail Jewelers Association.
9. The road to communication success is not paved with good intentions but with effort genuine effort.
10. Among her published works, one is a historical novel; another, science friction; and another, an autobiography.
11. A writer must have a knowledge of punctuation rules a thorough knowledge.
12. Ida is a receptionist; Beth, a stenographer; and Sue, a secretary.
13. How well acquainted are you with the Federal Insurance Contributions act?
14. However angry he might have been, he concealed it well.
15. You can obtain this information from The Treasury Department.
16. There is as you are well aware, a good reason for this decision.
17. Some persons want the government to support the new proposal.
18. Although our product is new, it is giving satisfaction, and it is paying off.
19. Have you read the latest biography of the Great Emancipator?
20. Please give me your inventory of stamps, envelopes, form postcards etc.

EDITING PRACTICE

The Editorial Supervisor The italicized words in the following sentences are words that your writers are overusing. Suggest two synonyms for each of the words.

1. Your *patronage* is important to us.
2. We shall be interested to hear what your *reaction* is.
3. Yours is indeed an attractive *proposition*.
4. Maybe we can make a *deal*.
5. Personality is definitely an *asset* to all business workers.
6. Martin *runs* his business very efficiently.

Spelling and Pronunciation Many words are misspelled because writers mispronounce them and therefore write what they hear, rather than the correct spelling. Study this paragraph and indicate any misspellings that might have been caused by mispronunciation.

> Thank you very much for sending us a notice of your special sale on piston rings. For the past six months, however, our stock of piston rings has been accumalating to the extent that we are grieviously concerned about storage space. Although we are not interested in your June 2 sale, we would appreciate your letting us know whenever you have any other good buys.

CASE PROBLEM

Making It Clear and Simple You have been asked to revise and simplify a memorandum that contains the following paragraph. Rewrite the paragraph in everyday, clear language.

> Subsequent to April 10, Mr. Lawrence terminated his contract with this organization after completing a considerable amount of years of continuous and exemplary service. Apropos to his decision to sever relations, Mr. Lawrence stated that he had procured an infinitely superior contract that was the quintessence of betterment. We must employ perseverance in endeavoring to replace this lost contract with one of comparable caliber.

Abbreviations

If the business writer's primary aim is to communicate clearly, surely it should be permissible to use shortcuts, or abbreviations, to further that aim. The danger in using shortcuts is that by reducing the word count, the writer may also bypass some of the amenities of communication. However, if the writer knows how to use abbreviations correctly—and when it is appropriate to use them—business messages can be brief and direct, and still invite the reader's goodwill. For instance, in the sentence "David works for the FBI," the abbreviation is entirely in order. Study and apply the following principles of using abbreviations and you will create business communications that are clear and to the point.

ABBREVIATING PERSONAL TITLES AND FIRM NAMES

For reasons of courtesy, a title usually accompanies a person's name, be that title just *Mr.*, *Mrs.*, *Miss*, or *Ms*. It is important for you to know the rules for abbreviating, or not abbreviating, those personal titles.

Titles After Names

The following titles written *after* names are always abbreviated: *Esq.*, *Jr.*, and *Sr.*, as are the academic, professional, and religious titles *B.A.* (Bachelor of Arts), *M.D.* (Doctor of Medicine), and *D.D.* (Doctor of Divinity). Consult your dictionary for the correct abbreviations of other familiar and unfamiliar titles.

Titles Before Names

When the title is used *before* the name, spelling it out or abbreviating it depends on whether the title precedes the full name or only the surname. However, the following titles are always abbreviated: *Mr., Messrs., Mrs., Ms.,* and *St.* for "Saint." Note that *Miss* is not included in the list; *Miss* is not an abbreviation. Note also that *Mesdames* is never abbreviated.

Titles Before Surnames Only A title written before just the *last name* of a person is written in full.

Governor Reed	Doctor Fernandez
Professor Green	Superintendent Adams

Titles Before Full Names A *full name* is a surname with a first name or an initial. When a title precedes a full name, practice differs. In formal usage, such titles should be spelled out. In business correspondence, technical writing, tabulations, or wherever brevity is desirable, abbreviated forms are commonly used.

Supt. T. Alan Chu   Prof. S. David Rowe

Titles of Respect and Dignity *Reverend* and *Honorable* are titles of respect and dignity used in addressing clergymen and government officials of any rank. Spell out such titles, except in addresses, lists, and notices. *The* precedes the titles in formal usage. Note that a given name or a title must follow either *Reverend* or *Honorable.*

The Reverend Doctor Newby   The Honorable Thelma Wright

Note: You can also refer to the *Forms of Address* section at the back of many dictionaries or to the listing in the Appendix of this book.

Firm Names

The name of a firm is not abbreviated unless that company prefers the abbreviation. In case of doubt, try to check the name against the company letterhead or other *official* source.

⊙ **CHECKUP 1** Correct any abbreviation errors in these sentences.

1. Any request for a salary advance must be approved by Miss. Roseman.
2. The speaker for the winter convocation will be Professor Walter Subarski.
3. Debbie is working in the office of Sen. Hawkins.
4. There are now two drs. working in the factory dispensary.
5. The Rev. Dr. Wood has been transferred.
6. Send the statement to Frank J. Adamo, Junior.

PUNCTUATING ABBREVIATIONS

This section discusses the use or the omission of periods in abbreviations.

Names of Associations and Government Agencies

Abbreviations for names of associations and for various agencies are in increasing use and are considered correct. A marked trend is to write lettered abbreviations "solid"—with no periods and no spacing. Call letters for radio and TV stations have always been written solid. This timesaving practice may be used for almost all lettered abbreviations, provided the writer is sure that the reader will know what the abbreviations mean.

AAA	American Automobile Association
AFL-CIO	American Federation of Labor and Congress of Industrial Organizations
AT&T	American Telephone and Telegraph
FBI	Federal Bureau of Investigation
IRS	Internal Revenue Service
NASA	National Aeronautics and Space Administration
NEA	National Education Association
UAW	United Auto Workers
USDA	United States Department of Agriculture

Chemical Symbols

Chemical symbols and formulas, which today are used frequently in business communications, are not followed by periods.

O (oxygen)   Fe (iron) H_2O (water)

IOU and *SOS*

Contrary to popular belief, *IOU* and *SOS* are not abbreviations. They do not "stand for" anything; therefore, no periods are used with them.

Letters Substituted for Names

Sometimes letters are used to designate persons and things, as in *Mr. A, Exhibit D, Madame X,* and so on. In such cases, no period follows the letter, unless the letter is an actual abbreviation; for example, Mr. Aldenty, shortened to "Mr. A.," would require a period after the *A*.

Shortened Forms

Through long and frequent use, some shortened forms have become accepted as complete words. For instance, *ad* is now used for *advertisement; gym* for *gymnasium; phone* for *telephone; lab* for *laboratory;* and *percent* for *per-centum.* Such shortened forms are regarded as complete words and are not followed by periods.

She is now a high-salaried ad writer for Pet Products.

Our company has a gym on the fifth floor of our main building.

Please answer my phone while I am in the meeting.

Biology lab was always fun in high school.

The percent of return from our consumer mailing was very low.

Geographical Names It is preferable to spell out names of counties, states and possessions, provinces, and countries.

Days and Months Names of days of the week and months of the year are preferably spelled out. In a table or a list, abbreviating may be necessary because of lack of space.

⊙ **CHECKUP 5** Correcting these sentences will check your understanding of the "always," "never," and "avoid" rules for abbreviating.

1. Our fire loss claim, No. 151-9335, had been settled by the insurance company.
2. The state of N. Hamp. has many beautiful forests.
3. That boiler explosion occurred at exactly 3:05 a.m. Saturday morning.
4. The city of Northport in Suffolk Co. has voted to abolish residence requirements for policemen.
5. We asked for a price on 25 sq. ft. of floor tile.
6. Fred is several years my jr., although he does not look it.
7. Enclosed is Policy Number 96754, which covers fire insurance on your office equipment.
8. I know that Mr. Dodd lives on Euclid Blvd., but I am not sure of the number.

Communication Projects

PRACTICAL APPLICATION

A In the following sentences, correct any incorrectly written abbreviations. Write *OK* for any correct sentence.

1. All traffic is being detoured to Centennial Blvd. while the highway is being widened.
2. In Ireland, both Catholics and Protestants claim Saint Patrick as their patron saint.
3. The Golden Age of Greece was about 500 B.C., wasn't it?
4. I expect to save 15 gals. of gas a month by joining a car pool to get to my office.
5. Did you know that Mnpls. is just across the river from Saint Paul?
6. The U.S.D.A. is coordinating efforts to stamp out foot-and-mouth disease.
7. Station W.P.A.T. has recently been sold by N.B.C. to a newly formed company.
8. Alison has enrolled in a training course for lab. technicians.
9. An invitation should have been sent to Prof. Scott.
10. The personnel manager prefers to be listed as Ms. Eileen Farley.
11. No. 46899 is missing from our files.
12. Make your appointment for the p.m., if at all possible.
13. We expect to ship your order Tues. a.m.
14. Mr. Hunt is secretary & treasurer of Blair Company.
15. We have yet to hear from the Reverend Doctor J. B. Greeley.
16. Na. and Cl. are the two elements in salt.

17. Exhibit H is powerful evidence for the prosecution.
18. Is Pt. Arthur on the coast of Texas?
19. Were the V.I. ceded to us, or did we buy them?
20. An office on Main Street has been opened by Eugene Ferry, Doctor of Dental Surgery.

B Correct all errors in the following sentences.

1. The City of Saint Petersburg claims to be the oldest in the US.
2. Until actual proof is found, I will never believe he is not trustworthy, completely trustworthy.
3. The large response to a small ad in the neighborhood shoppers paper surprised us.
4. Do you know how much money was received from the sale of U.N.I.C.E.F. Christmas cards?
5. Please send only c.o.d. orders to Mister Marsh.
6. The new Fall fashions seem much more conservative than expected.
7. The farthest west of Canadian provinces is the Prov. of Brit. Col.
8. The no. of deaths over the long holiday weekend was much lower than predicted.
9. In England a "roundabout" is what we know as a traffic circle.
10. His resignation is to take effect Apr. 30.
11. "The words "embarrass" me," he said facetiously.
12. Everybody knows whose home was at Mt. Vernon.
13. Did you know that the president of this company is the possessor of the Navy cross?
14. This statue dates back to 200 B.C.
15. Although the book is called *All about Insurance*, it gives little practical information.
16. Since World War II, West Ger. has made a remarkable recovery.
17. The weather in the south is sometimes cold.
18. A mysterious Madame X called this morning.
19. The inscription read "Obedience to Law Is Liberty".
20. We should like to know the name of the largest mfg. concern in your city.

EDITING PRACTICE

Plurals and Possessives Rewrite any sentences that contain errors. Write *OK* for any correct sentence.

1. Do you think that Janet keeping cosmetics in her desk is good business practice?
2. The paper cutter is not in it's usual place.
3. Orders for banjoes increase just before Christmas.
4. Mr. Ames said that your progressing very rapidly.
5. The German's economic recovery is a tribute to that nation.
6. They realize that their is still more planning to be done.
7. There is no precedent for are system of billing.
8. The Davises' financial standing is very sound.
9. Because highly specialized knowledge is needed, editors in chief's positions are not easily filled.
10. Whose going to manage the new branch office?

11. Our tenant's committee is chaired by Ann Morrow, a shrewd lawyer.
12. Are their any copies of the report left?
13. Both court-appointed attorney's, Rodriguez and Hamilton, claimed a conflict of interest.
14. We all agreed that the better system is her's.
15. Its foolish to believe that they will accept these price increases.

The Evaluator Would you OK this paragraph? If not, why not?

> You may expect a visit from our electrical expert on Monday morning, June 4. As you know, we guarantee our washing machines for three months after purchase; and we are only too glad to give you prompt service. That is why you really should of reported immediately that the rinsing cycle on your washer is not working satisfactorily. If your experience parallels that of other Launderquik users, your machine will need no further adjustment; but please remember that we are standing by and will be happy to help in any way we can.

CASE PROBLEM

A Ticklish Situation Mr. Noble is one of the best customers of the Paterson Electrical Supply Company. On March 15, he sent payment for an invoice dated March 1, with terms of 2/10, n/30. Mr. Noble deducted the cash discount to which he was not entitled. When the credit manager at the Paterson Electrical Supply Company called the matter to his attention, Mr. Noble indicated that he always makes payment within the discount period but that someone in his office slipped up and forgot to mail this month's payment on time.

1. What should the credit manager for the Paterson Electrical Supply Company do about this situation?
2. Suppose Mr. Noble made a habit of deducting the cash discount whenever he paid after the expiration of the discount period. What might you, as credit manager, write Mr. Noble in your letter refusing to accept the deduction?

30 Numbers

Specific details are the backbone of business communication. Often, such details require the use of numbers to indicate sums of money, to specify order quantities, to quote prices, to adjust claims, to make appointments, and to perform a host of other business activities. Making an error in numbers can not only cause confusion and uncertainty but can also be expensive and time-consuming. Therefore, learn well and apply carefully the rules that govern writing numbers.

NUMBERS WRITTEN AS WORDS

Numbers That Begin Sentences

Always write in words any number that begins a sentence. If it is awkward to spell out the number, rephrase the sentence.

> Seventy-five percent of the students passed the examination.
>
> One dollar opens your savings account at our bank.
>
> With only $1, you can open a savings account at our bank. (The sentence has been rephrased to make the amount stand out.)

Numbers One Through Ten

Numbers *one* through *ten* should be written in words when those numbers are used in isolated instances—either singly or with one other number.

> Mr. Penn has been our accountant for ten years.
>
> Mr. Penn has been our accountant for eight or ten years.

The "one-through-ten" rule also applies to names of numbered streets. They, too, are written as words.

> Many bargains are available at Third Avenue stores.
>
> The Tenth Street station is being enlarged.

Fractions Standing Alone; Mixed Numbers

When a fraction stands alone (is not used with a whole number), that fraction is written in words: *one-half, three-fourths*. When a mixed number (a whole number and a fraction) is spelled out, the word *and* should separate the whole number from the fraction: *two and one-half, three and one-third*. A mixed number is spelled out only at the beginning of a sentence; otherwise, it is expressed in figures.

> Approximately three-fourths of the registered voters cast their ballots in this year's primary.
>
> Five and one-half rooms is the size of my present apartment.
>
> My 5½-room apartment is more than enough for one person.

Time of Day

You learned in Section 29 to use figures with the abbreviations *a.m.* and *p.m.* With the term *o'clock*, use words for the time. When expressing time on the hour without *a.m., p.m.,* or *o'clock*, spell out the hour.

> We arrived at three o'clock.
>
> They always have dinner at eight. (Not *at 8.*)

Round Numbers

Round numbers can be either spelled out or expressed as figures. Where the writing is formal or literary, spell out round numbers that require no more than two words (a hyphenated compound number such as *twenty-six million* counts as two words). In business correspondence, however, round numbers are often expressed as figures.

> We have received two hundred requests for samples. (In business correspondence, the figure *200* could be used.)
>
> More than 750 students attended the rally. (Figures are used here because more than two words would be required to spell out the number.)

When spelling out numbers over one thousand, express the numbers in the fewest possible words.

> fifteen hundred (Not *one thousand five hundred.*)
>
> twenty-five hundred (Not *two thousand five hundred.*)

Ages

When expressed in years only, ages of persons are most often written as words. However, when the age of a person is given as a significant statistic—for example, in a news release or in matters pertaining to employment—figures are used.

> Surely Jane is more than twenty-five years old!
>
> Dr. Boggs, who is 56 years old, is a leading authority on conservation. (Item in a news release.)

Centuries and Decades

In formal writing, numbers referring to centuries and decades are written as words. However, there are instances where the use of figures is acceptable.

> This antique dates back to the seventeenth century. (Do not use *17th century.*)
>
> This antique dates back to the sixteen hundreds. (Here *1600s* would also be acceptable.)
>
> The unemployment rate in the United States was high in the nineteen-thirties. (Here *1930s* would also be acceptable; however, do not use *'30s.*)

⊙ **CHECKUP 1** Find and correct any errors in the following sentences.

1. She has already typed 10 pages of the final report.
2. The missing volume was on social conditions in the 19th century in France.
3. Your appointment with Dr. Tarrant is for 2 on Friday afternoon.
4. At age 30 a man's life expectancy is 35 years; a woman's, about 8 years longer.
5. Please run off two thousand two hundred copies of the form.
6. Brian said that he is able to save 1/5 of his income.
7. 12 items in the shipment were damaged.
8. When questioned by the committee members, the nominee proudly stated that she had donated over 1/3 of her annual income to charitable causes.
9. In New York City, 1 Fifth Avenue and 1 Park Avenue are considered prestigious addresses.

NUMBERS WRITTEN AS FIGURES

Numbers are usually written as figures in the instances mentioned on pages 222 to 224.

Numbers Higher Than Ten

In business correspondence, numbers from *11* to *99* and numbers over *100* are usually written in figures. However, numbers *11* to *99* may be written as words when the writing style is formal.

> We have had 11 transfers during the past year. (This is correct.)
>
> We have had eleven transfers during the past year. (The writer wishes to use a more formal style.)

When writing a series of numbers, use *all* figures or *all* words so that the form will be consistent.

> The shipment consists of 18 chairs, 6 desks, and 12 tables. (Note *6 desks*, not *six*.)
>
> Included in the group were fourteen students, three professors, and two parents. (Note *fourteen students*, not *14*.)

Sums of Money

In business communications, sums of money are written in figures. Only in specialized writing, as in legal documents, is money written both in words and in figures. Remember that the period and the two zeros are not used with even amounts of dollars: *$25*, not *$25.* or *$25.00*. In tabulations, of course, the period and zeros are used to even the columns.

When writing sums of money in a series, the dollar sign must be used with each member of the series.

> Our new handbags are priced at $5, $7, and $10.

Age in Years, Months, Days

Age expressed in years, months, and days or in years and months is written in figures.

> On June 1, Fred's age will be 25 years 7 months and 5 days. (Because the age is considered as a single unit, no commas are used in the series.)

Time Connected With Discount or Interest Rates

For clarity and emphasis, periods of time mentioned with terms of discount or interest rates are written in figures.

> If you pay within 10 days, you will receive the usual 2 percent discount. (The figures make the discount terms stand out.)

House, Street, ZIP Code Numbers

In business correspondence, house numbers are written in figures, with the exception of the number *one*. The abbreviation *No.* or the sign # should not be used with house numbers or with RFD numbers.

> The package was addressed to One Park Place, not 14 Park Place.
>
> Please change my address to RFD 2.

Spell out numbered street names from one through ten. Use figures for numbered street names over ten. When figures are used, the ordinal ending *st, th,* or *d* may be omitted so long as a word such as *East* or *West* separates the street number from the house number. If no such word intervenes, use the ordinal ending for clarity.

505 Fifth Avenue	340 East 72 Street
155 Eighth Street	1205 34th Street

The postal ZIP Code number follows the name of the state, without punctuation. A single space separates the state and the ZIP Code: *Chicago, Illinois 60604.* These rules also apply when the two-letter abbreviation for state is used: *New York, NY 10011.*

Decimals

Decimals are always expressed in figures, without commas: *4.5; 1.3456.* In technical writing, where exactness is imperative, a zero is written before the decimal point when there is no whole number: *0.2546.*

⊙ **CHECKUP 2** Check your understanding of the rules for writing numbers by correcting these sentences.

1. Of the seven hundred and fifty questionnaires mailed, only two hundred have been returned.
2. What rate of interest does your bank charge for a ninety-day loan?
3. Each service call costs $18.00, plus the cost of any replacement parts.
4. Try as I will, I can get no answer but 0.4368.
5. We ordered 90 tulip bulbs, ten rose bushes, and 20 dahlias.
6. Depending on quality and workmanship, we can offer you bedspreads at $10, 15, and $20.
7. The house at 1 Main Street is for sale.

Numbers Used With Words

Percentages Percentages that appear in isolated instances in sentences are written in figures followed by the word *percent*: *a 6 percent increase.* In technical writing, fractional percentages are expressed in decimals with the percent symbol: at *4.5%.* In business correspondence, they are written as fractions or as decimals: at *4½ percent* or at *4.5 percent.*

When percentages occur in pairs, they are written in figures with *percent* following the second figure: *from 2 to 10 percent.*

Note: The percent symbol (%) is used only in technical and statistical copy and in tables, invoices, and interoffice memorandums. When the percent symbol is used in a series, repeat the symbol with each figure of the series.

Money Expressed in Cents Isolated amounts of cents that appear in a sentence are written in figures followed by the word *cents*: *only 50 cents.* In a series, to be consistent, the dollar sign and the decimal point are used for cents: "I spent $4 for stamps, $2 for envelopes, and $.60 for cards." The symbol ¢ for cents is used only in price quotations and in technical communications: *250 blocks @ 75¢ and 4 bags of cement @ 98¢*.

Million, Billion Present practice in writing extremely large numbers is to spell out *million, billion,* and so on. Such sums can be written as follows: *more than 2 billion dollars* or *more than $2 billion*. Note that the number of millions or billions is expressed in figures.

Consecutive Numbers

When two numbers come together and one is a compound modifier, one number is written as a word; the other, as a figure. As a rule, spell out the first number unless the second number would make a significantly shorter word.

> Our order called for ten 30-inch strips. (Note that this is shorter than *10 thirty-inch strips.*)
>
> Get me 75 six-cent stamps. (Contrast this with *seventy-five 6-cent stamps.*)

⊙ **CHECKUP 3** Make any necessary corrections in these sentences.

1. In Wellsville, one egg now costs 12 cents.
2. The complete experiment required 3 hours 20 minutes 15 seconds.
3. The price of rice has increased by as much as 5 percent to 7 percent.
4. The deficit is expected to exceed $2 billion next year.
5. To fill a special order, we need 210 five-pound boxes.
6. The quotation was taken from page 1010.
7. Is it true that the entire trip takes no more than 2 hours, 15 minutes?
8. The only petty cash expenses for the week were $1.49 for glue, $1.98 for a calendar, and 25 cents for an eraser.
9. Banks are offering special discounts to all holders of six percent mortgages.

WRITING DATES

The *ordinal endings* mentioned in this section are the *st, d,* and *th* that follow figures: *1st, 2d, 3d, 15th,* and so on. Note particularly *2d* and *3d*. Writing them as *2nd* and *3rd* is out of style. Writing dates correctly is simply a matter of using or not using ordinal endings. The following rules represent current business practice.

Day Following Month

When the day follows the month, that day is written in figures, *without ordinal endings*: *April 15, January 2, July 17,* and so on.

Day Preceding Month

When the day precedes the month, the day may be written either in figures or in words. When figures are used, they must be used *with ordinal endings: 15th of April, 2d of January,* and so on.

Communication Projects

PRACTICAL APPLICATION

A Correct any errors in the use of numbers in the following sentences. Write *OK* for any correct sentence.

1. In New York City all 2d Avenue traffic moves in a southerly direction.
2. Did the Spanish Inquisition begin in the 16th or the 17th century?
3. At least 2/3 of the miners are significantly underpaid.
4. The Arlington Shopping Mall can accommodate over two thousand five hundred cars.
5. Young people think their elders are "over the hill" at 30.
6. Miss Walter phoned to say she will be here by 10 o'clock.
7. He asked Sally to meet him when she left her office at 5.
8. Although he had paid each of 12 installments on time, he received a curt "payment overdue" notice.
9. The employees submitted 55 pieces of art for the spring art show.
10. The printed program indicates a closing time of 4:30 o'clock.
11. There were 315 sales representatives present at the meeting.
12. Remember to order 100 seven-cent stamps.
13. All schedule changes must be made before the 5 of June.
14. Mortgage rates were once as low as 5½ percent.
15. We asked for ten boxes of stencils, 15 reams of paper, and three styli.
16. The cost of the submarine exceeded $5,000,000.
17. These manila envelopes sell for 7 cents each.
18. We have a wonderful selection of dresses at 25, 35, and $50.
19. 111 clerks are employed in our shipping department.
20. Profit on the sale of groceries is said to range from 13% to 15%.

B Correct all errors in the following sentences.

1. It is estimated that there will be five thousand five hundred surplus teachers by next September.
2. The Golden Age Club is the name of our group, all of whom are in their 70's.
3. The student world of the nineteen sixties has been called "The Rebel Years."
4. The mill has notified us that your order of thirty-two 6-foot steel pipes was shipped the twelfth of Feb.
5. The house on the back of that property is oddly numbered as #60½ Ardmore Place.
6. Have you read President Voorhees' amusing report, "No shortage of Shortages?"
7. There are no exceptions to our stated policy of 2% 10 days, net 30 days.
8. The inflation rate in the coming year is expected to be 7% to 9%.
9. Every petty cash expenditure must be covered by a voucher, even if the expenditure is only for five cents.
10. One rigorous weight-reducing plan urges brisk daily walks of up to fifteen miles.
11. The atomic weight of platinum is one hundred ninety-five and nine-hundredths.
12. Roger was 6 years 3 months and 16 days old on the opening day of school.

13. The typist at the first desk (the one who shared his lunch with us,) is our most skilled operator.
14. Please duplicate page 1,555.
15. The Company gave a party to celebrate Mr. Kain's thirty-fifth anniversary.
16. We shall be glad to discount your note in thirty days.
17. His doctor recommends that Mister Ross walk 5 miles each day.
18. We must make provision for an audience of 375 persons, exclusive of our staff members.
19. The Governor has set May 3rd as the opening day for the centennial celebration.
20. Do you think that the cashier is good for a "touch"?

EDITING PRACTICE

The Rewrite Editor Edit and rewrite the following paragraph.

> As promised in our letter of May 10th we are sending you a list of panelists for our W.B.S.B.—T.V. program. From the nominations received from you and from other authorities we have selected the following: Sen. Coulter, Gen. Alton B. Burrows, Professor Ely, and Mr. John C. Stock, who is the proprietor of a chain of laundrys. We hope you can attend the organizational meeting to be held next Friday at eight p.m.

Spelling Notebook As a means of self-improvement, Joan Ganin keeps a notebook in which she writes correctly any words she misspells. What entries would you suggest as a result of proofreading this paragraph taken from one of her letters?

> We were very much impressed with your written application for the position of junior bookeeper with our firm; and, as we do have an opening, I should like to talk with you and learn more about you. How about droping in to see me on Monday morning, May 1, at 10:45? My office is on the second floor, directly in front of the elevator.

Editing for Context Edit these sentences and rewrite any sentences containing words that do not fit the context.

1. As everyone accepted, Mr. Harmon did not show up for the meeting.
2. An expert speaker, Miss Pei never has trouble establishing a report with her audience.
3. The prosecution never fully proved its belief that there was collision among the three defendants.
4. Although it has been called "the architectural accomplishment of the decade," the new 50-story stricture is not as functional as the building it replaced.
5. If management had explained that the new machines will not replace any workers, none of us would have been apprehensible.
6. In retaliation to the scathing editorials in our local newspaper, Mayor Williams is suing for definition of character.
7. All of us thanked Ms. Gary for referring to March the due date for our term papers.
8. The livelihood of seeing Bert elected is very slim.
9. I have spent years trying to develop good spilling habits, but I still rely on the dictionary.
10. The coroner listed "inhalation of poisonous substances" as the official cause of death.

CASE PROBLEM

The Difficult Caller Marie Gallagher, secretary to Gorden Howell of the Lakeland Insurance Company, receives a telephone call for Mr. Howell from William Best, a customer who is a representative of a business machine firm. Mr. Howell often purchases equipment from Mr. Best. Marie tells Mr. Best that Mr. Howell is out of the office for the day. Mr. Best insists on telling Marie his troubles. He is irate because the Lakeland Insurance Company purchased three new adding machines from a competing firm. He wonders why, since he is both a policyholder of and a supplier for the company, he was not given the opportunity to make the sale. He even threatens to cancel his insurance.

1. What should Marie say to Mr. Best?
2. What should Mr. Howell do about the situation when he returns?

CHAPTER 5
WRITING SKILL

31 Structuring the Thought Unit

Children read word by word. Adults read in thought units. A *thought unit* is a combination of words that properly interconnect, words that properly belong together. When writers structure thought units correctly, readers can understand the message quickly and completely. When writers do not structure thought units correctly, readers are distracted from the message and sometimes must guess at its meaning. For example, if we say "Mr. York made the sale to Mr. Ames just before he left," we are asking the reader to guess if *he* stands for Mr. York, or for Mr. Ames.

The thought unit must be restructured to avoid this confusing pronoun reference. One more example: "Carrying the cat, the dog started to chase us." This tells the reader to believe that the dog was carrying the cat. Properly structured, this sentence would read "While we were carrying the cat, the dog started to chase us."

Writing is an art, and artistic skills must be developed. This chapter will provide you with the training you need to develop your writing skill. You will master advanced writing techniques and acquire know-how that will give you writing power. In this section you will concentrate on the first step in developing your writing skill, structuring thought units correctly.

WORDS IN THOUGHT UNITS

Sometimes a confusing, laughable, or even incorrect picture is formed because a single word is not connected with its proper thought unit. For example, read the following newspaper advertisement:

> Long ladies' gloves on sale Saturday.

Short ladies would not be able to take advantage of this sale, would they? The thought unit *long ladies* is incorrect. The proper thought unit is *long gloves,* and the copywriter should have written the advertisement as shown below.

> Ladies' long gloves on sale Saturday.

Failure to place an adverb correctly in a sentence is a frequent error. Note the placement of *only* in the following sentence:

> Ray only has one more payment to make on his car.

The thought unit *only has* is incorrect; the correct thought unit is *only one more payment.*The sentence should read as follows:

> Ray has only one more payment to make on his car.

Be sure to look at the thought units your words create.

PHRASES IN THOUGHT UNITS

Incorrectly placed phrases, as well as incorrectly placed words, can change the meaning of a message completely. This fact is known to expert writers, who edit their work carefully to see that they have placed phrases correctly. For instance, an expert would not write this sentence:

Most guests came to call on President and Mrs. Truman in taxis.

Placing *in taxis* with *President and Mrs. Truman* indicates that the President and his wife were in taxis. Actually, the writer meant that most *guests* used taxis as their means of transportation when they came to visit the President and his wife. To convey that message, the sentence should have been written this way:

Most guests came in taxis to call on President and Mrs. Truman.

Now read the following classified advertisement and see what happens because of the incorrectly placed thought units.

For Rent: Large furnished room only for gentleman with attached bath.

Surely, a *gentleman with attached bath* would be unique! A *furnished room with attached bath*, however, would present a familiar picture. The revised advertisement should read:

For Rent: For gentleman only, large furnished room with attached bath.

CLAUSES IN THOUGHT UNITS

Rather surprisingly, some writers have little difficulty in applying the thought-unit rule to the placement of words and phrases but do not apply the same principles to the placement of clauses. No trained writer should be guilty of writing such a confusing sentence as this:

We will release the financial report when the time comes to the newspapers.

The clause *when the time comes to the newspapers* is confusing. But when you apply the thought-unit rule to the placement of clauses, the sentence correctly reads:

When the time comes, we will release the financial report to the newspapers.

A misplaced clause may so alter the meaning of a sentence that it says something entirely different from what was intended, as in this sentence:

Mr. Burr placed the vase on the desk that was given to him by his wife.

Desk that was given to him by his wife means just that—the *desk* was given to him by his wife. However, suppose it is the *vase*—not the desk—that was given to Mr. Burr. In that case, the sentence would have to be written as follows:

Mr. Burr placed on the desk the vase that was given to him by his wife.

AMBIGUOUS *WHICH* CLAUSES

Expert writers understand the specific function of *which* clauses and therefore they use them correctly. These writers have no trouble placing a *which* clause with the word it modifies, explains, or amplifies.

Less adept writers sometimes place a *which* clause with a wrong word, but more often they use such a clause to modify an entire idea. Too, some writers think that the solution to many of their writing problems lies in using a comma followed by a *which* clause; this solution, however, is often incorrect. The following sentences illustrate and explain some common misuses of the *which* clause, and the revisions show the correct usage.

> We have a pamphlet dealing with government bonds, which we will send you on request.

Placing the *which* clause with *government bonds* means that the *bonds* will be sent on request. Actually, the writer of that sentence intended to say that the *pamphlet* will be sent. Unless the writer is prepared to give bonds away, the *which* clause should be used this way:

> We have a pamphlet, which we will be glad to send you on request, that deals with government bonds.

The same sentence gains polish when the *which* clause is deleted:

> On request, we shall be glad to send you our pamphlet dealing with government bonds.

Another misuse of a *which* clause is shown below.

> Further delay in payment will impair your credit, which neither of us wants.

In this sentence the *which* clause modifies a complete idea, *further delay in payment will impair your credit.* In terms of thought units, however, the ambiguous, if not insulting, meaning is *your credit, which neither of us wants. Which* clauses must not be used to refer to a complete idea; therefore, the sentence should read, "Further delay in payment will impair your credit, and both of us are interested in maintaining your good standing."

Do not assume that *which* clauses should be avoided altogether. When correctly used, they are an aid to effective writing. A *which* clause may be essential to message clarity, as in the sentence shown below.

> Read page 5, which contains the complete information about your department.

⊙ **CHECKUP 1** Keeping thought units in mind, revise the following sentences to make their meanings clear.

1. These machines are intended for trained operators because they are fully automated.
2. I found that giving the customer a chance to speak while selling typewriters often helped close the sale.
3. Sale on Summer Girls' Slacks!
4. People often borrow money from banks which they do not need.
5. Inflation and economic unrest are conditions that will continue in all probability.

WHO DID WHAT?

In business communications, as in any other kind of communication, it is essential that the writer make it absolutely clear *who* has done or will do a specific thing. Sometimes, however, the writer confuses the thought by having the wrong person or thing connected with an action, so the meaning intended is not conveyed to the reader. Such a violation of the thought-unit principle can cause doubt or uncertainty as to *who* did *what*.

> If not satisfied, we will return your money.

Consider the thought unit *If not satisfied, we*. The meaning here is that *we* are the ones who might not be satisfied. If a customer returned the goods and asked for a full refund, the manufacturer could refuse on the grounds that the manufacturer was well satisfied with the customer's money. The correct meaning is immediately apparent to the reader when the sentence is revised.

> If you are not satisfied, we will return your money.

Occasionally, if the who-did-what principle is violated, the sentence becomes ridiculous, for an object, not a person, seems to be performing an action.

> Entering the room, the typewriter was seen teetering on the edge of the table.

The thought unit *entering the room, the typewriter* pictures the typewriter as entering the room. This kind of phrasing shows a serious lack of communication know-how. In this revision, a person performs the action:

> Entering the room, Mr. Fosnough saw the typewriter teetering on the edge of the table.

Here is another illustration of this type of error:

> After climbing to the top of the tower, the whole city lay spread before us.

What does the thought unit *after climbing to the top of the tower, the whole city* mean? How could a city climb to the top of the tower? Revised, the sentence would read:

> After climbing to the top of the tower, we saw the whole city spread before us.

A who-did-what violation, sometimes called a *dangler*, does not necessarily occur at the beginning of a sentence. For example, note the error in the following sentence:

> Mr. Paine saw the expected caller glancing up from his desk.

As written, the thought unit is *caller glancing up from his desk*. Was the caller at his own desk, and did he glance up from that desk? Was the caller glancing up from Mr. Paine's desk; and if so, what physical contortions were necessary to perform the act? Most likely, it was Mr. Paine who glanced up from his own desk. In order to eliminate the confusion, the sentence should be written like this:

> Glancing up from his desk, Mr. Paine saw the expected caller.

INDEFINITE, CONFUSING PRONOUN REFERENCE

As everyone knows, a pronoun is used to substitute for a noun. However, unless the noun the pronoun stands for is clearly indicated, the message will not present a clear and correct thought unit. The careful writer makes all pronoun references definite and unmistakably clear.

Confusing *He* or *She*

When you use the pronouns *he* or *she*, you must be certain that the reader knows who *he* or *she* is. The antecedent of the *he* or *she* must be clear. Consider the confusion that could arise from a statement like this:

> Miss Simon promoted Jane to supervisor just before she took her vacation.

Who took her vacation—Miss Simon, or Jane? The *she* in this sentence is indefinite and, consequently, confusing. If it is Miss Simon who took her vacation, the sentence should read:

> Just before she took her vacation, Miss Simon promoted Jane to supervisor.

If it is Jane who took her vacation, the sentence should read:

> Just before Jane took her vacation, Miss Simon promoted her to supervisor.

Indefinite *It*

Using the pronoun *it* to refer to something that is not immediately clear is a common offense. For example, read the following sentence:

> I will place the pigskin in punt position, and when I nod my head, kick it.

Kick what? This indefinite *it* could result in a painful injury, wouldn't you say? The indefinite *it* must be replaced by the noun to which it should refer; and the revised sentence reads:

> I will place the pigskin in punt position, and when I nod my head, kick the ball.

Inept writers tend to use the pronoun *it* as a catchall word, even if there is no antecedent to which the *it* can refer. Consider the use of *it* in this sentence:

> It is the positive sales approach that is the effective element in these letters.

In this example the *it* reference is vague and serves only to make the sentence wordy. Consider how much more effective the sentence would be if it were written like this:

> The positive sales approach is the effective element in these letters.

Other Indefinite Pronoun References

Speakers who are uncertain of their sources frequently use the careless "they say" as a reference. Writers who use the same vague reference are considered amateurish; in written communication references must be definite and exact. For example, read the following sentence:

> They say that sales will decrease during the next six months.

Who is meant by *they* in this sentence? A lack of definiteness earmarks a poorly trained writer. A precise writer would present the information this way:

> *Market News* reports that sales will decrease during the next six months.

Another type of indefinite reference that is puzzling and annoying to a reader is illustrated in this sentence:

> Although I dictated all morning on Tuesday, my secretary typed only two of them.

The slipshod *two of them* is vagueness carried to an extreme. Two of what? stories? letters? reports? news releases? A clear and explicit thought could be communicated by writing:

> Although I dictated all morning on Tuesday, my secretary typed only two of the letters.

⊙ **CHECKUP 2** Test your understanding of the who-did-what and the pronoun-reference rules by revising the following sentences.

1. They expect fuel supplies to be critically short this year.
2. The puppy was found by John while he was chewing the slippers.
3. There is always a mob jammed around the booth selling tickets.
4. Will the owner of the car with license AX3083 please remove it.
5. Even after consulting five reference books, the problem remains unsolved.
6. Running for the elevator, my briefcase fell on Mr. Anderson's foot.
7. While Pat was dialing Joan's number, she was leaving for work.
8. Looking out the window, the Statue of Liberty was clearly in sight.

Communication Projects

PRACTICAL APPLICATION

A All these sentences contain violations of thought-unit rules. Revise them.

1. Come to the sale of the year on double-knit women's pantsuits!
2. Icy rain caused many schools to close, which was a safety measure.
3. Rest areas are provided for motorists who want to stop awhile on Route 80.
4. On television, it gives a whole hour of news beginning at 6 p.m.
5. Such rapid fluctuations in the prime interest rate almost seem suspicious.
6. Examined from all angles, John saw that the situation was not hopeless.
7. She told me to expect a 10 percent cut in salary, which depressed me.
8. If defective, you are covered for the replacement part by our guarantee.
9. If you are a good bowler, teach it to the new members of the League.
10. When our boss talked with the caller, he told him that he would be invited to speak at the meeting.
11. To make a hole in the dough, use a thimble rather than your thumb. Of course, you should boil it first.
12. To develop typing speed, time must be spent in intelligent practice.
13. The electrician installed a light over Mr. Lord's head that was recessed.
14. To reserve rooms at a hotel, a telegram should be sent at least three days in advance.
15. The group watched the elephants file by on our narrow balcony.
16. While climbing the stairs, the clock struck two.
17. With errors clearly marked, Ms. Whipple returned the letter to her secretary.
18. The president spoke to the old man, and he praised his work.
19. To make the sale, the car should be polished brightly.
20. Drag racing is a favorite pastime in this city, but not very many of them result in serious accidents.

B Revise any sentences that do not conform to thought-unit rules. Write *OK* for any correct sentences.

1. He found the screw that he lost lying on the floor.
2. Any handicraft is eligible for the prize which has not been exhibited before.
3. The new sorter can almost handle 500 cards a minute.
4. She bought a waterproof man's raincoat for her father.
5. While writing adjustment letters, courtesy is all-important.
6. They will pay moving expenses if the company transfers me to Lawrenceville.
7. In getting out of the taxi, Miss Knott's handbag fell to the pavement.
8. My brother only has two weeks' vacation this year.
9. The pilot taxied out to the oil truck in a small plane.
10. The men sailed out to meet the great liner in the small boat.
11. David is always pleasant, which makes him very popular.
12. Only the Board of Directors can nominate the three new officers.
13. In your reference manual, it says to use open punctuation.
14. Our sales manager is satisfied with only first-class service.
15. Don's boss will give him the assignment when he returns from Chicago.
16. I only have been to Vermont once before.
17. I could see the old office building where I used to work in the distance.
18. When October comes, we often take long walks in the woods.
19. Maurice will go if an emergency arises for the medicine.
20. After traveling all day, our destination was still miles away.

EDITING PRACTICE

Editing for Context Edit these sentences and rewrite any sentences containing words that do not fit the context.

1. This sale was dated in accordion with the instructions in your letter.
2. As far as we know, the firm you inquire about is solvent.
3. Are you buying this stock for speculative purposes?
4. The York Hotel offers a prodigy of social events.
5. The securities you mention are not listed on the Board.
6. Our golf course is considered idly constructed for beginning players.
7. You should receive your rights on May 1, one right for every share of stock.
8. Please have a redcap meet Mr. Ward at the airport.
9. There is a thrill to a game played on a coarse overlooking the ocean.
10. Our grill provides food for the hunky golfer.

Proofreading a Memo Even though memos are sent to fellow employees rather than to customers, the messages should be correctly written. What, if any, corrections would you make in this memo?

> Installation of esculators in our store will be completed on May 15. In preparation for this Blanton innovation, I am asking Merchandise Managers for the different floors to give some thought to rearranging departments and displays. For instance, I think we can increase sales by featuring our "leaders" in the arrear at the top of the moving stairs. As they are riding from floor to floor, customers have time to look; and an eye-catching display could motivate them to stop off—and buy! Please feel free to call on me if you think I can be of help.

CASE PROBLEM

The Annoyed Customer Judy Lawrence is temporarily employed in the curtain and drapery section at Robeson's Department Store. An angry customer comes into the department with a pair of curtains that she purchased from another salesclerk, who said that the curtains would not fade or shrink when they were washed. Apparently, this information was not correct. The customer proceeds to vent her anger on Judy.

1. What should Judy say to the customer?
2. What can the store do to retain the customer's business?

32 Advanced Writing Techniques

What is it that makes the performance of any activity—in music, art, dance, sport, writing—seem flawless? Whatever the medium, the flawless performance has the distinction of appearing effortless; it is smooth, polished, inevitably beautiful. Thus the observer (or listener or reader) of such a performance is deceived into thinking that it is easy, that anyone can achieve the same kind of performance. What is not evident in the finished production is the hard work of perfecting a technique; once the technique is mastered, the performer is free to become an artist, a creator.

If you view every written communication as a performance, or a production, you will soon realize that the finest performances come from the writers who have worked hardest at perfecting their writing techniques. The highest praise is reserved for these artist-writers, the writers who have mastered the most advanced writing techniques and are able to perform flawlessly. These are the writers to emulate.

WORD USAGE

To perform acceptably as a writer, you must use synonyms, antonyms, and homonyms with ease. You must avoid trite expressions, repetitious wording, and negative words. You must communicate precisely. These techniques of good written communication were discussed in Chapter 1.

To perform professionally as a writer, however, you must know the advanced techniques that make the difference between a good production and a polished one. Here are some of these advanced techniques.

Positive Words

Positive words are pleasant to hear and to read. They are words that create a receptive, pleasant glow in the mind of a reader. Consequently, the master writer deliberately uses words that produce this desirable psychological effect. The words in the following list evoke a positive response.

advancement	courage	genuine	satisfaction
agreeable	eager	gratify	success
attractive	earnest	happy	trustworthy
cheerful	easy	integrity	valued
comfortable	encourage	liberal	victory
compensation	enjoy	pleasure	warmth
confident	fortunate	profit	welcome
cordial	generosity	progress	willingness

Planned Repetition of Words

Although careless repetition of words is a mark of the poor writer, *planned* repetition is a technique of the master writer. Intentional repetition is sometimes used to emphasize a single idea; for example, repeating the word *same* in the following sentence shows Stuart to be in an abysmal rut.

> Stuart does the same things every day, at the same time, in the same way, and with the same lack of enthusiasm.

Repetition is one of the cardinal principles of advertising; therefore, an ad writer must be adept in using deliberately repeated words. The following ad may seem repetitious, but the repetition is a clever and purposeful transposition of words.

> HEALTHTONE will add years to your life, and HEALTHTONE will add life to your years.

Words and the Sound of Music

A sentence "sings" when the words in that sentence flow smoothly in pleasant sounds. To compose melodic sentences, avoid the following.

Too Many Harsh Sounds In our language there are many unpleasant-sounding consonants: *j, dj, ks, qu, nk, sh, s*. Listen to the sound of these words: *gesture, satchel, tragic, illegible, church, cabbage, virtue, anxious, bushel*. Listen to the harsh music produced by a too lavish use of the unpleasant *s* and *sh* sounds in the tongue-twister "She sells seashells by the seashore." Now listen to the following sentence and "feel" the effect of too many harsh, unpleasant sounds.

> Be assured that there will be no change in our existing policy with regard to future orders, charges, and exchanges.

Too Many Similar Sounds Many words, although different in meaning and in spelling, have similar sounds. An expert watches for these sounds and does not use too many sounds in any one sentence. Listen to the following sentence, which contains too many *ee* sounds, and note its lack of pleasing musical quality.

> When you steer your weary feet here to our restaurant, you have a treat awaiting you.

Correcting the *This* or *Thus* Fault

A rather common writing fault is the use of *this* or *thus* to refer to an entire preceding thought. This lack of definiteness sometimes forces a reader to reread, or to recast, a sentence in order to comprehend the writer's meaning. The slipshod, inexact use of *this* and *thus* can spoil an otherwise fine writing performance.

> Our stockroom is overcrowded. This has existed since we moved to the new building on Juniper Street.

To what does the *this* refer? To the overcrowded *condition* of the stockroom. An accomplished writer would have stated the point specifically, as in the following:

> This condition has existed since we moved to the new building on Juniper Street.

Now read the following sentence, which shows another example of unclear word reference.

> Mr. Burr has passed the CPA examination, thus proving that he is competent to open a set of books for you.

Thus, as used here, is ambiguous. The thought could have been expressed more clearly and more directly as follows:

> The fact that Mr. Burr has passed the CPA examination is proof of his ability to open a set of books for you.
>
> Mr. Burr has passed the CPA examination and therefore is competent to open a set of books for you.

Correcting the *So* and the *And So* Faults

Another of the polished writer's techniques is to avoid writing sentences in which *so* or *and so* is used to introduce a clause. For instance, note how awkwardly *so* is used in this sentence:

> Ronald Clark has been in our employ for only one month, so we are unable to tell you much about him.

So in this sentence is used to connect a result-giving clause with the reason-giving main clause. Although *so* is an accepted conjunction, hack writers have overworked it and destroyed its usefulness. *Because* is a better choice for relating cause- and result-giving clauses. The following sentence shows how the same thought may be expressed in a more polished fashion:

> We are unable to tell you much about Ronald Clark because he has been in our employ for only one month.

The following sentence shows the *and so* fault:

> Mr. Flynn has had much experience in personnel work, and so we recommend that you talk with him.

In this sentence, *and so* introduces a clause, but *and so* does not appear in any list of conjunctions. The sentence could have been written correctly in either of the following ways:

> Mr. Flynn has had much experience in personnel work; therefore, we recommend that you talk with him.
>
> We recommend that you talk with Mr. Flynn, who has had much experience in personnel work.

ADVANCED BALANCING TECHNIQUES

In Chapter 3, Section 21, part of the presentation focused on parallel structure, the balancing of elements used with coordinate and correlative conjunctions. For example, the sentence limps if you say, "Our portables are light, smooth-running, and won't stain," but it sails smoothly as "Our portables are light, smooth-running, and stainless." Using like elements with conjunctions is an important balancing technique.

The advanced techniques of balance are concerned with the flow and the rhythm of writing. Ideas of equal value must be expressed in parallel constructions. In the following examples, compare the imbalanced sentences with the corrected, balanced versions. Note how thoughts are thrown out of balance because words are omitted.

Balancing Comparisons

Comparisons are balanced only if they are complete, and they can be complete only if they include all the necessary words. The omission of one necessary word can throw a comparison out of balance, as in the example below.

> Research shows that men spend more time looking at window displays than women.

As written, the sentence could mean that men spend more time looking at window displays than they do looking at women—a somewhat doubtful statement. The comparison lacks balance, as well as sense, because an essential word is omitted. One word can make the meaning of the sentence clear.

> Research shows that men spend more time looking at window displays than women *do* (or *spend*).

Here is another imbalanced comparison:

> Mr. Boyd's status in the Elko-Haber Corporation is more than a clerk.

This sentence lacks sense because essential words are omitted. An expert would write:

> Mr. Boyd's status in the Elko-Haber Corporation is more than *that of* a clerk.

An imbalanced comparison like the one below provides a chance for skillful revision.

> Owen can write just as well, if not better, than Allen.

Disregarding the words set off by commas, the sentence reads as follows: *Owen can write just as well than Allen.* Of course, no one would say "as well than." In the following revisions, the first is acceptable, but the expert will write the second, more polished sentence.

Owen can write just as well as, if not better than, Allen.

Owen can write just as well as Allen, if not better.

Balancing Modifiers

Omission of single-word modifiers can destroy balance in several ways. Such an omission can produce, for example, this illogical message:

We need a traveling sales representative and stenographer.

Failure to write "*a* stenographer" makes "a traveling sales representative and stenographer" the same person. Dim, indeed, is the prospect of hiring a person who can serve in the dual capacity of traveling sales representative and of stenographer.

Please get me a black pen, file folder, and envelope.

Since the modifier is not repeated with each member of this series, *a* is the modifier for all three members of the series. However, "*a* envelope" would never be considered polished writing. For balance, the series should read "*a* black pen, *a* file folder, and *an* envelope."

Do you see why the next sentence is out of balance?

Mr. Taylor speaks often of his parents, wife, and children.

The modifier *his* is the correct modifier for all three members of the series and is technically correct; however, a writer with a "feel" for language would repeat the modifier *his* to achieve a fullness and roundness of tone. See how much better the sentence reads this way:

Mr. Taylor speaks often of *his* parents, *his* wife, and *his* children.

Balancing Verbs

Structural balance demands that whenever the parts of verbs in compound constructions are not exactly alike in form, no verb part should be omitted. In the following sentence, this rule has been broken.

I never have, and never will, file a dishonest tax return.

Failure to include the past participle *filed* with the auxiliary *have* causes the meaning to be "I never have file and never will file. . . ." Since the verbs in this compound construction are not exactly alike in form, no verb part should be omitted. The sentence should read:

I never have *filed,* and never will file, a dishonest tax return.

The following sentence shows the same kind of error.

Your check was received yesterday and the garden sets shipped by express.

The omission of the auxiliary verb after *garden sets* structures the sentence like this: "Your check was received, and the garden sets was shipped." The plural noun *garden sets* requires a plural verb; therefore, the sentence must read:

> Your check was received yesterday, and the garden sets *were* shipped by express.

Balancing Prepositions

The omission of a preposition can also throw a sentence off balance. You learned in Section 20 that some words must be followed by specific prepositions. When two prepositional constructions have the same object, you must use, in each construction, the preposition that is idiomatically correct. Failure to supply the correct preposition results in a mismatch; note the following example:

> Office workers should have confidence and respect for their supervisors.

In this illustration, *confidence and respect* is a compound, both parts of which are modified by the prepositional phrase *for their supervisors. For,* then, is the preposition used with both *confidence* and *respect.* But would anyone ever say or write "confidence *for* their supervisors"? The correct preposition to use with *confidence* is *in.* To be balanced, the sentence should read:

> Office workers should have confidence *in* and respect *for* their supervisors.

Balancing Conjunctions

In oral communication, subordinate conjunctions, particularly *that* and *when,* can often be omitted without causing any confusion. In written communications, however, such omissions may destroy the balance of the thought units of a sentence and thus confuse the reader. Read the following example aloud:

> Mr. Williams frequently talks about the time he had neither money nor position.

If this were an oral communication, the speaker could make the meaning clear by pausing slightly after the word *time.* The reader, however, might see the thought unit as "Mr. Williams frequently talks about the time he had," with the result that the words following *had* would not make sense. Therefore, the sentence should be written like this:

> Mr. Williams frequently talks about the time *when* he had neither money nor position.

The following sentence may also be misread:

> We investigated and found the furniture was shipped on May 2.

The reader may see "We investigated and found the furniture" as one thought unit. The subordinate conjunction *that* adds clarity and comprehension to the sentence:

> We investigated and found *that* the furniture was shipped on May 2.

In informal writing, however, subordinate conjunctions may be omitted if their omission will not confuse the reader.

Yes, we do have the book you mentioned.

The omission of *that* in this sentence does not confuse the reader; therefore, the writer may omit the word.

Balancing Clauses

Another mark of writing distinction is to avoid incomplete (elliptical) clauses whenever failure to write the complete clause would confuse the reader. In the sentence "You are a better skier than I," the meaning "than I am" is clear. But listen to this:

Did Mr. Wilson pay the bill or his wife?

This sentence could be interpreted as follows: "Did Mr. Wilson pay the bill, or did he pay his wife?" Both of the following revised sentences make the meaning clear; the second sentence, however, is more polished than the first one.

Did Mr. Wilson pay the bill, or *did* his wife pay it?
Who paid the bill, Mr. Wilson or his wife?

Communication Projects

PRACTICAL APPLICATION

A Some of these sentences contain too many harsh sounds; others, too many similar sounds. Rewrite them.

1. February inflation figures force us to feel that the effectiveness of the tough new price controls was only fancied.
2. A summary of some of his serious misconceptions scarcely seems necessary.
3. The proofreader missed the error; so, "Mr." remained misspelled.
4. Of course, the coarse mesh can stand more force and pressure.
5. Research shows that hodgepodge word usage produces messages that dissolve into unintelligible gibberish.

B Rewrite any sentence that violates an advanced writing technique. Write *OK* for any correct sentence.

1. Unions had an important role in this process and will continue to.
2. I saw the teenagers in trouble were the same ones I had seen earlier.
3. The company cannot afford to buy a computer, so it uses the time-sharing plan offered by Data, Inc.
4. Should Miss Simpson sign the letter or Sally?
5. Ruth ignored the whispered comments, thus proving that she was not going to be distracted.

6. The meeting adjourned without any action taken or decisions made. This was most unsatisfactory to all of us.
7. Laurie invited each guest to bring a friend and record.
8. Miss Winton said that Anne's poster was more original than the other contestants.
9. When we transferred the files, several folders were misplaced. This was not Janet's fault.
10. We all must work on this vital problem—and work, and work, and work!
11. The order was for a box and carton.
12. Our high school burned down my last term.
13. The staff has great admiration and faith in Mr. Lewis.
14. Now that a sane Fourth has become a tradition, we must think about planning for a sane Christmas.
15. We need help with the typing, the checking, and the assembling.
16. After the suit was altered, the customer would not take it nor pay for the alterations.
17. Our product is better, not equivalent, to the best.
18. Miss Clifford never has, and never will, be able to understand the procedure that she should follow.
19. Shall I report for duty next week?
20. The manufacturer was concerned about the high cost of the raw materials that went into his product, so he raised the price of the goods he sold.

C In these sentences, correct any violations in thought-unit construction or in advanced writing techniques. Write *OK* for any correct sentence.

1. He was one of our most trusted leaders, so we expected more of him.
2. Subtracting losses resulting from cost overruns, the net annual profit has dropped sharply.
3. Ed shows more interest in Ellen's project than he does Barry's.
4. He appears nonchalant but all the others nervous.
5. We have bought books at that store ever since they first opened.
6. Compared with the others, Lance seems a paragon of excellence, thus qualifying for the job.
7. They huddled in the wrecked plane, trembling and moaning.
8. Beth understood the blunder she had committed suddenly.
9. Did you order the steak rare or your husband?
10. Any one who works for that company is trained for just one job.
11. Having a broken arm and nose, we returned the statue.
12. The cost of buying the machine would be less than renting it.
13. Mr. Bond told Fred that he would need help to meet the six o'clock deadline.
14. Adam lives in Bronxville, which is a suburb of New York.
15. It stresses in your July 8 letter that check marks must be placed on forms that have been proofread.
16. Did Bob win the game or Steve?
17. Having put the car in the garage for repairs, walking or taking the bus was the only way to get there.
18. Joan was hurt in the accident, but all the others uninjured.
19. George and Harry learned the value of setting goals and working toward them at an early age.
20. That's the good news that I was speaking about.

EDITING PRACTICE

Editing the News Edit and rewrite the following excerpts from news items to be published in a local paper.

1. Some scouts came upon an unknown lake hiking through the woods.
2. The high school drum corps is on its way to the exhibition in a bus.
3. The following article is one in a series written by Peter Bessette, a Mohawk Indian priest for the Evening Standard.
4. The Academy band will give its last concert before taking its annual leave at Jones Field.
5. Mr. Lane became owner of the farm on which young Abe Lincoln helped his father in 1922.

Spelling and Pronunciation Can you find any spelling errors that were probably caused by mispronunciation?

> The pulleys on our Order 675 of May 9 are being returned to you today. Our maintainance supervisor reports that he cannot use these pulleys because they are 4½ inches in width, instead of the 4⅝ size specified on our order. When you bill us for this order, please credit us with $5.68, the shipping charges we paid to return the goods.

CASE PROBLEM

A Better Plan Bill Carpenter keeps the payroll records at the Barrett warehouse. Previously he had performed the same work for the Moore Transfer Company. Bill thought the records at Moore's were set up much better and that the system of keeping records at Barrett's, therefore, should be changed.

1. Should Bill present these ideas to his present employer?
2. How can he do so without being offensive?

33 Writing Power

Writing power is the culmination of writing skills that empowers the writer to influence the thoughts and actions of readers. The writer who has mastered the craft of writing, who has become adept at using all the advanced writing techniques, is the one who will create the most compelling written messages.

In the business world, communications must be attention-getting, logical, interesting, and persuasive to elicit increased profits and increased goodwill. The power of the written word is incalculable. Writing power is a strength everyone in business needs, and it is limited only by the communicator's expertness in applying the guides for developing writing power.

THE MAJOR WEAKNESSES

Two specific pitfalls that weaken communications are using the passive voice instead of the active voice and shifting voice, tense, person, or number. Study the examples in the following paragraphs so that you can easily recognize these writing faults. When you understand how they occur, you will be better able to avoid them.

Active Versus Passive Voice

Voice is that property of a transitive verb that shows whether the subject acts or is acted upon. Any verb phrase composed of a past participle with a "being" verb helper is in the passive voice: *will be shipped, has been sent, was done, is frozen*. In the active voice, the subject is the doer of an action; in the passive voice, the subject is acted upon.

> Gibson sent us a message. (Active voice.)
>
> A message was sent to us by Gibson. (Passive voice.)

The active voice expresses thoughts in a stronger, livelier way than does the passive voice. Compare these two sentences:

> Your order will be shipped on Monday, July 8. (Passive voice.)
>
> We will ship your order on Monday, July 8. (Active voice.)

Both sentences relate the same information, but the second sentence is more direct because it uses the active voice. In the following pair, note that the sentence using the active voice makes a stronger selling point than does the weak passive sentence.

> Last year our machines were sold to 75 out of every 100 business firms in Detroit. (Passive voice.)
>
> Last year, we sold our machines to 75 out of every 100 business firms in Detroit. (Active voice.)

Use the active voice to help strengthen your business communications.

Shifts in Voice, Tense, Person, Number

Whenever a sentence contains two or more clauses or whenever a paragraph contains closely related sentences, the expert writer is careful to see that there is no shift, no variation, in voice, tense, person, or number. Not only is the shift technically incorrect, but more important, it weakens communications.

Shift in Voice When one verb in a compound or a complex sentence is in the active voice, the other verb or verbs must also be in the active voice. Using the active voice in one clause and then shifting to the passive voice in another clause, or vice versa, weakens the communication.

> In winter the file clerks freeze with the cold, and in summer they are stifled with the heat.

The shift from the active voice in the first clause to the passive voice in the second clause diminishes the strength of the statement. Both verbs should be in the active voice, or both verbs should be in the passive voice. Since the active voice is the stronger, the sentence should read:

> In winter the file clerks freeze with the cold, and in summer they stifle with the heat.

Shift in Tense A verb has six principal tenses—present, past, future, and the three "perfects"—each tense showing the time of an action. Writers can make their communications stronger by avoiding a shift in tense unless an actual difference in time must be indicated.

> Edelman uses such simple language that any reader will easily understand his meaning.

This sentence shows a shift in tense, from present tense in the first clause to future tense in the second clause. The statement can be strengthened by avoiding the shift as follows: "Edelman uses such simple language that any reader easily understands his meaning."

Shift in Person A shift in person within a sentence is such a glaring weakness that any reader notices it immediately. For example:

> I should like to know the name of a branch store where you can get service within twenty-four hours.

The first person *I* is the subject of the first clause; the second person *you* is the subject of the second clause. The shift is weak because it is illogical. Why should *I* want to know where *you* can get fast service? The sentence should read:

> I should like to know the name of a branch store where I can get service within twenty-four hours.

Shift in Number A shift in number from singular to plural, or vice versa, weakens a message because this type of shift, like the shift in person, conveys an irrational message.

> A communicator must be well trained, or they will not be able to build goodwill.

Communicator in the first clause is singular in number, but *they*, which refers to *communicator*, is plural in number. To add strength to the sentence by avoiding this shift, you should write:

> Communicators must be well trained, or they will not be able to build goodwill.

SENTENCE AND PARAGRAPH CONTROL

A written communication can be only as strong as its weakest component, for if the sentence structure is faulty, or if the paragraph organization is unwieldy, the entire communication falters and becomes ineffectual. Since the components of the business communication are sentences and paragraphs, the writer must be able to shape them at will so that they perform their assigned tasks successfully. In short, to perform with writing power, the writer must have sentence and paragraph control.

Sentence Control

For the purpose of developing writing power through sentence control, the writer must learn that (1) each sentence must contain only one main thought, and (2) each sentence must be the proper length, neither too long nor too short.

One Main Thought In Chapter 4, Section 22, you learned not to use a comma to join two separate and distinct thoughts. From the viewpoint of writing power, the comma-for-period fault weakens a message because more than one main thought is expressed in a single sentence, such as the following example:

> We are interested in your views on merchandising, we need to do some more research before we can present our own opinions.

The correct punctuation, of course, is a period. However, other alternatives for correcting the comma-for-period fault include (1) using a coordinate conjunction, (2) using a semicolon or a semicolon and a transitional expression, and (3) using a subordinate conjunction to make one of the thoughts dependent on the other. These methods are more advanced techniques than the one of simply writing two separate sentences, and expert use of them produces more effective communications. For example, compare the following revisions of the example given above, and note how the relationship between the two thoughts is clarified in the last three revisions.

> We are interested in your views on merchandising. We need to do some more research before we can present our own opinions.
>
> We are interested in your views on merchandising, but we need to do some more research before we can present our own opinions.
>
> We are interested in your views on merchandising; however, we need to do some more research before we can present our own opinions.
>
> Although we are interested in your views on merchandising, we need to do some more research before we can present our own opinions.

More about the use of transitional expressions is given on page 249, and the proper subordination of thoughts is explained on page 250.

Proper Length An overlong sentence is ineffective and weak because it buries any message it contains. The reader gets lost in its maze of words.

> We were sorry to learn from your letter of March 4 that you failed to receive the February and March issues of THE BANNER; and since it is apparent that the magazines, which were forwarded in the regular course of mailing, bearing your correct name and address, were lost en route, we are glad to supply duplicates.

Whew! Such a spate of words to say that the writer is sorry and will send duplicates. The writer was correct in making the point that the fault was not the publisher's; but this point should have been written as a separate sentence. Study the following revision:

> We were sorry to hear that you did not receive the February and March issues of THE BANNER, and we are glad to supply duplicate copies. The magazines, bearing your correct name and address, evidently were lost en route.

On the other hand, a succession of short sentences weakens writing power because the reader is jerked along from thought to thought.

> We received your letter. It arrived this morning and was most welcome. All the sales representatives read it; they liked your suggestions. Your letters are always friendly. We enjoy hearing from you.

An expert would never write such a stop-and-go, stop-and-go communication. Instead, the expert would smooth out the bumps like this:

> Your welcome letter arrived this morning, and all the sales representatives liked your suggestions. Your letters are always so friendly that we enjoy hearing from you.

In some situations, the planned use of short sentences can be very effective. Short sentences are useful to bring out a series of important facts, to emphasize a point, and to break up a series of longer sentences. The following excerpt from a sales letter illustrates the planned use of short sentences.

> The Eureka camera is made especially for quick-moving action photography. Its motorized film-advancer prepares you for your next shot a fraction of a second after you press the shutter. You just focus and shoot! And its easy-open back permits you to insert a new cartridge faster than you can in any other camera. You can reload in 15 seconds! Best of all, the Eureka is equipped with a computerized flash that works on a rechargeable battery. You have a built-in flash! See your dealer for complete details.

Paragraph Control

The writer who structures the paragraph has control over it and over its direction. Paragraph control is achieved by presenting only one main thought in a paragraph, by avoiding overlong paragraphs, and by moving smoothly from one paragraph to another.

Proper Length In general, a paragraph should not be longer than six to eight lines. If the development of one thought requires more than six to eight lines, the writer should carry that thought over to another paragraph. To help the reader bridge the gap between paragraphs, the writer can make use of the transitional words and expressions listed below.

Smooth Transitions The reader of a polished business communication is carried along by interest in its message, by the rhythm and momentum of its words, and by the seamless transitions between paragraphs. The knowledgeable writer ensures the smooth flow of ideas by using appropriate transitional expressions. Here is a partial list of such expressions:

accordingly	however
after all	in addition
again	likewise
also	meanwhile
at the same time	moreover
besides	nevertheless
consequently	notwithstanding
equally important	on the contrary
for this purpose	on the other hand
further	similarly
furthermore	still
hence	therefore

STRUCTURING FOR EMPHASIS

Written communications are more effective when the writer emphasizes the salient points of the message. Once these points have been determined, the writer's problem is to structure sentences so that the reader, too, recognizes the important part or parts of the communication. What enables a business writer to write forceful and effective messages are the principles of emphasis.

Proper Subordination of Ideas

Proper subordination of ideas depends on the ability to determine the difference between an important idea and a lesser idea. The important thought is expressed as a main clause, and the lesser idea is properly written as a subordinate clause. The principle can be remembered as follows: "Main idea—main clause; subordinate idea—subordinate clause." Consider the following sentence:

> I had just started to write up our bids when your revised specifications arrived.

Which idea is more important, the fact that "I had just started to write up our bids" or the fact that "your revised specifications arrived"? The arrival of the revised specifications is the more important idea; therefore, it should be expressed as the main clause. The sentence should read:

> Your revised specifications arrived just as I started to write up our bids.

Coordination Versus Subordination When a sentence contains two ideas of equal importance, divide the sentence into two main clauses. For example, consider the following:

> The work is difficult, but the rewards are great.

On the other hand, writing power is diluted when the writer fails to see that the thoughts belong, not in two main clauses, but in a main clause and a subordinate clause. Note the following example:

> There were other candidates, and Bruce received the promotion.

This sentence places equal stress on what the writer considers to be two main ideas. The emphasis should properly be placed on Bruce's receiving the promotion, even though there was competition. For force, as well as for clarity, the sentence should be written:

> Although there were other candidates, Bruce received the promotion.

Interrupting Expressions Unwittingly, some writers destroy the forcefulness of proper subordination by writing the lesser idea as an interrupting expression. For instance, read this sentence:

> You are, considering the risks involved in such an investment, very fortunate.

The main thought, *you are very fortunate*, is interrupted by the lesser idea, *considering the risks involved*. This interference with the flow of the main thought is so distracting that the force of the statement is completely lost. Properly written, the sentence reads:

> Considering the risks involved in such an investment, you are very fortunate.

Variety in Sentence Structure

Communications that lack variety lack emphasis. Expert writers vary the structure of their sentences so that some are simple, some compound, some complex. These writers vary their connectives and transitional expressions to create writing that is interesting and forceful. Study this sentence:

> Your car was brought to our repair shop and has been here for two days. We looked it over carefully and found that the trouble was dirt in the carburetor, and we gave it a good cleaning. The car is now ready for you to pick up when you return from your vacation, and we shall be waiting to see you smile when you press the accelerator and hear the smooth hum of the motor.

This communication has no force because the writer uses too many compound sentences and too many *ands*. An expert would write something like this:

> Your car has been in our repair shop for two days. After looking the car over carefully, we found that the trouble was caused by dirt in the carburetor. Naturally, we cleaned the carburetor thoroughly, and now the engine is as good as new. We shall be waiting for you to pick up the car when you return from your vacation. Also, we shall be waiting to see you smile when you press the accelerator and hear the smooth hum of the motor.

Emphasis by Climax

In any series—of words, of phrases, of clauses, or of complete thoughts—you can emphasize the most important member of the series by building the series from the least to the most important member. Study the following illustration:

> The successful executive is industrious, wide-awake, and honest.

The word sequence is carefully planned. To be successful, the executive first of all must be industrious, then wide-awake, and then—most important of all—honest.

Emphasis by Mechanical Aids

Oral communication lends itself to dramatic gestures that emphasize important points. Shouting, pounding on a desk, and stamping a foot are effective only if they are seldom-used devices that contrast with normal conversation. Even changes in tone or pitch—whispering, for example—can be used to create striking emphasis. However, overuse of emphasis can make so much noise, can be so distracting, that the listener cannot hear the words. Thus overemphasis can destroy the message.

Written communication, too, lends itself to ways of emphasizing important points. Because the means are entirely mechanical, the writer must decide what to emphasize—and also the degree of emphasis desired. To emphasize a point, the writer can:

> Underline.
> Tabulate.
> Use dashes or a series of dots.
> Use exclamation points.
> Set words or expressions in all-capital letters.
> Type important words in red (if available on the typewriter ribbon).

If the mechanical means of creating emphasis are used excessively, contrast—and therefore emphasis—is lost. Knowing this, expert writers rely more on writing power than on mechanical devices to shape their thoughts and convey their messages.

THE PRICE OF POWER

Now that you have studied writing power, a word of warning to prevent power failure: Mastery of craftsmanship techniques will not make your writing effective unless you use language that is simple, direct, and clear. The purpose of communication is to convey a message, not to parade an extensive vocabulary.

Although the writings of individual correspondents are sometimes embellished to the point of utter confusion, government letters and publications are generally considered the ultimate in "way-out" communications. This old illustration of government gobbledygook at its worst appeared in the July-August 1964 issue of *Think* magazine.

> The records are crowded with speeches made and letters written as if they had no other purpose than to be incomprehensible. . . . In fact, (one) could do worse than study two communiques about air raid precautions, the first written by an aide to President Franklin D. Roosevelt, and the second written by Roosevelt himself.
>
> The aide's memorandum read: "Such preparations shall be made as will completely obscure all Federal buildings occupied by the Federal Government during an air raid for any period of time from visibility by reason of internal or external illumination. Such obscuration may be obtained either by blackout construction or by termination of illumination. This will, of course, require that in building areas in which production must continue during the blackout, construction must be provided that internal illumination may continue. Other areas may be obscured by terminating the illumination."
>
> A mildly exasperated Roosevelt suggested this revision: "Tell them that in buildings where they have to keep the work going, they should put something across the windows. In buildings where they can afford to let the work stop for a while, they should turn out the lights."

Communication Projects

PRACTICAL APPLICATION

A Rewrite the following items according to the directions given in parentheses.

1. Filing is an essential office activity. It should be done properly. Accurate filing means accurate finding. (Combine into one sentence, with proper subordination.)
2. The defendant is only eighteen years old and has not been proved guilty. (Give major importance to the fact that the defendant has not been proved guilty.)
3. An electronic calculator is a triumph of technology. They were originally large and cumbersome, but today they are small enough to fit in your hand. (Correct any shift in voice, tense, person, or number.)
4. My Spanish is still reasonably fluent; this is my first visit to Mexico in ten years. (Give major importance to the first clause.)

5. I was walking to the parking lot after work, and I heard a loud crash behind me. (Subordinate the less important idea.)
6. When conferring with the caller, the dean told her that college students sometimes take courses they did not like; but study them faithfully, and you will get increased knowledge. (Correct any shift in voice, etc.)
7. Is your car out of commission, and does it need some small repairs? Bring it to us, and we will give it special attention. We are most thorough, and our prices are reasonable. (Rewrite and vary sentence structure.)
8. Miss Leach occupies a commodious office. It is on the seventh floor of our building. This office is very quiet. (Combine into one forceful sentence.)
9. Bill had been warned by Mr. Foley that the excuse would not be accepted again. (Change to active voice.)
10. My plane was late, and I missed my first appointment. (Subordinate the less important idea.)

B Rewrite the following sentences, rewording them to make them more powerful.

1. The accusation having been made by Miss Thompson, she should explain it.
2. Everyone thinks that being successful depends on getting a lucky break.
3. We are all, being convinced that Dave is innocent, more than willing to defend him against those charges.
4. This new microwave oven will be discovered to be the best investment for your new home.
5. Susan's willing attitude was pleasing to her supervisor, and he complimented her on it.
6. The broker saw before him disaster, ruin, and defeat.
7. The customer comes into the store and orders his suit. Afterward, he spent an hour discussing our credit regulations.
8. Our expert mechanic removed pieces of rust from the radiator, and your car is now as good as new.
9. You asked for immediate delivery of the signed contract; nevertheless, we are sending it today by special messenger.
10. Important communications must first be outlined, or it will be ineffective.

C These sentences review the writing techniques presented in Sections 31 and 32. Rewrite all the sentences.

1. We have all been reading and been dismayed by the increasingly serious food shortage.
2. To sell burglar alarms, we found that newspaper ads resulted in more leads than using direct-mail letters.
3. Demand for recreational vehicles will increase yearly, which is the forecast of experts in the travel field.
4. We noticed the reservation was for the wrong date.
5. Totalitarianism has and always will be notorious for its suppression of freedom of the individual.
6. Before buying a dishwasher, the dealer should give a demonstration.
7. Mr. Eads told us that his father died before he was born.
8. Our firm has built a beautiful building on Main Street that is so light and airy.
9. We went trout fishing, but caught only one of them.
10. Office conversation is enjoyed by Jim as much, if not more, than by the other clerks.

D Choose the word that best completes each of the following sentences.

1. The (officious, official) version bears a distinctive logotype on the copyright page.
2. His claim is that (no body, nobody) of employees may represent him without his consent.
3. Infant (morality, mortality) is on the rise because parents neglect to have their children given the necessary immunization shots.
4. The federal government regulates (interstate, intrastate) commerce; (interstate, intrastate) commerce comes under the authority of each state.
5. Our budget for (capitol, capital) expenditure for next year has been cut in half.
6. The land in which we invested is on the (border, boarder) of Lexington and East Jewett.
7. Even though Ms. Forte is out of town, someone should (apprise, appraise) her of these developments.
8. After three days of substituting for John, I am thoroughly (board, bored) with working with figures.
9. Matilda's (ingenuous, ingenious) solution to the perplexing problem was a surprise to all—even to Matilda!
10. A six-foot (partition, petition) separates Harria's office from mine.
11. The findings of the two independently conducted (poles, polls) were exactly opposite!
12. The defense attorney later confided to the reporters her fear that the only (veracious, voracious) witness might not be believed.
13. Please make up your mind—this is no time to (waver, waiver)!
14. The box included (thorough, through) instructions for assembling the model ship.
15. Every time Fred chairs the meeting he (wastes, waists) half an hour with his corny jokes.
16. When I see her (pouring, poring) over her books, I do my best to remain quiet.
17. The committee will, we hope, use our recent report for (reverence, reference).
18. In our haste to (expand, expend) our operations, we overlooked some important economic indicators.
19. Please include a postage-paid return (envelop, envelope) with the letter to Ms. Harcourt.
20. From her remarks, we (implied, inferred) that she will soon choose her assistant.

EDITING PRACTICE

The Correspondence Supervisor Edit and rewrite the following paragraph.

> Just this morning I returned from a vacation in the far west and your letter is receiving priority first to be answered. Yes, we do publish Mr. Haltons book *Have You A Problem Situation?* We are sending you the requested information about this book as well as prices for all other books written for foremen in factories (see the enclosed brochure.) You must be very proud of your in-service training program.

Power Failure The following sentence is an illustration of power failure. How would you have written this message?

> Your anticipatory behavior at the first flash of St. Elmo's fire will be changed when Safety lightning rods are installed on the roof of your domicile.

CASE PROBLEM

Remembering Names How well do you remember names after an introduction? Six of your classmates will select assumed names and will introduce themselves to you. You may ask one question of each as you try to fix the name in your memory. Then, using their pseudonyms, introduce each student to another student.

CHAPTER 6

CREATIVE BUSINESS WRITING

34 The Psychology of Business Writing

"What's in it for me?" is our reflex response to any number of suggestions, proposals, plans, and requests. Psychologists consider this a "normal" response, as basic as our instinct for self-preservation. If the answer to "What's in it for me?" is favorable, then—and only then—do we act to comply with the proposal or request.

In business, as in other areas, we can capitalize on this psychological principle by learning to provide a built-in affirmative answer whenever we elicit "What's in it for me?" For example, the advertising copywriter who plays up the vitality and charm of milk drinkers, overlooking the numerous calories in every glass of milk, is making a sales pitch *and* supplying the consumer with a favorable answer to that automatic "What's in it for me?" question.

Understanding that this psychological principle is observed in successful business writing, as well as in selling and advertising, should help you write better letters. The more you learn and understand about human behavior, the more effective will your business writing become.

In the remaining sections of this textbook, you will study the various types of business writing. In this section, you will learn basic principles which, when applied, will lend a master touch to every bit of writing you will ever do. Your success as a writer, then, will be enhanced by your study of the following topics.

"WHAT'S IN IT FOR ME?"

You will be able to supply built-in answers to this question if you know and understand the areas of self-interest discussed in this section.

Financial Gain

Increasing Income Most people who work for a living are interested in earning more money. Therefore, if what you propose to a client or customer is a money-making opportunity, emphasize that in your letter. For example, if your business is selling stocks or mutual funds, you might include in your sales letter a sentence or two that will provoke action. Clients reading the following would not be likely to resist such a great "track record."

> If in 1970 you had invested $5,000 in Probity Capital, your investment would today be worth $10,230—more than double your money! (The figures, of course, must actually be true.)

Making Money by Saving Money Business people are aware that they can make money by saving money; for example, in some cases they can take advantage of special discounts and thereby save money. In writing, you should always emphasize that *you* are offering this special discount, that *you* are saving money for the reader. For example:

> Take advantage of our special discount terms, and you will realize savings that will boost your profit.

In other instances, your readers might not realize how much they could save by acting favorably on the subject of your letter. Therefore, you should tell them in simple, direct, and forceful terms. For instance, if you want to sell an office machine, the financial-gain incentive might be:

> The GAIN-110 computer will reduce payroll preparation time by as much as 40 percent—a significant cut in your personnel costs.

Quoting Dollars and Cents Whenever you quote amounts of money, use your knowledge of psychology. If the figures you quote mean income for the reader, present them in the largest possible amount; if the reader is being asked to pay out money, quote them in the smallest amount. For instance, suppose that you write for a real estate firm and one of your listings is a six-apartment building, each apartment renting at $200 a month. The figures you quote in promotional pamphlets, newspaper ads, or letters should be presented like this:

> Your yearly income from this property will be a comfortable $14,400. (*Not* "Each apartment will bring you an income of $200 a month.")

However, when you quote figures on mortgage *payments* for this building, you should quote the lowest terms possible.

> The amount remaining after the down payment can be financed by a 30-year conventional mortgage that will cost you only $188.73 a month.

Health and Security

Health and security are major concerns of most people, and buying incentives that are based on these concerns appeal to people's instincts for self-preservation.

Advertisements for many products—in particular, for medicines—appeal to a common desire to preserve and to promote our own good health. Therefore, be alert for opportunities to use this incentive in your writing. If, for instance, you are promoting the sale of a dishwasher, you should stress facts that relate to good health, such as:

> Your dishes, glasses, and silverware will be germ-free, because the final cycle makes them hospital-sterile (as proved by actual laboratory tests).

An appeal to people's desire for security can also be a part of your promotion efforts. Suppose, for example, you are promoting a new car, the Puma, and can emphasize any one of several buying incentives. Knowing the importance of the security motivation, however, you would emphasize that factor in your promotional material. Your letter or ad might then read:

> You and your family will be safe in a Puma. Merely press a button on the dash, and all doors will immediately lock. You need not fear that a child will fall out, nor need you fear that anyone from the outside can reach the occupants of your car.

Personal Comfort

Another facet of human behavior is the innate and universal desire for comfort and beauty in daily living, both at home and at work. For some letters, then, the built-in answer to "What's in it for me?" will be "more comfort," "more beauty," or "more relaxation." The spur to action here is a deliberate appeal to the senses, the emotions.

You can undoubtedly think of many goods or services that can be sold by using this approach. For example, the following sentence could be used to promote the sale of mattresses:

> Each morning you will wake up rested and refreshed, ready for a productive and happy day.

Here is an illustration of the appeal to the comfort incentive, as applied to a business situation:

> The comfort of this Executive Chair will see you pleasantly through the entire working day—no aches, no pains, no three-o'clock fatigue.

Comfort sometimes results from making the work load easier and quicker. For instance, consider how these picture-making sentences could motivate a homeowner to buy a minitractor:

> In summer, your TuffJob tractor will mow your lawn for you quickly and evenly, freeing your weekends for poolside fun. In winter, your TuffJob tractor will shovel your snow away effortlessly and return you to your fireplace in minutes.

THE DRIVE FOR PERSONAL RECOGNITION

Like the instinct for self-preservation, the drive for personal recognition is universal. This drive may be partially satisfied by acquiring possessions that society recognizes as status symbols, such as a car, a beautiful home, or expensive clothes.

Within each of us, then, is the "me," yearning to be recognized and properly acknowledged—whether you call it ego or soul or the dignity of self. It is essential that the business writer understand that the need for recognition is universal, for writing success is largely dependent on how well the writer can sustain the reader's sense of self-importance. Study the guidelines presented in the following paragraphs.

Focusing on the Readers

Cater to your readers' egos by emphasizing that your readers are your first concern. You can safely assume that your readers will agree that they are of primary importance—both to themselves and to you. Therefore, slant your communications so that they will have a *you* flavor, not an *I* or a *we* approach. Compare the following illustrations of *we* and *you* approaches.

> **We:** Please send us your check for $16.89, so that we may balance our books.
>
> **You:** Your check for $16.89 will balance your account and will maintain your fine credit standing.

We: We know from experience that our Airflo oil burner is not only a great timesaver but also a moneysaver as well.

You: You will be delighted with the saving afforded you by the Airflo—a saving in both time and money.

We: We are firmly of the belief that . . . .

You: You will undoubtedly agree that . . . .

We: The timely articles that we print in *Tomorrow* are chosen to attract intelligent, interested readers.

You: Research shows that you are the kind of intelligent, interested reader who will be attracted by the timely articles in *Tomorrow*.

Using the Readers' Names

Our names are extremely important to us because they mark each of us as an individual, set each of us apart from the rest of humanity, and gain for us the personal recognition we seek. To avoid detracting from the importance of each reader's "me," the knowledgeable writer will be sure to spell all readers' names correctly.

When you use the addressee's name in the body of a letter, you confirm that person's importance. In the following illustration, note how the use of direct address warms and personalizes the message of the letter.

> Answering your inquiry has been a pleasure, Miss Roberts. I hope you will always feel free to call on me whenever you think I can be of help.

Because it is *her* name, *her* claim to personal recognition, the sight of that name gives Miss Roberts satisfaction and pleasure. However, do not use the reader's name more than once in the body of any letter. If you fail to heed this warning, your letters will give the impression of fawning on the reader.

Being Courteous

Writing courteous letters is a "must" for the business communicator. Although readers may not always notice how polite you are, they would certainly notice it if you failed in so simple a matter as saying "please" and "thank you." Your courtesy should make each reader feel important and respected.

Answering Letters Promptly

Everyone resents being made to wait. Having to wait makes us feel that we are considered unimportant. Therefore, don't risk arousing resentment by not answering your correspondence promptly. You should make every effort to answer letters within twenty-four hours after receiving them.

Of course, some letters cannot be answered immediately. You might need time to look up the facts upon which your reply will be based; you might have been away from the office when the letter arrived. In such cases, be sure to let the correspondent know that the delay was unavoidable. For example, you might write an explanation like the following sentence:

> The price list requested in your May 9 letter came off the press this morning, and you will find it enclosed with this letter.

When you receive an angry letter from a customer, however, the best thing is to delay answering the letter until you no longer feel like writing an angry reply. Or write the letter, get it out of your system, and then tear it up. Suppose, for example, you had written a letter questioning a customer's deduction of shipping charges. You then receive a caustic, rude reply telling you that you had already agreed to this deduction. In the heat of anger, you might reply as follows:

> All right, so we made a mistake, but you don't have to get nasty about it.

But if you give yourself a cooling-off period, your letter might read:

> Thank you very much for your letter of June 17, in which you explain the deduction of $13.87 from our May 31 statement. Your account now shows no balance due.
>
> We are sorry that we did not record the fact that the May 15 shipment was to be sent prepaid. You may rest assured that we will make every effort to prevent any such incident in the future.

Using Status Appeal

You have learned that the drive for personal recognition can sometimes be satisfied by attaining status—by owning something or doing something that the general public will notice and will perhaps admire or envy. The appeal to everyone's desire for status is a standard sales "persuader"; this appeal may be either the main selling point or a strong supporting one. Whenever you see a sentence like the following, you will know that the writer is appealing to your desire for status.

> Be the first in your neighborhood to enclose your property with an artistic Colonial picket fence.

However, the letters you will be writing will be on a variety of topics and for different purposes; you will not be writing sales letters only. Now that you know the strength of an appeal to the desire for status, you will use that appeal whenever it lends itself to any type of writing. Suppose, for example, that you are writing an announcement of the reopening of the Mayfair restaurant. You would naturally stress the delicious food, the comfort and luxury of the new furnishings, and possibly the reasonable prices. You might also add a sentence like this:

> You will feel very much at home in the restful elegance and distinctive atmosphere of the new Mayfair.

MAKING AND KEEPING FRIENDS

To be successful, a business must have customers. Building a large following of customers, however, involves an intangible known as goodwill, good public relations, or simply making and keeping friends. It is this intangible, the psychological factor, that motivates customers to do business with one particular company, rather than with its competitors.

Generally, you can make friends for your firm by writing communications that would give *you* pleasure and satisfaction were you to receive them. The actual writing of such communications, however, depends on your knowledge and your use of the specific guidelines explained in the following paragraphs.

Using a Conversational Tone

Suppose you went to a store to make a purchase and the clerk, who was waiting on another customer, looked at you and said, "Your entrance has been duly noted, and careful attention will be accorded you within a few minutes." Wouldn't you wonder how that person ever got a job? Yet some business writers make the mistake of sending letters just as stilted and old-fashioned.

The result-getting writer uses a conversational tone that talks *to,* not *at,* the reader. In the illustrations below, note the difference between the *talking at* and the *talking to* approaches.

> **At:** Please reply at your earliest convenience.
>
> **To:** You will be doing us a real favor by sending this information soon.
>
> **At:** Please mark your reply for the attention of the writer.
>
> **To:** If you mark your reply for my attention, we'll be able to give you quicker service.

Being Cordial and Pleasant

Stop for a moment and think—are you drawn to people who are pleasant, who meet you more than halfway, who *show* that they are happy to be with you? "Yes," you say. "Of course." Your letters, too, can evoke friendly feelings if their wording draws readers to you and your firm.

For an example of what can be done to make a message pleasant and cordial, study the following alternate illustrations.

> Your application for charge-account privileges has been cleared, and your charge plate is enclosed.

Although the message is perfectly clear and is slanted toward the reader, it lacks a cordial tone. Compare it with this revision of the same message.

> Welcome to the ranks of Blanton charge-account friends! Your charge plate is enclosed. We are looking forward to your visiting us often.

Showing Concern for the Customer

As a business communicator you may write to hundreds of customers; thus you will need special skill in conveying the impression that each reader is important to you. If you have this skill, you can excel in the competition for customers.

Business communications of a social nature—letters of appreciation, of congratulation, of sympathy—usually reflect the writer's interest in individuals. The wide-awake correspondent makes use of every opportunity to write letters that express a concern for the customer.

Even when writing letters strictly for business, an expert recognizes possibilities of wording them in a way that shows interest in the reader's affairs.

Study the following pairs of sentences and note how the second version of each turns an ordinary communication into a message that shows interest in and concern for the reader.

1. In answer to your letter of May 4, the sale of children's socks can be increased by displaying them in the shoe department as well as in the children's department.
2. When we read your May 4 letter, we could see that you do indeed have a problem; but we think we can help you solve it. (The letter goes on with the suggestion made in the first example.)

1. We are sending you a list of the special discounts we are prepared to offer you on goods purchased for your August sale.
2. Knowing that your August sale is the big event of your business year, we are sending you well ahead of time a list of special discounts on goods that can be purchased for that sale.

Being Helpful

A writer who is quick to extend a helping hand, whether or not the firm will derive any profit from it, is earning dividends in goodwill and friendship. If your readers benefit from the extra time and effort you have voluntarily spent on their behalf, you are winning—for yourself and for your company—steadfast and permanent friends. The following illustration shows how a request for information might be handled by an untrained writer, by an average writer, and by a master writer.

Untrained: We are sorry to inform you that we do not carry tile flooring.

Average: Our company does not sell tile flooring, but the information you request can be furnished by Pratt & White.

Master: Our company does not sell tile flooring; but we have made inquiries and have learned that you can obtain the information you need by writing to Pratt & White, 75 Broad Street, Dart, Ohio 05725.

Keeping Friends

All business writers know that their letters must have the overall purpose of making friends. However, a fact not so generally recognized is that keeping old friends is just as important as making new ones. It could hardly be considered profitable to gain a new customer if, at the same time, you lose a faithful, steady customer.

All the psychological factors discussed here apply to letters written to customers already on your books, but the real secret of keeping friends is to *tell* them occasionally how much you appreciate them and how important they are to you. The way to keep your customers is not by lavishly flattering them, but by using sincere expressions such as these:

Doing business with you, Miss Flanagan, is always a pleasure.

Our long-time friendship is a source of great satisfaction.

We appreciate your friendship, and we are glad that you feel free to call on us for help.

Without good friends like you, Mr. Frome, our business could not prosper.

Communication Projects

PRACTICAL APPLICATION

A Read this letter and list the sales principles applied by the writer.

Dear Mrs. Carlson:

You will soon receive your set of beautiful Pilgrim cookware. We believe that when you see this fine ovenproof ware, you will be pleasantly surprised.

Since the Quartette assortment you ordered is no longer available, we have substituted the Homemaker set. This set contains all four pieces you ordered plus two more pieces—a 9- by 13-inch baking dish and a 10-inch pie plate. Rather than disappoint you, we have sent you the more expensive Homemaker set at no extra cost to you!

We are sure you will enjoy using your new Pilgrim set, and we wish you all the pleasures of serving fine food—with pride.

Cordially yours,

B Rewrite the following sentences with a *you* point of view.

1. We need to know immediately the arrival time of your group before we can reserve a block of rooms.
2. We believe our Accent line of stainless steel cookware can be sold at a good profit.
3. We stress that our pickup trucks are both dependable to drive and economical to service.
4. As soon as we refinish the desk you left with us, we will mail you a notice.
5. We are pleased to include you among the suppliers invited to an open house to view our new research and testing lab.
6. We think you can cut your price on china and still make a fair profit.
7. We wish to announce that for the month of May we are offering a 10 percent discount on all our dining room furniture.
8. Quickwit products are superior to the products of our competitors.
9. We think that our beautiful city is an ideal vacation spot.
10. Our sale next Tuesday will offer bargains to charge-account customers.

C Reword the following messages to give them a conversational tone.

1. Requirements for sending orders are listed on page 113, together with an order blank.
2. This special closeout-sale catalog lists many bargains for the customer who appreciates saving money.
3. A complete price list will be sent, upon request, to any qualified dealer.
4. We appreciate your efforts on our behalf more than we can say.
5. The patronage of our customers is an important factor in our success.
6. Please be assured that your complaint will receive a thorough investigation.
7. Assembly instructions can be obtained by sending your request to the manufacturer.
8. Charge-account privileges are extended only after credit references have been reviewed.
9. Interest in our endeavors is always appreciated.
10. Keep in mind the fact that our advertising rates will be increased starting January 1.

D Here is the opening sentence of a form letter sent by a mail-order catalog firm to customers who have not ordered for the past year. How would you rewrite the sentence?

> Our records indicate that we have not received any orders from you for some months.

EDITING PRACTICE

Plurals and Possessives Indicate the correct plural or possessive forms of the words enclosed in parentheses.

1. The (alto) voices were too loud for good musical balance.
2. All (ellipsis) in these sentences must be listed on your paper.
3. The (Stewart) office building was sold last week.
4. Have the (Perry) decided to move their factory equipment to Idaho?
5. The principal item of exchange after Christmas is (men) ties.
6. Do you think that the (Fritz) should be accorded credit privileges?
7. We are so proud of our drum (corps) performance in the competition!
8. How many (cupful) of coffee do you drink at lunch?
9. We are sorry that we cannot give you a three (month) extension of credit.
10. Mr. McKenna shot two (moose) while on his hunting trip.
11. The sale will be held at (Harvey & Manning) store.
12. We went for a ride in the (Jones) new sports car.
13. Mr. Williams gave his three (son-in-law) stocks for Christmas.
14. Several (passerby) stopped to look in the window.
15. The store manager spent the day listening to (customer) complaints.

Spelling Pitfalls This paragraph contains some of the words most frequently misspelled in business writing. Test your own spelling ability by making any needed corrections.

> We consider it a privilege to recommend William Keogh for the position of administrator of your hospital. Mr. Keogh has just completed his ninth year with us, and we believe that our growth and development during those years are due largely to his brilliance and hard work. Although we will find him difficult to replace, we realize that our operation is too small to challenge a man of his capabilities. Any institution or firm lucky enough to obtain William Keogh's services is to be congratulated.

CASE PROBLEM

A Compounded Error Dorothy Cary typed a stencil, proofread it quickly, and ran off a thousand copies. Then Dorothy spotted it—a misspelled word on each of the thousand copies. This material should not be mailed, should it? But what about all the paper and time lost?

1. Should Dorothy say anything about the error or let the material be sent without mentioning it?
2. If she decides to say something, what should she say to her boss?

35 Planning for Effective Writing

If you were participating in a seminar on the principles of administering a successful business operation, you would expect that planning and organizing would certainly be discussed. You would be right, because the success of any venture, business or personal, depends in large measure on good planning and organizational know-how.

Written communications are an essential part of business operations. Every year, business correspondents write the equivalent of 300 letters for every man, woman, and child in the United States and Canada. This figure does not include the millions of direct-mail advertising pieces, nor does it include the millions of interoffice memorandums and reports.

In your role as a business writer, in order to promote the success of your employer's operations—and your own personal advancement too—you will need the planning and organizing skills upon which success largely depends. The purpose of this section of your textbook is to equip you with these skills.

THE MECHANICS OF PLANNING

Writing business communications is not a "soft" job that involves merely sitting down and dashing off a few words. Before experts do any writing at all, they get organized. They know *why* they are writing, *what* they are going to write, and *how* they can make their writing most effective.

Determining Your Purpose

If you didn't have a reason for writing, you wouldn't write. Therefore, every letter you write must have a purpose, and before you consider anything else, you must ask yourself, "Why am I writing this letter?" Experienced writers can mentally answer that question, but beginners should jot it down and keep it in view while plotting a course of action. For instance, a beginner might make notations like the following:

Get credit information from Dunn about Dart, Inc.
Ask for bid on 500 reams of duplicating paper.
Allow 30 days' credit, instead of the 90 requested.
Answer inquiry about our Executive line of office furniture.
Refuse Grossman extra credit.
Request quote on 2,000 tons of ¾-inch tubular stock.

Assembling the Information

Once you have defined the purpose of your letter, your next step is to assemble the facts and any information that will enable you to write a letter that is clear, correct, and complete. If you omit this step in the letter-planning process, you may have to go through the extra step of writing again, this time in response to questions about your omissions. Don't let that happen.

For example, suppose you are writing to ask for a bid on 500 reams of duplicating paper. This type of communication is generally considered routine and would probably be assigned to a beginning writer. You write the following:

> Please quote us your best price on 500 reams of duplicating paper.

Obviously, the manufacturer will need more information before attempting to quote a price. To save the manufacturer's time—and yours—write the needed details in your first letter, not your second. To be sure that your letter will be clear, correct, and complete, jot down the points you wish to make, possibly like this:

Request bid. (1)
Ask for prompt reply. (6)
Delivery to be staggered—100 reams each month for 5 months. (5)
Specify that paper is for *ink* duplicator. (2)
20-lb. weight. (4)
8½" x 11" size. (3)

Orderly Presentation The above notations cover the information you need, but you jotted them down as they occurred to you. If you were to write the letter in the order in which you made the notes, you would not convey a very clear message.

Consequently, the final step in assembling the information you want to relay is to number your notes in the order that would make for a logical presentation. (This step is illustrated by the numbers in parentheses following the items listed above.)

Visiting by Mail

You now know *why* you are writing and *what* you will say, but *how* you say it depends on planning and organizing the material so that the communication flows smoothly from start to finish. To insure a smooth flow, a writer must work from an outline.

There is, however, no need to outline separately every letter you write, because you can form a broad, ready-made outline by comparing a letter to a visit by mail. If you were to call on your reader in person, your procedure would be as follows:

1. Greeting: "Good morning, Mr. Gray."
2. Purpose of the call: "Miss Robinson asked me to drop in and talk with you about . . . ."
3. Business of the call: Introduce the specifics you have come to discuss.
4. Leave-taking: "Good-bye, Mr. Gray, and thank you for giving me your time."

This procedure is the outline for a personal visit. It could also be the outline for a visit by mail.

Greeting The salutation is the greeting of a letter. If the letter is written to an individual, the salutation should be *Dear Mr. Bond* or *Dear Mrs. Baker,* not the cold *Dear Sir* or *Dear Madam. Gentlemen* or *Mesdames* is the salutation used in a letter to a company.

Purpose of the Visit When making a personal visit, you follow the greeting with a statement of the purpose of the call. Similarly, after the salutation, the opening paragraph of a letter tells the reader what will be discussed in the letter. Here are three examples of opening paragraphs that state the purpose of the call:

> We were pleased to learn from your letter of June 18 that you are interested in knowing more about our Executive line of office furniture.
>
> We think there must be some misunderstanding about terms quoted for our Order 867, placed on July 6.
>
> We are considering the purchase of a building that could be used as a warehouse, and we would like information about your listings.

Business of the Call This is the "meat" of your call, the place for your message. For instance, if you were writing that letter ordering 500 reams of duplicating paper, here is where you would make the orderly presentation of the notes you jotted down.

Leave-Taking Sometimes a letter has another paragraph that becomes a part of the leave-taking. Consider the following examples:

> We know that, as usual, you will ship promptly.
>
> Thank you for giving us an opportunity to explain the apparent discrepancy in your May 31 statement.
>
> We are looking forward to filling many more of your orders.

If you plan to use a final paragraph, there are two pitfalls to avoid. First, never use a participial closing, an *ing* expression, such as *Wishing you the best of luck in your new venture, we are . . .* or *Looking forward to seeing you at the conference, I am . . . .* Instead, simply write, *We wish you the best of luck in your new venture. Or, I am looking forward to seeing you at the conference.* Second, never offer thanks in advance. To do so would be presumptuous. Express gratitude for a favor or a service when you can acknowledge it, not before.

In all letters, the complimentary closing completes the leave-taking and affords the writer a last chance to set the tone of the communication. The choice ranges from the cold *Very truly yours* to the warm *Cordially.* An incongruous closing can be confusing, as shown in the following examples:

> Unless we receive your check by March 15, we will turn your account over to a collection agency.
>
> Cordially yours,

> We are looking forward with much pleasure to having you and Mrs. Cole with us at our anniversary banquet.
>
> Very truly yours,

IMPLEMENTING THE MECHANICS

Although a mastery of the mechanics of planning is necessary for effective business writing, it takes us only so far. If we stopped there, our letters would be routine, dull, and ineffective. We need additional training to implement these mechanics; consequently, those special skills are presented in the following discussion.

Atmosphere Effect

All of us have had the experience of meeting someone and immediately responding with a judgment like "I'll bet he's smart" or, on the other hand, "Oh, what a bore!" If asked the reasons for our judgment, we probably couldn't offer any. We know only that something about that person registered an impression and we cannot reason it away. For want of a better term, we might call it the "atmosphere effect."

Let's see if we can make impressions, or atmosphere effect, work for us in our business writing, so that our readers will think, "I'd like to do business (or I like doing business) with this company."

First Impression The reader's first impression on opening a letter might be "a quality firm," "a very ordinary company," or even "a shoddy operation." To create a desirable atmosphere effect, the stationery must be of good quality, the letterhead design attractive, the typing imprint uniform, the right-hand margin even, and the erasures not discernible.

Further Acquaintance After registering the first impression created by your letter, the reader looks for confirmation. Correct and polished grammar, spelling, punctuation, word usage—all these are needed to solidify the "quality firm" first impression. Avoid using clichés like *attached hereto, the writer, under separate cover*; otherwise, the atmosphere effect of your letter would be that of a stale, unprogressive business operation.

Paragraph Length Paragraph length is a key factor in creating a good first impression. However, the length of paragraphs in a letter is so important to atmosphere effect that it merits special treatment (Section 33).

As you plan your letter, remember that reading can be *hard work*. You do not want your reader to open your letter, see a densely packed page, and think "What a job to wade through this!"

If you are a trained writer, your readers won't have to wade through the communications you write. Your paragraphs will not exceed eight lines. Writing more than eight lines will not be necessary if, after you have written five or six lines, you are alert to a shift in thought that would justify starting a new paragraph.

An added advantage is your command of the transitional words and phrases presented in Section 33. These expressions enable you to carry your reader smoothly from sentence to sentence and from paragraph to paragraph. For instance, where would you "break" the following overlong paragraph and how would you edit it for smoothness?

> We are sorry to hear that you have had some difficulty with the heating system we installed for you in July. We are glad that you took the time to tell us your story. You know that we guarantee our work for one year, but you may not know how eager we are to see that you get maximum comfort and satisfaction from your new heating system. You may not know that sometimes a newly installed heating system needs a minor adjustment. Our heating engineer, Mr. John J. Nolan, will call at your house at 9 a.m. on Monday, October 3. He will very quickly make the minor adjustment your heating system evidently needs.

There are various editing possibilities for this paragraph, but one revision might go like this:

> We are sorry to hear that you have had some difficulty with the heating system we installed for you in July. However, we are glad that you took the time to tell us your story.
>
> You know, of course, that we guarantee our work for one year, but you may not know how eager we are to see that you get maximum comfort and satisfaction from your new heating system. Also, you may not know that sometimes a newly installed heating system requires a minor adjustment.
>
> Our heating engineer, Mr. John J. Nolan, will call at your house at 9 a.m. on Monday, October 3. He will very quickly make the minor adjustment your new heater evidently needs.

Now that you know why you should not write long paragraphs, be careful not to overcompensate and create letters full of short, choppy paragraphs, like the following letter:

> We'd like your best price on 500 reams of paper for ink duplicating.
>
> The size is 8½" x 11". The weight is 20 lbs.
>
> Delivery is to be staggered as follows: 100 reams on the first of each month for five consecutive months.
>
> We must have your bid by Friday, July 9.

Unquestionably, the paragraphs are short; in fact, they are so short that the reader gets quite a bumpy ride. With minor changes, the writer could have written the letter as follows:

> Please quote us your best price on 500 reams of paper for *ink* duplicating—size, 8½" x 11"; weight, 20 lbs.
>
> Because of a storage problem, delivery must be staggered as follows: 100 reams on the first of each month for five consecutive months.
>
> We would appreciate receiving your bid by Friday, July 9.

Facilitating Action

Would you agree that most of us have a tendency to do immediately the tasks that are easy and to put off those that will take time and effort? And would you also agree that making it easy for a person to act will increase your chances of getting a favorable and a prompt response? Here are some devices for facilitating action that will enable you to get better and quicker results from your letters.

Courtesy Carbon A courtesy carbon is a duplicate that is sent with the original copy of a letter. This device is effective when the reader can reply by writing answers in the margin of the carbon. The reason for its effectiveness is that the reader is relieved of the chore of planning and composing a reply.

For example, suppose you are president of a statewide photography association and are writing to give one of your colleagues a choice of dates for the annual meeting and to ask for recommendations for a speaker for that meeting. If you send a courtesy carbon, your colleague can answer your letter by writing in the margin *January 21* and *Dr. Crouch, Professor of Graphic Arts Technology at City College.* What do you think are the odds that you will get a quick answer?

When you assemble information for a letter that will be accompanied by a courtesy carbon, one of your notes should be *Call attention to courtesy carbon.* When you are composing that letter, be sure that you convey to the reader the no-work-involved idea. For example, say something like this:

> Just jot your comments in the margin of the enclosed carbon and drop it into the mail.

Enclosed Card or Return Slip Another method of obtaining a favorable and quick response is to enclose a card or a return slip with the letter. Suppose your firm, Universal Products, is planning a drive for new customers. A mailing list has been purchased; all high-level decisions have been made; and you are writing the promotional material that offers each reader a free copy of the latest edition of your special-discount catalog. You know that a self-addressed return card will be enclosed and that the company will pay for the postage.

The psychological motivation for your letter will be financial gain—making money by saving money—and the spur to action will be a final paragraph such as this:

> You will start to save money just as soon as you fill out and return the enclosed card. No postage is necessary.

Preparing copy for the return card is also part of your job, and even here you can promote action by your choice of words; for example, *money-saving,* rather than *special discount.*

Universal Products
147 State Street
Bath, Maine 04530

Gentlemen:

Please send the latest edition of your money-saving catalog to:

Name ______________________________

Street ______________________________

City ______________ State ______________ ZIP ______________

Attached Perforated Form Still another means of facilitating action is to use a perforated return form that can be detached from the letter. This method can be just as effective as a separately enclosed slip.

When you write this type of letter, be sure to include a paragraph that calls attention to the form. For instance:

> To renew your subscription—and to receive a bonus of six free issues!—fill in the form at the bottom of this page, tear it off, and mail it *today.*

Watch That *If!* Whenever people are given a choice of doing or not doing, they will very probably choose not to do. Therefore, never give your readers a choice of acting or not acting. Always assume confidently that they will act—and act favorably.

If is the word that indicates a choice; and *if* is the word to watch. Perhaps we can best illustrate this bit of psychology by rewording the last two examples.

> If you would like to receive the latest edition of our money-saving catalog, just fill out and return the enclosed card. No postage is necessary.
>
> If you wish to renew your subscription—and win the bonus of six free issues!—fill in the form at the bottom of this page, tear it off, and mail it *today.*

The *if* in each of these examples suggests to your readers that they might *not* like to receive or wish to renew—and the chances are that they will go along with the *not.* Be aware that the *if* in each of these paragraphs is the word that risks losing the order.

Rereading Your Letters

Many employees never climb from the bottom of the salary heap because they do not add extra polish to the work they do. There is no future for people whose philosophy is "That's good enough."

A business writer's extra polish is the final check of each communication. After you finish your letter-writing stint for the day, reread the letters as if they were addressed to you, not sent by you. From this fresh and different viewpoint, you should be able to spot any errors you have made, either in language or in psychology. And although you may regret the additional time and effort involved in making a final check, your intelligence tells you that only by so doing can you produce a top-notch job.

Communication Projects

PRACTICAL APPLICATION

A You are writing to a customer who has inquired whether your store, Marston's, carries all-wool blankets, twin-bed size, and if so, what colors are available.

You have jotted the following notes; now number them in the order you should present them in your letter.

Twin size ok
All-wool no longer available
Excellent part-wool, part Orlon, $14.95 each, twin size
Choice of colors: rose, blue, green, yellow
Fast delivery
Use order slip at foot of letter

B Using notes you have just arranged, write the letter.

C You have been assigned to write a form letter to be sent to cash customers to induce them to open charge accounts. Using the following properly arranged notes, write the letter.

Invitation to open charge account
List advantages:
1. Need not carry large sums of money when shopping
2. Merchandise needed now can be purchased now—no waiting
3. No finance charge if balance paid in 30 days
4. No red tape or delay on exchanges or adjustments

Final paragraph designed to win friends

D Choose two business situations in which the use of a courtesy carbon would be an effective device for facilitating action on a letter. Give reasons for your choices. Also, discuss two situations in which an enclosed card would promote action.

EDITING PRACTICE

Editing for Redundancies Edit and rewrite the sentences below, and eliminate all unnecessary repetitions.

1. Perishables depreciate in value very quickly.
2. We are glad to hear of the final completion of Order 845.
3. Payment of bills within ten days is the customary practice of our firm.
4. My boss rarely ever travels by air.
5. I do not remember of telling Bill to file the letter under *state of.*
6. Please bring with you notebook, pen, eraser, and etc.
7. Before it can be cashed, every check must be endorsed on the back.
8. Bruce may perhaps be able to solve your communication problem.
9. Since the original order has been lost, please resubmit an order for the same quantity again.
10. Please write to Miss Simpson and thank her for her very unique design of our new package.

Making the Headlines You work for the editor of a daily newspaper, and you are responsible for writing and revising headlines. How would you rewrite the following?

STUDENTS REEK HAVOC AT GAME
OPERATION ON TRAIN SAVES MAN'S LIFE

CASE PROBLEM

A Personal Matter Roberta Greene is busy typing a report for her supervisor when she receives a telephone call from her friend, Ruth Evans. Ruth wishes to find out about a dance that is being planned by their sorority. Roberta knows that Ruth is on her first job and may not realize that personal calls during office hours are not looked on with favor by management.

1. What should Roberta say to Ruth?
2. Why are personal calls usually taboo during office hours?

CHAPTER

WRITING BUSINESS LETTERS

36 Style in Business Letter Writing

What do we mean when we talk about *style*? We use the word to express many different things, in many different contexts, but the underlying flavor of the word remains "a certain quality." You are familiar with remarks like "Her painting has a special style," or "It is a deceptively simple style of writing," or "That is a typically French style of cooking." In each of these examples, "style" means a distinctive or a characteristic manner and refers either to appearance or method.

Since the success of a business depends largely upon its written communications with the public, the style of those communications is of paramount importance. The reader's first impression of any business communication is visual; before reading the message, the reader reacts to its appearance. Often this first impression so influences the reader that it affects the kind of reception the message will receive. For this reason, the mechanics of preparing a business letter—or any other kind of business communication—must be carefully adhered to. The writer's first aim is to make the communication so attractive that the recipient will want to read the message. Then, once the reader's interest is engaged, the message itself must hold the reader's interest.

The principles of developing a style of writing that is pleasant and interesting and the mechanical aspects of writing are both discussed in this section. Learn them well, for they are important to the success of all written communications.

THAT FIRST IMPRESSION—APPEARANCE

In Section 35 you learned about the appearance factor or "atmosphere effect," which influences opinions. You should apply this knowledge to the format of business letters in order to create and solidify the impression that your company is a fine firm with which to do business. Correct business-letter mechanics and format are presented first; then style of writing.

Balanced Format

You know that an attractive letterhead printed on good-quality paper, a message typed in proportion to its balanced margins, and a pleasing format all combine to make your letter inviting to the reader. Sloppy letters, like sloppy people, have a negative effect on the reader.

White Space The symmetry of a well-placed letter invites the reader's attention. A letter placed too high, too low, or too far to either side upsets the balance of white space that frames the picture, or message. All letters, however long they are, should have a generous margin of white space on all sides.

Typewriting Quality Whatever the choice of letterhead, letter format, or punctuation style, a letter can be visually pleasing only if it has been attractively typed. The quality of the typescript is governed by three factors: the evenness of touch, the quality of the typewriter ribbon, and the neatness of erasures. An even touch will produce typescript of even density—not a sprinkling of light and dark letters across the page. A well-adjusted electric typewriter guarantees consistent density of typescript, since each key strikes the paper with the same force, regardless of how much or how little pressure the typist uses. The type keys should be cleaned regularly to prevent dust-and-ink-clogged letters from marring the appearance of the typescript.

A good-quality ribbon should be used, one that is suited to the kind of typewriter—standard or portable, manual or electric. When the ribbon has been used so frequently that there is not sufficient ink to produce clear typescript, the ribbon should be replaced. Ribbons come in a variety of colors, but black is the color most frequently used. With tinted stationery, however, a colored ribbon of the same hue might be more attractive. For example, a florist who uses light-green stationery might like to use a dark-green ribbon.

Of course, erasures should be kept to a minimum, and if the erasures are noticeable, the letter should be retyped. Many erasures can be made so neatly that they are not noticeable. Good erasing tools are as essential to the typist as good carpentry or plumbing tools are to the carpenter or the plumber. A good typing eraser and a typing shield that will prevent the smudging of adjacent letters help to make the erasing process easier. Liquid paper usually is not acceptable for original copies of correspondence, although correction paper (such as Ko-Rec-Type) may be used if the erased strokes are covered with other strokes.

The Letterhead

Most letterheads are printed. Some examples of well-designed, printed letterheads are shown on page 280. The selection of size, shape, and quality of paper as well as the selection of the letterhead design should be made with the advice of a stationer, a printer, or an advertising agency. In seeking this advice, consider the following points:

> Quality stationery suggests that the firm considers its letters—and its readers—important.
>
> The usual letterhead size is 8½ by 11 inches, but special sizes may be used to create special impressions. For example, physicians, lawyers, and other professional people often use the smaller, baronial (5½ by 8½ inches) stationery because it is more prestigious than the larger size.
>
> Tinted paper is sometimes used for special effects. A garden shop may, for instance, select green paper.
>
> Business people believe in the power of a picture—"a picture is worth ten thousand words." Artwork and photography are used increasingly in letterheads, especially in promotional letters. Of course, the letter's second page should be of the same quality, size, and color as the letterhead. Although many companies prefer that the second-page stationery be blank, without any printing, others are using a printed second page with the company name in small print. Information copies or file copies are usually typed on onionskin paper.

Courtesy of the organizations above

The Envelope

Business envelopes are usually printed with a return address designed to echo the letterhead being used. It is essential that the information contained in the envelope address be identical with that in the inside address. The following guidelines, illustrated in the envelope below, should always be observed:

Begin typing the mailing address on line 14, about 4 inches from the left edge for a regular-size—No. 10—business envelope. The blocked style, single-spaced, is preferred by the U.S. Postal Service.

Always include the ZIP Code number. Leave one space between the state and the ZIP Code number.

On-arrival or addressee directions (*Please Forward, Confidential,* and so on) should be typed about four lines below the return address.

Indicate special mailing services, such as *Special Delivery* or *Air Mail,* below the stamp.

The U.S. Postal Service prefers that no information be placed below the ZIP Code number.

Punctuation Styles

The two commonly used punctuation styles for business letters are (1) open and (2) standard, or "mixed."

It is important to remember that the punctuation of the *message* is the same, regardless of which style is used for the other letter parts.

Open Punctuation Style This style, shown on page 284, requires that *no* punctuation be used after any part of the letter except the message. Open punctuation is frequently used with full-blocked arrangements, as both styles are considered time-savers for the typist.

Standard Punctuation Style In the standard punctuation style, only the salutation and the complimentary closing are followed by a mark of

Anthony Grillo, Inc.
Taylor Court
Sante Fe, New Mexico 87501

Attention Manager, Sales Department

The Lewison Agency
263 North Michigan Avenue
Chicago, IL 60654

punctuation. The salutation is followed by a colon, and the complimentary closing is followed by a comma. The standard style, which is more commonly used, is shown on page 285.

Letter Arrangement Styles

You may select from among five commonly used styles of letter arrangement. There is no standard by which the appropriateness or inappropriateness of a specific style can be firmly established. However, some companies adopt one particular arrangement, and all employees are expected to use it. In all other situations—as in selecting clothing, for example—it is up to the writer to make an appropriate choice from the letter styles discussed and illustrated in the following pages.

The arrangement of a letter depends upon the horizontal placement of the various letter parts. The vertical sequence in which the parts are positioned, as illustrated on page 283, is fixed in a logical pattern that is normally not altered to suit individual tastes.

Full-Blocked Letters In the full-blocked style, letters are written with *all* the parts beginning at the left margin. This style, which is illustrated on page 284, saves typing time because the typist does not have to use the tabulator in setting up the letter. Frequently, open punctuation (see page 281) is used with the full-blocked style.

Blocked Letters A letter in blocked style, as illustrated on page 285, follows the format of a full-blocked letter except in the position of the dateline, complimentary closing, company signature, and writer's identification. All these parts usually start at the horizontal center of the page. However, the date may be aligned to end at the right margin, and the subject and attention lines may be either centered or indented five or ten spaces.

Semiblocked Letters A semiblocked letter, as shown on page 286, generally follows blocked style. However, first lines of paragraphs are idented five or ten spaces.

Square-Blocked Letters In a square-blocked letter, as illustrated on page 287, the date is typed in the upper-right corner margin and the reference initials and enclosure notation are typed in the lower-right corner margin in order to save space. The result is that more copy may be typed on a page, possibly eliminating the necessity of a two-page letter.

Simplified Letters The Administrative Management Society has developed and advocates the use of the simplified letter style, as shown on page 288. The arrangement of the simplified letter is the same as the arrange-

PARTS OF A TYPICAL BUSINESS LETTER

1 **MADISON OFFICE EQUIPMENT CORPORATION**
1789 Lexington Avenue
New York, New York 10022

2 April 3, 19--

United Insurance Company
3 200 West 61st Street
New York, NY 10019

4 ATTENTION MR. RALPH JACKSON

5 Gentlemen

6 Subject: Secretarial Desks

Thank you for your recent letter requesting information regarding secretarial desks for your new offices. We have recently added several new models to our extensive line, so that you have a wide choice of styles available to fill your needs.

7 Our newest catalog in color is enclosed. To help you in selecting the desks best suited to your needs, we have checked several designs that have proved most popular with other insurance firms. Complete details regarding sizes, colors, and various individual features accompany each photograph. You will note that we also carry large stocks of office filing equipment and supplies.

We look forward to hearing from you and hope you won't hesitate to call on us for any further information you may need. A reply card is enclosed for your convenience.

8 Cordially yours

9 MADISON OFFICE EQUIPMENT CORPORATION

Lawrence Spanswick

10 Lawrence Spanswick
Vice President, Sales

11 LS/tr
12 Enclosures
Catalog
Reply card
13 cc Mr. John Somis

1. Printed letterhead
2. Date line
3. Inside address
4. Attention line
5. Salutation
6. Subject line
7. Body
8. Complimentary closing
9. Company signature
10. Signer's identification
11. Reference initials
12. Enclosure reminder
13. "cc" notation

Note that the vertical sequence in which the parts are positioned is normally not altered.

Full-Blocked Letter Style
Vigorous, Aggressive
With Subject Line and Open Punctuation

March 6, 19--

Mr. Roger S. Patterson
Western Life Company
2867 East Fourth Street
Cincinnati, Ohio 45202

Dear Mr. Patterson

Subject: Form of a Full-Blocked Letter

This letter is set up in the full-blocked style, in which every line begins at the left margin. A few companies modify it by moving the date to the right, but most firms use it as shown here. Because this style is the fastest to type, it is considered very modern. It is natural, although not necessary, to use "open" punctuation with this style of letter.

This letter also illustrates one arrangement of the subject line, which may be used with any style of letter. Like an attention line, a subject line may be typed with underscores or capitals. In a full-blocked letter, it must be blocked; in other letter styles, it may be blocked or centered. It always appears after the salutation and before the body, for it is considered a part of the body.

Legal firms and the legal departments of companies sometimes prefer to use the Latin terms Re or In Re instead of the English word Subject.

Yours very sincerely

Mary Ellen Smith
Mary Ellen Smith
Reference Department

urs

ment of the full-blocked style. However, the simplified letter is different in the following ways:

1. The salutation and the complimentary closing are eliminated.
2. The subject line, which is standard in the simplified style, and the writer's identification line are always typed entirely in capital letters.
3. Listings in the message are indented five spaces, except when the items in the listing are numbered or lettered. Items identified by letters or numbers are blocked, but no periods are used after the numbers or letters.

The chief purpose of the simplified letter is to save time. The claim is made that the use of this style saves 10.7 percent of the time required to type a

Blocked Letter Style

The Most Flexible
With Direct Address, Quotation, and Postscript

March 10, 19--

REGISTERED

Mr. Philippe Vargos, Gerente
El Aguila, S.A.
1242 Avenida Insurgentes
Mexico D.F.
MEXICO

Dear Mr. Vargos:

It is current practice in American business letters to display price quotations and similar special data in a special paragraph, like this:

> The paragraph is indented five spaces on both sides and is preceded and followed by one ordinary blank linespace.
>
> If it is necessary to use more paragraphs for the quotation, then a standard single blank line is left between paragraphs.

We indicate the mail service (a double space below the date) only if we are sending the correspondence by some special service, such as "special delivery" or "registered"; and we do so only to get the fact indicated on our file copy of the correspondence.

Yours very sincerely,

David I. Collins

Assistant Director
Bureau of Information
and Public Relations

DIC/urs

P.S. We treat postscripts in the same way that we treat other paragraphs, except that we precede each postscript by "PS:" or "P.S."

96-word letter in some other style. However, efficiency is not the sole criterion. Many writers consider the simplified style cold and impersonal, and as a result, they prefer to use one of the traditional styles.

USING APPROPRIATE WORDS—PERFORMANCE

Jonathan Swift, author of *Gulliver's Travels,* once said, "Proper words in proper places make the true definition of style." This statement holds true today, after two hundred years; proper words in proper places is the key to *performance,* the second aspect of style. Together with appearance, per-

Semiblocked Letter Style

Conservative, Executive
With Attention Line and cc Notation

March 7, 19--

Grant, Stone & Company
171 Westminster Street
Providence, RI 02904

ATTENTION TRAINING DIRECTOR

Gentlemen:

For a letter design that is both distinctive and yet standard, try this style: semiblocked (one of the two most popular styles) with the paragraphs indented ten spaces (instead of the usual five).

This letter also shows you an alternative arrangement for the attention line: centered, in all capitals (instead of being blocked at the left margin and underscored). In two regards, however, the use of the attention line is standard: It is accompanied by a "standard" salutation, such as "Gentlemen," "Mesdames," "Ladies," or "Ladies and Gentlemen"; and it is typed above the salutation.

Worth noting also in this letter are the following: (1) positioning the date at the margin, as an alternative to starting it at the center; (2) the use of "standard" punctuation, which calls for a colon after the salutation and a comma after the complimentary closing; and (3) the use of the "cc" notation at the bottom to indicate to whom carbon copies of the letter are being sent.

Yours very truly,

Melissa Cory

Melissa Cory, Director

URS
cc Ms. J. Lambeau
Dr. H. Moon

formance determines the effectiveness of our writing style and is important to the success of our written communications.

To create communications worthy of the reader's attention and action, the writer must make words, the tools of writing, *perform expressively*. You have been developing a vocabulary that will equip you with the tools you will need to write successful business communications. To make these tools perform expressively, use modern words, contemporary words; eliminate unnecessary words and repetitious words; express your ideas clearly and simply; and avoid using jargon or "shop talk."

Square-Blocked Letter Style

The Efficient Space-Saver
With Subject Line and "Corner Fillers"

Mrs. Joann Woods
Director of Training
Omega Corporation
Lincoln, Nebraska 68451

March 7, 19--

Dear Mrs. Woods:

SUBJECT: THE SQUARE-BLOCKED LETTER

A square-blocked letter like this one is simply the familiar full-blocked letter with (1) the date moved to the right and typed on the same line with the start of the inside address to square off that corner and (2) the reference symbols also shifted to the right to square off that corner.

This arrangement has many advantages. It is almost as quick to type as the full-blocked style. Because it saves lines of space that are otherwise given to the drop after the date and below the signer's identification, you can get seven or eight additional lines of typing on a page. You can see why this is popular among secretaries whose employers dictate rather long letters. Any letter looks shorter when typed in this style. It permits any kind of display, either centered or blocked.

When using this letter style, make it a rule not to use less than a 50-space line; otherwise, the first line of the inside address might run into the date at the right margin. For an ordinary letter, where you do not need to save space, you must remind yourself to start two or three lines lower on the page, lest your letter look too high on the stationery.

One limitation of the square-blocked letter style is the way it restricts the enclosure notation. If you use Enclosure by itself, you can put it below the initials (as shown below). If you want to enumerate the enclosures, however, the display would have to be at the left, and then the perfect balance of the squared corners would be lost.

Cordially,

Elsie Dodds Frost

Mrs. Elsie Dodds Frost

urs
Enclosure

Use Modern Expressions

Expressions, like fashions, change. Few people today would choose the cumbersome, confining clothes worn a few generations ago. In letter writing, fashions change, too. Some expressions are just as old-fashioned as celluloid collars and high-buttoned shoes, but many people continue to use them in business letters. Make sure that you know the expressions that are out of date so that you can avoid them; but also make sure that you know and use modern expressions in your letters.

Simplified Letter Style
The Efficiency Expert's
With Open Punctuation and Full-Blocked Design

March 6, 19--

Mr. Richard W. Parker, Jr.
Humphrey Lumber Company
520 Southwest Park Avenue
Portland, Oregon 97208

THE SIMPLIFIED LETTER

You will be interested to know, Mr. Parker, that several years ago the Administrative Management Society (formerly NOMA) designed a new letter form called the "Simplified Letter." This is a sample.

1 It uses the full-blocked form and "open" punctuation.

2 It contains no salutation or closing. (AMS believes such expressions to be meaningless.)

3 It displays a subject line in all capitals, both preceded and followed by two blank lines. Note that the word "Subject" is omitted.

4 It identifies the signer by an all-capitals line that is preceded by at least four blank lines and followed by one--if further notations are used.

5 It seeks to maintain a brisk but friendly tone, partly by using the addressee's name at least in the first sentence.

Perhaps, Mr. Parker, as some say, this form does not really look like a business letter; but its efficiency suggests that this style is worth a trial, especially where output must be increased.

Ralph E. Jones
RALPH E. JONES, TRAINING CONSULTANT

Use	Do Not Use
say, tell, let us know	advise, inform
now, at present	at this time, at the present time, at the present writing
as, because, since	due to the fact that, because of the fact that
letter	favor
regarding, concerning	in re
if, in case	in the event that
please	kindly
a specific word	same
for	in the amount of
according to	in accordance with

Eliminate Redundancy

Redundancy in writing or in speech results from using words that are unnecessarily repetitious; for instance, using *free gratis* for *gratis*. Since *gratis* means "free," *free gratis* means "free free." The following list includes some common redundancies that should be avoided.

Use	Do Not Use	Use	Do Not Use
about	*at* about	converted	converted *over*
above	*up* above	enter	enter *into*
alike	*both* alike	experience	*past* experience
beginner	*new* beginner	identical	*same* identical
check	check *into*	practice	*customary* practice
cooperate	cooperate *together*	otherwise	*as* otherwise
connect	connect *up*	repeat	repeat *again*
continue	continue *on*	together	*both* together
		et cetera	*and* et cetera

Use Plain, Simple Words

The purpose of a business letter is to convey a clear, easily understood message, but this purpose cannot be achieved by writers who insist on parading their extensive vocabularies. The proper words for business writing are plain, simple words that will be intelligible to any reader, regardless of educational background.

For example, suppose you wrote a letter expressing your dissatisfaction with a company's product and said:

> Your lawn mower has proved to be a baneful piece of equipment in my yard.

Would you really expect the reader to know what you meant, particularly if the reader didn't have a dictionary handy? The sentence might be rewritten by someone who is less of a vocabulary "show off" as follows:

> Your lawn mower has proved to be a detrimental piece of equipment in my yard.

Most likely you would understand this statement. But why take chances when simpler words would ensure the clarity of the message? You wouldn't need a dictionary or any other help to understand the following sentence:

> Your lawn mower has proved to be a nearly useless piece of equipment in my yard.

Avoid Jargon

Most trades develop a technical vocabulary that is likely to be unintelligible to anyone outside the trade. This vocabulary is called *jargon*. You should learn and use the special words of your trade, but remember that jargon is COIK (Clear Only If Known). For example, if you are writing to shoe store managers about *findings*, they'll know that you mean the merchandise other than shoes, such as polish, shoelaces, hosiery, and accessories. This is shoe store jargon and is understandable to them. However, no manager would talk to customers about buying *findings*. Why? The term is COIK—Clear Only If Known.

Related to jargon are the numerous words coined by writers and speakers. These invented terms often creep into the letter writer's vocabulary and, like any habit, are repeated monotonously. For instance, an accountant afflicted with this habit may write the following:

> *Accountingwise*, Sharpo sales have not stabilized our standing *profitwise*. If we can maintain our prices, our position can be improved *marketwise*.

Use jargon and self-coined expressions with caution, for they are COIK. Select a mode of expression that is fresh and simple—words and phrases that will be understood by your reader, the simple words discussed earlier in this section.

WRITING SKILL

Every writer should use appropriate words, but the business writer must combine these appropriate words in a way that will make friends and, at the same time, will facilitate action. The effective business letter must be concise, clear, cohesive, and complete.

Be Concise

A concise style implies brevity, compactness, just enough words to say what you wish to say without being rude. But do not confuse brevity with curtness or abruptness. The business worker appreciates concise wording because it saves time; and in business, time is money.

The principal enemy of conciseness is repetition. For instance, note how needlessly wordy the following is:

> In your letter of September 18, you asked for a 60-day extension in which to pay your account. In compliance with your request for this 60-day extension, we are happy to grant your request to extend the due date 60 days.

The reader already knows the nature of the request. If not, the sentence that follows the repeated information will serve as a reminder. However, the sentence that follows is too wordy. The following examples not only eliminate the repetition but also express the same thought much more effectively.

> We have extended the due date on the balance of your account 60 days. *Or:* The due date of your balance has been extended 60 days.

Another enemy of conciseness is irrelevancy. For instance, note how much of the following is irrelevant to the subject of the letter.

> One of our best customers got pretty annoyed today because we didn't have any bean sprouts in stock. Usually we do, but my partner thought I had ordered them, and I thought that he had.
>
> Now I would like to order two cases of bean sprouts. And from now on, I will do the ordering . . . .

At times, whole paragraphs can be eliminated without destroying any pertinent information. Be sure that whatever you include in your letters is relevant to your purpose.

Be Clear

A clear style is a vivid, unambiguous manner of writing. It tells what the reader wants to know in specific, not general, terms. A skilled business letter writer would never be guilty of making an obscure statement like the following example:

> We have many satisfied customers of our typewriters, and they have found that they seldom need repairs but when they do they service them quickly.

As bad as the ambiguity in the example above is the running together of ideas. Short sentences tend to be clearer than long, involved ones. See how much clearer the message is when it is written as two precise sentences.

> Thousands of satisfied customers use Sayre typewriters. These customers are satisfied because seldom, if ever, do Sayre typewriters need repair.

The revised statement is not vague, as the first is. Instead of dealing in vague generalities, a clear style deals in specifics. For example, *Your order will be shipped in the very near future* is too general a statement to be clear. *Your order will be shipped on May 15* is specific and, therefore, quite clear.

Be Cohesive

Cohesiveness in style refers to the way a letter holds together. In the cohesive letter, there is unity of thought—each sentence and paragraph flows smoothly into the next. The business writer should use connecting or linking words to lead the reader from one idea to another. Here are some examples of linking words and phrases:

since	as a result
naturally	on the other hand
however	nevertheless
thus	therefore
for instance	of course
for example	as a matter of fact

These linking words help to hold the message together. Keep in mind, though, that clear, orderly thinking in organizing a letter, as discussed in Section 35, is the most important factor in writing a cohesive letter. Linking words simply make the logic of the letter more quickly apparent to the reader.

Be Complete

Suppose you received the following letter and nothing more.

> Gentlemen:
>
> Send us our order.
>
> Sincerely yours,

Such a letter is almost rude in its curtness. At least, the writer could have said "please"! However, the letter is rude for another reason also: it is not complete.

A complete letter gives all pertinent information: whose order? what order? when to ship it? where to ship it? why? how? Revised to answer these questions, the complete letter would look like this:

> Gentlemen:
>
> Please refer to our Purchase Order 70315, dated February 3. Your salesman, Mr. Cannon, promised delivery of this order not later than March 18. If the mattresses do not arrive before March 30, they will not be available for our After-Inventory Sale.
>
> Have the mattresses been shipped? If not, can you send them by truck instead of by freight? Please wire us immediately how you plan to get the order to us in time.
>
> Sincerely yours,

Communication Projects

PRACTICAL APPLICATION

A Using the letter style you prefer, write a letter to your instructor discussing the pros and cons of each letter style discussed on pages 282–285.

B Using the simplified style illustrated on page 288, write a letter to your instructor indicating what you feel are your strengths and weaknesses in writing letters.

C Modernize the following expressions.

1. Due to the installation of our computer . . . .
2. Please advise as to the method of shipment of . . . .
3. We received the defective motor to be replaced and will rush same to you.
4. We appreciate your favor of May 10.
5. In re your telephone call yesterday, we . . . .

D Eliminate any redundancies in these sentences.

1. Repeat again what you told him.
2. Check into the situation as soon as possible.
3. The arrangements in the two offices are both alike.
4. We will cooperate together to do the work.
5. We are using the same identical procedures.

E Revise these sentences, using plain, simple words.

1. Their silence was tantamount to consent.
2. He was dilatory in completing the work.
3. His plenitudinous figure resulted in his having his clothes custom made.
4. The problem was so enigmatic that he had great difficulty in solving it.
5. Her voice is so strident on the telephone.

EDITING PRACTICE

Updating Vocabulary Rewrite these excerpts from business letters, eliminating all outmoded words and expressions.

1. Your favor of May 1 reached us today.
2. Hoping to see you soon, I am . . . .
3. Kindly let us know by May 10.
4. Please write us at your earliest convenience.
5. Thank you in advance for your advice.
6. Please advise regarding your wishes.
7. In the event that you have an accident, this policy will cover your liability.
8. Enclosed please find our order.
9. Thank you for your order for ten typewriters; we are shipping same today.
10. At the present writing, we are refurbishing our offices.

Analysis of Spelling Errors Correct the spelling errors in this paragraph and, in one sentence, tell why they were made.

> Because of limited storage space, we keep our inventory of office supplys to a minimum. We have only one storeroom, where boxes are stacked to the ceiling; and passageways are narrow allies barely wide enough to permit a person to slip in and out. However, please continue to send us notices of any special sales that you think would interest us.

CASE PROBLEM

Carbon Copies In some firms it is a practice to make a carbon copy of a reply to a routine letter on the back of the letter being answered. Suggest some possible advantages and disadvantages of this procedure.

In business, time is money—and the need to get accurate information in the least amount of time is also money. Hence millions of dollars are spent annually to find newer and faster ways of producing the information needed by businesses. For example, less than a hundred years ago, requests for money owed were handled by writing letters. Today even small offices request payment by means of a printed monthly statement—either typewritten or prepared by other manual means. Increasingly, billing has become a completely mechanized procedure; high-speed computers now calculate and print each hour thousands of requests for money owed. Without new technological methods of handling information, business as we know it today could not function effectively.

In spite of great labor-saving advances, writing request letters is still an important business function. Why? Some businesses are less mechanized than others, and some forms of request are too infrequent to mechanize. More important, however, is the fact that mechanized requests lack the personal touch that can build good human relations and goodwill for a company.

Everyone in business has occasion, at one time or another, to write a request letter. Business people need all kinds of information and services in order to operate efficiently—price lists, catalogs, specifications for raw materials and finished products, repair and maintenance services, samples of products, bids and price quotations, and much more. Typical reasons business people write request letters are these: (1) to reserve a hotel room or a conference room, (2) to obtain an appointment, (3) to obtain printed materials, such as catalogs, price lists, magazines, books, and reports, (4) to ask for special favors—permission to quote from copyrighted publications, permission to use a company's library or special book collection, (5) to order merchandise, (6) to ask for information missing from a letter, (7) to seek technical information about products or services.

Writing request letters is often considered a routine matter. Usually, request letters ask for something that the reader will be happy to give because the letter provides an opportunity to sell a product or service as a result of granting the request. Therefore, some writers of request letters feel that they are doing the recipient a favor and that they do not have to expend much effort in writing the letter. While this may be the case in writing *some* request letters, most of them require much planning and thought if the letter is to accomplish its objectives. The following guidelines should be observed in writing all request letters, whether they are of a routine nature or are more complicated:

Give complete information.
Give accurate information.
Be sure the request is reasonable.
Be courteous.
Be brief.

Note how these guidelines are followed in the request letter illustrated on page 295.

Give Complete Information

A letter of request should give the reader all the facts needed to answer the writer. In general, the letter should answer the following questions: Who? What? How many? When? Where? Why? Note how the following letter answers these questions.

Gentlemen:

Please send me 100 copies of your brochure, *Supervision in the Office*, which was advertised in the March issue of *Supervisory Management*. I have enclosed my check for $50 to cover the cost, including mailing.

I should like to have these brochures by May 25 for our management conference to be held in San Francisco. If there will be an extra charge in order to get them to me by that date, please let me know.

Very sincerely yours,

8745 Shelton Drive
Monroe, NY 10950
May 13, 19--

Cold Temp Refrigeration Company, Inc.
17896 Lake Boulevard West
Chicago, Illinois 60613

Gentlemen:

I am interested in the Cold Temp air conditioner that you advertised in the April issue of Home Furnishings magazine. To help me decide whether this is the air conditioner that best suits my needs, I should appreciate your answering the following questions:

1. What are the various capacities of air conditioners that you manufacture?

2. How large a room can be cooled effectively by the unit you advertised?

3. What is the price of this unit and what are the prices of your other units?

4. Who in my area is the local distributor of your products?

Since I plan to make a decision regarding the air conditioner I will purchase not later than June 5, I hope to hear from you before that date.

Very truly yours,

Mrs. Tito Arnaz

Mrs. Tito Arnaz

Since letters of this type are nearly always on company letterheads, it is not necessary to include the address of the writer inside the letter. However, if the letterhead contains the addresses of several offices, or if the writer wishes the reply to be sent to a different address, the specific address should be indicated.

The writer, of course, should allow the supplier sufficient time to handle the request by writing well in advance. If the writer who is requesting the brochures is not sure there is enough time, he or she should include a statement similar to the last sentence or to the following:

> Please rush these brochures to me by airmail special delivery, and bill me for the extra cost.

In the example on page 294, the writer has given the reason for the request. Although it is not always necessary to do so, giving the reason will sometimes enable the reader to serve you more satisfactorily. For example, a supplier who knows that the brochures are to be used in a management conference might suggest other printed materials that would be of interest to the group. Knowing why in this case also gives the reader an incentive for rushing the materials. In the example below, the writer gives the reason why special hotel accommodations are needed, so that the hotel manager can use good judgment in selecting an appropriate room or suite. A request for a hotel reservation is normally quite routine, but the details must be clearly stated if, as in this case, special requirements must be met.

> Gentlemen:
>
> Please reserve a suite for Ms. Helen C. Ryan for October 10–13. Ms. Ryan, executive vice president of Larwex Enterprises, Inc., will arrive at the hotel at approximately 4:45 p.m. on October 10.
>
> During her stay, Ms. Ryan will be conducting a series of seminars for eight regional sales managers. Therefore, she would like to have a suite with an adjoining conference room large enough for a table and nine chairs. She will also need a portable chalkboard. If an appropriate suite is not available, then please reserve a large double bedroom for Ms. Ryan and a small conference room in which luncheon may be served on both October 11 and 12. The conference room will be needed on October 13 as well; but the meeting will end at 11 a.m., so luncheon will not be required.
>
> Please confirm this reservation and let us know what type of accommodations you are holding. Would you also send some sample luncheon menus.
>
> Very truly yours,

Not all request letters require as much detail as the preceding example. Note how the following letter, though brief, supplies all necessary information.

> Gentlemen:
>
> I am enclosing my check for $13.50 for a two-year subscription to *Tennis News*. Please send the magazine to the following address:
>
> Mrs. Jennifer C. Price
> 13 New Hampshire Court
> Detroit, MI 48215
>
> Very truly yours,

A letter requesting an appointment must also carefully spell out all necessary information. The reason why an appointment is requested is usually stated in order to convince the executive that the appointment should be accepted. In addition, giving the reason for the appointment also enables the executive to make any necessary preparations for talking with the visitor. All other necessary information—who, when, where—must, of course, be included also. Note how the information is given in the following example.

> Dear Mr. Felton:
>
> I expect to be in Phoenix the week of May 15. May I see you sometime during that week to show you our new training film on safety in the aircraft industry? This film, with sound and in full color, was made with the assistance of the country's foremost aircraft safety engineers. I think you and your inspectors will find the film worthwhile.

An hour is all that is needed to show the film and to describe some of the other training films we have recently released. Any day of the week will be satisfactory to me. Please let me know your preference so that I may complete my itinerary. Incidentally, will your projection room be available? If not, I will bring my projector and screen.

Sincerely yours,

Give Accurate Information

Before it is mailed, each letter of request should be checked for accuracy of information. It is easy to give a wrong date, an incorrect amount, or an incorrect title or address. Accuracy is particularly important in letters ordering goods or services.

Although larger companies use a special purchase order form for most purchases, they sometimes order merchandise by letter; and smaller companies may place all orders by letter. Complete and accurate information is doubly important in these cases.

Gentlemen:

Please ship the following by air express:

Quantity	Catalog No.	Description	Unit Price	Total
3	A825-L	Table lamps; green base	$72.00	$216.00
5	Z938-X	Floor lamps; brass base	96.00	480.00

I should appreciate your rushing this shipment so that I can get this order to my customer by July 7, in time for a Tenth Anniversary Sale. Bill me at the usual terms of 2/10, n/30.

Very truly yours,

Make Reasonable Requests

Although most people do not knowingly make unreasonable requests, a surprising number of writers are guilty of such thoughtlessness. Suppose you were a correspondent for a manufacturer of computers. What would you think if you received a letter from a college student with a request like the following:

> I am writing a report on computers, so I should appreciate your telling me all you can about computers.

Surely, you would think that such a request is unreasonable! First, the student could have obtained a great deal of information from library resources but obviously did not take the time to search for the information. Second, the writer didn't have sufficient knowledge of the subject to know its scope and therefore could not ask for specific information. Third, "all" that a specialist in any field knows about that field probably could fill several volumes.

Before you request information, ask yourself these questions: "Do I know what I want to find out? Is there some place where I can find the information without imposing on someone else? Am I making a reasonable request—one that the reader will have the time to fulfill? Am I allowing the reader enough time to give my request adequate attention?" The answers to these questions will make it unnecessary to write some letters, and those that are written will be specific, pertinent, and reasonable.

Be Courteous

Closely related to the unreasonable request is the discourteous one. Often the writer of a discourteous request is confused about both the writer's and the reader's obligations. The letter writer may feel, "I am conferring a favor by making this request"; or "The reader owes me this and should comply with my request. I don't have to say 'please' or 'thank you'."

The discourteous request is likely to sound like this:

> Frank Adler
> Local Printers, Inc.
> 145 Service Street
> Garden City, NY 11535
>
> Dear Sir:
>
> Send your price list and stationery samples to me.
>
> Yours truly,

Mr. Adler will, of course, send the price list and samples regardless of whether he is given the courtesy of *Mr.* in the inside address, whether his title of *Office Manager* is included, whether the friendlier salutation *Dear Mr. Adler* is used instead of the formal *Dear Sir*, or whether the writer says "please." Yet Mr. Adler would be more favorably impressed (and more inclined to be helpful) if the letter were written in a courteous manner, as the following letter was.

> Mr. Frank Adler, Office Manager
> Local Printers, Inc.
> 145 Service Street
> Garden City, NY 11535
>
> Dear Mr. Adler:
>
> Since you have always been so helpful to me in the past, I should appreciate your sending me your latest price list and stationery samples.
>
> We are in the process of revising our letterheads and will find this information and the samples helpful.
>
> Very sincerely yours,

Making it easy for the reader to act is another form of courtesy. One method is to use courtesy carbons (described in Section 35). Another is to number the questions or requests when there are several. For example, read the following letter:

> Dear Mrs. Guitterez:
>
> Thank you for the samples of Durasheen and Fibreglow drapery materials. I am delighted with the wide range of colors and textures. To help me in making a selection for the executive offices, would you please answer the following questions:

1. Is the Durasheen material fire-resistant?
2. Does the Durasheen line come in a darker brown than the samples supplied?
3. The nubby texture of the Fibreglow fabric is ideal for the conference room. Is it also available in a smooth finish for the adjoining library?
4. Do you have local representatives who might be available to counsel us on color harmony?
5. What local firm do you think would give us the best job (and price) on making draperies from your materials?

As soon as I have the answers to these questions, I shall be able to make a decision. Your help will be appreciated.

Sincerely yours,

Be Brief

Another important aspect of courtesy is brevity. It is discourteous to waste the reader's time with rambling thoughts and irrelevant details. Too much information is sometimes a fault of request letters. If the letter is complete and contains all the necessary information discussed earlier in this section, that is all that is necessary for an effective request letter. A letter of request should be complete enough to give the reader whatever information is needed to serve you properly—yet brief enough to be able to serve you quickly.

Communication Projects

PRACTICAL APPLICATION

A Members of your Consumer Awareness Club were discussing aids to consumers, particularly the periodical *Consumer Reports*, published by Consumers Union, Mount Vernon, New York 10962. One member had heard that a group of people could subscribe to the magazine and the *Annual Buying Guide* at a substantial savings over the individual subscription price of $8 a year. You volunteer to request information from Consumers Union about group subscriptions. Write the letter.

B Select two newspaper or magazine advertisements that invite you to write for additional information about products or services. Write a letter to each of the companies and ask for a catalog, sample, brochure, or other descriptive information.

C Write a letter to Maxwell's Department Store, 1788 Eastgate Boulevard, Garden City, New York 11530, to order a briefcase. You make the following notations to guide you in organizing and writing the letter.

Why? To order a briefcase.
What? No. 178B, four-pocket, black cowhide, $17.95.
How? Send by United Parcel and charge to my account; gift wrap.
When? Immediately.
Where? Send to writer at address on letter.

D Write to the Circulation Department of *Finance Business News*, 120 Dexter Road, Chicago, Illinois 60632, to notify them of a change of address. You have moved from 4543 Lake Drive, Cleveland, Ohio 44106, to 980 Market Street in Ann Arbor, Michigan 48104, and you would like to have your subscription transferred to the new address.

E Write a letter to the Rug Makers Council of 1876 Bushwick Drive, Topeka, Kansas 66604, asking for a copy of their pamphlet *Care and Cleaning of Rugs,* written by Julia Foster. Enclose your check for $1 in payment.

F Request a single room with bath at the Hotel Barton, 165 Shore Drive, Grand Rapids, Michigan 49502. You plan to attend the convention of the Sales Management Society on March 15–17 at the Hotel Barton. Request the special convention rate and a written confirmation of your reservation.

G Write a letter to the Daley Electronic Corporation, 10 Third Avenue, New York, New York 10017, requesting the names and addresses of dealers in your city who carry their products. If they have a catalog, you would also like to receive a copy of it.

H How many different ways can you express "please" and "thank you" without using the actual words? Consider yourself *good* if you know five different ways; *excellent* if you know eight; *expert* if you know ten!

EDITING PRACTICE

The Correspondence Supervisor Edit and rewrite the following paragraph, correcting all errors.

> Please check to see if my name has been accidentally removed from you're files. In addition, credit my account for $1.50, the cost of 2 selections. I would apreciate you checking to see if my supscription was cancelled and weather I will receive the remaining copys.

Rewrite Desk Improve the following first lines taken from request letters.

1. Here is the booklet.
2. This is to notify you that your check has not yet been received.
3. Referring to your quotation for bid on typewriter ribbons which you mailed on July 15 and was received July 19, you failed to indicate the type of material the ribbon would be made of.
4. We wish to call attention to the fact that the certificate which you said was enclosed was not enclosed.
5. We would like to notify you that the service contract which you say expires at the end of the year does not expire until March.

CASE PROBLEM

Positively Friendly Since positive statements are more likely to win friends than negative ones, rewrite these statements to make them sound more friendly.

1. Really, Mrs. Dvorak, you can't blame us because you didn't follow the printed instructions that came with each coffee maker.
2. I'm very sorry, but we just can't make an adjustment unless merchandise is returned in a reasonable length of time.

38 Writing Letters of Response

Among the most important business letters are those written to acknowledge the receipt of correspondence and to respond to requests made in that correspondence. Such letters are usually written for the following reasons: (1) to acknowledge an order received and to give the date and method of shipment and the terms of payment; (2) to transmit printed materials, such as a catalog, a price list, or a booklet; (3) to agree to or to confirm a meeting or an appointment; (4) to express regret that an appointment cannot be made or kept, and perhaps to suggest another date; (5) to answer questions about the company's product or service; (6) to explain a delay in shipping or an accounting error; (7) to acknowledge receipt of information, materials, money, or merchandise; (8) to follow up on decisions reached at meetings and during conversations.

THE IMPORTANCE OF RESPONSE LETTERS

In many respects, letters of response are sales letters. In most cases, they provide an opportunity for the company to give service, develop goodwill, and build sales. In no other type of business letter are the positive outlook and the *you* attitude more important. Response letters should be looked upon as opportunities to gain new friends (or to keep old ones); they should never be written grudgingly or matter-of-factly.

Five basic rules should guide the writer of response letters.

1. Be prompt.
2. Be helpful.
3. Be sales-minded.
4. Be complete.
5. Be specific.

Be Prompt

Every inquiry, every request, and every favor should be acknowledged promptly. Many companies require that every letter be answered within forty-eight hours of its receipt; some organizations allow only twenty-four hours for a response.

Even when an inquiry cannot be answered in detail, common business courtesy dictates that some kind of reply be sent promptly. The letter of inquiry should be acknowledged, and the inquirer should be given some specific indication of when to expect the information sought. For example:

> Dear Mr. Aish:
>
> Your request of May 3 for a quotation on bulk orders of No. C432 Fibreglass insulation is being handled by Mr. Les Abrams. He is looking into the matter with the manufacturer and expects to have a response by May 10. Mr. Abrams will write you just as soon as he has the information you requested.
>
> Sincerely yours,

The writer of the letter on page 301 has acknowledged the inquiry and has informed the inquirer that action on his request is being taken by a specific person. The inquirer has also been told that he can expect an answer soon after May 10. Not only will a carbon copy of this letter be sent to Mr. Abrams, but also a copy will be placed in a tickler file for May 10 so that the writer will follow up on Mr. Aish's request.

If a correspondent receives many similar requests, one letter can be used as a guide in answering all the requests. Such a letter is shown on page 303. Sometimes the same letter may be used to answer all or nearly all the requests; in this case, the letter could even be duplicated, with space left for the typist to fill in the inside address, the salutation, and any other variables. In other cases, the letter may need to be modified to suit each inquiry.

For example, the following form letter could be used whenever an item is out of stock. The words that are underscored would vary from letter to letter, depending on the inquiry.

> Dear Mr. Carver:
>
> Requests for our booklet, Lawn Planting and Care, have been much greater than we expected; so we are temporarily out of stock. We have ordered another printing and expect a new supply on March 15. As soon as the shipment arrives, your copy will be mailed to you.
>
> We certainly appreciate your interest in our lawn products. You will find our booklet very helpful in developing the type of lawn in which you will take pride and from which you will derive much personal enjoyment. We have had many enthusiastic letters from those who have used our products.
>
> Very sincerely yours,

Promptness is particularly important when you need to acknowledge a gift. A delayed response implies lack of appreciation, whereas a prompt thank-you assures the donor that you truly do appreciate the gift. The acknowledgment, like the one below, need not be long, but it should, of course, be sincere and cordial.

> Dear Ms. Ortiz:
>
> Thank you for the very helpful book on travel in Europe that I received today. I know the book will be very useful in planning my trip to Europe next summer. Since I am hoping to begin my planning this week, the book arrived just in time.
>
> I very much appreciate your thoughtfulness, and you may be sure that I will be sending you postcards from the many interesting places I plan to visit.
>
> Cordially,

Since customers and potential customers are pleased and impressed by prompt responses, capitalize on your promptness by mentioning how quickly you have acted. Usually you need only indicate when you received the letter you are answering, as shown by the following illustration: "When I received your letter in today's mail, I checked immediately into the availability of a private banquet room for your May 30 dinner meeting, and I am pleased to report that . . . ."

November 9, 19--

Mr. John Hill
The Collector, Inc.
38-31 Bell Boulevard
Bayside, New York 11361

Dear Mr. Hill:

Thank you for requesting additional information about the Auto-typist.

If repetitive typing enters into your word processing plans (and our field surveys show it does in three out of four offices), then you owe it to yourself to investigate Auto-typist performance and compare its cost with any other word processing unit on the market today.

There are several Auto-typist models, all priced under $2,000. The Model 71 reproduces a one-page letter. The Model 76 will store a series of complete letters or up to 50 or more form paragraphs. The enclosed folder describes these and other models in detail.

The Auto-typist is not an experimental development. It is a dependable piece of equipment, proved through years of use by insurance companies, banks, mail order firms, fund raisers, and other organizations that have depended upon low-cost, individually typewritten letters long before word processing became a well-known term.

For additional information, please call our representative for your area, Mr. William Schulz, at 555-0870. Mr. Schulz will be pleased to make an appointment at your convenience to answer all your questions.

Cordially yours,

James Schulz
Sales Manager

JS:at
Enc.

Courtesy American Automatic Typewriter Company

When you go out of your way to give prompt service, you should let the reader know what you have done; otherwise, the reader simply cannot be impressed by the special effort. Note how the following letter does this.

Dear Miss Hawkins:

Generally, our drapery shop needs about two weeks to make up draperies of the type you ordered from us yesterday.

However, because your need for these draperies is urgent, we have given your order top priority. We expect to complete your draperies by Wednesday of next week and will hang them for you on Thursday, in time for your reception.

Yours sincerely,

Be Helpful

The thoughtful letter writer gives more than a bare minimum of help when responding to an inquiry or a request. For example, in the letter on page 303, the writer has responded by enclosing a folder, by describing the usefulness of the automatic typewriter in answering routine correspondence, and by telling the reader where to obtain additional information.

Going beyond the minimum to help does not mean verbosity in responding, but it does mean being aware of a customer's total needs and designing a letter to satisfy those needs. For example, the writer of the following letter not only fills the request made but also anticipates the inquirer's interest in a closely related item. Yet, to go beyond the minimum, the writer did not have to write a long, long response.

> Dear Mr. Wiggins:
>
> We are delighted to enclose the booklet you requested, *How to Decorate Your Office*. There is no charge for this booklet, and we hope you will find it as useful as many of our customers claim it has been to them.
>
> You mentioned in your letter that you are also planning to redecorate your employee lounge. Though we do not carry the type of furnishings you would want for this job, we thought you might be interested in the reprint from *Plant Facilities* that describes some innovative practices in planning employee facilities. We should also be happy to recommend a local firm that can be of assistance to you in doing this work.
>
> Very sincerely yours,

Even though you may not always be able to provide what the reader desires, you should be as courteous and as helpful as possible. For example, the letter below probably won a friend for the writer's company, even though the correspondent could not give the customer what she wanted.

> Dear Mrs. Kniss:
>
> I wish we were able to supply you with the same upholstery material that we used for the chairs we covered for you two years ago. Unfortunately, we do not have any more of this material available, and the manufacturer tells us that they have discontinued the color and the pattern.
>
> I would suggest that you try Rodney's in the hope that they might have a sufficient quantity of the material still in stock. In case they do not have it, I have another suggestion. Pattern No. 167-red, a sample of which is enclosed, is quite similar to the one in which your chairs are covered and certainly would blend well. Since we have only a limited quantity of this material available, please let us know as soon as possible if you would like us to hold it for you.
>
> Cordially yours,

Be Sales-Minded

Today, competition in business is very keen. Often, competing products are very similar, so a company must rely on superior service in order to win and retain customers. Therefore, everyone employed by a firm—from the salespeople, the receptionist, the secretary, the messenger, the manager, the mail clerk, the switchboard operator, the correspondent, to the president—is expected to treat the public in a manner that will make and keep friends for the company. This calls for employees who demonstrate an interest in, and a helpful attitude toward, the buying public. Such behavior helps create an image of friendliness, reliability, and efficiency.

Sales-minded people convey the idea that they are more interested in having satisfied customers than in merely making a sale. They do not allow their letters to sound routine. Each letter is as individualized as time permits, and each sounds special.

One way of making response letters seem special is by varying the expressions used. If each day you must respond to many requests, you may be inclined to make them all sound alike; for example:

> This is to acknowledge receipt of your request for . . . .

The danger does not lie in the fact that two customers may find out that they have received exactly the same letters. The danger is that the writer becomes bored, and this boredom results in a mechanical indifference that shows in the letters. On the other hand, if the writer tries to create different letters, correspondence will become more interesting to write and more interesting to read. In how many different ways can you express "This is to acknowledge receipt of your request for . . ."? Here are a few:

> Thank you for your order for . . . .
> Your order for Bakit is appreciated and . . . .
> We are grateful for your interest in Bakit, and . . . .
> Your request for Bakit arrived this morning, and I . . . .
> The Bakit you asked for is being . . . .
> Many thanks for your confidence in Bakit . . . .
> This morning I had the pleasure of sending you . . . .
> I know you will be pleased with the new Bakit that . . . .
> You made a wise choice when you . . . .

You, of course, can add to this list. The point is that you shouldn't allow your letters to sound like a broken record. By varying your wording of the same ideas, you will make your letters sound fresh, and you will give the reader the feeling that you are writing especially for that reader alone.

Of course, the ultimate purpose of every business activity is to make a sale. Most response letters, if they are well written, give the writer an opportunity to accomplish this goal. Unlike most sales letters, however, the letter of response is in answer to a direct request. In other words, it is in answer to an invitation to sell something to the reader!

As you read the following effective response letter, don't you get the feeling that the writer is sales-minded?

> Dear Mr. Carlisle:
>
> Thank you for asking about FINANCE WEEKLY, the publication prepared especially for business executives like you.
>
> As a subscriber to FINANCE WEEKLY, you will receive every Friday valuable information about significant business changes throughout the nation. The enclosed form will bring you three months of this helpful financial service on a special introductory

basis. The fee? A very low $5 for three months, or 12 issues—less than 50¢ an issue.

FINANCE WEEKLY not only keeps you abreast of present trends and developments in the financial world but also provides you with the kind of information you need from the world of politics and government . . . the world of banking . . . the world of stocks and bonds . . . the world of foreign trade . . . everything that affects the financial picture in *your* world—in your business and in your personal life.

To take advantage of this special introductory offer and to benefit from FINANCE WEEKLY's keen judgment and helpful advice, complete and return the enclosed form today. You need not send any money now. If, after reading the first issue, you don't agree that FINANCE WEEKLY will help you save much more money than the cost of a subscription, just let us know and we will cancel your order without charging you one cent!

Remember, too, your fee for this informative service is a tax-deductible business expense. This introductory offer is a huge saving over the annual subscription rate of $48—the rate at which 9 out of 10 regular FINANCE WEEKLY readers renew our service year after year.

We will start your service just as soon as we hear from you. Once you learn to depend on FINANCE WEEKLY to help you make business and personal decisions, we know that you will look forward eagerly to receiving each Friday's issue.

Sincerely yours,

Note the chatty narrative style of the letter. Adding ellipses (. . .) in this instance contributes to the easy flow of the letter. This device is not recommended for all response letters, but it can be used effectively in some letters.

Remember that the good response letter offers an excellent opportunity to be of service as well as to make a sale. You can see these points in action in the following response letter.

Dear Music Lover:

Here is the brochure on quadraphonic sound that you recently requested. It describes this outstanding, new, four-channel music system that you may own and enjoy in your home for just slightly more than you might spend on an ordinary stereo system.

Quadraphonic sound does more than just add two speakers to your present two-channel, twin-speaker stereo system. It is as close to concert-hall realism as any home system can hope to be. Plan an early visit to our showroom in your city to hear a demonstration of this miracle of sound.

To broaden our market for quadraphonic records, the Classic Music Library has made it possible for you and your family to enter this fascinating new world of sound. And you don't have to make any of the time-consuming and costly mistakes that many people make when they buy stereophonic equipment and records.

We have taken care of all details for you in this superb Classic Quadraphonic system, assembled by the world's leading sound engineers. These artists of sound have created and assembled for you a finely engineered and matched set of stereophonic components; a complete 50-record library of the world's best music; a remarkable 10-record audiovisual encyclopedia of music, the first of its kind; a full set of beautiful library cases; and a custom-designed, hand-rubbed hardwood cabinet for displaying the entire library.

Yes, simply because Classic wants to broaden the market for these new quadraphonic records, you can now have the Classic Music Library installed in your home for only $50 down and $16.50 a month until the low total price of $875 is paid. This price is only a few dollars more than you would pay for ordinary stereo records and an ordinary stereo system. Look—and listen to—how much more you get for just a little more money!

To order your Classic Music Library, simply fill out the enclosed postage-paid card and mail it today. It will bring you a selection of records to choose from and samples of wood finishes to match the type of cabinetry that will best suit the decor of your home.

Sincerely yours,

Even though Classic's letter may be a printed form letter, it has been written with the personal touch that combines all the essential qualities of the well-written response. Note the effective use of the *you* attitude, the use of word-picture images, and the logical presentation of benefits that the product has for the reader. This letter of response, therefore, provides an excellent opportunity to persuade a customer to buy.

Be Specific

In all letters of response, the writer should specifically identify the subject of the letter being answered. In the examples given here, notice how the writer has taken pains to be specific.

In acknowledging receipt of money, you should refer to the amount and to the purpose for which the money was paid. For example:

> Thank you for your check for $82.90, which we will apply to the balance of your account.
>
> We appreciate receiving your check for $196.88 in payment of Invoice No. 50402.

In confirming appointments, repeat the time and place of the meeting so that there will be no misunderstanding. Note these examples:

> We are pleased to accept your invitation to attend the Market Sales Conference on November 10–12 in the Santa Ana Room of the Chancellor Inn.
>
> I was delighted to have the opportunity of chatting with you this afternoon. As we discussed, I shall meet you in Anaheim at 2:30 next Tuesday afternoon in the lobby of the Ramsdale Hotel.

When acknowledging the receipt of important business papers (and they should always be acknowledged), the paper or the document should be specifically named—contracts, policies, checks, stocks, bonds, and so on. For example:

> The Notice of Completion for the new Arroyo Branch of your store has just been received. We will have our officers sign it and return your copy to you.
>
> The 300 shares of IBM stock have been received and will be sent to the Tiburn Trust Company the first thing in the morning.

Frequently orders for merchandise are acknowledged by letter. These acknowledgments should specify the date of the order and the purchase order number. The acknowledgment should also refer to the date and method of shipment, as well as to any special instructions concerning the order. For example:

> We are delighted that you are taking advantage of our end-of-year sale on furniture. Your Order 437, dated December 18, will be shipped by United Parcel this afternoon. As you requested, we will deliver to your Sansone Street store.

Another form of response letter is the follow-up letter, which should always be written to thank a customer for an order, to confirm a meeting date, to formalize a business agreement, or to verify information exchanged during a telephone conversation. Follow-up letters must be specific in enumerating the major points of the agreement or conference, as shown by the following letter:

> Dear Mark:
>
> This letter will confirm our telephone conversation of this morning regarding the proposed Credit Manager's Conference to be held June 10–15 in Dallas. The following points summarize the major aspects of our discussion:
>
> 1. Hank Meyes will look into hotel arrangements in Dallas and Fort Worth for the conference site.
> 2. A questionnaire will be used to poll the members of our organization to determine desirable topics for the group meetings. Bill Atkins will handle this matter.
> 3. You will prepare a proposed agenda for each of the five days, which will also include excursions to nearby entertainment spots and a no-host cocktail hour to wrap up the conference.
>
> As you suggested, we will have a planning meeting in your office on January 8 at 3 p.m. Thanks for your assistance in helping to organize this important meeting!
>
> Cordially,

Be Complete

An important quality of every business letter is completeness, and the letter of response is no exception. "Have I included all the information the reader needs?" is the question everyone must ask before mailing a response letter. The writer who is not able to answer all the questions asked should direct the inquirer to a source where the answers can be found.

To make sure that complete answers are included in response letters, some writers underline the important points in the letter of inquiry; others jot comments in the margins of the letter. These underscored words and marginal notes then serve as an outline to help the writer prepare a complete response letter.

This technique is illustrated by the letter of inquiry shown on page 309 and the response to that letter shown on page 310. Note how the writer, in responding to the questions, answers them in the order they were asked and uses the same numbering system. Note, too, that *every* question is answered, even though the folder enclosed will answer the same questions. By personalizing the letter in this way, the writer has made it more effective.

1783 Lincoln Boulevard
Westwood, Virginia 23205
April 2, 19--

Electrostatic Cleaner Company
896 Kingston Avenue
Chicago, Illinois 60613

Gentlemen:

I am very much interested in the Electrostatic electronic air cleaner that was advertised in the March issue of Home Products. There are some questions I would like answered about your air cleaner to help me decide whether yours is the make that best suits my needs.

1. Under what principle does your air cleaner work? *agglomerate*
2. Where does the unit have to be mounted? *vertical, horizontal, underneath*
3. How often does the collecting cell have to be washed? *18 mos.*

I should appreciate your answering these questions in time for me to make a decision by May 10.

Send folder T86-74

Very truly yours,

James A. Daughtrey

James A. Daughtrey

PRINTED RESPONSES

One advertisement in a national magazine can cause a deluge of request letters, especially if a free booklet or a free sample is offered. Such an advertisement may draw hundreds of thousands of pieces of mail, all of which must be answered. Obviously, this many requests cannot be promptly or efficiently answered by writing individual letters; individual letters would be impractical, much too costly, much too time-consuming.

When such a great response is anticipated, a form letter or card is printed in advance, before the advertisement appears, and is ready to be mailed as

Electrostatic Cleaner Company 896 Kingston Avenue · Chicago, Illinois 60613

April 24, 19--

Mr. James A. Daughtrey
1783 Lincoln Boulevard
Westwood, Virginia 23205

Dear Mr. Daughtrey:

Thank you for your interest in the Electrostatic electronic air cleaner. I am delighted to answer the questions you have asked about the model advertised in Home Products.

1. This model, FL-190-A, operates on the agglomerator principle. The dirt particles are charged and collected on the cell plates in the conventional way, but as they build up on the cell, they "agglomerate" or break off in chunks, which are easily retained by the special pad on the clean-air side of the cell. This method of air cleaning, used successfully for many years in commercial installations, eliminates the need for frequent washing of the cell.

2. The unit may be mounted either horizontally or vertically in any forced-air system, or it may be placed underneath a furnace.

3. The cell may have to be removed and washed in a good nonsudsing detergent once every 18 months or so. This procedure will be necessary only if the cell is especially sticky or greasy.

I am enclosing a folder that describes the unit in more detail, gives price information, and lists the dealers in your area who carry this model. You will find that there is no finer air filter on the market, that its installation is flexible, and that its price is competitive.

Please let us know if you have any further questions.

Very sincerely yours,

Robert G. Golden

Robert G. Golden
Sales Manager

RGG:rej
Enclosure

requests are received. This letter or card is carefully planned so that it will answer most of the inquiries prompted by the advertisement and will keep to a minimum the number of individual responses that will be needed. If the printed response is too specific, its use will be limited; if it is too vague, it will not be useful in answering most of the requests. Its planning, therefore, is a major consideration.

The writer's first step is to try to anticipate the questions that will be asked; the next is to answer each one clearly. The form letter may itself provide the information, or it may simply refer to an enclosed booklet or pamphlet that answers the questions. But no matter how well the writer anticipated the readers' queries, some individual replies will usually have to be written to answer questions not covered in either the form letter or the booklet.

A reply card may be included (usually postage paid), to facilitate the reader's ordering the product, asking for a free demonstration, requesting inclusion on a mailing list, making an appointment with a sales representative, and so on.

The printed response card shown below was accompanied by "a handy postpaid card" and an explanatory booklet. This response card is not too specific; its use will not be limited. On the other hand, the hotel reservation confirmation form on page 312 is very specific, but because it fits a highly standardized situation it suits its purpose very well.

Here's the Material
You requested

And we hope you'll find some ideas in it that you can use to profit . . . If you would like to know how our products might be used in your business, you'll find a handy postpaid card enclosed in the booklet. Mailing it will bring a prompt response. Thank you for your interest.

Sincerely yours,
R. C. Lawrence, Jr.
Vice President

Courtesy Pitney Bowes

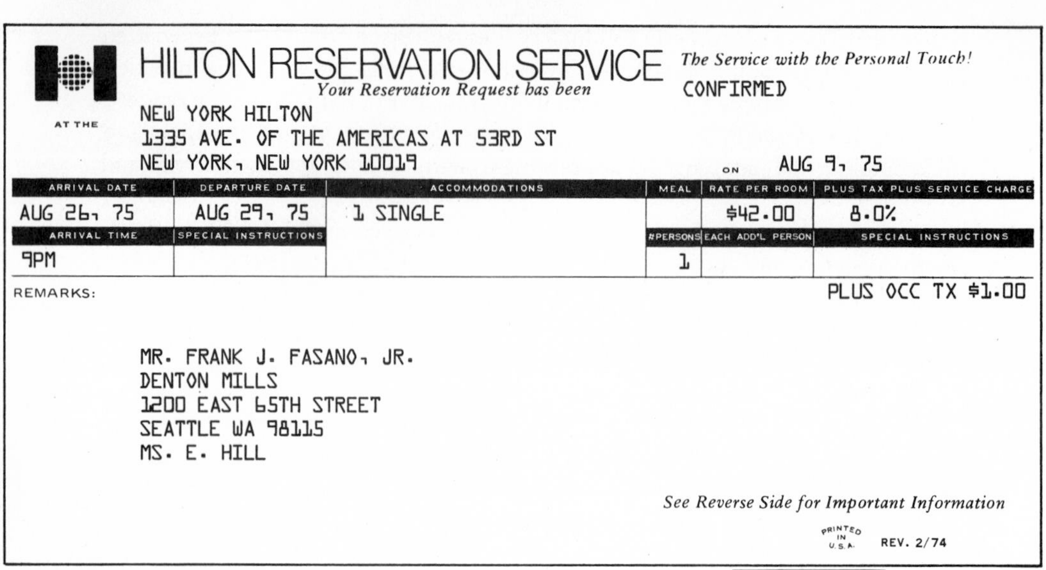

HILTON RESERVATION SERVICE *The Service with the Personal Touch!*

Your Reservation Request has been CONFIRMED

AT THE NEW YORK HILTON
1335 AVE. OF THE AMERICAS AT 53RD ST
NEW YORK, NEW YORK 10019 ON AUG 9, 75

ARRIVAL DATE	DEPARTURE DATE	ACCOMMODATIONS	MEAL	RATE PER ROOM	PLUS TAX PLUS SERVICE CHARGE
AUG 26, 75	AUG 29, 75	1 SINGLE		$42.00	8.0%
ARRIVAL TIME	**SPECIAL INSTRUCTIONS**		**#PERSONS**	**EACH ADD'L PERSON**	**SPECIAL INSTRUCTIONS**
9PM			1		

REMARKS: PLUS OCC TX $1.00

MR. FRANK J. FASANO, JR.
DENTON MILLS
1200 EAST 65TH STREET
SEATTLE WA 98115
MS. E. HILL

See Reverse Side for Important Information

PRINTED IN U.S.A. REV. 2/74

Courtesy The Detroit Hilton

A word of caution about printed responses: Make sure that the letter sent really answers the request. In the rush to respond to a large number of requests, you can easily make errors, either because you read the request carelessly or because you are not thoroughly acquainted with the contents of the form letter. For example, suppose that a dealer who is not now a customer requests information about costs of factory repair service from Bakit and receives the following form letter.

> To Service Engineers of Bakit:
>
> The Bakit service and parts manual that you requested is enclosed.
>
> Normal repair procedures are described opposite each subassembly. However, if you have any problems, you may either write to or telephone our Service Department (555-9878, Extension 4398).
>
> Please note that factory repair service is also available to your customers—and at minimum cost. For information about factory repair service, please request Bakit Factory Service Manual KZ1975.
>
> Cordially yours,

First of all, the dealer is not a service engineer and has no use for a manual of service and parts. Furthermore, a careful reading of the request letter would have told the correspondent that the information wanted was contained in Bakit Factory Service Manual KZ1975. The correspondent then could have sent this manual or could have referred the request to someone else who could have sent it. Lost: one potential customer because of an inappropriate form letter.

Communication Projects

PRACTICAL APPLICATION

A As a new manufacturer of toys, you have received a large order from Denton's Department Store, 1983 Stuart Avenue, Appleby, Iowa 51430. This order is the first one you have received from Denton's. They would like to know how and when the merchandise will be shipped, as well as the terms of payment. How would you reply to Denton's?

B Kenneth Rowan, 18 Greenhouse Drive, Springfield, Illinois 62701, requested an annual report from your company, Merit Publishing Company. Unfortunately, you have run out of copies and you do not plan to reprint last year's report. Since it is almost the end of the year, you will soon be preparing the new annual report. You might indicate to Mr. Rowan that you will put his name on the mailing list to receive the new report and that, in the meantime, if he would like any information relating to last year's report, you would be happy to provide such information.

C Henry Jackson, Director of Public Relations for Desmond Manufacturing Company, 114 Fargo Avenue, Peoria, Illinois 61601, telephoned Donna Peters, Advertising Consultant for the Markam Stores, 789 Front Street, Springfield, Illinois 62701, to ask her to participate in a panel discussion on the topic "Getting the Most from Your Advertising Dollar" at the convention of the Advertising League. The meeting will be held on August 10 at the Adams Hotel in Springfield, Illinois, from 10 a.m. to noon. Ms. Peters is to make a 15-minute presentation and then participate in a 30-minute discussion period. The meeting will be held in the Empress Room and will be followed by a luncheon from 12:30 to 2 p.m. Ms. Peters is invited to the luncheon as a guest of the organization. Compose the letter Mr. Jackson should write to Ms. Peters to confirm all the details of the meeting.

D Refer to Practical Application A. Because of a breakdown in one of the machines in your factory, there will be 10-day delay in making shipment of Denton's order. Write a letter to them, tactfully explaining the reason for the delay and assuring them that they will receive delivery on the rescheduled date.

E You are employed as a correspondent for the Kold Refrigeration Company, 90 Gate Street, Appleby, Iowa 51430, and have been asked to compose a form letter that will accompany a brochure, "Make a Refrigerator Comparison Test." Requests for the brochure will come from a coupon advertisement that will appear in all of the leading home magazines next month. Keep in mind that a good response letter offers an excellent opportunity to be of service as well as to make a sale.

EDITING PRACTICE

Updating the Correspondence Rewrite these letter excerpts to improve the wording.

1. I send you herewith the catalog you requested.
2. In the event you will be unable to attend, please advise.
3. I am enclosing an invoice in the amount of $685.
4. The books are going out to you today under separate cover.
5. Up to the present writing, we have had no reply from you.
6. We wish to offer our thanks to you for taking the time to complete the questionnaire.
7. I have before me your letter of June 1.
8. The information in your letter has been duly noted.

CASE PROBLEM

Right Meeting—Wrong Report Don Farrell is employed in the sales department of the Reynolds Shoe Company. His supervisor asked him to attend an important meeting of the advertising department staff to explain how the two departments can work together more effectively in obtaining a better sales situation in the year ahead. Don misunderstood the subject he was to discuss and, instead, prepared a talk on the function of the sales department. During the chairman's introduction of Don, Don realized that he had misunderstood the topic.

1. What should Don do when he is called upon?
   a. Give the report he prepared?
   b. Admit his mistake and ask that the meeting be rescheduled?
   c. Blame his supervisor for giving him the wrong information?
   d. Bluff his way, hoping that no one will notice?
2. How could this situation have been prevented?

39 Writing Claim and Adjustment Letters

The customer who feels that money, merchandise, or a service has wrongly been withheld—that only an apology, an exchange of merchandise, or improved service can rectify matters—may write a letter explaining this view. Such a letter is called a "claim letter." The letter written in reply to the claim letter is called an "adjustment letter." Of course, the best policy is to conduct such an efficient business operation that no claim letters need be written; and adjustment letters will thus be eliminated.

However, the elimination of claims is wishful thinking. Situations are bound to occur, whether through the fault of the company, the customer, or both, that will result in some customers' writing claim letters. It is also possible that a third party may be at fault or even that there is no basis for a claim. The astute writer of business letters must first be able to determine if there is a basis for making a claim, and then how to effectively write a claim letter. If employed by a firm against whom a claim is made, the writer must be skilled in writing effective adjustment letters.

THE NATURE OF CLAIMS

If you order and are billed for merchandise that you fail to receive, you have a just claim against the company that sold you (or your firm) the merchandise. You might write the following claim letter to the company.

Billing Department
Hastings Office Supply Company
1832 Riverside Drive
Terre Haute, Indiana 47804

Gentlemen:

According to your Invoice 6704-B, dated June 10, we were billed for 10 cans of spirit duplicator fluid. However, we received and acknowledged receipt for only 6 cans.

We would appreciate your verifying your records to determine whether the other 4 cans have been shipped, whether they are being placed on back order, or whether an error was made on the invoice.

As soon as we learn the status of the additional 4 cans of fluid, we shall be happy to send payment.

Sincerely yours,

There are, of course, many additional situations from which claims arise: A product received may be defective or may not meet specifications. Merchandise that was not ordered may be delivered. Goods may be damaged in transit. A customer may claim the right to an adjustment under a warranty or guarantee. Someone may be billed incorrectly for goods purchased, or perhaps there is a misunderstanding about the price, the terms of payment, or the date of delivery. Policyholders may write letters to their insurance companies to present claims for damages sustained by fire, smoke, or windstorm.

As a business correspondent, you will find it necessary from time to time to send claim letters. In behalf of your company, you want to express annoyance, anger, or hurt at the mistake or misunderstanding that has occurred. But, although you can be thought of legally as the "injured party," it is a mistake to show in your claim just how "injured," annoyed, or angry you are. Most claims—approximately 98 percent of them—are due to accident rather than intention. Furthermore, most businesses recognize just claims and want to settle them fairly. There is no reason to assume that a claim letter, to be effective, must be a belligerent letter.

For example, suppose that a claimant (a person who makes a claim) had written the following claim letter instead of the one you just read.

Gentlemen:

I don't understand why you can't get a simple business transaction straight!

Last month, I ordered 10 cans of spirit duplicator fluid. When the shipment arrived, I got only 6 cans and I signed for only 6 cans. Isn't this perfectly clear? Doesn't anybody look at the shipping ticket before they make up bills?

As if that isn't bad enough, now you're trying to collect for the 4 cans you never shipped. You'll have to take me to court for that! Furthermore, if I don't hear from you within 5 days, I refuse to pay you for anything.

Yours truly,

Such a letter only exposes the writer's lack of sympathetic understanding. How does such a letter affect you? Certainly it does not endear the writer to you. An angry letter is far more likely to make the reader want to fight, rather than settle, a claim.

The point should be clear. When you write a claim letter, recognize that the person who will receive your claim is a human being too. Adopt a positive attitude toward the reader—assume that your reader will want to know about your claim and will want to make any necessary adjustment. In most instances you will find that this assumption will be the correct one.

WRITING CLAIM LETTERS

In addition to maintaining a positive attitude toward the business or person addressed in your claim letter, observe the following rules:

1. Be sure of your facts.
2. Describe your claim completely and concisely.
3. Suggest reasonable solutions.
4. Avoid threats and demands.
5. Avoid accusations.

Be Sure of Your Facts

The successful claim must state clearly all the facts about the claim. If, for example, part of your order is missing, it is important to establish that the portion of the order was missing on arrival. You must be certain that every item has been weighed, counted, checked, and rechecked so that you know exactly what was received and what was not received. Many slipups can happen on your side, the claimant's side—errors in ordering, misplacing a shipping or acknowledgment copy, miscalculating extensions on bills, misunderstanding verbal instructions on an order—even errors made at the receiving dock or in the storeroom. As the claimant, you will be doubly embarrassed to find that the error is yours! Be sure of your facts before writing a claim letter.

Describe Your Claim Completely and Concisely

Give the details necessary to establish your claim, such as dates, styles, catalog order numbers, and purchase order, invoice, or check numbers. Only then can the recipient of your claim determine how the error occurred. More important, only in this way can the recipient determine the source of the error and fix responsibility in its own company so that the mistake cannot occur again.

Suppose, for example, that the insurance company that handles your automobile insurance notifies you that your policy is no longer valid because you have failed to pay your premium. You recall that you wrote the company a note on the back of their notice stating that your policy would be canceled if your premium was not paid within 10 days. In that note, you explained that your check No. 186 had been mailed January 4 for the full amount of the premium. Since you had no further word from the insurance company, you assumed that they had located the check and that everything was all right. Now the claim letter that you write might read as follows:

Gentlemen:

I was distressed to receive your notice of March 1 indicating that you have canceled my automobile insurance policy No. AZ1843687 for failure to pay the premium of $350 due on January 15.

On January 4, I mailed my check No. 186 for $350. On January 17, the check, endorsed by your company and stamped "Paid," was returned to me. I reported this information to you on the back of a notice of cancellation mailed to me January 30. Since I received no further word from you, I assumed that the matter had been straightened out satisfactorily.

I am enclosing a photocopy of the front and back of my canceled check. Would you please send me a notice of the reinstatement of my insurance.

Very truly yours,

Note that the letter gives *all* details, completely but concisely, so that the insurance company can quickly rectify the situation.

Suggest Reasonable Solutions

The claim letter that suggests a reasonable solution strengthens your chances of gaining a just settlement. For example, if you placed an order and received only part of it, one solution might be to indicate that you will accept the missing portion if it arrives by a specific date, as shown by the following statement:

> We shall be happy to accept the 6 lamps if they reach us before February 5, the first day of our Anniversary Sale.

Or suppose that you were overbilled $50 on an order. In this case, you might say:

> Our records indicate that we were billed $250 for the merchandise on our Purchase Order 3290, dated July 7. The figure should have been $200. Therefore, please credit our account for $50 and send us a credit memorandum for this amount.

It is usually best to suggest the type of solution you will accept. For example, if you received defective merchandise, you might request replacement of the merchandise, cancellation of the order, a credit of the amount to your account, or substitution of a similar item meeting your needs. By suggesting a solution, the company will know exactly what action you want taken and, if it is reasonable, it will often follow your suggestion.

Avoid Threats and Demands

Give the receiver of your claim the benefit of the doubt. Of course, no courteous person would use such phrases as *you must, I want you to, I demand, unless you,* or *I must insist.* Furthermore, a claimant who makes threats and demands will only alienate the reader. Rather than use such strong language, a good writer will use a positive approach and will give the reader sound reasons to support the claim. The chances are that this approach will result in a faster settlement of the claim.

Suppose that the letter you write to the insurance company is not answered within a reasonable length of time. You may want to send a follow-up claim to the president of the agency that handles your insurance. Here is an example of the kind of letter you could write:

> Dear Mr. McDonald:
>
> I am enclosing a photocopy of a letter I wrote to the main office on March 5.
>
> My letter has not yet been acknowledged, and I am concerned about whether my automobile insurance is in force.
>
> I should very much appreciate your looking into this matter for me and providing written notification regarding the status of my automobile insurance.
>
> Very sincerely yours,

By selecting and addressing the follow-up claim to a higher official, you indicate you are concerned about a reply, yet your letter doesn't threaten or blame or accuse.

After you, as claimant, have exhausted all your letter-writing resources, your attorney may want to write in a more threatening tone.

Avoid Accusations

You should also make certain to avoid accusing tones whenever you write claim letters. Suppose that Mr. Witmer, a customer, owed you $300, less a cash discount of 2 percent ($6) if paid within 15 days after the date of the invoice. His check for $294 was not mailed, however, until 30 days after the invoice date—15 days after the discount period. Should you claim the $6 due you or forget about it? The decision is one that each company has to make. Often, a company may allow three to four extra days for the mails to clear, but not an extra fifteen days! Obviously, a claim letter is necessary in this case. Here is one that might be written:

> Dear Mr. Witmer:
>
> Thank you for your check for $294, dated September 30, in payment of our invoice of September 1 for $300. We appreciate your business, Mr. Witmer, and we hope that you found the merchandise up to our usual high standards.
>
> We know that you, as a businessman, realize the purpose of granting discounts for prompt payment of invoices. We both know very well, with so many records to process, how easy it is to overlook—or perhaps even misread—a statement when it is approved for payment. You will notice that our terms of 2/15, n/30 are more generous than most businesses allow. Therefore, you will realize that we cannot extend discount privileges for invoices paid 30 days after the date of the invoice.
>
> We can either credit your account for $294 and carry over to your next statement the $6 still remaining, or if you prefer, you can mail us the $6 balance to complete your payment.
>
> We are planning to introduce a new line of jewelry in time for Christmas sales and believe that you will be interested in looking through the enclosed attractive brochure. By October 15, we will have a complete stock on hand.
>
> Sincerely yours,

This letter meets the test of an effective claim letter. It is positive in tone, and the facts are clearly and concisely presented. Two acceptable solutions are suggested to the customer. Instead of accusing, the writer is courteously appreciative; in addition, the writer tries to develop goodwill.

In writing claim letters, remember that you're writing to people—people who are just as human and just as reasonable as you are. Calmly explain your facts; suggest reasonable alternatives; and avoid any discourteous threats, demands, or accusations. A claim letter written in this manner is likely to produce a favorable and prompt adjustment.

MAKING SATISFACTORY ADJUSTMENTS

Here are some everyday business situations involving dissatisfied customers: (1) An order for printed personal stationery is filled with the address incorrectly printed. (2) A customer makes a claim against an out-of-town retailer for overbilling, forgetting that the account also showed a previous unpaid balance. (3) A customer seeks damages from an appliance manufacturer for a defect in a newly purchased electric blender. In each instance, the customer feels justified in writing a claim letter to ask the appropriate person for an adjustment.

To handle adjustment letters satisfactorily, you, the writer, must use language skillfully; you must also have a sound understanding of the psychology involved in handling and settling claims. Because all claims are somewhat distasteful and irritating to the claimant, the adjustment-letter writer should soothe the claimant's feelings. To the extent possible, you should try to retain or rebuild the claimant's goodwill as a future customer. Finally, within the limits of company policy, you must provide an adjustment that is equitable.

Any person responsible for making adjustments must be familiar with the company's policies. Policies, of course, are the guide rules for the actions of a business. Such rules ensure that a business will act in a consistent manner in all of its transactions. These rules provide guidelines for arriving at adjustments that are fair both to the customer and to the company.

Equitable Adjustments

Equitable adjustments mean reasonable, right, fair, honest, or impartial decisions in dealing with claims. As a writer of adjustment letters, you must act as a judge. You must collect all the facts for and against the claim, weigh the evidence, and arrive at a decision that is right both for your business and for the customer. Therefore, before replying to a claim letter, you must consider all aspects of the situation and be satisfied that your decision is equitable.

Making the Right Decision

Even the most clever writer of adjustment letters will be unable to write a letter to retain goodwill and future sales if the basic adjustment decision is unfair or unjust to the customer. The writer of adjustment letters can, however, rely on certain guides in weighing the evidence and arriving at wise decisions. Three sources of evidence that the adjuster should tap are the company, the claimant, and the transaction itself.

The Company You may assume that your company, like most other companies, is ethical in its dealings. (You would not want to be associated with a company that is not.) Ask yourself the following questions to determine the extent of your company's responsibility in causing the claim. Do you know, without a doubt, that the company is not at fault? Could anyone in the company have made a misleading statement? Could the advertising be misinterpreted? Could your records be at fault? Is it possible that someone in the company made a mistake? If such questioning reveals an element of blame on the part of the company, you, the adjuster, will probably decide to honor the claim, at least in part.

The Claimant To help you evaluate the claimant's share in causing the claim, ask questions like these: Could the claimant be mistaken? Is the claim, if true, the kind that a reasonable person would make? Has the claimant provided all the information you need to check the claim and fix responsibility for it? Does the claimant have a record of fair dealings with your company?

The Transaction The answers to the following questions will help you arrive at an equitable decision about the transaction. Were there any implied contractual obligations peculiar to the nature of your business that were not carried out? For example, does your company guarantee "Double your money back if you are not satisfied"? Could there have been faulty parts in, or faulty assembly of, the product? Was the use of the product explained fully at the time of sale? at the time of delivery? during the tryout? If you find a defect either in the product or in the transaction, you should arrive at a decision favorable to the claimant. Most business people want to please their customers.

The facts from such a study of the claim, in relation to your company, the claimant, and the transaction, provide the evidence you need to arrive at an equitable decision. At times you may have to write inquiries to your claimant to determine some of the facts. For example, read the following letter:

> Dear Miss Fitzgerald:
>
> Thank you for your letter of May 8 concerning an adjustment on your Dutton 2001 wristwatch. When we checked our files, we were unable to locate a certificate of purchase to validate the period of the guarantee. Therefore, would you please let us know the number in the top right corner of your receipt. If you do not have the receipt, please give us the name of the dealer from whom you made the purchase and the approximate date of purchase.
>
> As soon as we receive this information, we shall be happy to proceed with the adjustment.
>
> Very sincerely yours,

When you, the adjuster, have the needed additional information, you will be able to arrive at an equitable decision on the claim.

WRITING ADJUSTMENT LETTERS

Arriving at a just decision is one matter; communicating this decision in a way that will satisfy the claimant is another. The least difficult adjustment letter to write is one for a case in which the claim can be allowed as requested. The most difficult is a letter for the claim that must be disallowed. The letter for the claim in which some compromise is found equitable is between these extremes.

An Allowable Claim

Mistakes occur even in the best-regulated businesses. When the fault is your company's or your own, admit the error freely. The claimant will respect you if you are big enough to admit a mistake, especially if you have erred for the first time. You should accept the responsibility of correcting your error without quibbling over the added cost or effort caused by it. Remember that the writer's aim is to keep the claimant as a customer. Note how the writer of the following letter attempts to retain the customer's goodwill.

> Dear Mr. O'Brien:
>
> A shipment of the parts you ordered for your Kit A33 Faucet Assembly was sent to you by air freight this morning. These parts will replace the Kit Z31 parts you received in error.
>
> Our order department has a wonderful record for efficiency and accuracy; apparently something went wrong this time. Mistakes do occur, unfortunately; but we will do our best to determine the cause of this error and prevent its happening again.
>
> At your convenience, please return the Kit Z31 in the shipping container, and send it by railway express collect. Please let us know, Mr. O'Brien, how we may be of further service to you.
>
> Sincerely yours,

Some companies will allow a customer's claim, even on questionable evidence, if the cost of doing so is not too great and if, by so doing, a customer will be retained. In such a situation, future sales will often compensate for any loss that may occur in settling a minor claim.

A Partially Allowable Claim

A more difficult letter to write is the one in which a compromise solution is necessary. If the negotiation concerns an item of high value, the company may want to send an adjuster to talk to the claimant in order to seek a compromise.

For example, suppose a customer writes your company requesting that a newly bought microwave oven be repaired because the chrome trim on the door was dented slightly. The dent does not affect the performance of the oven and is not very noticeable. To remove the oven and return it to the manufacturer for replacement of the strip of chrome would be extremely costly. You believe that a compromise, something much less drastic than returning the oven, is in order.

How much of an adjustment a company makes may vary from one company to another because of differences in company policy. However, weighing the evidence in light of your company's policies, you believe that a $40 adjustment is equitable. More important, you feel that this adjustment is likely to keep your claimant as a satisfied customer. Your letter describing your proposed adjustment might read as follows:

> Dear Mrs. Freeman:
>
> We are unable to tell whether the small dent on the chrome strip along the door of your Thermowave oven occurred during shipment or installation or whether it was damaged in the retail store where you made your purchase. Because we pride ourselves on the quality of our products, we hope that our inspection report was correct in indicating that the oven was in perfect condition when it left our factory. Still, Mrs. Freeman, we want you to be satisfied with your purchase of our product.
>
> Since the dent is not so noticeable that it would mar the appearance of your oven and does not affect either the operation of the oven or the opening and closing of the door, we question the advisability of replacing the chrome strip. For one thing, you would be inconvenienced because the repair would take approximately six weeks, including shipping time; in addition, the delicate mechanism that operates the oven could be damaged in removal or in transit. In fairness to you, though, we are prepared to make an adjustment of $40 to show our sincerity and good faith.
>
> If this adjustment is satisfactory, please call your dealer, Mr. Linton, to let him know. Our check will be sent to you through the dealer.
>
> We are sure you can look forward to many years of fine service from your new Thermowave oven.
>
> Sincerely yours,

A Nonallowable Claim

Perhaps the most difficult letter to write is the one in which you must refuse to grant an adjustment. Sometimes the refusal is necessary just to avoid setting a precedent for allowing unjustified claims. The cost of settling one such claim might be small, but a business cannot afford the cost of settling many unjustified claims.

For example, assume that you are a fabric manufacturer. Unless you handle fabrics on consignment, you cannot permit every retail outlet to return yard goods just because the goods don't sell. Suppose, however, that you receive a request from Mr. Trevino to return the unsold goods. Of course, you must disallow the claim; but you should do so in such a way that you will retain Mr. Trevino as a customer. Your letter to him should protect your company's position and, at the same time, should show interest in the customer's point of view. For example:

> Dear Mr. Trevino:
>
> Thank you for writing us about the summer suiting materials you wish to return for credit. We checked our records and we find that you received the goods on March 1, in plenty of time for your presummer sales.

Of course, we can see why the fabric weights that you bought must be sold during a particular season. We wish we were in a position to absorb your materials into our stock. Unfortunately, we have no outlet for them and our warehouse space is limited.

May we recommend that you cut your price to 10 percent above cost and include them in your midsummer clearance sale. Most stores do this most successfully when a fashion item fails to move. Lawrey's Department Store used a novel way of disposing of similar materials last year—they featured the fabrics as drapery materials rather than as suiting.

Our Mr. Aikin will be in your store on August 1 to show you our new winter and spring patterns. If you have not sold the material by that time, Mr. Trevino, Mr. Aikin may have some additional suggestions for you.

Sincerely yours,

Note that this letter accomplishes the following purposes:

1. It starts with a positive tone, and the tone throughout the letter is friendly and courteous.
2. It acknowledges Mr. Trevino's claim and sympathizes with his problem.
3. It offers suggestions that Mr. Trevino may follow, and gives as an example the name of a well-known department store that was successful in solving a similar problem.
4. It helps maintain goodwill and good public relations by indicating that there will be follow-up by a company representative.

Communication Projects

PRACTICAL APPLICATION

A Review the letter of adjustment addressed to Mrs. Freeman (page 322). Suppose that in your judgment of the problem, you consider it preferable to let Mr. Linton, the dealer who sold the oven to Mrs. Freeman, call to make the compromise offer. Assume further that your claims adjuster, Mr. Mark Harmon, has called at the home of Mrs. Freeman to inspect the damage. Write to Mr. Linton and give him the information he needs in order to talk with Mrs. Freeman. Mr. Albert Linton's address is Linton's Home Appliance Center, 8763 Market Street, Lexington, Kentucky 40506.

B The Home Telephone Company, 189 Reed Place, Warsaw, Ohio 43844, has billed you for a long-distance call to New York City on May 15, 4:34 p.m., in the amount of $6.74, including tax. The call was made to 555-8787. You did not place this call, and no one was at your home during the afternoon of May 15 to make the call on your telephone. Write to the telephone company, explaining the situation and asking them to adjust your bill accordingly.

C Mary Witherspoon, the Personal Representative who handles your account with the Home Telephone Company, receives your communication regarding the long-distance call to New York City on May 15 (see Practical Application B). She looks into the matter and finds that the call was placed from a number different from yours. Compose the letter that Mary should write in response to your claim.

D You are employed in the office of ABC Television Stores, Inc., a large retail chain. In checking a purchase order and receiving a report against a sales invoice of May 1, you find a $75 discrepancy. You ordered a Mark Television Set, No. C18-75, at $189.50 net. The sales invoice shows a net charge of $264.50 for this item. You prepare a check for $189.50. Write a letter to the Mark Television Manufacturing Company, Inc., 8530 River Street, Chicago, Illinois 60607, and explain the $75 deduction in your check. In shipping you the order, Mark Television was a full ten days ahead of schedule, so be sure to thank them for this quick delivery service.

E Assume now that you work in the office of the Mark Television Manufacturing Company, Inc., and that you have received the check and letter of explanation from ABC Television Stores, Inc., 89 State Street, Minneapolis, Minnesota 55404 (described in Practical Application D). When you check with the shipping department, you find that No. C18-85, which is in a mahogany cabinet, and not No. C18-75, which is in a laminated plastic cabinet, had been shipped to ABC. The error is your company's, but you feel that they should know (if they have not yet sold the set) that they have the more expensive model on their floor. It would cost you almost all of the $75 difference to ship the correct one and return the one shipped in error. Write a letter to ABC and explain the error. Try to phrase your letter so that ABC, if they have not suffered a loss, will be willing to send you the additional $75.

F The complaint shown below has been forwarded to you in the Claims and Adjustment Department. You are authorized to send a check for twice the retail price of $1.75 to any dissatisfied customer and, at your discretion, to send a new can of Ted's Barber Lather to replace a faulty one. You talk with Mr. Fernandez in the product-quality control department. He is unable to explain what caused the situation described in the letter. The research and product development department would like to have the can in question returned. Answer the claimant's letter, making an effort to retain his goodwill.

> Dear Sirs:
>
> For ten years I was a satisfied customer. Ted's Shaving Soap has provided me with several thousand clean shaves.
>
> Just last week I bought an aerosal can of Ted's Barber Lather. Quite frankly, I don't like it. Three shaves and the fizz is gone. There's still plenty of lather in the can, but I can't get it out.
>
> What shall I do?
>
> Sincerely yours,
> George H. Indie

EDITING PRACTICE

Applied Psychology As written, these sentences would create ill will. Rewrite them from the viewpoint of good public relations.

1. We have already written you once about this matter.
2. You made a mistake of 50 cents on our invoice of July 18.
3. You neglected to indicate the number on our invoice.
4. You complained that Order 32A failed to arrive on time.
5. We were surprised to learn that you found the merchandise unsatisfactory.

6. We will repair the chair that you claim was broken in transit.
7. Your failure to reply has made the problem even worse.
8. Your recent letter fails to explain satisfactorily your delay in paying.
9. We are returning your Check 189 because you were careless and forgot to sign it.
10. There is no possibility that we will be able to deliver your order on time because a number of more alert customers placed their orders ahead of you.

CASE PROBLEM

Attending to Customers Fred Anson is a salesman in the men's furnishings department of Carter's Department Store. Early on Saturday morning his supervisor came by and said, "Fred, see if you can get your new merchandise marked and put on the shelves as quickly as possible. It's going to be a busy day, and I have several special things for you to do." While Fred was rushing to complete the job, a customer, Mr. Jackson, entered the department. Even though Fred was the only available salesman, he continued marking the merchandise and let the customer wait. Just as Fred finished his marking and went to wait on his customer, Mr. Jackson left the department.

1. Was Fred justified in ignoring Mr. Jackson in order to finish marking the new merchandise? Why or why not?
2. What should Fred have said to Mr. Jackson as soon as he saw him?

40 Writing Credit and Collection Letters

Doing business on credit is a fundamental characteristic of our system of private enterprise. In a competitive system, the buyer is king. Buyers ask for and get many services from sellers. One of the services buyers receive is the privilege of buying on credit. Sellers invite the use of credit because they know that charge customers buy more and are more loyal customers.

Can you imagine a world without credit? If it were not for our credit system, many consumers would not own homes, automobiles, and such large appliances as refrigerators and television sets. Credit is both a necessity and a convenience. It is a necessity because most consumers could not amass a sum of money large enough to purchase costly items. It is a convenience because many people do not like to carry large sums of money on their person, particularly when traveling. In addition, credit purchasing gives them the added benefit of an accounting for, and a verification of, their monthly purchases.

Today, the use of credit is widely encouraged by business firms and retail stores. Rare is the adult who does not have at least one credit card for charging such purchases as gasoline, hotel accommodations, airline tickets, car rentals, restaurant bills, and other kinds of merchandise and services. Businesses also make use of the credit privilege for similar reasons.

The most common type of credit is open-account credit, which usually means that the customer has 30 days in which to pay for purchases. Consumers buy on open account from those who deliver their daily newspapers, from utility companies, and from retail stores. Business firms also buy on open account from many of their suppliers. To encourage prompt payment of an account, suppliers often grant retail stores and other large-buying customers a discount when an invoice is paid within a certain period. Typical terms are 2/10, n/30, which means that 2 percent may be deducted from the total amount of the bill if it is paid within 10 days of the date of the invoice; otherwise, the entire amount is due in 30 days. Retail customers do not generally enjoy this discount privilege.

THE THREE C'S OF CREDIT

Credit privileges for both consumers and business people are granted or refused on the basis of character, capacity, and capital—the three C's of credit.

Character

Character refers to the honesty and integrity of people or businesses. People with good character are ethical and trustworthy. They have a strong desire to meet their obligations and are not satisfied until their debts have been paid.

Capacity

Capacity is the ability of people or businesses to meet their financial obligations. A person may desire to pay a $1,000 debt; but without sufficient income, it will be impossible to meet those bills. Questions such as the following help to determine capacity: Is aggressiveness a characteristic of the individual or of the business? Is good judgment exercised by the individual or by the management of the business? Is the individual intelligent? healthy? well trained? Is the business stable?

Capital

Capital refers to personal or business assets—cash, securities, real estate, and personal property. Creditors consider capital assets the most important of the three C's because these assets determine whether the business has the ability to pay if legal action to obtain payment should be required.

INVESTIGATING CREDIT APPLICATIONS

Credit managers of business firms or stores have the responsibility for determining the character, capacity, and capital of applicants for credit. Obviously, they can't trust everyone; they can grant credit only to those who give reasonable assurance that they will pay their bills when due. To do otherwise is business suicide. At the same time, credit managers have learned through experience that they can trust most people. They want to offer credit to those who are eligible, because such practice means more sales for the company. The successful credit manager is both discerning and sales-minded. These two qualities must be kept in balance.

Each applicant for credit must be investigated. Usually applicants must fill out written applications, which include information regarding their assets, their debts, their income, and their character references. Retail stores sometimes require an interview with the applicant.

Credit investigators use various sources—firms and stores with which the applicant has done business, banks, and credit rating bureaus—to obtain information about an applicant. For example, the letter on page 328 was written by a wholesaler to a bank to ask for information about a credit applicant. On page 329 the bank's reply to the credit inquiry is illustrated. Note that the bank provides accurate answers to the questions asked without divulging the specific account or loan balances.

Letters sent to the other business references supplied by the credit applicant would be similar to the one illustrated; only the questions asked would vary. For example:

1. Approximately how many years has the credit applicant had an account with you?
2. What is the maximum amount owed you at any one time?
3. What is the maximum amount of credit you would be willing to grant the applicant?
4. How would you consider the applicant as a credit risk? (Please check) Excellent___Average___Questionable ___

GRANTING CREDIT

A majority of those who apply for credit are granted this privilege. When an investigation reveals that an applicant is a good risk, the business firm or store writes a letter of welcome. In this letter the seller should explain the terms of credit and should encourage the customer to use the new charge privileges. Because the granting of credit signals a new source of business, the welcoming letter is frequently signed by an officer of the company. The letter granting credit provides an excellent opportunity to establish a good business relationship with a new customer. For this reason, many large businesses resist the temptation to send form letters to new charge customers.

Business people recognize that an individually typed letter, even one that is prepared by automatic typewriter, provides a desired personal touch that will lead to good customer relations.

WHOLESALE HARDWARE, INC.
1398 Acme Street Fort Worth, Texas 76111

March 5, 19--

Fort Worth Bank of Commerce
65 Century Boulevard
Fort Worth, Texas 76111

Attention: Credit Manager

Gentlemen:

Mr. William Ross, owner of Ross Hardware Store, 934 Republic Avenue, Fort Worth, Texas 76111, has applied to us for credit. He has given your bank as a reference.

We shall appreciate your answering the following questions about Mr. Ross' financial dealings. Any information you provide us will be held in strict confidence.

1. What is the average monthly balance in his checking account(s)?
   What balances, if any, are there in his savings account(s)?

2. On what basis (secured or unsecured) have you extended credit?
   Is any amount outstanding?
   On what basis?

3. Has your lending experience been satisfactory?
   Have there been any overdrafts?
   Have there been any drawings against uncollected funds?
   What has been the maximum amount of loans made by your bank to him?

We are considering extending credit up to $3,500 on terms of 2/10, n/30. We should appreciate your opinion as to whether such a limit is a reasonable one for this firm.

Yours very truly,

Frank Ciulla

Frank Ciulla
Credit Manager

FC:rl

The letter illustrated on page 330 grants credit to Ross Hardware Company and is addressed to the owner, Mr. Ross. Note how the letter spells out both the credit terms and the personal services Mr. Ross can expect to receive.

In recent years, businesses have developed many new types of retail credit, such as revolving accounts and a wide variety of installment plans. The retail customer should, therefore, receive a specific description of the credit terms of the account. The letter illustrated on page 331 grants credit to a customer of a retail store.

Fort Worth Bank of Commerce

65 Century Boulevard
Fort Worth, Texas 76111

Office of the Credit Manager

March 10, 19--

Mr. Frank Ciulla
Credit Manager
Wholesale Hardware, Inc.
1398 Acme Street
Fort Worth, Texas 76111

Dear Mr. Ciulla:

This letter is in reply to your inquiry of March 5, 19--, regarding Mr. William Ross, owner of the Ross Hardware Store. We have done business with Mr. Ross for the past 15 years and are pleased to supply the information you requested in your letter.

Mr. Ross maintains both a regular checking account and a savings account with us. Balances average in high four figures and low five figures, respectively.

During last December, unsecured loans reached a yearly high of high four figures. At the present time, nothing is outstanding; and our experience has been entirely satisfactory. Seasonal credit was extended in August, 19--, on a secured basis up to a high of low five figures. All payments have always been made promptly according to terms.

We have a high regard for Mr. Ross' character and his business ability. You should experience no difficulty in extending credit up to $3,500 on the terms you indicated.

Please let us know if you have any additional questions regarding Mr. Ross' financial capacity.

Very sincerely yours,

Arthur T. Middleton

Arthur T. Middleton
Credit Manager

ATM:trr

REFUSING CREDIT

Perhaps the most difficult letter to write is the one in which the writer refuses credit. Some credit managers believe this matter is so delicate that it should be handled in person rather than by mail. Others believe that a delaying tactic should be used; that is, the customer should not be told directly that credit is being refused. They prefer to say something like this:

> On the basis of the information we have received regarding your credit standing, we feel that we cannot give you a definite decision at this time.

WHOLESALE HARDWARE, INC.
1398 Acme Street Fort Worth, Texas 76111

March 17, 19--

Mr. William Ross
Ross Hardware Store
934 Republic Avenue
Fort Worth, Texas 76111

Dear Mr. Ross:

Thank you for your recent request to extend open account credit to you. We are pleased to extend you credit in any amount up to $3,500, with terms of 2/10, n/30.

We look forward to a long, pleasant business association with you, Mr. Ross. Our local representative, Mr. Arnold Frascati, will call on you every three weeks to make sure that you are getting the merchandise you need when you need it. Please feel free to review with Mr. Frascati your current stock to make sure that you have an adequate inventory to meet your needs at all times. He will also keep you up to date on new products as they come on the market.

Please let us know whenever we can be of service to you.

Yours very sincerely,

Frank Ciulla

Frank Ciulla
Credit Manager

FC:rl

Still other credit experts believe that the refusal can be handled effectively by letter without serious injury to the customer's pride. For example, the following letter of refusal was written by a credit person who believes in "leveling" with the customer. To avoid a negative response on the part of the rejected customer, however, the writer has presented the factual, nonemotional information that caused the application to be rejected. Also, the writer has counterbalanced the refusal by adding positive statements.

Dear Mr. Shartle:

You have complimented us by requesting credit privileges at Anderson's.

R. J. Thompson and Company
17 Wilshire Terrace
Reno, Nevada 89503

August 16, 19--

Mrs. Kenneth Glover
189 Toledo Road
Reno, Nevada 89503

Dear Mrs. Glover:

R. J. Thompson and Company takes great pleasure in adding your name to our long list of credit customers. We sincerely hope that our association will be a long and mutually pleasant one.

As one of our privileged charge customers, you will enjoy so many benefits at Thompson's in addition to the pleasant shopping atmosphere we have provided in our newly decorated store. For example, our charge customers receive advance notice of all special sales, so that you may take advantage of some wonderful bargains before they are announced to the general public. Charge customers automatically become members of the Thompson Travel Club, entitling them to special reduced rates on any of 10 fabulous tours to Europe and the Orient we offer throughout the year. Your account plate also may be used to charge meals in our exciting new TOP OF THE THOMPSON revolving restaurant and for beauty treatments in ADRIAN'S SALON. Your account plate opens the door to every department in our main store and our two branch stores at Amberton and at Willow Lawn.

On the tenth of each month, you will receive an itemized statement of all purchases made through the last day of the preceding month; purchases made after that date will appear on the following month's bill. Remittances are expected not later than the 25th of each month.

We hope that you will make regular use of your new charge account. THOMPSON'S looks forward to your visits and to being of service to you.

Cordially yours,

Roberta R. Randolph

Roberta R. Randolph
President

RRR:tl
Enclosure
Account plate

As in the case of all those who apply for credit, Mr. Shartle, we have made a careful investigation of your ability to handle additional credit. However, your present credit obligations are substantial, and we feel that you should not endanger your credit reputation by taking on additional credit obligations.

Please continue to allow Anderson's to serve you on a cash basis until such time as you are able to reduce your present obligations. When the circumstances are more favorable, you may be sure that we shall welcome the opportunity of considering your application again.

Cordially yours,

Airwork
CORPORATION

CITY AIRPORT • DETROIT, MICHIGAN • AREA CODE 313-LA 1-2300

November 20, 19--

Mr. William Barker
Aviation Services Inc.
Cleveland Hopkins Airport
Cleveland, Ohio 44109

Dear Mr. Barker:

We would very much like to establish Aviation Services on an open account basis. Unfortunately, the credit investigation concerning Aviation Services has indicated to us that we will be unable to do so, at least at the present time.

While we realize that practically all of us in the aviation industry are faced with the problem of high receivables and operating costs, we still cannot increase our open accounts if there is an indication that our terms of 30-day payments could not be met.

For the present time, we would like to handle Aviation Services on a C.O.D. basis. This, of course, is by no means a reflection on your own integrity or the integrity of your associates. At some future time, whenever you suggest, we will be glad to re-check credit references in the hope that your account can then be put on an open basis.

We are geared to make prompt shipments to many companies on a C.O.D. basis, and we do hope that you will keep us in mind whenever you have requirements that we can fill. We will do our best to give you top-notch service.

Regards from Airwork,

Credit Department

DM:bsw

Courtesy The Dartnell Corporation—Gold Medal Award Letter

The credit manager who refuses credit to an applicant, whether in person or by letter, has one objective—to convince the customer to buy on a cash basis. This effort calls for the highest form of communication skill. Note how this is done in the example above and in the letter on pages 330-331.

COLLECTION LETTERS

The more thorough the credit investigation, the fewer the losses from bad accounts. However, even the best regulated credit department will grant credit to some customers who will not pay their bills. Charge customers who do not meet their obligations must be reminded to make payment.

Collecting an overdue account is not an easy task. No one likes to ask for money. Yet businesses must ask—or lose money. The trick is to get customers to pay without losing their goodwill. The collection of overdue accounts will be greatly simplified if the following rules are observed.

Be Sure Customers Understand Your Credit Terms

The terms of credit should always be explained to the customer at the time credit is granted. In commercial credit (between wholesaler and retailer), it is also advisable to review credit terms pleasantly, but firmly, when you acknowledge a new customer's first order. If your terms are 30 days net, you expect your money in 30 days. Do not hedge with weak statements like *We hope you will send your check in 30 days.* You should instead say, *Our terms are 2 percent discount if you pay within 10 days; the net amount is due in 30 days.*

Assume That Customers Will Pay

When a customer fails to pay a bill on the date the payment is due, you should assume that this failure is an oversight. Most of your customers are honest, but they may tend to forget or to procrastinate. And psychologically, a distasteful task such as separating oneself from money tends to be delayed to the last moment. If the usual monthly statement does not produce results, send the customer a second statement a week or ten days later. You can write or stamp *Second reminder* or *Please remit* on the statement. Some credit departments use a rubber stamp with a humorous reminder, such as a drawing of a finger with a string tied around it or a cartoon face drawn with a very sad expression. Some companies use printed forms, usually impersonal, sometimes humorous, like those illustrated on page 334. Most customers will respond to gentle hints that their accounts are overdue and that you want your money. Remember, the first follow-up is not an attack; it's a gentle nudge and is highly impersonal.

Send Additional Reminders Frequently

If a customer does not respond to the second statement, it's time to go into action. An account that is 120 days overdue is usually much more difficult to collect than one that is only 40 days overdue. Therefore, if you haven't received payment within ten days after sending a second statement, you should write a letter to the customer. Thereafter, send frequent reminders until the account has been paid.

THE COLLECTION SERIES

Suppose you have sent Ronald L. Dooley, a charge customer, both a monthly statement and a reminder. Ten days have elapsed since the reminder was sent, but you have not received a response. Your first follow-up letter, though written in unequivocal terms, should still give Mr. Dooley the benefit of the doubt.

Sherlock Holmes' Easiest Case

WATSON: Mr. Holmes, here's a most interesting mystery. It's about a very good customer of ours.

HOLMES: It is obvious that the customer likes music and owns a tape cartridge system.

WATSON: Then why doesn't he pay his bill?

HOLMES: Elementary, Dr. Watson — he's just waiting to hear from us.

Is the case solved? it's up to you!

COLUMBIA STEREO TAPE CARTRIDGE SERVICE

Just a Reminder

Possibly you overlooked paying the minimum due on your most recent credit card statement.

Your payment for the amount shown below will be appreciated. If it has already been mailed, please accept our thanks and excuse this reminder.

Credit Card Number

Minimum Amount Due

Mobil Oil Corporation

P.O. Box 600, Kansas City, Mo. 64141

Courtesy of the organizations above

First Follow-Up Letter

Dear Mr. Dooley:

The balance due us on your account is $147.38. To date you have not responded to two statements mailed to you.

Does the balance shown agree with your own records? If not, please let us know at once. If our records and yours agree, please send us your check for $147.38 to clear your account.

Sincerely yours,

Suppose Mr. Dooley does not respond to the first follow-up letter. When should the next letter be sent? Practice will vary from company to company. In general, the second letter should be sent not later than 15 days after the first. The tone of the second letter, though friendly and courteous, should be firmer and more insistent than the first.

Second Follow-Up Letter

Dear Mr. Dooley:

We are having difficulty understanding why we still have not received the $147.38 balance that you owe us or at least some word of explanation for the delay in making payment.

Let's review the facts. The net amount was due on April 20. We did not hear from you. A second statement, therefore, was sent to you on May 1. Still we did not receive your check. We then wrote you on May 12 asking you if there was an error or some other reason why you did not make payment. As of today, June 1, we have had no word from you. In all fairness to us—and to yourself, Mr. Dooley—will you please let us hear from you by return mail?

Sincerely yours,

How many letters will be sent to Mr. Dooley before legal action is taken? Practice will vary, of course, but most companies will send from three to five letters before turning the account over to a lawyer or employing the services of a collection agency. Turning an account over to a collection agency or an attorney is a costly and time-consuming matter; thus all steps should be taken to collect from the customer before resorting to legal action.

In a five-letter follow-up series, the third letter to Mr. Dooley will be more insistent than the second. The fourth letter will demand payment; the fifth letter will indicate legal action, which will be necessary to collect a few accounts. It is, of course, only fair to warn of this impending action and to allow one last chance to pay. Note the increasingly stern tones in the following letters.

Third Follow-Up Letter

Dear Mr. Dooley:

Help us save your reputation.

Your account is now 75 days overdue. Two statements and two previous letters have been ignored. You still owe us $147.38.

You received the merchandise. You knew our credit terms. Still you have not sent your check for $147.38. At this point, your credit standing is in doubt; your reputation is in jeopardy.

Help save your credit rating and your reputation. Send us your check for $147.38 now.

Sincerely yours,

Fourth Follow-Up Letter

The tone of the fourth letter in the collection series is still more severe. Note, however, that the writer is still trying to appeal to the delinquent customer's self-interest.

> Dear Mr. Dooley:
>
> This letter is the sixth reminder that you owe us $147.38—two statements and four letters. Your account is now fully 90 days overdue!
>
> We believe that these six reminders represent a maximum of patience on our part. But patience grows thin—especially when you have failed either to answer our previous letters or to send us your check.
>
> Please help us, Mr. Dooley, to maintain your credit standing. To do so, we must insist that you send us your check for $147.38 within the next seven days.
>
> Sincerely yours,

Fifth Follow-Up Letter

Before Mr. Dooley's account is turned over to a lawyer or a collection agency, the following letter might be sent:

> Dear Mr. Dooley:
>
> Unless we receive your check for $147.38 within ten days, we shall have to turn your account over to our attorney for collection.
>
> We regret the need for this action. Yet, in all good conscience, what more can we do? This letter is the seventh reminder of your overdue balance. The $147.38 is now 100 days overdue.
>
> Of course, we want our money; we do not want to embarrass you with a legal action. We do not want to add legal fees to what you now owe us. All we want is a check for $147.38.
>
> Please help us avoid this action and help yourself maintain your credit standing.
>
> Sincerely yours,

Each of these collection letters had two objectives: (1) to collect the money due and (2) to retain the goodwill of the delinquent customer. As it becomes clearer and clearer that the customer is not "playing fair" with the creditor, however, the tone of each succeeding letter becomes more and more insistent and, finally, demanding. By the time the last collection letter in the series is sent, it is obvious that the customer is not going to pay. The principal function of this final letter is to scare the reader into paying the bill in order to avoid legal action.

Communication Projects

PRACTICAL APPLICATION

A As credit manager for a large manufacturer of furniture, you are responsible for either writing or approving all correspondence related to credit and collection. Criticize the following piece of correspondence that reaches your desk. Then rewrite the correspondence as you think it should be written.

Dear Mr. Shaw:

Your application for credit has been approved. Thank you.

Very truly yours,

B In your capacity as credit manager (see Practical Application A), you must refuse credit to one of your customers, Mr. Ingram, for $5,000. He has been a customer for several years and has never charged more than $2,000. Mr. Ingram has always paid his bills, but he has been a "slow pay"; hence you do not feel that he should be granted credit for as much as $5,000. Write Mr. Ingram your refusal, but attempt to retain his goodwill.

C Assume that you are employed in the credit department of Campbell's Department Store. Mrs. Lester Carson has been a charge customer for five years. Although she is usually slow in paying her bills, she has settled within 45 to 60 days of purchase. This month, however, Mrs. Carson has not paid the balance of $189.67, even though you have sent her two statements and two letters. Write the next letter that should be sent to Mrs. Carson. Appeal to her sense of fair play. The account is now more than 90 days past due.

D The first reminder of an overdue account is usually a gentle nudge. Prepare three such reminders to be included with the second monthly statement. Make the first one a humorous reminder. In the second reminder, inquire whether or not there has been a mistake. Use your imagination for the third reminder—assume that the customer has forgotten; show that you have confidence in the customer, or develop other similar ideas.

E Write a series of three collection letters that may be used as form letters by Brighton's Department Store. The first letter is to be mailed 15 days after the second statement has been mailed. The remaining letters will be mailed at 15-day intervals. The third letter should warn of legal action.

EDITING PRACTICE

Editing the News Edit and rewrite the following excerpts from copy submitted by the police court reporter.

1. Police found the man who had been struck by an automobile in a hotel on Avenue D.
2. The sheriff captured the bandits who attempted to rob the National Trust Company within 10 days.
3. The officer hastened to the restaurant where the thief was last seen on his motorcycle.
4. The defendant entered a plea of *nolo contendere* to the reduced charge through his attorney.
5. An automobile reported stolen yesterday morning by Jack Desmond was found this morning abandoned on Highway 85.

CASE PROBLEM

The Social Graces What would you say to each of the following people under the circumstances indicated?

1. George Franks has just been promoted to the position of supervisor of your department.
2. Grant Sommers, an attorney with the firm of Myers and Sommers, has recently passed away. His surviving partner, Amanda Myers, will handle the legal problems for your firm.
3. Joan Greco has just returned to the office after a long illness.
4. Mary Thompson asks you to have lunch with her, but you have already promised to have lunch with Jean Lester, who doesn't like Mary.

41 Writing Letters That Say "No"

Almost every business decision involves either a direct or an implied "Yes" or "No." When a purchasing agent decides to buy a particular brand of computer, the agent has in effect rejected all other brands. When five contractors bid on a construction job, the awarding of the contract to one of them constitutes a refusal of the other four contractors. When a consumer buys a new refrigerator, the customer is in effect saying "No" to every other make on the market.

Choosing a product and choosing a course of action are comparable. When one salesperson is selected from ten who apply for a position, the other nine must be turned down. Similarly, many customer claims and requests for credit must be refused by businesses. In fact, some businesses annually receive thousands of requests, and when a favorable decision is not in the best interests of the business, the request must be refused. Every business writer, therefore, must know how to say "No" and still retain the goodwill of the person who is being denied.

REQUESTS THAT MUST BE REFUSED

To understand the reasons for "No" letters, consider some of the typical requests that a business receives and must refuse. Requests that are opposed to a basic company policy are frequently received. Wholesalers, for instance, receive numerous requests from consumers who wish to buy their products at the wholesale price. Book publishers receive requests for unauthorized discounts on their products. Manufacturers often are asked to sell their product direct to the consumer or to unauthorized retailers. Sometimes requests ask for information that may actually be a company secret, such as a product plan, formula, or trade secret. Other requests for information may be unreasonable because of the time and cost of collecting and sending the facts asked for. Endorsements of political figures or support for controversial ideas are often requested and usually must be refused. Some requests for speeches or requests to attend meetings may also have to be refused because of lack of time or conflicts in schedules. Requests for confidential information about company personnel are nearly always refused.

In addition, every business receives more requests than it can honor for donations to welfare agencies, to educational institutions, to religious groups, to medical research organizations, to service clubs, and to civic and professional groups of all kinds. As good citizens, most business people do contribute generously to various worthy causes. Yet there is a limit to the amount that can be budgeted for such contributions, no matter how much the assistance is needed and warranted. Although we may want to fulfill every request, often we must refuse many requests.

In short, businesses must say "No" to many requests; however, they must say "No" for good reasons, reasons that will not offend the person or company making the request. To do otherwise would not be in the best interests of a company that wishes to retain the goodwill of its customers.

WRITING "NO" LETTERS

Since "No" letters are necessary in some instances, correspondents must learn how to say "No" both gracefully and in a way that retains goodwill. To be able to write such refusal letters requires an understanding of these five basic guidelines:

Be positive.
Show appreciation.
Don't slam the door.
Don't recall past sins.
Give reasons.

Be Positive

People tend to reflect toward others the attitudes displayed toward them. If you are negative in your approach to others, they are likely to be negative toward you. If you are positive in your approach, people are likely to react toward you in a positive manner. For example, if you frown when you meet someone, the chances are that the other person will frown too. On the other hand, put a pleasant smile on your face, and the odds are that the other person will respond with a smile. Psychologically, then, if you want your reader to respond in a positive manner, you must write in a positive manner—even when you are saying "No." Consider the contrast between the following examples of negative and positive statements:

Negative	Positive
Your product does not meet our specifications.	Our engineers believe that the brand we selected is closest to our specifications.
You do not meet our standards for this particular job.	Although your qualifications are excellent, we feel that we must continue to search for someone who meets all the unique qualifications for this job.
In view of your poor payment record, we are unable to grant you credit.	We shall be glad to evaluate your credit record after you have settled some of your obligations.
We must say "No."	Unfortunately, we cannot give you a "Yes" at this time.
Your prices are too high.	Perhaps, when you have adjusted your prices to make them more competitive, we shall be able to do business with you.
We cannot give you the information you want.	We should like to send you the information you request, but we know you will understand why this is not possible.

The letter on page 341 illustrates how positive words and a positive attitude may soften a refusal and help to retain the goodwill of the customer.

Show Appreciation

When the answer to a request must be "No," another way that the writer can soften disappointment and pave the way for future friendly relations is to show appreciation. A "No" letter that shows appreciation will help to retain goodwill that might otherwise be lost.

For example, assume that each of five contractors has presented a detailed bid for a new office building your company is contemplating constructing. When the company has made its final selection of a contractor, common courtesy dictates that a letter be written to the unsuccessful bidders who have spent time, effort, and money to prepare their bids. Notice how the following letter shows appreciation and softens the negative response.

> Dear Mr. Higgens:
>
> We very much appreciate the time and effort spent by you and your engineers to prepare the bid for the office building we plan to construct next year.
>
> The contract for this building has been granted to Excel Construction Company because we felt that their bid was the best for the type of construction required and for the materials specified.
>
> Although we have granted this contract to Excel, we sincerely hope you will bid for us again when future contracts are offered.
>
> Sincerely yours,

Don't Slam the Door

There is little reason for slamming a door when it can be gently closed or even left ajar. Too firm or too final a refusal in a letter is like slamming a door in someone's face—and there is no need to anger anyone by such

COMPANY

570 LEXINGTON AVENUE, NEW YORK, N. Y. 10022 . . . TELEPHONE PLaza 1-1311

MARKETING and

PUBLIC AFFAIRS

September 24, 19--

Miss Mary Smith
YZR Association
Program Committee
300 Madison Avenue
New York, New York 10017

Dear Miss Smith:

Thank you for your nice letter of August 30 regarding the YZR Annual Charity Ball.

As a matter of policy, our corporate operations do not advertise in souvenir programs. The number of proposals we receive in this area is, as you might imagine, very substantial.

We do appreciate your thinking of General Electric, however. Please accept our best wishes for this very worthy project.

Sincerely,

R. O. Stratton, Manager
Institutional Advertising

ROS:cr

Courtesy General Electric Company

rudeness. If you feel strongly that you do not want the services or products offered by a particular person, refuse what is offered, not the person. A gentle refusal usually does not anger. Instead, it holds out hope and keeps open the lines of communication, as shown in the following examples:

Perhaps at some future time we shall . . . .

Maybe, when our needs expand . . . .

We are keeping your application on file for . . . .

We wish that we were able to consider your request, but . . . .

It is possible that next year . . . .

We shall certainly keep your proposition in mind when . . . .

The following letters illustrate the impact of both slamming the door (the first letter) and saying "No" in a gentle manner (the second letter). Suppose you were the applicant who received the following refusal:

> Dear Ms. Carillo:
>
> We are sorry we can't consider your application for a position as executive assistant in our firm. Only a few applicants for this position can be accepted. Therefore, those we accept must have the highest aptitudes for, and interest in, our kind of business.
>
> Frankly, we do not see in your application the qualities we need in our organization. Therefore, we believe it would be a waste of your time and ours, too, to interview you.
>
> Because we already have so many more qualified applicants, we are returning your application and résumé. We can't consider you for this position; sorry.
>
> Yours very truly,

Slam! Even if you may not be qualified, you certainly would be angry at having the door slammed in your face. In contrast, consider the more tactful and friendly tone of this letter:

> Dear Ms. Carillo:
>
> We very much appreciate your interest in a position with the Carter Corporation. Thank you for taking the time to submit your application for a position as executive assistant.
>
> We require a minimum of five years of experience for all of our executive assistants, and we note that you have had only three years of experience at the present time.
>
> We shall be pleased to retain your application and résumé on file should you wish to apply at a later time for an opening for someone with your qualifications.
>
> Very sincerely yours,

As an applicant, you would not be so disgruntled by this gentle refusal, nor would you blame the company, for it has given you a face-saving reason for the refusal. Remember that applicants may also be customers or friends of customers, so it is to the advantage of the company to retain their goodwill even when turning them down for a job.

Don't Recall Past Sins

Closely related to slamming the door is blaming the reader for the "No" decision you must make. Little can be gained by recalling your reader's past sins, sins that cause your refusal. Basic kindness should prevent any but the most naïve writer from writing the following:

> Under no circumstances would we ever make a purchase from your company. The last order we gave you arrived a month late, despite the fact that you promised faithfully to get it to us on time.

You will help your reader save face when you avoid statements that suggest fault or blame. Here are additional examples of sins that should not be recalled when you write "No" letters:

Because of your mistake, we cannot . . . .

Since we were dissatisfied with your previous service . . . .

You neglected to let us know that . . . .

Because of your unsatisfactory repair of . . . .

Since you failed to . . . .

Suppose that bidders for a contract had been notified that the bids would be opened at 3 p.m. on June 5. Suppose that one contractor did not submit a bid until the following morning. You have heard from business associates that this contractor has in the past submitted bids after the deadline to undercut the lowest bidder. For ethical reasons, you cannot accept the late bid. However, you should certainly not write a letter like the following.

Dear Mr. Miles:

You failed to submit your bid at or before 3 p.m. on June 5. You have been known in the past to follow such a practice in order to undercut the bids of your competitors. Submitting bids after the deadline is unethical and unfair to other bidders. We cannot, therefore, condone such unethical procedures.

It goes without saying that we must reject your bid.

Very truly yours,

Instead, the letter to the unsuccessful bidder should be worded something like this:

Dear Mr. Miles:

Your bid on our proposed office building was received at 11 a.m. on June 6.

Since all bids were opened at 3 p.m. on June 5, the deadline indicated, we are returning your bid unopened.

We know that you will understand why the bid must be returned to you.

Sincerely yours,

Such a letter should cause this contractor to make sure that he submits future bids on time.

Give Reasons

In refusal letters, it is important to avoid emotional outbursts that cause the reader to seethe or boil over in anger. Refusals should be based on factual and objective reasons. Obviously, the reasons should be true, as well as convincing. Consider the following illustrations of logical reasons for a refusal.

Because our margin of profit is so small, a further reduction in our selling price would result in a loss to us.

Our budget for charitable donations for this year has been exhausted.

Our dealer agreement gives Marlin's the exclusive right to sell our products in your city.

To collect the information you request would require several weeks, and we simply cannot afford to devote so much time to doing the job.

The All-Aide line we are now carrying has proved to be a very successful item for us, and we do not think a change at this time would be a wise decision.

If you must refuse a specific request, sometimes you can propose another course of action that may bring a favorable response. Notice the attempt to achieve such a goal in these communications.

> I regret that another engagement makes it impossible for me to speak at your April meeting. However, I would be happy to do so at your May or June meeting. I would appreciate your giving me a month's notice.
>
> Why not put your suggestions in writing and send them to us? After we have had an opportunity to carefully consider your suggestions, we can get together to discuss them further.

Note how the writer of the letter illustrated below has carefully explained why the request must be refused. Note also that the policy of the company

Davies Furniture Company
7100-7150 Drexel Drive Phoenix, Arizona 85033

September 1, 19--

Mr. Alan Drinkwater
Director of Development
Desmond College of Art
189 Marvin Gardens
Phoenix, Arizona 85033

Dear Mr. Drinkwater:

Thank you for your recent letter requesting a contribution to the Desmond College of Art. We have always admired the work of your college in turning out many outstanding graduates who have achieved national recognition in the field of art.

For the past ten years, we have made donations to many worthy institutions like yours through our Mutual Participation Donation Plan. Under this plan, our company matches dollar for dollar the cash gifts made by its employees to support worthy causes in which they have an interest. We feel that members of a community have an obligation, as do the businesses in the community, to support worthwhile activities that contribute to the growth and welfare of that community.

Since we do have such a plan, Mr. Drinkwater, we are sure that you can understand why we must limit our contributions to those that comply with our policy. I do hope that the employees in our organization who are friends or alumni of the Desmond College of Art will choose to give your development fund their support. In that way, we can also make a contribution of equal value.

Thank you again for writing us. Best wishes to you in your drive for funds. Desmond is such a fine school that it deserves support for its outstanding program.

Very cordially yours,

Margaret A. Livingstone

Margaret A. Livingstone
Director of Public Relations

MAL:iw

has a built-in alternative—if the employees contribute, the company will match their contributions.

Now assume that you work for a wholesaler who sells only to retail outlets. A consumer (not a retailer) has sent you a rather large order. You must refuse because it would not be fair to your retail-store customers for you to sell directly to consumers at wholesale prices. Note how the reasons given in the following letter soften the refusal because they show that the writer's decision is factual and objective.

> Dear Mr. Hamasaki:
>
> We are forwarding your order, with a copy of this letter, to Lee's Department Store, 131 Grant Avenue in Danville. Lee's is the nearest retail outlet to you that sells Electra products to consumers in Danville.
>
> We refer you to Lee's for these additional reasons.
>
> 1. Lee's has the exclusive franchise to sell Electra products to consumers in Danville.
> 2. Lee's is the only dealer in Danville with a complete service department for all Electra appliances.
> 3. Lee's carries a complete line of Electra products, and they would be happy to demonstrate any of them for you.
>
> Since we are prohibited by the franchise agreement to handle your order, we hope that you will visit Lee's Department Store soon.
>
> Sincerely yours,

Notice how considerate the writer of this letter has been by forwarding the order to a nearby retailer so that Mr. Hamasaki's order is placed immediately without any delay or inconvenience to him. This letter makes its refusal by using only tones that are positive—assistance, appreciation, and action!

Communication Projects

PRACTICAL APPLICATION

A The following refusal letter is poorly written, particularly from the standpoint of tone. Rewrite the letter.

> Dr. Kenneth Bronson
> 1043 Rockland Road
> Cleveland, Ohio 44118
>
> Dear Sir:
>
> We have received your order for a Martel Tape Recorder. Since we are strictly in the manufacturing business, we do not sell directly to consumers. We cannot fill your order, obviously. We looked up your nearest dealer of Martel products. The Franklin Electronics Company, 987 Front Street, Cleveland, Ohio 44118, carries a complete stock of our products. Write us again if we can help.
>
> Yours truly,

B The following letter was written by a tile manufacturer to Mr. Gordon, a consumer who had written to ask for wholesale prices on their tile. Criticize the letter, and rewrite it as you think it should be written.

Dear Sir:

As a consumer, you are not entitled to know the wholesale prices of our tile. Wholesale prices are the personal business of our firm, our authorized dealers, and tile layers. Obviously, if we told you our wholesale prices, you'd know the retail markup. Frankly, we are surprised that you'd make such a request!

Yours truly,

C You are employed by the publisher of business textbooks for schools and colleges. Your firm has been asked by the Redfield Teachers Association to exhibit books at the next meeting of the city teachers. The exhibit fee is $50. About 400 teachers will be in attendance, but only about 60 of them teach in the field in which you publish books. Your company policy is to exhibit only at national meetings and state meetings where there will be at least 350 teachers in the subject area of your publications. Write the letter to Ms. Amy Roberts, President of the Redfield Teachers Association, P.O. Box 5378, Dallas, Texas 75222, explaining why your firm cannot accept her invitation to exhibit at their meeting.

D As president of Baxter and Ward, Inc., you have received a letter from the Ajax College Forensic League asking you to contribute $100 to help defray travel expenses so the debating team can attend a national conference in St. Louis. As an individual, you are willing to contribute $25. Your company, however, has a policy limiting its contributions to national and community causes. This request does not comply with company policy, so the $25 contribution is a personal one you are making. Write the letter that will accompany your contribution to Miss Lucy Marks, 75 College Drive, Tenafly, New Jersey 07670.

E The Office Stenographers Association has invited you to speak at its meeting on April 10. It is April 2 when you receive the invitation, and you feel that you have not been given sufficient time in which to prepare your speech. Write a note of refusal to Mrs. Donna Andrews, the president, 17 Avenue D, Rockford, Illinois 61106.

EDITING PRACTICE

The Editing Desk Edit and rewrite the following paragraph; correct all errors.

The carbon copy of your statement of April 1, shows that you were quite right to question the price of the coat you bought on March 15. The correct amount is $80.00 as you note not the $90.00 charged on the statement. A directive has been issued to all our typists forbidding the xing out of any typed material words or figures. In the name of the company I thank you for telling us about the incorrect amount on your statement, and for calling our attention to the xd-out figures.

CASE PROBLEM

The Chronic Complainer Leandra Faraday works at the desk next to Marla Regis. Marla is a chronic complainer. She complains about everything—

EASTERN AIR LINES INCORPORATED / 10 ROCKEFELLER PLAZA / NEW YORK, NEW YORK 10020 / 212-986-4500

September 20, 19--

Mr. Michael Angura
District Sales Manager
National Imports, Inc.
200 Concord Street
Brooklyn, New York 11201

Dear Mr. Angura:

We have a great executive pick-me-up for you when you travel for business this fall from New York. It's called Triangle Travel, and it works like this.

Take your wife along on a business trip. When your work is finished, fly to a vacation resort. Then, after you've thoroughly relaxed, fly directly home. That's a Triangle Travel trip.

Now, resorts in the Bahamas, Florida, Puerto Rico and Mexico become easy extensions of your business trips. You combine hard work with relaxation, return home physically and mentally refreshed.

The cost? Far less than two separate trips. On a business trip to Atlanta, for instance, you can take your wife, fly on to a vacation in the Bahamas and return to New York--all for just $324 total fare for two (tax not included).

We've mapped out some trips from New York, including fares and hotel accommodation costs, in a full-color Triange Travel booklet. We'll send you a copy if you'll mail us the enclosed reply card.

Cordially,

K. A. Fraser
District Sales Manager

KAF:jb
Enclosure

Courtesy Eastern Air Lines Incorporated

supplied by the purchaser, may be addressed by the broker and returned to the purchaser for mailing. Available lists include such specialized groups as former subscribers to magazines, buyers of mail-order merchandise, licensed pilots, and purchasing agents.

Some large companies rent mailing lists containing hundreds of thousands of names. Before renting the entire list, however, they usually test the list by sending letters to a selected sample of names. If the response is satisfactory, they rent the entire list. Before sending letters to the entire list, the firm may test two or three different letters to determine which one gets the greatest number of responses.

Triangle Travel

☐ I would like to receive a copy of Eastern's Triangle Travel booklet.

Mr.
Mrs.
Miss
Name ______________________________

Address ______________________________

City ______________ State ______________ Zip ______________

The business-like way to fit a vacation into a full schedule.
Triangle Travel
EASTERN
We make it easier to fly

Courtesy Eastern Air Lines Incorporated

Determining Buying Motives

Why do people buy? People buy products and services to satisfy needs or wants. Although the people's needs are relatively simple—food, housing, clothing, and transportation—their wants are endless. They want not just food but delicious food; they want smarter clothing, a newer car, a nicer house than the people next door have. They want security, status in the community, approval from their friends and loved ones. They want modern conveniences that help them avoid exertion; they want more fun out of life.

In some cases, people may not be aware that they want or need something. This lack of awareness is where sales expertise enters the scene—the job of the sales representative, the advertiser, and the sales-letter writer is to satisfy wants and to stimulate the sale of a product.

A number of years ago, outdoor cooking for the average family was limited almost exclusively to roasting hot dogs and hamburgers over a wood fire. Today nearly every kind of food is cooked outdoors on home grills and barbecue spits. All kinds of special equipment—asbestos gloves, turning forks, long-handled salt and pepper shakers, automatic barbecue spits—have been developed to meet the needs of America's outdoor chefs. Enterprising salespeople and persuasive advertisers created these new sales opportunities by appealing to an interest in leisure activities, to the need for outdoor activity, and to the idea of families doing things together.

Inducements to buy, as described above, are called sales appeals. Advertisers spend hundreds of millions of dollars every year searching for the answer to this question: What sales appeal will have the greatest pulling power on the consumer?

See how the following excerpts tempt readers by appealing to their buying motives. What different kinds of wants are the advertisers seeking to satisfy?

Product or Service	Want-Creating Appeals
Packaged spaghetti dinner	*Your family* will give *you rave notices* when you serve Venezio Spaghetti. All the *color* and *vigor* of the Italian Riviera are captured in this *zesty* dish.
Dog food	*Be good to your dog.* TASTY is now *flavor-primed.* Makes your dog an *eager eater.*
Soft drink	Now it's *Bubble-Ade* for those who *think young.*
Postage meter	*Thousands of small businesses* have replaced *old-fashioned* stamp sticking with this *compact, low-cost, desk model* postage meter.
Newspaper	The *Star* is much more *interesting*—and *you* will be, too.
Living-room furniture	Enjoy the dramatic beauty of Continental Sofas, the symbol of *true elegance.*
Record club	Let music take you on a world tour of *beauty, romance,* and *adventure.*
Fences	Frame your home and grounds in *intimate privacy* and *safety.*
Telephone service	Isn't there *someone somewhere* who would *love to hear your voice* tonight?
Gift shop	*Thrilled* is the bride who receives a *distinctive* gift from Sylvia's.
Wristwatch	A name you can *trust* . . . *winner* of six *professional awards.*
Blender	*Performance! Value! Durability!*
Cutlery set	Hot-forged carbon *steel* blades honed for *razor-sharp* edges—this is truly "*butcher sharp*" cutlery.

QUALITIES OF SALES LETTERS

There is no such thing as a standard sales letter, just as there is no standard advertisement. Sales letters vary in length (some are less than a single page; others may be as long as six pages), in organization, and in the appeals used. Many letters that experts would consider "poor" have proved highly successful; and many letters written by professional advertising specialists have proved unsuccessful.

The real test of a sales letter's effectiveness is its *pulling* power; that is, the number of positive responses it receives compared to the number of letters mailed. The response may be in the form of a returned coupon, a request for a free sample, or an actual order. A "perfectly written" letter employing the most subtle sales strategy must be considered a poor letter if it does not result in a response from the reader—it did not do the job it was supposed to do.

Generally speaking, an effective sales letter has these three qualities:

It attracts the reader's attention.
It arouses the reader's interest and creates a desire to buy.
It convinces the reader to buy.

Although achieving these qualities might sound easy, no sure-fire formula for writing a successful sales letter has been found. The wastebaskets that are filled daily with thousands of unread sales messages attest to that fact. Yet sales letters are used successfully and extensively by thousands of business organizations. Probably no two sales letters written about a product are alike; business is always experimenting with different approaches, different appeals, different want-satisfying devices.

Attracting the Reader's Attention

A sales letter is like a door-to-door sales representative—it is seldom invited to call. As a caller without an invitation, the sales letter must attract favorable attention immediately. As in door-to-door selling, a favorable appearance and approach can create the proper sales atmosphere.

The appearance of a sales letter can make the difference between whether the letter is read or whether it is deposited in the nearest wastebasket. Although there is no single format guaranteed to make a sales letter appear interesting to a prospective reader, certain qualities have proved interest-provoking when applied carefully to particular audiences. Superior-quality stationery and an engraved letterhead give an appearance of dignity and importance; a newsletter format looks informative; an attached free sample appeals to the desire to receive something for nothing; a short, spaced-out letter is easy to read.

Experienced sales representatives know that they must keep the prospect's door open if they are to complete their sales presentation; sales-letter writers know that they must keep the prospect reading in order to create a desire to buy. The lead phrase, sentence, or paragraph may pique the reader's curiosity, pay a compliment, or "shake" the reader; it may dangle a promise to save time, to offer something for nothing, to improve the reader's status. The device used to attract the attention must convince the reader that he or she will benefit by finishing the letter. Some examples of attention-getting openings are these:

Opening	**Product or Service**
How many dos and don'ts of great salad making do you know?	Salad dressing
What are you doing this weekend? The usual? Again? One of these days you're going to get fed up with TV, crabgrass, barbeque smoke, that same old dull story.	Personal airplane
Are your child's school grades just "satisfactory"?	Encyclopedia
WANTED—FOR SPEEDING	Office machine
Up-to-the-minute enjoyment at an old-fashioned price. That's what you get . . .	Magazine
Will your family sleep safely tonight?	Insurance
2 OUT OF 5 FARM ACCIDENTS LAST YEAR COULD HAVE BEEN PREVENTED	Safety guards
Brahms? Berlioz? Bartok? Cash? Midler? Reese? Who is your favorite?	Record club
Who *wouldn't* love you?	Perfume
FREE-FREE-FREE!	Household cleanser
Now you can look ten years younger!	Reducing machine

Fresh approaches to attract attention must constantly be sought. However, writers must be careful not to use tricks. Sales representatives who put their foot in the door to keep the door from being closed in their face are not likely to have much luck selling their product. Marking a sales letter "Personal" or making scare statements is like putting a foot in the door. These devices will fool no one and are certain to speed a letter into the wastebasket.

Arousing Interest and Creating Desire

Once you have captured the reader's attention, you should aim to create a desire for the product or service. To do this, you must first arouse the reader's interest in what is being sold. To become interested in and desire a product, the reader must recognize that the product is capable of satisfying a want or a need. The letter may hint that the product or service will help the reader attain a longer life, beauty, economy, security, romance, a youthful appearance, enlightenment, smart appearance, wealth, or freedom from drudgery.

The following appeals may be used to arouse interest and create desire for a product or service:

Comfort (reclining rocker)	Physical attraction (cologne)
Profit (stocks or bonds)	Satisfy appetite (pastry)
Save money (insulation)	Enhance reputation (contribution)
Save time (electronic oven)	Avoid effort (power mower)
Health (mouthwash)	Cleanliness (shampoo)
Enjoyment (stereo)	Gratify curiosity (gadget)
Safety (burglar alarm)	Recognition (exclusive dress)

In creating desire to buy, the writer selects each word, each phrase, for its power to appeal to a want. Note in the following examples and in the letter shown below how desire-creating words and phrases are used.

> Marx is the *latest* in *high-speed, moderately priced* copiers. *Fully automated,* it delivers 850 to 1,000 *sharp* black-on-white prints per hour and *handles copies up to 18 inches wide.*
>
> Examine the swatches carefully; note the *close weave,* the *subtle pattern* that *complements your finest sport jacket.* The fabric not only *sheds wrinkles* but also has the *look of costly imported worsted.*

Why are these words and phrases helpful in creating desire? They so vividly describe the product that the reader can almost feel, see, taste, or

Courtesy IBM Office Products Division

IBM

International Business Machines Corporation

590 Madison Avenue
New York, New York 10022
212/PLaza 3-1900

October 10, 19--

Miss Sally Jones
Secretary to
Mr. Albert Chang
XYZ Corporation
110 Main Street
Tenafly, New Jersey 07670

Dear Miss Jones:

Close your eyes just a moment and picture working eight hours a day by candlelight. Flickering shadows. Sputtering flames. Definitely harder on the eyes than modern lighting.

Aren't you glad we have all the modern inventions of today--including those that smooth and speed your work? But there is still another important office convenience that could help both you and your dictator.

IBM Input Processing Equipment is so advanced that, using it, the dictator can pause . . . review . . . make a change . . . and re-record, instantly erasing unwanted material. You will receive error-free dictation.

For you, this makes draft copies as old-fashioned as gaslight. You can transcribe faster from precorrected material, too. You'll type your work once and be proud to have your boss sign the neat results. Altogether, it sounds good because it is good . . . for you and your boss.

If you'd like to know more about IBM Input Processing Equipment before discussing it with your employer, I'll be glad to send you literature describing the many special features . . . including IBM error-free dictation and transcription.

Sincerely,

J. N. Smith
Sales Representative

mcw

smell it. Here are some additional examples of how words can be used to achieve this goal:

> A mustard that is shy, retiring, is no mustard at all. A great mustard should manage to be a delightful contradiction of emphatically hot and delicately mild.
>
> X shampoo makes your hair so satin-bright—satin-smooth too!
>
> Our electric typewriters will help produce letters that are a pleasure to type, a pleasure to sign, a joy to read.

Driving for Action

In a baseball game, only the runs scored count—not the number of times the batter gets on first, second, or third base. Many a sales letter is stranded on base because the writer does not understand the strategy of scoring—making the customer say, "Yes, I'll accept your offer."

The strategy for scoring with sales letters starts with the first attention-getting question and infiltrates every sentence of the letter. Throughout the letter, the writer must develop a "Yes" attitude in the reader.

Developing a "Yes" Attitude From the opening sentence, the sales letter should try to put the prospect in a "Yes" frame of mind and to keep this attitude to the final "Yes" decision. Only a very inexpert salesperson would put a customer into a "No" frame of mind by asking, "You don't want to buy my lawn mower, do you? (The natural answer: "No, I don't.")

Throughout the sales letter, sentences and questions should be phrased so that the reader has to agree with what is said. Many sales letters begin with an obvious "Yes" question, such as: "Do you want to save 15 minutes a day?" Questions that demand "Yes" answers put and keep the reader in a positive frame of mind and make the big "Yes" easier to get. Read these examples and see how easy it is to answer "Yes!"

> Do you want your child to earn better grades in school?
>
> Would you like to cut your gasoline consumption by 20 percent?

Making It Easy to Act When writing sales letters, keep to a minimum the decisions that the reader must make. Follow the example of a shoe-sales expert, one who shows a customer no more than two or three pairs of shoes at one time. If it's necessary to show more, the sales expert usually puts away the first pairs before bringing others to the customer. Why? The more pairs of shoes a customer sees, the more confusing and difficult it is to make that all-important decision: "This pair of shoes is the one I want." The fewer the decisions, the easier it is to say "Yes."

Other techniques also make it easy for the reader to respond with an affirmative act. Note how this is accomplished in the letter on page 356 and in these examples:

> Just write your initials in the box on the enclosed postpaid reply card and drop it in the mail now.
>
> Just print your name and address on the coupon—SEND NO MONEY.

MUTUAL BENEFIT LIFE
INSURANCE COMPANY · NEWARK, NEW JERSEY · 07101

Executive Offices

Reply Card

Mrs. Grace Hamilton
1442 Billows Avenue
Wilmington, Delaware 19899

You'll literally earn a fortune before you reach retirement age!

Your ability to earn an income is your most valuable asset. Yet, a disabling accident or illness can rob you of those future earnings--leaving you without an income!

Mutual Benefit Life has recently introduced a series of disability income policies which are uniquely designed to replace income lost by an accident or illness. These benefits are Tax Free. As a Mutual Benefit Life policyholder, you can have an early opportunity to learn more about this valuable form of essential protection and how it can work for you.

For more information and a free gift of a Johnson and Johnson First Aid Kit, just mail the postage-paid card in the window of this letter. Naturally, there is no obligation.

Cordially,

Senior Vice President

WEH/pd

Courtesy The Mutual Benefit Life Insurance Company

THE SALES LETTER CAMPAIGN

A series of sales letters will often be written to prospective customers, particularly to sell higher-priced items. In such follow-up letters, professional writers sometimes use a different appeal in each letter, with the hope that one of the appeals may ultimately convince the reader to take action to buy the product or service.

In the sales campaign, as many as eight letters may be sent, depending upon the nature of the product, its cost, and the nature of the market. The letters in such a series should be spaced about ten days apart, and they should be kept relatively short.

Communication Projects

PRACTICAL APPLICATION

A You are the owner of a shop that sells infants' clothing and other items for infants. List sources of mailing lists of prospective customers.

B Make a list of at least ten different sales appeals you find in advertisements in magazines, newspapers, sales catalogs, and on television. Prepare your list under these headings:

Type of Product *Trade Name* *Sales Appeal*

C Select some product you would very much like to buy, such as a sports car, a portable typewriter, a motorcycle. Write a sales promotion letter that might be written by a dealer for this product. Try to get prospects to come to your place of business for a free demonstration of the product.

D Write three eye-catching openings for each of the following products: (a) an electric portable typewriter, (b) a garbage compactor, (c) an electric blanket, (d) a news magazine, and (e) a trip to Hawaii.

E Select some current issue in which you are interested, such as ecology, getting the 18-year-olds out to vote, or some other issue. Prepare a letter to an audience that might be swayed to accept your point of view.

EDITING PRACTICE

Applied Psychology Change the following letter excerpts into sentences that will maintain good public relations.

1. You made a mistake by shorting us 28 cents in your check dated June 8, so please send us that amount immediately.
2. Because you neglected to send us the $84.75 you owe us, you'll be hearing from our attorney shortly.
3. Since you failed to tell us which model number you wanted, we can't do anything for you.
4. Your delay in paying your bills is not good business policy.
5. You claim that the motor was not inspected after it was repaired.

CASE PROBLEM

Etiquette for Social-Business Situations Analyze the following statements to determine whether they are correct or incorrect. If you need help, consult a book of etiquette.

1. To place a call, always have your secretary get the other party on the telephone first.
2. At a luncheon, if the host orders an alcoholic drink, the guest, too, must have an alcoholic drink.
3. At a formal dinner, you should never begin eating until the host begins.
4. When introducing an older person to a younger one, the older person's name is mentioned first.
5. The person being called on the telephone is the first one to terminate the conversation.

43 Writing Public Relations Letters

The dictionary defines *public relations* as "the business of inducing the public to have understanding for and goodwill toward a person, firm, or institution."[1] Therefore, letters that seek to develop favorable public opinion, to influence thinking about a particular company's policies, products, or actions, or simply to make new friends are called *public relations letters.* To a large extent, every business letter that is written is a public relations (PR) letter. The writer of an adjustment letter attempts to make a settlement that will be fair to the company represented and that will, at the same time, satisfy the customer. Such a letter shows that the company has concern for the customer. And that is what public relations letters are all about: "We are not just interested in making a sale; we are interested in knowing that you are satisfied."

Indirectly, public relations letters are sales letters; primarily, they are written to influence public opinion. While the ultimate goal of a PR letter may be to promote a sale sometime in the future, the immediate goal is to promote a favorable company image. This image may be one of friendliness, fair play, reliability, prestige, or efficiency—or any combination of these qualities. If the firm has a favorable image in the eyes of the community, then this image should help to create sales.

CREATING A FAVORABLE COMPANY IMAGE

Many companies spend millions of dollars each year to favorably influence public attitudes toward their enterprises and toward the people who work for them. Some companies sponsor special television shows, on which the only advertising is a mention of the company's name. Some firms run newspaper and magazine ads that are intended primarily for public enjoyment or enlightenment. Large grants for research are given to medical and educational groups by some companies. Others make large endowments to universities and colleges and offer scholarships to worthy students. Although nearly all companies feel an obligation to offer such services for the benefit of society, they are at the same time very much aware of the public relations value of such actions.

In an effort to create a favorable company image, many large organizations employ public relations specialists whose function is to see that the company has its "best foot forward" at all times. PR specialists are trained to use all communication media—letters, newspapers, radio, television, magazines, films—to influence public opinion. They prepare countless news releases, radio announcements, and articles; they arrange for press conferences, speaking engagements for top executives of the company, public receptions, and so on. They seize every opportunity to develop a favorable feeling toward the organization for which they work. For example, when a downtown build-

[1]*Webster's New Collegiate Dictionary*, G. & C. Merriam Co., Springfield, Mass., 1973, p. 932.

ing is being remodeled or expanded, causing some inconvenience to shoppers and pedestrians, the alert PR specialist arranges to install a colorful sign, which may read something like this:

Please excuse the noise and dust as we hurry to complete a bigger and brighter housewares department. Come to our grand opening party on September 1!

Jackson's . . . **Growing to Serve You Better**

The public relations person is also likely to be the one to see to it that peepholes are installed at strategic points so that "sidewalk superintendents" may observe the progress of the construction.

Every business is judged daily in the courts of public opinion. And public opinion is powerful! If opinions are favorable, the way is usually smooth; if they are unfavorable, the going can be rocky indeed. Following are typical situations in which public relations specialists seek to influence public opinion.

1. A manufacturer in a small city finds it necessary to build a new power plant to handle expanded production. After careful study, management has come to the conclusion that the best location for the new plant is on the river near the city park. For obvious reasons, the company expects that there will be some objection from the public to locating the new plant near the park—a few trees must be cut down, the view of the river from the park will be obstructed, the typical power plant is not a thing of architectural beauty, and so on. Even though the company has permission from the City Council to go ahead with its plans, management knows that it must also have support from the public—from customers, friends, employees, and neighbors. The PR department uses every available communication medium to persuade the public that the company's proposed action is justified.
2. A commuter railroad is operating at a deficit. Although fares have increased 200 percent in the past five years, the company is still losing money and must ask for another increase. Of course, the railroad is sensitive to the opinions of its customers; it needs their understanding and their support. The PR department of the railroad may place advertisements in newspapers, may purchase radio time, may issue circulars to riders, and may write letters to leading citizens in order to explain why the railroad has found it necessary to seek authority to raise fares.
3. During the past year, an automobile company has fallen from its position as one of the top three producers, and profits are down. Management knows how important it is for the stockholders to understand the situation. They know that faith is easily shaken when the facts are not clear. The PR department is given the responsibility of preparing a letter to stockholders, to explain the company's position and plans and to assure stockholders of the bright future ahead.

4. The manager of the local airport writes to homeowners who live near the landing field to apologize for the noise created by the jet engines and to assure these people that improvements will be made soon.
5. A university has changed its name from Oxford Teachers College to Oxford University of Arts and Science. The PR department writes a special letter to the alumni of the institution in order to inform them of the school's new name.
6. A large public school system plans to use modular scheduling starting next fall in all of its schools. A news release is issued to newspapers, and a letter is written to parents and to various civic organizations to inform the public of this new development.

A local dairy that was forced to reduce home deliveries from daily to every other day handled the situation by sending customers a letter of explanation like this:

> Dear Mrs. Rosen:
>
> For twenty years Dino's has been delivering its fine dairy products to its customers in Lincoln every day of the week. Even though the cost of delivery has increased threefold during the past two years, we have continued to offer the same service at only a fraction of this cost.
>
> Unfortunately, the expense has now become so great that we are faced with the problem of either cutting the frequency of delivery or increasing the prices of our products. We believe that most of our customers would prefer that we reduce delivery service to every other day and maintain our prices at their present level.
>
> Therefore, after June 1, Dino's will deliver your dairy products every other day, beginning on ——. So that you will not be without milk and other dairy products you use, you will probably want to increase your order on delivery days. On the postage-paid reply card that is enclosed, please indicate the changes you would like to make in your present order.
>
> We appreciate your business, Mrs. Rosen; and we pledge to continue supplying you with the high-quality dairy products you are used to receiving from Dino's—and at the lowest possible costs.
>
> Sincerely yours,

PROMOTING A NEW BUSINESS

Promoting a new business requires a combination of public relations and sales techniques. Suppose you work in the sales-promotion department of the Tres Chic Couture, which manages a chain of women's specialty shops. Tres Chic has recently opened a new boutique in Chalon Hills and has hired Janiece McGregor as manager of this shop. As part of the promotional efforts—and to help Janiece get off to a good start—you want to create an atmosphere in the community that will bring customers to the new store. In addition to running a number of newspaper ads, sponsoring spot announcements on the local radio station, and distributing thousands of circulars, you write the following letter that will be duplicated and mailed to a list of two thousand telephone subscribers in Chalon Hills. The image that is being created for this new business is built mainly around Janiece McGregor—local resident who made good.

MAY WE INTRODUCE YOU TO—

Janiece McGregor,

manager of Chalon Hills' newest and most unusual specialty shop for women:

TRES CHIC BOUTIQUE

located in El Camino Real Shopping Square, Devonshire Road and Pillar Drive.

Perhaps you already know Janiece and her husband, Ron. Both of them grew up in your city and were graduated from local schools. They both attended Southeastern University, where Janiece majored in Fashion Arts and Ron in Business Administration. Janiece and Ron represent a winning team, with her original ideas in dress designing and his business expertise.

You may recall that Janiece is past president of the Parent-Teacher League of the Chalon Hills Elementary School, where her 6-year old Jason and 8-year old Jaime attend school. Janiece was instrumental in our civic drive to save the trees along Highway 7, and she recently was appointed Den Mother for Scout Troop 540. She plans to continue in this capacity and to continue taking an active role in community affairs. For the past two years, Janiece served as buyer for the Fashion Court Department at Manderville's Department Store, in addition to participating in community activities.

Many of the new fashions you will find at TRES CHIC BOUTIQUE were designed by Janiece herself. Her staff of seamstresses will be on hand at all times to ensure that you always get the proper fitting and the styling that most becomes you. You'll also find a large selection of ready-made fashions in the latest styles to suit every occasion.

Do drop by to say hello to Janiece at TRES CHIC BOUTIQUE. She will be glad to see her old friends and to meet new ones at Chalon Hills' loveliest new shopping spot.

Cordially yours,

Of course, the PR image this letter is trying to create will not emerge unless Janiece and her staff give customers excellent merchandise and service. Customers must find at TRES CHIC BOUTIQUE the quality merchandise and friendly service that the letter promises.

Building an Image

The first months for Janiece McGregor are crucial. Once the image has started to emerge, she must keep building it. The TRES CHIC BOUTIQUE chain wants to help Janiece get firmly established, because her success will, of course, benefit the company as well. In your campaign to build an image, you prepare this form letter to mail to everyone who visits the shop.

Dear ———:

Thank you for visiting TRES CHIC BOUTIQUE this week. We are pleased to welcome you as a new customer, and we are delighted that you gave us an opportunity to show you some of the newest designs in women's wear.

Whatever your needs in women's wear, be assured that your choices from TRES CHIC will always be of superior quality. Careful attention by an efficient, courteous staff, including expert seamstresses, ensures you of clothes that fit you perfectly. Whatever your needs—a street dress, a pants suit, or an exclusive gown for a special occasion—we are prepared to cater to your every fashion wish.

Stop by frequently and browse. You will see new selections each time you visit, for only by moving our stock quickly can we keep one step ahead of the fashion market.

Cordially,

Recognizing a PR Moment

Timing the PR letter is important; the precise time when the public will listen to and accept an idea is a *PR moment*. Obviously, the PR moment for creating a business image occurs when the business first opens. Another PR moment is immediately after a new customer's first visit. The two letters illustrated on page 361 are examples of good timing.

A new item or service in a business can also provide a PR moment. Suppose that TRES CHIC BOUTIQUE has, by popular demand, started daily fashion showings at the Larkspur Restaurant in Chalon Hills. Janiece and Ron take advantage of this public relations moment to announce this new feature. The opening paragraph of their announcement might start like this:

> In response to popular demand, TRES CHIC BOUTIQUE is pleased to announce a daily fashion showing of its latest creations. While dining at the Larkspur Restaurant in Chalon Hills, between 12 and 2 p.m., watch the lovely models who will circulate throughout the dining room, showing the newest TRES CHIC fashions.

In a similar way, anniversaries and special dates in the life of a business often provide appropriate PR moments. For example, at the end of one year of operation, a gasoline service station might capitalize on the occasion by writing an "anniversary" letter that begins like this:

> From zero to 3,500 gallons of gasoline per day. That's the sales story of the Calkins Service Station during the past twelve months.
>
> We opened our service pumps just one year ago, June 5. Now, more than 750 friends like you stop regularly for gasoline and service. In the months and years ahead, we pledge to continue to give you the complete automobile service that you want and that your car deserves . . . .

PUBLIC RELATIONS—OTHER PROMOTION OPPORTUNITIES

The opportunities for writing letters to friends and customers of a business are limited only by the imagination. Of course, many such letters have a definite sales objective. Yet they also enhance the image of the firm. The following are typical subjects for promotion letters:

An invitation to open a charge account.
An announcement of a special privilege or service to preferred customers.
An incentive to charge customers to use their accounts more frequently.
A welcome to new residents and visitors.
A congratulatory message.
An invitation to a demonstration, lecture, or reception.
A reminder of a holiday or special occasion.
A thank-you for business patronage.

Inviting Charge Accounts

A cash customer of a store or a firm is often invited to open a charge account. The following charge-account invitation includes an application form. All the customer needs to do, as indicated by the statement at the top of the application, is fill in the form, fold and seal it, and drop it into the mail.

THIS STRIP IS GUMMED — READY TO SEAL. NO ENVELOPE NECESSARY

SHOP THE EASY WAY . . . SAY CHARGE IT!

Neiman-Marcus offers the following credit services —

- 30 Day Account: You are billed once a month and payment is due upon receipt.
- Pivot Account: A convenience for budgeting everyday needs. Pay as little as 1/6 of your statement balance — or more if you like. A nominal service charge is added monthly.
- Special Account: Take as long as 6 months to pay for special "investment" purchases such as coats, suits, luggage, and jewelry. Even longer for china, silver, and antiques.
- Trousseau Account: Assemble all of your needs on one account and divide your payments over 6 to 12 months. A nominal service charge is added after the sixth month.
- Furs — Jewelry: Choose a beautiful Neiman-Marcus fur or fine jewelry and divide your payments over 6 to 12 months.

Please Print Neiman-Marcus

application for charge account

Name Mrs. Henry Moran

Address 546 Ridge Dr. City Dallas Zone 75214

Name of Firm Moran & Son State Texas

Title or Position architect

Business Address 4641 Greenview Avenue, Dallas 75214

Name of Bank First National Branch

Have Accounts at Sanger-Harris, Fitches, Dreyfuss

Signature X *Mrs. Henry Moran*

Preference: ☑ Regular 30 Day Date August 8, 19--

☐ {Pivot (6 mos. Plan) Credit limit desired $

Courtesy Neiman-Marcus

Giving Charge Customers Special Privileges

Giving special attention to charge customers is good business. Generally speaking, these customers are loyal patrons; they buy more than cash customers, and they return to the store again and again. Most stores make a point of creating occasions when charge customers are given special privileges or attention. Here is such a PR letter:

> Dear Mrs. Metaxas:
>
> As a select customer of Hayden's, you are invited to a preview showing of the latest fashion creations by Armanda. Please circle this date on your activities calendar right now: Friday, October 19, at three-thirty in the afternoon. Your Hayden Charg-card will serve as your ticket of admission.
>
> The preview showing will be held in the Century Room on the sixth floor. The very latest in gowns, cocktail dresses, furs, and hats will be modeled by students of the Amerida Modeling School. Tea and coffee will be served to all our guests both during and following the showing.
>
> The fashions to be modeled will not be placed on our selling floors until November 4. However, you may place your advance orders during the preview showing. We want you, a preferred customer of Hayden's, to have first choice.
>
> Sincerely yours,

Encouraging Charge Customers to Use Their Accounts

Charge customers who have not made frequent use of their accounts can be encouraged by letter to use their charge privileges more often. Here is a clever letter that may prove irresistible to the "delinquent" charge customer

Dear Customer:

You've Earned	
10¢	Is it worth 10 cents a line to you to read this
20¢	letter?
30¢	We'll gladly pay you that amount—but only if
40¢	you read the entire letter.
50¢	Now, we reason this way: You really are a valued
60¢	customer. But lately you haven't been in even
70¢	to say "Howdy." We would like you to come back;
80¢	we would like to see you often; we would like
90¢	you to reopen your account. We think that it is
\$1.00	better for us to have a long-time customer like
\$1.10	you on our books than a new customer whom we
\$1.20	don't know. And since it would cost us at least
\$1.30	\$2.50 to open a <u>new</u> account, we would rather pass
\$1.40	this amount to you.
\$1.50	So we say, "Here is a \$2.50 check on the house."
\$1.60	Come in and select anything you wish, to the value
\$1.70	of \$25 or more, from our extensive stock of nation-
\$1.80	ally advertised clothing and shoes for the entire
\$1.90	family. Invest in that household appliance—pop-
\$2.00	up toaster, steam iron—you have been dreaming
\$2.10	about. Or do your gift shopping early for such
\$2.20	items as diamonds, watches, radios.
\$2.30	The enclosed check, worth \$2.50, is your down
\$2.40	payment.
\$2.50	Why not come in tomorrow.

Cordially yours,

DALLAS, TEXAS 75201

WELCOME TO DALLAS . . .

for the meeting of the Association of School Business Officials on October 14 through October 20. We hope you are planning to attend this meeting and to bring your family. We know that you will have a delightful visit in our city.

Please plan to make Neiman-Marcus your unofficial headquarters, and if your busy schedule permits, plan to have lunch in our famous Zodiac Restaurant, which features informal modeling from 11:30 A.M. to 2:00 P.M.

A warm welcome awaits you at Neiman-Marcus . . . and an invitation to see our collection of Winter fashions.

If you do not already have an account with us, please fill in and return the convenient application card. As a charge customer you will receive our fashion brochures, notices of coming events, and our world-famous Christmas Booklet.

Sincerely yours,

Stanley Marcus

Courtesy Neiman-Marcus

Welcoming New Residents and Visitors

Hotels, department stores, and various businesses often obtain lists of the visitors who are expected to attend conventions in their city in order to write them letters of welcome. The letter illustrated above is an example of such a welcome.

When a new family moves into a community, many alert business firms write a letter of welcome. Naturally, the purpose of the letter is to win friends and customers. Note the technique employed in this letter:

Welcome Neighbor:

Dolan's—Boise's favorite cleaning establishment—welcomes you to the community. We hope that you will like our friendly people, our modern stores, our lovely city parks and playgrounds, and our exciting cultural and entertainment centers. We are definitely a proud, growing, and bustling community.

Dolan's has grown up with Boise. We were the first cleaning establishment in the city, having opened our doors for the first time in 1902. As a family-owned business, we have been serving the cleaning needs of the community ever since. Our cleaning plant was remodeled with the most modern equipment just two years ago, and we now have five pickup outlets throughout the city for your convenience. But best of all, we have the friendliest, most efficient staff of employees.

We are enclosing a certificate entitling you to a 20 percent discount on your first cleaning order. We would like to show you why Dolan's is Boise's most popular cleaning establishment. There IS a reason!

Sincerely yours,

Writing Congratulatory Letters

Any occasion for congratulations is a PR moment. For example, some businesses write letters to congratulate parents on the arrival of a new baby. The list of names is usually obtained from hospital notices in the local newspaper.

Enclosed with the following letter is a pair of miniature long trousers.

Dear Mark:

You're a mighty discerning young man to have chosen the parents you did, and that's why I'm writing this letter to you instead of them. Congratulations!

Here's your first pair of long pants. A little early, perhaps, but I want you to get used to coming to Hayden's for all your clothing needs. Your dad has been a friend of ours for some time now. We like to think he is well satisfied with his purchases, and we hope you'll bring him in to see us often.

Tell you what: If you'll come in with your dad one year from now (I'll remind you), I'll have a present for you that you can really use.

Sincerely,

Sending Special Invitations

The following letter is typical of those that are used to invite customers to special demonstrations or receptions. Note that such a letter may also serve a sales function.

Dear Mrs. Simpson:

Artist Norman Wyeth, who paints some of the most widely acclaimed seascapes, will be at Maximo's Art Shop on Saturday, April 10, from one until three in the afternoon. Prints of his "Storm on the Shore" will be on sale. A limited number of copies, only 50, will be available for sale at our shop exclusively, and each copy will be numbered and signed personally by Mr. Wyeth.

You are invited to come and meet Mr. Wyeth and, if you are among the lucky, to purchase one of these prints of his most famous work. While you are here, you might want to look around our gallery for other paintings and prints that may "catch your eye."

Cordially yours,

Writing Letters for Special Occasions

Holidays and other special occasions provide opportunities to build goodwill and to promote sales. Study the techniques employed in the following examples:

Dear Dad:

Mind if we sneak a small string around that middle finger of your left hand?

Not that we think you're absentminded. Far from it. But just in case the press of business has caused you to suffer a temporary lapse of memory, we thought it would be helpful to remind you that May 12 is Mother's Day. You hadn't forgotten? Good!

What we don't want you to forget is that Loman's is the store from which she would purchase her gift if she were doing the shopping. Leather-crafted desk sets, luggage, luxurious handbags, jewelry, manicure sets, boudoir sets, oil paints, and crafts—everything and anything she could possibly want.

Why not drop in this week? Ask for Mrs. Barnes; she will be pleased to help you choose just the right gift for the occasion.

Cordially yours,

Dear Mrs. Rockwell:

Let's talk about golf. Yes, I know that there's snow on the ground and nary a leaf on the trees. The fairways aren't fair, and the temperature doesn't budge above 40 degrees.

But even December is golden weather at the Sportsman's Shop. If you could see our fantastic selection of golf balls, clubs, bags, shoes, carts, jackets, caps—everything you can imagine—you'd know what I mean. No, we aren't stuck with an overambitious order placed last summer. We intentionally stocked up because just about this time of year every golfer longs to hike out to the club and smack a few. That's why nothing would please your golfer more this Christmas than a new set of clubs, a new bag, a couple dozen new golf balls, or a good-looking pair of golf slacks. Arnold Palmer Championship clubs? Wilson's K-77? We've got 'em!

The best part of the story is that all golf equipment is on sale at 25 percent off. Why not come in to the Sportsman's Shop and take care of that special man of yours now?

Sincerely yours,

THANKING CUSTOMERS FOR THEIR PATRONAGE

There is a saying that "the squeaky wheel gets the oil." Some customers, too, feel that they will get attention only if they complain and make trouble for a firm with whom they are doing business. Loyal customers who never complain and who quietly and promptly pay their bills may receive no attention at all. An increasing number of business firms, however, are trying to remedy this situation. The letter of the Lily-Tulip Corporation, illustrated on page 368, is an excellent example of how one company attempts to show its appreciation to its loyal customers.

LILY-TULIP CUP CORPORATION

PACKAGING, VENDING, SERVICE PRODUCTS IN PAPER AND PLASTIC

1100 North Glenstone Avenue, Springfield, Missouri 65801 UNIVERSITY 2-2744

June 29, 19--

Dallas Paper Company
1876 Water Street
Dallas, Texas 75205

Gentlemen:

THANK YOU!

Yes, we most certainly owe you a special word of thanks. Normally we are so busy with our problems we seldom take time to express our appreciation to customers such as you who pay their accounts, month after month, year after year, quietly and regularly, with no effort on our part.

It has been said, and it is true, a credit man is so busy saying "Please remit" he overlooks the opportunity to say "Thank you." So we are forgetting the problems for the moment to express our gratitude to you and your entire organization for your acceptance of our product and the fine manner in which you have consistently maintained your account.

The success of our efforts depends entirely upon the cooperation of our accounts; so it is to you we feel most indebted. Our appreciation is great--our thanks sincere.

Cordially yours,

LILY-TULIP CUP CORPORATION

J. A. Patterson
Regional Credit Manager

JAP:wh

Courtesy The Dartnell Corporation—Gold Medal Award Letter

Another example of how some businesses attempt to show their appreciation to customers is this letter, thanking the customer for making prompt payment.

Dear Mr. Dexter:

Today is a red-letter day for you! No more car payments—your Dodge is all yours! The enclosed canceled note is evidence that all payments have been made.

We appreciate that you have made all your payments promptly, Mr. Dexter. It has been a pleasure doing business with you, and we hope that you will call on us again whenever you wish financing.

The enclosed certificate entitles you to preferred credit privileges at the lowest available rates. Just present this certificate to any of our branch banks for fast service on loans of any kind. We shall be pleased to help you.

Cordially yours,

Note that in addition to thanking the customer, the writer of the letter also uses this communication to serve a sales function by encouraging future business.

Communication Projects

PRACTICAL APPLICATION

A As manager of Jorgen's Superior Markets, you must explain to your charge customers that because of rising costs, you must discontinue your policy of permitting customers to charge purchases and you must reduce your delivery service. Deliveries will be made only after 2 p.m. and only for purchases totaling more than $20. It will be necessary to charge 50 cents for this delivery service. Explain these new store policies very tactfully because the customers to whom the letter will go have been used to these services for over 15 years.

B Assume that you have been graduated from college and that you have also had five years of business experience either as (a) a tax accountant in a public accounting firm or (b) a secretary in an attorney's office.

You have now decided to set up your own (a) tax accounting business or (b) public stenographer's office.

In promoting the new business, you choose to announce your venture by writing a letter that will be sent to 100 businesses in the community. The fact that you have had both business experience and excellent training in college should be emphasized. Write a letter that includes all the details that will improve your chances of selling your services.

C Develop a letter that encourages charge customers of a retail store to use their charge accounts. Use your ingenuity in making the letter different from others you have seen.

D In many cities, a service called *Welcome Wagon* greets new residents and relays to them greetings from each of the businesses interested in making contact with potential new customers. Assume that you are employed by a business engaged in dry cleaning and laundry service, Bradley Cleaners and Laundry. In addition to regular cleaning and laundry service, you specialize in cleaning or laundering draperies and curtains. Not only do you come to the home and take down the draperies or curtains, you also rehang them after they have been cleaned or laundered. Write a form welcome letter (to be distributed by the *Welcome Wagon*) to newcomers to your city. Assume that the letter will be accompanied by a set of five coupons, each worth $2, that may be applied to cleaning or laundry brought to one of your ten pickup stations in the city.

E Shoji Motors, manufacturer and dealer of compact Japanese-made automobiles, is about to introduce, for the first time in your city, the Shoji 6, their 6-cylinder car, in four different styles. A special preview showing, accompanied by light refreshments, is planned for all customers, including family and friends, of Shoji Motors. The showing will be held at the Shoji Motors showroom, 189 Delecorte Place, August 28, from three until five in the afternoon. Admission will be by ticket only, which you will include with the letter of invitation you are writing. The general public will not see the new car until the following Monday.

EDITING PRACTICE

Editing to Improve Writing Techniques Edit the following sentences to remove all evidence of poor writing techniques.

1. He felt the facts should determine his reply.
2. Marlene is one of the best if not the best secretaries in the office.
3. Jess always has and always will be late for meetings.
4. In his writing, Don consistently uses big words, thus making his communications ineffective.
5. The group must complete the research, assembling of facts, and writing the report.
6. Our engineers have made many improvements in design, and so we shall be able to produce a better product.
7. The mail would lie in the out-basket for hours and sometimes days.
8. There is no future for the business communicator who is careless or indifferent to the techniques of writing.
9. Within two days after I sent my complaint to Mr. King, a reply was received from him.
10. In order to prepare his invoice, all the figures will be needed by you.
11. You may use either of these four typewriters on which to practice.
12. Carl said he couldn't find any stamps for the letters after looking in the desk drawers.
13. Marge borrowed the stapler which was on my desk.
14. Did you learn why the customers returned their monthly statement?
15. Arriving at 10 a.m., I suggested that Joan plan to allow more travel time to get to work.

Plurals and Possessives Indicate the correct plural or possessive forms of the words enclosed in parentheses.

1. The (Lynch) are not remodeling their downtown store.
2. Many (chintz) are used for making curtains.
3. All notices of employment opportunities are posted on (it) bulletin board.
4. Dr. Ralston is a man (who) experience is highly regarded.
5. (Children) excess energy often gets them into trouble.
6. For good investments, buy stock in public (utility).
7. The (President-elect) room was provided without charge by the hotel.
8. Each choir member sang two (solo).
9. Have they made the (analysis) of the three reports yet?
10. Each employee received a box of (handkerchief) at Christmas.
11. My (boss) desk is always cleared at the end of the day.
12. The two (general manager) reports were in agreement.

13. All the (secretary) in this company can speak Spanish fluently.
14. (Mary and Joan) telephone, which they share, is on Mary's desk.
15. The Muir Building has only (attorney) offices on the first 10 floors.

CASE PROBLEM

Making Statistics Meaningful As an employee of the public relations department, Paul Edison is responsible for taking visitors through the company plant and for telling them facts and figures about the company. Here is part of the talk he uses on his tours: "Five years ago, we had only 127 production workers. Today, we have 1,270. Five years ago, we produced 19,550 clocks each year. Today, the workers produce 247,000 clocks annually. Five years ago, we were losing $1,000 a week. This year, our profits will be about $250,000." These facts are an important part of Paul's presentation, but they are difficult for visitors to grasp because of the way in which Paul presents them.

Can you present the facts in such a way that visitors will grasp them more readily?

44 Writing Social-Business Letters

Many letters written by business people serve a dual purpose. They are not strictly business letters; that is, they do not involve the day-to-day business operations. These letters are more personal—even semisocial in nature.

Business executives do not lose their personal identity simply because they hold responsible positions in their organizations. In fact, they often participate in even more activities than the average individual does, and these activities may be only indirectly related to their jobs.

Typical executives are members of professional organizations in their fields, such as the National Sales Executives Association, the American Institute of Certified Public Accountants, or the Administrative Management Society. They may continue to be active in their college fraternities or sororities; they may hold office in their college alumni associations; and they may belong to several civic or church groups. Companies consider these activities desirable, even though they are not strictly related to business, because active, outgoing employees make important contributions to the company image.

As a result of their professional and personal associations, executives are obligated to write letters of a semisocial nature: congratulatory letters to friends and business associates who have received promotions; thank-you letters for favors, gifts, hospitality, and special services; condolence letters to those who have suffered misfortunes; letters involving the affairs of professional, social, and civic organizations to which they belong; and formal social communications. These are social-business letters; they are, in effect, public relations letters of individuals who are employed in business organizations.

FORMAT OF SOCIAL-BUSINESS LETTERS

For social-business letters, a smaller-size stationery—baronial or monarch—is preferred by most executives. Of course, the regular company stationery also may be used.

Basically, the format of a social-business letter is the same as the format of a regular business letter. However, the salutation in a social-business letter is often followed by a comma, rather than by a colon. In addition, the inside address may be written at the foot of the letter, like this:

Cordially yours,

Ms. Laura Desmond, President
Bank of Commerce and Trust
1735 Lincoln Boulevard
Cincinnati, Ohio 45202

LETTERS OF CONGRATULATION

Job promotions, honors bestowed by groups or organizations, appointments or elections to office, and other achievements of a business or of its employees are all appropriate occasions for writing congratulatory messages. In fact, such occasions are excellent PR opportunities. Since everyone wants to be respected and admired, a cordial letter of congratulation on such important occasions will always build the reader's goodwill toward the writer, and such goodwill, of course, is a valuable asset to business people.

Congratulating Individuals

Many social-business letters are written to congratulate someone on an important career achievement. For example, suppose that you are a business executive and you read in the local newspaper that a fellow member of the Administrative Management Society has just been promoted to an important position in his company. As a thoughtful person, you might write a congratulatory letter like this one:

Dear Ron,

I was delighted to read in yesterday's *Herald* of your promotion to the position of comptroller with Continental Tours. Your many years of hard work with the company merited this promotion, Ron.

I am so pleased that your ability has been recognized. Congratulations and best wishes for continued success in your company.

Sincerely,

An astute businessman and businesswoman should take advantage of the opportunity to promote goodwill on any occasion when a friend, a business associate, or an acquaintance has been honored by a group or an organization. Of course, the warmer and more friendly the letter, the more effective it will be. However, the wishes expressed must be sincere if the reader is to accept the gesture as something more than just a means of promoting business. The following letter sincerely expresses the writer's pleasure in the honor bestowed upon a friend:

> Dear Ethel,
>
> The Soroptimists made a wise choice in naming you "Business Teacher of the Year." I know that this recognition is well deserved, and I cannot think of anyone more deserving than you to receive it. Over the many years of our friendship, I know how dedicated you have been to your work and to the welfare of the students in your classes. Please accept my sincere congratulations.
>
> This occasion also provides an excellent opportunity for me to offer my personal thanks, too, for your many expressions of friendship over the years. May I thank you, too, for your many hours of work serving on several committees and particularly for your leadership and accomplishments on the Education Committee. I am always confident that a committee's work will be done efficiently and promptly when you are its leader. It is indeed a pleasure knowing you and working with you.
>
> Cordially,

Sometimes, however, the business person wishes to write to extend congratulations to someone only casually known or perhaps to someone not known at all. Such a letter will necessarily be somewhat more formal in tone than one written to a friend, but nevertheless it should be cordial and sincere. Because such letters are often used to build valuable business contacts, they require extra care and skill in writing. Letters like the following should achieve the desired purpose without offending the reader:

> Dear Mrs. Bradley:
>
> Please add my congratulations and good wishes to the many I know you have already received on being elected Mayor of Brentville. Our city is fortunate to have such a dedicated, hard-working citizen in this most important position.
>
> I know that you will live up to your many campaign pledges and will work hard to improve conditions not only for the businesses in Brentville but also for every resident of our great city.
>
> My sincere best wishes for a most successful term of office.
>
> Cordially yours,

Some occasions call for letters of congratulation that are more personal in nature. For example, a social honor, an important anniversary, special recognition, or some other personal achievement usually calls for congratulatory letters to be written. Here is a letter that could be written on one such occasion:

> Dear Marion:
>
> How happy I was to be in the audience last night at the Chamber of Commerce Awards Banquet when you received the "Executive

of the Year" award! You have contributed so much to improving the business climate in our city that I know of no one who deserves this recognition more than you do.

You have done so much to improve business practice and to stimulate business in the downtown area in just the past year alone. I know that we will feel this influence for many years to come. Your influence in getting Minibus service in the downtown area is but one of the aspects of your fine work—and one for which I am particularly grateful.

If there is any way that I may be of assistance to you in your efforts, I hope that you will feel free to call on me.

Cordially yours,

Another excellent opportunity for a personal letter of congratulation is any important achievement by the children of friends or business associates. Such a letter may be written to the parents or, especially if the writer knows the family, directly to the son or daughter of the business associate. Note the example below.

Dear Richard,

I was happy to learn from your father today that you have been selected as the valedictorian of your high school graduating class. I know that you have worked very hard over the past four years to achieve this distinction and that your parents are very proud of you, and justly so. I have taken much personal pleasure in watching you grow into such a fine young man over the many years I have enjoyed the friendship of you and your family.

My sincere best wishes, Richard, for continued success during your college career.

Sincerely,

Not only are letters of congratulation written to customers and friends outside the organization, but they are also frequently sent to fellow employees in the company. In fact, some executives consider these letters among the most important they write. There are, of course, many occasions to write letters of congratulations to co-workers; one obvious occasion for such a letter is a job promotion. Here is an example:

Dear Miss Hatachi:

I was both pleased and proud to learn of your promotion to the position of administrative assistant to the president. This position is one of the most important in the company, and I know that no one is better qualified than you to fill it.

How long has it been since you and I first joined this company? We were among the first employees, as I recall, shortly after it was formed more than ten years ago. I have very much enjoyed our association, and I look back with pleasure at what has often been a very close working relationship.

Even though your new position will reduce the opportunities for such a working relationship, I hope that you will call on me if there is any way in which I may be of assistance to you. I also hope that we will get to see each other from time to time at some of the company social functions. Good luck to you!

Cordially yours,

An important anniversary with the company provides another occasion for writing a congratulatory letter, as illustrated here:

> Dear Bob,
>
> Congratulations on your fifteenth anniversary with American City Bank. Where has the time gone? It seems like just yesterday when you started as a teller. You have made remarkable progress in your years with us, and all of us who have worked with you marvel at your ability to handle difficult jobs so smoothly. We've learned much from you, my good friend!
>
> I hope to be around on your twentieth to congratulate you again. Of course, by then you'll be so high up in the bank that I will need to get special permission to contact you. However, it will be worth it!
>
> Warm wishes for continued success, good health, and happiness.
>
> Sincerely,

A letter of congratulation may also be appropriate when an employee retires. The tone of such a letter, however, depends primarily on the attitude of the person retiring. Some look forward to retirement; others do not. If you don't know the feelings of the retiree, use a style similar to that used in the following example:

> Dear Mrs. Lopez:
>
> I, among several hundred other employees here at Robinson's, will miss your pleasant smile and cheerful voice over the telephone. It hardly seems possible that you have been with us 18 years and that after next week you will be retiring. It will be difficult finding a replacement who will contribute as much as you have to the friendly feeling among employees and customers.
>
> All good wishes to you in your retirement. I hope you will enjoy many, many years of good health and happiness with your friends and family. Please visit us whenever you have the opportunity and desire to do so.
>
> Sincerely,

Congratulating Other Companies

A slightly different kind of letter of congratulation is that written by one business firm to another. Of course, such a letter very often has sales overtones.

> Dear Mr. Kaplan:
>
> How pleased I was to have had the privilege of attending the open house for your new store in the Northridge Shopping Center. It is one of the most beautiful stores I have ever seen. The architectural design is absolutely brilliant, and the furnishings are magnificent. Your store will certainly be the envy of the trade! In any event, I know that it is certain to attract many customers and that business will be equal to, if not better than, that enjoyed by your other fine branch stores.
>
> Please let me know how our company—or how I, personally—may serve you in your new location. We want to be the best of neighbors, and we welcome the opportunity to prove our intentions. Congratulations!
>
> Cordially yours,

THANK-YOU LETTERS

Occasions that call for thank-you letters often arise; for example, to acknowledge receipt of a gift, to express appreciation for thoughtfulness, for special favors, and so on. Thank-you letters in business are just as necessary as the "bread and butter" notes sent to friends who have entertained you in their homes or who have done something especially nice for you. In fact, failure to write a thank-you when it is called for can lose goodwill, because people expect their gifts and special efforts to be appreciated and are displeased when appreciation is not shown.

Promptness in sending a thank-you note is as important as what is said, because any delay in sending the letter may be taken to imply a lack of sincere appreciation.

Writing Thanks for a Gift

Business executives often receive gifts from suppliers and from others with whom they do business. Although some business firms deplore this practice, it nevertheless exists. Some companies prohibit the acceptance of gifts by individuals, as indicated tactfully in the following example:

> Dear Mr. McNamee:
>
> The beautiful six-volume set of *Treasures of Art* arrived this afternoon. It is a magnificent set, and I have never seen more beautiful color reproductions anywhere. I am amazed at how well the publisher has captured the brilliance and detail of the original paintings.
>
> You may be sure, Mr. McNamee, that we shall make very good use of this set in our company library. Each copy will bear this inscription on the inside front cover: "Presented to the Camelot Company library by the Rockwell Corporation."
>
> On behalf of all the employees at Camelot who will derive much pleasure from your thoughtful gesture, may I express our deepest appreciation to you.
>
> Sincerely yours,

Writing Thanks for Hospitality

When hospitality has been extended to you, common courtesy calls for a thank-you. For example, suppose that you visit a supplier's factory in another city to discuss the purchase of his product. He makes reservations for you at a hotel, takes you to dinner, and in other ways looks after your physical comfort—he even entertains you in his home. Of course, a "bread and butter" note is a must.

> Dear Mr. Erickson:
>
> Thank you for the many courtesies extended to me on my recent visit to Mill Valley. My stay was certainly much more pleasant because of your thoughtfulness in arranging for my comfort.
>
> The high spot of the entire visit was the evening spent in your beautiful home. You and Mrs. Erickson are most gracious hosts. The food was excellent; the conversation, stimulating; the people, delightful. The time passed so quickly that I was embarrassed to find that I had stayed so long—so engrossed and comfortable was I in being part of such good company.

I have mailed a small package to Mrs. Erickson as a little token of my appreciation for the many kindnesses shown me. I shall not soon forget my visit to Mill Valley.

Sincerely yours,

Writing Thanks for Courtesies

When you receive a letter of congratulation upon a promotion, a special recognition, or an achievement, you should acknowledge it with a thank-you letter. For example:

Dear Roger:

You were very thoughtful to write me about my recent promotion. One of the most satisfying things about being promoted is that one often gets such pleasant letters from the nicest people! I already like my new job very much, and I know that I will enjoy it even more after I have really become accustomed to this completely different work.

Thank you, Roger, for all your good wishes and your thoughtfulness. About that offer to be of assistance—I may be calling on you sooner than you expect, so be prepared!

Sincerely,

Writing Thanks for Special Favors

Often friends or business acquaintances go out of their way to do a favor. Someone, for example, may have recommended a friend for membership in a club, another may have recommended a particular firm to a customer, or still another may have been of special service in a business situation. A special favor of this kind deserves a thank-you; for example:

Dear Mr. Martinez:

This morning we were visited by Mr. Alvin Cooper of Alvin's Restaurants, Inc. We were delighted that he placed a very large order for restaurant equipment and supplies for his new chain of ten restaurants he will be opening later this year. Mr. Cooper told us that you recommended us highly to him.

We are extremely grateful to you, Mr. Martinez, for this very special favor. While we appreciate the order immensely, we appreciate equally as much your confidence in us. It is a compliment of the highest order.

I hope that we will have the opportunity of returning this favor in some way before too long. In the meantime, we want to say "thanks."

Cordially yours,

FORMAL INVITATIONS AND REPLIES

From time to time, business people receive formal invitations to such events as an open house, a special reception to honor a distinguished person, a special anniversary, or a formal social gathering. Such invitations are usually engraved or printed and are written in the third person.

The examples below and on page 379 show the formal printed invitation, the formal handwritten invitation, the handwritten acceptance, and the handwritten refusal. An acceptance or a refusal is occasionally typewritten; however, this practice is not recommended. Handwritten invitations and replies are written on personal stationery or special note-size stationery. Plain white notepaper may also be used.

Printed Invitation

The Sales Executives' Club

requests the pleasure of your company
at a formal showing
of its new film
"Selling the American Dream"
Tuesday, the tenth of May
at eight o'clock
Cavalier Room of the Century Hotel

R.S.V.P.

Handwritten Invitation

Mr. and Mrs. Delbert Anderson
request the pleasure of
Mr. and Mrs. Peter De Merrit's company
at a dinner party
on Saturday, the Fourth of July
at eight o'clock
5208 Lupin Drive

R.S.V.P.

Telephone 555-7116

Acceptance

Ms. Audrey Brennan
accepts with pleasure
the kind invitation of
The Sales Executives' Club
for Tuesday, the tenth of May

Refusal

Mr. and Mrs. Peter De Merrit
regret that a previous engagement
prevents their accepting
Mr. and Mrs. Anderson's
kind invitation
for the Fourth of July

LETTERS OF CONDOLENCE

Just as you would write a note or send a card of sympathy to one who has suffered the loss of a close relative or friend, so do business executives write letters to friends and associates upon learning of misfortunes and tragedies in their lives. Naturally, letters of condolence should be genuinely sympathetic. It is not easy to comfort those who have suffered losses; letters of condolence, therefore, are among the most difficult letters to write. Although handwritten condolence letters are preferable, typed letters are acceptable. If you are unable to write a really personal note of sympathy, you may send a printed sympathy card. Following is a letter of condolence.

> Dear Clark:
>
> I was saddened to learn of the death of your father this week. Please accept my sincere sympathy for your loss.
>
> When my mother passed away last year, a friend sent me a copy of the enclosed essay by Forest Holiday. I received much consolation from reading his thoughts, and I hope they may also offer you some comfort.
>
> My thoughts are with you and your family in your time of grief.
>
> Sincerely yours,

You do not have to wait until you enter the world of business to take advantage of the suggestions made in this section. Because of the personal nature of the correspondence discussed, much of the material will apply to you even now.

Communication Projects

PRACTICAL APPLICATION

A Harold (Hal) Malone was in a number of classes with you in college, and you became close friends. You read in the local newspaper that Hal, who was graduated last year, was awarded a trip to Europe by his employers, Atlas Insurance Company, because Hal's insurance sales were the highest in the state. The newspaper article also reported that Hal is being named Assistant District Manager after only one year with the company. No wonder the college yearbook indicated that Hal was "The Most Likely to Succeed." Write a short letter to your old friend to congratulate him on both his award and his promotion.

B You are the executive assistant to the president of your company, Samuel Dean, Jr. Mr. Dean asks you to compose a letter to be sent to a retiring employee, Alan Rowe, who has been with the company, McKnight Manufacturing Company, for 30 years. A gift of a $200 check is to be included with the letter you will write, thanking Mr. Rowe for his service as supervisor of accounts receivable and wishing him well in his retirement. A plaque will be presented to Mr. Rowe at the annual Christmas banquet.

C You have just returned from a business trip to Louisville, Kentucky. During your three-day stay in Louisville, you were the house guest of Mr. and Mrs. Albert Allende, long-time friends of your family. Mrs. Allende (Anna) even met you at the airport and insisted on personally driving you to your business appointments, rather than having you experience the difficulty of getting around a strange city in a rented car. (Taxi drivers were on strike during the time you were in Louisville.) Write a note of thanks to the Allendes, who live at 87 Mark Twain Drive, Louisville, Kentucky 40204. Today you ordered a gift to be sent them as a small token of your appreciation.

D You are employed by the Westgate Bank of Commerce, which has over 30 branch banks in your area. One of the branch managers, Marvin Brody, has been named Assistant Vice President. His office will be in the headquarters office at Sixth and Spring Streets in Westgate. It is customary to have a reception honoring newly appointed executives and to formally announce the event. Prepare a formal announcement of the appointment that will be sent to all executives throughout the system and to every employee of the branch from which Mr. Brody comes. The reception will be held in the president's suite on the fortieth floor of the headquarters office building on April 10, from 4:30 until 6:15 p.m. Include an RSVP, by telephoning Extension 908.

E Recently you purchased a home through Mrs. Lois Frisch of the Larkin Real Estate Agency. The day that you moved into your new home, a gift basket of fruit, a beautiful house plant, and a bottle of champagne were delivered to your home. The gifts were sent by Mrs. Frisch, accompanied by a card thanking you for buying the home through her and wishing you well. Write a note to Mrs. Frisch to thank her for her thoughtfulness.

F You have just learned of the illness and death of Mrs. Alex Swenson, the wife of one of your best customers and long-time friend. Mrs. Swenson (Dora) leaves, in addition to her husband, a married daughter (Anne) and two young grandchildren, Mary and Lyle. Write a letter to Alex, vice president in charge of purchasing for Coordinated Industries, Hannibal, Missouri 63401, to extend your sympathy.

EDITING PRACTICE

Editing for Redundancies Correct these sentences by eliminating all unnecessary repetitions.

1. Clean your typewriter keys daily, as otherwise you will not get sharp copy.
2. The desk will fit just inside of the entrance.
3. The instructor will not repeat her instructions again.
4. The inspection was over with by the time I arrived.
5. Past experience shows that Mary is habitually late.
6. The booklet was sent free gratis.
7. The monthly reports submitted by Tracy and Art are both alike.
8. We are planning to convert over to a word processing system in the office.

CASE PROBLEM

Listening for Essential Ideas Your instructor will read an article to you. Listen carefully; then summarize the article in as few words as possible.

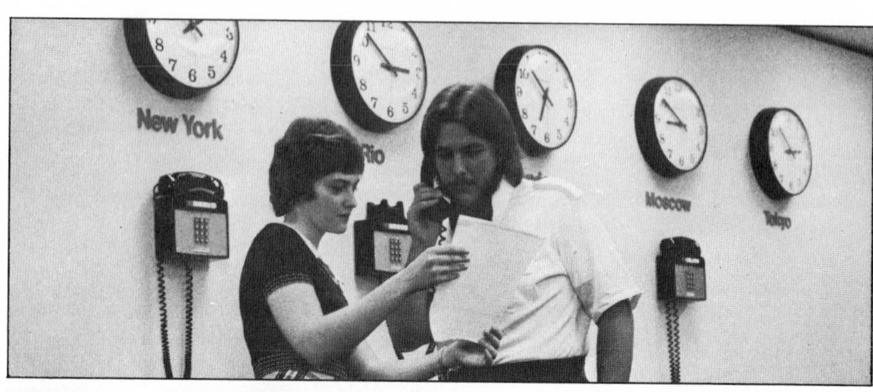
New York
Rio
Moscow
Tokyo

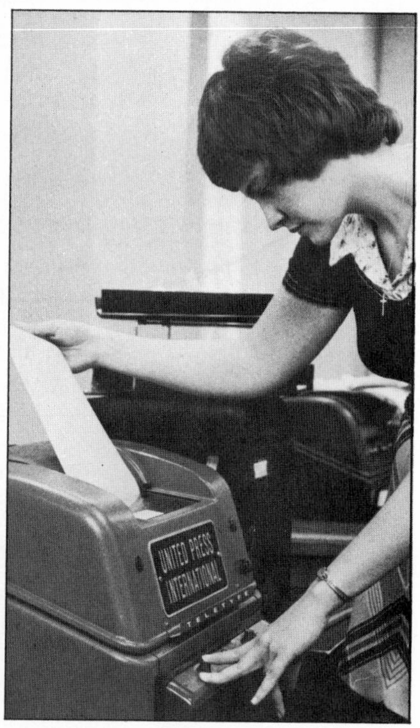
UNITED PRESS
INTERNATIONAL

CHAPTER 8

OTHER WRITTEN COMMUNICATIONS

45 Memorandums

A memorandum, usually referred to by the short form *memo,* is the primary means of corresponding with another employee (or with several or many employees) within an organization whenever the situation requires that the message be put in writing. Memos serve the same purpose *within* an organization that letters serve outside it: memos are used to give or to request information, to transmit documents, to announce company policies, to recommend promotions, and so on. Often, as discussed in Section 46, memos are used to make informal reports.

FORM OF THE MEMO

Preparing and transmitting in-house messages can be accomplished most efficiently and economically if printed interoffice memo forms are used. Most companies use interoffice memo forms printed on stationery 8½ by 11 inches or 8½ by 5½ inches. Like invoices, purchase orders, and other commonly used business forms, memo forms are often packaged as snap-out forms—that is, preassembled carbon packs that provide an original for the addressee, one or more carbon copies ("cc"), and a file copy. However, a few companies—usually very small offices—create interoffice memos on the typewriter as needed.

Whether the memo form is printed or typewritten, the headings provide for essentially the same basic information. The heading of a printed memo form, such as the one on page 385, usually includes (1) the name of the company, (2) the title *Interoffice Memorandum* (or *Interoffice Memo*), and (3) the guide words *To, From, Subject,* and *Date*. If the company has several divisions or has offices in several locations, the heading might include the additional guides *Department, Location,* and *Telephone Extension.* Another example is shown on page 410; memo forms with typewritten headings are shown on pages 387 and 395.

The *To* Line

The *To* line is usually filled in with the addressee's full name and an appropriate courtesy title (*Dr., Mrs., Miss, Mr.,* or *Ms.*).

TO: Mr. Louis T. Como
TO: Dr. Alicia Johnson
TO: Mrs. Pat Boyd

It is appropriate to include the addressee's job title when:

1. The writer wishes to show deference to the addressee:
   TO: Mr. Jorge Sanchez, Chairman of the Board

HARRISON OFFICE PRODUCTS, INC.

Interoffice Memo

To: All Sales Representatives

From: Howard L. Chester, Sales Supervisor

Date: June 10, 19--

Subject: Ratio of Customer Calls to Completed Sales for the Month of May

Since you are always interested in comparing your sales efforts with those of the other sales representatives in Territory 4, I've compiled the following data from your daily reports.

CUSTOMER CALLS PER SALE MADE

Territory 4 Averages

Representative	May, Last Year	May, This Year	Year to Date
A	3.8	2.3	3.9
B	3.9	3.6	3.5
C	8.5	6.8	6.7
D	9.6	8.9	8.3
E	5.7	4.7	4.3

Territories 4, 5, and 6 Averages

Territory	May, Last Year	May, This Year	Year to Date
4	6.3	5.3	5.9
5	4.2	3.7	4.3
6	6.9	5.8	7.1

Notice that the ratio of customer calls to sales in Territory 4 for May of this year (5.3) is better than a year ago (6.3) and than the year to date (5.9). Although our ratio is improving, we have not yet reached the low averages reported from Territory 5. Perhaps all of us should study the methods used by Sales Representatives A and B to increase the number of sales per call.

HLC

bt

2. The name of the addressee is the same as, or could easily be confused with, that of another employee.

   TO: Miss Patricia Lindberg, Sales Correspondent
   (Mrs. Pat Lundberg is administrative assistant to the sales manager.)

3. The addressee has several job titles, and the message pertains to the duties associated with only one of those titles.

   TO: Ms. Elvira T. Allen, Director, Employee Benefits Committee
   (Ms. Allen is also the director of marketing.)

To assist in the prompt and accurate delivery of interoffice memos, particularly in large offices, many writers include appropriate address information.

For example:

TO: Mr. Jacob Toppen, Room 1610, Accounting Department
TO: Ms. Julia Perez, Personnel Department, 5th Floor

Distribution and *CC* Notations When a memo is being sent to a number of people, it is appropriate to type "See below" on the *To* line and to include a *Distribution* notation at the bottom of the memo.

DISTRIBUTION:
Mr. David Bernstein, Accounting Department
Miss Anne Davis, Purchasing Department
Mrs. Louise Garofalo, Personnel Department
Mr. Frank C. Green, Manager, Accounting Department
Mr. George Harris, Vice-President, Personnel
Dr. R. S. Vincent, General Manager

If space permits, the *cc* notation may be placed below the name of the addressee, as illustrated below; otherwise, it may be typed below the typist's initials, just as in a business letter.

TO: Mrs. Phyllis Dunbar
cc: Mr. K. T. Raymond
Mr. L. A. Kirsch

The *From* Line

The writer of a memo does not use a courtesy title with his or her name. For identification purposes, the writer may include a job title, department affiliation, office location, or telephone extension.

FROM: Barbara Fisher, Secretary, Legal Department,
Room 1660, Ext. 3204

The *Date* Line

Just as in letters, the date should be written in full, not abbreviated or expressed in figures.

DATE: February 4, 19— (*or* 4 February 19—)

The *Subject* Line

The subject of the memo should be stated as briefly as possible, preferably so as to fit on one line; for example:

SUBJECT: Request for Additional Clerk-Typist

The Body, or Message

Unlike a business letter, a memo ordinarily does not include a salutation. Therefore, the body, or message, of the memo begins three or four lines below the subject line. Unless the message is very short, the body should be single-spaced. Paragraphs may be indented, but frequently they are blocked.

The Signature

Many writers prefer to have their initials—or their full name—typed below the message, to align with the fill-ins at the top right of the memo (see the illustration below). However, others feel that it is unnecessary to repeat information that already appears in the *From* line; therefore, they simply initial the memo near their typewritten name or below the message.

Reference Initials and Enclosure Notation

The initials of the typist and, when appropriate, carbon copy and enclosure notations, are typed just as they are in a regular business letter.

INTEROFFICE MEMORANDUM

TO: Mrs. Donna Gregus FROM: Jorge C. Torres

SUBJECT: National Sales Conference DATE: August 15, 19--

As requested in your August 12 memo, here are my suggestions concerning the forthcoming national sales conference:

1. I recommend that we hold our meeting in the Midwest this year. My choice is Springfield, Illinois, because of its central location.

2. Most of the representatives prefer to hold meetings away from the city. Several motels with excellent room, meeting, and other accommodations are located on the outskirts of Springfield. I believe that any one of the motels listed on the enclosed sheet would be a good conference site.

3. Because a number of people have joined the staff since the last national sales conference, I recommend that all representatives with less than one year's service be asked to attend a special one-day indoctrination session to be held before the other sales representatives arrive.

4. A number of our representatives are not so familiar with our advertising and general sales-support policies and procedures as they would like to be. Therefore, I suggest that this year's agenda include a panel discussion of these topics.

Please let me know whether you would like to discuss these suggestions or any other aspect of the conference.

JCT

urs
Enclosure

TONE OF THE MEMO

There is no hard-and-fast rule for determining the tone of a memo; however, there are some guidelines. The tone of the memo does depend on and should reflect (1) the relationship between the writer and the addressee, (2) the nature of the subject, and (3) company policy on memos. Most companies trust the discretion of the writer to dictate the "right" tone for each memo.

In actual practice, the tone of the memo is largely determined by the position of, and the writer's relation to, the person to whom the memo is addressed. Generally, memos addressed to top management or to those above the writer's rank are more formal than memos addressed to the writer's peers. Some top executives insist on formality; some do not. If you do not know and you are not given specific instructions, find a middle way—not too informal and not too deferential. Avoid using contractions like *you'll* and *here's*. For example:

> Here is the tentative schedule of space advertising you requested for next year. You will notice that two new publications have been added . . . .

The subject matter also helps to determine the tone of the memo. For example, a memo announcing the schedule of the company's softball team would obviously have a tone different from a memo justifying costs that ran over budget. The more important the topic, the more formal the memo.

ORGANIZATION OF THE MEMORANDUM

Regardless of the form and the tone of the memorandum, its main purpose is to convey a message. It should be as brief and to the point as possible without being curt or skimpy. Like a letter, a memorandum attempts to sell a point of view; for example, a memo may be used to "sell" a superior on the need for more personnel or for new office equipment. A memo, however, is usually more economical in its use of words than a letter.

A typical memo contains three elements: (1) a statement of purpose, (2) a message, and (3) a statement of future action to be taken.

Statement of Purpose

Always explain your reason for writing the memo. You may refer to a memo written or received previously, to a meeting attended, to a telephone conversation, and so on. Never assume that the subject line alone is enough to indicate the purpose of a memo. The purpose of a memo may be stated in one of the following ways:

> As you requested in your memorandum of August 17, I am sending you a report of employee turnover during July.
>
> You will recall that at our last meeting of the Advertising Committee I was asked to investigate the cost of special shipping tickets for our new Diamond line. Here is what I found.
>
> I am attaching a photocopy of a letter I received this morning from Claude Jenkins. I believe Claude's comments give further evidence of the need for improving our billing procedures.

On December 9, Mary Hertz will have been on the Carlson staff for ten years. I recommend that we arrange a special anniversary luncheon in her honor on that date.

Message

State the main points of the message so that the reader can grasp them easily and quickly. One way to make a message clear immediately is to enumerate the important points. For example:

After making a careful study of the traffic situation on the eighth and ninth floors, I recommend that:

1. The work hours for the Circulation Department staff be staggered. Half of the group could report for work at 8:30 and leave at 4:30; the other half could report at 9 and leave at 5.
2. The elevators be reserved from 8 to 9 each morning for passengers only. The use of elevators for mail and freight during the morning rush hour delays employees going to their offices.

If the memorandum covers several major topics, side headings can be used. For example:

The need for additional shipping-room personnel varies by branch office. Some offices appear to be overstaffed, while others are seriously short of personnel.

Rochester. In the Rochester plant, two additional people are needed at once. Business in that area of New York State is growing very rapidly, and in recent months serious bottlenecks have developed in getting out customers' orders.

Scranton. The staff in Scranton is adequate at present. The problem here is not one of quantity but of quality. With the new training program, however, this problem should soon be overcome.

Boston. In this office, the shipping room is overstaffed. This overstaffing is the result of the decline of shipping from the Boston plant since the Springfield warehouses were completed.

Statement of Future Action

The memorandum should usually end with a statement of future action to be taken or with a request for further instructions, as illustrated in these examples and in the memo on page 387.

Do you wish me to follow up on these suggestions?

Our committee will meet again on June 21, and at that time I will report on the decisions reached.

Please let me know whether the solution I have recommended is satisfactory to you.

I shall be glad to give you more details on my meeting with Mr. Frankheimer if you wish to have them.

The memo on page 385 illustrates effective organization. Note that the purpose is stated in the first sentence and that the detailed information is carefully presented and is displayed in tabular form. The implications of the table are summarized in the first part of the last paragraph, and a suggestion for future action is made in the last sentence.

Communication Projects

PRACTICAL APPLICATION

A One of the field engineers in your office has told your manager that it would save time and prevent errors to have a portable electronic calculator on field trips. The manager, James G. Gannon, has asked you to find current prices for a suitable model. You have found the following are available locally: (1) The MC10 Calculator, with 12 digits and percent and memory keys, a bit large to be portable but very well made, $128.95 (discounted from $159.95); (2) the HE Microcalculator, 8 digits, $108.95; (3) the BA Slide Rule Calculator, with 8 digits, "total memory," very compact, $99.95. All have carrying cases and battery-charging units, and all operate on both AC and DC. Present this information to Mr. Gannon in an organized, concise, readable memorandum, following the style presented in this section. Supply the names of the local stores.

B Since your company moved to its new offices on the ground floor of a new building in an urban renewal area, there has been a rash of losses. Items have been disappearing at an alarming rate from the stock room, which has a "blind" opening at the end of a long corridor. New ceramic ash trays on reception desks have vanished. Even purses and coats have disappeared. Your boss, Miss Janet Mason, has been asked to call a meeting of all office personnel to discuss the matter and to explain new security procedures the company is considering. Miss Mason, in turn, asks you to prepare a memo announcing the meeting in Conference Room 4 at 9:30 Friday morning, November 25. Attendance is mandatory except for those who are to answer the phones during the meeting. Encourage suggestions and ideas to be offered at the meeting.

C As administrative assistant in the personnel department and an officer in your company's Vacationers' Club, you are to look into group travel opportunities for interested club members. To begin with, you are preparing a memo to all employees asking them to indicate whether they prefer a trip (1) to Europe, the Caribbean, Mexico, or Hawaii; (2) of one, two, three, or four weeks; (3) during winter, spring, summer, fall, or Christmas holiday. Write the memo with a sales flair; emphasize "Take the trouble out of travel," "have a fling at fun," "buy the economy tour package," or other similar incentives. Also prepare the brief questionnaire for the bottom of the memo.

D Your company has announced a policy of paying one-half the tuition for courses completed in local evening schools when such courses are directly related to the employee's work. In order to take advantage of this program, each employee must submit a request in writing to the personnel director, Mr. Keith J. Blount, at least one month before the anticipated registration. Assume that you are interested in taking a course called Introduction to Electronic Data Processing at a local evening school. Write a memorandum to Mr. Blount, state your reasons for taking the course, and show how your work would benefit. Fill in all the necessary details.

E The Superior Tool Company Employees Association, of which you are secretary, has accumulated $1,000 over the past two years to be used for charitable purposes. In order to determine what would be worthwhile causes, the Association has decided to ask all supervisors to discuss the matter with their subordinates and to submit to the Association's secretary by Monday, December 5, a list of five suggestions for using this fund. Write a memorandum to all supervisors of the company, and ask for their suggestions for using the money. Ask that the memorandum be posted on all departmental bulletin boards. Inasmuch as this topic might seem to lack urgency or a sense of great importance within the departments, do your best to dramatize your appeal. In short, sell the reader on the importance of a speedy response.

EDITING PRACTICE

The Correspondence Supervisor Edit and rewrite the following paragraph.

> We are very sorry to learn, that the coffee table you purchased from us did not arrive in perfect condition. A replacement table will go out on the very, first delivery scheduled for your section of the city which should be on Wednesday. It is our sincere wish to give service, quality, and to satisfy our customers, therefore, we are greatful to you for writing us about the table. You have helped in the maintainance of the reputation, that we value so high.

CASE PROBLEM

A Confidential Matter The office is buzzing with news that the new office manager is to be appointed today. Will it be Janet Anson, Fred Marshall, or someone from outside the firm? Glenda Knox, secretary to the vice-president, Jerome Anshen, knows who has been appointed because her boss made the selection. However, Mr. Anshen has asked that she keep the matter confidential until an official announcement is made. Frances Lucas, Glenda's best friend in the company, would like to know who has been appointed and asks Glenda at lunch, "Please tell me who got the job; I won't breathe a word to a soul, I promise."

1. Should Glenda tell Frances? Why or why not?
2. What should she say to Frances?

46 Informal Reports

In the world of business, the report is the primary medium for distributing important information. Marketing managers, sales people, secretaries, department heads, and many others receive reports that supply them with essential business information, and many of them write reports to supply others with essential business information.

A report is almost always written, but it may, of course, be given orally. If the information is important enough to report, it is important enough to put in writing—even if only for the record. Anything worth reporting is important; therefore, "Put it in writing" is the basic principle behind all reports.

The values of a written report, compared with an oral report, are obvious. An oral report may be misunderstood. Much of an oral report may be quickly forgotten, especially statistical data. Even a forceful oral report will grow weaker and weaker each day. A written report, however, can be referred to again and again, so that the reader reinforces the message with each reading. Moreover, a precise and permanent record exists in the report itself.

Reports can be broadly classified according to their lengths—*informal* (shorter reports) or *formal* (longer reports). Formal reports usually require extensive research, documentation, investigation, and analysis, and they usually fill considerable space, as you will see in Section 47. But first you will study informal reports, the type you will handle most often.

MECHANICS OF WRITING INFORMAL REPORTS

The first step in writing any report, formal or informal, is to prepare an outline. For informal reports, you have a ready-made preliminary outline, the memo form you learned in Section 45, which is as follows:

To:
From:
Date:
Subject:

Whether you use this exact form or whether you adapt it will depend upon the circumstances under which you are working at any given time. *How* you use the outline will also depend on a number of variables, as discussed below.

To

The way you write the addressee's name depends partly upon the degree of formality or informality of your office atmosphere. For instance, if everybody is on first-name terms with the boss, if the boss expects to be called by his or her first name, and if you know that the report is a personal one, you might write this:

To: Tom Blaine

But suppose you know by its content that the report will be read by other persons, as well as by the boss, or you know that the report will be placed in the files for future reference. In this case, you would write:

To: Mr. Thomas Blaine

From

The *From* line should match the tone of the *To* line. For example, the first two lines of a very informal report written only for the personal information of the boss would look like this:

To: Tom Blaine
From: Pat Cray

A different *From* line is needed for a report that is not for the exclusive information of the boss or for a report that will be filed. Keeping in mind the fact that all readers will know the boss but may not know who you are, you would write your opening lines as follows:

To: Mr. Thomas Blaine
From: Pat Cray, Secretary

Subject

The *Subject* line should be a comprehensive, yet clear and precise, statement that will prepare a reader for rapid assimilation of the information given in the report. Composing a good subject line, therefore, requires a high degree of skill. Let's look at some illustrations. Here is a subject line for a sales representative's report to the sales manager.

Subject: Sales

This line would be meaningless to the sales manager. He or she would have to read the report in order to grasp its subject. The following line, however, would orient the reader immediately.

Subject: Sales Report for Week of May 10, 19—

Now suppose that you are a personnel director and you receive a report with a subject line like this:

Subject: Employee Turnover

Quite possibly you have forgotten that you asked for a report on some phase of employee turnover. If so, the above subject line does nothing to refresh your memory or to prepare you to quickly grasp the facts presented in the report. But how about the following revision?

Subject: Statistics on Employee Turnover for the 19— Fiscal Year

Date

Absolutely without exception, every report should carry the date on which it was written. Conditions change so rapidly that facts presented on one date may not be valid for long. And frustrating indeed is the experience of finding in the files a report that could be valuable—provided you knew when it was written.

Wherever dates are given in the body of a report, those dates must be specific. You would not write, "On Wednesday, we received 117 inquiries about . . . ." You would write, "On Wednesday, December 16, 19—, we received . . . ."

Adaptation of Memo Form

Although the memorandum form is your outline for writing informal reports, in many cases you would not use the exact memo format. One of the possible variations would be the following:

Pat Cray
September 8, 19—
Statistics on Employee Turnover for the 19— Fiscal Year

This adaptation shows that Pat Cray wrote the report on September 8, 19—, and the subject is stated as a heading, or title. The assumption is that this report would go only to Mr. Blaine and therefore requires no additional name. However, if an addressee's name is necessary, the body of the report could start like this:

> Mr. Blaine: Statistics on employee turnover for the 19— fiscal year are as follows:

Carbon Copies

Whenever you write an informal report, no matter how minor you think it is, be sure to make a carbon copy for your own files, because anything important enough to put in writing is important enough to be retained. You may never need to refer to your file copy, but if you do, nothing else can take its place. The best precautionary measure against lost or misaddressed reports is to have in your files a folder marked "Reports," which contains a carbon of every report you write.

PLANNING AND WRITING INFORMAL REPORTS

Many people, including some correspondents, think that writing involves merely sitting down and dashing off a few words. This is a false notion that accounts largely for the fact that good business writers are scarce and therefore are very much in demand.

Actually, a topnotch writing effort of any kind represents hard work and is the result of much thought, careful planning, and excellent training. For the know-how that will enable you to write informal reports of the very best quality, you need to study, think about, and apply the following principles.

Being Clear, Complete, Correct, and Concise

As you know, writing that is *concise* is not writing that is incomplete. To be concise, you must say everything that needs to be said, but you must say it in the fewest possible words.

You are also well aware that your writing must be clear and complete. You would not write a "fuzzy" sentence like this:

> Mr. Wright spoke to Mr. Klein about the vacation schedule for the Accounting Department, and he said he would have it ready sometime next week.

Instead, you would write a clear, complete, definite message, such as the following:

> Mr. Klein reported to Mr. Wright that the Accounting Department vacation schedule would be set up by Thursday, March 4, 19—.

All reports must be correct in every detail. Perhaps we should use the stronger term *accurate*, because any information important enough to be reported must be more than substantially correct, it must be completely accurate. For example, if you are asked to report the number of free-sample requests that come in on a given day, you'd better be sure that you give an exact, not an approximate, count.

INTEROFFICE MEMORANDUM

TO Mr. Martin A. Lindberg FROM Pat Cray

SUBJECT Suggestion for Improving Customer Service DATE February 9, 19--

We receive approximately 2,000 purchase orders for small printing jobs each week. Most of these purchase orders are typed by our customers on their general purchase order forms. This typing is time-consuming for our customers (some customers send in about 100 orders each week), and in typing many of the orders they often forget to indicate such vital information as printing quantity, folding details, delivery instructions, and so on.

I suggest we create a standard form that our customers can use to save typing time in their offices and to help us obtain complete, accurate information on every order, so that we may better serve all customers. The benefits both to our customers and to us are great:

1. Our customers will save typing time. This will help build customer goodwill.

2. The standard form guarantees that the typist will not leave out essential information. This will help our plant fulfill their orders faster and more accurately, and it will help our billing department to determine charges precisely, which will certainly please our plant, our billing department, and our customers.

3. Our order department can use the form to take telephone orders and thereby save time and assure accurate order-taking.

Our plant could print and distribute these forms economically, of course; perhaps we could even imprint the individual customer's name on the forms.

I suggest that we arrange for the managers of our plant, our billing department, and our sales department to meet and discuss this in detail.

PC

cc Mr. W. Johnson
Mrs. V. Woods
Mr. J. Kurbs

Wording

The wording of reports differs from that of letters. A letter is designed to do more than convey a message, for its accompanying purpose is to win new customers or clients for the company and to retain old ones. Therefore, the tone of a letter is warm and friendly. A report, on the other hand, is a straightforward, factual presentation—and it should be worded as such.

As an illustration, read the following opening paragraph of a letter answering a request for information about your company's in-service training courses.

> In response to your request of April 2, we are very glad to tell you that our company presently has a schedule of three in-service training courses. (The second paragraph would give the titles and other details of the courses.)

Now, note how the wording changes when the same information is given in a report.

> Our company presently conducts three in-service training courses: (1) History and Policies of the Company; (2) Report Writing; and (3) Inventory Control Methods and Procedures.

TYPES OF PRESENTATION

How brief or how detailed should your informal report be? Should you give the requested information in a single paragraph? Should you present the information in outline form? For the most effective presentation, should you tabulate the information?

Because you are preparing the report, no one but you can answer these questions. Only you are close enough to the situation to know why the report was requested, to be able to project the probable uses of the information, and so on. To be able to make a wise decision about the form your report should take, though, you must know the types of presentations and the purposes that each best serves.

Paragraph

The paragraph form is used for the presentation of a simple fact. For example, if your boss has asked you to report on how many days were lost last week because of absence—and if you know for sure that the only statistic your boss wants is the total number of days—you might write the following in a memo-style report:

> In the Sales Department during the week of March 11, 19—, absences totaled 7 days.

Or, if you wanted to give a little extra information, you might write:

> In the Sales Department during the week of March 11, 19—, four employees were absent for a total of 7 days.

Outline

If, however, you know that your boss has a personal interest in the staff, you might correctly guess that you should list *who* was absent. Therefore, you might write:

> Information regarding absenteeism in the Sales Department during the week of March 11, 19—, is as follows:
>
> 1. Total days of absence: 7
> 2. Number of employees absent: 4
>   a. John Anderson, 2 days
>   b. Vincent Lanzo, 2 days
>   c. Willard Starr, 1 day
>   d. Angela Vargas, 2 days

Tabulation

In some cases, the most effective way to present information is to tabulate it. The advantage of the tabulated form is that the reader can see everything at a glance and need not wade through a river of words. Obviously, the decision to tabulate would be influenced by the amount and kind of information to be given and by the writer's projection of the uses to which the information may be put.

For example, suppose you have been asked to give a report on absenteeism. You might set up a table like the one shown below.

Sales Department Absenteeism
Week of March 11, 19—

Employee	No. Days Absent	Reason for Absence
Anderson, John	2	Illness (cold)
Lanzo, Vincent	2	Illness (cold)
Starr, Willard	1	Illness (cold)
Vargas, Angela	2	NSA Conference

Total Days of Absence: 7
Total Employees Absent: 4

UNSOLICITED REPORTS

An unsolicited report is, quite simply, one that you make on your own initiative rather than one you are asked for. In business, any idea that you might have for increasing efficiency, productivity, or profit-making will usually be welcome. And, more than likely you will want to put your idea in writing so that you may present it in the most complete, logical, and generally effective manner.

How do you go about preparing and submitting an unsolicited report? Here are some details that you should consider before you begin to write.

To

You will want to direct your suggestion or idea to the person who has the authority to put it into effect. Usually this person will be your boss; but even if it happens to be someone else, courtesy and protocol demand that the suggestion be routed *through* your boss *to* that other person. For example:

To: Ms. Johanna F. Blaine (your boss)
Mr. Paul C. Booker (the "authority person")

Subject

In any report, the subject line must tell the reader what the report is about. In an unsolicited report, though, you probably will want to slant the wording of the subject so that it will appeal to the reader's particular interest. For example, if you know that your boss is particularly interested in providing customers with fast, accurate service, you might select a subject line like the one used in the informal report on page 395.

Communication Projects

PRACTICAL APPLICATION

A Which of the following questions would require a written, rather than an oral, report? Write a report on your choices; address the report to your instructor.

1. Where is the best place to keep all the reference books we've been accumulating in this department?
2. What complaints have we received about our new Product H-55?
3. What matters should be covered at our next staff meeting?
4. How should the "Pending Projects" be filed so that we can find them more readily?
5. What kind of photocopying machines do the company's secretaries prefer?
6. How many vacation days have you taken this year?
7. Do all the departments in the company have formal arrangements for noontime telephone coverage?
8. Who's on the exhibits committee for the Housewares Show?
9. Would a centralized stockroom or individual supply closets on each floor be more efficient?
10. When do you think we should have the next sales meeting?

B Write a subject line for each of the selections you made in the preceding assignment.

C Your boss is interested in the following stocks: Dow Chemical, IBM, and American Telephone and Telegraph. You are asked to find out the closing prices of these stocks for Monday and Friday of the previous week. Consult a newspaper for the information you need, and write an informal report on this information.

D Under the subject line "Statistics of Employee Turnover for Fiscal Year 19—," write a report that includes the following data:

> At the beginning of the fiscal year there were 4,241 employees. During the year, 466 new appointments were made; 26 employees were transferred from other branches; 46 former employees were reinstated—making 538 additions to the staff. During the same period, 582 employees were separated: 230 by resignation, 24 by death, 25 by transfer to other branches, 7 by removal for cause (discharged), 6 by retirement, and 290 for miscellaneous reasons. At the close of the fiscal year, there were 4,197 employees, a decrease of 44 for the year.

E Write an unsolicited report to present an idea you would like to see put into effect.

EDITING PRACTICE

Preferred Spelling Some of the words in this paragraph do not conform to preferred spellings. Identify and respell them.

> As your counsellor and as advisor to the staff of the school yearbook, I should like to talk with you about the inadvisability of cancelling our plan

for including an acknowledgement section in this year's book. Can you find time to drop in to see me sometime this week? I shall be in my office every afternoon from two to four.

CASE PROBLEM

To Ask or Not to Ask Questions One of the most important things new employees must learn is when to ask for help and when to use their own judgment in trying to solve a problem. People who solve their own problems are appreciated only when their work is correct. On the other hand, new employees who make mistakes because they are afraid or hesitant to ask questions may very well find themselves in serious trouble. What would you do in the following situations?

1. During Evelyn's first week on the job, her boss asks her to make five copies of an interoffice memorandum. On the list of those who are to receive the memo is a Mr. Allen. Evelyn knows that there are two Mr. Allens in the company—one is the vice-president in charge of manufacturing and the other is the purchasing manager. Because the memo concerns the purchase of new equipment, Evelyn decides that the purchasing manager is the one who should receive the memo. Accordingly, without asking her boss, Evelyn addresses the memo to the purchasing manager.

   a. Do you agree with Evelyn's decision?
   b. What alternative action would you suggest?
   c. Is it possible that both Mr. Allens should receive a copy of the memo?

2. Linda's boss, Mr. Adams, is in a meeting in Mrs. Collins' office. He has telephoned Linda from there and asked her to find a report in the file and to bring it to him immediately. Linda knows that Mrs. Collins is the treasurer, and she knows her telephone extension; but the company occupies a very large building, and she does not know where her office is located.

   a. What steps might Linda take to locate Mrs. Collins' office?
   b. Will Linda's boss be embarrassed if she takes too long to deliver the report?

3. Dan has just started to work as an order-editor and finds on his desk an order for an item that he has not heard of. He knows that recently many items were declared out of stock, and he assumes that this is one of them. Therefore, he notes this information on the order.

   a. Do you agree with Dan's action?
   b. Should he have checked further?
   c. What could be the consequences of his action?

47 Formal Reports

Formal business reports are usually concerned with complicated problems or questions necessitating investigation, analysis, research, and documentation. For instance, here are some typical report subjects: an analysis of the methods of marketing a company's products; a study of the various advertising media used by a business and the rate of return for each type of advertising; a plan for reorganizing a department of a business; a study of future needs for factory space for a manufacturing enterprise; an analysis of working procedures in several departments of a business, with recommendations for simplifying these procedures; an experiment to test a new product for durability.

The writing of a formal report may require weeks or even months of exhaustive study, and the completed document may contain anywhere from several pages to more than a hundred. Regardless of length, formal reports must be expertly written, because they are the bases upon which a company may make decisions involving thousands of dollars.

Interestingly enough, there are some brilliant investigators who can do the research and can compile the facts but who simply cannot write a report. Therefore, some companies may employ a specialist whose sole function is to take the material assembled by the researcher and put it into report form. These writers, of course, are in the top salary bracket.

In this section you will receive specialized training in writing formal reports. Fortunately, you have a head start because your knowledge of informal reports is an excellent background for writing the more complex formal reports.

PREPARING THE REPORT

Most business organizations have their own style and form for reports. Even within a company, the form may vary, depending on the department and the nature of the subject being treated. A technical report, such as one specifying requirements for manufacturing radio-tube components, may be organized in outline form with little text. Similarly, the reports of chemists, engineers, pharmacists, and other scientists are likely to include considerable tabular material, such as tables and graphs, with a relatively small amount of written interpretation. On the other hand, many business reports are mainly narrative, with a minimum of tabular matter. Though the style and form of the report may vary, most formal reports include these main sections:

Introduction
Summary
Body
Conclusions and Recommendations
Supplementary Material

Before any of these sections can be written, however, there is much work to be done. To be able to determine the purpose and scope of the report, the investigator must first gather reliable facts, assemble and analyze them, then draw conclusions from the factual analysis, and make recommendations that are reasonable in view of company needs.

Defining Purpose and Scope

Why is the report being written? The answer to this question must appear in the introductory section of the report. In a study of the current letter-writing practices of the Ajax Company, for example, the purpose of the report might be stated as follows:

1. To determine the present letter-writing styles being used in Ajax Company.
2. To select as a model a letter and punctuation style for company-wide adoption.
3. To make recommendations for improving letter-writing practices throughout the company.

The report writer can easily undertake a topic too large to be treated effectively. The experienced report writer clearly defines the scope of the problem and sets up boundaries. Think, for example, how difficult it would be to write a 1,000-word paper on "Correspondence Practices of Office Workers." This topic is so broad in scope that any attempt to treat it in one report would be foolhardy. Therefore, the scope of the report should be limited to one specific phase of a general topic. For example:

Too General: Correspondence Practices of Office Workers
More Specific: Letter and Punctuation Styles Currently Used by Stenographers in the Ajax Company

Gathering Information

"No report is stronger than the facts behind it." Computer specialists, in speaking of the preparation of reports by machine, emphasize this statement vividly with their term *GIGO* (pronounced *GUY-GO*), standing for "garbage-in, garbage-out." The value of any report depends on the quality of the material going into its production. If "garbage" goes in, "garbage" is bound to come out. With reliable facts behind it, a reliable report can be written; with questionable data, only a questionable report can result.

In gathering information and documenting it, writers should be familiar with the authoritative references in their fields. There are, of course, many general references that everyone needs. Such standard sources as the *Writer's Guide to Periodical Literature, The Business Periodicals Index, Facts on File, The World Almanac,* and *The New York Times Annual Index* are invaluable helps to nearly any writer.

In each field of business, such as accounting, marketing, or office administration, there are basic references as well as current periodicals that should be reviewed frequently by report writers. Naturally, anyone doing research must first learn how to find and use books, periodicals, card catalogs, and various indexes. When data are to be obtained in other ways, such as through questionnaires or personal interviews, other research techniques must be mastered.

Working Bibliography In consulting the various reference works pertinent to the subject, the writer should make up a list of the books, periodicals, reports, and other sources to be used as references in the report. This preliminary list of sources is called the *working bibliography*. If the writer makes each entry of the working bibliography on a separate card (5 by 3 or 6 by 4 inches), the cards will make it easier to assemble the final bibliography of sources actually used. The writer will also find the bibliography cards useful when footnoting material in the report.

A book card for a working bibliography should contain all the following information:

Author's full name (last name first)
Title (and edition, if there is more than one)
Name and location of publisher
Date of publication (latest copyright date)

In addition, it is helpful to include for the writer's own use the library's call number for the reference.

The following illustration shows a bibliography card that has been prepared for a book reference. Note the library's call number in the upper right corner.

658.4
Dr

Drucker, Peter F.

Management

Harper + Row, Inc.
New York, 1974

When consulting a magazine, newspaper, or other periodical, the writer prepares a bibliography card like the one on page 403. This card should show the full name of the author, the title of the article (in quotation marks), the name of the publication (and location, if a newspaper), the date, volume, and number of the publication, and the page numbers.

Henn, James D.

"Some Basic Elements of a Vital Records Program,"

Records Management Quarterly,

July, 1974, pp. 24-29

Vol. 8, No. 3

Note-Taking The writer also uses cards for taking notes. Cards are much more practical for this purpose than sheets of paper because they are sturdy and can be sorted and resorted easily.

The ease with which material can be organized and a report can be written depends to a large extent on how well notes have been made from reading. Most good writers take more notes than they need. This practice gives them a great deal of information, which they can "boil down" to the essentials before writing the report.

When you take notes from your reading, be sure to carefully identify each source. Always use a new card for each new source or topic. Normally, summary statements or phrases with page references are sufficient for note cards. Whenever you use a quotation, however, be sure to copy the statement exactly, enclose it in quotation marks, and list the number of the page from which the quotation was taken. Later, when you are organizing the material for writing, you may find it helpful to include a brief subject reference at the top of each card; for example, if you are tracing the development of a product, you might identify references by "year," "developer," or "site of development."

STRUCTURING THE REPORT

After collecting and studying the material relating to the topic, the writer can begin to organize the report. This is the time to revise note cards, sort them by topic, and tentatively organize them into a logical sequence for the report.

Outline

Using organized note cards as a guide, the writer next makes an outline to serve as the structure, or framework, of the report. The outline should be kept as simple as possible. While determining the outline, the writer should keep in mind the kinds of topic headings the report requires. If outline entries are carefully thought out, many of them can be used as topic headings in the final report. The writer should keep in mind the following points in making the outline:

The purpose of the report is to convey information efficiently.

A good report structure gives the reader a sense of movement; one thought naturally reads into another.

The outline is a time-saver when the writer starts writing.

The outline should be arranged to present material in logical units and in logical sequence.

Headings

Most books, articles, and business reports utilize headings to indicate the organization of the material. Headings of equivalent weight should be styled alike. For example, the main divisions of an article, a report, or a chapter in a book may be centered, and the subdivisions of each main heading may be typed as paragraph headings. When there are more than two divisions, however, the following arrangement of headings should be used:

CENTERED FIRST-ORDER HEADING

Centered Second-Order Heading

BLOCKED THIRD-ORDER HEADING

Blocked Fourth-Order Heading

Indented Fifth-Order Heading

If the report writer is consistent in the use of headings, the reader will better understand the report's organization and content. Consistency should be observed in the form as well as in the style of the headings. In general, a topic form is preferred to a sentence form. For example, "How to Write Reports" is preferable to "This Is How to Write Reports."

WRITING THE REPORT

There are considerable differences between the informal writing style of the business letter and memorandum and the writing style commonly found in the formal report. These differences will be pointed out in the following discussion.

Style

Long business reports are important documents upon which management bases many of its high-level decisions. Consequently, such reports tend to be written in a serious, formal style, usually in the third person. The impersonal style helps the writer avoid interjecting a personal tone, which might weaken a report by making it seem merely a statement of one person's opinions and beliefs, instead of a sound evaluation of the data gathered for the report. Of course, usually only one person, the writer, is evaluating the facts, but the more the writer can de-emphasize the *I* and cite facts to back the evaluation, the more objective and more persuasive will the report sound.

A poor report writer presenting a report on letter-writing practices might make these statements:

> It seems to *me* that we are too old-fashioned in our letter arrangement styles.
>
> *Personally, I* would *prefer* to use the modified-block letter style for all company correspondence.
>
> Even though most of the other departments prefer close punctuation, *I* have a strong *preference* for open punctuation and think we ought to adopt it as our standard.

Even though the facts may provide a sound basis for the evaluations given in the examples above, these sentences do not seem objective because the writer has used so many personal references. In addition, the writer has shown how judgments are drawn from the data gathered.

On the other hand, the good report writer knows that merely stating a judgment will not persuade anyone to accept it, no matter how soundly based on fact and reason the judgment may be. Therefore, the expert writer uses an impersonal style and relates all evaluations to the facts found in the study. This writer carefully avoids any expressions that may imply that the evaluations are based on personal opinions instead of sound reasons and facts. Instead of the sentences given above, the expert writer would write the following:

> The evidence gathered in this survey shows that the letter styles used by Ajax Company are not so up to date as those of other similar organizations. (The facts would then be cited.)
>
> Use of the modified-block letter style would be appropriate for Ajax Company because the style has the modern look of simplicity and also is faster and easier to type.
>
> Five of the eight departments studied use standard punctuation; however, adoption of open punctuation would have the following advantages: . . . . (Explanation of advantages would follow.)

This same impersonal writing style should characterize all sections of the report. Remember that reasoning from facts is an important factor in the success of any business report.

Title Page

The title page usually includes the complete title of the report, the name and title of the author, the name of the person for whom the report is prepared, and the date the report is submitted. Each of these items should be attractively arranged on the page. A typical title page is illustrated on page 406.

Table of Contents

This section is prepared after the report has been completed. One commonly accepted form is shown at the bottom of page 406.

LETTER-WRITING PRACTICES

OF THE AJAX COMPANY

March 6, 19--

Prepared for: Bernard Fisher
Prepared by: Phoebe Atkinson

TABLE OF CONTENTS

Introduction

The introductory section of a long report is designed to tell the reader why the report was written, how the data were gathered, and what the report does (or does not) do.

Suppose that Bernard Fisher, the general manager of the Ajax Company, has asked Phoebe Atkinson, office manager, to investigate the letter-writing practices in each department, with a view toward improving the company correspondence function and cutting costs. In such a report, Miss Atkinson would include in the introductory section the *purpose and scope* of her report and the *procedure* she followed to collect and analyze data.

Purpose and Scope First, the writer should explain why the report was written. The next point is to clearly enumerate the basic objectives of the report.

> This report was prepared at the request of Mr. Fisher, general manager of Ajax Company. The purposes of the report are:
>
> 1. To determine the letter-writing styles being used in each department of the Ajax Company.
> 2. To determine what punctuation styles are being used in each department of the Ajax Company.
> 3. To identify correspondence problems in each department.
> 4. To seek ways of improving correspondence practices in the company.

A brief statement of scope may be included in this section.

> This report does not include grammatical practices, spelling problems of stenographers, tone, word-choice, or problems of writing technical articles.

Procedure The introductory section of the report should also describe the method used to collect and analyze the data. An example follows:

> To collect valid information for this report, all supervisors responsible for correspondence in each department were interviewed. The questionnaire shown in Appendix A of this report was sent in advance and was filled out by each supervisor. Later, the questionnaires were reviewed briefly and were checked during the final interview conducted by Mrs. Bratowski. In addition, all current periodicals in business communications were consulted so that the results of the company survey could be compared with recommended present-day practices.

Summary

For the busy executive, the summary is placed early in the report (following the introduction). This section contains the most significant information in capsule form, which is helpful to the reader who cannot take time to read the entire report. When time permits, the reader can complete the reading of the report. The length of the summary may range from one paragraph to four or five pages, depending on the material that has been gathered. The following is an opening paragraph of the summary in the Ajax letter-writing practices report.

SUMMARY

This study shows that there is considerable variation in the correspondence practices within the Ajax Company. The data gathered, when analyzed, show the following significant trends:

1. Little use is made of the correspondence handbook.
2. All departments use at least two different letter styles.
3. Department heads do not consider standardized letter styles important.
4. The correspondence supervisor for the company, Mr. Walt Camden, will require the support of top management in order to put his recommendations into practice.

Body

The body is the report proper. In this section the writer tells what was done, how it was done, and what the writer found. Writing this section should present no great difficulties if the writer follows a carefully prepared outline and has good notes. The writer should stick to accurate, verifiable facts and present them in a clear, concise manner. The suggestions given in Chapter 5 for forceful, clear writing apply to the writing of reports.

Conclusions and Recommendations

This section can easily be the most important one in any report, for it is here that the real results of the report appear. The writer's conclusions tell the busy executive, on the basis of the most reliable data available, "Here is what the report shows."

Personal observations should be reduced to a minimum—conclusions should be drawn from the facts only. In the light of the conclusions and from experience with the company, the writer can make recommendations. (Note: As a guide to making worthwhile recommendations, the writer should glance back at the listed purposes of the report. As a rule, there could well be at least one recommendation for each stated purpose.)

By referring to the purposes stated in the introduction of the report on letter-writing practices, the writer might include the following conclusions and recommendations:

CONCLUSIONS AND RECOMMENDATIONS

From an analysis of the data gathered in the study, the following conclusions are drawn:

1. The authority of the correspondence supervisor is being undermined.
2. Most departments do not use the correspondence manual.
3. Old-fashioned letter styles are widely used within the company.
4. Punctuation problems are not adequately solved.
5. Correspondence is not standardized within the company.

With these conclusions in mind, the following recommendations are made:

1. Have top management write a strong letter of support for the correspondence supervisor's work.
2. Bring the correspondence manual up to date, and provide copies for each department supervisor.
3. Choose a standardized correspondence format for the entire company.
4. Call a meeting of all supervisors to explain the new correspondence policy.

Supplementary Information

Supplementary information, which is given after the conclusions and recommendations, provides substantiating data for the report. One or both of the parts discussed below may be included.

Bibliography This section is an alphabetic listing of all the references used in the report. Bibliographical entries are listed in alphabetic order by author. Forms for book and periodical entries are shown below.

Books

Harvey, Walter E., *American Business Practice*, International Book Publishers, New York, 19—.

Roberts, Jane, and John Franciscus, *Written Communications in Business*, Morgan Book Company, Boston, 19—.

Periodicals

Gluckman, Joyce, "Correspondence for Secretaries," *The Office Worker*, Vol. XVII, No. 12, 19—, pp. 143–150.

Piedro, Anthony P., "Personal Problems in the Office," *The Office Administrator*, Vol. IX, No. 1, 19—, pp. 29–46.

Appendix The appendix consists mainly of supporting information to back up the material in the body of the report. Long tables, charts, photographs, questionnaires, letters, and drawings are usually placed in this section. By including such material at the end of the report, the body of the report is freed from the kinds of detail that make reading difficult.

Letter of Transmittal

A short letter of transmittal (see page 410) composed after the report has been completed, accompanies the report. It is written in the form of a memorandum and usually contains such information as:

A reference to the person who authorized the report.
A brief statement of the general purpose of the report.
Appropriate statements of appreciation or acknowledgment.

MECHANICS OF REPORT WRITING

An immaculate physical appearance, expert placement, and meticulous attention to the mechanics of English, spelling, and punctuation emphasize the importance of the finished report. For this reason, mechanics, as well as organization and writing style, are important in preparing the report.

Of course, all the mechanics of English, spelling, and punctuation discussed in earlier chapters apply to report writing. Some suggestions for setting up a report are necessary, however, and they are presented in the following paragraphs.

1. Use common sense and show variety in paragraphing; take care to avoid too many long and too many short paragraphs. Keep in mind that the topic sentence, telling what the paragraph is about, very frequently appears first. Also, the closing sentence is often used to summarize the meaning of the paragraph.

AJAX COMPANY
Interoffice Memorandum

To: Mr. Bernard Fisher, General Manager

From: Phoebe Atkinson, Office Manager

Date: May 2, 19--

Subject: Attached report on letter-writing practices

The study of our company's letter-writing practices, which you authorized on April 2, 19--, has now been completed. The results of the study, together with my conclusions and recommendations, are contained in the attached report.

These results are significant; I hope they will be of value to you. Much credit should be given to Nora Bratowski, my assistant, who contacted each department head personally to verify the data shown. If you wish, I shall be glad to discuss the report with you in person.

PA

ck
Enclosure

2. Be generous in using headings. Take care to leave plenty of white space around major headings, tables, and other display materials. Be sure that all headings of the same value within a section are parallel in wording. For example:

Nonparallel	**Parallel**
Writing the Introduction	Writing the Introduction
The Body	Writing the Body
How to Write the Closing	Writing the Closing

3. Use footnotes to give credit when the ideas of others are used, either verbatim or modified. A footnote may be placed at the bottom of the page carrying the footnoted item, or all the footnotes may be listed at the end

of the report. Footnotes should always be numbered consecutively, whether they appear at the bottom of each footnoted page or are grouped at the end of the report. The information usually given in a footnote includes the footnote number, author, book or periodical title, publisher, place and date of publication, and page numbers. Since footnote styles may vary, it is advisable to consult the company's reference manual or a standard reference manual.

4. Select carefully any tables, charts, diagrams, photographs, drawings, and other illustrated materials used to supplement the writing. To promote better understanding of the contents, choose the items that contribute most to the report. Try to eliminate any items that are not pertinent.
5. Bind the report attractively. Many types of binding, from the single staple to an elaborate sewn binding, can be used. Reports that are subject to frequent, rigorous use should be placed inside a special hardback report folder for protection. Do not rely on a paper clip to bind the report; with only a clip, the chances of losing part of the report are very high.
6. Observe these rules of good manuscript form:
   a. Type all reports on standard 8½- by 11-inch paper. Legal-size paper will not fit standard office files.
   b. Use double spacing except for long quotations (usually three or more lines), for which single spacing is preferred. Of course, type on only one side of the sheet. Consult a standard style manual for other spacing details.
   c. Leave ample margins. Commonly accepted are these:

      Left margin: 1½ inches to allow for side binding
      Other margins: 1 inch
      First page only: When it contains the title, allow a 2-inch top margin.
   d. Always prepare at least one carbon copy.
   e. Traditionally, the first page is not numbered when it contains the title. All other pages, beginning with 2, should be numbered in the upper right corner.
   f. Follow this pattern for any material presented in outline form:

      I.
        A.
          1.
            a.
              (1)
                (a)

Communication Projects

PRACTICAL APPLICATION

A Your supervisor, William J. Whitson, asked you, as his substitute, to attend an important meeting while he is out of town. The purpose of the meeting was to discuss employee turnover—a subject that is of growing concern to the company management. From the notes you took, prepare a report to Mr. Whitson in which you give him the full details of the meeting. Supply other data that you think might be appropriate. Here are your notes:

1. Annual turnover rate: Clerical employees, 35%; supervisory, 15%.

2. Reasons given for leaving the company (in order of frequency): Clerical—Working conditions undesirable, higher salary in another company, commuting too difficult, friction with supervisors, no opportunity for advancement.
   Supervisory—Better salary, no opportunity for further advancement, working conditions disliked, friction with managers, company fringe benefits inadequate.
3. Recommended actions: Improve facilities by (1) redecorating offices and installing air conditioning and (2) replacing old furniture and equipment with modern and efficient articles; encourage frequent departmental meetings that will give employees an opportunity to express their opinions; institute training program for supervisors; initiate a salary survey of similar businesses; study promotion policies; obtain services of a management consultant to make recommendations concerning fringe benefits; consider the possibility of designating a personnel relations counselor to handle grievances.
4. Department managers are to consider the turnover problem with reference to their experiences with employees under their supervision, are to be prepared to discuss the problem further, and are to make recommendations at a special meeting to be held on May 14. Prior to this meeting, by May 9, managers should submit a memorandum on morale in their departments.
5. In the discussion, it was brought out that there seems to be an atmosphere of unrest and that morale is generally low. It was also pointed out that the commuting problem may be eased shortly, when the proposed new bus route (direct from the Lackawanna Park district) goes into effect.

B You are the assistant to the sales manager of the Kleen Air Company, manufacturers of central vacuum cleaner systems. Each week the company's thirty-five sales representatives send your boss handwritten notes on the number of calls they made during the week, the number of call-backs (return calls), the actual sales made, the referrals received from customers, and their own comments, including customers' comments. Create a standardized report form that all representatives can use to send in sales information. Then prepare a memorandum for your boss suggesting the new form be used and explaining why it is an improvement over the present system.

C In Chapter 7, Section 36, several styles of business letters were discussed. Refer to this discussion and study the characteristics of each letter style and its merits as you see them. Then write a report in which you describe each style, listing its advantages and disadvantages, and present your recommendations. Use illustrations. Refer to other sources if you wish.

D Write a brief memorandum to your instructor in which you describe the function of each of the following parts of a report:

1. Title page
2. Table of contents
3. Introduction
4. Summary
5. Body
6. Conclusions and recommendations
7. Supplementary material

EDITING PRACTICE

Editing for Writing Power Edit and rewrite these sentences for the purpose of improving writing power.

1. Confident of his ability, the position was eagerly sought by Allen.
2. The opinions expressed in your letter of June 9 have been carefully studied.
3. Mr. Lane is our new supervisor, and he is a specialist in writing all kinds of business communications.
4. We revised the news release. The original was ambiguous. We needed to be more explicit.
5. One of the motors developed a knock, when all plans for a record flight had to be abandoned.
6. We specialize in quality goods; but price, too, has been considered by us.
7. Go to Edson's, and there one can find many outstanding bargains.
8. Not having been able to obtain, through banks or agencies at his disposal, any information concerning your credit rating; and as he did not know the rules governing such cases as yours, the new manager sent the goods c.o.d.
9. Although he couldn't really spare time away from the office, but wanting to visit the new plant, Jack's plans were indefinite.
10. The report to management, about the new accounting system that was started recently for the plant in Cincinnati, was very long and complicated so then the accounting manager had to call a special meeting to explain it.

Vocabulary and the Report Writer Identify and correct the vocabulary errors that weaken the effectiveness of this report writer's opening paragraph.

> This report on sight possibilities for the construction of a new warehouse was authorized by Mr. James E. Walsh on June 8, 19—. The information presented here is the result of frequent conferences with the ten leading reality agents in this city. A personal inspection trip was made to every lot offered for sale, and each parcel was evaluated in terms of its suitability for the location of a warehouse.

CASE PROBLEM

The Avid Conversationalist Harry Walker, the mail clerk at Robins, Inc., is supposed to complete his daily delivery of mail by 11 a.m. and then return to the mail room in time to process the outgoing mail for an 11:40 a.m. pickup. However, when Harry gets to the credit department, Max Miller usually engages him in a lengthy one-sided conversation. As a result, in one or two instances Harry has not completed processing all the outgoing mail on time. Today Harry is late in getting started on his deliveries, and Max tries to engage him in another lengthy conversation.

1. What can Harry say to Max so that he will not offend him?
2. What should Harry do if Max persists in talking?

48 News Releases, Minutes, Telecommunications

News releases and minutes of meetings are two common types of written communications that you, as a business writer, may be expected to prepare. In addition, you will frequently be expected to write messages that will be dispatched either by teleprinter or by another form of telegraphy. A knowledge of how to write each of these communications is essential for the business writer. Let us consider news releases first.

NEWS RELEASES

Publicity, advertising, public relations, goodwill—all these terms denote the effort of a business to get its name, its reputation, and its product before the public. In fact, large companies—even schools and colleges—today employ publicity directors whose job it is to attract favorable public attention to their organizations.

An important means of getting the planned publicity of business into the hands of the public is the news release. Whenever a business plans an event that it considers newsworthy or capable of enhancing its public image, its public relations personnel prepare and submit a news release to various news outlets for publication. Such a news announcement may concern the appointment of a new company president after a meeting of the board of directors; it may tell of a large local expansion in a company's plant, which will increase the work force and have a great impact on the economy of the community; it may publicize the introduction of a new line or new product; or it may concern the awarding of some honor (perhaps for long, faithful service) to a member of the organization; and so on. Any item that will interest the public and create goodwill for the organization is an appropriate subject for a news release.

Any news story sent by a company must, of course, be approved for publication. In large companies, the director of public relations would have this responsibility. In small companies, individual department heads might handle their own news and distribute it in keeping with company policy, or releases might be issued from the office of the president or of one particular executive.

In order to be published and thereby serve its purpose, the release must be newsworthy; that is, the contents of the release must be of sufficient interest to the public to justify being published. Naturally, the writing style of the news release, as well as the form in which it appears, will have a strong effect on the newspaper editor who will decide whether or not it is to be published.

Form of the News Release

With hundreds of releases coming to their desks each week, newspaper editors will select for publication the items that require the least amount of rewriting, everything else being equal. Therefore, the news release must give complete, accurate information in a "news style" of writing that presents the facts in a clear and interesting way.

News releases may be typewritten, duplicated, or printed, but carbon copies should never be sent. A carbon copy suggests that the original copy was sent to someone more important.

Many organizations use a special form for issuing news releases. These forms are arranged so that editors can get to the heart of the story without wasting time. Like a letterhead, a news release form usually contains the name and address of the company or organization and the name, address, and telephone number of the person responsible for issuing the release to the public.

A well-written news release is illustrated on page 416. Observe the following points about the preparation of this release and also of longer news releases.

1. The news release is double-spaced and has generous margins for possible changes by the newspaper editor.
2. The writer includes a tentative headline to identify the story. An editor, of course, may change this title to fit the style and space requirements of the publication.
3. The news release indicates the time when a story may be published. In the example, note the prominence of the phrase *For Immediate Release.* A release may be sent to newspapers before an event occurs so that news will reach the public at almost the same time the event takes place. For example, if a company plans to announce a million-dollar gift to a local hospital at a banquet on Saturday, June 25, the release might read *For Release after 6 p.m., Saturday, June 25.*
4. In a long release, subheads may be inserted between parts of the release to relieve the reading monotony and to guide the editor who wants to scan the story.
5. If there is more than one page to the release, the word *MORE* in parentheses is added at the end of each unfinished page. At the end of the last page of the release, the symbol *-xxx-, ###, oOo,* or *-30-* is typed to indicate "the end" (adapted from the telegrapher's abbreviation *30,* which means "the end").

Writing the News Release

However good the form of a written communication, it is its words that determine whether it will be read and used. In writing a news release—just as in writing letters, memorandums, and reports—certain guides will help the writer develop an effective writing style and will improve the chances of getting the release printed. Especially important is the arrangement of paragraphs in the news release.

The opening paragraph of a news release should summarize the entire story and should present the most newsworthy information first. In this opening section, the writer should give the *who, what, why, how, when,* and *where* of the news story in such a form that this paragraph can stand

NEWS RELEASE

Sterling Furniture Company Westwood, New Jersey 07124

Frances A. Sellers, Director of Public Relations

James Simpson
Manager
Sterling News Bureau
(201) 986-9300

For Immediate Release 3/19/--

VIRGINIA MARRITT NAMED ADVERTISING DIRECTOR

OF STERLING FURNITURE COMPANY

Westwood, March 19, 19--. Virginia Marritt has been named advertising director of Sterling Furniture Company, Westwood, N.J., according to Alex Prior, president.

Miss Marritt succeeds Pat Buono, who was promoted to vice president of sales.

The new advertising director joined Sterling in 19-- as a junior executive trainee. A year later she was assigned to the sales division in charge of product information; and in 19-- she was appointed assistant director of advertising. Miss Marritt is a graduate of the University of Pennsylvania.

-xxx-

by itself. If, for example, an announcement is to be made of the appointment of Sterling's advertising director, Virginia Marritt, an amateur news writer might lead off this way:

> Alex Prior, president of the Sterling Furniture Company, Westwood, N.J., announced the appointment of Miss Virginia Marritt as his advertising director.

However, since Alex Prior is not the person the release is about (Virginia Marritt is the subject), the lead should read:

> Virginia Marritt has been named advertising director of Sterling Furniture Company, Westwood, N.J., according to Alex Prior, president.

Each succeeding paragraph should supply background facts in the order of decreasing importance. Editors who need to cut part of the release because of space limitations will "kill" it from the bottom up. For example, note how the last paragraph of the news release shown on page 416 can be omitted without making the first two paragraphs of the release an incomplete news story:

> Virginia Marritt has been named advertising director of Sterling Furniture Company, Westwood, N.J., according to Alex Prior, president.
>
> Miss Marritt succeeds Pat Buono, who was promoted to vice president of sales.

MINUTES OF MEETINGS

Nearly every business has a number of committees that meet periodically, perhaps weekly, biweekly, or monthly. In addition, special meetings are called from time to time for the purpose of settling important matters that arise. In most cases, a written record—called *minutes*—of the proceedings is required. The minutes serve as a permanent record of the decisions reached and the actions that are to be taken and inform those who were not present at the meeting about what took place. Nearly every business employee, at one time or another, may serve as secretary to a group or committee and thus be responsible for keeping an accurate set of minutes.

Recording the Minutes

The faithful recording of the proceedings of all meetings is an important function, for the minutes usually serve as the only historical record of a meeting.

There is probably no one best way to record what happens at a meeting. The secretary of the meeting must be the judge of what is unimportant (and hence not worth recording). If an agenda of the meeting has been prepared beforehand, the secretary should receive a copy. The agenda lists briefly the business to be transacted and acts as a guide to the person who presides at the meeting. The agenda also helps the secretary check to be sure that all scheduled items are accounted for in the minutes. Much of the success of good note-taking revolves around the personal efficiency of the secretary. However, any secretary preparing to record the proceedings of a meeting should find the following general guides helpful:

1. Record the time and place of the meeting.
2. List the persons attending and those absent. In a small group, actual names can be given; in a large group, however, it is usually sufficient to state the number of people present, such as "Forty-five members were present."
3. In the opening section of the minutes, mention the fact that the minutes for the previous meeting were read and approved, amended, or not approved.
4. Develop the art of recording the important points in the discussion of each item on the agenda. Why? Sufficient supporting facts are required so that those who were present can recall the discussion from reading the minutes

and those who were not present can be informed. Papers read during the meeting are often attached to the final typewritten minutes, because it is usually not possible for the secretary to record verbatim all such information.

5. Record verbatim all resolutions and motions, as well as the names of the persons who introduced and seconded the motions. If there is difficulty in getting such information when the motion is first made, the secretary should request that the motion be repeated or even put in writing so that the exact motion is recorded.
6. Type the minutes first in draft form so that they can be edited before being typed in final form. Sometimes, too, the secretary may want to get another person's approval before typing the minutes in final form. The secretary signs the minutes, thus certifying their accuracy. Sometimes the presiding officer countersigns them.
7. Normally, make one copy of the minutes and file it in the folder, notebook, or binder used for this purpose. Sometimes minutes are duplicated and sent to each person present at the meeting or to designated officers who would be interested in the business of the meeting.

Form of the Minutes

Various formats are used for the minutes of a meeting. The secretary's main job, however, is to make sure that all the essential information appears in a neat, well-arranged form. Some organizations prefer to emphasize the main points on the agenda by using a standardized format.

The minutes on page 419 illustrate one acceptable format. Notice the standard pattern and the topical headings that are used for all meetings of this group and the way in which the motions and discussion are concisely summarized.

Other groups use a more traditional format in which the proceedings of the meeting are written out in rather complete detail. The example on page 420 illustrates this style.

TELECOMMUNICATIONS

Telegrams are the most common form of message sent or received by teleprinter equipment. Growing out of the wireless telegraph invented by Samuel Morse, telegraphy has had a long and exciting history as the fastest method of transmitting written messages prior to the development of electronic data communications equipment.

Telegrams, however, continue to be important in today's business. In fact, so important is this type of message that many large companies maintain teleprinter equipment in their various divisions in order to provide for rapid transmission of messages to plants and divisions that may often be widely dispersed across the country. The best-known equipment used in this field is *Teletype*. Some telephone and telegraph companies maintain a service that connects teleprinters. With this service, customers call as they would by telephone but actually communicate through the teleprinter equipment. *TWX* (teletypewriter exchange service) and *Telex* are exchange services of Western Union.

EMPLOYEES' RECREATION CLUB OF THE ASHLEY COMPANY

MINUTES OF MEETING OF FEBRUARY 1, 19--

TIME, PLACE, ATTENDANCE	The regular monthly meeting of the Employees' Recreation Club of the Ashley Company was held in the auditorium at 5:15 p.m. The president, Pat Corey, presided. All members and officers present.
MINUTES	The minutes of the last meeting (January 4, 19--) were read and approved.
OFFICERS' REPORTS	Treasurer: The treasurer's report showed receipts of $585.15, disbursements of $432.16, and a balance in cash of $309.10, as of January 31, 19--. Ana Cardone moved that the treasurer's report be received and placed on file for future audit. Eli Rusk seconded the motion. Motion carried. Secretary: The secretary indicated a 10 percent average increase in attendance at club functions last year. (The secretary's report was informal; hence no motion to accept it was necessary.)
COMMITTEE REPORTS	Chairperson Berry presented the report of the nominating committee. Nominated were: President: James Bradley Vice President: Anne Morrison Secretary: Joseph Prior Treasurer: Cora Hart The president called for nominations from the floor. No additional names were suggested. Al Pitt moved and Pat Jahn seconded the motion that nominations be closed and that a unanimous ballot be cast for the committee's slate of officers. Motion carried.
OLD BUSINESS	Plans for the Easter Dinner Dance, to be held at the Nicole Hill Manor on April 14, were discussed, but action was not taken.
NEW BUSINESS	James Barlow introduced a motion to increase the annual club dues from $5.00 to $6.50. The motion was seconded by Elaine Burke and passed by a majority of the members.
ADJOURNMENT	The meeting adjourned at 6:10 p.m.

Respectfully submitted,

Jonathan Blakeley

Jonathan Blakeley, Secretary

Writing Teletype Messages

For purposes of economy, teletype messages should be as brief as possible. Any redundancy in the messages should, therefore, be eliminated. However, the word *redundancy* has a special meaning in reference to teletype messages; it includes not only repetitiveness but also *any* part of a message that can be omitted without loss of meaning. Brevity in teletype messages is important because the cost of sending a message is based on the number of words. The fastest but most expensive Western Union message, the telegram, is based on a minimum charge for a 15-word message, plus an additional charge for each word over 15.

MINUTES OF THE MEETING

of the

M A R K E T I N G C O M M I T T E E

National Products Corporation
April 14, 19--

Presiding: Craig Cordero

Present: Harold Bodega
Stephanie Browne
Martha Sanchez
Arnold Smith
Andrew Wise
Frank Yu

Absent: Lois Ellis

The meeting was called to order at 9:30 a.m. by Mr. Cordero. The main discussion of the meeting concerned the feasibility of providing giveaways at conventions.

Among the proposals were these:

Mr. Wise suggested a spiral-bound memo pad, approximately 5 by 3 inches, with an imitation-leather cover imprinted with our logotype. The idea was considered favorably, and Miss Browne was instructed to determine cost estimates for 4,000.

Miss Sanchez showed a sample of a combination plastic letter opener and ruler that would carry an advertising message. From the discussion, the majority agreed that the memo pad would be more effective.

Other proposals included plastic pencil sharpeners and paperweights, but all were discarded in favor of the memo pad.

The Committee expects to see a sample memo pad and complete cost estimates at the next meeting, Wednesday, April 21. Meeting adjourned at 10:30 a.m.

Respecfully submitted,

Arnold Smith

Arnold Smith, Secretary

It would, of course, be false economy to sacrifice completeness and clarity for brevity; that is, it would be a waste of money to write a 15-word message that might be misunderstood if just three additional words would ensure its clarity. The skilled composer of teletype messages, however, can usually express a thought in surprisingly few words by eliminating unnecessary words.

The composer of the teletype message, unlike the letter writer, does not always need to use complete sentences and may dispense with some typical courtesies of the business letter. Contrast the following paragraph from a letter with a telegram that means the same thing.

Letter	Telegram
We should appreciate your checking our Purchase Order 6651 for delivery date. The order was promised to reach our store by Monday, May 31. To date, it has not been received. We must have the men's suits for our summer sale, which will begin at noon on Monday, June 7, 19—.	Must have our Order 6651 before June 7.

Note that the telegram writer states in 8 words what the letter writer says in 50 words.

Teletype messages are frequently sent to change travel plans. The following telegram explains a change in plans because of bad weather.

> United Flight 346 grounded because of bad weather. Will arrive on Amtrak Pennsylvania Station 4:48 p.m. Tuesday.

The message is concise but it contains 17 words, two more than the minimum charge for a telegram. However, the writer can eliminate the redundant words and convey the same message to the reader in only 12 words.

> Weather grounded United Flight 346. Arrive Amtrak Pennsylvania Station 4:48 p.m. Tuesday.

Another common means of saving time and money in sending teleprinted messages is through the use of abbreviations and codes; for example, LA for Los Angeles, ATL for Atlanta, DTR for Detroit. Standard lists of such address abbreviations are used by telephone and telegraph companies, airlines, and other organizations. Some companies develop common code abbreviations that are used to exchange teleprinted messages within the company. However, the cost to encode or decode a message of nonstandard language is a deterrent to the frequent use of codes unless the code is a computer language.

From a study of teletype messages, you can see that considerable difference exists in purpose—and thus writing style—between business letters and teletype messages. As a rule, the well-written teletype message has these features:

1. Only necessary words are included. For instance, in the telegram example above, the phrase *because of*, the words *bad*, *will*, and *on* were easily eliminated without loss of meaning.
2. Explanatory information is usually omitted. In the telegram about the purchase order, the date the order was promised was not mentioned and the time of day that the suits were needed was not stated. Only vital information appeared.
3. Information understood by both sender and receiver is omitted. When writing the telegram expediting the order for suits, the writer did not have to say "*our Purchase* Order 6651" as this information was understood by simply saying "Order 6651."

Teletype Message Forms

For teletype messages, details regarding the sending of the message, the word count, and the charge per word vary according to the particular service and the utility offering the service. Current costs of the different kinds of teletype services can be obtained from your local Western Union or cable office.

western union **Telegram**

NO. WDS.—CL. OF SVC.	PD. OR COLL.	CASH NO.	CHARGE TO THE ACCOUNT OF	☐ OVER NIGHT TELEGRAM UNLESS BOX ABOVE IS CHECKED THIS MESSAGE WILL BE SENT AS A TELEGRAM
			Sender	

Send the following message, subject to the terms on back hereof, which are hereby agreed to June 9, 19--

TO Horace Mendez, Report Delivery
Wayne, Denver & Corde, Inc.
CARE OF OR APT. NO.
STREET & NO. 711 Fortune Drive
TELEPHONE (615) 555-7263
CITY & STATE Knoxville, Tennessee
ZIP CODE 27901

Submit revised bid. Deadline midnight June 15, 19--.

Alice Prendergast
Dover and Company

SENDER'S TEL. NO. (414) 555-2938
NAME & ADDRESS Dover and Company
150 Rutherford Avenue
Milwaukee, Wisconsin 53216

Courtesy Western Union Corporation

Details about format remain rather constant, however, and should be understood by anyone who is responsible for preparing a teletype message.

Teletype forms may vary slightly from one company to another, but you should usually fill out the form in the following manner, as shown by the properly completed telegram above.

1. Make at least one carbon copy. Additional copies may be made so that a confirmation copy can be sent to the addressee and copies can be sent to other departments as needed.
2. Single-space the message and use ordinary punctuation as you would in any other business writing. (For many years, typists attempted to simulate teleprinter type by typing the message in all-capital letters and by spelling out punctuation; for instance, using the word *STOP* to indicate a period. Such practice is now obsolete.)
3. Type the signature of the sender and the name of the company.
4. Follow instructions for filling in appropriate sections on the form. Thus, in the sample telegram above, since the message is to be charged to *Dover and Company*, the word *Sender* is typed in the box titled *Charge to the Account of*. If the telegram were to be charged to a telephone number, that number would replace the word *Sender*. Were the telegram to be sent collect, the word *Collect* would be typed under *Pd. or Coll.* In addition, the class of service should be checked.

Communication Projects

PRACTICAL APPLICATION

A At last evening's organizational meeting of ESPA (Environmental Study and Protection Associates), a new group on your campus, Dale Jensen was elected president and you, secretary-treasurer. Faculty sponsor is Professor Robert Stanton, of the physics department. The group plans to meet monthly on the second Tuesday. Its aims are to publicize instances of local pollution, to investigate possible conservation measures on campus, to recommend publicity (films, posters, and so on) to make the college community more conservation-oriented. Write a news release (supply the facts needed) about the organization—its officers, aims, plans—for your school newspaper *or* for the "College Corner" column in the local paper, the *Courier*. How would your release differ for the two publications?

B Write the minutes for the second meeting of ESPA (see Application A). Assume various projects were proposed at the meeting—recycling drive, bikeways in local parks, field trips to local industrial plants, film on "The Air We Breathe," poster contest, etc. Supply all the specifics, such as motions passed or defeated, and so on.

C As public relations director for Wadsworth Manufacturing Company, Oakland, California, you are responsible for writing all news releases for the company. Your president, Mr. John Yates, tells you that he will announce to the board of directors on Friday, December 9, 19—, the promotion of Harold S. Wier to advertising manager. He asks you to prepare a news release that can be published after the board meeting, which usually adjourns about 4 p.m. Wier has been with your company for ten years—as a representative (five years), then as sales supervisor (three years), and currently as assistant advertising manager (two years). He lives in Manchester, a suburb of Oakland, with his wife and three children. He is a graduate in business administration from Briarwood College. At Briarwood, he earned school letters in football, basketball, baseball, and swimming. In talking with you about his new position, Wier paid tribute to the fine work of his predecessor. Later, you learn that Donald H. Sheldon, former advertising manager, resigned a month ago because of a misunderstanding with the president. Wier stated, "Our basic advertising policy remains unchanged. We shall continue to stand for new media and new methods; but for the time being, we will concentrate our efforts in trade magazines and newspapers." Using an acceptable format, write a news release for this story. (Your telephone number is 555-3415.)

D As secretary to the standing committee on office procedures, your principal responsibility is to take minutes of all meetings. These minutes are distributed to committee members only; hence, a concise form may be used. From the following information, prepare minutes of the latest meeting of this committee.

1. The meeting, held in Room 2310, Administration Building, was called to order by Mr. Reston at 2 p.m., November 25, 19—.
2. Correction made in minutes of preceding meeting (October 25) as follows: Revised procedure manual will be ready January 15, not December 15. Approved as corrected.
3. Dryerson reviewed employee suggestions for September. Awards of $50 each for two accepted suggestions were approved. Dryerson to make arrangements for presenting the awards at the next board of directors' meeting.
4. Revised written procedure for handling purchase orders presented by Raydon. Accepted with editorial revision.
5. The meeting adjourned at 4:15 p.m., with the understanding that the next meeting would be held at the same time and place on December 15.
6. Amburn, Dryerson, Egan, Raydon, Reston, and Simpkins were present; Bergman was absent.

E Your employer, Mr. Hiram Reavis, will speak to the Young Executives Club at the Hotel Superior in Seattle on July 7 at 7 p.m. He has asked you to wire the hotel for reservations for July 6 and 7 and to request a two-room suite with bath. (While in Seattle, he is interested in interviewing young sales representatives to work with your company.) Choose the most economical telegraphic service and compose the message, asking for (1) a confirmation and (2) information regarding the availability of a chalkboard, a 35mm projector, and a screen to be used for Mr. Reavis's talk.

F Revise the following full-rate telegrams. Aim for brevity, clarity, and completeness. Limit each telegram to 15 or fewer words.

1. We are shipping by air express the parts you ordered for Machine 8462 except for Part 17F21, which will be shipped to you next Tuesday.
2. Proposed contract for reconstruction of fire-damaged Plant 15 received. Must also have target dates for completion of each section of contract. Wire dates in time for board meeting Thursday morning.
3. Raymond Haskins expects to arrive in Atlanta on Delta Flight 491 on Monday morning. Please arrange to meet him and brief him on Vita-Hard contract on way to board meeting.
4. Our Purchase Order 6189 for six blue luggage sets and two dozen umbrellas has not arrived and our inventory is almost depleted. If the order has not yet been shipped, arrange shipment by express.
5. The duplicate computer printout of the monthly sales forecast was accidentally damaged during shipment, so please airmail another copy immediately.

EDITING PRACTICE

Supply the Missing Words Indicate a word that you think would make sense if inserted in the blank space within each sentence.

1. If this booklet does not give you the . . . you desire, please write us again.
2. Thank you for being so . . . about the delay in filling your order.
3. We are happy to tell you that your . . . has been established at the Hotel Worthington.
4. We hope that we shall have the pleasure of serving you whenever you have . . . to use hotel facilities.
5. Once you know the . . . of a charge account, you will never shop without your charge account plate.
6. Please sign the original copy and return it to us in the enclosed envelope, retaining the . . . for your files.
7. We understand that you will probably . . . to purchase as much as $100 worth of merchandise monthly on your account.
8. We hope that your clerical staff will . . . some means of checking purchases made by persons of the same name but of different addresses.
9. We have taken steps to see that there is no . . . of this type of mistake.
10. We hope that our business dealings will be . . . pleasant and profitable.
11. The report . . . the data that had been gathered by the newly elected subcommittee.
12. The new inventory system was . . . just before the Christmas rush began.
13. An office worker's . . . is judged not only by the volume of work completed but also by the accuracy of the work.

14. All the payroll . . . were noted on the check stub.
15. Government . . . are available to many different groups in many parts of the country.

Proofreading for Homonym Errors Identify and correct any homonym errors you find in the following paragraph.

> The principal task of report writing is not the report itself; it is the assembling of facts that are the bases for statements made therein. The value of a report, then, depends upon the thoroughness with which all aspects of the situation have been studied. Any supervisor can cite numerous instances of poor reports that were due solely to a slapdash job of assembling facts.

CASE PROBLEM

Should She Bluff? Donna Gregus, a new assistant office manager, was at a personnel meeting where merit ratings were being discussed. Unfortunately, Donna knew very little about merit ratings because she had never rated anyone on the job. Soon after the meeting began, the manager asked Donna to give her opinion about changes in the merit rating procedures and forms.

1. Should Donna bluff her way through or admit that she knows very little about merit ratings?
2. What should she say?

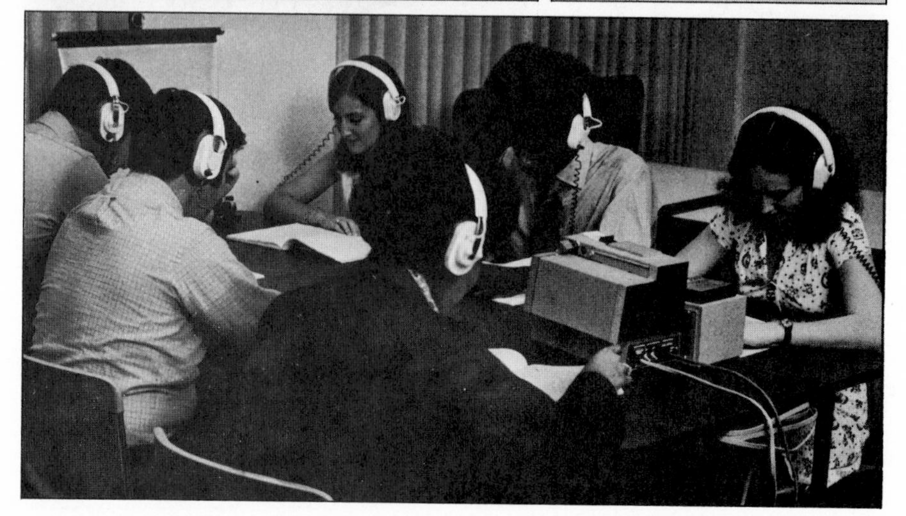

CHAPTER 9

COMMUNICATING ORALLY

49 Communicating Orally in Business

You have just entered the reception area of the impressive building occupied by the Brookfield Insurance Company and are greeted by the receptionist's warm smile and friendly voice asking, "May I help you?" You reply, "I have a ten o'clock appointment with Mr. Leeds." The receptionist tells you, "Mr. Leeds' office is on the seventh floor, Suite 715 A. May I have your name so that I may telephone Mr. Leeds that you are here?" After you give your name, the receptionist directs you to the correct elevator. As you move toward the elevator, you overhear her telephoning Mr. Leeds' secretary that you are on your way. You realize that you have already formed an impression of the Brookfield Insurance Company, a very favorable impression created by the brief oral contact you have had with just one employee of the company.

On the seventh floor, you enter a tastefully furnished office where some forty or fifty employees are busily engaged in different kinds of activities. A young woman approaches you and announces, "Good morning; I'm Mr. Leeds' secretary. He will be with you just as soon as he completes a long-distance telephone call. Won't you have a seat and make yourself comfortable."

While you are waiting, you glance around the office. Several employees are quietly engrossed in telephone conversations. In one corner of the room, one man is explaining to another how to operate a duplicating machine. In a glass-enclosed conference room, a small group is gathered around a table listening to an explanation of some figures on a flip chart. A young executive in another office is using her dictating machine. On the bulletin board opposite where you are sitting is a notice of a sales training conference for the sales representatives in District A; another notice announces a meeting of the Office Employees' Association next Wednesday.

For a moment, you reflect on the importance of oral communication in the work going on around you. Then, as you are ushered into Mr. Leeds' office, you think you are fortunate to have had some training in oral communication. Why do you consider it so fortunate? You are here to be interviewed by Mr. Leeds for a position with his firm that you very much want. You are about to make your training in oral communication work for you.

ORAL COMMUNICATION IN BUSINESS IS IMPORTANT

From the moment you begin to work in the world of business, your conviction will grow stronger each day about the vital role of oral communication in all business activities. From the receptionist in the lobby to the president on the top floor, information is constantly being transmitted orally from one employee to another, from employees of the firm to customers and vendors on the outside, and from these and other outsiders to employees of the firm. The success enjoyed by any business organization depends, to a very large degree, upon the success of its members in making themselves understood and in persuading others to accept their ideas.

Though written communication is important in transacting business, oral communication is used more often and by more people. Some business positions require the use of oral communication almost exclusively, and the people who fill these jobs are hired on the strength of their ability to speak well. The sales representative, the office receptionist, the switchboard operator, the person who handles customer service or complaints—all these people must be highly skilled in oral communication. The office or factory supervisor, the public accountant, the personnel manager, the bank teller, the business executive, and the secretary are only a few of the other workers who make extensive use of oral communication in carrying out the responsibilities of their positions.

If you aspire to a position of leadership in business, your ability to speak forcefully, persuasively, and convincingly will play a vital role in helping you achieve your goal. At meetings and conferences, speakers will include all levels of employees, top management people, and outside consultants. On many occasions, you will do much of the talking. You will seek to solve grievances of employees; you will conduct meetings and small group discussions; you will give talks to employees, to the public, and to business and professional groups. In your daily contacts with supervisors and co-workers, you will use oral communication for reporting, instructing, reprimanding, giving information, and asking for information. This power to communicate orally is important to every business leader.

HOW BUSINESS USES ORAL COMMUNICATION

Business uses oral communication in many different ways. Some ways in which business employees depend upon oral communication are:

To sell goods and services. All salespeople, whether they are selling goods or services, rely on their oral communication ability to help them make sales. Whether it is an insurance agent who canvasses you at home or the retail salesperson who asks, "Would you like a tie to go with that shirt?" both use their oral communication abilities to sell. Even the airline ticket agent uses oral communication to assist you in arranging your proposed business or vacation trip.

To give instruction to an individual or to a group. The teacher, whether he or she performs in a school situation or in special business or industrial classes on the job, is dependent on oral communication; the sales manager who conducts special training classes for sales representatives must be an effective oral communicator; even the computer programmer who must instruct a new assistant relies heavily on oral communication.

To explain or report to supervisors, to subordinates, and to those on the same level. The sales manager may report orally to the vice president in charge of sales; the supervisor in the office interprets a new company policy for employees; an employee explains a grievance to the supervisor; the general manager's secretary tells the file clerk to pull all correspondence with the Evans Manufacturing Company.

To give information to customers and potential customers. A customer calls a department store for information about the sizes, colors, and prices of vinyl tile; another customer telephones for advice about the best method of cleaning recently purchased rugs.

To give formal speeches before groups. The president of a company is asked to give a speech before the members of the Rotary Club; an accountant is asked to talk to a college class in advanced accounting; the secretary to the president of a large manufacturing firm is asked to address a group of college students on "The Advantages of Becoming a Secretary."

To participate in social-business conversation. The office manager telephones the secretary of Kiwanis to cancel a reservation for the luncheon meeting tomorrow; a sales representative congratulates two former associates who have gone into partnership.

To interview employees and prospective employees. The personnel manager and the section supervisor interview applicants for an accounting position; the supervisor discusses an employee's merit rating at the end of the probationary period.

To acquire information necessary to conduct the everyday affairs of business. The credit manager of a department store calls the local credit bureau to determine the credit rating of a new customer; the mail clerk telephones the post office to find out which class of mail to use for a special mailing the company is planning; the accountant visits the Internal Revenue Service office to discuss methods of figuring depreciation on equipment; a secretary telephones a travel agency to get information about hotel accommodations in Portland.

To purchase goods and services. A homeowner asks a department store sales person many questions about a rug she would like to buy; the purchasing agent telephones a local stationer to order file folders; the manager of a truck fleet inquires about a truck-leasing plan.

To provide service for customers and potential customers. The credit manager explains to a customer the procedure for opening a charge account; the section manager in the bedding department tells a customer why bedding can't be returned for exchange or refund.

To participate in meetings. A sales manager conducts a meeting of the Sales Executives Club; a secretary contributes ideas for the convention of the National Secretaries Association to the members of the planning committee.

To participate in informal discussion with fellow employees. The receptionist takes up a collection to buy a gift for a fellow employee who is in the hospital; the mail-room supervisor organizes a committee to plan the office Christmas party; the sales promotion manager gets all the employees in the office together for lunch.

These are a few of the activities that may be witnessed daily in business—activities that rely for their success almost wholly upon effective oral communication.

VARIETIES OF ORAL COMMUNICATION USED IN BUSINESS

Oral communication in business takes various forms, some more frequently used than others. Among the most commonly used methods of communicating orally are the following:

Face-to-face conversation—interviews, sales, social-business situations, informal discussions between supervisors and employees.

Telephone conversation—with another office, with customers, with suppliers.

Conversation via interoffice communication devices—between executive and secretary-receptionist, between sales representative on selling floor and clerk in stockroom.

Dictation and recording—dictating a letter to a secretary, using a dictating machine for dictating letters, recording meetings on tape.

Radio and television appearances—giving interviews or reporting information.

Formal speeches—debates, panels, addresses to employees, the public, customers, or professional groups.

Leadership of, or participation in, group discussions or meetings—leading employee group discussions, participating in stockholders' meetings and in meetings of business and professional organizations.

Instruction—teaching training classes for sales representatives and retail store employees.

Each of these methods of communication requires a slightly different technique. The difference may be in the amount and kind of prior preparation, the manner in which the voice is projected, or the style in which the speaker makes the presentation. For example, speaking over the telephone requires a knowledge of how far the telephone mouthpiece should be held from the lips and how much the speaker's voice should be projected. A radio or telephone presentation may be read from copy and, therefore, requires a knowledge of how to read without giving the impression that you *are* reading. Leading a meeting requires a knowledge of parliamentary procedure. Teaching a class requires that the teacher know how to ask questions properly. Participating in a panel or in a group discussion requires the ability to think quickly and to put thoughts into understandable language without hesitation.

ORAL COMMUNICATION FOR EFFECTIVE EMPLOYEE RELATIONS

Effective oral communication is essential to good employee relations. Through oral communication, a free flow of information and ideas can be maintained between management and employees and within the company's various levels of authority. It is generally found that when employees have frequent and easy means for discussion and expression of their ideas, morale is high. Personal conferences, committee meetings, group conferences, and speeches that allow for question-and-answer periods are among the means of oral communication used for improving relations between management and employees.

If morale is high, employees generally have better communication relations with the public. Oral communication with the public in one form or another frequently is part of the job of almost every employee. Public relations is considered so important that many businesses train their employees in such areas as public speaking and proper telephone technique.

ORAL COMMUNICATION FOR EFFECTIVE PUBLIC RELATIONS

To a great degree, the success of a business is based upon customer satisfaction, which is the result of good customer relations. To keep customers, business spends considerable time and money to plan and create carefully worded letters that will not offend. To win new friends, it spends thousands of dollars annually to develop advertising copy. However, often the oral contacts with customers and potential customers are overlooked. The manner in which a customer is treated over the telephone or in person is as important in developing goodwill as is the written communication—perhaps more so. All employees—whether sales people, secretaries, switchboard operators, or cashiers—create a public image of the company they represent by the manner in which they speak to customers. A curt or rude employee can cause a business to lose many sales—and even lose customers of long standing. To customers, each employee they come in contact with *is* the firm. If customers are made to feel that their interests are important, they will most often be satisfied; on the other hand, if they are given the impression that the firm is not interested in its customers' satisfaction, they are very likely to take their business elsewhere.

In the remaining sections of this chapter, you will learn techniques for improving your oral communication that will assist in making you a better business employee and will help you upgrade your position in the business world.

Communication Projects

PRACTICAL APPLICATION

A For each of the following business positions, indicate the oral communication activities that you think would be typical in that position:

1. Accountant
2. Retail sales clerk
3. Secretary
4. Personnel interviewer
5. Receptionist

B Be prepared to discuss each of the following topics:

1. How Effective Communication Skills Help College Students Succeed.
2. How Effective Communication Skills Help Business Teachers Teach More Effectively.
3. How Effective Communication Skills Help New Business Employees Climb the Ladder of Success.

C Be prepared to take the affirmative or negative side in a debate on this topic: *Resolved: That business relies more on effective written communications than on oral communications.*

D List as many business positions as you can that require the use of oral communication almost exclusively.

E Practice reading the following instructions for talking on the telephone as though you were going to read them for a radio broadcast. Try not to sound as though you are reading the material or have memorized it.

> Clear enunciation is a must. Every word and syllable should be spoken distinctly. Strive to keep your voice well modulated, and move your lips, tongue, and jaw freely to form your words. Hold the mouthpiece about an inch away from your mouth, and speak *directly* into the transmitter. Be sure to keep gum, candy, and pencils out of your mouth so that they don't affect your pronunciation or cause you to slur your words. You can tell if your words are coming through clearly by the number of times you are asked to repeat what you have said.[1]

F Without using gestures or written diagrams, *orally* give directions for the following:

1. How to reach the nearest department store by automobile or by walking.
2. How to reach the school library (or cafeteria) from the classroom in which this subject is taught.
3. How to fold a letter for mailing in a No. 10 envelope.

G Be prepared to describe an object orally without telling the class what the object is. If you have described the object clearly, the class should be able to identify it from your description.

EDITING PRACTICE

Spelling and Vocabulary Some of the following sentences contain spelling errors; some test vocabulary; some are correct. For each correct sentence, write *OK* on your paper. Correct each incorrect sentence.

1. Robinson's will celebrate the occassion with a storewide sale.
2. The specifications for the building are accurate.
3. Not even a millionnaire likes to waste money.
4. If you are wise, you will heed the advise of your supervisor.
5. Mr. Green's position in the company precludes any argument.
6. Ms. Lee was favorably effected by the increase in salary.
7. The company has benefitted from the installation of the computer.
8. You are not to breath a word about the change in organizational structure.
9. Each company is equiping its offices with push-button telephones.
10. Our president was formally a college teacher.

Editing for Context Rewrite any sentences containing words that do not fit the context. Write *OK* for any correct sentence.

1. Please sign the affidavit before May 1.
2. We must addend to a set of rules established by the directors.

[1]Albert C. Fries et al., *Applied Secretarial Procedures*, 7th ed., McGraw-Hill Book Company, New York, 1974, p. 51.

3. To countenance serious inflation, drastic legislation is needed.
4. We did not receive the article listed on the manifest.
5. We are affiliated with the largest manufacturer of toys in the country.
6. Your failure to make prompt payment demented our confidence in your integrity.
7. Mark purchased an annuity policy for his own protection.
8. Your actions do not ward our taking any steps to improve the situation.
9. We purchased the goods at a tremulous saving, which we are passing on to you.
10. We hope you will not comply us to take the matter up with our attorney.

CASE PROBLEM

The Rude Caller When Mr. Ryan's secretary, Peggy, answered the telephone and was asked by the caller to speak to Mr. Ryan, Peggy responded, "May I ask who is calling?" The voice at the other end abruptly said, "No, you may not," and the telephone receiver was noisily slammed. "What a rude person," thought Peggy, with a perplexed expression on her face.

1. Was the caller the only rude participant in that brief telephone conversation? Why not?
2. What should Peggy have asked the caller in order to get the information she wanted? Why?

50 Elements of Effective Oral Communication

Two business executives were discussing the candidates for an important management position in their organization.

"Both Alice and Maria have had similar training and experience. How are we going to determine which one should get this position?"

"We obviously need to look at some other important aspects of the job. The woman we select for this particular job has to represent us at meetings of a number of groups in the territory, doesn't she?"

"Right—she does. Besides, she must make many contacts on the telephone as well."

"Then which of these two women do you feel will better handle these two important aspects of the job?"

"There's no doubt in my mind that Alice would be far superior in making presentations, in leading group discussions, and in talking over the telephone to our customers. She knows how to speak effectively; she has a large vocabulary; and she certainly makes a very good impression in terms of appearance."

"Well, there's little doubt in my mind that Alice is the person for this job. Do you agree?"

Certainly you would have to agree with their decision, too. It is unfortunate that so many candidates for good positions fail to get them because they are weak in oral communication. For most positions in business, oral communication is used more frequently than written communication. Furthermore, obtaining a good position and succeeding in it depend so heavily upon persuasive oral communication. That is why it is so important to be aware of the two major factors that determine one's effectiveness in communicating orally—physical appearance and the qualities of speech.

APPEARANCE

In most situations requiring oral communication, the speaker can be seen by the audience. (Important exceptions are, of course, talking on the telephone and using recording devices.) Because the speaker is first seen, then heard, the audience gets some kind of impression even before the speaker utters a word. This first impression is based primarily on posture, use of hands, facial expression, eye contact, body and head movement, and overall personal appearance.

A speaker's physical appearance often sets the stage for acceptance or nonacceptance of what is said. A speaker who makes a good physical impression quickly gains the interest of listeners. Of course, a speaker must have something interesting and worthwhile to say to hold the attention of the audience for any length of time; but the first barrier to effective oral communication will be overcome if the speaker has good posture, is dressed appropriately, is well groomed, and knows how to make each listener feel that he or she is being spoken to directly.

Posture

Many speakers underestimate the importance of posture to good physical appearance. This is a serious mistake. Regardless of how short or tall you are, you should stand up to your full height. You'll find that as you develop good posture, you will develop better breathing control. You will appear more confident and so give your audience the feeling that you know what you are talking about and that your message is important. Of course, no speaker should appear stiff or pompous and all-knowing. You should develop a natural posture, constantly reminding yourself to stand erect, with shoulders back and stomach in.

Hands

What should you do with your hands when you speak? As a speaker, you will distract your audience by picking imaginary lint from your clothing, putting your hands to your face, or toying with some article you are holding. The listeners will automatically direct their attention to your physical maneuvers and soon lose track of what you are saying. If you are standing, place your arms and hands in a relaxed position at your sides (rather than behind your back or folded in front). From time to time make natural gestures. If there is a lectern in front of you, you may place your hands on either side of it; but remember never to lean on the lectern.

When you are talking from a sitting position, you will be heard better if you sit slightly forward in your chair. You may rest your arms and hands in your lap, on the arms of the chair in which you are sitting, or partially on the edge of the table or desk in front of you. However, never use the desk or table as a place to rest your head and elbows. A lazy-looking speaker encourages disinterest on the part of the audience.

Facial Expression

A speaker's facial expression influences the listeners' impressions. A relaxed, pleasant, interested expression will create a better atmosphere for communicating, of course, than a wrinkled brow and turned-down mouth. As you look in a mirror from time to time, see whether you can capture your personality as others see it. Are your facial muscles relaxed? Is your smile natural, pleasant, and genuine? What characteristics in your facial expression are appealing to those around you? See if you can develop animation and show enthusiasm in your facial expression. Above all, you must look alert and interested if you want to impress your listeners.

Eye Contact

One of the best ways to appear interested is to look at your audience, whether that audience is composed of just one person or of more than a hundred. Everyone likes to feel directly addressed by the speaker. Therefore, your eyes should never leave your audience for any extended period of time; it's hard for your listeners to stay interested when you are looking constantly at your notes, the wall, the ceiling, or out the window. When talking to one or two persons, look squarely into the faces of your listeners (without, of course, staring them down) unless you are directing their attention to an object such as a chart. When speaking to a large audience, move your eyes over the entire audience; look into the faces of your listeners and not over the tops of their heads.

Body Movement

Body movement also contributes a great deal to the physical effect created by a speaker. The effective speaker never paces back and forth because excessive movement will distract an audience. It is permissible to move your body from the hips in order to turn from side to side or to move your body in a forward motion in order to emphasize a remark. Of course, if you are using a chart or other illustrative material, you must move from time to time to the visual device. However, when speaking, you should stay in the same spot as much as possible.

Grooming and Dress

Personal appearance—grooming, cleanliness, and attire—is also an important factor in effective communication. How a speaker looks and dresses expresses personality just as much as speech and conduct. There are so many factors involved in personal appearance that not all of them can be considered here in depth. But if you are interested in better oral communications you should be aware that you communicate best when you appear your best. Good appearance breeds confidence. Appearing clean, being dressed neatly and conservatively, avoiding extremes in personal grooming and clothing styles, and selecting attire and accessories that are tasteful and in harmony with one another and with your personality are some of the factors of personal appearance that you must consider in business. A speaker who is weak in any one of these factors cannot hope to be very persuasive as an oral communicator—whether speaking merely to one person or to a thousand.

SPEECH

Although a speaker's physical appearance creates the first impression on the audience, the quality of speech may have an even greater influence on the audience. The quality of speech is determined by the following factors:

Force or volume of voice	Rate or tempo of speech
Pitch or level of voice	Enunciation
Tone	Pronunciation

The force of a speaker's voice and the pitch and the tempo of speech depend, to a great extent, on the speaker's breath control. The volume of air that is taken into the lungs and breathing control help determine how much force a speaker's voice will have; both factors also affect the voice pitch. The rate of speaking will be determined by how frequently a speaker must breathe more air into the lungs. The speaker should talk only when breathing air out—never when taking air into the lungs. Good posture can help a speaker breathe in the maximum amount of air and can help to control the amount of air expended.

Force or Volume

To communicate orally, a speaker must be heard. Sufficient volume, therefore, is necessary; and good breathing control is important for sufficient volume. If you have trouble being heard, you should practice breathing deeply and controlling your breath with diaphragm and abdominal muscles, just as a singer does. The large abdominal cavity should be used to store a supply of air that can be released evenly to produce a clear, sustained tone. How much force you must use will, of course, be determined by such factors as how good the acoustics are in the room in which you are speaking, how large your audience is, and whether or not you are using a microphone or other electronic device to amplify your voice.

Pitch or Level

A speaker's voice will be more audible if it has a pleasing pitch. Pitch refers to the level of a sound on a musical scale. Practice can help correct the shrillness of a voice that is pitched too high or the excessive resonance of a voice that is pitched too low. Equally in need of correction is the constant pitch that results in a monotone. An effective speaker varies the pitch. The rising and falling of voice pitch is called *intonation.* Intonation can indicate that a statement is being made, that a question is being asked, or that a speaker is pausing. A drop in pitch indicates finality or determination and is, therefore, used at the end of a declarative sentence. For example, in reading the following sentence you should close with a drop in pitch.

> It is *impossible* for me to be there, *especially on Friday.* (Emphasize the word *impossible.*)

A rise in pitch is used for a question or for suspense, doubt, or hesitation. The following sentences should close with a rise in pitch.

> How *can* I be *more emphatic*? (Emphasize *can.*)
> I'm *sure* I can go, *but I'll phone you anyway.* (Emphasize the words *sure* and *anyway.*)

Gliding the pitch up and down or down and up usually expresses sarcasm or contempt, as in the slang expression "Oh, yeah?"

The most important aspect of pitch is variation. Variation of pitch not only helps hold the audience's attention but also helps listeners know the exact meaning intended. Important words can be stressed by a rise in pitch. Comparisons can be stressed by using the same pitch for each element; contrasts, on the other hand, can be made by pitching the first element high and the second low.

Notice the different shades of meaning that emerge as you read the following sentences and emphasize the italicized words.

> *He* gave her the package. (He did, not someone else.)
> He *gave* her the package. (It was a gift.)
> He gave *her* the package. (Only she got the package.)
> He gave her *the* package. (That particular package.)
> He gave her the *package.* (Not something else.)

Tone

The tone of your voice often reveals your attitudes and feelings. Naturally, a pleasant and cheerful tone is more desirable because it will have a better effect on your audience. On the telephone, the tone of your voice must substitute for your facial expression. Hence, the expression, "The voice with the smile." In addition, variation in tone, as well as in volume and pitch, can be used to add interest to your speaking voice. The tone you use should match the words and ideas you are expressing.

Rate or Tempo

Tempo, too, should be varied to avoid the extremes of speaking so rapidly that words are not understood or speaking so slowly that the audience does not pay close attention to what is being said. Regulate your rate of speaking so that you can enunciate each word clearly and so that the listener can hear each word without difficulty. A good rate for speaking is 125 words per minute; oral reading rates and radio speaking tend to run slightly higher—about 150 words per minute. To determine what 125 words per minute sounds like, read aloud the following paragraph in a half minute. If you read too rapidly or too slowly, read it over until you achieve the correct rate. At the end of a quarter minute, you should be at the diagonal line. Use the diagonal line as a guide for determining whether you should increase or decrease your speaking rate.

> A good speaker is one who talks slowly enough to be understood by the audience and speaks in a pleasant voice, articulating and pronouncing each word correctly and distinctly. To/develop a good speaking voice, you must spend sufficient time in practice. An effective speaker is an asset to business and will find more opportunities for moving ahead than the person who cannot speak effectively. (65 words)

Changing the tempo contributes to variety, as well as to clarity. Important words may be spoken slowly; unimportant words or phrases, more rapidly.

Try to speak in thought units so that you can assist the listener in interpreting your words. If the sentence is short, obviously the thought unit will consist of the entire sentence, as in "My office is very pleasant." When there are several thought units within a sentence, then the speaker should pause slightly after each thought group, as in "My office is very pleasant;/ but I must agree,/ some days are much more hectic than others."

Use pauses to stress major points. By pausing between major points or after important statements, you add variety and emphasis to the points you want the audience to remember.

Enunciation and Pronunciation

Because both of these elements are of particular importance in effective business speaking, they will receive special treatment in Section 51.

Communication Projects

PRACTICAL APPLICATION

A If you were one of the candidates for the position discussed at the beginning of this section, would you qualify for the job in terms of your oral communication abilities? Prepare a list of your strengths and weaknesses. Include such factors as your overall personality, the first impression you make on others, your personal appearance, your facial expressions, and your mannerisms. Comment on each of these factors.

B Select three prominent individuals (in politics, sports, or the arts) who frequently appear before the public in some type of speaking role. List the factors—pro and con—that affect their speaking effectiveness.

C Read each of the following sentences in three ways so that the meaning is changed by your emphasis.

1. Jean mailed the package this morning.
2. Paris is the city I enjoyed most on my trip.
3. Is Marla coming to the office party again?
4. If it is possible, please report to work earlier on Monday.
5. Please forgive me; I didn't expect to be so late.

D Read the following sentences twice. Then, standing before the class, read them aloud. Try to keep your eyes on the audience as much as possible as you read the material.

1. She never comes to work late, if she can help it.
2. I doubt very much that I will be able to come to the picnic.
3. No, they are not very efficient typists.
4. What difference does it make whether or not I am at the meeting?
5. Do you really think he will be able to complete the work by Friday?

E Read the following paragraphs twice. Then, standing before the class, read them aloud. Try to keep your eyes on the audience as much as possible as you read the material.

1. To be an effective speaker, you must be aware of your audience at all times, not only in selecting and preparing your topic but also in giving your speech. Audiences respond favorably only to speakers who talk directly to them and who smile occasionally. The speaker who looks at the ceiling, at notes, or into space quickly loses rapport with the audience.
2. Nearly every speech of any length is brightened considerably by touches of humor and by human-interest narratives. Of course, such stories should not dominate the speech. Observe the following rules: Use stories and jokes that add interest to the subject or illustrate a particular point. Before telling a joke to an audience, test it on friends to make sure it has a punch line. Make sure that stories and jokes do not offend or embarrass the audience. And time your stories to make sure that they are not too long.
3. When you are talking to an audience, pretend that you are carrying on a face-to-face conversation with just one person. Remember that the audience is just as eager for you to perform well as you are to do so. Don't be upset if you are nervous—even experienced speakers and actors are! Feeling nervous is a result of anxiety about doing a good job, and most authorities feel that a little stage fright provides needed tension.
4. Most people take telephone usage for granted—and this is one of the reasons why so many office workers are ineffective telephone communicators. Too many employees assume that a business tele-

phone conversation is the same as a personal telephone call. Actually, the telephone is one of the most important communication media in business; and it must be used with great skill, especially when talking with outside callers and with superiors in the office.

F Present a short talk to the class on some topic of your choice. Try to make each person feel as though you are talking individually to him or to her.

EDITING PRACTICE

Synonyms or Antonyms? In each item below, two words are synonyms or antonyms. For each item, identify the pair by letter and indicate whether the words are synonyms or antonyms.

1. (a) slander (b) reference (c) equality (d) disparity (e) excellence
2. (a) opener (b) glamor (c) candor (d) hypocrisy (e) sagacity
3. (a) hunt (b) perform (c) discipline (d) start (e) chasten
4. (a) estranged (b) reconciled (c) old (d) erudite (e) odd
5. (a) affable (b) garrulous (c) gracious (d) loquacious (e) joyous
6. (a) blissful (b) clever (c) happy (d) boisterous (e) busy
7. (a) respiratory (b) sordid (c) involuntary (d) stolid (e) phlegmatic
8. (a) excusing (b) modest (c) faultless (d) extraneous (e) pretentious
9. (a) convex (b) solid (c) harrowing (d) cadaverous (e) concave
10. (a) contrive (b) death (c) action (d) undershirt (e) demise

Editors' Alert The following sentences require thorough checking. Make any needed corrections, and if necessary, rewrite any poorly worded sentences.

1. Starting Monday all typists offices will be locked at the end of the day.
2. There's no other reasons for this delay.
3. She ordered 25 boxes at $4.25 a box, making a total of $106.25.
4. Why don't you and he think that the plans we made will be acceptable?
5. They will continue on with their work next week.
6. Please complete the questionairre and return it in the enclosed envelope.
7. Please follow-up the requests made in each peice of correspondents.
8. Our company has always in the past—and always will—be notorious for its promptness in paying its bills.
9. The work was only given to Marcus and I on Monday, and we have hardly had time to organize the materials.
10. 200 trainees attended the special orientation classes that began last month.

CASE PROBLEM

Placing the Blame Jean Garret and Ellen Post both typed for Mr. Yost. One day Mr. Yost came to Jean with a typed letter in which there were many errors. He was quite irritated because of the careless proofreading and requested that it be retyped. Jean noted that the reference initials were those of Ellen Post and that, therefore, the letter was not her work but Ellen's.

1. What should Jean say to Mr. Yost?
2. What should Jean say to Ellen?

51 Enunciation and Pronunciation

Fred Locke is employed in the shipping department of Reed's Quality Furniture Company, Inc., in High Point, North Carolina. One day the manager of his department called Fred into his office and severely reprimanded him for making a costly error. Fred had shipped forty end tables to Martin's Furniture Store in San Francisco, California. "I'm sure that they were the correct table style and wood finish," Fred informed his boss.

"Yes, they were, but Martin's wanted fourteen end tables, not forty. Now we have to absorb the cost of returning twenty-six tables. How could you make such an error?"

Fred remembered that Martin's needed the tables in a hurry, so they telephoned the order. He shipped the tables the same day, and when their confirming purchase order arrived later that week, he really did not notice that the quantity was different. "I was positive that the person who telephoned the order said 'forty,' not 'fourteen,'" explained Fred.

Apparently, the caller enunciated the *fourteen* so poorly that Fred thought it was *forty*. Unfortunately, Fred neglected to repeat the figure; so this one seemingly innocent error cost Fred's company its entire profit from this sale. Furthermore, the error caused Martin's a great deal of bother in sending the extra tables back to North Carolina.

There are many other instances in business—and even in social situations—where poor enunciation leads to costly delays, unnecessary expense, and the loss of goodwill. Therefore, it is important for all business employees, particularly those who have either face-to-face or telephone contact with customers and venders, to both enunciate and pronounce words clearly and correctly.

DISTINGUISHING BETWEEN ENUNCIATION AND PRONUNCIATION

The terms *enunciation* and *pronunciation* are closely related. However, they have slightly different meanings, and it is important that you understand each term to improve your speech.

Enunciation

Enunciation refers to the distinctness or clarity with which each of the sounds of a word is uttered. For instance, saying "runnin" for *running* or "gonna" for *going to* are examples of our careless enunciation. Enunciating difficulties often occur in *ing* words, such as "feelin" for *feeling* and "typin" for *typing*. Also, when we speak rapidly, we often tend to run our words together, dropping some of the sounds. Saying "dijago" instead of *did you go* and "meetcha" for *meet you* are other examples. A person who slurs too many words is difficult to understand, particularly over the telephone. Naturally, both the speaker and the listener will become annoyed if the listener must ask the speaker to repeat something several times. Much of this kind of difficulty can be avoided if we simply speak more slowly.

Pronunciation

Pronunciation refers either to the sound that the speaker gives to the various letters or combination of letters that make up a word or to the way in which the speaker accents the word. A person who says "pro*noun*ciation" instead of "pro*nun*ciation" is guilty of a pronunciation error. Should you say "libary" or "lib*r*ary," "com′•par•able" or "com•par′•able"? The dictionary indicates that the pronunciations are *library* and *com′•par•able*; and these are the pronunciations used by most people.

Of course, there are regional differences in pronunciation; and in addition, a number of words have more than one acceptable pronunciation. In the latter case, the dictionary lists first the pronunciation used most widely in the country.

Many difficulties in pronunciation arise because some letters or combinations of letters are pronounced one way in some words and another way in others. For example, the combination *ow* is given a long "o" sound in *know* but an "ow" sound (as in *ouch*) in *now*. Other difficulties in pronunciation arise because a letter may be sounded in some words while in other words the same letter is silent; for example, *k* is sounded in the word *kick*, but it is not sounded in such words as *know* and *knee*. Because of these inconsistencies in our language, it is essential to consult the dictionary whenever you are in doubt about the pronunciation of a word.

Though errors in pronunciation are less likely to cause misunderstandings than errors in enunciation—you would know what was meant if someone said "com•par′•able" instead of "com′•par•able"—such errors tend to distract the listener and may even cause the listener to consider the speaker careless or uneducated. The business worker eager to succeed does not wish to be branded with either of these labels.

Furthermore, since so many words are written according to the way they sound, you can improve your spelling ability by carefully and correctly pronouncing and enunciating each word you use. Many words are misspelled because letters that should be sounded are overlooked. Those who repeatedly say "goverment" instead of "gover*n*ment" probably overlooked the *n* in this word. Some words, on the other hand, are misspelled because extra sounds are inserted where they do not belong; for example, by pronouncing "ath*a*letic" instead of "athletic." In still other instances of mispronunciation, the sequence of letters in the word may be rearranged. How many people do you know who say "ir*rev*elant" when they really mean "ir*rel*evant"? You can easily see how taking sufficient care in pronunciation will help prevent other errors, such as "quite" for *quiet* and "praps" for *perhaps*.

Most business workers have to give and to receive information and instructions over the telephone or in face-to-face conversation. To prevent the costly misunderstandings that are often caused by improper pronunciation and enunciation, every business worker must try to develop and practice intelligible speech.

SUGGESTIONS FOR IMPROVING ENUNCIATION AND PRONUNCIATION

The following four-step plan will help you to improve your enunciation and pronunciation:

1. Use the dictionary to check the preferred pronunciation of words you are uncertain about.
2. Speak slowly enough and with sufficient care so that each letter in a word is sounded as it should be sounded and words are not run together.
3. Learn to use the physical organs of speech properly.
4. Practice proper enunciation and pronunciation, particularly of words that are frequently mispronounced or poorly enunciated.

In Section 1 you learned how to use the dictionary to determine the preferred pronunciation of words; in Section 50 you learned how to control your speaking rate. Now you will learn how to effectively use the speech organs over which you have control. You will also practice correct enunciation and pronunciation of words that frequently cause difficulty.

DEVELOPING A FLEXIBLE JAW

A rigid jaw leads to muffled speech. Many sounds are oral sounds and should, therefore, be made by the mouth. If they are forced through a locked jaw, they are certain to be muffled and indistinguishable. Keep your jaws locked tight and try to pronounce these words—*either, able, buy*. Can you understand yourself? Obviously you can't, and you would not expect any listener to understand words pronounced in this manner.

To be an intelligible speaker, you must move your jaw freely between an open and a closed position. Say each of the vowels and notice the different positions of your jaw as you say *a, e, i, o, u*. Compare your jaw positions as you say first the sound "ow," as in *how*, and then the sound "oo," as in *room*. When you say "ow," your jaw is dropped. However, when you say "oo," you move your jaw only slightly if at all.

Practice will help give you the free-moving feeling of a flexible jaw. First, stand before a mirror and practice the following words to be certain that your jaw is unlocked.

open	going	around	ninety-nine
buy	able	arrival	one nine eight
mine	morning	ideal	responsible

Now practice the phrases shown below. This exercise will help you develop a flexible jaw.

going to buy	around and around	high in the sky
down and out	up and down	up and around

Finally, practice these sentences to prove that your jaw is flexible and that it moves sufficiently.

She put the pen down on the table.
Many men have power, prestige, and ability.
Telephone 469-4589 as soon as possible.
My flexible jaw makes me a better speaker, does it not?

DEVELOPING MOBILE LIPS

As you were practicing the words, phrases, and sentences in the preceding section, you probably noticed that in addition to your jaw moving up and down, your lips were assuming many different positions. Six consonant sounds are made by action of the lips. The lips are closed for the sounds of "m," "b," and "p." The lower lip touches the edges of the upper front teeth for the sounds of "v" and "f." The lips are rounded for the sound made by *w*, as in *woman*.

Poor enunciators do not move their lips very much; as a result, their speech is often unintelligible. The good speaker, on the other hand, uses a variety of lip positions. In addition to the lip movements for the six consonants previously mentioned, the "oo" sound in *who, lose, shoe,* and *do* requires rounded lips. The lips are widely stretched for the "e" sound in *me, we, key,* and *see.* In words like *few, boys, use,* and *how,* the speaker is required to use two different lip positions. The sound for "ow," as in *how* and *now,* requires that the jaw be dropped and the lips be rounded to form a circle.

While using proper lip positions, practice these words. First read across and then read down the columns.

me	my	be	by	pen	pound
vase	very	voice	vest	vine	violent
first	fine	forest	fence	few	file
waste	when	why	wary	west	winter

Now practice the following phrases. Be certain that you avoid lazy lip movements.

friend in need	rapidly weighed	wintry weather
office manager	very fine work	answer the phone
mimeograph stencil	watered stock	empty the wastebasket
ditto master	economic waste	lose the shoe

Are your lips sufficiently mobile, so that you can enunciate clearly each word in the sentences given below? Practice the sentences until every sound is clear.

Peter Piper picked a peck of pickled peppers.
She sells seashells by the seashore.
How, now, brown cow?
The rain in Spain falls mainly on the plain.
Which witch was the wickedest witch?
Hickory dickory dock, the mouse ran up the clock.
The whistling west wind whipped the whispering trees.
Who picked up the bale of mail this morning?

DEVELOPING A LIVELY TONGUE

Repeat several times the phrase *the tip of your tongue*. As you say the words, notice the lively movement of your tongue. Try saying the same phrase with your tongue held loosely in your mouth, using a minimum of movement. Did you notice the lack of clarity? In order to speak clearly and with precise enunciation, you must move your tongue to several positions—the front of your mouth, the back of your mouth, and the roof of your mouth—and even between the top and bottom rows of teeth for the "th" sound, as in *this, either,* and *that*.

Now that you know what a lively tongue feels like, stand before a mirror and practice the following words:

feed	food	seed	sad	sod	sued
main	men	so	saw	peel	pale
twist	train	late	law	pad	port

Did you notice the movement of your tongue? Now practice these words, which require that the tongue be placed between the teeth.

thigh	thy	ether	either	loath	loathe
then	the	with	whether	wrath	through

Using an active tongue, practice the following phrases and sentences until every sound is clear.

actually colder
attempted assault and battery
health, wealth, and happiness
through thick and thin
this and that and those and them
seesaw at three-thirty
Linger a little longer, lovely lady.
The third-rate theaters appealed to the holiday crowd of shoppers.
Thirty thousand thermos bottles were sold there.
The sixth and seventh letters were so smoothly dictated.
Nothing gained, nothing lost, but nothing accomplished either.
This number is 336-3154, but Miss English is not here.

You have been given several suggestions for improving your enunciation and pronunciation. It is important for you to continue to be conscious of the way you enunciate and pronounce words, to use your dictionary to check the pronunciation of words about which you are in doubt, and to continue to practice good speech habits. If you will follow these suggestions, you will find that your speaking will improve and that the improvement will quickly become easy and natural for you.

Communication Projects

PRACTICAL APPLICATION

A The following phrases are frequently run together even though each word should be enunciated separately and distinctly. Practice saying these phrases properly, first in isolation and then in an original sentence that you create for each phrase.

give me	did you	going to	do you	got to
used to	want to	kind of	come here	will you
over and over	didn't you	don't know	going to go	have to

B From one of your textbooks, select a paragraph that you think will be of interest to the class. Read the paragraph aloud to the class, and be careful to enunciate words clearly and to pronounce them correctly. Each member of the class will list every word you enunciate poorly or mispronounce.

C You wish your secretary to place a number of long-distance telephone calls for you. Dictate the following names and telephone numbers, making certain that the names and numbers are intelligible. Spell the difficult or unusual names; for example, "Setliff Furniture Company (S-e-t-l-i-f-f) of Poughkeepsie (P-o-u-g-h-k-e-e-p-s-i-e), New York. I want to talk with Mr. Setliff personally. The number is (914) 555-6658."

Person to Be Called	Company and City	Telephone Number
1. Yves Piaff	St. Laurent Travel Club New York City	(212) 555-3250
2. Will speak with anyone	Linton and Bremer Law Offices Ventura, California	(805) 555-3329
3. Ms. Andrea Rifkin	Galaxy Employment Services 15 Century Drive Sioux City, Iowa	Don't know the number
4. Gregory Jones, Jr.	Bona Fide Electronics, Inc. Worcester, Massachusetts	(617) 555-7346 Extension 193
5. Claims Manager	Freedom Insurance Company Biloxi, Mississippi	Don't know the number

D You wish to send the following message by telegraph to one of your customers. You telephone the message to the telegraph office. You will be called on in class to read all the information as you would read it over the telephone.

To be sent to: Mr. Marcus Asbury, Wilkes-Barre Manufacturing Company, 22 Shrewsbury Lane, N. W., Wilkes-Barre, Pennsylvania 18701.
The message: Returning 756 Rattan Lamps, No. 934. Replace with 89 in blue, balance in assorted colors.
Sender: Your name and address.

E As office manager, you find it necessary to order a number of items from a local stationer. Since you need the items in a hurry, you telephone the information to the stationer. Assume that you have dialed the number and that the person at the other end says, "Wilson Stationery Company; may I help you?" Pick up the conversation from this point, and place the order for the following items.

1. 6 boxes of medium-hard carbon paper, No. 880, 8½ by 11½, Stock No. 2-105-19
2. 4 boxes 20-lb. white typewriting paper, 8½ by 11, Stock No. 13-1276
3. 2 quire stencils, Stock No. ABD-1379
4. 1 dozen No. 2 pencils, Stock No. 54-927

EDITING PRACTICE

States, Capitals, Principal Cities In each item below, there are two states, capitals, or principal cities that are misspelled. Spell them correctly.

1. Lincoln Colombia Cheyanne Pierre Jefferson City
2. Racine Laramie Pittsburg (Pa.) Bethlahem Portsmouth
3. Michigan Idaho Arizona Montanna New Jersy
4. Honalulu Allbany Richmond Charleston Indianapolis
5. Seattle Spokane Hoboken Scenectady Cincinatti
6. Wichita Clevland Agusta Duluth Butte
7. Olimpia Providence Topeka Frankfourt Helena
8. Minnesota Colarado Pensylvania Virginia Rhode Island
9. Minnapolis Juneau Trenton Charleston Jeferson City
10. Brooklyn Pasedena Brockton Levenworth Lowell

Editors' Alert Check the following sentences and make any improvements they need. Note every detail carefully.

1. This television set is far from portible, since it is too heavy to lift.
2. The number of items we carry are truly amazing in terms of variety.
3. Whatever you would like us to do to correct the error is agreeable, however, we must set a cost limit of $100.
4. Your assistance will be greatly appreciate by all of us in the office.
5. We considered the investment a year ago and decided against it at that time but perhaps the situation has changed and you can tell us how the venture would now be worth while for us.
6. Under any other circumstances we would be glad to have a speaker represent us at your conference, but as I explained, circumstances do not permit anyone to contribute the time right now.
7. Ten men and 12 women spent from one p.m. to three testing the experimental on the job training courses.
8. Even though the mistake is your's, we will be glad to make the change you request.
9. I think we need a system of industrial awards, presented each year by the president of the United states, as an incentive to increase industrial research in these particular areas.
10. I do not mean to accuse American Industry of lack of initiative but to recognize that there is need for encouragement, as there is in all human endeavors.
11. Really, I cannot comprahend how you can tolerate such sloppy procedures; certainly we would never under any circumstances first loose a customer's check and then claim that he sent a check for the wrong amount.
12. Most of all we would like to honor the laurence's, who have tirelessly contributed of their time to this extremely important fund raising drive.
13. On January 10 175 items disappeared before they could be loaded on the trucks, which we are at a loss to explain.
14. If it was three hundred cases or even 350 cases instead of 452, I would suspect a mathematical error in our paper work; however I think we must assume they are lost somewhere within the plant.
15. Garcia and Valdez have a law office in the north-east corner of the first floor.

CASE PROBLEM

The Helpful Co-Worker Martin Franks had been working at the Pelham Tax Service Bureau for about one month, under the supervision of Jed Grant. One day, while he was working on a report for which Jed had given him specific oral instructions, Martin was told by Dale Lowery, who sat at the desk next to him, that he was doing the report incorrectly. Dale had been with the company over twenty years and had prepared many similar reports.

1. What should Martin say to Dale?
2. How would you feel if you were in Martin's place and had been told that you were doing the report incorrectly?

52 Communicating With Individuals

Near the top of the list of communications activities of business employees—if not at the top—is talking with individuals. Business workers talk with their fellow workers—with colleagues in the department in which they work, with their supervisor and various department heads, with top management, and with service employees such as messengers and custodians—many times during the day. In addition, most employees talk, either on the telephone or face-to-face, with individuals outside the company—customers, sales representatives, suppliers, visitors, and various people soliciting or giving information. In fact, many business employees depend largely on their oral communication skill to earn a living—the sales representative, the switchboard operator, and the receptionist are examples. Everyone who has contact with the public plays an important role in developing and promoting the company image. When the agent at the airline ticket counter speaks to passengers, it is not as an individual, but as a representative of the company. The same is true of a receptionist, a secretary, or a credit clerk. In one sense, those who speak for the company *are* the company to those who do business with it.

GUIDELINES FOR INDIVIDUAL COMMUNICATION

The following suggestions should serve as guidelines for communicating effectively with individuals, whether face-to-face or over the telephone.

Listen Carefully

Listening is one of the most important skills connected with effective oral communication. Attentiveness and interest, just two attributes of the good listener, can often lead to better communication than talking can. For example, if the secretary is attacked verbally by an irate customer for something over which the secretary has no control, the secretary can go a long way toward soothing the customer by merely listening attentively. Often the secretary need not say anything, because what the customer most wants is an attentive and sympathetic listener.

Permit Others to Talk

Don't do all the talking. Give the other person a chance to talk, while *you* listen attentively. Watch for signs that the other person wants to say something or is becoming bored and not listening carefully. No matter how interesting you think the conversation is or how well informed or articulate you think you are, you must give your listener a chance to speak. Otherwise, you will not keep your listener's attention and respect.

Encourage Others to Talk

Sometimes the other person seems to prefer listening to talking. Remember, however, that a good conversationalist is one who not only talks well but also encourages the listener to contribute to the conversation. Ask frequent questions to let the other party know that you are interested in listening too. And prove your interest by listening with interest.

Look at the Speaker

Of course, this guideline applies only to face-to-face conversation. A speaker likes to have the listeners' complete attention. When you speak, you like to feel that your listeners are focusing on what you are saying and not being distracted by objects or sounds coming from other directions—conversations in another part of the office or something that is happening outside the building, for example. So when you listen, make eye contact with the speaker; look at the person who is talking.

Compliment When Appropriate

Many people with whom we communicate are seeking approval. Compliment when the occasion demands it. This is especially important in tense conversation situations. If a valued employee has a complaint that you cannot eliminate, put that person in the right frame of mind for a "No" answer by complimenting his or her work or loyalty. The same technique will work with customers. In tense situations with customers, try to find a way to compliment their taste, their promptness in paying their accounts, and so on. In all conversations, be generous with praise when it is timely and when it is deserved. Never pay a compliment, however, unless you can do so convincingly and honestly.

Keep Conversations Concise

Except in social situations, it is not wise to prolong conversations unduly. If you're asked for opinions, give them quickly and clearly. Not everyone wants to hear the story of your life or every detail about your weekend or a blow-by-blow account of why you were late getting to work. Keeping to the point doesn't mean that you have to be brusque. Try to sense what the situation calls for and act accordingly, but when you are in doubt, the best rule to follow is to keep your conversations short.

Address a Person by Name

Be sure you understand the name of a person whom you have met for the first time. Repeat the name as you are introduced: "I'm happy to meet you, Mr. Busché." If you aren't absolutely sure of someone's name, ask that person to repeat it for you; you can say "I didn't hear your name clearly" or "How do you pronounce (or spell) your name?" Then pronounce the name aloud to fix it in your mind, and when appropriate, use the name in the course of the conversation. Finally, always be sure that you use the person's name when you say good-bye. If you follow these steps, you should have no difficulty remembering the person's name the next time you meet.

Get on the Same Level

It is said that Napoleon had his desk raised so that he could look down upon everyone who came into his office. Not long ago most executives sat behind a huge desk when they talked to visitors; at the desk, these executives appeared more important, more courageous, more domineering.

The trend today is toward a more relaxed atmosphere. Executives who are effective communicators move from behind their desk and face their visitor without a barrier between them. This makes possible a better give-and-take atmosphere and therefore better communication.

RECEIVING VISITORS

Although in most companies the receptionist greets all visitors, nearly every employee meets the public. This is especially true in small offices and in retail stores. You should, therefore, be familiar with the basic rules for meeting the public.

Give Prompt Attention to Visitors

Recognize a visitor's presence immediately. Even if you are busy, you can interrupt your work for as long as it takes to smile and say to the new arrival, "I'll be with you in a moment. Won't you sit down?"

Greet Visitors Pleasantly

Be pleasant and friendly when you greet visitors, and use their names in your greeting whenever possible. Add a personal touch to your greeting, such as "Good morning, Mrs. Talbot. How are you on this lovely day?" or "It's good to see you again, Mrs. Talbot." These friendly greetings make callers feel that they are getting special treatment.

Be Courteous to Everyone

Every visitor should receive friendly and courteous treatment. Even if the visitor is upset about something or is just plain grumpy, you must overlook this discourtesy and show that you are understanding. Perhaps your visitor is annoyed about "unfair treatment" from your company. If this is the case, there may be justification, and you have an opportunity to mend a business rift. Treating such a person discourteously will tend only to make the situation worse. Usually a person responds well to pleasant treatment, and your courteous attitude will help to calm the visitor and will give your company a chance to make amends.

Apologize for Delays

If an appointment cannot be kept promptly by the person who is to receive the visitor, you should tell the visitor why ("I'm sorry, Mr. Sheldon, Mr. Whitehead has been delayed at a meeting with the president"); and you should tell him about how long he may have to wait ("Mr. Whitehead should be able to see you about 11:30"). Make the visitor comfortable (a selection of current magazines and today's newspaper should be available, or offer him a cup of coffee if it is available). You might ask, "Shall I telephone your office and tell your secretary that you will be delayed a half hour?"

You may have some visitors whose shabby appearance leads you to believe they could not possibly have business of interest to one of the company executives. Don't be too sure! Sometimes the one who scorns that well-groomed look is a VIP—perhaps even the most important stockholder in the company. However, everyone is, of course, entitled to your most courteous treatment.

Find Out the Purpose of the Visit

Almost every caller will have an appointment with an executive or other member of the company. For example, a visitor may say to you, "I am Ralph Winter; I have an appointment with Mr. Whitehead," and you will usher him to the appropriate office or telephone the host that his visitor has arrived. If you do not know, however, whether the visitor has an appointment, you must ask, "May I help you?" or "Whom do you wish to see?" If he has no appointment, take his name, the name of the company he represents (if any), and the purpose of his call. Relay this information to the person who you think can be of most help to the caller. After getting permission to show the visitor in, invite him to follow you to the appropriate office. Then present him like this: "Mr. Massey (host), this is Mr. Winter (visitor)."

Be Discreet and Tactful

Protect both your employer's and the company's interests by being discreet in your comments to visitors. For example, if your employer is late coming to the office in the morning or returning from lunch, it is not necessary to supply unnecessary details to the visitor. Instead of saying, "Mrs. Avery is late getting in this morning," say, "I expect Mrs. Avery about 9:15." If she is late returning from lunch, you might say, "Mrs. Avery had an important luncheon meeting and should return shortly." Avoid making conversation about company business or personnel. If the subject comes up, be noncommittal and change the topic of conversation as quickly as you can. Never engage in negative statements, such as "Hasn't business been poor lately?" or "We have a terrible time getting good secretaries."

Be discreet in giving any opinions solicited by the visitor. The person the visitor will see may have a different opinion from your own. For example, the visitor may want to show you certain products and ask whether you think your company might be interested in buying them. Unless you are responsible for company purchases, however, you should not give an opinion about the company's possible interest in buying the products. Of course, you should not be rude even though you are pressured for comment. Simply say pleasantly, "I am sorry, but I do not purchase our company's supplies."

MEETING THE PUBLIC BY TELEPHONE

Meeting the public by telephone requires techniques that are different from those used in meeting the public face-to-face. Usually, those engaged in telephone conversations are unable to see one another and must depend entirely on their voices to communicate friendliness, interest, and a willingness to be helpful.

Most people take telephone usage for granted—and this is one of the reasons that so many office workers are ineffective telephone communicators. Too many employees assume that a business telephone conversation is the same as a personal telephone call. Actually, the telephone is one of the most important communication media in business; and it must be used with great skill, especially when talking with outside callers and with superiors in the office.

The following tips may seem elementary to you. Nevertheless, you should review them carefully:

Talk directly into the mouthpiece.

Talk slowly and naturally. Exaggerate your enunciation slightly. Shouting is never necessary.

If a caller must be transferred to someone else in the company, say, "If you will hold on just a moment, I will have your call transferred." Then depress the telephone plunger twice, very slowly, and repeat until the operator returns to the line. Then say, "Will you please transfer this call to Mr. Branch Lee on Extension 4103."

If, while talking, you must put down the receiver, place it on a book or magazine rather than drop it on a hard surface. In this way, you will protect the caller's ear from irritating noises.

Place the receiver gently in the cradle when you hang up.

Guidelines for Telephone Courtesy

Courtesy is the key to telephone effectiveness. Greet all callers pleasantly. If you know who the caller is, you might say something like this: "Good morning, Mrs. Abrams," or "Hello, Dick." If you do not know who the caller is, identify yourself first—"Turner" or "Miss Gilbert" or "Rossi speaking." When answering the telephone for a department, be certain to identify both the department and yourself—"Mailing Department, Mr. Alonzo" or "Shipping, Alonzo." A secretary usually answers the employer's telephone like this: "Mrs. Cord's office" or "Mrs. Cord's office, Miss Carter speaking."

Your voice should be friendly and your manner courteous, regardless of who is calling. This manner is *especially* important when talking to outside callers. Remember that the impression created by your voice should be that of a friendly smile. Show the caller that you want to be helpful; always listen attentively and don't interrupt. So that the caller will know you are listening, occasionally acknowledge comments with a "Yes" or with some other simple verbal response. Use the caller's name at least once before hanging up, and conclude the call with a remark like "Thank you for calling us, Mrs. Fredericks" or "We will look into the matter for you right away, Mr. King."

Originating Calls

The telephone company makes the following suggestions for originating calls:

1. Plan the conversation before you call. A little forethought will save both time and money. If your conversation will be an involved one, jot down notes in advance.
2. Place your own calls. Not only is it faster and easier to do so, but it is also more courteous. No busy executive likes to be greeted with "Hold on, Mr. Gomez, I have Mr. Carpenter on the line." Mr. Gomez then has to wait until Mr. Carpenter gets on the line. Since Mr. Gomez is the person being called, it is discourteous to keep him waiting.
3. To avoid delays, identify yourself promptly and state the purpose of your call. For example, say, "This is Jack Archer of Litton and Warren. I would like to speak to the person in charge of adjustments."

Receiving Calls

To ensure efficient use of the telephone when you receive a call, observe the following suggested procedures:

1. Answer promptly and identify yourself immediately. You should answer at the first ring, if possible, and not later than the second ring.
2. Respond to inquiries graciously, take appropriate notes, and verify important details. "Yes, we should be glad to send you a duplicate copy of last month's statement. You want the December, 19—, statement; is that correct?"
3. At the close of the conversation, take the required action. Be certain that you keep all promises you make to the caller.
4. Allow the caller to hang up first.
5. If you are going to be away from your telephone, let someone know; and indicate how you would like calls handled that are directed to you during your absence.

Answering for Others

Two special suggestions are appropriate when you are answering telephone calls for other people in your firm.

1. If the person called is not available, offer to be of help or to transfer the call to someone who can help.
2. If the caller wishes to speak to only one individual and that person is not available, obtain the caller's name and telephone number and record the caller's message, if any.

Handling Complaints

One test of your ability to handle telephone calls will be revealed if you must deal with an annoyed customer who has a complaint. You must remember that you represent your firm and that little or nothing be gained by allowing yourself to become angry. Your task will be made considerably easier if you follow these suggestions in handling telephone complaints.

1. Listen carefully to the caller's complaint. Take careful notes of all important details.
2. Express interest in and an understanding of the caller's problem. "Yes, I can see why you were annoyed by the mistake in your bill, Mr. Hayakawa, but I am sure we can correct it right away."
3. Tell the caller what action you will take. If you cannot make the adjustment yourself, refer the caller to someone who can. Don't make the caller repeat the entire story to someone else; each time the message must be repeated to another person, the caller becomes angrier.

Communication Projects

PRACTICAL APPLICATION

A You are administrative assistant to Donald Beckman, vice president of Model Furniture Manufacturing Company, Inc. Mr. Beckman will hold an important conference in his office during the next two hours and has told you that he does not want to be disturbed under any circumstances. The following situations occur during this time. What would you say to each of the individuals involved?

1. Mr. Franklin, plant manager, telephones and says that it is urgent that he speak to Mr. Beckman.
2. Mrs. Beckman, the vice president's wife, telephones and asks to speak to her husband.
3. Mr. Lawrence, a customer from another city, arrives an hour early for an appointment with Mr. Beckman.
4. The president of the company, Mr. Cardoza, telephones and says that it is important he speak with Mr. Beckman at once.

B The office services manager, Mrs. Josephine Lee, has asked you to prepare a one-page memorandum to all secretaries on each of the following subjects.

Choose one subject and then write the memorandum.

1. How to place outgoing telephone calls.
2. How to receive incoming telephone calls.
3. How to handle delays in telephoning.
4. How to say "No" gracefully to a caller.
5. How to handle complaints by telephone.

C List five "dos" and five "don'ts" for receiving visitors in an office.

D What essential qualities must the good listener have?

E Suggest three greetings a receptionist might use to find out the purpose of a caller's visit.

F Give examples of how a good communicator can make use of a compliment in order to score a point.

EDITING PRACTICE

Editing to Improve Writing Techniques Rewrite the following sentences, and correct all evidence of poor writing techniques.

1. Martin will continue on with the task assigned him.
2. Mildred did not loose the material she transcribed, as was thought.
3. The tray is empty and all the letters in the mail.
4. Because Mr. Abbott came to the meeting does not mean that he will consent to the plan.
5. Your competitors are outselling you because they use a less costly and newer method of manufacturing.
6. Feldman can handle the situation as well, if not better, than me.
7. This particular function is general performed by the marketing department.
8. Mr. Gerson joined the staff 1974.

CASE PROBLEM

The Negligent Employee Horace Brady, the sales department head, receives the following written report from Mike Carr, a supervisor. Accordingly, Mike must talk with Julie about the quality of her work and the reason for her failure to receive a salary increase. What should Mike say to Julie when she comes to his office?

> I cannot recommend Julie Newland, my secretary, for a salary increase at this time. During her first six months on the job, she tried very hard to do good work, but she soon lost interest. Now my work is taking second place to her long coffee breaks and her personal visits and telephone calls. Yesterday, for example, it took three hours to get three short letters typed.

53 Communicating With Groups

If you were to ask some typical executives how many meetings they attend in the course of a week, they are likely to reply "*Too* many!" Their responses would be based on the fact that many executives attend from two to as many as twelve or even more meetings every week. As a result, they may have to do much of their work at home. Although the meeting is one of the most important media of communication in business, the frequency of meetings is decried by almost everyone. Such might not be the case if meetings were better organized and run and if more were accomplished as a result of each meeting.

As a responsible business employee, you may have frequent opportunities to participate in group meetings. You may be selected as a member of a *standing* (permanent) committee that meets regularly, such as a finance committee, a publicity committee, or a social committee. You may also be called upon to sit on a committee formed for a particular purpose only, such as a committee appointed to study commuting problems of employees or to plan a company dinner-dance. These temporary committees, formed for a special purpose and then disbanded once that purpose is achieved, are called *ad hoc* (pronounced "ad hock") committees.

Because meetings consume so much time and talent in the typical organization, they must be organized and run efficiently. In the average company, the time spent in meetings adds up to many thousands of dollars a year. In addition to attending meetings during business hours, the business worker often goes to many meetings and serves on a number of committees outside the company—for example, in professional, social, religious, political, and civic groups.

PARTICIPATING IN GROUP MEETINGS

Everyone who is invited to join a group discussion has an obligation to contribute his or her best thinking and suggestions. Time and money are wasted because employees take meetings for granted and do not contribute their maximum efforts to the discussion. They often come to a meeting unprepared, uninterested, and uninspired. The six basic rules for participating effectively in a meeting are explained in the following discussions.

Prepare for the Meeting

The first rule for effective participation in a meeting is to come prepared. Find out in advance all that you can about the topic to be discussed at the meeting. If there is an agenda (see page 458), study each item carefully and learn more about those topics you are not familiar with. For example, if the subject of personnel evaluation is to be discussed, be sure that you know what

NOLAND MANUFACTURING COMPANY

Meeting of the Employee Personnel Committee

June 15, 19--, 9:30 a.m.
Board Room

AGENDA

1. Call to order by Chairperson Sutcliff.
2. Approval of the minutes of the last meeting.
3. Approval of the agenda.
4. Announcements.
5. Old Business:
   A. Report of the subcommittee on employee evaluation procedures.
   B. Discussion of the proposed merit rating plan.
6. New Business:
   A. Discussion of personnel needs for new fiscal year.
   B. Recommendations for promotions.
   C. Selection of new chairperson.
   D. Other items.
7. Adjournment.

the current company procedures are for evaluating personnel and the advantages and disadvantages of these procedures. You may wish to refer to books or articles dealing with this topic or to examine company forms that are currently in use. In addition, it is often useful to get the opinions of knowledgeable people who will not be present at the meeting. If there is to be a discussion of a revision of the evaluation form, study the form thoughtfully, try it out, and ask various people who use the form what they like and do not like about it.

Being prepared means coming to a meeting with a set of well-founded opinions. Opinions that are worth listening to in a business meeting are the ones backed up by facts. People are often opposed to a new idea merely because they don't know enough about it. The old saying, "You're down on what you're not up on," applies to participation in a meeting. Make certain that this saying never applies to you.

Express Opinions Tactfully

When someone asks you for your opinion or when you volunteer an opinion, be tactful in expressing yourself. Often, opposing points of view can cause strong disagreement. No matter how strongly you may feel that you are right and that the other person is wrong, your chances of winning that person's support are no better than your tactfulness in presenting your views. For example, don't say, "You're wrong, and here's why." Instead, you might say, "Your point of view certainly has merit, Frank, but I have doubts because . . ." Never tell him he is wrong—*wrong* is a strong term, and your right to use it requires indisputable evidence. In selling your point of view, the "Yes, but . . ." technique is effective; that is, acknowledge the other person's point of view and show your respect for it. Then present your own ideas. For example, "Yes, I agree that the solution seems simple and that your idea represents one way to approach the problem, but. . . ."

In expressing yourself, separate facts from opinions. Label as facts only those statements for which you have solid evidence. Opinions should be signaled by such words as "it seems to me," "as I understand it," or "in my opinion."

Be Positive

One of the most unwelcome participants in a group meeting is the person who thinks "No." This person's primary mission seems to be that of killing the ideas and proposals that others voice. Such a participant seldom presents a positive idea but is always quick to say of someone else's idea, "That won't work."

Most meetings are held for the purpose of solving problems, and problems cannot be solved in a negative atmosphere. Participants must be willing to approach a problem with the attitude that the only way to solve it is to present as many ideas as possible. No one immediately vetoes an idea someone else has presented; instead, each person tries to see the idea's merits and to enlarge upon the idea's possibilities, no matter how weak it may seem at first. To smother ideas before they are fully aired is not only rude but also extremely disheartening to those who are genuinely trying to reach intelligent decisions.

Show Courtesy to Other Participants

The ideal meeting is one in which everyone participates freely. The over-aggressive speaker who monopolizes the discussion will discourage the participation of others. Even though you may be more knowledgeable about the topic than anyone else in the group, you should never display your intelligence in an offensive, overbearing manner. You may win the skirmish and lose the battle—the too-sure, know-it-all person often does.

More victories have been won in group discussion by modesty and tact than will ever be achieved by overaggressiveness. Don't jump in while others are speaking; wait your turn patiently. Show interest in what others are saying. You will win more friends by listening and taking notes on remarks by others than by interrupting their remarks—regardless of how inane the remarks may seem to you. Acknowledge that others may have as much information as you have or perhaps even more.

Courteous group members do not (1) resort to sarcasm when they disagree with someone, (2) interrupt the person who is talking, (3) fidget, (4) gaze into space, or (5) carry on side conversations with other members of the group while someone else has the floor.

Keep Remarks Short and Pertinent

Some participants in a meeting take a circuitous route to reach the point they want to make. They ramble endlessly and indulge in frequent side excursions. If you have something to say, get to your point quickly. Meetings become boring and unproductive mainly because some participants insist on relating personal preferences, experiences, and opinions that have little or no bearing on the discussion at hand.

Take Notes

As mentioned earlier, it is good to develop the habit of taking notes. The act of taking careful notes (1) keeps you on your toes, (2) tells the speaker that you consider his or her remarks worth recording, and (3) provides a valuable reference source during and after the meeting. Take notes not only on what the speaker is saying but also on what you want to say when it is your turn to speak. Jot down your key remarks in advance (especially if you know shorthand) so that your presentation is both well organized and complete.

LEADING A GROUP DISCUSSION

Without a doubt, the most important person at a meeting is the group leader, or chairperson. By skillful direction, the leader can turn an ordinary meeting into a rich and profitable experience for everyone. Without good leadership, the most promising discussion can become worthless. The good discussion leader follows the basic rules outlined here.

Make Advance Preparation

A good leader prepares thoroughly for meetings and conferences. When you are the group discussion leader, be sure you know the time and place of the meeting, the names of those who are to attend, and in general what the meeting is to accomplish. Notification of a meeting of a standing committee usually takes the form of an agenda (a list of the topics to be discussed and the names of those who are to lead the discussion). The agenda is sent as far in advance of the meeting as possible. For a monthly meeting, those who are to attend the meeting should receive the agenda at least a week ahead of the meeting date. This advance notice will give the participants an opportunity to prepare themselves for the discussion. For a weekly meeting, it is sufficient to have the agenda in the hands of the committee members a day or two before the meeting. A sample agenda is shown on page 458.

Generally, the topics on the agenda are listed in the order in which they will be discussed. Under new items, those that are most important should be listed first in case there is not sufficient time to cover them all.

Prepare the Meeting Room

The room in which the meeting is to be held must be properly set up in advance. This is the responsibility of the group leader, and it should not be entrusted to just anybody—too often the job just doesn't get done. The result is that there is an insufficient number of chairs, there are no ashtrays (or the ashtrays are overflowing), the room is poorly ventilated, there is no chalk for the chalkboard, and so on.

A meeting should start promptly; one way to avoid delays is to have the meeting room in order beforehand. If visual aids are to be used, someone should check well in advance to make sure that the proper equipment is on hand and is in working order. If an operator is required for projection equipment, the meeting date should be confirmed the day before the meeting. Many meetings with a program featuring a motion picture have been fiascoes because the film didn't arrive, the operator forgot the day and time, there was no electrical outlet, or the extension cord was too short to reach the outlet.

Arrive Early

The chairperson of the meeting should be at the meeting place a few minutes early to check the facilities and to set an example for the others. Arriving early also gives the leader a chance to distribute the agenda. (Even though everyone has received an advance copy of the agenda, not everyone will remember to bring it to the meeting.) The leader or the leader's secretary should also bring along a few extra pencils and pads (there will be some participants who will have neither) and extra copies of reports or other papers to be discussed, even though copies may have been distributed in advance.

Establish a Down-to-Business Atmosphere

The chairperson sets the tone of the meeting. If the leader begins late or is apathetic about getting the proceedings under way, the participants are likely to lose whatever enthusiasm they may have had when they entered the room. Generally it is best to start a meeting precisely at the hour for which it is scheduled, even though there probably will be latecomers. If the members of a group realize that the meeting will start without them, they are likely to make an effort to be punctual.

Guide the Discussion

The good leader talks as little as possible and draws out the opinions of the participants. Unfortunately, some people think that *leader* and *talker* are synonymous terms when it comes to running a meeting. The skillful leader brings out each participant's best thinking. The leader's function is not to show how much he or she knows but to steer the discussion in the proper direction. The experienced leader knows that the greater the participation—that is, the more minds at work on a problem—the better the chances are of accomplishing the objective of the meeting.

Encourage Participation

Everyone should be able to make some contribution to a meeting. Some people, however, are shy and will not say anything unless they are encouraged. Call on these people in a manner that encourages them to participate; for example, "Marie, you have had a lot of experience in advertising. What do you think of Bill's suggestion regarding spot announcements on radio?" or "Mr. Carter, we would be interested in having the benefit of your experience in data processing. Do you think we can readily convert our billing process to a computer system?"

A leader encourages participation by saying something complimentary after a speaker has made a contribution; for example, "Thank you, Mark. That's certainly a suggestion worth considering," or "Good idea, Mrs. Gershon. Could you tell us more about the outcome of that plan of operation?" Such types of comments are preferred to comments that evaluate the ideas and suggestions of others.

Squelch the Orators

In any group there will always be one or two people who want to do all the talking. Certainly they have a right to be heard, but unless they are listed on the agenda as the principal contributors, they should not be permitted to monopolize the discussion. Only a strong leader can prevent a loudmouth from taking over the meeting. The chairperson should be tactful but firm. "That's very interesting, Joe, but I think we ought to hear from Miss Jennings," or "Let's get back to you a little later, Irene. I think we would all be interested in having as many points of view as we can get."

Keep the Discussion on the Track

Meetings have a tendency to get off the track, and if the chairleader is not careful, the main problems to be solved at the meeting will be bypassed entirely. All too often, a subject comes up that is of genuine personal interest to all those present at the meeting but has little or no bearing on the main topic. People just naturally like to tell about their personal experiences, likes and dislikes, and amusing anecdotes. These digressions should be permitted now and then because they lighten the discussion; we can't be completely serious all the time. However, when side issues begin to waste valuable time, they must be cut off. The leader can do so tactfully. "That must have been an unusual experience for you, John. I don't know how you managed to stay so calm and collected under the circumstances. But let's get back to our discussion of the revision of the office manual. Mr. Warren, how complete do you think the discussion on report style should be?" Generally you can keep the discussion on the track without being rude, but bluntness is justified as a last resort. "Joe, time is getting away from us, and we are nowhere near a solution to our problem. Let's see if we can't bring this discussion down to specifics. Carl, what are your recommendations?"

Summarize From Time to Time

As already mentioned, it is neither necessary nor desirable for the chairperson of a group discussion to evaluate everyone's remarks as soon as they are presented. The group leader listens attentively and makes no comment except, perhaps, to stimulate further discussion. "Good, Tom. That's an interesting point of view. I gather that you are opposed to any change in the procedure at this time. Right?" Above all, the leader does not tear down ideas or argue with the speaker; doing so will only discourage other participants from expressing themselves. The leader of the meeting is only one person, and it is usually not within his or her province to judge every idea expressed.

Now and then, the chairperson should summarize the major points that have been presented up to that time. "We are agreed, then, that we should not open a branch office in Richmond at this time. You believe that for the remainder of this year, at least, the Virginia territory can be serviced adequately from Washington. Right? Well, let's move on, then, to the problem of warehouse space in Washington. Is it sufficient, or will additional space be needed? Charlie, you've had more recent contact with the situation than anyone else here. What do you think?"

Know How to End

If the leader has prepared the agenda carefully and has run the meeting efficiently, there is no reason why the meeting cannot end at the hour scheduled. If the discussion seems likely to extend beyond the closing hour and it is important to continue, get the approval of the group; for example, "Ladies and gentlemen, it is five minutes of twelve, and it looks as though we won't get out of here by noon. Shall we continue the discussion, or would you rather schedule another meeting for this afternoon?"

After the meeting, the secretary should write up the minutes and distribute them as soon as possible. Memorandums should be written to those who are assigned special responsibilities at the meeting. Such a memorandum is illustrated on page 464.

Know How to Conduct Formal Meetings

Many groups conduct their meetings on a formal basis, following parliamentary rules. If you are elected to office in such a group, you should read *Robert's Rules of Order*, the standard guide to parliamentary procedure.

Interoffice Memorandum

To	Mr. Edward M. King	**From**	Albert Wallin
Subject	Company Contributions to Employees Medical and Dental Plans	**Date**	May 25, 19--

This memorandum is to remind you that the Executive Committee, at its meeting yesterday, requested that you investigate a number of medical and dental plans available to our employees and that you prepare a report on the comparative merits and costs of each plan.

When you have obtained your data, I would like to see the information so that I can begin determining whether it would be feasible for the company to contribute the full cost of these programs.

Thank you, Ed, for your help in this worthwhile project.

AW

iti

Communication Projects

PRACTICAL APPLICATION

A Evaluate the following statements made by group discussion leaders. If the statement is not an appropriate one, what should have been said?

1. "I don't think that idea would work."
2. "We'd like to hear more about the plan."
3. "Anne, what has been your experience with this problem?"

B If you had been asked to participate in a meeting concerned with ways of improving the services of the college library, how might you prepare yourself for such a meeting?

C How do standing committees and ad hoc committees differ?

D What steps would you take to prepare a meeting room for an all-day discussion?

E Explain what is meant by the expression *be positive* in reference to participating in a meeting. What are three reasons for taking notes at a meeting?

F Prepare an agenda for an ad hoc committee meeting for which you are to act as chairperson. Select a discussion topic, such as "Improving Procedures for Receiving Callers in the Blank Company." Then develop a list of topics concerned with phases of this subject and assign them to individuals in your class.

G At a meeting of the Anniversary Celebration Committee of the Abrams China Company, George Davis was given the responsibility of gathering information regarding facilities for the fiftieth anniversary dinner-dance. Write a follow-up memorandum to Mr. Davis to remind him of the assignment. Supply any details you think appropriate.

EDITING PRACTICE

Applied Psychology The wording of the following letter excerpts does nothing to cement good human relations. Revise the sentences.

1. The complexities and subtleties of this onerous obligation will be apparent to any institution not eleemosynary in character.
2. You must have had the merchandise since before Christmas—Christmas, 1910!
3. We cannot accept your application for credit because investigation indicates that you are a "late pay."
4. Why aren't you using the charge account we took the trouble to open for you?
5. Although we fail to understand why you say the wood doesn't match, we are sending you a new table leaf.
6. Because you failed to give us your telephone number, we had to delay delivery of the item for almost a week.
7. You made an error of $1.89 in the total of our May 30 statement.
8. When we asked for delivery by February 10, we meant this year—not next!

CASE PROBLEM

The Poor Chairperson As chairperson of the social committee, Margaret was greatly discouraged after the first meeting. She couldn't understand why so many committee members were late. Hadn't she telephoned all the members that very morning to ask if they could meet at 2 p.m.? She waited until 2:30 before enough members were there to start the meeting. When she asked the group what social activities they wanted to discuss, she got little response. Those ideas suggested did not seem practical to Margaret, and she quickly discouraged them. The meeting adjourned at 4 p.m. with nothing decided other than that another meeting would be called soon. What went wrong with Margaret's meeting?

54 Preparing and Delivering a Speech

Nearly everyone is called upon at one time or another to "say a few words" to an audience. Since active people belong to one or more business, professional, civic, church, or social groups, they are bound to be asked to express themselves in public. The more active a person is in these organizations, the greater the opportunity to speak before groups. The responsible business executive may frequently speak before professional organizations, at company meetings, and before many different civic, religious, and educational groups.

Even people who do not participate in extra-business activities find that they must be prepared for public appearances—introducing a speaker, explaining a procedure to a group of clerical workers, extending greetings to visitors to the company offices, making a presentation at a meeting of company sales representatives, and so on.

A speech is like a letter in that it reflects an image of the company that employs the speaker. An effective speech, like an effective letter, conveys a message clearly and convincingly and at the same time builds an image of goodwill.

The first step in delivering an effective speech—whether it is a two-minute introduction, a five-minute commentary, or an hour's discourse—is to plan it carefully. Planning involves previewing the speaking assignment, gathering and organizing material, outlining, and rehearsing.

PREVIEWING THE SPEAKING ASSIGNMENT

Regardless of whether the speech topic has been selected for the speaker or whether the topic is the speaker's own choice, every speaker must answer three basic questions before gathering and organizing material: (1) What is the purpose of the speech? (2) To whom is the speech to be given? (3) How much time is allowed for the speech?

What Is the Purpose of the Speech?

Every speech has a purpose—to explain something, such as a company procedure; to describe something, such as the features of a new product or an experience; or to report on something, such as a market survey. The purpose may be to present a point of view, to inspire, or to win support for a proposal. Every speech must be organized to fit its purpose.

Assume that you have been asked to tell the company sales representatives about the engineering features of a new pocket-size electronic calculator your company has just started manufacturing. If your talk is entitled "How the MiniBrain Calculator Is Made," obviously, you are not expected to dwell on how to sell the product, how much money has been allocated to promote the sale of it, or how much it costs to transport the raw materials to the factory. The purpose of the talk is to give the sales representatives product information that they can use to persuade prospects that their calculator is superior to the competitors'. Your remarks should center on the materials used for the various parts of the calculator, the engineering features that permit the calculator to be operated so easily, the features it has that the others do not have, and so on.

To Whom Is the Speech to Be Given?

The effective speaker finds out everything about the audience before gathering material for the speech. If you are to discuss dictation techniques before a group of executives, your emphasis will be quite different from the one you would use in discussing the same topic with a group of secretaries. If your speech is one of several that are to be given, you should inquire about the rest of the program so that you can put your topic in perspective with the others. You should find out as much as you can about the interests, occupations, and age level of the audience. In addition, it is helpful to know the expected audience size and the general background of the people expected. The program chairperson can supply this and other useful information. With this help, you can find out what the audience already knows about the subject and what the audience expects to learn from the presentation. With such knowledge at hand, you can avoid rehashing facts already known and can give particular emphasis to areas of most interest to the audience.

How Much Time Is Allowed for the Speech?

The speaker must know precisely how much time is allowed for the speech. Obviously, you should not try to crowd into thirty minutes a topic that requires an hour. Therefore, once you know the amount of time you have been allotted, you should plan your speech so it can be adequately presented in this time period.

The shrewd speaker, when assigned thirty minutes, takes only twenty-five. If you have been assigned a very broad topic like "Electronic Data Processing," you should select the facet of the subject that best fits the audience. For example, your speech may deal with "Computers in Credit Transactions" for an audience composed of credit managers, or it may deal with "Word Processing Affects the Executive Secretary" for an audience composed of executive secretaries.

GATHERING AND ORGANIZING DATA

There is no substitute for preparation. Even the most gifted speakers always prepare carefully beforehand, whether they are to speak for only a few minutes or for an hour. If your topic is one that you can prepare for by reading, read as widely as possible. Find a good library that has up-to-date magazines, books, and bulletins on your topic, and get as many points of view as you can. Check and double-check on facts—especially statistical information. Take notes—more than you can possibly use in your speech.

Put the notes on cards and start a new card for each new subject or source. Be sure to identify on the card the source of your information in case you want to refer to it later.

The advantage of writing notes on cards is that it is easy to discard unwanted material and to arrange and rearrange the remaining material in the best order for the preparation of your speech outline. In fact, if your notes are prepared well, your final arrangement of the cards will represent an outline.

For some topics, valuable information can be obtained from talking to other people. If you are speaking on "What Accountants Like Most About Their Jobs," for example, talk to as many accountants as you can. Again, take notes on your findings, and make use of this information in preparing your speech. First-hand information always adds interest to any presentation.

OUTLINING AND ORGANIZING THE SPEECH

After selecting the topic and gathering and organizing the data, the speaker is ready to begin outlining the speech. The following is a guide to preparing an outline:

1. Speech Title— Time Allotted—
2. Purpose of Speech—
3. Introduction (arouse interest and give purpose)—
4. Body of Speech—Principal ideas to support purpose
   a. Principal idea No. 1
      Supporting information and material
   b. Principal idea No. 2
      Supporting information and material
   c. Principal idea No. 3
      Supporting information and material
5. Conclusion
   a. Summary of principal ideas
   b. Plea for action (if applicable)

The Introduction

The introductory remarks should be brief and should arouse the interest of the audience in the speaker and in the subject. Various methods of introducing the talk may be used; for example:

1. A direct statement of the subject and of the importance of that subject to each member of the audience.

   The title I have selected for my talk to you is "Automation and You—Assistant or Replacement?" Each of you has a stake in automation because your future in your chosen field may depend upon how well you understand this important development.

2. An indirect opening that is of vital interest to the audience, with a statement connecting the subject with this interest.

   Tomorrow your job as accountant may be abolished or changed so drastically that you won't recognize it. Why? Because so many of the things that you are now doing by hand can be done much more efficiently by machine.

3. A striking example or comparison that leads up to the purpose or subject of the speech.

   One of every three businesses today makes some use of data processing equipment, whether on its own premises or through some type of service operation.

4. A strong quotation relating to the subject.

   "There is nothing in this world constant but inconstancy." So said Swift many years ago. This statement has more meaning today than ever before . . . .

5. Important statistics related to the subject.

   In the past three months in this city, more than three hundred office workers were replaced by machines.

6. A brief anecdote.

   Last week my secretary handed me a clipping from a local newspaper. It was about experiments that are now being made with a "machine stenographer." The manufacturers hope to perfect it so that the dictator merely dictates into the machine, and the letter comes out all transcribed, ready for mailing. My secretary never once thought about being replaced by such a machine but was worried only about whether it could straighten out the grammar and punctuation that I insist on mangling!

The Body of the Speech

Once audience interest is aroused, you are ready to provide the principal ideas that will support the purpose you have established for your speech. How many ideas you will present and develop will depend wholly upon the amount of time you have been allotted for the speech. It is better to develop each idea fully enough to be convincing than to present many ideas that are weakly developed and therefore not fully accepted or understood by the audience.

How is an idea communicated? First, it must be stated in a brief but clear and interesting way. Then the idea should be developed by explanation and illustration. Finally, the idea should be summarized.

Among the techniques available to the speaker for developing ideas are those in the following list. Which techniques the speaker selects will depend upon the nature of the data to be presented.

Giving examples.
Making comparisons.
Quoting statistics.
Quoting testimony of a recognized authority.
Repeating the idea in different words.
Defining terms used in stating the idea.
Using descriptive language that makes the listener "see" the situation.
Using narration to relate a story connected with the idea.
Using audio and/or visual aids.

Here is an example of how one idea used in a speech might be communicated, following the suggestions that have been presented. Suppose a speech was designed to try to persuade an audience of business executives that air travel is best for business purposes.

Principal Idea: Air travel saves your business time and money.

Development:
1. Tell the story of two business executives traveling from and to the same cities to conduct their business. One went by air and returned home the same day. The other went by train and had to remain overnight.
2. Show a chart of figures comparing the cost of travel between two cities by private automobile and by air transportation.
3. Give several examples of travel time between your city and another heavily visited city nearby, making comparisons in time by air, automobile, bus, and train.
4. Quote presidents of leading corporations who say they use air transportation exclusively for all business trips for themselves and for other executives of their companies. They find that both time and money are saved.

Audiovisual Materials Many speakers use such audiovisual materials as charts, slides, filmstrips, overhead projectors (transparencies), and motion pictures to enrich their presentations. Before deciding to use a visual aid, be certain that you have determined whether or not the material will be visible to the entire audience. The size of the audience and the type of room in which you make your presentation will be the principal determinants. Good visual aids can make your presentation more interesting by providing a change of pace. Talks dealing with figures can be made clearer and much more effective by using well-prepared charts and diagrams. If the situation is such, however, that mechanical means would prove ineffective, then consider the possibility of using duplicated handout materials.

Motion pictures should be previewed to determine whether they are appropriate. Above all, facilities and equipment should be checked prior to the presentation so that there will be no delays after the talk has started.

The Conclusion

The conclusion of a speech should be brief and to the point. A summary of the major points made in the speech and a plea for action, if applicable, are all that is needed. The summary may repeat key words or expressions already used or may restate the principal ideas in different words. Sometimes an example, a comparison, or an effective quotation serves as an appropriate summary. In any case, the final statement should tell the listeners very specifically what they should do, believe, or understand as a result of the presentation.

PRACTICING THE SPEECH

The inexperienced speaker should write out the entire speech from the outline developed, *not* for the purpose of reading the speech but for refining expressions, improving the choice of words, and timing the presentation. By recording this preliminary speech and then playing it back, the speaker can determine how the words will sound to the audience. Appropriate changes can then be made.

After you have refined the speech, have read it through several times, and have timed the reading, you should prepare an outline on index cards. This outline should include phrases, quotations, and statistics. If possible, it should be prepared in large, clear handwriting or in jumbo typewriter type so that you can refer to the notes casually from a distance of two or three feet. Supplementary materials should be keyed into the outline in some way (underlined, solid capitals, or color) that will make them stand out.

Using the final outline, you should practice delivering your speech and should try to anticipate the conditions of the actual talk. A beginning speaker often finds the following practice suggestions helpful. Stand erect—before a mirror if possible—and imagine your audience before you. Watch your posture, facial expressions, and gestures as you deliver the speech. If you can practice before an audience of family or friends who will be sympathetic but frank in their analysis, so much the better. If you can record your presentation, you will be able to hear how clearly you speak and to judge the overall effectiveness of your presentation.

DELIVERING YOUR SPEECH

Though *what* you say in your speech is extremely important, *how* you say it is equally important. The best talk ever written can put an audience to sleep if it is poorly delivered. On the other hand, an average speech can bring an audience to its feet if the speaker is poised, dynamic, and persuasive. To deliver a speech effectively, you must possess the following important characteristics: confidence in your ability to deliver an effective message, a pleasing personal appearance, and good stage presence and delivery.

CONFIDENCE

"I don't have a knack for public speaking." "Speakers are born, not made." "I'll make a fool of myself if I try to give a speech." "I'll get stage fright and forget everything I'm supposed to say." These are typical reactions of a novice speaker. If you believe any of these statements, then you, like so many other people, underestimate yourself. You're better than you think!

When you are talking to an audience, pretend that you are carrying on a face-to-face conversation with just one person. Remember that the audience is just as eager for you to perform well as you are to do so. Don't be upset if you are nervous—even experienced speakers and actors are! Feeling nervous is a result of anxiety about doing a good job, and most authorities feel that a little stage fright provides needed tension. However, try not to show the audience any signs of your nervousness.

One way to develop confidence is to make sure that the conditions under which you are going to speak are as favorable as you can make them. Try to arrive fifteen or twenty minutes before you are scheduled to speak. If you speak best standing behind a lectern—and most people do—ask your host to provide one. Even an improvised lectern, such as a cardboard box covered with a cloth and set on a table, is better than no lectern at all. If possible, get the feel beforehand of the space you are going to occupy when you do address the group. Know in advance how you will approach the podium. If you think your approach will be awkward for you or for others on the stage or distracting to the audience, ask your host to change the arrangement. Check the ventilation, the lighting, the public-address system, and the seating arrangement. In short, make all the advance preparations you can to assure a feeling of familiarity with your surroundings. This is another big step in building confidence.

APPEARANCE

One of the most important elements that will contribute to your confidence as a speaker is your appearance. If you can eliminate any concern about how you look to the audience, then you can concentrate on other aspects of your presentation. In preparing for your speech, spend a little extra time on personal grooming and the selection of clothing to assure yourself that your appearance will be as good as it can be. Clothing should be freshly cleaned and pressed, and shoes should be polished and in good repair.

Special advice to women speakers:

> Choose jewelry that is tasteful and that will not be distracting. Above all avoid jewelry that makes a distracting jangling noise when you move your hands and arms.
>
> Choose makeup suitable to your appearance, and apply it skillfully.
>
> Although a touch of bright color is appropriate—even desirable—be careful not to overwhelm your audience with bizarre color combinations or dazzling prints or stripes. You want the audience's attention on what you are saying—not on what you are wearing.

Special advice to men speakers:

> Wear a dress shirt and appropriate tie. Make certain that the style and color are currently acceptable.
>
> At least one button of the suit coat should be fastened, whether or not a vest is worn.
>
> Because in most cases the speaker is seated before the audience while waiting to be introduced, wear long socks, even if you do not ordinarily wear them, so that at no time are bare shins visible.
>
> Don't be too conservative with the necktie you choose—some experts recommend bright flecks of color. Make sure that your socks harmonize with your suit.

Knowing that you are immaculately and tastefully groomed builds confidence in yourself and establishes the audience's confidence in you.

GOOD STAGE PRESENCE AND DELIVERY

Speak Out

You have a responsibility to make sure that you are heard by each person in the audience. Any person who can't hear will become disinterested, bored, and annoyed. If possible, before you deliver a speech, check the volume of your voice in the room where you will speak.

Keep your chin up when speaking so that your words will be directed out to the audience rather than down to the floor. Vary the pitch of your voice so that the audience is not lulled to sleep by a monotone. When you want to emphasize a point, raise your voice; when you wish to stir emotions, drop your voice so that it is barely audible to the audience. Either extreme of tone, of course, will lose its desired effect if prolonged.

Be Poised

If you have stage fright, take a deep breath before you begin to speak; this will relax your vocal cords. Stand with your weight distributed evenly on both feet, and don't shift from one foot to the other excessively. Don't stand too stiffly or too leisurely—appear alert but at ease. If your listeners think that *you* are comfortable, then they are more likely to be comfortable.

Be Aware of the Audience

To be an effective speaker, you must be aware of your audience at all times, not only in selecting and preparing your topic but also in giving your speech. Audiences respond favorably only to speakers who talk directly to them and who smile occasionally. The speaker who looks at the ceiling, at notes, or into space quickly loses rapport with the audience.

As you speak, look slowly back and forth over the entire audience, and pause here and there to "take in" a particular segment of the crowd. Smile frequently. Train yourself to watch the audience carefully and to be sensitive to its changing moods. If, as you are talking, you see blank or disinterested expressions on the faces of your listeners, you will know that your talk is dragging and that the audience has tuned you out. This situation may call for an amusing story, a personal anecdote, or merely a change in the pitch of your voice. If you are using visual aids, you might direct the audience's attention to a chart or other illustration when the talk seems to pall.

If your audience seems tired because the hour is late or too many speakers have preceded you, be quick to sense its boredom. If you aren't sure you can reawaken its interest with a sparkling performance, cut your talk to the bare essentials. Usually it is better to omit a portion of your speech than to run the risk of boring an already weary audience. The audience will be grateful to you.

Avoid Objectionable Mannerisms

A good speaker avoids objectionable mannerisms. When you talk, for example, do you toy with an object such as a paper clip, rubber band, or watch? Do you clear your throat, wet your lips, or remove your eyeglasses frequently? Do you punctuate your remarks frequently with an "uh," "ya know," or "anda"? Do you have pet expressions or slang that you overuse? If you are not aware that you have any such mannerisms, ask some of your friends to listen to a rehearsal and to criticize. A speaker who has even one annoying habit cannot give a completely successful talk, for mannerisms distract an audience.

Don't Read or Recite From Memory

Never memorize or read your speech to the audience. Only a gifted actor or actress can make a memorized speech sound unmemorized, and nothing is more boring to an audience than a singsong recitation. In addition, if you memorize your speech, you may become so flustered when you forget a line that you will find it difficult to continue. A memorized speech often does not follow a logical order because a speaker has omitted something important or has mixed up the parts.

Reading a speech so that the ideas sound convincing is also difficult. If you try to read your speech, you will lose eye contact with your audience every time you refer to your notes.

Instead of reciting or reading your speech, become sufficiently familiar with your material so that all you need is a brief outline with key words and phrases to make your speech flow in logical sequence. Use a conversational tone. Imagine that you are conversing with your audience, not giving an oration. Your voice should reflect the warm, easy tone that you would use if you were talking to a group of very good friends.

Use Notes

Most speakers—even the most experienced—rely on notes to guide them in their presentations. There is nothing wrong with using notes. It is a greater crime for a speaker to dispense with notes and to give a rambling, disorganized speech than to use notes and to present an organized speech. Even if the notes are not actually used, having them on hand gives you confidence because you know you have something to fall back on if you should have a temporary lapse of memory.

Look at your notes only when absolutely necessary, and return your attention quickly to your audience after each glance at your notes. Keep your notes out of sight as much as possible while you are giving your talk, and turn the pages or cards as inconspicuously as you can. An audience is quickly discouraged by a large, slowly dwindling stack of notes.

Plan Distribution of Material

Often the speaker will have duplicated material to distribute to the audience. As a general rule, such material should not be distributed at the beginning of a speech. If it is, the audience will be too busy examining the "giveaway" to pay attention to the speaker. The important points of a speech should be made before any material is distributed to the audience.

Use Stories and Anecdotes Discreetly

Nearly every speech of any length is brightened considerably by touches of humor and by human-interest narratives. Of course, such stories should not dominate the speech. Observe the following rules in using humor and human-interest stories:

Make Sure They Are Relevant Use stories and jokes that add interest to the subject or illustrate a particular point.

Make Sure They Have a Punch Line The story should have a point. Before telling a joke to an audience, test it on friends. Many stories and jokes fall flat because they are too subtle for a mass audience, because they are not well told, or because they have weak punch lines.

Make Sure They Are in Good Taste Make sure that stories or jokes do not offend or embarrass the audience. Avoid risqué stories or jokes that make fun of physical handicaps, religious convictions, or racial or religious groups.

Make Sure They Are Short A story or joke that lasts more than a few minutes is likely to pall. Only the most skillful storyteller can get by with longer accounts. Rehearse stories carefully before delivery, and time them to make sure that they are not too long.

INTRODUCING A SPEAKER

One of the most important speaking assignments is introducing a speaker. A good introduction sets the stage for the main address. If the introducer does an outstanding job, the main speaker's task is greatly simplified. In introducing a speaker, observe the following points.

Make the Introduction Brief

The audience has come to hear the speaker, not the person who is introducing the speaker. Therefore, keep the introduction short—not more than two or three minutes in length.

Set the Stage for the Speaker

Do some research on the speaker. Find out from the speaker's friends, associates, or secretary some personal traits or achievements that do not appear in the usual sources. A human-interest story about the speaker's hobby, family, or generosity will warm the audience. Although you should have complete details about the speaker's experience, education, and attainments, you do not need to use them all. An audience is quickly bored, and sometimes a speaker is embarrassed, by a straight biographical presentation, no matter how impressive the speaker's background is. Only the most significant dates, positions, and accomplishments should be given. You need only to convince the audience that the speaker is qualified to speak on the topic assigned, is worth knowing, and has something important to say.

Avoid Trite Openings

When introducing a speaker, avoid such trite expressions as "The speaker for the evening needs no introduction," "I give you Mr. Gordon Brandt," or "Without further ado, I present Mrs. Patricia Anderson."

Keep Your Eyes on the Audience

Don't face the speaker you are introducing—face the audience. Then wait until the speaker is at the lectern before seating yourself.

Save the Name Until Last

Many successful toastmasters recommend not mentioning the speaker's name until the very end of the introduction. During the introduction refer only to "our speaker." Then at the end of the introduction, say something like this: "It is my pleasure to present Mr. David Randolph."

CLOSING REMARKS

At the end of the main speaker's remarks, someone on the platform or at the speaker's table has the responsibility for closing the meeting. If the speech was a particularly good one, you may say, "Thank you, Mr. Carlson, for your most enlightening and inspiring message. We are indeed grateful to you. Ladies and gentlemen, the meeting is adjourned." If, however, the speech has been average or even disappointing, as indicated by the reaction of the audience, you may close by merely saying, "Thank you, Mrs. Jordan, for giving us your ideas on new horizons in office procedures. Ladies and gentlemen, thank you and good night."

In any event, never prolong the closing remarks. If the speech was good, there is nothing you may say that will add to its effectiveness. If it was poor, the audience is usually tired and wants to be dismissed.

Communication Projects

PRACTICAL APPLICATION

A List three topics on which you feel qualified to speak. For each topic, give two reasons you feel qualified to speak on this topic. Indicate one audiovisual aid that you might use in presenting each topic before a group. For each topic, suggest one attention-getting title for a twenty-minute speech.

B Select one of the topics you listed in Practical Application A for a five- or six-minute presentation before the class. Prepare an outline for this speech, and follow the format suggested on page 468.

C After your outline has been approved by the instructor, write out your speech in full. Then read, refine, and time the speech. Finally, following the suggestions made in the text, make an outline of the speech on no more than four 5- by 3-inch index cards.

D Suggest two ways that a beginning public speaker can overcome the common problems enumerated below:

1. Excessive verbalizing (using "uh," "ya know," "anda," and so on).
2. Nervousness.

3. Annoying mannerisms, like scratching your head or toying with your speech notes.
4. Reading all or most of the speech.

E As president of your business fraternity or sorority, you have been asked to serve as master of ceremonies at your school's Graduation Banquet. The after-dinner speaker will be the mayor of your city. Compose a unique, tailor-made message of introduction for the mayor from information you have gathered from various sources. Supply any additional details about the speaker that you feel will add interest to the introduction.

F Indicate two ways you might close the meeting referred to in Practical Application E.

G From the list of job classifications below, select one that you believe is of special interest to your class. Research this topic and make an outline for a five-minute talk. Outline your talk and be prepared to present it to your class.

bookkeeper or accountant
stenographer or secretary
receptionist
administrative assistant
word processor
retail salesclerk
sales representative
punch-card tabulating machine operator
computer operator

EDITING PRACTICE

The Editorial Supervisor Edit and rewrite the following paragraph.

We are indeed happy to add your name to the list of Lionel distributors. Your's will be a large territory for you are our only outlet in the buckeye state. We are sending the booklet requested by you, "Lionel Cleanser —101 Home Use"; and we shall of course be glad to amplify any of the topics presented therein. Good luck to you.

CASE PROBLEM

Playing Fair Doreen, a co-worker and friend, confides to you, "I don't think Mrs. Fields likes me. I was late twice this week and only fifteen minutes each time, but she warned me that if I'm late just one more time, she will deduct an hour's wages from my salary check." Your experience with Mrs. Fields (who is also your supervisor) has led you to believe that she has always been fair to the employees and that she was merely carrying out her responsibility in seeing that employees report to work on time. In discussing the matter with your friend, however, you don't want to appear to be an "apple polisher."

1. Do you think Mrs. Fields played fair with your co-worker?
2. What would you say to Doreen?

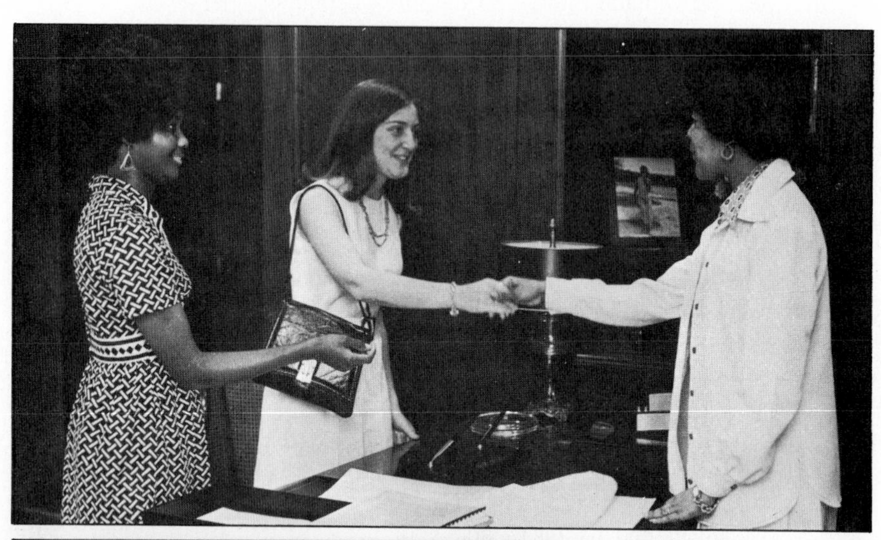

CHAPTER 10

OBTAINING A JOB

55 Writing to Get the Job

The writing, reading, listening, and speaking skills you mastered in the first nine chapters of *College English and Communication* have prepared you to fulfill all the communication requirements a new job may demand of you. These are marketable skills; they are skills that employers look for in job applicants, skills that job applicants are sure to impress on prospective employers.

YOUR FIRST OPPORTUNITY

As a job applicant, your first opportunity to inform a prospective employer of your skills comes when you write your letter of application. You write a letter of application when you are applying "blind" for a position, when you are answering a newspaper ad, when you have been recommended by someone for a position, when the employer requests a letter of application.

Arouse the Employer's Interest

The letter of application is a sales message. Just as an effective sales letter stimulates the consumer's interest in a product or service, so the effective letter of application stimulates the employer's interest in the applicant and prepares the way for an interview. It is obviously a most important letter. But a prospective employer cannot judge your skills, your qualifications for a job, from the letter of application alone. Most applicants send with the letter of application a detailed résumé listing their work experience, educational background, and references.

Together, the letter of application and the résumé give the employer a valid picture of your job potential. Together, they are powerful opportunity-makers. This section will show you how to prepare an effective letter of application and résumé. Mastering these principles of *writing to get the job* will pay off in many ways—including financial!

Submit Well-Prepared Samples

When you write to apply for a job, you are giving the prospective employer a preview of the product you are selling—your work skills. You will, therefore, take extra care in preparing the letter and the résumé. Both should be neatly typewritten on a good grade of white bond paper, 8½ by 11 inches. (Never use company letterhead stationery or hotel stationery!) Leave ample margins on all sides. Before mailing the letter, double-check your spelling, grammar, and punctuation. Be prepared to rewrite your letter or résumé several times to ensure that it is as nearly perfect as you can make it.

Because the résumé should be prepared before the letter of application is written, it will be discussed first.

THE RÉSUMÉ

A résumé is a brief account of a job applicant's background and qualifications. It summarizes specific facts and specific information in a distinctive format so that a prospective employer may find in one source all the information needed to decide whether an applicant is worth interviewing. During the interview, the résumé may serve as an agenda of topics to be discussed.

When the résumé accompanies the application letter, most of the details regarding the applicant need not appear in the letter itself. The letter then serves the functions of selling the applicant's job qualifications and of obtaining a personal interview. The résumé, on the other hand, saves time for the reader by presenting the facts in summary form. In a well-prepared résumé, the applicant emphasizes those qualifications that best meet the requirements of the specific job sought.

To type an original copy of a résumé for each letter of application may not be practical. You may plan to mail dozens of letters of application; moreover, some personnel departments may request more than one copy of your résumé so they can distribute them to key people in their companies. Duplicating résumés, therefore, is very often practical. However, since your résumé reflects you, it must always look professional. Never submit a carbon copy of your résumé, and never use a duplicating method that produces poor-quality copies. You may have résumés printed (by the "offset" process) on good-quality bond paper for less than you might think. Consult your telephone directory for a small-job printer and inquire about the cost.

Format

Although one résumé may vary from another in organization and layout, most are commonly divided into these sections: (1) work experience, (2) education, (3) personal information, and (4) references. Each section should be arranged to show clearly the qualifications of the applicant. The typing should be clean and even, the margins should be well balanced and uncrowded, and the headings should stand out. In choosing a format, try to select one that best fits the information you will include. In doing so, keep in mind these points:

1. State the facts; leave interpretation of these facts to the reader.
2. Be sure the facts are complete. For example, say *when* you were graduated and from *where*; *when* you resigned from a position and *why*.
3. Be neat and orderly; there should be no typographical errors, smudges, or other evidence of sloppy work. Within each section of your résumé, list the most recent information first.
4. Use brief phrases rather than complete sentences. For example, say "Took legal dictation" rather than "I took legal dictation each day from Mr. Mahoney, an attorney."
5. Limit the résumé to one page if possible. By doing so you will be forced to organize well and to list only important details.

An effective résumé is illustrated below. In the illustration, note the prominence of the name, address, and telephone number of the applicant.

Work Experience

Although the most important job qualification for a new graduate is educational preparation, do not underestimate the value of any kind of work experience, part-time or full-time. Almost everyone has held some type of job during vacations or on a part-time basis after school. Such jobs as paper carrier, soda jerk, filling-station attendant, filing clerk, gardener, or even

Elizabeth Testa
1420 Bellewood Drive
Jackson, Michigan 49202
Telephone (193) 826-2198

POSITION APPLIED FOR — Secretary, with opportunity for advancement to Executive Secretary or Administrative Assistant.

EXPERIENCE

July, 1975, to Present — Blakely Products Company, 8740 Westwood Street, Jackson, Michigan--Secretary

Duties: General secretarial duties in marketing department, including taking and transcribing dictation; filing; operating adding, duplicating, and other office machines.

Reason for leaving: Moving to Ames, Iowa

Starting salary: $125 Present salary: $135

Summer, 1974 — Martin's Department Store, 1240 State Street, Jackson, Michigan--Stenographer

Duties: General stenographic duties

Salary: $100

EDUCATION — Jackson College, Jackson, Michigan--1973-1975. Awarded Associate in Secretarial Science degree.

Jackson High School, Jackson, Michigan--1969-1973. Graduated with honors upon completion of the college preparatory curriculum.

PERSONAL — Date of birth: March 10, 1955

REFERENCES

Mr. James L. Blakely
Director of Marketing
Blakely Products Company
8740 Westwood Street
Jackson, Michigan

Mrs. Alice M. Bloomquist
Office Manager
Martin's Department Store
1240 State Street
Jackson, Michigan 49201

Prof. Harold Justin
Secretarial Science Department
Jackson College
Jackson, Michigan

baby-sitter are experiences that speak well for the young man or woman seeking a job. Such experiences should be reported; they demonstrate that the applicant is industrious, has initiative, and is dependable. If you worked to pay for your education, state this fact.

In organizing the work-experience section of your résumé, list the latest work experience first; that is, list work experience in reverse chronological order. For each job give inclusive dates, as well as the reason for leaving. For example, an applicant might write "Wesco Drugstore, 1972–1974, Assistant Manager; left for advancement." On the other hand, a lack of experience in the area of work for which you are applying should not be emphasized on the résumé. Rather, it might be better to take the positive approach and say, "While attending school, I had a number of part-time jobs, such as baby-sitting and soda-fountain clerking, to help earn my tuition." When you write your letter of application, you can then show how your knowledge *of* the job for which you are applying will more than compensate for your lack of experience *on* the job.

Education

Your educational background will count very heavily in job hunting. Make the most of your presentation by including the following facts. First, list any colleges you have attended and the dates of attendance. List any degrees or diplomas you have obtained. Detail here information such as the following:

> Your major course of study (accounting, secretarial administration, advertising).
>
> Special subjects you have had that will enhance your value as an employee. For example, a course in office management or business communication will be of interest to the prospective employer even though you are applying for a job in the accounting department. Be specific about subject titles. "Accounting IV" tells the employer nothing; "Corporation Accounting" is more specific.

Second, name the high school from which you were graduated and the date of graduation. If you took subjects that relate to your qualifications for the position, list them.

Stress leadership qualifications, extracurricular activities, and special honors. Business managers want employees with a wide range of interests; they want people with social poise and with leadership potential. Therefore, in listing both hobbies and interests, show that you have varied interests and that you have developed social graces and leadership qualities through extracurricular activities.

Personal Information

Under the personal information section of the résumé, give your date of birth. If you wish, you may also include your height, weight, state of health, and other personal facts; however, employers may not legally request information about your race and religion.

References

Three to five names of references are recommended; at least one of these should be a character reference, such as a minister or lawyer. If you have had little or no job experience, you might include as references instructors who know your scholastic ability and preparation. If you have had job experiences, however, list one or two former employers who know you and your work. Always include the job title of each person you list. For instance, you might write "Mr. J. J. Walsh, Office Manager"; "Dr. I. J. Kingston, Professor of Marketing"; or, if you are listing a character reference, "Mrs. Maybelle A. Di Falla, personal friend." Give the complete address of each person, as shown on the sample résumé on page 482.

Of course, you should always obtain permission—either in person, by telephone, or by letter—from each individual whose name you use as a reference. Answering inquiries for prospective employers is a time-consuming task, and the people who agree to this task do so because they have confidence in you, like you, and want you to succeed. In return, you owe them the courtesy of keeping them informed about your progress in getting a job.

THE LETTER OF APPLICATION

After you have completed your résumé and you can see clearly how your qualifications fit the job you seek, you are then in a good position to organize your application letter. The letter of application is your sales message. Although the résumé that accompanies the letter helps the employer determine whether or not you have the education and skills required for the job, the application letter presents a better picture of you as a person. In other words, the résumé is factual and rather formal; the application letter is a sales message and can be personalized. Study the letter on page 485. The following guidelines should help you in writing a letter of application.

Get to the Point Immediately

The first paragraph of the application letter should state the following:

Your intent to apply for the position.

The position for which you are applying.

The source from which you learned about the vacancy (if it is not a "blind" application).

There is no one "best" opening for a letter of application. The following opening sentences are suggestions that have been used successfully.

For Newspaper Ads

Please consider me an applicant for the position of credit correspondent, as advertised in today's *Tribune*.

I am applying for the cost accounting clerk position that was advertised in the *Tulsa World* on Sunday, October 5.

322 North Kline Street
Buffalo, New York 14209
May 27, 19--

Mr. David Loo, Personnel Manager
Endicott Manufacturing Corporation
416 East Euclid Avenue
Buffalo, New York 14220

Dear Mr. Jackson:

I would like to apply for the position of administrative assistant to the editor of your company magazine, Endicott Quotes. This vacancy was called to my attention by Professor H. C. Callans of Tremont College. Professor Callans believes that my qualifications are suitable for this position.

My college training, I think, provides an excellent foundation for the position. I have always been interested in writing, and you will see from my resume that I have concentrated heavily on English and journalism. I have held editorial positions in both high school and college. During my sophomore year I studied shorthand and typewriting; I have continued to use these skills in my college work. A summary of my qualifications is enclosed.

As an administrative assistant to your editor, I would welcome the opportunity to assist in an editorial capacity as well as to use my secretarial skills. I have had experience in proofreading and in layout. My secretarial skills are well above average, and I find it easy to work with others. Although I certainly don't know all the answers, you will find me eager to learn. I am happiest when I am busy!

If you wish to telephone me about an interview, you can reach me at Tremont College (555-8000, Extension 338) any weekday. My last class is over at 3 p.m., and I could arrange to come to your office after that time.

Sincerely yours,

Diana P. Harley

Diana P. Harley

Enclosure

The position of administrative assistant to the sales manager, which you advertised in yesterday's *Sacramento Bee,* is one for which I feel well qualified. Please consider me an applicant.

I am interested in the position of systems analyst listed in the Help Wanted section of last night's *Kansas City Star.* I should like to apply for that position.

For Referrals

A mutual friend, Mr. Gerald P. Gates, has suggested that I write you concerning a position as secretary in your company.

Your company has been recommended to me by Mrs. Flora Addington, placement director of Phillips College, as one with exceptional opportunities for a person interested in advertising. I should like to inquire about a possible opening in the art department.

Attorney Frieda E. Larsen, a friend of my family, has told me of an opening for an assistant editor on your company magazine. May I be considered an applicant? (In this opening, it is assumed that the employer is acquainted with Ms. Larsen.)

For "Blind" Applications

I believe my qualifications for a position as adjuster will interest you. May I tell you what they are?

I have chosen your company's personnel department as one in which I would like to work. Perhaps you will be interested in my skills and abilities.

Here are five reasons why I think you will be interested in interviewing me for the position of traffic supervisor in your company.

Tell Why You Should Be Considered

The second paragraph of your letter should convince the employer that you are a desirable candidate for the position referred to in the first paragraph. For example:

Undoubtedly, Mr. Johnston, you want a secretary who can take dictation and transcribe rapidly and accurately, a secretary who has a thorough grasp of secretarial procedures—filing, telephone duties, letter writing, and mail routines. My training at Bryant College (detailed on the enclosed résumé) has prepared me to handle all aspects of secretarial work competently and confidently. You will be proud to sign the letters I place on your desk.

Here is another example of a second paragraph in which you demonstrate your qualifications.

A summary of my qualifications is enclosed. As you will see, my training at Lockyear's Business School was very comprehensive. Not only did I complete all the accounting courses offered by the college, but I also studied personnel management, economics, business psychology, office supervision and management, typewriting, and statistics. In all my courses, I consistently ranked in the upper 25 percent of the class.

Of course, the nature of the second paragraph will depend on what you have to sell. If your business experience is limited and unlikely to impress the employer, you will have to emphasize your educational background. In such a case, you might follow the above paragraph with a statement such as this:

Of particular interest to me in the accounting course was machine accounting. In this class we learned the applications of accounting theory to automated procedures and equipment. I am especially eager to work in a large organization, such as yours, where EDP is used on a wide scale.

Here is another example of capitalizing on achievements in school:

You will notice from my résumé that English and business communication were among my favorite subjects. In addition, I was a member of the debating team, was on the journalism staff, and was president of our speech club. You will find my written and oral communication skills well above average.

The following applicant admits lack of business experience; however, this is compensated for by the applicant's interest and enthusiasm.

> I must confess the lack of first-hand experience as a bank teller, Mr. Green. Compensating for this, however, has been my interest in your bank and in the work your tellers do. Several times in the past year, I have talked with Jim Yaeger, who started his teller training with you a year ago, about the interesting duties he performs. These discussions make me even more certain that banking is the kind of work I want to do. I am convinced that within a short period of time, I can learn to perform effectively as one of your tellers.

If you have had business experience that is related to the position for which you are applying, make the most of it.

> I am particularly interested in machine accounting in which automated equipment and procedures are employed. Last summer I was a temporary employee in the systems department of Jones-McComb Corporation, where I had an opportunity to become acquainted with EDP techniques. This experience was valuable, and I have decided to do further study in the field in evening school after I have obtained a position.

Show Willingness to Work and Learn

The employer who hires you is taking a risk—a risk that you may not be fitted for the position. One of the best assurances you can give that you are a safe risk is your willingness to learn and your genuine interest in the job. For example:

> Obviously, there will be many routines and procedures that will be new to me. You will find me eager to learn and to improve.
>
> I shall bring to the job a willingness to work and an eagerness to improve. Let me prove that statement to you.
>
> I am not afraid of hard work; in fact, I enjoy it.
>
> I have no illusions about my lack of experience; yet I am quick to learn and I enjoy learning.
>
> I pride myself on my punctuality, accuracy, and dependability.
>
> I learn fast and I remember what I learn.

Make It Easy for the Employer to Ask You for an Interview

The last paragraph of your letter of application should be the action-getting paragraph—aimed at obtaining an invitation for an interview. Make it easy for the employer to contact you.

> I can come to your office for an interview between 9 a.m. and 5 p.m. on any weekday. My telephone number is 555-7613. If you would prefer to write, please use the address at the top of this letter.

Some job-hunters are more direct; they prefer to follow up on the letter rather than wait for the employer. For example:

> I can come to your office for an interview between 9 a.m. and 5 p.m. any weekday. After you have had a chance to review my qualifications, I shall call your secretary for an appointment.

Some successful applicants enclose a postage-paid return card containing information such as the following:

Dear Miss (Applicant's Name):

Please come to my office on ____________________
(Date)

at ____________________ for an interview.
(Time)

Very truly yours,

(Interviewer's Name)

If a postal card is enclosed, you might include the following statement in your letter.

> Just complete the enclosed postal card and ask your secretary to drop it in the mail. I am available at any time that is convenient for you. If you would prefer to telephone, my number is 555-2518.

Send the application letter in an envelope of the same good-quality bond paper as that on which the letter is written. Here again, the rules for neatness, good style, and placement apply. Choose a plain (unprinted) white business envelope such as a No. 10 (4⅛ by 9½ inches). Include your return address in the upper left corner of the front of the envelope.

OTHER EMPLOYMENT LETTERS

Requesting Permission to Use Someone's Name as Reference

As mentioned earlier, it is common courtesy to request permission to use someone's name as a reference. Although permission may be requested by telephone or in person, it is often requested in writing.

> Dear Reverend Roberts:
>
> As you may know, I was recently graduated from the Roanoke College of Business, and I am now making application at several firms in the Richmond area for a position as a management trainee. May I list your name as a reference on my application forms? I should be most grateful for this privilege.
>
> You may jot your answer at the bottom of this letter, if you wish. I am enclosing an envelope for your reply. Thank you.
>
> Sincerely,

Thanking Those Who Helped You

After you accept a job, make sure to thank personally each one who helped you—and say it in writing.

Dear Reverend Roberts:

You'll be pleased, I am sure, to learn that I have accepted a position as management trainee with the A. S. Harrison Company in Richmond. The job is exactly what I wanted. It gives me an opportunity to learn retail-store management from the ground up; some day, perhaps, I will be a manager of a branch store for the company. At least, this is my ambition.

Thank you very much for allowing me to use your name as a reference. I know that your recommendation was a help in my obtaining the job.

Sincerely,

Letters Following Up the Interview

After you have been interviewed, it is good strategy (as well as courtesy) to write to the interviewer, especially if you have reason to expect that a decision will not be made in a short time. Your thank-you letter gives you another opportunity to do a selling job. The letter might follow this form:

Mr. Jack DeLorenzo
Personnel Director
Worldwide Sporting Goods Corporation
San Francisco, California 94112

Dear Mr. DeLorenzo:

I enjoyed meeting you and talking with you on Tuesday. Certainly, I came away with a much clearer picture of the work of a mail-room supervisor in the Corporation. The work sounds very exciting and challenging, and I am more convinced than ever that it is something I would like to do.

Thank you for your time and the many courtesies you showed me. I was especially glad to meet Mrs. Hamm; please convey my best wishes to her.

Cordially yours,

Accepting the Position

If you have been notified that you have been chosen for a position, it is wise to accept in writing, especially if the firm is out of town or if your reporting date is a week or two away. You might use the style illustrated in the following letter.

Dear Ms. Stein:

I am pleased to accept the position as your secretary. I know that I shall enjoy working with you in the field of public relations and communications. The salary of $97.50 a week, plus benefits, is quite satisfactory to me.

As you have asked, I shall report to your office on Monday, March 9, at 8:45 a.m.

Sincerely yours,

Declining a Position

Occasionally it is necessary to decline a job after it has been accepted. Naturally, you need solid, justifiable reasons for doing so. In such an event, give the reasons for your action. The following example illustrates a letter giving an acceptable reason for declining a job.

> Dear Mr. Aaron:
>
> This morning I received some distressing news. My mother, with whom I have been living and who depends on me to look after her, was told by her doctor that she would have to move from this area to a milder climate for reasons of health. She has now completed arrangements to leave Hartford at the end of this month, and I must accompany her.
>
> I am sorry that I shall have to decline the position that you offered to me. It was a wonderful opportunity, and I shall always be grateful to you for your kindness. Thank you.
>
> Sincerely yours,

Communication Projects

PRACTICAL APPLICATION

A Scan the "Help Wanted" ads of your local Sunday newspaper for a position similar to the one you aspire to upon graduation. Write a letter of application answering the ad and attach a résumé you have prepared specifically for this job.

B Jim Amunds, a friend, tells you of an opening in the printing company where he works—Fotographics. The firm is expanding into the production of high school yearbooks. Several new jobs will be open, including one that involves corresponding with various high schools about the scheduling of the company's photographers at their schools, the dates for getting proofs out and back, and other arrangements. The job seems to have good potential for advancement, and the company seems to be going places. The job especially appeals to you because you worked on your own school annual and had responsibility for the photography and helped with the page makeup. Write a "blind" letter (use Jim's name if you wish), applying for the job. Attach a résumé that you have slanted especially for this position.

C Write a letter to one of the people listed on the résumé you prepared for Practical Application B to ask permission to use his or her name as a reference.

D Assume that you have accepted the position for which you applied in A or B above. Write a letter to thank one of the people who served as a reference.

E Two weeks ago today you accepted a position as management trainee in the transportation firm of Rapid Transit, Inc., Marlboro and Mayberry Streets, Memphis, Tennessee 38112. You are to begin work next week. Today, however, you were offered a comparable position with their chief competitor. This position has greater potential, a higher starting salary, and considerably better fringe benefits. You decide to accept the latter position. Write a letter to John H. King, Director of Training at Rapid Transit, declining the position that you originally accepted.

EDITING PRACTICE

Editors' Alert Here are more sentences on which you can sharpen your editing skills. Try to develop an all-seeing eye that doesn't miss a detail. If necessary, rewrite the sentences.

1. As of March 28, we have accredited your account in the amount of $62.95 as shown by the enclosed reciept.
2. According to the latest bulletin, the new technical manual that has been in progress for the passed 4 years will not make its debit until June.
3. We are reluctant to acknowledge that a price raise is necessary but we can no longer postphone the decision.
4. I have asked Henderson to develope the leads suggested in your memo, and will personally take on the matter of discussing the matter with key executives here.
5. Having done everything possible to expedite the schedule, the laying of the cornerstone can now be moved up to the first of the month, instead of being held on the 10th.

CASE PROBLEM

Office Grooming Richard Foster was quite concerned when Marcia Spivak, his secretary, arrived at the office with her hair in curlers and a scarf over her head. There has always been an unwritten rule that both men and women in his office dress in a manner acceptable for business.

1. What should Richard say to Marcia?
2. Should Richard send Marcia home as a disciplinary measure? Under what conditions?

56 The Employment Interview

Perhaps no other single occasion offers young men and women a better opportunity to use oral communication to advantage than the job interview. In an interview, every time you speak you are selling yourself. Your response to questions, your description of experiences and situations, your explanation of procedures and methods—all contribute to the interviewer's impression of you. Regardless of how skillful and knowledgeable you are as an applicant, how impressive your résumé, or how persuasive your letter of application, all may fall flat if you fail to sell yourself when you meet a prospective employer face-to-face. A job interview can be either a frightening or an enjoyable experience, depending largely upon the amount of advance preparation and planning you give to it.

PLANNING FOR THE INTERVIEW

Preparation for the interview begins long before it actually takes place. Before applying for a position, you must choose the type of work you want to do and train rigorously for it. Later you must choose the type of company for which you want to work, then compile a résumé, write a letter of application, and obtain an interview. Such long-range planning is necessary, of course. The following discussion will be helpful in preparing for a job interview.

Know What You Have to Offer

Good sales representatives know their products thoroughly—better than anyone else does. They have analyzed their products from every conceivable angle; they know their strengths and their weaknesses. They understand fully what features of their products are most likely to appeal to prospective buyers, and these are the features they emphasize in their sales presentations.

As a job applicant, you are a sales representative, and your product is yourself. Preparing a résumé gives you an opportunity to put down on paper what you have to sell—to see your strong points and compare them with those that your competitors for the position may have. The items emphasized on the résumé are those every employer is interested in—education, experience, and special interests and abilities. You should know these qualifications so well that you can communicate them orally without hesitation.

The first step in planning for the interview, therefore, is to anticipate questions that you may be asked about your education, experience, and personal qualities. Here are examples of some of these questions:

> What subjects did you concentrate on while attending college?
>
> Which of these subjects did you like best? Why?
>
> Tell me something about your course in __________ (personnel administration, business communications, office management, or other subjects).
>
> I see by your application that you worked at Blank's for two summers. What kind of work did you do? What did you like most about your job? What did you like least?
>
> What do you most enjoy doing outside of working hours—hobbies and other activities?
>
> Were you active in school organizations? Which ones?
>
> Do you consider your skills (a) about average? (b) above average? (c) below average?
>
> Do you like to write? Do you consider yourself strong in English?

Answers to such probing questions will tell the interviewer a great deal about you and about how well you would fit the position, how quickly you would adjust to the job and to the people around you, and what your potential is for growth. In preparing for a job interview, then, you might ask yourself this question: What would I want to know about me if I were the interviewer?

Plan How You Will Look

On no other occasion is it more important to look your best than at an employment interview. Plan ahead, therefore, to make the most of your appearance. Knowing that you look well will help to make you feel more at ease.

Wear clothes that are becoming and that are conservative. Make sure that they fit properly and comfortably. Do not wear anything in which you feel ill at ease—you should be able to concentrate completely on the interview itself without being distracted by such things as shoes that are tight, a hat that slips off your head, or a suit that is too small. When dressing for an interview, give special care to the items in the following checklist.

GUIDE TO GOOD GROOMING

✓ **Women**

- __ A tailored dress or suit, freshly cleaned and pressed (no frilly party dresses).
- __ A simple, stylish hat that coordinates with dress or suit (optional).
- __ Well-brushed or polished shoes that are in good repair and that match apparel—no flats or extreme styles.
- __ Gloves (optional, but if worn, clean).
- __ Hose.
- __ A simple purse that complements apparel.
- __ A fresh hairdo.
- __ Careful attention to nails, makeup, and general grooming. (The word *conservative* should dictate appearance.)
- __ A clean coat, free from lint.

✓ **Men**

- __ A conservatively cut suit, freshly cleaned and pressed (no sports jackets or extreme styles).
- __ A hat (optional).
- __ Freshly shined shoes in good repair. No flashy styles.
- __ A conservative tie that complements suit.
- __ Socks to match tie. (Long socks are preferred. If short socks are worn, be sure they are not at "half mast.")
- __ A clean, long-sleeve dress shirt. (Watch for frayed collar or cuffs.)
- __ A fresh shave and a recent haircut.
- __ Careful attention to nails and to general cleanliness.
- __ A clean coat, free from lint.

Your appearance will control the interviewer's first impression of you, and it is likely to be a lasting one. People who dress carelessly inevitably leave the impression that they are careless workers. Those whose style of dress is too casual may give the impression that they do not take business seriously or that they are not capable of exercising good judgment. Do not give the interviewer an opportunity to make a negative judgment about you.

If your interview is to take place in the early morning, plan to arise early enough to give yourself time to dress carefully. Always allow yourself extra time for reaching the place of interview. You can read or window-shop if you arrive too early, but you cannot erase the negative impression you will make if you are late.

Plan What You Will Say

Interviewers operate in different ways. Some will do most of the talking and will ask only a few questions about your education and experience. Others will draw you out as much as possible and say very little. Anticipate in advance such general statements or questions from the interviewer as these:

> Tell me about yourself. (This request will give you a chance to emphasize your most salable features. The interviewer doesn't want to know about your childhood but wants you to answer such questions as these: What do you do best? What do you like best?)
>
> Review your college work and your experience. (Here you will emphasize the college courses that will best implement your qualifications for this particular job. The same is true of your experience.)
>
> What do you think your strongest points are? your weakest?
>
> Tell me why you think you should be hired for this position.

Anticipate also some personal questions, such as:

> What kind of person do you think you are?
> Do you like to work?
> What do you enjoy doing in your leisure time?
> Do you read a great deal?
> Where do you live?
> What salary do you expect?
> Are you punctual in your appointments?
> Do you have financial obligations?

Although you should anticipate the questions you are likely to be asked, it's a good idea also to think of questions you would like to ask the interviewer. Not only will you receive information, but your asking questions will also show the interviewer that you have given careful thought to the position. Be prepared, therefore, to ask such questions as:

> What duties are required in this position?
> Does the company provide opportunities for further education?
> What are the opportunities for advancement?
> What type of insurance is available through the company?
> What about employee social and recreational facilities?

Anticipate the Salary Question

More often than not, the salary paid for a position—at least the general range—is known to the applicant before the interview. If the salary is not known, however, and the interviewer has not mentioned it, you should say, near the end of the interview, "I understand that the beginning salary for this position is $_______ a month. Is this correct?" (Base the figure you mention on knowledge, not whim. Find out from employment agencies or newspaper ads what the salary range is for the jobs you apply for—before you apply.)

Sometimes information about the salary is withheld, or the salary is listed as *open*. This means that the company has set a general salary range for the job, but the specific amount paid will depend upon the qualifications of the applicant.

If the interviewer asks you, "What salary do you expect?" be prepared to give an honest, straightforward answer. Find out in advance what similar jobs are paying; then say something like this: "I understand that similar jobs in this area range from $_______ to $_______ a month. I had expected to receive about $_______." (Mention a figure somewhere in the middle or, if you consider yourself unusually well qualified, near the top.)

Plan What You Will Take With You

Every applicant for a position should bring the following items:

A filled fountain pen or a good ball-point pen.

A pencil with a good eraser.

A résumé. (This may be put in a plain folder, in a large envelope, or in a special acetate folder. The résumé should never be folded and put in a pocket or purse.)

A small pad on which to take notes.

Applicants for stenographic positions are usually given a typewriting and shorthand test. In addition to the items listed above, they should also take a clean stenographer's notebook, a good typewriter eraser, and possibly an eraser shield. Although these items are usually supplied by the company, it is well to be prepared in case they are not.

If you are applying for a position in which samples of your work would be helpful, take some along. Put them in a folder or in a clean envelope.

On the day of the interview, give yourself plenty of time to arrive at the interviewer's office on schedule. Take no chances on delayed trains, taxis, and buses; start early. Last-minute dashes to make an appointment are likely to find you disheveled and breathless. Plan your schedule so that you can walk into the receptionist's office with calm assurance.

You'll usually be asked to fill out an official application form, and arriving ten or fifteen minutes early will give you a head start on this task. You will want to complete the application blank slowly and carefully (it will be part of your permanent record if you get the job). Try to get a copy of this application blank before arriving for the interview. In this way, you can be sure to give it the attention it deserves.

Find Out All You Can About the Company

There are two main reasons for finding out in advance all you can about the company. First, knowing something about the organization will help you to decide whether it is a place in which you would like to work. Second, you should have a strong answer to the often-asked question, "Why did you choose our company?" Too many applicants have no ready answer to that question beyond the weak "I just heard it is a nice place to work," or "It's close to my home." It is much more effective to say, "I have always been interested in investments, and I know that your company is one of the leading investment firms in this area."

How should you research facts about a company? You might talk to the person, such as your placement counselor, who referred you to the organization. You might ask this person or an instructor for the name of an acquaintance who works there; then talk to the employee. If you have an opportunity, pick up copies of employee magazines, booklets, or advertising brochures.

Above all, learn the exact spelling of the name of the person who is to interview you. If you are not absolutely sure, telephone the interviewer's secretary or speak to the company receptionist.

THE INTERVIEW

When you arrive at the office, you will be greeted by a receptionist. Give your name and the purpose of your visit. "I'm (your name). I have an appointment at nine with Mr. Wilkinson." If you have to wait a few minutes, review your résumé, check over the completed application blank, read the literature that will probably be available in the reception office, or otherwise occupy yourself. Don't engage in conversation with the receptionist unless you are invited to do so.

When you are ushered into the interviewer's office, try to be relaxed (though not casual or arrogant) and to look pleasant. Do not extend your hand unless the interviewer does so first. It is enough to say, "How do you do, Mr. Wilkinson." You do not need to give your name; the secretary or receptionist will have announced your arrival.

Seat yourself only when you are invited to do so. Keep with you the materials you have brought. Don't place anything on the interviewer's desk unless you are invited to do so. The interviewer may or may not ask to see the application blank and the résumé. The moment will come, however, when you are asked about your education and experience. This is the time to give the interviewer your résumé if you haven't already done so. Say something like this: "Here is my résumé, on which that information is summarized. I also have completed the application blank." (Hand both to the interviewer.) Wait for the interviewer to make the first move. You will know at once how the interview will be conducted—whether the interviewer is going to ask most of the questions or prefers that you take the initiative. Usually the interviewer will direct the proceedings.

Don't smoke. Even if you are a smoker, it is probably best to refuse a cigarette if it is offered to you. Say simply, "No, thank you; not just now." If you are a nonsmoker, you merely decline with "No, thank you."

Face and speak directly to the interviewer. Don't stare at the floor or out of the window while either of you is talking. Of course, you should take your eyes from the interviewer's occasionally, but leave no doubt that you are talking and listening to him or her. Speak slowly and enunciate carefully. Give your answers and statements in a straightforward manner; show that you have thought them through and that you can speak with precision. Give short answers; the interviewer doesn't want your life story or your complete personal philosophy in answer to every question. At the same time, a mere "Yes" or "No" is not sufficient. For example, if you are asked this question, "I see you had one course in accounting. Did you like it?" it is not enough simply to say "Yes" (assuming that is how you actually feel). You might add, "I enjoyed the course very much, and I plan to take more accounting in evening school."

Be specific about your special qualifications. If you are asked about your skills in shorthand and typewriting, give the results of your last tests. Say something like this: "I can write shorthand at 100 words a minute fairly consistently on new material. My typing speed on the last few tests was in the upper 60s." Or "My accounting courses consisted of principles, cost, intermediate, and departmental. In the departmental course we were introduced to automation as it relates to accounting, and I especially enjoyed that." Or "I consistently made top grades in communications courses, and I particularly liked writing credit and collection letters." Or "One of the most interesting things I did during my summers at Blank's was to verify the cash balance each day. It wasn't easy to make everything balance, since we had so many people handling the cash, but I was successful at it and learned a lot from the experience."

On the other hand, be noncommittal about controversial matters. If you are asked what you thought of Blank's as a place to work and your opinion isn't especially favorable, say something like this: "My work there gave me some valuable experience, and I enjoyed much of it." If you are asked for your opinions about people for whom you have worked and for whom you feel no special fondness, say something like this: "Miss Lodge was often helpful to me; I believe I profited from working with her."

The interviewer will usually be interested in why you left other positions, especially when you have indicated on your application blank that you left because of unsatisfactory working conditions or for other negative reasons. If you complain to the interviewer about the people or about the company policies, however, you may give the impression that you are a chronic complainer. Try to be objective and to say something like this: "I found it difficult to adjust to some of the procedures and to the unusual hours at Blank's. Many of the people were extremely pleasant and helpful. There were some with whom I didn't seem to have much rapport, but I am sure some of the fault was mine." The interviewer will appreciate your frankness as well as your discretion.

Try to be at ease; smile occasionally. Remember that the interviewer needs someone to fill a position that is open and is just as eager as you are to make a decision in your favor. Most interviewers are pleasant, friendly, and understanding. Try to display an air of confidence. Above all, don't fidget. Nervousness often shows up in such habits as brushing imaginary lint off clothing, straightening and restraightening a tie, fussing with hair, toying with an object such as a purse or a paper clip, and putting hands to the face. Avoid such habits; give your attention to the interviewer.

The interviewer will let you know when the interview is over. The usual sign is to rise. As soon as the interviewer does so, you should also rise. The exchange that takes place might be something like the following conversation.

> *Interviewer (rising):* I enjoyed meeting and talking with you.
>
> *You (rising):* Thank you, Mr. Wilkinson. I appreciate the time you have given me.
>
> *Interviewer:* We have your telephone number, and we will call you just as soon as we have reached a decision.
>
> *You:* Thank you. I shall look forward to hearing from you.
>
> *Interviewer:* Good-bye.
>
> *You:* Good-bye.

Leave as quickly as possible and thank the secretary and the receptionist as you leave.

FOLLOWING UP THE INTERVIEW

As soon as possible after the interview, make a written summary from notes and memory of the facts you learned in the interview and the opinions you have formed about the company and about the job for which you were interviewed. If you are being interviewed for jobs in several different companies, this written summary will prove an excellent way to refresh your memory about the interview when you are trying later to make your final job choice.

Whether or not you follow up the interview with a thank-you letter to the interviewer will depend on how much you want the job. If the position is an especially desirable one, you will want to thank the interviewer for his or her time and to reemphasize some of your special qualifications. For other suggestions relating to follow-up letters after interviews, refer to Section 55.

Communication Projects

PRACTICAL APPLICATION

A Prepare written answers to each of the following questions and statements likely to come up in an employment interview.

1. Why do you wish to work for our company?
2. What kind of work do you enjoy doing most?
3. What kind of work do you enjoy doing least?
4. What salary do you expect?
5. What are your job goals for the next ten-year period?
6. Why have you selected this type of work?
7. Tell me about yourself.
8. Why did you leave your last position?
9. How do you spend your spare time?
10. What do you do in the summer?

B List ten "Dos" and "Don'ts" for the job applicant *preparing* for an interview. Then list ten "Dos" and "Don'ts" to be observed *during* the interview.

C Your interviewer mentions a person for whom you worked one summer, saying: "I see that your department supervisor at Blank's was Myra London. I know Myra through my work in AMS. She is a tough person to get along with. Did you find her so?" Write down what you would answer (assume that you feel exactly the same way as your interviewer about Myra London).

D Assume that you are interested in an office position in the U.S. Civil Service Commission. Find out all you can about the tests that are scheduled for your region in the near future. Then prepare a three-minute talk on this subject to be given to your class or write a brief report on your findings.

E Answer the following questions:

1. Why do you think that you should thank the secretary and the receptionist when you leave the interviewer's office?
2. It is suggested that you take a small notebook along with you to the interview. What notes might you want to make?
3. Why is it important to choose carefully the company for which you would like to work?
4. In large companies, the applicant for a position is interviewed at least twice; first by a personnel specialist, and later on by the person for whom the applicant will work. What do you think is the main purpose of the first interview? How might the two interviews differ?

F Assume that you have been interviewed for an office position in the Haynes Manufacturing Company. Your interviewer, Mr. Horace Willson, was very pleasant and seemed favorably impressed with your qualifications. However, he said that he plans to interview several other applicants before making a decision and that it will probably be two or three weeks before a decision is reached. Write a letter to Mr. Willson and thank him for the interview. (It's a job you especially want.) Emphasize special points or additional facts that may improve your chances for getting the job.

EDITING PRACTICE

The Rewrite Desk Edit and rewrite the following paragraph.

> Will you please except our sincere apology for failing to return promptly the merchandise that we were unable to use? The shipment arrived during our rush season, and our stock clerks, therefore, were concerned with goods that could be placed on the shelves rather then with those that should be returned. We assure you that a delay such as this, will not occur again.

CASE PROBLEM

Courtesy to the New Employee Dale Rogers is a new auditor assigned to the desk next to Bert Cone. When Dale first reported for work, the auditing supervisor, Mrs. Hidalgo, had intended to introduce Dale to all the members of her staff. However, Mrs. Hidalgo was unexpectedly called to a meeting before she could introduce Dale to Bert or to any of the other employees in the office.

1. What should Bert do?
2. What should Dale do if Bert does nothing?

CHAPTER 11 ADVANCING ON THE JOB

57 Communication Duties on the Job

The purpose of an interview is to determine if you, the prospective employee, are qualified for a specific position. The interviewer will make a decision based on your letter of application, your résumé, and the interview with you. You will get the job if the interviewer is convinced that you are well prepared for the job and have the "right" personal qualifications.

Indeed, you *are* well prepared! As a result of your experiences in your business communications class, you should be well equipped to handle most communication problems that will confront you in your work. You will read all types of communications that cross your desk, listen to customers in face-to-face conversation and over the telephone, speak to your boss or to customers to give them information they have requested, and write all types of effective communications.

Remember, though, that all other employees in your company were hired because they, too, were considered well prepared by their interviewers. How, then, are promotions decided? Obviously, the workers that are promoted are not selected at random. They are selected on the basis of their "extras"—those business skills and personal qualities that distinguish one employee from all others.

This section discusses those extras you will need to distinguish yourself for promotion.

YOUR FIRST PROMOTION

Many people begin their careers as stenographers and are promoted to secretarial positions when they have proved their ability to perform in more demanding positions. Sometimes, college-trained applicants are hired as stenographers; but they must know, and must be able to perform, secretarial duties that involve communication.

What are the differences between the duties of the secretary and those of the stenographer? A stenographer's principal responsibilities are to take and to transcribe dictation, and to type from rough drafts or from dictating machines. Shorthand and typewriting skills, though, are not the only skills needed by the stenographer; they must be supported by a strong background in English. The stenographer must have a sound knowledge of spelling and of the rules of grammar and punctuation, in addition to familiarity with the correct form for business letters, reports, and other documents. The stenographer must show ability in all these aspects of communication to be considered for a secretarial position.

The secretary, too, must be proficient in all these areas. As a secretary, you must be able to accept greater responsibility for the communication activities of the office. If you are initially employed as a secretary, your responsibility in this area begins on the first day of work; if you start out as a stenographer, you must prove that you are of secretarial caliber by taking the initiative to handle additional responsibilities on your own whenever the opportunity presents itself.

THE SECRETARY'S COMMUNICATION RESPONSIBILITIES

As a secretary, you will probably work with a busy executive who has many communication responsibilities. If you can accept some of these duties and free your boss for more important tasks, you will make yourself valuable to the firm and particularly to your boss! The areas that you should be able to handle include taking dictation and transcribing it, processing incoming mail, preparing outgoing mail, writing letters, signing letters, and preparing messages.

Dictation and Transcription

Techniques of taking and transcribing dictation are not within the province of a book on communications. Certainly the secretary prepared to enter the business world has acquired and perfected these skills. Most employers look for more than these basic skills; they expect their secretaries to know the finer points of grammar, punctuation, capitalization, and spelling. Many executives rely on their secretaries to edit and correct their dictation; some also expect their secretaries to verify the facts, figures, and names used in their dictation.

Editing How much editing should the secretary do on the letters the boss dictates? That depends almost entirely on the boss. Some administrators dictate very methodically, indicating punctuation, unusual spellings, and new paragraphs. Usually these executives are so sure of themselves that they want very little editing done. Others dictate only the barest outline of a letter and say to the secretary, "Fix it up." Most bosses, however, are somewhere between these two extremes; if the dictator makes errors in grammar and punctuation, the secretary usually can feel free to make the necessary changes. Obviously, the secretary must be positive of the correction before proceeding. If not, the secretary may say to the executive, "You mentioned April 11 as the first day of the meeting. Did you mean April 12?" or "In my notes I have 'I don't want to set any precedents in this decision.' I believe you actually said, 'I don't want to set *a precedent*.'"

Finished Letters After transcribing the letters, the secretary should proofread them carefully while they are still in the typewriter. In this way, errors can be corrected without running the risk of misaligning the correction. A letter that is not correct or that contains unclear sentences should not be placed on the employer's desk for signature. The secretary should never try to pass over an error or a garbled sentence.

Transcribed letters should be accompanied by the addressed envelope and the enclosures when the letters are presented for signature. The envelope should be placed over the letterhead so that the flap faces the letterhead; by so doing, you won't obscure the message. If the executive is not in the office when the letters are brought in to be signed, place the letters on the desk, face down or inside a folder.

Incoming Mail

An important part of the executive's business day is spent reading the morning mail. Most executives give the mail their first attention each morning. The alert, efficient secretary gets to the office early enough to open and sort the mail and have it on the executive's desk when he or she arrives each day.

Sorting the Mail In a small office, all incoming mail may be picked up and distributed by whoever arrives at the office first: the secretary, the receptionist, an office assistant, even the boss. In a large office where a great deal of mail is received, the mail is picked up and distributed by a special staff in a central mail room. In either case, letters addressed to individuals or to departments are usually delivered unopened. Letters addressed to the company without specific reference to individuals or to departments are opened, read, and then distributed to the appropriate persons.

Usually, the secretary is responsible for receiving and opening the employer's mail. The mail is handled in the following manner:

> Letters marked "Personal" are placed *unopened* in the executive's IN basket or on the desk.
>
> All other letters are opened, read carefully by the secretary, and placed on top of the executive's desk or in the IN basket. If passersby can look into the office, place the letters inside a folder so that they cannot be seen.
>
> The mail should be arranged in order of importance. A commonly accepted arrangement is as follows (in order from top to bottom):
>
> > Telegrams
> > Letters marked "Personal"
> > Other first-class mail
> > Circulars and advertisements
> > Magazines and newspapers
>
> If there is a great deal of mail, it may be separated into three folders marked "Telegrams," "First-Class Mail," and "Other Mail." Some secretaries separate the mail according to the urgency with which it must be handled (some telegrams are not important, while a particular newspaper item or a circular may be). In this case, folders are labeled "First Priority," "Second Priority," "For Reading Only—No Action," and so on. Of course, the secretary must know enough about the employer's business to know which pieces of mail are in most urgent need of attention.

Opening the Mail Use a letter opener. Never rip mail open or cut it open with scissors, because the contents might be damaged. Check each envelope carefully for enclosures.

If the mail contains checks or other important papers, slit open the envelope on three sides (so that it opens as flat as a sheet of paper) to make sure that you do not overlook enclosures. Also, because addresses are frequently given only on the envelope, make sure that you have a record of the address before destroying the envelope.

Outgoing Mail

The secretary's responsibility for outgoing letters does not end when the letters are placed on the executive's desk for signature. First, you should make certain that the executive knows that the letters *are* ready to be signed so that they will be mailed that day. Check to see that every letter is signed and that any enclosure mentioned in a letter is actually with that letter. And, double-check to see that each letter goes into its proper envelope. Nothing is more embarrassing than to have one person receive a letter that should have gone to someone else.

After preparing the letters for mailing, the secretary should make sure that the mail goes out on that day. If the outgoing mail collection has been missed, the secretary should either deliver the mail to the mail room or drop it into a mailbox after the office closes.

Writing Letters

Many letters that an executive might ordinarily dictate do not require careful thought, technical knowledge, or decision-making. These are the letters that a secretary could write for the employer, and these are the letters that are discussed in this section. Your training in communications will enable you to write routine letters to lighten your employer's work load; tactfully suggest that you undertake the job of answering such letters.

The types of letters most often written by the secretary include letters making reservations, letters requesting something, letters of referral, thank-you and acknowledgment letters, letters about appointments, and transmittal letters. Most of the letters were discussed in Chapter 7. Some are so important to the secretary, however, that they will receive additional emphasis here.

Reservation Letters For letters making hotel and travel reservations, either the employer's signature or the secretary's signature may be used. Refer to Chapter 7 for additional information on writing reservation letters. The letter that follows has been written for the employer's signature.

> Gentlemen:
>
> Please reserve a single room with shower for me for September 15 and 16, at a rate not to exceed $20.
>
> I shall arrive about 3 p.m. on September 15 and expect to check out before 2 p.m. on September 17. Please send me a confirmation of this reservation.
>
> Very truly yours,

Request Letters Request letters, too, may be written either for the employer's or for the secretary's signature. Here is an example of a request letter written for the secretary's signature.

> Gentlemen:
>
> Yesterday Mr. Robert van Schaik, treasurer of our firm, attended the annual Controller's Institute sponsored by your organization. He bought back with him a pamphlet entitled How to Improve Your Records, which we feel would be especially interesting to all our accounting supervisors.

We should, therefore, appreciate receiving 25 copies of this pamphlet if they are available. We would be very happy to pay for the postage necessary to send them to us, as well as to pay any charge you may make to cover the cost of printing.

If you have exhausted your supply of these pamphlets, may we have permission to reproduce a sufficient number of copies for our use? Mr. van Schaik would be most grateful to receive these pamphlets or to have your permission to reproduce them.

Sincerely yours,

Referral Letters Often executives may not be able to give personal attention to letters sent to them but really meant for someone else. In such cases, secretaries usually write an acknowledgment letter for their own signature and attend to any necessary follow-through. The following letter would be sent in answer to the request; at the same time, a copy of the original letter and a carbon copy of the reply would be sent to the person who can fulfill the request.

Dear Miss Anderson:

Thank you for asking us to send you 50 copies of our booklet, Secretarial Tips, for distribution to students in your class in secretarial procedures. We are pleased that you think so highly of our pamphlet.

Unfortunately, our office supply of this pamphlet is exhausted. However, I am referring your request to our Chicago office, from which the pamphlet was originally distributed. You should receive the 50 copies within ten days.

Sincerely yours,

Letters While the Boss Is Away Even though the secretary may not be requested to write letters while the boss is in the office, while the boss is away the secretary may be expected to acknowledge important letters received and to explain any delays caused by the boss's absence. Letters written for these reasons are usually brief, courteous, and noncommittal—that is, the letter does not reveal private company business such as where the boss is or why the boss is away.

Sometimes the correspondence cannot await your employer's return. Such letters are referred to someone else in the company. Only urgent or highly important letters are routed in this way.

Dear Mr. Carrington:

Thank you for your letter of May 10 to Mr. Mattell.

Mr. Mattell will be out of the office for about three weeks, so I am referring your letter to our credit manager, Mr. Martin A. Glendening. You will be hearing from Mr. Glendening just as soon as he has had an opportunity to review your application.

Sincerely yours,

Georgia Esterbrook
Assistant to Mr. Mattell

After writing the above reply to Mr. Carrington, Georgia Esterbrook writes the following memo to Mr. Glendening, transmitting the letter to him.

TO: Mr. Martin A. Glendening FROM: Georgia Esterbrook
Assistant to
Mr. Mattell

SUBJECT: Attached letter from George A. Carrington DATE: May 13, 19—

As you know, Mr. Mattell is in Philadelphia this week attending the convention of the National Credit Unions. I am attaching a letter that came today from Mr. George A. Carrington that requires an immediate response. I am also sending you a carbon copy of my letter to Mr. Carrington.

Would you please take care of this request, Mr. Glendening? I would be grateful if you will send me a blind carbon of your letter to Mr. Carrington.

GE

In your letter, do not express opinions that may disagree with those of your employer or that may be embarrassing. For example, if a job application was sent to a personnel director who is out of town, the personnel director's secretary would *not* write the following reply:

Thank you for your application for a management trainee position. Your qualifications seem to be excellent, and I know Mr. Gardner will be much impressed by them.

The personnel director may feel otherwise about the applicant's qualifications, or the company may not be able to make use of the applicant's services at the present time. Therefore, a noncommittal letter like the following would be more appropriate.

Dear Miss Carr:

Thank you for your application for a management trainee position.

The personnel director, Mr. Wesley Gardner, is out of the office this week. When he returns, he will write you at his first opportunity.

Sincerely yours,

This letter does not commit Mr. Gardner beyond getting in touch with the applicant. Note, too, that the letter does not provide any confidential information regarding Mr. Gardner's whereabouts.

Signing Letters

When your boss is away or is in a hurry to leave the office, you may be asked to sign his or her name to dictated letters. Or you may be asked to sign all routine correspondence, even when your boss is in the office. If such is the case, write your initials immediately below your boss's "signature," as shown here:

Cordially yours,

Paula K. Laughton
J.G.

Paula K. Laughton

Some employers, however, prefer that their signatures be faked—especially when the letter is written to people whom they do not know personally.

Messages

Whenever the boss is out of the office or is in conference, the secretary must take messages of telephone calls received or of in-person visits during the boss's absence. The efficient secretary writes down these messages as they are received, checks them to make sure they are accurate and complete, and submits them—in writing—to the boss.

The messages are written because the secretary knows better than to entrust messages to memory and because the written messages also serve to remind the boss to follow through. The secretary should keep a duplicate copy as a reminder to follow up on the boss. The written message precludes the boss's saying "You didn't tell me that Mrs. Stapleton wanted me to return her call last Wednesday"; the duplicate reminds the secretary on Wednesday to check that the boss does call Mrs. Stapleton.

The illustration shown below is typical of the message forms used in most offices. Notice that only a few words are used in the message, yet the message is clear and complete.

To: Ms. Jeannine Saunders

Here is a Message for You

Mr. Henri Engel

of Engel Office Supplies

Phone No. 555-3783 Ext. —

☑ Telephoned
☐ Returned Your Call
☑ Please Phone
☐ Will Call Again
☐ Came To See You
☐ Wants To See You

Do you need the shipment before Friday? If you do, Mr. Engel will send it by special delivery. Please let him know today.

Taken By E. B. Date 6/29 Time 11:10

Communication Projects

PRACTICAL APPLICATION

A Your employer, Donald Thuesen, is on vacation and will not return to the office for another ten days. As his secretary, you acknowledge all letters that are received in his absence. Write a letter that you could use with little or no change to acknowledge most of his correspondence.

B A letter from Mr. Donald Bennett to your employer requests a decision within two weeks regarding Mr. Bennett's proposed schedule for redecorating your company's offices. Your employer, Mr. John Kenyon, is out of the office for a month and cannot be reached. Since you cannot give an official answer, you refer this letter to Thomas Rooney, the vice president. Write an appropriate letter to Mr. Bennett to let him know what you are doing.

C You are secretary to Miss Loise Roualt, director of the office services department. Miss Roualt has asked you to get information on photocopiers from two companies. The first, Koppee Corporation, 151 Hill Drive, Denver, Colorado 80214, manufactures two new models, the P-15 and the Mini-14. The second, CopyQuick Corporation, manufactures the Exacto-21 and the Exacta-99 models. Miss Roualt is interested in knowing the cost per copy for each machine and the cost of renting or buying each machine; the paper sizes that each machine can take; whether collating equipment is available, and if so, its cost; and the maximum number of copies each machine can make per minute. Write to the companies and request this information for Miss Roualt.

D As the secretary in each of the following situations, write the appropriate letter for your boss.

1. Your boss, Miss Ardis Svensen, a real estate broker, was called out of town yesterday by the sudden death of her father. She is not expected to return for at least two weeks, as she must attend to family matters. Today a letter arrives from Mr. Ronald Cleverdon, president of the County Realty Board, asking Miss Svensen to serve on the planning committee for the spring conference of the Board, of which she is a long-time member and former officer. Her acceptance (or refusal) is needed within one week, since the first meeting of the committee is planned for two weeks from today.
2. Before leaving on a business trip, your boss, Hugh Hadden, asks you to write Econo-Products for 25 copies of the pamphlet *Are Your Human Relations Human?* He doesn't say whether the pamphlet is free or not.
3. A new monthly publication, *The Corporate Tax Letter*, favorably impressed your boss, Leonard Lindsell, chief counsel of Metropolitan Baking Co., when he saw it on the desk of a business friend he was visiting recently. He asks you to write for a sample copy. The magazine is published by The Clearing House, 20 N. Wacker Drive, Chicago 60608.
4. On September 29, your boss, Mrs. Leona Romarty, plans to meet her sister in Chicago to attend their uncle and aunt's fiftieth wedding anniversary the next day. The two sisters wish to stay two nights at the Hotel Lincoln Plaza, 1 Oak Lane. They prefer a twin-bedded room, with bath, on an upper floor, with a view of Lake Michigan. Write the letter of reservation and ask for a written confirmation.

EDITING PRACTICE

The Supervising Editor The following sentences lack writing polish. Edit and rewrite them.

1. Our sales catalog contains many items priced far below those of any other company. This offers you a very considerable saving.
2. Nothing must go wrong. Our business is to see it doesn't.
3. We have instructed our representative in your city that he should make a satisfactory adjustment and to live up to our policy of giving customers satisfaction.
4. The reason Jeffrey did not finish the report on time was because he was to change some statistics at the last minute.
5. Please order at once a thesaurus, book of synonyms, and abridged dictionary.
6. I am sure Miss Bernard will be delighted to interview you when she returns from her vacation in Canada. I will give her your résumé and letter of application and ask her to call you.
7. Many young business communicators hope to become supervisors because of the prestige they have.
8. Under the last line of the letterhead is to be printed our telephone number.
9. Mr. Cole's confident manner, his wide experience, and his friendliness—all combine to make him an unusually effective executive.
10. We do a wholesale business only; therefore, we cannot supply the vacuum cleaner you ordered, but we have three representatives in your town, any one of whom will be glad to demonstrate our vacuum cleaner, so we urge you to get in touch with one of the stores listed below.

CASE PROBLEM

Signing for the Boss Often employers must leave the office before signing outgoing letters; so they instruct their secretaries to complete the letters and mail them. Mr. Hicks asks his assistant, Jo Conly, to sign his name and place her initials below the signature. Miss Tyler tells her secretary, Ann Wyeth, to sign Miss Tyler's name but not to bother with initials, since most people "won't know the difference." Mr. Sanford instructs his secretary, Pat Anderson, not to sign his name but to place the following notation below the typewritten signature: "Dictated but not read." What are the pros and cons of each method?

58 Communication and Advancement

The rewards for office workers who prove themselves competent are salary increases and advancements to better job positions. The successful secretary, for example, may be advanced all the way to the top secretarial job, *executive secretary* or *administrative assistant.*

This section will give you the training you need to advance to higher secretarial positions and to do the job once you get there.

THE ADMINISTRATIVE ASSISTANT AND THE EXECUTIVE SECRETARY

In some businesses, the highest level secretarial title is *executive secretary.* As the name implies, this person is actually an executive who has many decisions to make and who often supervises the work of typists, clerks, stenographers, and/or secretaries. In some businesses, a person with similar responsibilities may be called an *administrative assistant.* The executive secretary and the administrative assistant have similar communication responsibilities; both are, in reality, assistants to an executive. In this discussion, the term *administrative assistant* will be used to refer to this top secretarial position.

Whatever the title, the top secretarial job in any company is demanding and requires expert communication skills. The job is also challenging and rewarding—rewarding in responsibilities and in salary.

THE ADMINISTRATIVE ASSISTANT COMMUNICATES

The administrative assistant will, of course, be required to perform the communication activities described in Section 57. In addition, the administrative assistant must assume other responsibilities.

Incoming Mail

The incoming mail is an important part of the executive's day, as discussed in Section 57. Besides opening and sorting the daily mail for the executive, the administrative assistant usually takes on these duties:

Reading the Mail Usually the administrative assistant is expected to read the mail before placing it on the employer's desk. There are two important reasons for reading the mail: (1) to keep informed of matters that have a bearing on the executive's work and (2) to make the executive's job of answering the mail an easier one.

Suppose the executive receives a letter from Gaylord Taylor, a business acquaintance in another city. Mr. Taylor writes that he will be visiting your city on a certain date and hopes to see your boss. The assistant reads the letter, checks the executive's calendar, and makes the following notation on Mr. Taylor's letter: "You will be in Birmingham during that week." Or suppose the executive receives a letter from Mr. Harry Felton, a supplier, in which Mr. Felton refers to a specification sheet he received from the executive. The assistant attaches to Mr. Felton's letter a copy of the specification sheet referred to so that the executive will have on hand the information needed to reply to Mr. Felton. The assistant may also be called on to perform the following tasks in order to ease the load of the executive:

> Underline important dates, amounts, or statements on incoming letters. Place notations in the margin of incoming letters, such as "I will answer this request" or "He refers to a telephone call from Mr. Chalmers" or "She means June 11 (instead of June 10)."
>
> Place a routing slip on letters that probably should be handled by another department. Of course, if the letter is addressed to the executive, he or she should be given the opportunity to read it even though someone else will reply. The routing slip, however, makes it easier to handle the letter if the executive agrees with the recommendation to route it elsewhere.
>
> Read and flag for the executive's attention magazine or newspaper articles of special interest. This may be done by clipping to the publication a memo slip containing a notation such as "See pages 43, 44, and 76."

Digesting the Mail The busy executive who receives a large amount of correspondence may expect an assistant to prepare digests (summaries) of important messages. An executive who is planning to be away on an extended business trip may ask the assistant to send summaries once a week or perhaps more often.

Digest of Important Mail Received October 3

Mr. J. C. Fairchild	Accepts your proposal on the refurnishing of the Monkton office. On his way there now; will write when he returns.
Mrs. Agnes Moran (Arlington Mills)	Can't speak at the Interior Decorators Association meeting as previously agreed. Going into hospital for major surgery.
Ms. Yolanda Barca	Can you come to Providence on November 8? Her London representative will be there. They want to discuss Liverpool situation with you. (Your calendar is clear.)
G. O. Brooks (memo)	Wants you to introduce the guests of honor at the president's reception on October 19.
Mr. George Phillips (Phillips Originals)	Appreciates your help on the Calvert Memorial Room. Board bought everything you recommended. Can you have dinner at his club on November 2? (Your calendar is clear.)

Writing Letters

An executive often depends on the administrative assistant to write letters and memorandums and to follow up on those that require future action. The initiative for writing letters for the executive may come from the assistant or from the employer, who might write on an incoming letter a notation such as "Tell him I'll see him." The assistant who takes the initiative may do one of the following:

1. Write a rough-draft reply and attach it to the incoming letter that goes on the employer's desk.
2. Make notations on the incoming letters, such as "I will answer" or "I'll tell him you will be away that week" or "Will send today."

There is no hard-and-fast rule about the duties of the administrative assistant in handling the employer's correspondence. Whether the assistant writes letters for the employer depends entirely on the executive's wishes and the assistant's ability. In any event, the assistant should never be presumptuous. The assistant should turn over *all* incoming letters, routine or not, until the employer decides that the assistant is able to originate correspondence.

Communication Follow-Up The efficient administrative assistant assumes responsibility for following up on the employer's communication activities. For example, if certain letters must be answered by a specific date, the assistant should remind the employer when an answer is due. The assistant can either maintain a tickler file or record reminder notes on a desk calendar pad.

Follow-up is needed, for example, for incoming letters that arrive with enclosures omitted, for outgoing letters that request appointments and that have not been answered, for materials requested that have not arrived, or for some other action referred to in incoming or outgoing correspondence that has not materialized after a reasonable time. Here are some examples of such follow-up letters:

Dear Mr. Burton:

Mr. Gregory left Monday on an extended trip to our branch offices. He asked that if we did not receive a letter from you by today regarding the appointment he requested, I inquire of you whether March 11 at 1 p.m. is satisfactory. I am to let him know before he leaves Oakland on March 9, so that he can plan the remainder of his trip accordingly.

I expect to telephone Mr. Gregory at 4 p.m., March 8. Therefore, would you wire or telephone me (555-9175) collect before that date and tell me whether you can see Mr. Gregory when he is in Minneapolis?

Sincerely yours,

Dear Mrs. Taylor:

We received your letter of March 12 with 24 vouchers enclosed. However, the voucher made payable to Gloria Sanchez for $75, dated February 16, was not included even though this voucher was on the list of vouchers being sent.

We would appreciate your sending this voucher to us by airmail special delivery so that we can complete our posting before March 25.

Very truly yours,

Business correspondence must be answered even while the employer is away from the office. Incoming mail must be handled; urgent mail must be acknowledged or answered; and routine mail should be answered. The assistant should, therefore, set up a procedure for taking care of correspondence while the executive is away. Here are some practical suggestions:

1. If the boss will be away for more than two or three days, acknowledge all letters to which a correspondent might reasonably expect a prompt answer. An example of such an acknowledgment letter is given on page 507.
2. Forward mail to a knowledgeable person in the company if the incoming letter indicates that some action must be taken immediately.
3. If the employer is on an extended trip, send copies of letters requiring action before he or she is expected to return to the office. Be certain to send any necessary supporting materials.
4. Answer all letters that you would be expected to handle if your boss were in the office.
5. Place in folders all mail received—letters awaiting the executive's attention, photocopies of letters forwarded to others for reply, carbon copies of letters that you or others have answered, advertising mail, newspapers, and so on.

Signing Letters In Section 57 you learned how a secretary signs a letter for an employer. An administrative assistant, however, sometimes writes a letter for his or her own signature, as shown in the following examples.

Very truly yours,

(Miss) Catherine Wilson
Administrative Assistant to
Mr. Latimer

Cordially yours,

Warren Jackson
Assistant to the Controller

MEETINGS AND CONFERENCES

A very informal meeting may require little preparation, but the success of most meetings depends on someone's taking the responsibility for planning and arranging them. The administrative assistant usually has this responsibility and attends to these details: (1) reserves and sets up the meeting room and restores it to order after the meeting; (2) prepares an agenda—a list of topics to be discussed at the meeting; (3) makes definite assignments for each participant; and (4) takes notes on the discussion and prepares minutes of the meeting.

The Meeting Room

The assistant to the person chairing the meeting usually has the assignment of preparing the meeting room and returning it to order after the meeting. The assistant must, therefore, take care of the following details:

Seating Arrangements Many meetings start poorly because seating arrangements are inadequate. The resultant delay, confusion, and milling around could take the sparkle out of even the most carefully planned conference. There should always be a sufficient number of chairs for participants and a few extra chairs for unexpected guests.

If possible, conference members should be seated around an oval table. Such an arrangement takes the stiffness out of a meeting and gives everybody an opportunity to see, hear, and concentrate on the contributions of each participant.

Other Details On the table in front of each chair, place a copy of the agenda, several pencils, and a writing pad. Ashtrays, too, should be provided. When a chalkboard is to be used, make certain that it is clean and that a clean eraser and plenty of chalk are on hand. If audiovisual aids are to be used, make certain that the proper facilities are available. If an operator is needed to run the equipment, be sure to remind the operator *well before the time of the meeting*. A smoothly run meeting depends largely on how well the advance preparations are made—nothing should be left to chance.

Final Clean-Up After the meeting is over, make certain that all equipment and unused supplies are returned and that the meeting room is restored to its original order. Report any problems involving borrowed equipment. Check all seating locations to be sure that no personal possessions have been left behind. Inspect chairs, tables, windows, drapes, and so on, to be sure that everything is left exactly as it was found.

The Agenda

The form of the agenda varies greatly. The agenda illustrated below is typical for an informal committee meeting. When parliamentary procedure is followed in a meeting, the agenda is more formal and includes such information as the name of the presiding officer, the specific time at which each topic is to be presented, the resolutions to be considered, and the like.

AGENDA

Meeting of the Forms Control Committee
August 14, 19—
10:30 a.m. — Board Room

Mr. Bentley . . . . Customer Service Department's proposal to redesign all its forms

Miss Caesar . . . . Purchase of Vari-typer for use in preparing personnel forms

Mr. Ruiz . . . . Snap Forms Company's offer to provide free consultant on forms design

Mrs. DeCaprio . . . . How new data processing equipment is affecting sales of office forms

Mr. Orr . . . . No report

Mr. Scott . . . . No report

Miss Levy . . . . No report

Usually the agenda is sent to all participants in advance of the meeting so that they have time to prepare their comments, suggestions, or questions. At the meeting room, make sure to supply a copy of the agenda for each participant—nearly always someone misplaces an agenda or forgets to bring it to the meeting.

The Notes and Minutes

The administrative assistant of the person who conducts a meeting is usually the one who makes a record of what took place. A stenographic notebook is best for taking notes of the meeting because the center rule on each page separates the names of the speakers from their remarks.

The assistant should transcribe the notes of the discussion as soon as possible, preferably the same day. Section 48 gives specific suggestions for preparing minutes.

RESEARCH ACTIVITIES

Some of the communications an executive writes may involve research. The research work may consist merely of looking up information in the department's own files, of telephoning and writing to other departments to gather facts and figures, and of consulting one or more periodicals or reference books. The executive depends on the assistant to help with this research.

Some executives are engaged in activities that require more formal research. The marketing department of a large oil corporation will have a staff of research specialists—people who carry on dozens of studies simultaneously to determine where and how the firm's products are being used, the need for new products, and the need for improvements in existing products. A personnel department may research wage and salary trends, employee benefits offered in various industries, and labor contracts. A construction engineer may research causes of collapse of buildings and bridges. Some executives are editors, and one type of research they must do is that of checking the accuracy of statements made by authors of the articles in their company publications. Many executives write articles for magazines and other periodicals; some write books.

In all these cases, the administrative assistant's responsibility for research is likely to be heavy and to require frequent use of the company library and of nearby public and college libraries. In some instances, the administrative assistant may even maintain a small library for the executives' or the department's exclusive use.

Many executives are often asked to deliver speeches. For example, a sales manager who is active in various national organizations dealing with marketing, selling, and advertising will be on the lookout for speech materials to keep up to date. The responsibilities of an assistant to such an executive often encompass reading current periodicals and keeping a speech file for the employer.

Basic References

Every administrative assistant should be familiar with basic reference sources. The following are recommended.

A Good Dictionary The dictionary is probably the most important reference source. For most writing purposes, a dictionary such as *Webster's New Collegiate Dictionary* (G. & C. Merriam Company) or *The American Heritage*

Dictionary of the English Language (American Heritage Publishing Co.) is sufficient. Executives who do a great deal of writing or editing should have available an unabridged dictionary.

A Secretarial Handbook A secretarial handbook contains such information as the following: rules for the use of English grammar, capitalization, spelling, punctuation; guides for transcribing, mailing, and filing business correspondence; aids to proofreading; styles and formats for typing; and information relating to postal, express, and telegraphic services.

Secretarial handbooks provide references for most general types of secretarial duties. Several are available. Among the most popular are *Standard Handbook for Secretaries*, by Lois Hutchinson, and *A Reference Manual for Stenographers and Typists*, by Ruth E. Gavin and William A. Sabin (both, McGraw-Hill Book Company).

A Reliable Fact Book Most assistants find frequent use for a fact book such as *The World Almanac* (Newspaper Enterprise Association Inc.). This fact book contains such varied information as names and addresses of colleges and universities, population figures, baseball records, names of members of congress, senators, Academy Award winners, and much, much more.

An Authoritative Grammar Reference An assistant whose boss writes a great deal should keep a good grammar reference at hand. One such reference is the *McGraw-Hill Handbook of English*, by Harry Shaw (McGraw-Hill Book Company).

Special References

An administrative assistant needs special references that pertain to the business of the executive. For example, the assistant who works for a lawyer may need a good law dictionary, such as *Black's Law Dictionary* (West Publishing Company), and a handbook for the legal secretary, such as *Legal Office Procedures*, by Marjorie Dunlap Bate and Mary C. Casey (McGraw-Hill Book Company). Other examples of special references follow:

> Administrative Assistant to a Doctor. A medical dictionary, such as *Blakiston's Gould Medical Dictionary*, edited by A. Osol and C. C. Francis (McGraw-Hill Book Company); a medical secretary's handbook, such as *Medical Office Procedures*, by Miriam Bredow (McGraw-Hill Book Company).
>
> Administrative Assistant to a Publisher. Various stylebooks, such as *A Manual of Style*, University of Chicago Press Staff (University of Chicago Press); *Writer's Guide and Index to English*, by Porter G. Perrin (Scott, Foresman and Company); *The New York Times Style Book for Writers and Editors*, edited and revised by Lewis Jordan (Quadrangle); *Words Into Type*, by Marjorie E. Skillin and Robert M. Gay (Appleton-Century-Crofts); *Roget's International Thesaurus*, by P. M. Roget (Thomas Y. Crowell Company).
>
> Administrative Assistant to a Chemist. *Lange's Handbook of Chemistry*, compiled and edited by J. A. Dean (McGraw-Hill Book Company).
>
> Administrative Assistant to an Accountant. *Accountant's Handbook*, edited by R. Wixon (Ronald Press Company); *Office Management Handbook*, edited by H. L. Wylie (Ronald Press Company).

Use of the Library

To use library facilities efficiently, the assistant should become acquainted with the librarian and should seek the librarian's help. The librarian will be able to point out the available sources of information and special reference works as well as the library's auxiliary services, such as the interlibrary loan system and the library's reference services. Often, too, when the assistant is not acquainted with the titles of books or articles or the names of authors, the librarian's help is a great time-saver.

Once you have found all the references you need, you should follow these practical suggestions for recording the information.

1. Be systematic and orderly in all note-taking. Most researchers use cards for this purpose.
2. Always check to make sure you have the latest edition of the book.
3. Be careful to record, for each reference, the author's full name, the title of the book or periodical, the title of the article (if a periodical reference), the volume and number (if applicable), the publisher's name, the date and place of publication, and all page numbers referred to.
4. Write on only one side of the card and limit each card to one subject. (See Section 47 for further suggestions for taking notes.)

Reading and Writing Reports

Reading and writing of reports often occupy a major portion of the business executive's working day. A well-trained administrative assistant should be prepared to read some of the reports normally read by the boss and be able to write a brief summary of the highlights of each report. Always take care to summarize skillfully so that no important aspects of the report are omitted and no facts misrepresented. To avoid misinterpretation, cite the exact page references of important items. For example:

> Sims gives five reasons for requesting the new equipment in the accounting section. (See page 10.)

The administrative assistant may also be called upon to write reports. For example, your boss might ask you to request that all office supervisors submit information regarding absence and tardiness of the employees under their supervision. The boss might want you to tabulate the information and to summarize it so that he or she will know how many absences and latenesses there have been in each department, the reasons for them, which members of the staff are the most frequent offenders, what steps are being taken to reduce absenteeism, and so on. Because of the training provided in Sections 46 and 47, you are ready to tackle any type of report assigned to you.

Contributing Ideas

Business is hungry for good ideas that will reduce overhead, increase sales, promote new products, and make and keep friends. Many companies have suggestion boxes for employee ideas and periodically award cash bonuses for the best ideas contributed.

To reach the level of top management, you must be someone with imagination, someone who can make constructive suggestions. In Section 46 you learned to put your ideas in writing and to present them effectively. Therefore, you will be interested in the accompanying illustration of an administrative assistant's proposal for saving time and materials.

THE TRIDENT AGENCY, INC. Interoffice Memorandum

To Mr. William Bray, Office Manager

From Sally Stephenson, Administrative Assistant to the President

Subject Suggestion Regarding Carbon Copies of Correspondence

Date June 8, 19--

My suggestion is that carbon copies of replies to incoming letters be placed on the backs of those letters instead of on separate sheets of paper. Advantages of using this procedure are as follows:

1. The reply cannot be lost or become separated from the letter to which it belongs.

2. Paper will be saved because a second sheet of paper will not be needed for the carbon copy. The back of the incoming letter carries the carbon copy.

3. Filing space will be saved because only one sheet of paper needs to be filed.

If you think this suggestion is workable, I should be happy to discuss it with you at your convenience. My extension is 3886.

SS

HUMAN RELATIONS

The administrative assistant reflects the "voice, mind, and personality" of the employer; that is to say, other workers look upon the assistant as a representative of the employer's point of view. The administrative assistant sets the tone of the office; his or her attitudes, moods, and actions affect the morale of the entire office staff. If the assistant is disagreeable to someone, the person with the injured feelings can easily get the impression that the assistant's unpleasantness is a reflection of the boss's attitude.

Acting as the representative of the employer to the office staff and to the general public, the administrative assistant must try to promote good human relations at all times. A good assistant knows and observes the following guides to good human relations.

Be Discreet

An assistant to an executive is in a position to learn about matters of the utmost secrecy. You employer may discuss with you such confidential matters as salaries, personal feelings about employees, plans for reorganizing the department (which may involve releasing certain employees), and personal family matters. An employer who can't trust an assistant needs a new one! Even the slightest leak by the assistant assumes greater proportions than it may actually deserve. The best rule to follow is this: Reveal nothing about the employer's feelings, attitudes, and habits.

It is especially difficult when dealing with other company executives or with VIP's from outside the company. Because of their position, these men and women may feel that they are entitled to know everything that happens in the office. Usually the only way to satisfy these people is to say that you know nothing about the matters in question. For example, suppose a young department head says, "I hear the company is setting up a new branch office in Denver and that Goldberg is to be the manager. Is this true?" Even though you may know that the rumor is correct, you have no authority to confirm it. You merely say something like this: "I wasn't aware that any announcement had been made; I haven't seen anything on it." If the person persists, you may have to say, "You'll have to ask my boss, Mr. Blair. I don't have the information."

Be Impartial

We all have our pet likes and dislikes regarding people. There are all kinds of people in an office—some are easy to like, some are not. As an administrative assistant, however, you can't afford to show partiality. Although one cannot be "all things to all people," an assistant can't afford to choose sides. You must try to weigh your actions and attitudes on the basis of facts rather than emotions. The employer has the authority to hire, promote, and fire; and this power can cause anxiety on the part of employees. Because the boss is an important figure to everyone who works for him or her and because the administrative assistant has "inside information," the assistant must be objective, noncommittal, fair, and impartial.

Avoid being too friendly with anyone in the department. Don't join office cliques. Being too friendly with certain individuals puts the assistant on the spot insofar as gossip and tale-bearing are concerned. Resist the petty pastime of gossip.

Be Loyal

One way of demonstrating loyalty is by keeping confidences. There are other ways, too. Because the boss represents authority, your employer is a target for criticism. When you hear the boss criticized, whether justly or unjustly, either rise to the executive's defense or say nothing. Never agree openly with criticism. Nothing shakes the faith of loyal employees more than an assistant who confirms unfavorable rumors about the boss.

Loyalty to the employer is absolutely essential. But just as important is loyalty to the employees. Employees often share many confidences with the assistant—their health, pet dislikes, love affairs, feeling toward the company, family squabbles, and so on. Anything told in confidence should be kept from everyone else—even the employer. One of the surest ways to jeopardize morale in an office is to carry everything to the boss. If employees can't trust you, they will have nothing to do with you. Under such conditions, a spirit of teamwork is difficult to obtain.

Be Businesslike

Human relations in an office are affected by the amount of work that is accomplished. Unless employees can contribute something worthwhile to an organization, they are not likely to be satisfied, productive workers. Many people have the mistaken notion that if a country club atmosphere prevails in the office, everyone is happy and more productive. Such is not the case! Certainly everyone likes a little sociability, some fun, and some periods of relaxation. If this atmosphere predominates, however, the purpose of work is lost.

As administrative assistant, you should be businesslike in your attitude toward the job and toward all other workers. This does not mean that you are disagreeable. It means simply that you are aware that there is a job to be done and that the job demands hard work and efficient methods.

Here are a few "don'ts" for the administrative assistant seeking a businesslike attitude:

1. Don't visit among employees for social purposes. Stay at your desk unless you have business to attend to elsewhere.
2. Remember that the telephone is a business instrument—not a social one. If friends persist in calling you at the office, tell them that you are too busy to talk and that you will telephone them in the evening.
3. Don't joke about business matters or about office "characters." It is easy to take business matters—and some employees—lightly. Joking about company matters destroys purpose and takes away the genuine satisfaction that employees receive from doing their jobs well.
4. Don't let employees monopolize your time. Some employees like to visit and are constantly finding excuses to come to the assistant's desk (they may really want to see what the boss is doing). Show by your businesslike attitude that employee visits should be completed quickly.
5. Avoid extremes in clothing and accessories. Dress for business.

Avoid these "don'ts" and you will be taking the first step toward advancing on the job!

But Be Pleasant

The foregoing suggestions might give the impression that the assistant should be a piece of furniture—cold, hard, and indifferent. Nothing could be further from the truth. The assistant should smile easily and should be friendly to everyone. Never let a bad mood show. Be cool, calm, and collected in all situations. Remember, the assistant often sets the tone for the atmosphere of the whole office as well as for job performance. Being pleasant and friendly is just as important to good human relations as being businesslike is to productivity.

Communication Projects

PRACTICAL APPLICATION

A You are administrative assistant to John Aliano, office services manager of the Lewis Office Equipment Company. Mr. Aliano is scheduled to make a speech to a local chamber of commerce on the subject "Effects of Automation in the Office," and he has asked you to compile some specific information on these topics:

1. How automation will affect the secretary-stenographer.
2. How automation will affect the general clerical worker.
3. How automation will affect the records manager and the file clerks.

Mr. Aliano has told you that there are three sources from which reliable information may be obtained: for the secretary-stenographer, the National Secretaries Association, Kansas City; for the general clerical worker, the Life Insurance Association of America, New York; for the records manager and the file clerks, the National Records Management Institute, Cleveland. Supplying necessary details, draft a letter to each of the respective groups.

B As administrative assistant to Jennifer Romanov, industrial relations manager for the Lampston Textile Company, you are asked to handle routine communications for your employer. Recently the company purchased an excellent film, *Improving Production in Offices*, for use within the company. Write a memorandum to all department heads, and suggest the use of this film as a means of achieving more productivity from the workers; mention a preview showing of the 30-minute film for all department heads. The showing will be held at 4 p.m. on Tuesday, May 4, in the employees' cafeteria. You are to coordinate the use of the film.

C Your employer, Dave Loo, is the public relations director of the Union Light and Power Company. Mr. Loo and the advertising staff have written a colorful brochure, *What to Look For in Buying Home Appliances,* the first in a series of publications that have been made available in limited quantities to the general public. During the last week, you have received the following requests, and Mr. Loo has asked you to send a personal letter (for his signature) and a copy of the brochure to each inquirer.

1. Dear Sirs: Please send me information on buying appliances. Yours truly,
2. Gentlemen: Do you have any free information you can give me on what safety features to look for before purchasing appliances? Sincerely yours,
3. Gentlemen: I have heard about your fine booklet on buying electrical appliances for the home. Please send me 250 copies, which I intend to use in a mailing to all my electrical appliance customers. Connors Electrical Appliances Store. (The request must be refused.)
4. Sirs: Would you permit me to duplicate certain sections of your fine brochure on buying electrical appliances for the home? I am interested in making this information available to my customers and will be sure to give you credit for the authorship. Sincerely yours, (The request is granted.)

D Occasionally, your employer, Mr. Ross Leopold, must leave rather suddenly on an out-of-town trip for several days. When this happens, you as his assistant must compose many letters canceling all appointments for those days. Such letters must be definite, referring to the time and place of the original appointment. Often, they must express regret for the inconvenience caused and suggest another time for the appointment. Write a form letter that generally may be used for canceling Mr. Leopold's appointments.

EDITING PRACTICE

The Rewrite Desk Edit and rewrite the following paragraph.

> In your letter of August 17th, you ask for a reference for Chas. Wood. We have never employed a Chas. Wood; but a Thomas Wood worked here as receiving clerk from the third of April, 1971 to the first of January 1974. If this is the Mr. Wood about who you inquire we can save the writing of 2 or 3 letters by telling you that Thomas Wood's work was most satisfactory and that we found him industrious and cooperative.

CASE PROBLEM

Supervising Others You supervise the work of ten stenographers at the Blake Company. Jane Aire, one of the stenographers, has made an error on an important letter that must be mailed today. It is now ten of five, and five o'clock is quitting time. When you ask Jane to please make the correction before she leaves so that you can get the letter in the last mail, she says, "But if I'm late, I'll miss my ride." What would you do in this situation?

Appendix

FORMS OF ADDRESS

The following list, which offers the correct forms of address for government officials and religious dignitaries, is based on the Forms of Address section of the *Reference Manual for Stenographers and Typists, Fourth Edition,* by Ruth E. Gavin and William A. Sabin (McGraw-Hill Book Company, 1970).

The salutations in the right-hand column are listed in order of decreasing formality. Note that *Mr., Miss, Mrs.,* and *Ms.* are on the same order of formality, as are *Madam* and *Sir.* However, *Madam* should be used in salutations such as "My dear Madam Secretary," not "My dear Mrs. Secretary"; "Dear Madam Mayor," not "Dear Miss Mayor."

Government Officials

President of the United States

The President The White House Washington, DC 20500	Mr. President: The President: My dear Mr. President:

Vice President of the United States

The Vice President The United States Senate Washington, DC 20510	Sir: Mr. Vice President: My dear Mr. Vice President:

United States Senator

The Honorable John H. Glenn, Jr. The United States Senate Washington, DC 20510	Sir: Dear Sir: My dear Senator: Dear Senator Glenn:

Member of Congress

The Honorable Barbara Jordan House of Representatives Washington, DC 20515	Madam: Dear Madam: My dear Miss Jordan: Dear Miss Jordan:

Chief Justice of the United States

The Chief Justice of the United States Washington, DC 20543	Sir: My dear Mr. Chief Justice:

Cabinet Member

The Honorable Henry Kissinger Secretary of State Washington, DC 20520	Sir: Dear Sir: My dear Mr. Secretary:

Governor

The Honorable Ella T. Grasso Governor of Connecticut Hartford, CT 06115	Madam: Dear Madam: My dear Governor: Dear Governor Grasso:

State Senator

The Honorable Mervyn Dymally The State Senate Sacramento, CA 95814	Sir: Dear Sir: My dear Senator: Dear Senator Dymally:

State Representative or Assemblyman

The Honorable Stanley Fink The State Assembly[1] Albany, NY 12224	Sir: Dear Sir: My dear Mr. Fink: Dear Mr. Fink:

Mayor

The Honorable Janet Gray Hayes Mayor of San Jose San Jose, CA 95110	Madam: Dear Madam: My dear Madam Mayor: Dear Madam Mayor: Dear Mayor Hayes:

Jewish Dignitaries

Rabbi With Doctor's Degree

Rabbi Louis Baruch, D.D. *or* Dr. Louis Baruch *Full address*	Reverend Sir: Dear Sir: My dear Rabbi (*or* Dr.) Baruch: Dear Rabbi (*or* Dr.) Baruch:

Rabbi Without Doctor's Degree

Rabbi Samuel Wesler *or* Reverend Samuel Wesler *Full address*	Reverend Sir: Dear Sir: My dear Rabbi Wesler: Dear Rabbi Wesler:

[1]For state representatives, substitute *House of Representatives.*

Protestant Dignitaries

Methodist Bishop

The Reverend Harold J. Stone Bishop of *(place)* *Full address*	Reverend Sir: Dear Sir: My dear Bishop Stone: Dear Bishop Stone:

Protestant Episcopal Bishop

The Right Reverend John Ames Bishop of *(place)* *Full address*	Right Reverend and dear Sir: My dear Bishop Ames: Dear Bishop Ames:

Protestant Episcopal Dean

The Very Reverend Walter Scott Dean of *(place)* *Full address*	Very Reverend Sir: My dear Mr. Dean: My dear Dean Scott: Dear Dean Scott:

Clergyman With Doctor's Degree

The Reverend Dr. James Aspen *or* The Reverend James Aspen, D.D. *Full address*	Reverend Sir: Dear Sir: My dear Dr. Aspen: Dear Dr. Aspen:

Clergyman Without Doctor's Degree

The Reverend Donald Fried *Full address*	Reverend Sir: Dear Sir: My dear Mr. Fried: Dear Mr. Fried:

Roman Catholic Dignitaries

Cardinal

His Eminence Francis Cardinal Amato *Full address*	Your Eminence:

Archbishop and Bishop

The Most Reverend John Baxter Archbishop (*or* Bishop) of *(place)* *Full address*	Your Excellency:

Monsignor

The Right Reverend Monsignor Anthony J. Costa	Right Reverend Monsignor: Dear Monsignor Costa:

Priest

Reverend Scott Brady, S.J. *Full address*	Reverend Father: Dear Father Brady:

Mother Superior

The Reverend Mother Superior Convent of *(name)* *Full address*	Reverend Mother: Dear Reverend Mother: My dear Reverend Mother *(name)*: Dear Reverend Mother *(name)*:

WORDS OFTEN MISSPELLED

A

absence
accessible
accidentally
accommodate
accrual
accumulate
accurate
acquire
acquisitive
across
actuarial
adaptability
adequate
adhere
adjacent
adjoining
adjourn
adjunct
admissible
advisory
affiliate
aggressive
agreeable
allege
alleviate
allocated
altogether
amateur
amortize
analogous
analysis
anonymous
anxious
apostrophe
apparatus
apparel
apportion
appraisal
appreciable
appropriate
approximate
aptitude
arbitrary
architect
around
arrears
ascend
ascertain
assistance
assumption
athlete
attorneys
authoritative
authorize
auxiliary

B

bankruptcy
becoming
beginning
believing
beneficiary
benefited
bookkeeper
boundary
brilliant
brochure
bulletin

C

calendar
campaign
canceling
cancellation
capacity
carburetor
career
careful
carried
carrying
centralized
chargeable
charging
choose
chose
chronological
cipher
coincidence
collapsible
collectible
column
commensurate
commercial
committee
comparable
comparative
comparison
compel
compelling
competent
competitive
compilation
comptroller
concise
concurred
conferred
conscientious
consensus
conspicuous
contemporary
contingency
continuous
contribute
controlled
convenient
coolly
coordinate
correlate
correspondence
corroborate
courtesy
credentials
criticism
criticize
crystallize
cumulative
cycle
cylinder

D

dealt
deceased
defensible
deficit
delinquent
demurrage
depreciation
descend
dilemma
director
disappear
disappoint
disapprove
discipline
discretion
diseased
disillusion
dispel
dissatisfied
dissension
dissolution
distributor
dividend
doubtful
dripping
dropping
durable
dutiable

E

economical
efficiency
electrical
elementary
elevate
eligible
eliminate
embarrass
eminent
emphasize
endeavor
enforceable
enumerate
enunciation
envelop (v.)
envelope (n.)
environment
equaled
equalize
equally
equipping
equivalent
erroneous

especially
essence
etiquette
evaluation
exaggerate
excellent
excerpt
excessive
excusable
exercise
exhaustive
exhibit
exorbitant
expeditiously
expendable
explanation
extension
extraordinary
extravagance

F
facilitate
facilities
facsimile
familiarize
fascinate
feasible
February
finally
financier
flight
flourishing
forcibly
foreign
forfeit
forty
fragile
fraudulent
freight
friend
fulfill

G
gasoline
gauge
generalize
genuine
gorgeous
government
governor
grammar
grievance
grieve
grievous
guarantee

H
handicapped
harass
height
heretofore
hesitant
hindrance
hyphen

I
illegible
imaginary
imminent
imperative
implement
impossible
impromptu
inadvertent
incapable
incessantly
incidence
incidentally
inconceivable
incredible
incredulous
indispensable
inexhaustible
inferred
insurable
intelligence
intelligible
intercede
interrupt
intricate
invalidate
investigator
invoicing
irrelevant
irreparable
irresistible
itemize
itinerary

J
janitor
jeopardize

K
knowledge
knowledgeable

L
laboratory
lavatory
legible
leisure
liaison
likable
likelihood
linoleum
liquefy
loose
lose
lucrative
luxurious

M
machinery
mahogany
manageable
mandatory
marital
mathematics
measurable
measurement
mechanical
mediocre
mileage
millionaire
misapprehension
miscellaneous
monopolize
mortgage
mutually

N
naïve
necessarily
necessitate
negligible
negotiate
neutralize
nickel
nonsense
notarize
noticeable
nucleus
numerical

O
objectionable
obligatory
obsolete
obtainable
occasional
occupant
occurrence
omission
operator
ordinarily
original
overrated
oxidize

P
pamphlet
panicky
parallel
pardonable
parity
participant
pasteboard
pastime
peaceable
perceptible
permissible
personnel
persuasive
pertinent
phenomenal
Pittsburgh (Pa.)
politician
possession
potential
practical
precise

precision
prerogative
prohibition
pronunciation
prorate
prosperous
psychology

Q

quandary
quantity
questionnaire

R

readily
reciprocate
recollect
reconciliation
reimburse
remembrance
renewable
repetition
resources
restaurant
retrieval
retroactive
ridiculous
revenge
routine

S

sabotage
safety
schedule
scientific
scrutinize
seize
sense
sensible
serviceable
siege
similar
sincerely
situation
sizable
solely
specifically
specimen
sponsor
statistical
statistician
status
substantial
summarize
superficial
superfluous
supervisor
surgeon
susceptible
symmetry

T

tariff
technical
tenancy
thorough
through
traceable

U

unscrupulous
until
urgent
usable
utilize

V

vacuum
vague
valid
validate
valuable
velocity
vendor
vengeance
ventilator
villain
visitor
visualize
volume

W

waive
warehouse
weather
Wednesday
whereas
wherever
whether
wholly
wield
withhold

Y

yacht
yield

Z

zealous

ABBREVIATIONS OF STATES AND TERRITORIES

The following list shows both the traditional abbreviations of states and territories and the new two-digit abbreviations that were introduced by the U.S. Postal Service. Whether you spell out or abbreviate these names, always be sure to include the correct ZIP Code number.

State	Traditional Abbreviation	Post Office Abbreviation
Alabama	Ala.	AL
Alaska	. . .	AK
Arizona	Ariz.	AZ
Arkansas	Ark.	AR
California	Calif.	CA
Canal Zone	C.Z.	CZ
Colorado	Colo.	CO
Connecticut	Conn.	CT
Delaware	Del.	DE
District of Columbia	D.C.	DC
Florida	Fla.	FL
Georgia	Ga.	GA
Guam	. . .	GU
Hawaii	. . .	HI
Idaho	. . .	ID
Illinois	Ill.	IL
Indiana	Ind.	IN
Iowa	. . .	IA
Kansas	Kans.	KS
Kentucky	Ky.	KY
Louisiana	La.	LA
Maine	. . .	ME
Maryland	Md.	MD
Massachusetts	Mass.	MA
Michigan	Mich.	MI
Minnesota	Minn.	MN
Mississippi	Miss.	MS
Missouri	Mo.	MO
Montana	Mont.	MT
Nebraska	Nebr.	NE
Nevada	Nev.	NV
New Hampshire	N.H.	NH
New Jersey	N.J.	NJ
New Mexico	N. Mex.	NM
New York	N.Y.	NY
North Carolina	N.C.	NC
North Dakota	N. Dak.	ND
Ohio	. . .	OH
Oklahoma	Okla.	OK

State	Traditional Abbreviation	Post Office Abbreviation
Oregon	Oreg.	OR
Pennsylvania	Pa.	PA
Puerto Rico	P.R.	PR
Rhode Island	R.I.	RI
South Carolina	S.C.	SC
South Dakota	S. Dak.	SD
Tennessee	Tenn.	TN
Texas	Tex.	TX
Utah	. . .	UT
Vermont	Vt.	VT
Virgin Islands	V.I.	VI
Virginia	Va.	VA
Washington	Wash.	WA
West Virginia	W. Va.	WV
Wisconsin	Wis.	WI
Wyoming	Wyo.	WY

Index